THE SURROGATE
PROLETARIAT

WRITTEN UNDER THE AUSPICES OF
THE CENTER OF INTERNATIONAL STUDIES
PRINCETON UNIVERSITY
A LIST OF OTHER CENTER PUBLICATIONS
APPEARS AT THE BACK OF THIS BOOK

The Surrogate Proletariat

Moslem Women and Revolutionary Strategies
in Soviet Central Asia, 1919-1929

Gregory J. Massell

Princeton University Press, Princeton, New Jersey

Library of Congress Catalogue Card Number 73-16047
ISBN: 0-691-07562-X

Library of Congress Cataloging in Publication data will be found
on the last printed page of this book.

This book has been composed in Linotype Times Roman

Printed in the United States of America
by Princeton University Press

To
HARRY ECKSTEIN
gentle critic and sensitive friend

and the late
MERLE FAINSOD
wise counselor and dedicated teacher

ACKNOWLEDGMENTS

THIS study is a by-product of a general inquiry into the problems of strategy in planned social change. I have been engaged in this inquiry with the support of the Center of International Studies at Princeton University. I am grateful for the facilities the Center has placed at my disposal. In particular, I wish to express my appreciation to Klaus Knorr and Cyril Black, the Center's former and present directors respectively, who have given me generous encouragement and the opportunity to work in a stimulating environment where rugged individualists and devotees of collective intellectual endeavor coexist peacefully and with mutual benefit.

A Faculty Research Grant from the City University of New York helped me to complete this study. I also wish to thank Ruth G. Weintraub, formerly Dean of Social Sciences at Hunter College, C.U.N.Y., and Robert S. Hirschfield, Chairman of the Department of Political Science at Hunter, for their kindness in helping me to balance teaching duties and the responsibilities of research in a congenial way.

Over the past few years I have explored some of the issues examined in this book in a series of papers presented to professional meetings.* One of these papers, "Law as an Instrument of Revolutionary Change in a Traditional Milieu," appeared in *Law and Society Review* (II, 2, February 1968). The permission of the Law and Society Association to draw on portions of the article is gratefully acknowledged.

* These include "Law as an Instrument of Revolutionary Change in a Traditional Milieu," read at the Annual Meeting of the American Political Science Association and the Law and Society Association in Chicago, September 1967; "The Vulnerability of Islamic Society to Revolutionary Social Engineering: A Preliminary Balance Sheet," read at the Plenary Session of the Annual Meeting of the Middle East Studies Association in Austin, Texas, November 1968; "Family Law and Social Mobilization: A Comparative Analysis of Soviet Central Asia and Communist China," read at the Annual Meeting of the Association for Asian Studies in Boston, Mass., March 1969; and "Revolutionary Modernization and Stable Rule in a Multi-Ethnic System: Some Implications of Soviet Politics in Central Asia," presented to the Seminar on Soviet Nationality Problems at Columbia University, December 1969.

Acknowledgments

I have tapped the wisdom of many people in preparation of this book. A number of colleagues and friends at Princeton University read most or all of an early draft of the manuscript, and I gained much from their criticism and suggestions. Merely to mention their names—Eqbal Ahmad, Morroe Berger, Richard Falk, Ted Gurr, Manfred Halpern, Mancur Olson, and Stuart Schaar—is but a small token of my gratitude.

In exploring the larger issues on which this study impinges, I have profited greatly from ongoing discussions with Mohammed Guessous (formerly of Princeton University and now at the University of Rabat, Morocco) and Allen Kassof (member of the Department of Sociology at Princeton and Director, International Research and Exchanges Board). I was very fortunate in having them as friends and intellectual companions during the crucial stages of this work: one with a marvelous capacity for illuminating classical Islamic concepts and traditional life styles as well as a wide range of Western scientific ideas; the other with a special competence in relating Soviet social problems to broader issues of societal development and with an equally special gift for going directly to the heart of a particular matter.

Among the intellectual influences that strongly affected this study even before it took shape on paper are Alex Inkeles, Barrington Moore, and Richard Pipes. As my teachers in graduate school at Harvard, and later as colleagues at Harvard's Russian Research Center, they generously gave me the benefit of their specialized knowledge and rigorous scholarship. I owe them more than they probably realize.

A special debt of gratitude is owed to the late Merle Fainsod of Harvard and to Harry Eckstein of Princeton University whose intimate concern and kind advice were so important at each stage of this project, and to whom this book is dedicated. To Merle Fainsod I owe not only the inspiration for this study but also my original training in Soviet affairs. Harry Eckstein encouraged my interest in political sociology, provided a unique sounding-board for my arguments, and sustained my morale throughout. He also suggested the main title of this book. Both of these men helped to shape my intellectual experience to a far greater extent than can be documented here. Both drew upon an unending supply of patience and understanding to help me cope with perplexities and doubts. Both contributed much to whatever cogency this volume may have.

In the final stages of preparing this manuscript a number of persons have given me valuable assistance. My friends, Mrs. Joan

viii

Campbell Eckstein and Mrs. Jeannette Mirsky, both of Princeton, have kindly given much of their time to editing large portions of the manuscript. Mrs. Jane McDowall, Administrative Associate to the Director of the Center of International Studies, has never failed to supply help and advice beyond the scope of her official duties. My thanks are also due to Mrs. June Traube, Mrs. Maria Merrick, and Mrs. Joanne Weissman, who patiently typed several versions of this book. Mr. Steven Burg, Miss Nina Dinell, Mr. Richard Kagan, and Miss Oksana Kujbida—my students as well as graduate assistants at Hunter College, C.U.N.Y., at various times—cheerfully bore the burden of proofreading the manuscript and provided many useful comments. Miss Barbara Permut has been immensely helpful in expediting the manuscript through the successive stages of the printing process; she has invested painstaking care in correcting the galleys and page proofs and has also helped in resolving many of the attendant technical problems. Mrs. Clara B. Herzog has carried out the complex task of compiling a comprehensive index. Finally, but not least importantly, I wish to thank the library staffs of Harvard University, Columbia University, Princeton University, Hoover War Memorial Library at Stanford University, University of California at Berkeley, New York Public Library, the Library of Congress, and the British Museum for their courteous help.

The help of all these individuals and institutions has been very great. That of Sylvia Perera Massell has been at least equally indispensable and much more varied. Every page of this book bears the imprint of her keen questioning and patient prodding. She has helped in gathering and sifting masses of material. She has also helped me in dealing with the myriad of minor and major crises that inevitably plague the writing of a book. It is with the warmest thanks that I acknowledge her large share in the making of this book.

I know that I have not met many of the valid objections raised by colleagues and friends concerning many aspects of this study. All the more reason to make it quite clear here: while numerous individuals and institutions share responsibility for whatever virtues this book may possess, the responsibility for the actual contents, including opinions expressed as well as errors of fact or interpretation, is solely my own.

GREGORY J. MASSELL

Princeton, New Jersey
July 1972

ABBREVIATIONS

N. K. Krupskaia, *ORSZ*   *O Rabote Sredi Zhenshchin*
(sbornik statei) [*On Work Among Women* (collected articles)]

A. P. Kuchkin, *SKA*   *Sovetizatsiia Kazakhskogo Aula, 1926–1929 gg* [*The Sovietization of the Kazakh Village, 1926–1929*]

S. Liubimova, *VPG*   *V Pervye Gody* [*In the Initial Years*]

A. Nukhrat, *OZV*   *Oktiabr' i Zhenshchina Vostoka* [*October and the Woman of the East*]

A. Nukhrat, *VMV*   *Vosmoe Marta na Vostoke* [*The Eighth of March* (Woman's Day) *in the East*]

B. Pal'vanova, *DSV*   *Docheri Sovetskogo Vostoka* [*Daughters of the Soviet East*]

Kh.S. Sulaimanova, *ISGPU*   *Istoriia Sovetskogo Gosudarstva i Prava Uzbekistana* [*History of the Soviet State and Law in Uzbekistan*]

ZVR   *Zhenshchiny v Revoliutsii* (sbornik) [*Women in the Revolution* (collection of essays)]

CONTENTS

PART ONE

Revolution and Tradition: The Initial Confrontation

Contents

PART TWO

*Justification for Action: The Potential Use of
Women in Revolutionary Transformation*

Contents

xvi

INTRODUCTION

THE CONCERNS OF THIS BOOK

SOVIET politics and government have had, since the revolution's inception, an unparalleled fascination for Western students of politics. The Soviet political system has been perceived as novel (if not totally unprecedented), enigmatic (if not utterly beyond sure knowledge), and, depending on one's interests and values, supremely threatening or auspicious. The result has been an enormous literature, much of it of very high quality.

Yet there remain conspicuous lacunae, perhaps themselves resulting from the special allurements of the Soviet regime. For one thing, attention has been riveted upon the central loci of power, where, we think, great men have been working toward extravagant visions, sublime or evil, with extraordinary means. About the reaches of power to the peripheries of the vast Soviet land mass, to areas bound to be relatively inaccessible to central power for reasons of geography, technology, culture, and social structure, we know something, but much less than we should. Second, the largeness and explicitness of Soviet revolutionary aspirations—perhaps also the nature of readily available data—have led to an emphasis on ideology, overarching plans, programs, and party-lines. Again, about the grueling day-to-day business of putting visions to work, translating political programs into administrative activity, working in the villages and hamlets to integrate formed men and women into still unformed structures, we know something, but not enough —and much of what we know is only what has been most conspicuous: conflicts of wills and views, falls from grace, blood-letting, large administrative reorganizations. Moreover, the fascination of Soviet politics has led to a preoccupation with the Soviet Union *per se*, with who is who in its uncertain structure of power, and what is what in the kaleidoscope of Soviet ends and means. In the process, larger questions of social and political behavior, questions of comparative politics to which Soviet experience is highly relevant, have been, in the main, neglected,[1] to the joint detriment

[1] For one of the first comprehensive attempts to discuss this particular problem and some ways of dealing with it, see Frederic J. Fleron, Jr. (ed.),

of comparative politics and our understanding of the Soviet system. There are exceptions, of course, such as studies that relate Soviet experience to the larger phenomenon of totalitarianism or the Communist Party to the broader study of political parties, but these are noteworthy precisely because they are exceptional. Finally, political studies of the U.S.S.R. have focused, for the most part, on the institutional and behavioral patterns of the Soviet system as a distinct and integral entity, without differentiating significantly between its component (notably ethnocultural) parts. For example, revolutionary and developmental processes in Russia's Asian borderlands—which include one of the largest clusters of Islamic societies outside the Middle East—have received very little scholarly attention from students of Soviet affairs, and none at all from social scientists interested in problems of revolution, modernization, and directed social change.

This study may go a small way toward filling in these gaps. It is concerned with a problem central to comparative politics in a world of new nations pursuing unprecedented goals: how, and to what extent, political power may be deliberately used in the revolutionary transformation of societies, especially those we generally call "traditional" societies; conversely, how, and to what extent, traditional structures and life styles may serve as obstacles to engineered revolution. It pursues that concern through a study of the interaction between central power and local traditions in one of the peripheral areas of the Soviet land mass, Soviet Central Asia, an area about which reliable information is at present scant and data are quite difficult to gather. It examines the confrontation between highly developed, radical, determined, authoritarian communist forces and a cluster of traditional Moslem societies—hence between essentially modern political machines and traditional solidarities and identities based on kinship, custom, and religion. And it is most especially concerned with the meaning and impact of large, abstract political plans of great movements and figures when pursued by ordinary men and women in the small, concrete worlds of human relations in households, villages, and peer groups, on the manipulation of which the achievement of all revolutionary goals ultimately depends.

Thus, I am concerned here, in a special setting, with confronta-

---

Communist Studies and the Social Sciences: Essays on Methodology and Empirical Theory (Chicago, 1969).

tions that occur daily in innumerable settings in the present world: the confrontation of tradition and revolution, of vision and reality, of central plans and local mores, of impersonal social blueprints and intimate human relations.

The modernization process, even when relatively sedate, always contains elements of suspenseful confrontation. In few cases, however, has it been quite so dramatic as in the attempted modernization of Central Asia under Soviet auspices. One reason is that the drive toward modernization did not, by and large, come out of Central Asia itself, not primarily from a local elite or even a local counter-elite commanding the support of an "expectant people." The outside powers, moreover, had an exceptionally extravagant vision and explicit ideology, as well as remarkable revolutionary élan and impatience. *Per contra*, the societies to be transformed were at an especially low level of social and economic development, as different from that postulated by the Marxist theory of revolution as they could possibly have been; they were also, relatively speaking, highly intact and integrated, that is, lacking in relatively large, significant, and politically experienced groups that were both alienated and marginal. The drama of modernization in Soviet Central Asia thus arose from a huge gap between the social structures existing and those envisioned; from the lack of significantly disintegrated structures ready-made for refashioning; and from great verve and urgency on one side and a deep imperviousness to manipulation on the other.

This drama involved only partially, however, the confrontation of traditional society and revolutionary men. Equally dramatic were the conflicts engendered by that confrontation among the revolutionaries themselves, men and women whose ideology—originated, developed, and intended for application in Western industrialized societies—had not really prepared them for dealing with what existed in Central Asia. Their experiences there, even more than elsewhere in the Soviet Union, compelled them to rethink many problems and to reconstitute many organizations and instrumentalities, but since they were men of firm—and rapidly rigidifying—philosophy, and since there were vested interests in the organizations, this process did not come about without grave internal strains. In short, the choice of means and ends in Central Asia, even more so than in Russia proper, was never completely open-ended and arbitrary. Far from being able to act and to elicit desirable behavior at will, the Soviet regime found itself embroiled in a virtually continuous redefinition of required action, a redefinition in which the perceptions of upper echelons and field-workers interacted. Constantly tempted to ordain, the regime found itself, instead, needing to experiment, and that with a number of quite unorthodox propositions and techniques. Thus, Marxist-Leninist ideology, the Central Asian experience, and experiences elsewhere in the U.S.S.R. interplayed in a continuous process of impact and feedback that is marvelously intricate and exceedingly difficult to unravel.

Because of the huge intricacy of that process, this study is not intended to provide an exhaustive enumeration of all of its facets. Its purpose is to isolate and examine one sector of a revolutionary drive under authoritarian auspices. Broadly speaking, it concerns Soviet attempts to create reliable access-routes to Central Asia's societies, to subvert established native solidarities, and, simultaneously, to lay the groundwork for an efficient mobilization system. As we shall see, in its search for optimal means to induce and manage such a revolution, the Communist Party came to experiment with a number of approaches. One such approach—constituting action "from above," as visualized by communist organizers—involved the use of the regime's coercive power to excise the most openly obstructive elements (especially the local traditional elites), with the expectation that this would force the general population very quickly into compliance with revolutionary ways. Another approach—action "in depth," as Soviet activists referred to it—evolved after the former had largely failed to bring about desirable results and comprised a search for a weak link in society, for crucial actors whose deliberately engineered alienation could drain traditional institutions of vitality.

Who these actors might be, and how they might be effectively used, will differ among societies. My thesis here is that Soviet authorities, after much groping and many false starts, were led to an approach that was dramatically unorthodox. This approach was based on twin assumptions: that the key to undermining the traditional social order was in the destruction of traditional family structures, and that the breakdown of the kinship system itself could most speedily be achieved through the mobilization of its women. This approach explicitly stipulated that, regardless of any other aspects of social status, women could be assumed to be, in Moslem traditional societies, "the lowest of the low"—as a rule segregated, exploited, degraded, and constrained. It may be said, then, that

Moslem women came to constitute, in Soviet political imagination, a structural weakpoint in the traditional order: a potentially deviant and hence subversive stratum susceptible to militant appeal—in effect, a *surrogate proletariat* where no proletariat in the real Marxist sense existed. Through that weakpoint, it was thought, particularly intense conflicts could be engendered in society and leverage provided for its disintegration and subsequent reconstitution.

To be sure, the Soviet regime did not stake all on the use of women as agents of revolutionary transformation, but that use was essential to all facets of their approach and thus may be singled out, as it is here, for special emphasis. In other words, while the overall Soviet assault on the region's societies proceeded on many levels (and with widely varying degrees of success), we shall focus here on one essential facet of that assault: the deliberate attempt to stimulate and exploit in Moslem traditional societies sexual and generational tensions designed to induce an upheaval in a traditional system of values, customs, relationships, and roles, beginning with the primary cell of that system, the extended patriarchal family. By the same token, we shall focus largely on a single dimension of this process of radical social change: the development of female roles in revolutionary modernization.

We are concerned here, then, with a chapter in Soviet history that not only lays bare the evolution of Soviet activities in Central Asia, but also reflects the Soviet response to problems of making a revolution after the "successful" revolutionary act *per se*, that sheds light on the main paths revolutionaries may take anywhere when they try to consolidate their power and to realize their purposes, and that tells us something about the strengths and limitations of these alternative paths in general and in particular cases.

Soviet experience suggests three paths to making a revolution beyond the mere winning of political incumbency. These are "revolutionary legalism," "administrative assault," and "systematic social engineering." The evolution of Soviet policy in Central Asia may be said to have involved a progression from the first, to the second, to the third. It is true that there was much overlapping among these approaches, making neat compartmentalization by analytic constructs difficult. Moreover, the approaches themselves reflected changes in emphasis, even conflicting desires, in Soviet ranks, rather than abrupt shifts in orientation. But the overall pattern of Soviet actions is sufficiently clear to permit us to discern a learning process on the part of revolutionary elites, with each approach a learning experience in itself, showing the feedback mechanisms operative in this process. Commensurately, the use made of Moslem women affords an understanding, on a special dimension, of the trial-and-error progression from one revolutionary approach to another.

The study of Soviet experience from this perspective makes it possible to view revolution and modernization as consciously managed processes, as processes of deliberate social engineering. It provides an opportunity to analyze "revolutionary" strategies less as attempts by insurgents to topple a particular regime than as maneuvers by incumbents to install a new order, to transform society quickly and fundamentally—which is, in a sense, the essence of making "revolution," not just rebellion. If revolution only commences with the seizure of incumbent power, then a problem arises in all revolutionary processes which the Soviet authorities had to learn about slowly and painfully: how incumbents may themselves carry out insurgency, at least of a kind. In being both generated and controlled by the incumbents, any revolutionary action-scheme had to be governed by both the requirements of social revolution and the imperatives of incumbency itself; it had to induce a psychological and organizational revolution at the nerve-centers of a social order, as well as consolidate and legitimize the incumbent's power.

Borrowing from the relevant Soviet terminology of the period, we may understand such an attempt as part and parcel of a very much larger problem: How can the transitional march be forced from a "feudal-patriarchal mode of life" directly to "socialism"—thus "bypassing the agonies of the capitalist stage of development"—without, at the same time, endangering the mainstays of Soviet power? Or, to what extent can a social revolution be promoted by an incumbent without substituting, in the process, one "system of antagonistic contradictions" for another, and without exposing the incumbent to the corrosive influences of such a system? How can authority successfully legitimate itself, and carry on its routine business, while it is destroying and transforming the social bases on which legitimacy must rest?

THE STRUCTURE OF THIS STUDY

This study deals with the period of Soviet rule in Central Asia when these issues were most explosive (circa 1919-29), and when the regime was increasingly tempted to induce social transformation directly, suddenly, massively, and violently. Accordingly, I have attempted to structure the account of this period in a way that would reflect as closely as possible the changes in Soviet premises and actions as well as the shifts in local orientations and reactions. I have also avoided pure chronology, but tried to relate description, analysis, and conceptualization in a manner that would permit readers to keep in focus the basic *issues* at stake as well as the nuances of my arguments about them. The subject is, of course, historical. But since I attempt to present a discussion of abstract issues, straightforward narration has been modified by categorization that reveals the seams in the apparently seamless garment of the history of the period.

The study consists of four distinct parts each of which is built around a particular set of issues.

Part One is designed to provide background and stage-setting material. Much of the descriptive material assembled there will be familiar to the specialist in this field. But the organization of the material is especially designed to emphasize facets of Central Asian societies that are important for the study as a whole. Broadly speaking, Part One presents a synthesis and general interpretation of Central Asian history in a way that should permit us to relate the primordial political metabolism of local societies to their basic vulnerabilities and strengths. Specifically, Chapter One, while including a (necessarily brief) overview of the Central Asian setting, is intended to go beyond it in a special way. It seeks to isolate the distinctive properties of local traditional solidarities and evolutionary trends that made the native milieu vulnerable to outside intervention and conquest. Chapter Two discusses Soviet attempts to deal with a closely related issue: the relevance of power to intervene for the ability to transform. It examines the characteristic problems of social access and influence encountered by the Soviet regime in Central Asia, problems due largely to a salient (and unexpected) feature of local social units: the coincidence of marked susceptibility to outside conquest and tenacious resistance to direct political manipulation. In this context, the chapter reconstructs and evaluates the Soviet search for strategic factors in revolutionary transformation, factors that might provide social engineers with especially high leverage in undermining and radically changing a Moslem traditional milieu. In effect, then, this chapter seeks to determine the main stimuli impelling communist elites to turn to

Moslem women as potentially important allies in the revolutionary process.

Part Two, including Chapters Three and Four, carries this analysis further by examining in detail Soviet perceptions of female inferiority and of the revolutionary potential of women in a traditional Moslem social order. This part focuses on the spectrum of Soviet expectations[2] regarding actual operational imperatives and opportunities. It is thus intended to pinpoint quite specifically the premises underlying the Soviet action-scheme, premises that relate immediate means to ultimate ends and that constitute, in effect, a network of justifications for broad-scale action.[3]

The chapters (Five and Six) comprising Part Three provide an account of specific Soviet actions based on initial expectations. These actions ("revolutionary legalism" and "administrative assault") are considered in the context of the regime's experimentation with alternative strategies of engineered revolution. In each case, the determinants and objectives as well as the patterns of particular initiatives are reviewed, with the aim of providing a basis for evaluating the regime's subsequent attitudes and conduct.

The fourth, and last, part is also the largest one. It deals with the broad variety of responses and outcomes related to early Soviet actions. Chapters Seven and Eight, in particular, attempt to reconstruct and analyze the patterns of popular response and institutional performance in the course of an induced revolutionary upheaval. Thus, they are built around a set of questions that are crucial in this context: how resistant is the Moslem orthodox milieu, as a specific type of traditional society, and how vulnerable and adaptive is it in the face of a determined modernizing force that seeks to shatter

---

[2] As I shall make clear in the text, in referring to Soviet expectations I do not mean to imply the existence of a hard set of values and judgments that materialized spontaneously, simultaneously, and overnight, and that invariably commanded the adherence of every member of the Soviet apparatus.

[3] In dwelling at length here (as well as elsewhere in this study) on what might seem like minute particulars of Soviet reasoning, I have acted on an assumption which I share with Cicourel: building a base for comparative analysis across societies and cultures (which this study seeks to do) requires, among other things, "the study of practical reasoning and decision-making so that the particulars of action scenes in their course and ecological settings can be articulated with the general language categories, and policies or rules invoked for comparable or contrastive purposes." See A. V. Cicourel, "Kinship, Marriage, and Divorce in Comparative Family Law," *Law and Society Review* (June, 1967), esp. p. 111.

and transform the existing life style, and to challenge fundamentally the primordial *status quo*? Which of the traditional relationships and values in such a milieu are most and least sensitive to deliberate political manipulation, and why? What are the benefits and costs of such manipulation, from the sponsor's point of view, especially when it aims to alter drastically the relationships between the sexes?

Needless to say, in seeking answers to these questions there is the danger of imposing an overly rigid framework on available material. But we are dealing here with a mass of scattered human responses to particular experiences. Political generalizations about these responses, framed in particular categories, are warranted as long as it is remembered that we arrive at such generalizations, in effect, by aggregating diverse individual perceptions and actions into collectivized patterns.

Chapter Nine examines the Communist Party's perceptions of the consequences of (and problems engendered by) its own moves, and traces the roots of its wide-ranging reassessment of the needs, capabilities, and constraints governing its actions in a revolutionary situation. It also examines the pattern of official retrenchment emerging from the process of reassessment and leading to a new mode of revolutionary commitment: "systematic social engineering." Finally, Chapter Ten reviews and ties together the basic issues of this study. It evaluates the implications and limits of the revolutionary strategies we have discussed, and it does this from two perspectives: in the light of Soviet experience in Central Asia and in the light of some relevant insights available in the context of contemporary social science.

SOME LIMITATIONS OF THIS STUDY: PROBLEMS OF DATA AND INTERPRETATION

With the exception of Part One, the bulk of this study is based on materials, including primary sources, most of which have never been used by the scholarly community. Moreover, the analytical approaches employed and the interpretations offered here depart in some ways from established lines of inquiry into Soviet and Central Asian revolutionary politics. To that extent they are likely to be unfamiliar to specialists and generalists alike. While this unfamiliarity accounts, in part, for what might seem an inordinate stress on descriptive and evaluative detail, that stress should itself be helpful in orienting the reader in largely uncharted terrain.

The empirical research for this study is based primarily on official publications (including periodicals and daily press), of the Soviet government and the Communist Party, on proposals, appraisals, and debates evolving in the ranks of communist activists and field-organizers (especially as recorded in *Kommunistka*, organ of the Zhenotdel, the party's Department for Work among Women), on data supplied by Soviet historians, ethnographers, sociologists, and lawyers, and on available eyewitness reports.

This book is, for the most part, a case-study in micropolitics and political sociology. With its emphasis on the systematic analysis of the strategies and process of engineered revolution at the grassroots of society, it is designed to go beyond the general, though extremely valuable, historical overviews of the establishment of Soviet rule in the region, and studies of Central Asia's administrative network, intellectual history, and economic growth, available in the works of Allworth, Bennigsen and Lemercier-Quelquejay, Caroe, Conolly, Hayit, Nove and Newth, Park, Pipes, Rakowska-Harmstone, Rywkin, Wheeler, Wilber, Winner, and Zenkovsky. By the same token, the developmental and processual perspective of this inquiry makes relevant the findings of a handful of American anthropologists who have contributed to the study of the Central Asian milieu, especially Elizabeth Bacon, Stephen and Ethel Dunn, and Lawrence Krader.[4]

The fact that this is a study in micropolitics involves both advantages and disadvantages. The main advantage is obvious. A microsocietal study that focuses narrowly on particular instruments and targets of political action, and that probes the socio-cultural bases of political behavior at the subnational level—in particular local areas, social strata, and small groups—permits us to analyze social and political processes in depth.

But such an analysis also imposes special responsibilities and raises special problems. For one thing, it increases the risks of analytical discontinuity between peripheral and central loci of ac-

[4] For a full citation of these works, see Note 1, Chapter One. See also Serge A. Zenkovsky, "American Research on Russia's Moslems," *The Russian Review* (July, 1959), pp. 199-217. Of all of the cited works, that of Alexander Park probably comes closest to approaching the Central Asian milieu in a way I have myself chosen. But Park's study terminates in 1927, and it barely mentions the issues I regard as crucially important and examine in this book, issues concerning the costs and benefits of particular revolutionary strategies, especially those involving the development of female roles in revolutionary modernization.

xxviii

tion, between particular and general concerns, between special and overarching issues. In short—to reiterate a truism—it is all too easy, when studying a narrowly defined problem in great detail, to lose sight of the larger picture. Indeed, I deliberately skirted many topics and avoided confronting a good number of legitimate issues —for example, those concerning the possible connections between revolutionary processes in the Central Asian and Russian (i.e., European) milieus.[5] But proceeding in this fashion seemed to me a reasonable way of avoiding what might be an even more perplex-

---

[5] One such issue—obviously very important in itself—concerns the relationship between female mobilization (and the attack on the family) in Central Asia and the emancipation of women (combined with the downgrading of the role of the family) in the Soviet Union as a whole. It may be argued that the former was merely a local reflection on the latter, thus raising important questions about the uniqueness and significance of the Central Asian experience. While I chose not to deal with this issue here, it merits a few words of clarification at this point. As I have argued elsewhere in this study (see the initial section of Chapter Five), early Soviet policies concerning the family were designed largely within and for European Russia, where they were intended to legitimize a revolution in the relations between the sexes that was already well under way. In Central Asia, Soviet policies were designed, first and foremost, to induce such a revolution. In Russia the relevant policies were initiated immediately after the October Revolution, and were not terminated (in their special form) until the mid-1930's. In Central Asia, the policies discussed here were initiated much later (in mid-1920's) and were by and large terminated—and for very different reasons—by 1929. These variations alone make it very clear that we can distinguish between the functions of the Russian and Central Asian policy-models. In Central Asia, the Soviet action-scheme in this realm came to be far more specialized than in Russia, far broader in scope, far more self-conscious and autonomous. Indeed, it is fair to say that in Russia, female emancipation was a secondary issue, a by-product of broader revolutionary concerns. In Central Asia, it was, for a time, a primary issue *par excellence*, a lever for social destruction and reconstruction, an important catalyst for generating the revolutionary process itself. In this sense, we can indeed consider the Central Asian case as *sui generis*, making a systematic correlation of central and local policies not absolutely necessary in this context. For some excellent studies of overall Soviet family policy, including women (albeit primarily women in European Russia) see M. G. Field and D. E. Anderson, "The Family and Social Problems," in A. Kassof, ed., *Prospects for Soviet Society* (New York, 1968), pp. 386-417; M. G. Field, "Workers (and Mothers): Soviet Women Today," in D. R. Brown, ed., *Women in the Soviet Union* (New York, 1968), pp. 7-56; H. K. Geiger, *The Family in Soviet Russia* (Cambridge, Mass., 1968); and P. H. Juviler, "Family Reform on the Road to Communism," in P. H. Juviler and H. W. Morton, *Soviet Policy-Making* (New York, 1967), pp. 29-60.

ing alternative: entanglement in a larger context that would carry the argument too far afield and thus distend or distort the case-study as a whole.

However, yet another built-in problem was not equally susceptible to reasonable solution. Microsocietal studies generally require intimate proximity between analyst and milieu—not only the perusal of available documents but also, as much as possible, personal observation, interviews, and fieldwork. Needless to say, this kind of research has so far been out of the question in the U.S.S.R., especially, perhaps, in Soviet Central Asia, a region about which Moscow has been particularly sensitive as an area abutting the Middle East, China, and the Indian subcontinent, and containing what are probably the Soviet Union's least assimilated societies and cultures.

Accordingly, throughout this study it has been necessary to rely primarily on published Soviet materials. The informed reader need not be told in great detail about the attendant problems, and about the general difficulty of studying a relatively closed society. Suffice it to say that the scarcity, fragmentariness, qualitative unevenness, politically motivated tendentiousness and selectivity, and hence frequent unreliability of available data—especially the kind of data a political sociologist needs most—have imposed severe limitations on the scope and intensity of our analysis (as will be noted in the appropriate places, as a rule in footnotes,[6] throughout). It has been necessary to sift a vast amount of literature for what were often merely bits and pieces of meaningful information, while trying to avoid distortions for the sake of particular interpretations. All too often, personal judgments had to be made about the extent to which such information could be relied upon as accurate, or at least as intrinsically suggestive and significant. Indeed, putting together the available material had all the allure and difficulty of assembling a puzzle when one knows that many of the key pieces are missing.

One example may suffice to illustrate this problem. In discussing the commitments and actions of Soviet revolutionary elites—or simply elites serving the Soviet regime—it would have been very

---

[6] A word about my use of footnotes. They may seem unusually voluminous. This is due, in part, to the nature of the data: very often, only the juxtaposition of several documentary sources permits us to corroborate and clarify a particular point. But there is yet another reason. In order not to overburden the text with caveats and explanations I have relegated many of these to the notes. Thus, the footnotes contain a number of important qualifications that form a part of the argument as a whole, and should be consulted with this in mind.

valuable to determine the relationship between particular political initiatives and pressures and particular groups and views. Yet this task, so patently important to a balanced critical analysis, is often beyond our present capacity to undertake. We know, of course, that even case-studies of pressure-group politics in democratic systems (hence in relatively open societies) are frequently (and necessarily) restricted to sources that present the "official view" of a process, offering primarily the "visible" aspects of pressure machinery in action.[7] In the context of an incipient totalitarian system the problem is qualitatively and not just quantitatively different. Perhaps more in Central Asia than in other regions under Soviet rule, it is extremely difficult, and sometimes altogether impossible, to link particular attitudes and strategies of action with particular individuals, or with specific functional or factional groups. In the course of Stalin's victorious drive for power in the 1920's it becomes increasingly difficult to disentangle personal and official views, to know for sure just who speaks for what and for whom. This is not merely a matter of official secrecy—a "normal" condition, under the circumstances. Nor is it merely a problem of someone's voluntary or coerced (though unrecorded) change of mind in the heat of revolutionary confrontation. In Central Asia, the difficulties of such analysis and attribution become inordinately magnified by what is ordinarily a mundane problem: the problem of the political actor's *identity*.

Here, not only institutional affiliation and position in the hierarchy but also, often quite literally, the simplest details of personal background and attitude are quite obscure or altogether missing. One of the reasons for this surely has to do with the nature of the cadres' assignment. We know that, in Central Asia, the growing (and unforeseen) concern with Moslem women as potentially important revolutionary catalysts brought forth—from Russia as well as Central Asia—relatively or completely unknown revolutionary cadres. Moreover, the nature of their task—calling for practical political fieldwork, as close to the village-level and local grass-roots as possible, and commensurately far from the hubs of power and communication—tended to cast an especially long shadow of anonymity on those active in this network. Also, as it happens, many of these specialists and activists in the field were swept away by the purges, quickly and completely, sometimes almost as soon as they

[7] See, e.g., Harry Eckstein, *Pressure Group Politics* (Stanford, 1960), p. 113 ff.

assumed an important role in a given locale. Consequently there was hardly time for them to convey, in a way detectable now, the nature of their political convictions and personalities, before vanishing from the scene.

There is yet another reason for the problem at hand, perhaps transcending the others in importance. Native Central Asian cadres, including the highest party and government officials, no matter how long they managed to survive in the apparatus, were clearly secondary rather than primary political actors. Without a doubt, they were cast in this role by Moscow from the very beginning. They were neither trusted nor respected as leaders by the largely Slavic core of the communist apparatus. At times, the distrust barely concealed the ruling stratum's indifference or contempt. Hence, in Central Asia the issue of the cadres' ethnicity and culture tended to complicate immensely the issues of power and transformation. One of the manifestations of this state of affairs may be found in the inordinate circumspection and caution with which all but a few of the region's cadres spoke about their tasks, especially in public. It is also safe to assume that the cadres' cultural heritage itself reinforced the effect of these manifestations. Men and women steeped in the values of a Turko-Islamic civilization and in the norms of tribal and communal solidarities, and accustomed to informal networks of authority and communication, were bound to tread with special care in the unfamiliar, precarious world of revolutionary politics. They did so all the more because that world was dominated by the formal machinery of a powerful state that was itself controlled by aliens. Thus, the requisites of toeing the line in a distinctly subordinate role, and the responsibilities of balancing personal, communal, and family interests and the demands of a state machine, placed a special premium on political discretion, obliqueness, and dissimulation. Indeed, the art of survival itself came more than ever to denote here—and perhaps more than elsewhere in Russia—the capacity to shield a private world with an elaborate and elastic public face.

As a result, we know very little indeed about the Central Asian cadres, the men and women who were heavily involved in the events dealt with in this study, and who are frequently mentioned here. We do know some things: for example, that many of the initial field-organizers were dispatched from European Russia, and were single young women in their early twenties, for the most part of Russian, Jewish, or Armenian background. We know that most of them joined the Communist Party immediately before the Bolshevik Revolution or during the Civil War. We know that some of them were commandeered by the party's Zhenotdel (Department for Work among Women) directly from service as the Red Army's first female political commissars on the Central Asian front, while others were transferred from revolutionary assignments in Russian and Siberian factories and towns. We know that these young communists were charged with the task of making the first contacts with Moslem women, and recruiting among them the most likely collaborators. However, only in a handful of cases do we know anything at all about the first generation of native Central Asian female cadres emerging under the tutelage of the new arrivals, except that they tended to be orphans, runaway child-brides, young widows, or divorcées.[8]

For that matter, we know next to nothing about the motivations, propensities, and commitments even of men like Khodzhaev, Ikramov, and Aitakov, to mention but three of the highest native functionaries in the Soviet political apparatus. In many cases, their leadership in Central Asian republics (as prime ministers, presidents, or ranking party secretaries) spanned almost two decades of unprecedented change, from the Bolshevik Revolution to the Great Purges of the 1930's. Yet when they, and many like them, come to face the firing squad at the end of an era, having been accused of fantastic crimes, it is essentially faceless men who go into a pigeonhole of history, often without leaving so much as a trace behind them.[9] We know that they stood at critical junctions in the management of revolution, including the attempted strategic use of Moslem women. But, in all too many cases, we know best what tends to matter least: that they were recruited by the Communist Party at one or another time; that they were assigned to a number of successive posts; that, in the exercise of their official duties, they worded their speeches carefully, adapted themselves to the party

---

[8] There were good reasons for this. I discuss them in detail elsewhere in this study, especially in Chapters Three and Four.

[9] Most of them were executed after public or secret trials in the 1930's on what later proved to be fabricated charges ranging from wrecking and subversion to espionage and treason. Most of them were posthumously rehabilitated by the state in the 1950's, after Khrushchev's secret speech to the Twentieth Party Congress about the crimes of the Stalin era.

line adroitly, and accepted Moscow's orders without audible murmur.

To all intents and purposes, then, they were largely anonymous agents of power and change, filling temporarily some slots on the assembly line of a great social upheaval. They were used by a force much greater than themselves. This force they evidently failed to understand in time, and it unceremoniously discarded them when their usefulness was judged to be over. Beyond this, we cannot be sure of the role they played. Paradoxically, we cannot even be sure of the substance of what was seemingly the most dramatic issue of their political lives, and purportedly their cardinal sin from the Soviet point of view: their *nationalism*. For the most part, we must make the best of Stalin's and Vyshinsky's testimonials to this effect, though the record of the Soviet regime has taught us to be wary of such "evidence."

To the extent that I have tried to give an aura of "real life" to what were inherently complex and obscure events I have thus had to take calculated risks. Where the gaps in documentation were especially great, they had to be filled in with what one hopes is reasoned conjecture. It is fair to say, then, that this account is based as much on a reconstruction of what actually happened as on independently verifiable facts, as much on inference as on evidence.[10] By the same token, the marshaling of available data is intended to exemplify the texture of realities rather than conclusively "prove" our case, to illustrate but not yet validate the argument.

Having said this, there is no need for me to belabor this point: this is not, and cannot yet be, a definitive study. Nor is it intended to tell the whole story; the issues with which it deals constitute only a small part of the highly complex unfolding of a revolutionary process. The answers it formulates—even the questions it poses— are segmental, tentative, and partial. The analytical and explanatory scheme it develops rests on judgments that are critical and qualitative rather than quantitative.[11] And the period covered by

[10] My point is that the reconstructions can be made within acceptable limits of fancy, or anyway unavoidable ones. Historical study always requires them in some degree. In this case, the degree is rather large, but not so large as in much historical work, e.g., archaeology.

[11] It should be made very clear at the outset: there is as yet no way to determine the actual distribution of feelings and views among individuals and groups in Soviet Central Asia, and no way to ascertain the scope and intensity of popular and institutional actions. Notes by Zinger, a party analyst, in *Revoliutsiia i Natsional'nosti* [*Revolution and the Nationalities*] (6, 1937,

this study is relatively short, inasmuch as the dimensions of my analysis are made to conform to a specific, discernible cycle of political actions and outcomes in a particular case.

Thus, this inquiry does not pretend to go beyond the confines of

---

esp. pp. 101-102) may serve as an illustration of the difficulties in this matter. Zinger's comments on two Soviet statistical studies published in the mid-1930's (concerning women and youth in the U.S.S.R.) contain barely veiled allusions to the obliteration in public documents of all significant indications of attitudes and behavior. As the comments make clear, even those figures that were made public failed by and large to differentiate among specific nationalities. This meant that there were hardly any meaningful references, not only to the extent of popular adherence to religion and custom, but even to the representation of ethnic minorities in the occupational and educational framework.

A less direct but in some ways more telling argument may be found in an article by Vasilieva in *Sovetskaia Etnografiia* [*Soviet Ethnography*] (3, 1953, pp. 221-25), published at the end of the Stalin era. While making no direct references to the lack of quantitative studies of change in Soviet Central Asia, Vasilieva paints a grim picture of the state of Soviet ethnography of the region. As she puts it, so-called "field studies" limited themselves to "the description of the new socialist way of life" in the Central Asian village, i.e., to the description of houses, rugs, and shoes, and the counting of bicycles and samovars in native households. Such studies produced descriptions "which, with the exception of a very few lines, could be applied to just about any nationality in any of the Soviet republics."

While we are well aware of the reasons for this state of affairs, one recent note by M. N. Pak, a Soviet historian, places the matter in especially sharp focus. In 1965, Pak published a detailed review of the state of oriental studies in the U.S.S.R. While his comments formally concerned Soviet research on Asia and Africa, they may be taken as an indication of the problems affecting all Soviet scholarly work, beginning with studies of "Eastern" peoples in general, and including Russia's Asian minorities in particular. Pak's argument may be summarized as follows: The cult of personality under Stalin was responsible not only for undermining socialist legality in the U.S.S.R., but also for the closure of the more important orientalist institutes, and the physical annihilation of the Soviet Union's greatest orientalists. Moreover, the corollaries of this cult—"subjectivism," "dogmatism," "intellectual monopoly" in all fields—put an end to all theory-oriented initiatives in the social sciences. Most important of all, the grave repressions of the Stalin era led to a "peculiar psychological trauma" among Soviet social scientists, crushing their capacity for courageous intellectual self-assertion, and making them shun serious and controversial issues, avoid genuine scientific generalizations, and stick to "conventional thought following ready-made outlines and clichés." (See M. N. Pak, *Sovetskoe Vostokovedenie* [*Soviet Oriental Studies*], Moscow, 1965, esp. pp. 5-7.)

a historically and analytically delimited case-study.[12] As such, it does not, as a rule, attempt to look beyond Soviet Central Asia, in that it does not relate the experience of this milieu to comparable experiences in other regions of the Soviet Union and in other traditional societies—for example, those of the Middle East. Although such a comparison should be enormously instructive, the self-imposed limits of this case-study, the great diversity of cultural patterns and historical circumstances that would need to be taken into account, as well as the scarcity of hard data and of clearly applicable general theoretical constructs preclude, at this time, the kind of rigorous inquiry that systematic comparison implies.

Given such built-in limitations, the relevance of this study for broad comparative analysis and theory is intended, for the most part, to be implicit rather than explicit. Its purpose is to help in building an empirical and conceptual base for theoretical propositions rather than to produce readily testable generalizations. Thus, its findings—in the facts they present, in the questions they raise, and in the conclusions they offer—are presented primarily as a sensitizing tool, and are but a small step in the requisite direction. But, as such, they may serve to facilitate a task that is as important as it is new to the agenda of the social sciences: the evaluation of the implications of Soviet experience for the larger universe of revolutionary politics and processes, and for theories pertaining to that universe.

[12] For a helpful typology, and a splendid treatment of the limits and potentialities of case-studies vis-à-vis comparative studies in political inquiry, see Harry Eckstein, *Case-Study and Theory in Macropolitics*, mimeo, Center of International Studies, Princeton University, 1972, and Sidney Verba, "Some Dilemmas in Comparative Research," *World Politics*, xx (October, 1967), pp. 111-27. Using Eckstein's and Verba's definitions as a guide, it is probably fair to say that, while my inquiry is intended to go beyond a purely idiosyncratic case-study, it necessarily falls short of a disciplined configurative study. For, on the one hand, its analytical framework is made reasonably explicit, its facts (scarce and fragmentary as they are) are systematically presented, and its interpretations, while to some extent necessarily intuitive, are considered, whenever possible, in the context of broader theoretical concerns. On the other hand, the inadequacy of available data, the tentativeness of conclusions based on qualitative rather than quantitative judgments, as well as the scarcity of general theoretical constructs relevant in this case, preclude, at this time, the kind of rigorous consideration of the broad theoretical utility of our findings that a proper disciplined configurative study implies. In some respects, this inquiry comes closest to what Eckstein has termed a heuristic case-study, though the limitations cited above would apply here as well, making it less than "pure" as a case in point.

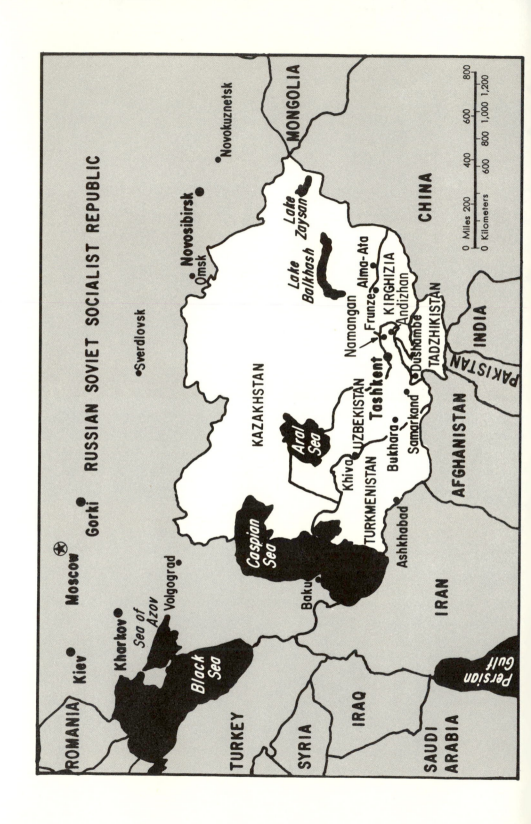

PART ONE

Revolution and Tradition:
The Initial Confrontation

ONE · *Imposing a Structure of Power in Central Asia: The Determinants of Soviet Success*[1]

The Setting: An Overview

Soviet Central Asia encompasses a vast area at the heart of the Eurasian continent, an area (about 1.5 million square miles) that is almost half the size of the United States. It is delimited by European Russia and Siberia in the north; it stretches southward to the Himalayas and the Pamir, where it borders on Iran and Afghanistan; and it is flanked by the Caspian Sea in the west and by Chinese Sinkiang in the east.

Its terrain and climate are varied and, in large part, forbidding. From north to south, arid or grassy steppes are followed by great expanses of desert-country, and then by high plateaus and mountain ranges, the deserts and plateaus studded with relatively few and far-flung oases and fertile valleys coterminous with rivers and

---

[1] The substantive materials presented in this chapter are, for the most part, available elsewhere (see this footnote, *infra*). Therefore, rather than covering again reasonably familiar ground, I have attempted to develop here a general interpretation of these materials, in a way that would be of help to the reader in following critically the major issues of the study as a whole. Moreover, in its emphasis on what seem to me some of the crucial dimensions in Central Asia's history and politics, this chapter focuses on a single problem: what accounts for the vulnerability of the region's societies to outside intervention and conquest?

By and large, I have not taken for granted in this chapter any previous acquaintance with the literature on the area. At the same time, though, I have restricted myself only to indispensable details of the region's physical and socio-cultural milieu and political evolution. Thus, the analysis that follows is necessarily concise and simplified.

For some recent general studies by Western scholars, dealing at least in part with Soviet Central Asia, see E. Allworth (ed.), *Central Asia: A Century of Russian Rule* (New York, 1967); S. Becker, *Russia's Protectorates in Central Asia: Bukhara and Khiva, 1865-1924* (Cambridge, Mass., 1968); A. Bennigsen and C. Lemercier-Quelquejay, *Islam in the Soviet Union* (New York, 1967); O. Caroe, *Soviet Empire: The Turks of Central Asia and Stalinism* (rev. ed., New York, 1967); H. Carrère D'Encausse, *Réforme et Révolution chez les Musulmans de l'Empire Russe* (Paris, 1966); V.

3

irrigation canals. Two great rivers, Amu-Daria and Syr-Daria, with a few tributaries between them, form the main water system of the region, flowing in the general northwesterly direction to the Aral Sea.

In so vast an area, only about ten million people lived in 1897, fourteen million in 1926, not fully seventeen million in 1939, about twenty-five million in 1959, and about thirty-three million in 1970. At the same time, the region's extraction potential in oil, coal, iron, and a host of non-ferrous metals was discovered to be enormous, and certainly large enough to rival such great Soviet extraction basins as Baku, Donets, Kuznetsk, and Bashkiria. This makes the region's mining potential, in absolute terms, among the highest in the Soviet Union, and, per capita, among the highest in the world. In addition to becoming one of the Union's chief suppliers of industrial raw materials, Central Asia has also come to serve as one of the U.S.S.R.'s prime food- and fiber-baskets, with contributions

---

Conolly, *Beyond the Urals: Economic Developments in Soviet Asia* (London, 1967); B. Hayit, *Turkestan im XX Jahrhundert* (Darmstadt, 1956); A. Nove and J. A. Newth, *The Soviet Middle East: A Communist Model for Development* (New York, 1967); R. A. Pierce, *Russian Central Asia, 1867-1917* (Berkeley, 1960); R. Pipes, *The Formation of the Soviet Union: Communism and Nationalism, 1917-1923* (rev. ed., Cambridge, Mass., 1964); T. Rakowska-Harmstone, *Russia and Nationalism in Central Asia: The Case of Tadzhikistan* (Baltimore, 1970); M. Rywkin, *Russia in Central Asia* (New York, 1963); G. Wheeler, *The Modern History of Soviet Central Asia* (London, 1964); C. K. Wilber, *The Soviet Model and Underdeveloped Countries* (Chapel Hill, 1969); S. Zenkovsky, *Pan-Turkism and Islam in Russia* (Cambridge, Mass., 1960).

The most thorough historical account of developments in Central Asia in the period on which this study concentrates (1920's) may be found in A. G. Park, *Bolshevism in Turkestan, 1917-1927* (New York, 1957).

Extensive ethnographic material on the area may be found in E. Allworth, *Uzbek Literary Politics* (The Hague, 1964); E. E. Bacon, *Central Asians under Russian Rule: A Study in Culture Change* (Ithaca, N.Y., 1966); V. V. Bartol'd, *Istoriia Kul'turnoi Zhizni Turkestana* (Leningrad, 1927); M. A. Czaplicka, *The Turks of Central Asia in History and at the Present Day* (London, 1918); A. E. Hudson, *Kazakh Social Structure* (New Haven, 1938); L. Krader, *Peoples of Central Asia* (The Hague, 1963); L. Krader (ed.), *Handbook of Soviet Central Asia* (3 vols., New Haven, 1956); V. I. Masal'skii, *Turkestanskii Kray*, vol. 19 of Semenov-Tianshanskii (ed.), *Rossiia* (St. Petersburg, 1913); T. G. Winner, *The Oral Art and Literature of the Kazakhs of Russian Central Asia* (Durham, N.C., 1958). S. P. Dunn and E. Dunn, "Soviet Regime and Native Culture in Central Asia and Kazakhstan," *Current Anthropology*, 8, 3, 1967.

ranging from fruit, vegetables, and wheat to livestock, wool, silk, and cotton, the latter group constituting by far the largest element in the Union's overall agricultural output. If nothing else, the very magnitude of these stakes explains, in part, both long-term Soviet commitment and recent, increasingly overt Chinese interest in the area.

The region's population includes three principal ethnic groups: Turkic (approaching twelve million in 1959 and seventeen million in 1970, with the latter figure including, in millions: Uzbeks, 9.1; Kazakhs, 4.8; Kirghiz, 1.4; Turkmen, 1.5); Iranian (mainly Tadzhiks, about one and one-half million in 1959 and over two million in 1970); and Slavic (Russians, Ukrainians, and Belorussians, altogether about eight million in 1959 and almost ten million in 1970). Among the smaller ethnic groups there are Karakalpaks, Arabs, Jews, Persians, Uighurs, Dungans, Kurds, Tatars, and Armenians. The Slavic component has risen from about seven percent in 1897 to almost one-third in 1970. The greatest increases in Slavic population have taken place in all of the region's larger cities and in its northern (Kazakh) territories, where Slavs now constitute an absolute majority, even though a veritable population explosion among Soviet Moslems in the 1950's and especially the 1960's has reversed this trend throughout Central Asia. At the same time, the region's urban population has grown at approximately the same rate and to similar proportions, with Slavs accounting now for the lion's share of the inhabitants of major cities. Formally, most of the indigenous population has been Moslem ever since the Arab invasions in the eighth century, with the Sunnite-Shiite division corresponding roughly to the Turkic-Iranian one.

On the eve of the full-scale Russian arrival in the area (in mid-nineteenth century), traditional occupations in the region were basically of two types: sedentary pursuits of the oasis, and nomadic pastoralism of the steppes, deserts, and high plateaus. In the first category, Uzbeks, inhabiting primarily oases and lowlands in the south-central part of the region, and (to a lesser extent) Tadzhik mountaineers in the extreme southeast tended to concentrate in sedentary agriculture, urban commerce, and artisan trades. In the second category, the bulk of Kazakhs in the northern steppe, Kirghiz on eastern plateaus, and Turkmen in the arid desert country of the southwest tended to combine nomadic stockbreeding with marginal agriculture and the caravan trade (as well as brigandage on caravan routes, especially in the case of Turkmen).

5

The rural proportion of the largest of the indigenous peoples ranged from about 90 percent for Uzbeks and Tadzhiks to over 99 percent for Kazakhs, Kirghiz, and Turkmen.

The social structure of indigenous communities tended to reflect basic subsistence patterns: the most pronounced residues of tribal organization were to be found among the pastoral nomads and, to a lesser extent, among the mountaineers. Yet, whether tribe- or village-oriented, whether nomadic or sedentary, local traditional societies were organized around kinship units in relatively self-sufficient communities, by and large along patriarchal, patrilineal, and patrilocal lines. Among other things, this meant that male and female roles were, on the whole, sharply differentiated, though elements of ritualized female inferiority tended to be more pronounced in sedentary communities than in nomadic-pastoral ones. Likewise, polygamy was sanctioned by both religion and custom, though it tended to be practiced more consistently in settled village communities and towns than in the nomadic-pastoral milieu, and was prevalent primarily among relatively well-off and privileged strata.

The educational pattern was overwhelmingly traditionalist in nature; most of the existing schools offered primarily religious instruction, and were staffed and controlled by Moslem clergymen. It is probably a safe inference that before the mid-nineteenth century the functional illiteracy rate of the indigenous population was never significantly below 100 percent. The highest concentration of those formally learned in Moslem religion, history, philosophy, and law was among the sedentary and relatively urbanized Uzbeks, especially in such ancient Islamic civilizational centers as Bukhara and Samarkand.

A highly complex pattern of social and cultural pluralism was reflected in the region's legal institutions. Two major categories of law were typically in operation here: codified Moslem law (*shariat*) and local customary law (*adat*). As a rule, *shariat* was administered by formal canonical courts staffed by qualified Moslem religious personages. In this form, the system was operative primarily in urban and sedentary-agricultural locales. The *adat* depended neither on a written code nor on formal administration; the resolution of disputes tended to be entrusted to tribal leaders, to clan and village notables, and/or to local Moslem clergymen. This system tended to be operative primarily in tribal, nomadic-pastoral milieus. In terms of Georges Gurvitch's legal typology, the legal systems of Central Asia's traditional Islamic principalities (such as Bukhara and Khiva) had a "theocratic-charismatic" base; the legal systems of primitive, "poly-segmentary" social organizations (especially among nomads and mountaineers) had a "magical-religious" base.[2] Yet even these two broad categories of judicial legitimation and arrangements were only ideal-typical in nature. Reality was considerably more complex. Central Asia was an extremely variegated patchwork of religious and tribal tribunals, usages, and laws. In such a context conflict resolution could be formal or highly informal, public or private, and the prevailing legal forms, norms, and practices depended to a large extent on the particular region, communal organization, and ethno-cultural milieu, as well as on the personal charisma of the particular judicial mediator.

After centuries of invasions and ethnic flux on a very large scale (including attempts at empire-building by Chingis Khan and Tamerlane), the region's largest political units in the mid-nineteenth century also reflected the basic sedentary-nomadic division. Nomads in the north, east, and west tended to group themselves under hierarchies of tribal chieftains and notables, the latter's authority depending both on personal influence and genealogical lines. The few major towns and agricultural oasis-clusters in central and southern sections, set in valleys and lowlands and at important junctions of the irrigation system (and in many cases separated by enormous stretches of steppe, desert, or mountains), served as bases for principalities ruled by princely-theocratic oligarchies: the khanates of Khiva and Kokand, and the emirate of Bukhara.

Thus, at a high level of generality, the region's ecology, social structures, ethno-cultural configurations, religious traditions, and patterns of political evolution (including colonization by a major—Tsarist Russian—imperial power) may be said to have shared a number of important features with large parts of what we regard as the underdeveloped, traditional world, especially with Chinese Sinkiang, the Near and Middle East, and North Africa.

THE SOVIET CONQUEST: CONDITIONING FACTORS

The Tsarist conquest of the region (concluded in the 1880's) had not been an especially difficult one. The Soviet military reconquest (1918-22) was carried out with even greater ease, once

[2] See G. Gurvitch, *Sociology of Law* (New York, 1942), Chapter Four. Cf. G. A. Almond and G. P. Powell, Jr., *Comparative Politics: A Developmental Approach* (Boston, 1966), Chapters VI and IX.

7

enough strength could be spared from the fronts of the civil war in the north, and from the victorious confrontation with Allied intervention. On the face of it, the relative ease of the Soviet conquest was due to the strength of what was, for that time and place, a large and modern Red Army, to the correspondingly rapid collapse of organized external and internal challenges to Bolshevik moves, and, *ipso facto*, to the erosion of viable alternatives.

The successive elimination of the preceding regimes—the Tsar's, the Bukharan Emir's, and the Khivan Khan's—secured the land physically, while the evaporation of counter-revolutionary threats from abroad permitted Moscow to secure its rule *de jure*. It was quite fortuitous, in this connection, that the consolidation of Soviet power coincided with shrinking competition all along the perimeter of Soviet penetration into the Near East and Central Asia. After some half-hearted attempts to challenge Soviet presence in the area —mainly by forces based in Turkey, Afghanistan, and British India—none of the surrounding nation-states could afford to assume other than a posture of nervous neutrality. Far from being able to influence events in Central Asia, they could only worry about the impact of these events on *them*. It was impossible to predict the effect of the rise of communist banners north of the Himalayas on British rule in India, on revolutionary potentials in the moribund empires of Turkey and China, and on the shaky tribal monarchies of Afghanistan and Iran.

By 1923, organized internal challenges in the region could also be considered broken. Moscow engaged and liquidated, one by one, the nascent movements and parties that had sprung to life during the collapse of the Tsarist empire. Contestants for local power organized on the basis of religious, tribal, communal, or nationalist ties succeeded but fleetingly in holding a corner of the stage of military and political combat. The orthodox (Ulema-Dzhemieti) and largely secular and liberal (Shurai-Islamiye) Moslem associations, as well as the nationalist and reformist groups of Alash Orda in Kazakhstan, of Young Khivans in Khorezm, and of Young Bukharans in Bukhara, all collapsed in fairly short order. The only serious attempts at guerrilla warfare by tribal and traditionalist elements also failed: the *basmachi* (mainly Uzbek and Tadzhik) revolt on the southern and southeasterly approaches of the region, and the Turkmen revolt in isolated desert-pockets of the southwest. Even though they festered for a number of years, and erupted spasmodically as late as in 1931, they were effectively contained, de-

8

prived of a mass-base, and reduced to minor banditry by the time Moscow was ready for the "national delimitation" of Central Asia into nominally autonomous republics in 1924.[3]

There were manifold causes for the fall of all of Moscow's indigenous competitors. The superiority of Russian arms and absence of support from abroad were but some of the short-term factors. Though apparently sharing a broadly defined ethnic and religious background, and facing simultaneously the threat of foreign domination, the contestants tended to act separately, sporadically, uncertainly, and often at cross-purposes. Community of purpose, and with it a modicum of shared will and of rational capacity to act in concert, was lacking, for reasons deeply rooted in the history and constitution of the region. The major conditioning factors in this case can be grouped under three headings: primordial cleavages and conflicts, Tsarist imperial politics, and native elite orientations in a revolutionary era.

Primordial Cleavages and Conflicts

It seems a safe inference that Central Asia was vulnerable to coordinated outside intervention and conquest primarily because, beneath the surface manifestations of overarching ethnic and religious unity, it was rent by primordial attachments of tribe, clan, and village community, as well as of linguistic and geographical separatism and localized micro-cultural life style.[4] Such a pattern of cleavages—involving both segmental and cultural divergences—could never be easily transcended here, not even in time of common crisis. It can be said that this basic incapacity had to do with what was surely one of the region's most widely shared characteristics: the primordial antagonistic pattern of its political relationships.

Even when confronted with a common challenge—such as the threat of an enemy's invasion of the region as a whole—local traditional elites (princely-theocratic, religious, tribal, and communal) were unable to abandon what appears to have been their

---

[3] For an excellent analysis of the entire spectrum of revolutionary, traditionalist, and nationalist currents at that time, in this and other areas of the Tsarist empire, and of their confrontation with Soviet forces, see Pipes, *The Formation*. For a very thorough account of specifically Moslem and Turkic currents, in this respect, see Zenkovsky, *Pan-Turkism*.

[4] For a discussion of primordial attachments, see "The Integrative Revolution: Primordial Sentiments and Civil Politics in the New States," in Clifford Geertz, ed., *Old Societies and New States* (New York, 1963), pp. 105-57.

9

customary political calculus. At the risk of oversimplification we can say that according to this calculus all other groups were considered in terms of narrowly personal, familistic, tribal, dynastic, or communal advantage, and almost invariably fell into one of the following categories: irrelevant strangers—to be avoided or ignored but to be always mistrusted; potential enemies—to be feared or courted, and ultimately destroyed; potential vassals—to be used but to be always suspected; or potential slaves—to be exploited yet kept at arm's length. These attitudes denoted the absence of the basic ingredients of collaboration and trust in relationships outside primary social units, such as a family or clan; in the quintessentially patriarchal world of Central Asia, they also ensured that interpersonal as well as intergroup relations, especially those transcending the confines of a local community, would tend to be characterized by persistent suspicion and rivalry (on sexual as well as political and other grounds) and that the very art of politics would be viewed here, to a large extent, as the art of conspiracy.

Needless to say, such political metabolism was not conducive to regional stability and integration. In fact, all coherently articulated socio-political units that had emerged in Central Asia before the Soviet arrival exerted continuous pressure on each other, and were perennially in a state of tension between federation and fragmentation, with cleavages running simultaneously along urban/rural, sedentary/nomadic, lowland/highland, religious, tribal, regional, ethnic, and dynastic lines. The principalities, such as Kokand, Khiva, and Bukhara (ruled primarily by Uzbeks)—in quest of an enlarged pool of subject-populations and taxes, and (as great Islamic cultural centers) in quest of an enlarged and more homogeneous community of believers—never ceased trying to extend their control to the surrounding countryside, including each other's as well as nomadic habitats. In turn, nomadic tribes (especially Turkmen and Kazakh)—in quest of booty, or tribute, or access to water in a rigorous terrain—exerted continuous pressure on the cities and on sedentary communities, even if they were themselves continuously affected by internal cleavages. Throughout the region's history, however, neither side commanded enough persistent strength to establish clear-cut dominion over the other.

Thus, for example, militant Turkmen clans, when faced with a sharpening water shortage in their realm, and with the Uzbeks' heavy-handed control of the irrigation system in Khiva, repeatedly engaged the Khivan khanate in internecine warfare. Similarly, the

10

gradual encroachment of cotton-growing Uzbek peasants upon Kazakh, Kirghiz, and Tadzhik pasture lands engendered continuous friction. The exchange of the nomad's harvest of meat, hides, wool, and cattle for the cotton goods, silk, metalware, and grains of the urban craftsman and sedentary cultivator was never free of suspicion or open conflict. At the same time, nomadic raids on towns and villages did not preclude raids of neighboring (for example, Kazakh) clans on each other—in search of pasture-and-water rights, booty, women, or vengeance. Also, the commercial proclivities of some Tadzhiks, Uzbeks, Tatars, Bukharan Jews, and Armenians often placed them rather precariously in the role of merchants and usurers in an ethnically alien sea, with resultant frictions that were not always peacefully resolved. As a result, more often than not the region's local communities and ethno-cultural groups tended to view each other with contempt or fear, as inferior or dangerous strangers. No wonder that even the arrival in mid-nineteenth century of Tsarist troops at the gates of the three surviving city-based principalities—Khiva, Bukhara, and Kokand—failed to diminish their mutual distrust and hostility.[5] Even though the response of individual nomadic and semi-nomadic groups to external threats was more coherent, the relations among these groups never really approached rational cooperation. As often as not, one betrayed the other to the Russians.[6]

Moreover, as a rule, the region's largest historical units made for a segmental rather than unitary political universe, while the smallest and primary communal structures were essentially segmentary rather than hierarchical in nature. In such a milieu, the vertical linkages between ruling elites (princely-theocratic, religious, military and mercantile) at the supra-communal level and the communal leadership of tribes, clans, and villages (including the mass of peasants and nomads) at the grassroots were decidedly weak. Large-scale horizontal connections were also very weak, in that conscious loyalties and purposive collaboration rarely went beyond the confines of primary social solidarities, based on kinship, culture, and village-community.

This meant that the successive supra-communal forms of emirates and khanates were themselves deeply and continuously

[5] For a history of the Tsarist conquest and occupation, see esp. Pierce, *Russian Central Asia*, and Becker, *Russia's Protectorates*.

[6] See Ryskulov, *NV*, 12, 1926, pp. 108-109. Cf. Bartol'd, *Istoriia*, p. 120; Masal'skii, *Turkestanskii Kray*, p. 378.

11

affected by internal cleavages wrought by dynastic, military, religious, ethnic, and communal tensions. The village-communities and diverse tribal enclaves within reach of such urban-based principalities tended to be viewed as fiefs by an emir or a khan and his designated local governors. Relations between ruler and ruled rarely went beyond the exaction of taxes or tribute, the recruitment of warriors, the collection of women for the harem, and the conscription of corvée labor by the ruler's personal representatives or military governors. To be sure, communal loyalties of faith, custom, and kinship were often transferable to the apex of a principality, even if the latter was a petty tyranny. But this was so primarily in instances when the ruler himself came from the particular community in question. More often, the bonds holding a supra-communal entity together were based on fear and awe in the face of a victorious military campaigner and a particularly cruel and efficient wastelayer of hamlets and towns. They could also be based on veneration of a ruler who was especially generous and pious.

But such allegiances could last only as long as brilliant victories, efficient cruelty, or pious generosity persisted at the top. In the highly competitive and splinter-prone world of Central Asian politics, and in a world where scarcity, greed, and familial and dynastic calculations were more pervasive than other motivations, such allegiances could not last very long. Commensurately, the withdrawal or transfer of loyalties—and the disintegration of a principality into its component communal parts—could come to pass with lightning speed, often upon the barest evidence of monarchic weakness or power-transfer at the top. Neither well-institutionalized political organizations nor a pattern of well-balanced and legitimized reciprocal obligations were there to hold a supra-communal structure together.[7]

Overarching tribal authority in the nomadic-pastoral milieu tended to be better legitimated, primarily because, unlike in principalities subsuming an urban and agricultural domain, it was based on recognized bonds of kinship and common descent. But this authority, too, was insufficient to ensure the viability of large tribal structures over the long term. It would seem that three prime factors were responsible for this: the pervasiveness of polygamy among traditional elites, the weak institutionalization of primogeniture in inheritance and succession, and the competitive pres-

[7] See, e.g., Becker, *Russia's Protectorates.* Chapter 1.

12

sure of component lineages and clans.[8] (To be sure, for the most part these factors were also operative in the region's urban-agricultural states. In turn, some of the legitimizing elements in a principality's oligarchic rule—such as an emir's wealth, victorious battles, and military might—played an equally important role in the tribal realm. But the problems connected with polygamy and primogeniture were probably more pronounced in nomadic-pastoral domains precisely because the integrity of tribal units depended very heavily on consanguinal bonds.) Thus, large tribal empires could hardly withstand the centrifugal pressures entailed in shifts of power from one father to many sons, in machinations of many wives and concubines on behalf of their respective male offspring, and in maneuvers of clan leaders and bands of relatives for relative advantage in the tribal domain. In short, even political solidarities that were ethno-culturally among the most homogeneous in the area (for example, Kazakh hordes and tribes) were subject to persistent fragmentation into smaller consanguinal units.

The divisive effects of such a pattern of relationships in the region as a whole were further compounded by the fact that the boundaries of established political structures (tribes, clans, khanates, emirates, and later Tsarist administrative subdivisions) were never coextensive with those of ethno-cultural units, and certainly not with those of incipient nations. In fact, the very idea of a nation-state materialized here as late as, or even later than, it did in most Asian and African milieus.

The fact that Islam had been assimilated in varying fashion and degree by different socio-cultural units also played a significantly disjunctive role in such a context. The ultra-sophisticated Bukharan orthodoxy of the largely sedentary Uzbeks contrasted with the varied beliefs and practices (including folk-Islam and shamanism) of the pastoral Kazakhs and Kirghiz. The prevailing Sunni orthodoxy of Central Asia's religious centers could be juxtaposed to the Shiite heresy of the Tadzhik mountaineers. The functions, role, and influence of Moslem religious personages differed widely from city to city, and from sedentary communities to mountain-villages and nomadic encampments.

[8] In attempting to clarify this matter, I have benefited greatly from discussions with my friend Jeanette Mirsky of Princeton. She places special emphasis on the weakness or absence of primogenitary principles as the main fragmenting factor in tribal societies. She explores broader issues of civilizational change in Asia in a forthcoming critical biography of Sir M. Aurel Stein.

13

Such heterogeneity, such a patchwork of mutually exclusive and often conflicting cultural configurations, loyalties, and interests, such pervasively parochial and micro-centripetal sensibilities had entailed a marked discontinuity between local concerns and supra-communal issues—consistently impeding both formation and retention of overarching, large-scale political solidarities in Central Asia. Human perceptions, expectations, and loyalties tended to focus on the ruler rather than the state; on the community rather than the corporate entity; on the judge rather than the court; on the locally respected elder or notable rather than on any formal institution; on intimate ties of custom, faith, and blood, not of citizenship.[9]

Thus (to paraphrase Clifford Geertz's apt characterization of another Islamic milieu[10]), while the clusters of urban and rural worlds were animated here by what were by and large shared ideals of an Islamic religious tradition, and were thus merely parts or variants of a single system, their interaction was basically non-collaborative. In effect, then, what characterized Central Asia's socio-cultural and political universe was a community of experience but not a community of interests, since incipient cleavages prevented the aggregation of elements of consensus into a consciously shared sense of citizenship in an overarching political order.

Tsarist Imperial Politics

The complex primordial pattern of actual or potential tensions contributed mightily to the incipient political fragmentation of the region. The Tsarist conquest and occupation (started full-scale in the mid-nineteenth century and concluded in the 1880's) helped to accelerate these centrifugal forces as well as induce new ones. The impact of Tsarist imperial presence was as diverse as it was, for the most part, unintended.[11]

Tsarist military might indeed succeeded in imposing a semblance of peace and order in the region, by curbing the war-making capacities of most local societies. As it turned out, though, official mili-

---

[9] For a very sensitive political analysis of the propensities current in the traditional Islamic world, and one that is quite relevant here, see M. Halpern, *The Politics of Social Change in the Middle East and North Africa* (Princeton, 1963), esp. Chapters 1-2.

[10] See his *Islam Observed* (New Haven, 1968), esp. pp. 4-9.

[11] See Note 5 in this chapter, as well as H. Carrère d'Encausse, *Réforme et Révolution.*

tary policies merely created a semblance of stable rule. The greater part of the colonized population (mainly in Kazakh-, Kirghiz-, Turkmen-, and some Uzbek-inhabited territories), while prevented from forming native military units, was also exempted from serving in the Tsarist army. Yet, at the same time, the vassal principalities of Khiva and Bukhara were permitted to keep some military contingents for internal use, while some (mainly Turkmen) tribal armed forces were not only encouraged but singled out (often on par with the Cossacks) for praetorian-guard roles in the empire. This kind of inconsistency and favoritism helped to exacerbate the frustration of communities deprived of the means of self-defense, as well as aggravate competitive tendencies within and between local political units. In effect, then, by failing to provide adequate alternatives for the expression of native militant energies Tsarist policies merely constrained these energies instead of dissipating them. Thus, when in 1916 the desperate situation on the Russo-German front caused St. Petersburg to order full-scale induction of Central Asians into military service, the resulting native revolt was as widespread as it was fierce.[12]

Without a doubt this denouement stopped or reversed, at least temporarily, the general trend toward socio-cultural differentiation and political fragmentation in Central Asia. For the first time in more than a century some Kazakh clans banded together into "khanates" and "patriarchal communities" and not only fought back for a time with a goodly measure of collaboration, but even attempted to form in the steppe fairly large, if only rudimentary, structures of sovereign political administration. But the Revolt of 1916 was too sudden and elemental, too unpremeditated, unstructured, and uncoordinated, to generate lasting cooperation on a regional or ethnic or even local supra-communal basis. The explosion of politicized despair was really a series of outbreaks of long-accumulated grievances. It was a reflection of the Central Asians' rising sensitivity to Russian rule rather than of their significantly growing awareness of, and political affinity to, each other.

New bureaucratic and pseudo-electoral procedures as well as administrative boundaries in occupied areas held out the promise of uniform representation and citizenship, but failed to provide

---

[12] For a brief account, see Pierce, *Russian Central Asia*, Ch. XVIII. For a full-scale treatment, see E. Sokol, *The Revolt of 1916 in Russian Central Asia* (Baltimore, 1954). Cf. Bartol'd, *Istoriia*, pp. 149 ff.; L. Klimovich, *Islam v Tsarskoi Rossii* (Moscow, 1936), pp. 290 ff., and 349 ff.

even a semblance of meaningful political participation. As a result, Tsarist policies merely succeeded in making traditional solidarities above the primary communal level increasingly insupportable—as inter- and intra-tribal competition for office and privileges in the new hierarchy became more intense, as the proliferation of self-serving factions and cliques proceeded apace, and as administrative reshuffling of rural districts delimited nomadic movement, repartitioned traditionally held territories, and aggravated friction between clans.[13]

Exposure of local communities to new patterns of production, trade, and transportation induced a series of spontaneous tendencies which none of the local traditional elites and largely agricultural and pastoral milieus was able to absorb quickly and easily. Russian economic penetration of the region brought in its wake mass-produced goods, a mass-distribution system, some industrial (mainly extractive) development, and emphasis on a single cash-crop (cotton). By World War I, these new economic patterns were well on their way to overwhelming the traditional native modes of production and exchange, without providing the indigenous population with viable (and accessible) alternatives. Thus, local urban artisans came to the verge of bankruptcy. Subsistence patterns in agriculture were disrupted. Formerly self-sufficient Uzbek and Tadzhik peasants became increasingly dependent on (and indebted to) local money-lenders and Russian banks. The rate of migration of impoverished peasants to towns or large farms in search of work rose dramatically. Traditional professions (including caravan trade) associated with economic exchange between town and country were threatened with extinction.[14]

At the same time, the Tsarist policy of singling out a new stratum of "honored natives"—mostly urban merchants—for preferential treatment gained for the imperial authorities a small stratum of commercial compradors; but it also accelerated social differentiation and aggravated local tensions, in that the newly privileged men enjoying foreign patronage came to be regarded with hostility and contempt by the mass of their countrymen.[15] Commensurately, a significant departure from some Islamic rules of conduct (especially on the part of the urban mercantile community) became

[13] See Ryskulov, *NV*, 12, 1926, pp. 108-109; Broido, *NV*, 6, 1924, p. 413.
[14] Ryskulov, *NV*, 12, 1926, p. 108; Bartol'd *Istoriia*, pp. 160 ff., 171; Masal'skii, *Turkestanskii Kray*, p. 342.
[15] See references in preceding note.

16

quickly apparent; the crime rate skyrocketed; and sporadic riots—as much against indigenous (especially Bukharan and Khivan) overlords as against Russian authorities—multiplied.[16]

Russian colonization of the land, at first largely spontaneous, became increasingly deliberate and officially organized. Land-annexations squeezed the native population into ever tighter corners, disrupted access-routes to pastureland, compounded the land-and-water hunger of the affected herdsmen, and further embittered their relations with other indigenous groups against whose domains they pressed when driven from their own lands. At the same time, growing economic insecurity tended to accelerate socio-economic differentiation within larger kinship units, and obliged a growing number of nomadic households to turn to agricultural pursuits, without adequate psychological preparation, requisite skills, and suitable material support. Such propensities were bound to affect adversely all larger solidarities based on lineage, kinship, and custom.[17]

It was one of the great paradoxes of the Russian presence that it served to expose local traditional communities and ethnic groups to new secular institutions and ideological orientations over which the occupying power had virtually no control. The Tsarist conquest helped to break Central Asia's intellectual isolation, an isolation that had been well nigh complete since the high Middle Ages.[18] In the process, it not only exposed indigenous societies to new models of secular education, achievement, and authority. It served to open local ethnic groups and disaffected social strata to the influence of Western political radicalism, Moslem cultural reformism, and Turkic nationalism (under the tutelage, respectively, of Russian, Tatar, and Young Turkish revolutionaries and reformers).

The most sharply articulated political confrontation engendered by this exposure was that between *dzhadidism* and *kadimism*. The

[16] See Masal'skii, *Turkestanskii Kray*, p. 532; Bartol'd, *Istoriia*, p. 209; F. Bozhko, *Oktiabr'skaia Revoliutsiia v Srednei Azii* (Tashkent, 1932), pp. 7-9, citing Galuzo, *Turkestan Koloniia*.

[17] For some telling illustrations, see A. I. Kastelianskii (ed.), *Formy Natsional'nogo Dvizheniia v Sovremennykh Gosudarstvakh* (St. Petersburg, 1910), pp. 579 ff., 583 ff., 590; Masal'skii, *Turkestanskii Kray*, pp. 351-52, 374; Bartol'd, *Istoriia*, pp. 121-22, 197-98; Ryskulov, *NV*, 12, 1926, pp. 106-107.

[18] For some detailed accounts of ideological, intellectual, and artistic currents in Tsarist and early Soviet Central Asia, see Pipes, *The Formation*; Zenkovsky, *Pan Turkism*; Winner, *The Oral Art*; and Allworth (both of his books cited in Note 1 of this chapter).

former called, first of all, for a secular, "new method" approach to education. It reflected a self-conscious appreciation of Western effectiveness and strength stemming from pragmatic utilization of ideas and techniques, and a concomitant revulsion from what was viewed as the root-source of all that was moribund and anachronistic in Islamic civilization: the Moslem educational system.[19] The latter constituted a conservative reaction to the secularist threat, and it embodied an equally self-conscious assertion of the values of Islamic orthodoxy. Needless to say, what started out as an argument about the goals and methods of education turned quickly into a confrontation regarding the structure of society and political authority, and it came to involve deeply—on both sides of the argument—the region's Moslem clergy and rising secular intelligentsia. The growing emotional gap between the forces of *dzhadidism* and *kadimism* in the ranks of local elites was fully matched by an emotional and structural gap between the secular intelligentsia and the tradition-bound rural masses, compounding the existing potential for distrust and fragmentation.

While helping to engender (by and large unwittingly) the forces of ideological change in the region, Tsarist policies also sought—after initial drift and hesitation—to arrest the new trends. Official attempts to do so proceeded on two levels: deliberate preservation of two of Central Asia's supra-communal political structures (Khiva and Bukhara) as substantially autonomous and tradition-bound vassal states; and equally deliberate preservation of (and, in some cases, growing support for) the status and functions of some traditional elites (princely-theocratic, clerical, and tribal) in the region as a whole. It goes without saying that the implications of these policies stood in direct contradiction to virtually all other tendencies—in the realm of politics, administration, culture, economics, and land colonization—ushered in under Russian auspices consciously or by default.

Of course, this contradiction merely reflected the conflicting motives and pressures within the Tsarist system itself. As Russia's colonial empire grew, a growing array of interest groups (military, political, bureaucratic, economic, and cultural) found it increasingly possible to pursue their own, often disparate, objectives in the interstices of an authoritarian but only nominally unitary state,

---

[19] For a striking variant of such attitudes, see Fitrat's "Rasskazy Indiiskogo Puteshestvennika," as quoted in Klimovich, *Islam*, pp. 209-12.

This, in part, accounted for the confusion of means and ends, and for the virtual absence of coordination between various lines of action. It was a measure of this confusion that, initially, both conservative and liberal opinion in Russia demanded the total subjugation and dissolution of Central Asia's remaining vassal states, as well as the removal of the region's traditional elites from most positions of influence. But such demands were made for very different reasons. Liberal (not to speak of radical) opinion was outraged by the unimpeded operation within the Russian fold of two vassal principalities, and of traditional life styles, viewed as representing (presumably far more prominently and flagrantly than Tsarist autocracy itself) the most pernicious forms of "reactionary orthodoxy," "medieval barbarism," and "oriental despotism." *Per contra*, conservative opinion, in championing essentially the same goals, reflected the pressures of Russian chauvinism, religious missionary zeal, and military, economic, and cultural imperialism. That is to say, it reflected the impetus of forces bent upon the unhampered absorption, assimilation, and exploitation of conquered milieus, and the elimination from positions of influence of those who might compete with (or obstruct the imposition and operation of) Tsarist imperial authority.

In the end—in the decade or two preceding war and revolution —official policies swung (albeit even then not always consistently) toward a conservative position of a special kind. Increasingly uneasy about the growth of revolutionary, reformist, and nationalist movements in Central Asia—movements as irrepressible here as in European Russia—and eager to obtain as many local allies as possible in the preservation of imperial rule, Tsarist authorities came to count ever more heavily on the good will and cooperation of local *status quo* forces: the princely-theocratic oligarchy of Khiva and Bukhara and, in the region as a whole, the tribal and communal elites of notables and elders as well as the conservative Islamic clergy. The reliance tended, of course, to be mutual, since local custodians of tradition perceived the threat of change at least as sharply as their unexpected allies in St. Petersburg. Thus, the Tsarist regime not only preserved the autonomous status of Bukhara and Khiva, but found itself duty-bound to send armies to the rescue whenever nomadic raids, sporadic peasant outbreaks, or urban reformist currents seemed to threaten the vassals' lives. Similarly, after some initial missionary forays on behalf of the Russian Orthodox Church, St. Petersburg found it necessary to assume

19

the unlikely role of a patron of Islam in Central Asia—surrounding the activities of the Moslem clergy with an aura of official solicitude and support, strengthening the clergy's preferred status (in civil and judicial authority as much as in education), and even contributing to the construction of new mosques and religious seminaries in the region.

Some of the consequences were as incongruous as they were unpremeditated. As a rule, traditional elites showed neither the will nor the capacity to assimilate the new social forces generated by the modernizing trends induced by Tsarist occupation. They were certainly disinclined to consider changes in the traditional system itself, so as to make it more responsive to changing needs and to the demands of new social strata and groups. Instead, when given a free hand, Bukharan and Khivan incumbents either hounded suspected reformers out of their domain or hunted them down for the kill. (Their methods of dealing with enemies were not noted for humanitarian constraints, and were, of course, easily borrowed from well-preserved medieval armories.) Thus, by being able to call on modern Tsarist armies whenever ethnic, tribal, communal, or reformist tensions within the principalities threatened to topple the traditional system of power, Central Asian oligarchies could in effect postpone indefinitely the need to face the imperatives of building a viable political community based on the recognition of, and reasonable compromise with, newly emerging social forces.

But, while temporarily successful, these efforts to preserve—artificially, as it were—what were increasingly anachronistic sociopolitical realms could do little or nothing to stem the tide of change. For example, anyone who successfully evaded the dragnets of emirs and khans, and crossed over into Russian-occupied territory, had a fair chance to find refuge (legally or illegally), likeminded men, and supportive institutions (such as "new method" schools, publications, and associations) in Central Asian cities. Similarly, conservative clergy and communal leaders throughout the region were encouraged by colonial authorities to denounce radical *dzhadids* to the Tsarist police, and they did so often and with alacrity. Yet even if temporarily unable to hold their own in Central Asia, budding nationalists and secular reformers could count on the welcome ideological tutelage and moral support of liberals as well as radicals (Tatars, Slavs, and others) in European Russia—or in Turkey, if necessary.

This, then, was the cumulative, and paradoxical, effect of Rus-

20

sian influence in Central Asia. While some Tsarist policies were calculated to preserve traditional polities and life styles, other policies, as well as a host of uncontrollable factors, continued to undermine the mainstays of the traditional order. Even though the full weight of Russian influence was never applied in planned and determined fashion, the forces unleashed by the Russian arrival were strong enough to sow doubt, estrangement, and fragmentation in what had been previously tradition-bound communities, and helped to erode the fragile edifices of all remaining large-scale solidarities, including theocratic principalities and nomadic tribes.

Native Elite Orientations in a Revolutionary Era

Though some dimensions of Tsarist policies or presence in Central Asia led to growing instability and anomie, others might have been expected to produce new foci of identity and collaboration. For example, the very concept of ethnicity in the region—and of citizenship in an overarching, secular ethnic collectivity—was in part a product of Russian (and, through Russia, Tatar and Turkish) mediation. Yet the political and existential situation of pivotal groups that could have supplied the necessary leadership for this purpose was hardly conducive to this end. To wit: a combination of imperial policies and spontaneously generated forces had led to the emergence in the traditional milieu of a new secular intelligentsia. The latter was, in effect, the first equivalent of a middle class in the region's history, and the first conscious carrier of secularism and ethnic/national awareness transcending tribal and communal loyalties. However, this new stratum was itself gravely handicapped in comprehending, and in dealing with, the opportunities (and problems) that materialized in the twilight years of the Tsarist empire. In fact, as was pointed out earlier, the nascent reformers and nationalists as a rule found it safer to live, work, and learn—and bide their time—in the Russian environment of Turkestan's or Russia's cities, or in Istanbul, than on their own home ground, where they were distrusted or hounded by incumbent custodians of tradition.

It seems safe to say, then, that in this sense Tsarist policies (and some unintended corollaries of these policies) helped both to preserve and to weaken all significant forces that ultimately aspired to provide an alternative to the colonial status quo. The same policies helped to make the traditionalist-modernist confrontation into an irreconcilable conflict. Quite inevitably, therefore, the moment

21

overarching Tsarist controls snapped everywhere in 1917, and before the Bolsheviks even tried to assert themselves in the region, local supra-communal structures were faced with immediate turmoil. Yet as the suppressed patchwork of ethnic, tribal, communal, and reformist energies erupted in 1917 in widespread conflagration, there turned out to be no basis whatsoever for mutual trust and cooperation among the available native elites, princely, tribal, religious, or secular. Not surprisingly, no idea proved attractive, legitimate, and relevant enough, and none of the indigenous claimants to power—from khans and emirs to tribal chieftains and nationalist reformers—proved imaginative, experienced, organized, and strong enough to provide acceptable leadership for the region as a whole or for any of its ethnic components. Thus, Tsarist departure and Bolshevik arrival were, in effect, triggers which served to reveal the archaisms and deficiencies of the local *ancien régimes*.

PRINCELY-THEOCRATIC AND TRIBAL ELITES

As the forces of rebellion (1916), revolution (1917-18), and ultimately Soviet military intervention (1918-20) intensified the turmoil in Central Asia, the region's princely-theocratic and tribal elites showed themselves utterly unequal to the challenge. Generations of exposure to the realities of new social and cultural trends in or around their domains seemed to make little difference. The requisite awareness of newly crystallizing issues and the will and capacity to deal with them were still lacking. The customary political calculus—based on suspicion and conspiratorial rivalry, and stressing narrowly personal, dynastic, tribal, or communal advantage—continued to take precedence over any other considerations. As revolutionary challenges and then Moscow's troops bore down on neighboring principalities and tribes, one by one, no significant initiatives materialized to find a common ground for accommodation, cooperation, and defense.

Thus, the briefly resurrected principality of Kokand, and then the Emirate of Bukhara and the Khanate of Khiva, fell separately and in rapid succession. No one, apparently, felt impelled to hasten to the other's assistance. The Bukharan incumbents, for example, evidently the strongest of the three, seemed more intent on hunting *dzhadids* within the city limits than on seeking potential allies in the surrounding countryside. (This helps to explain why, when the Red Army approached in 1920 for a final showdown, the assault on the walls of Bukhara and Khiva coincided with *dzhadid* uprisings from inside.)

If the principalities in the south-central portions of the region showed little interest in each other's survival, they showed no interest at all in the fate of the pastoral societies surrounding them on all sides. The performance of tribal and communal elites by and large replicated this pattern. In most cases, the clan-leadership of the region's nomads and mountaineers simply ignored the demise of Khiva, Bukhara, and Kokand. In one revealing case, tribal forces, even though themselves gravely endangered by the Soviet advance, in fact went so far as to reenact an ancient local conflict in the midst of the general conflagration. Thus, the Turkmen clans of Transcaspia (in the southwest), unable to resist the lure of an isolated and weakening enemy, initially invested most of their energies in settling old scores with Khiva's Uzbek overlords, and in the end contributed materially to the destruction of the khanate. (Of course, this left Turkmen communities all the more exposed and alone in facing later the Soviet onslaught.)

On the northerly approaches to the area, Kazakh clans at first groped for a broad tribal alliance (under the nominal, largely symbolic leadership of Alash Orda nationalists) that would permit the establishment in the steppe region of the equivalent of an overarching tribal state—in effect, the re-establishment of an ancient form of Kazakh supra-communal unity (the Horde) in the area.[20] But divisive tendencies proved insurmountable from the very beginning. For one thing, some clans were less enthusiastic than others in offering allegiance (and military assistance) to a central—in effect, national—government, and one run primarily by urban intellectuals and secular reformers. For another thing, the quickly shifting lines of battle in Russia's Civil War, the confusing appeals and claims emanating from the warring sides, and strictly local perceptions of short-term communal interests made some clans join the Whites and others the Reds. It is a safe assumption that this was done for practical rather than ideological reasons. The same factors induced a number of tribal units, and even some officials of the Alash Orda government itself, to change sides at short notice when circumstances seemed to demand it. As a result, the embryonic tribal state in the steppe soon wound up with at least two uncoordinated shadow governments that were constantly in transit and that claimed uncertain sovereignty over a multiplicity of elusive nomadic communities.[21] In any case, even in the most propitious moments of this ethno-tribal self-assertion, emerging Kazakh lead-

[20] See, e.g., Pipes, *The Formation*, p. 84.
[21] See, e.g., Zenkovsky, *Pan-Turkism*, p. 213.

23

ership manifested neither a clear desire nor a palpable ability to establish a basis for understanding and cooperation with other resurgent Turkic forces (Kirghiz, Turkmen, and Uzbek) in the region. Needless to say, once the Whites were decisively beaten, and pivotal Alash Orda leaders either defected to, or were captured by, the Bolsheviks, Kazakh resistance in the northern steppe evaporated virtually overnight.

In the southern and southeastern deserts, oases, and highlands, Uzbek, Tadzhik, and some Kirghiz *basmachi* detachments formed nuclei of the relatively strongest and most coherent native response to Tsarist collapse and the Soviet challenge. *Basmachestvo*—a guerrilla movement based on a combination of tribal, Islamic, and local traditionalist sensibilities—could count on a number of advantages in staking out a claim to self-determination. *Basmachi* had in their ranks some members of fanatical Moslem sects (mostly refugees from ravaged Kokand) who were able and eager to imbue the movement with a passionate missionary commitment to holy war. They had access to Bukharan money for the purchase of weapons and local popular support (which made them intermittently amenable to serve as mercenaries for the Emir of Bukhara). They had the (temporary) leadership of Enver Pasha, a brilliant and experienced, though by that time politically peripheral, Turkish general. Their operational terrain included the most remote and inaccessible portions of Central Asia (such as the mountain passes and high plateaus of the Pamirs), was inhabited to a large extent by their kinsmen (and by relatively few Slavs), was self-sustaining by virtue of its contiguity to one of Asia's richest plains (the Ferghana Valley), and was thus eminently well suited to guerrilla warfare. Last but not least, *basmachi* units had direct access to a sanctuary—in northeastern Afghanistan—where the sympathies of the ruling tribal oligarchy and the contiguity of ethnically kindred clans ensured, at least for a time, a safe haven.

However, even this confluence of highly favorable factors did not permit the *basmachi* movement to endure more than about two years after Central Asia's occupation by regular Soviet troops (1920) and the Soviet regime's first political approaches to the population.

For one thing, a measure of cultural heterogeneity and the pressure of tribal and communal interests quickly cancelled out the unifying effects of shared religious and traditionalist concerns. Personal rivalries and tribal feuds led to mutual sabotage and

24

assassinations on the part of clan elders and village notables who headed the movement, removed the most capable commanders from the field, and undermined the unity and efficiency of the fighting units. As it turned out, even Enver Pasha himself, the man entrusted with supreme authority over the entire *basmachi* military effort—"Commander in Chief of all Islamic troops, son-in-law of the Caliph, and representative of the Prophet," as he liked to call himself[22]—was not immune from the effects of the pervasive, incipiently conspiratorial distrust in traditionalist ranks. He incurred sufficient jealousy from the Bukharan Emir and rival *basmachi* leaders to find that his efforts, too, were sabotaged. (In the end, almost completely abandoned by his troops, he was killed by a Soviet patrol in the summer of 1922. With him went the last hope for concerted native action in the south.)

Second, while the forces of Islamic and traditionalist orthodoxy were clearly insufficient to ensure rebel unity, they were unquestionably instrumental in separating the *basmachi* from the most important political allies they might have had. In effect, the passions of orthodoxy precluded any cooperation between *basmachi* and *dzhadid* elements, even though they shared a highly valued objective (self-determination) and in many cases belonged to the same ethnic and tribal group. Moreover, the distrust and hatred were not merely a matter of intellectual principle. As it turned out, *basmachi* raiders who managed to overrun an oasis or town, or a Soviet garrison outpost, were not at all averse to consider a *dzhadid's* ear a legitimate trophy in battle, perhaps even more legitimate than a Russian or Bolshevik head, since the "new method" man could be viewed as a traitor to his people's primordial ties, customs, and beliefs. In a time of revolutionary turmoil and foreign intervention the implications of such behavior for any large-scale native solidarity and integration were, of course, disastrous.

A third set of factors responsible for the decline of the *basmachi* had to do with an important shift in Soviet policies at that time. After Lenin's and then Stalin's repeated warnings (concerning, precisely, the threat posed by the *basmachi* revolt), local depredations by Soviet emissaries and army units, and by Russian settlers, were brought to a halt. In particular, Moscow stopped the massive desecration and destruction of local mosques that followed Soviet occupation. It also abrogated the erstwhile draconic decrees concerning local religious observances and customs, private property,

---

[22] Pipes, *The Formation*, p. 258.

and Moslem educational, judicial, and communal institutions, decrees that had been issued here in the first flush of victory. The concessions to Islamic sensibilities and the curbing of the crudest of repressions served to calm native passions in very short order. As Richard Pipes has succinctly noted, "the entire resistance movement known as Basmachestvo had been not so much an embodiment of a positive political or social philosophy as a desperate reaction to ill-treatment and abuse of authority, and it collapsed as soon as these irritants were removed."[23] It would seem that this was true at least to the extent that the regime's timely actions served to deprive rebel leaders of a broad popular following.

By 1923, most of the remaining factors that favored a guerrilla war were no longer operative. With the Bukharan Emir and his court-aristocracy themselves refugees in Afghanistan, the flow of money and weapons to the *basmachi* dried up. At the same time, a sharp turn in the commitments of Afghanistan's princely-tribal oligarchy—following a series of internal coups and realignments— imposed an increasingly tight reign on guerrilla movements across Soviet-Afghan frontiers and deprived the rebels of their most important sanctuary. To all intents and purposes, this act spelled the end of armed resistance in Central Asia.

RELIGIOUS ELITES

As was the case with Central Asia's princely-theocratic and tribal elites, the region's religious intelligentsia found it impossible to transcend traditional political orientations and relationships. Local *ulema* and *mullahs* did make some (albeit abortive) attempts to construct a framework for societal collaboration. For example, they founded, at the time of the Tsarist collapse, a regional (albeit orthodox) Association of Clergymen (Ulema-Dzhemieti). They participated to some extent with relatively liberal and secular elements in the establishment of the first (albeit shortlived) Moslem Central Council (Shurai-Islamiye) and united Islamic organization (Ittifak-ul-Mislimin) in Turkestan, with a seat in Kokand. And they helped to form (in cooperation with mercantile interests and some liberal *dzhadids*) the ill-fated Government of Kokand.[24] But these were exceptions to the rule. Though Moslem religious personages commanded considerable prestige and authority in the area, both in formal communal administration and at the grass-

---

[23] See ibid., p. 260.
[24] See ibid., pp. 88 ff., and Zenkovsky, *Pan-Turkism*, pp. 227-33.

roots, they were by and large unable and disinclined to provide an impetus toward, and supply the leadership for, heterodox supra-communal initiatives. For that matter, the clergy not only could do little to hinder the imposition of a structure of Soviet power, but, paradoxically, in some ways even helped to ease the grafting of that power in the region.

There were at least four basic reasons for this. First, there was, of course, Islam's long-standing universalistic bias, a bias in favor of a general community of believers, and not of a particular nation of citizens. Second, a hierarchic clerical structure was absent in Islam, making it difficult for the clergy to evolve overarching po-litical leadership and an overall system of command. Third, the very diversity of clerical roles in Islam meant a similar diversity in intellectual and operational horizons. Thus, for example, the *ulema* —in the role of jurists, scholars, educators, and specially-desig-nated officials, among others—tended to be enmeshed primarily in urban and courtly politics. The bulk of religious functionaries in the countryside (*mullahs, ishans, imams*, or *tabibs*, with their widely varying yet intimate involvement in local life styles) tended to identify with the milieu in which they lived. At the same time, the assorted roaming dervishes and holy men of the Central Asian bazaars and countryside, like their brethren throughout the Middle East, tended to identify either with a purely religious locale—such as a place of miraculous healing where they presided—or with par-ticular religious sects and brotherhoods that cut across urban, rural, or ethnic loyalties. In the fourth place, the Moslem clergy had tra-ditionally accepted, and accommodated itself to, any locally pre-vailing power—as long as that power did not violate local customs and beliefs, dismantle socio-religious institutions, or remove the clergy itself from its primordial functions. Thus, even though the clergy insisted in theory on the essential unity of temporal and spir-itual authority, it was largely content to serve in essentially con-sultative and mediating roles in a given authority-system. Such a tradition of deference to *de facto* power-holders had, of course, led the bulk of Central Asia's *ulema* to collaborate with imperial Tsar-ist authorities without undue difficulty, even as some village *mul-lahs* in the hinterland, and some zealots and sectarians in villages and towns, tried from time to time to lead mobs in a "holy war" against the infidel.

This last proclivity, in particular—having to do with the clergy's traditional accommodation to a prevailing power—seems to have made the religious intelligentsia especially ambivalent in its responses to the Soviet arrival. The new regime was, after all, not only powerful but revolutionary (as well as alien). There seems little doubt that this ambivalence deepened when sharp (and largely unprecedented) competition materialized in the exercise of highly important social functions over which the clergy had a virtual monopoly since time immemorial, namely, the consecrative, educative, adjudicative, and welfare functions.[25] The challenge to this monopoly was undoubtedly all the more acutely perceived in that it was posed to a large extent by men (liberal and radical *dzhadids*) who had been previously hounded and denounced by orthodox clergymen, and who now enjoyed (albeit conditionally and temporarily) the support of the new regime. It is a safe assumption that in these circumstances the clergy felt both vulnerable and on the defensive.

The response of the religious intelligentsia to the unfolding challenge amply reflected its ambivalence. When, in the heat of Soviet takeover, Moscow indulged in, or condoned, in Central Asia acts that were brutally contemptuous of local religious sensibilities, the clergy tended to become the mouthpiece for popular grievances, and to move toward more or less violent (though uncoordinated) opposition. But when the Soviet regime, partly as a result of the *basmachi* revolt, moved in the early 1920's to redress some local grievances, and relaxed its grip on Moslem judiciary, educational, and endowed communal institutions, the clergy's response showed signs of confusion and fragmentation. This became especially manifest in a growing ideological split in clerical ranks. While this split led clergymen to take significantly differing positions across a broad spectrum, it was expressed most dramatically in the emergence of two main contending groups. Soviet authorities were content to refer to them (with evident satisfaction) as "red" ("progressive") and "black" ("reactionary") *mullahs*.[26]

The "reds" came to preach the convergence of communist and Islamic tenets on a number of grounds, including that of landtenure by those who till it; some demanded that they be allowed to join, and actually formed, Communist Party units; and some even

---

[25] With the partial exception of tribal-nomadic milieus, where its adjudicative functions were shared with tribal chiefs and village elders, and its welfare-oriented functions with local shamans.

[26] For a brief but highly informative account of the clergy's role in the 1920's, see Park, *Bolshevism*, Ch. v.

coolly declared Lenin to be a Moslem prophet. Their position, then, tended to be a logical extrapolation of reformist trends that had first materialized in Central Asia in the late nineteenth century, and that had found secular expression in the rise of the *dzhadids*. Accordingly, "red" *mullahs* were prepared to collaborate in some revolutionary initiatives both with the *dzhadids* and with their Soviet sponsors.

The "blacks" were steadfast in their opposition to what they considered (albeit not always overtly) spiritually blasphemous and politically dangerous attacks on the mainstays of Islam. And, understandably, they were in no mood to participate in common ventures with native reformers and foreign infidels, revolutionaries, and occupiers. Yet this was just about as far as the "black" *mullahs* were willing to go. Far from attempting to prod (and lead) their religious communities towards militant and concerted self-assertion, as a rule they behaved with consummate caution, adopting a politically neutral and accommodationist position: they came out, by and large, for order and tranquility, and for obedience to the new authorities, and restricted themselves to purely local pursuits. It would seem, then, that with their traditional political allies and protectors—including khans, emirs, tribal leaders, as well as colonial officials—gone or fighting for their own lives, Moslem clerical elites were reluctant or unable to act in autonomous political roles.

Needless to say, though Moscow was in no mood to change its basic attitudes toward religion in general and Islam in particular, it could not but welcome the neutrality of the "black" clergy and the zealous, if a bit startling, cooperation of the "reds." To be sure, given the Moslem clergy's centuries-old record of more or less skillful adaptation to various power structures, one could not know with certainty just where genuine cooperation ended and deliberate deception began. All the same, an opportunity to pit one clerical group against the other, and to hold up one of them as an example for all the faithful to follow, was too tempting to be missed. Accordingly, it was not missed.

But the implications of this denouement went beyond mere tactical advantage for Leninist cadres. The broad spectrum of clerical orientations—from left to right, from "red" to "black"—may be said to have had two related and immediately relevant effects. It tended to discourage the formation of a unitary pattern of popular response (even if this were otherwise possible) to the challenges

29

of foreign intervention and secular revolution. It also served to reduce the intensity of popular passions in the face of enormous dislocations accompanying Soviet victory. (In some respects, it even
tended to endow Soviet presence with a minimal measure of legitimacy, at least to the extent that "red" *mullahs* could win a hearing
at the grassroots.) Thus, the clergy's orientations clearly contributed to the pacification of the native population, providing the regime with a much needed breathing spell after the Civil War and
hence with an opportunity to consolidate its power in Central Asia.

SECULAR ELITES

Of all the forces moving to occupy the positions abandoned by
defunct rulers in Central Asia, the new secular intelligentsia was
perhaps most self-conscious, consistent, and deliberate. Its exposure to modernist trends in Russia and abroad had much to do
with this attitude. Yet the efforts of the region's budding nationalists and reformers were hopelessly fragmented from the very outset.
Revolutionaries or reformers, radicals or liberals, they were caught
in a crossfire of competing forces, none of which they were quite
prepared to handle. As the Russian Civil War unfolded along the
region's northern approaches, while the Bukharan and Khivan
states still held out in the south against Bolshevik insurgents in
Tashkent, the nationalist *dzhadid* groupings of Young Khivans and
Young Bukharans and the Kazakh Alash Orda found themselves
between the Scylla of native theocratic and tribal traditionalism
and the Charybdis of competing Russians, Reds and Whites.

To stake out a claim in these conditions, the secular intelligentsia needed at least some suitable allies, access to a popular following
and military force, a determinate political base, and an overarching
collaborative framework sustained by ideology, organization, and
leadership. As it turned out, none of these was readily available
at the time.

An alliance with Russian Whites proved out of the question, although some of the region's indigenous forces (for example, the
Alash Orda) at one time showed a definite interest in such an alliance. The Whites' jingoist, militarist, imperialist, and autocratic
past apparently weighed too heavily on their shoulders to permit
them to treat Central Asian nationalists as equals. Though increasingly hard-pressed by the Bolsheviks on all fronts, the Whites refused to consider seriously ideas of future local autonomy, even in
return for native armed support. The Bolsheviks showed, in this

30

respect, far greater political adroitness. Their ringing proclamations of national liberation and equality[27] persuaded a number of men in modernist ranks (even some who were uneasy about the Reds' revolutionary program) that collaboration with the Soviets was feasible and advantageous. But at least as many *dzhadid* nationalists (including some of their ablest leaders) had deep misgivings about the Bolsheviks' long-range plans and trustworthiness as allies. Their growing (though, in most cases, belated) awareness of the communists' ruthlessly monopolistic bias made them quite uncertain about the promise even of temporary cooperation with Moscow. At the same time, the secular intelligentsia could have had few illusions about help from kindred or likeminded groups abroad. Sun Yat-Sen's republicans in China and the Young Turks and Kemalists in Turkey were themselves fighting for their lives. And the Afghans, Persians, and Arabs of the Islamic world to the south, even if they *had* been motivated to help, were not only under colonial or semi-colonial tutelage but were badly torn by tribal, ethnic, religious, and communal cleavages, and were barely starting on the road towards national identity and independence.

For any chance of success, native nationalists and reformers needed access to some popular following, military force, and a political base. Yet the very factors that had always kept them from intimate contacts with the grassroots of their own societies militated against such access now. Most of the region's armed resistance forces were under the command of the *dzhadids'* sworn enemies, emirs, khans, tribal leaders, and *basmachi* chieftains. Rebel territory was, in effect, out of bounds for the secular intelligentsia. Even the countryside that was not affected by *basmachi* raids was dotted with aloof, suspicious, deeply traditionalist hamlets, where the intelligentsia's contacts were minimal and where primordial authority was exercised by local chiefs, elders, notables, and *mullahs*. Other parts of that countryside were settled by Slavic colonists who were either hostile or little inclined to have anything to do with native intellectuals. The latter's prospects in the city, on the other hand, were hardly less gloomy. For it was precisely in Central Asia's major *cities* (such as Tashkent) that Bolshevik organizational strength was greatest, Soviet administrative and military machines came to be most solidly anchored, and Slavic (and other Euro-

---

[27] See, e.g., *Lenin o Druzhbe s Narodami Vostoka* (Moscow, 1961), pp. 261-63. Cf. Pipes, *The Formation*, pp. 155 ff. and Zenkovsky, *Pan-Turkism*, pp. 161 ff.

pean) population segments were best entrenched. Thus, without a determinate *locus operandi*, and without access to a natural reservoir of popular following and armed force, it might have occurred to native nationalists that they could be speaking and acting in a void, representing no one but themselves.

Great as these difficulties were, they might have been at least partially overcome through unequivocal unity of action based on a coherent (and locally relevant) ideology, a cohesive organization, and overarching, authoritative leadership. Yet such a collaborative framework proved as unattainable to Central Asia's secular elites as it did to their tradition-bound kinsmen. Perhaps the most important reason for this had to do with a lack of suitable political experience. We know that, in the decades before a decisive revolutionary confrontation, the region's rising modernist elites could not easily maintain ties with their own countrymen, precisely when the imperatives of modernization and nation-building called for such ties most urgently. In their case, then, alienation may be said to have gone hand in hand with social and political isolation. Thus, these elites had had in effect no chance to apply their minds, and to try their hand, in the politics and management of their own societies—before the crucial test arrived, in 1917, requiring that they do just that.

This meant that, as political actors, native nationalists and reformers were mere fledglings, especially when compared with some of their competitors, particularly Soviet cadres. It is surely a political datum of the first order that Central Asia's first indigenous political parties came into being only a few years, and in some cases months, before they had to deal with the exigencies of revolution and self-determination, and were in turn challenged by Lenin's professional revolutionaries. The incoherence of organizational structures was fully matched by a confusion of objectives. Thus, while some leading members of the intelligentsia championed overarching unity based on a common faith (Pan-Islamism), others emphasized political designs based on a broadly shared ethnic background (Pan-Turkism). Still others preferred to concentrate primarily on local or micro-ethnic concerns, such as those embodied in the Young Khivan and Young Bukharan movements, and in Uzbek, Turkmen, Kazakh, Kirghiz, and Tadzhik nationalism.[28]

[28] For a thorough review of Pan-Turkic and Pan-Islamic trends in Tsarist and Soviet Russia, see Zenkovsky, *Pan-Turkism*. For a good example of Soviet views on Pan-Turkic and Pan-Islamic tendencies in the U.S.S.R., see

This made communication—not to speak of cooperation—among nationalists and reformers extremely problematic. It also ensured that the leadership of most large-scale political initiatives in the region would be, in large part, non-native (especially Tatar) in composition. As leading exponents, for example, of Pan-Turkic and Pan-Islamic ideas, Tatars enjoyed some natural advantages. They had the political and organizational experience their Central Asian kinsmen lacked. They could draw on an impressive record of (and thus base much of their prestige on) decades of intense intellectual and political proselytizing activity in the region. And, as outsiders, they could not be readily suspected of favoring some local groups at the expense of others. But, in the end, the very factors that tended to make their overarching (hence potentially unifying) leadership acceptable here—or simply less unacceptable than that of native Central Asians—also served to undermine their role and remove them from the scene. For example, their political dynamism ultimately made their intentions suspect: as a number of local Turkic nationalists came to see the situation (not wholly without foundation) Tatar ambitions to inspire a grand Turkic or Moslem union could go hand in hand with an ambition to dominate it.[29] At the same time, the distance of the Tatars' home-base from Central Asia, and its proximity to the centers of Soviet power in Russia, made the problems of political logistics insurmountable. As the battlelines of civil war and Soviet intervention cut the connections between Central Asia and Tatarstan (due northwest on the Volga), and as the Tatar intelligentsia was itself subjected to Moscow's early pulverizing pressures, the Tatars' chances to exert significant influence outside (and even inside) their own domain evaporated in short order.[30] The erosion of such a potentially unifying organizational and ideological impetus left Central Asia's secular intelligentsia in greater disarray than before.

Soviet policies certainly contributed to this disarray, and to the commensurate erosion of opportunities for unity. On the one hand,

---

A. Arsharuni and Kh. Gabidullin, *Ocherki panislamizma i pantiurkizma v Rossii* (Moscow, 1931).

[29] See, e.g., Zenkovsky, *Pan-Turkism*, pp. 156 ff.

[30] The case of Sultan-Galiev, a dynamic Tatar communist leader, furnishes a striking example of the fate of the Tatar radical intelligentsia. For a brief but excellent account of Sultan-Galiev's rise and fall and of his role in furthering a highly original nationalist-communist vision, see Pipes, *The Formation*, pp. 168 ff. and 260 ff.

Moscow's deliberate utilization of some non-Russian troops in re-conquering Central Asia—including the use of Tatar, Bashkir, Kazakh, Dungan, Uzbek, and Turkmen detachments in a way that pitted them against local rebels who were also their historic enemies[31]—further exacerbated local divisions and mutual distrust. On the other hand, the Soviet regime held out to secular elites the promise of new institutional arrangements designed to take local autonomist sensibilities into account. But these arrangements—involving the formation of separate, though only nominally autono-mous, republics and districts—emphasized the smallest rather than the largest ethno-cultural subdivisions in the region. This helped to reinforce the particularistic orientations of local reformers and nationalists, and permitted an all the more effective crackdown on Pan-Turkic and Pan-Islamic tendencies. At the same time, *dzhadid* politicians were invited to join the Communist Party and were of-fered responsible posts in republican and local administration, while teachers, doctors, publicists, writers, and artists among them were provided with unprecedented opportunities for putting mis-sionary aspirations and professional ambitions to work.

Given the Bolsheviks' steadily growing might and associational incentives, the Whites' barely concealed contempt, the hostility or ambivalence of traditional elites, the incipient fragmentation along ethno-cultural or communal lines, and the mute indifference of the bulk of traditionalist rural masses to the events around them, it is not surprising that an aspiring modernist intelligentsia ultimately found few meaningful alternatives to an association with the Soviets.

Once enmeshed in the network of Soviet power, however, the native secular reformers had little chance to hold their own. Those who may have harbored dreams of furthering other than Moscow's causes while entrenched in the Soviet apparatus surely had no chance for success in any foreseeable future. Even the most sophis-ticated men among them could have had but a very rudimentary understanding of the forces that were about to overtake them. To Moscow's determined, singleminded,[32] centralizing pull, and to the Bolsheviks' ultra-sophisticated political awareness, tight-knit and

[31] See G. N. Melnikov, *Oktiabr' v Kazakhstane* (Alma-Ata, 1930), pp. 30, 186.

[32] Single-minded at least where the retention of Soviet rule in the border-lands was concerned.

purposive organizational strength, highly self-conscious power orientation, and increasingly ruthless transformationist thrust, the indigenous intelligentsia could counterpose but quite inadequate resources.

As we have seen, the secular elites, having entered only recently the political arena, and having been consistently isolated from their natural societal constituencies, lacked the requisite background for cooperative and large-scale political designs. They were not only small in number but lacked a strong, unified, well-legitimated leadership and organizational framework. Their long-term separation from the grassroots could not be easily remedied, since they arrived at this juncture without clearly articulated and shared goals, without sufficient training in the intricacies of mass-oriented ideology and politics, and without solidly shaped and flexible designs for action. They were also divided by the diversity and uncertainty of their transformationist commitments. The latter ranged from vaguely liberal to radical, did not clearly relate immediate political imperatives and the realities of a traditional social order, and barely transcended the habituated small circles of parochial vision.

Perhaps most important in the short run, it turned out that the region's modernist intelligentsia was as afflicted by mutual suspicions, jealousies, and feuds—and as divided by lines of ethnicity, community, and kinship—as its traditionalist countrymen. This became especially evident on the eve of Central Asia's "national delimitation" in the early 1920's. It would seem that at that time leading native politicians, including radical *dzhadids* and members of the Communist Party, actively conspired to seize maximum political, economic, and territorial advantages on behalf of their new local constituencies, and apparently even came to blows on this account on the forum of the Sredazburo, the Central Asian Bureau of the Communist Party's Central Committee.[33]

For all these reasons, then, the intelligentsia's chances for coherent, cohesive, and autonomous self-assertion inside the Soviet fold were doomed from the outset. In this case, as in others, the classic communist treatment of tactical alliances led to a full-scale denouement in a very short time. In little over a decade following the consolidation of Soviet rule in the area virtually the entire *dzhadid* cadre initially co-opted by the Communist Party and the Soviet administrative hierarchy was methodically isolated with-

[33] See Liubimova, *VPG*, p. 62.

in the apparatus, purged with relative ease, and physically liquidated.[34]

DISCONTINUITY BETWEEN LOCAL CONCERNS AND SUPRA-COMMUNAL ISSUES: GENERAL IMPLICATIONS

As we have seen, the cumulative effect of endogenous and exogenous factors was to emphasize strongly the traditional discontinuity between local concerns and supra-communal issues. Indeed, it would seem that throughout the Soviet reconquest of the Moslem borderlands the mass of the local population remained, for the most part, mute and impassive spectators. Or, as Richard Pipes has pointed out, they tended to "[give] up the struggle . . . as soon as the Communist regime . . . made it possible for them to return to their traditional ways of life. . . ."[35] Given the pattern of primordial cleavages, and the customary modes of accommodation to successful conquerors, the arrival of Soviet forces in the urban hubs of Central Asia could indeed be regarded as still another exchange of urban masters. While such masters might be trusted even less than their predecessors, their arrival had clearly revealed the chinks in the previous incumbents' armor, and the weakness of all other current competitors for power in the region. Thus, their very arrival testified to their strength which, in turn, dictated caution and avoidance where possible. To be sure, the new masters, like their predecessors, had to be watched, but like all strangers they could be considered largely irrelevant to the life of a local community—until it became evident just how their presence would affect day-to-day existence in a given village, family, or clan.

Needless to say, this permitted Moscow to handle the foci of local political competition and military resistance one by one. However, what Soviet victories ultimately attained here was a peace of well-nigh universal withdrawal, turning Central Asia quickly into a vast conglomeration of self-imposed insularities. When faced with

[34] For the role of Peters, a Latvian communist and high-ranking Soviet secret police officer (and a protégé of both Stalin and Dzerzhinsky), in preparing the ground for this denouement in the 1920's, see G. Agabekov, *OGPU* (New York, 1931), pp. 12, 15. For an illustration of Lenin's early unease about Peters, as well as about Pravdin, who apparently stood close to him, see Lenin's letter to Yoffe, Sept. 1921, quoted in *Lenin o Druzhbe*, p. 325. Some brief supplementary accounts may be found in Zenkovsky, *Pan-Turkism*, pp. 246, 248, and Rywkin, *Russia in Central Asia, passim*.

[35] See Pipes, *The Formation*, pp. 259-60.

a systematically winning Red Army, and with a succession of indigenous leaders and groupings whose legitimacy was questionable, whose goals were hazy or incomprehensible, and whose actions were at cross-purposes, spasmodic, and ineffectual, nomads and peasants came to withdraw into the most natural of their social shells. They withdrew, that is, into those relatively small communal circles wherein ties of faith, blood, and custom could be depended upon for mutual understanding, protection, and support; where lifelong intimacy of tested affinal and consanguinal ties permitted one to expect a fair measure of security and solidarity; and where there was, by definition, hardly any need at all to get involved with strangers.

This meant that, at the inception of Soviet experiments in social engineering in the 1920's, the new revolutionary regime confronted in Central Asia a highly diverse and multilayered universe. In this universe, the largest (supra-communal)—and hence the most *heterogeneous*—historical subdivisions were on the verge of disintegration, while the smallest—and hence the most *homogeneous*, including clans, extended families, and village communities—were relatively intact. This social pattern made the imposition of a structure of Soviet power in the region in the period between 1918 and 1922 a relatively easy task, and also ensured that no serious and concerted challenge to that power would easily materialize. Yet as Bolshevik strategists were shortly to realize with growing unease, the very pattern of local traditional solidarities and orientations that had made the cluster of Central Asia's traditional societies so fragmented, communocentric, and insular, and thus so accessible and vulnerable to the determined thrust of modern Soviet power, tended also to make them particularly elusive to attempts not merely to "establish" a mechanism of power but to legitimize it and use it for rapid revolutionary transformation and efficient integration.

TWO · *Problems of Access and Influence in a Traditional Milieu: The Quest for Strategic Leverage Points*

PROBLEMS OF ACCESS AND INFLUENCE: THE RELEVANCE OF LENINISM

POWER to intervene vis-à-vis ability to transform: this was the crucial issue confronting the Soviet regime immediately following military victory and formal incorporation of the Moslem borderlands into the Soviet Union. It is a safe assumption that this dichotomy—the ease of military conquest and the difficulty of revolutionary engagement—affected most sharply initial Soviet perceptions in the area. Neither official ideology nor even the instrument that had been used by the party so successfully elsewhere—the organizational weapon—proved, at least at first, quite relevant and equal to the task in Central Asia. Here, the regime confronted a milieu that turned out to be far more elusive to direct manipulation than Russian society, and far less comprehensible in terms of Marxist-Leninist ideology.

To be sure, in Leninism the Bolsheviks had an ideological weapon that combined a strong voluntaristic and teleological bias with equally strong organizational, interventionist, and manipulative dispositions. But Leninism was also markedly ambivalent regarding specific transformationist strategies to be employed in the conquered societies, especially in the Central Asian context. In fact, if one was to point to at least one intrinsic tension within Leninism as an ideology, it would surely be the tension between the certainties of intervention and the uncertainties of transformation.

The critical importance of interventionism in Leninist orientations is well known.[1] A passion to make history, not wait for it to unfold, came to be the touchstone of Lenin's political imagination.

[1] Among the many full-length works on Leninism, A. G. Meyer's *Leninism* (Cambridge, Mass., 1957) is unquestionably the best. Excellent chapters on Leninist ideology and tactics may be found in M. Fainsod's *How Russia Is Ruled* (rev. ed., Cambridge, Mass., 1963); in L. Schapiro's *The Communist Party of the Soviet Union* (New York, 1960); and in B. Moore's *Soviet Politics—The Dilemma of Power* (Cambridge, Mass., 1950).

38

It formed the basis of his attitudes to all politics as well as to the strategy and tactics of a conspiratorial movement: the timing and execution of the conquest of power, the destruction of the old world of customs, relationships, and norms, and the construction of a new one. For Lenin, the political act became a creative act par excellence. The ends of history might be given, the tempi were not: they could be forced by the planned and systematic application of political violence, through the medium of a tough revolutionary vanguard.

Thus, a Leninist vanguard could supplant faith in historical determinism with a passionate emphasis on political artifice; instead of being bound by the uncertainties of revolutionary forecasting and mass-spontaneity, a revolutionary elite could actively master the flow of time through an assertion of political intelligence and will. In this way, men who had found the strength and insight to break with the world of feelings, and were not inclined to stand by and suffer helplessly while conditions "matured," could bring out and quicken that which was merely immanent and elemental in society's historical development. Through an act amounting to political alchemy, they could both telescope and improve upon the historical process; they could transcend the rhythms of history and, in doing so, transcend themselves.

Given the supreme importance of a revolutionary elite—in effect a group of men substituting themselves for history and its "progressive classes"—quite exceptional means were necessary to ensure its effectiveness. For Lenin, the means seemed obvious: a tightly knit, hierarchical, centralized—in effect, monolithic—organization, staffed by militant, unquestionably disciplined, professional revolutionaries. Such an organization—combining the characteristics of a religious sect and a military machine—had to be suited for conspiracy and combat, for agitation and mass mobilization. It had to be capable of destroying the old political society and providing the requirements of the new. In their relationship to the masses, members—and especially the high command—of a Leninist party would thus resemble a steeled, professional officers corps and priestly stratum leading the multitudes on a crusade. The party itself could claim to be an indispensable catalyst and guide—indeed, an infallible instrument—for transformation and development. While its success in particular actions depended on a pragmatic rather than doctrinaire approach, it could lay claim to a monopoly of power as much as to a monopoly of truth.

In this sense, a Leninist revolutionary disposition might be visualized as a radical modernizing disposition, an intense proclivity for deliberate and holistic social engineering. As such, it denoted a profoundly instrumental approach to nature, society, and history, a persistent disposition to seek, activate, and utilize optimum techniques and instruments for the mobilization of human and material energies on the road to an imagined promised land.[2] It thus implied a purposive and concerted effort to traverse great developmental distance toward authoritatively (and unilaterally) charted goals in deliberately truncated time.[3]

These were the implications, and the certainties, of intervention. But they reflected primarily an intensely perceived imperative, and an explicitly or implicitly stated vision and intent. They did not necessarily denote an ability to deal with the fruits of victorious intervention, i.e., to transform the conquered milieu in conformance with valued ends. While, in the conquest of power, Leninist revolutionary politics might indeed have been viewed as having the virtues of autonomy, the same could not be said for the period of actual social reconstitution. By forcing what would in effect be a *coup d'état* before socio-economic conditions were "ripe" enough for spontaneous mass insurrection, Leninist revolutionaries could not but confront these same incongruent conditions after victory. By substituting themselves for history and its "progressive classes," Leninists would be taking over, *ipso facto*, history's unfulfilled tasks.

Even before the Civil War was fully concluded, there were signs that Lenin's previously unqualified optimism was waning. Between 1917 and 1923—as Alfred Meyer has characterized this—the period of "exuberant optimism" in Lenin's expectations gave way, at first, to a period marked by an "emergence from utopian dreams," and then to one of "objective self-criticism," somber "stock-taking," and "strategic retreat."[4] The ruling elite was now faced with a number of painful problems affecting the whole of society, the

[2] For a strikingly articulated variant of such a disposition see Lenin, *Sochineniia*, Vol. 27, pp. 134-35, as quoted in K. Buslov, *Problemy Sotsial'-nogo Progressa v Trudakh V. I. Lenina* (Minsk, 1963), p. 167; cf. Meyer, *Leninism*, p. 263, including footnote (†).

[3] For a suggestive visualization of such an imperative (in the context of what Cyril Black has called "defensive modernization"), see Stalin's speech, "The Tasks of Business Executives" (Feb. 4, 1931), in his *Problems of Leninism*, pp. 365-66, as quoted in Fainsod, *How Russia Is Ruled*, pp. 102, 285.

[4] See Meyer, *Leninism*, pp. 187 ff.

solutions to which proved unexpectedly obscure.[5] Moreover, if Lenin's political imagination was taxed by such problems in the familiar realm of Russia proper, how was he to respond to those arising out of Soviet presence in Central Asia, a milieu belonging, on most counts, to the previous millennium? In the period between 1918 and his final incapacitation, Lenin's unease and bafflement on this account grew, and came to center on a cluster of interrelated and sharply perceived problems, most of which concerned quite directly Russia's Asian borderlands.

The Specter of a Chartless Voyage

Lenin's initial response to Central Asia was characteristic: it was a throwback to nineteenth-century European ethnocentrism; it was an amalgam of shock, frustration, and disgust. As he saw it, the social order in Russia's borderlands was characterized by "stubbornly habituated" institutions, by "ossification," "stagnation," "backwardness." It did not even deserve to be termed an "order of things"; it was a state of "disgrace and savagery."[6] It was bound to make Soviet attempts to tackle economic, social, and cultural institutions in the area most difficult. Trotsky concurred, though only in the characterization. Evidently he had all too little time or desire to concern himself with the implications: Central Asia represented "the most backward of the backward"; it meant "barbarity or patriarchal life"; it amounted to "prehistoric existence."[7]

Not satisfied with merely indicting the "savagery," Lenin was quite honest to admit utter ignorance where Central Asia's peoples were concerned, and he was quick to demand "[elementary] facts" about the region from his special emissaries there.[8] He pressed for information about local economies as much as about the quality of indigenous personnel; he wanted facts about local political associations and about the effectiveness of Soviet agencies in the field—as well as a delineation of the reasons for persistent tensions between Soviet Russian personnel and the indigenous population. He wanted to know most of all about local social structures, and, with

[5] For an excellent analysis of the early doubts, and of the confrontations on this account, between Bolsheviks and non-Bolsheviks alike, see Robert V. Daniels, *The Conscience of the Revolution* (Cambridge, Mass., 1960).

[6] Lenin, *Sochineniia*, Vol. 32, p. 139, as quoted in V. Bil'shai, *Reshenie Zhenskogo Voprosa v SSSR* (Moscow, 1959), p. 190.

[7] Leon Trotsky, *A History of the Russian Revolution* (Ann Arbor, 1932), Vol. III, pp. 46-47.

[8] *Lenin o Druzhbe*, pp. 324-25.

a persistence that bordered on the naive, he asked in a letter to Yoffe: "Is it true that the natives are being '*forcibly*' differentiated [into social classes by the representatives of the Soviet regime]?"[9]

Already, when addressing the Second Congress of Asian Communists (November 22, 1919), Lenin hinted at his own bafflement.[10] The fundamental question was this: How was one to build socialism under "Eastern conditions"—where there was no industrial proletariat to speak of, where peasants and nomads constituted the bulk of the population, where diverse primordial traditions were a guide to the norms of life, where the "Oriental masses" were barely reachable, "where one must solve the problems of a struggle not against capitalism, but against survivals of medievalism"?[11]

One of Lenin's answers (enunciated somewhat later and to a different audience)[12] to this question was stereotyped and probably largely hortatory. Given tough and self-reliant native revolutionary cadres, given peasant-soviets "[especially] adapted to the conditions of a pre-capitalist social order," and given the assistance of the victorious (i.e., Russian and generally European) proletariat operating from an "advanced" revolutionary center, "backward countries . . . [with feudal or semi-feudal systems could indeed] pass on to a soviet system and, via certain developmental stages, to communism, bypassing the capitalist stage of development." To be sure, precisely what means would be needed to accomplish this transition was something that was "impossible to point out in advance." Only "practical experience" would tell.[13]

But in his speech to the audience that included leaders of fledgling communist movements in India, China, and Indochina, Lenin was somewhat more straightforward about his expectations and uncertainties: "[The] majority of the peoples of the East find themselves in conditions [even] worse than those of the most backward European nation—Russia. . . . [Hence,] there stands before you

---

[9] Ibid.

[10] See Lenin's speech to the Second All-Russian Congress of Communist Organizations of Peoples of the East, *Izvestiya*, Dec. 20, 1919, and *Soch.* (4th ed.), Vol. 30, pp. 130-41, as quoted in *Lenin o Druzhbe*, pp. 273-84.

[11] *Lenin o Druzhbe*, pp. 281-83.

[12] See "Doklad Kommissii po natsional'nym i kolonial'nym voprosam," at the Second Congress of the Comintern, July 26, 1921, in Lenin, *Soch.* (4th ed.), Vol. 31, pp. 207-209, 215-20, as quoted in *Lenin o Druzhbe*, pp. 302-307.

[13] "Doklad Kommissii . . . ," ibid., pp. 305-306.

here a task that had never before confronted any of the world's communists . . . [:You] must adapt yourselves to conditions that are *sui generis*, [and unheard of in Europe; and] you must succeed in adapting [both] theory and practice [to these conditions]."[14] The problem, then, was both "difficult and original. . . . [The] teachings of communism that had been meant to apply to communists of more advanced countries [needed to be] translated [for the benefit of specifically Oriental, agrarian, tradition-bound milieus]."[15]

How, exactly, was all this to be done? While Lenin's answer was replete with suggestions about strategy and tactics (including a special emphasis on the revolutionary activization of the peasantry and on an alliance with "bourgeois nationalism"), it was coupled with a well-nigh extraordinary proposition. Ultimately, he said, communists of the Asian world would need both to formulate and to solve their concrete revolutionary tasks by drawing on their own independent experience. Why? Because "there is not a single communist book" where such solutions could be found.[16]

The Specter of General Indifference

As Lenin and some of his Asian lieutenants in the party—such as Mikoyan, Sultan-Galiev, and Safarov—were becoming all too well aware, the preoccupations of Russian, or generally European, communists during and immediately after the Civil War centered primarily on the political and economic survival of the "revolutionary center." Issues of power, order, and safety were seen as paramount. Asian borderlands, involving particularly Central Asia and the Caucasus, tended to be viewed as auxiliary to Russia proper.

Such attitudes among leading Leninist cadres were coupled both with ignorance of Russia's Asian borderlands and with an unwillingness to study the subtleties of local ways of life. The borderlands were presumably too insignificant in the hierarchy of power and status in the Union to merit much attention. They were too far behind even the most "backward" Russian peasant communities; too uninvolved in either making or consolidating the October Revolution; too unfamiliar, inhospitable, and exotic to lend themselves to grand political analysis and strategy. Thus they tended to be, in effect, ignored by the bulk of communist leadership and rank and file

[14] See Lenin's speech to Asian Communists in 1919, as quoted in *Lenin o Druzhbe*, pp. 281-83.

[15] Ibid., p. 283.　　　　　　　　[16] Ibid.

alike. For example, Trotsky, Bukharin, Kamenev, Rykov, Radek, Zinoviev, Sverdlov, Molotov, Bubnov, and Krestinsky—all of them pivotal figures in the party's high command in the early 1920's— had hardly anything significant to say on the subject. Other leading communists—such as Kuibyshev, Kaganovich, Tomsky, Kalinin, Ordzhonikidze, and Frunze—became involved on one or another occasion in issues concerning Soviet Asia, but only in the role of proconsuls sent down from the center to solidify a particular political or military position in the region or to grace a particular event. The only concern that was more or less intensely shared by all these men, with respect to Central Asia, was the role this region could play in securing Russia's strategic positions and in revolutionizing the Orient; and this had little or nothing to do with the nature of the region's societies or with the prospect of their transformation and development along socialist lines.[17]

Mikoyan sensed this quite early, and registered his unease at the party's Tenth Congress in March, 1921. He reminded his comrades that it was "impermissible [to lump] all eastern peoples" under a single set of largely stereotyped categories. "The East," he said, "is more varied than the European countries." It was imperative that "[Soviet] politics with respect to the eastern question . . . be subtle and well thought out." It was necessary "[to look carefully into the economic and class-structure of each Asian society . . .], to take local circumstances into account, and to accommodate oneself to them." Yet, in spite of this need, Mikoyan detected a peculiar reluctance on the part of most European communists to probe these matters: "We [sit here and] talk about [our] eastern nationalities, but I know that the notion many comrades have of the East is that of something fantastic, something rather dim."[18]

Safarov, a leading Turkic communist with apparently close ties to Lenin, was equally outspoken. "It is necessary to state honestly," he told the same party congress, "that until now our party has hardly interested itself in the national question." How was it possi-

[17] For a partial consideration of Central Asia's role in early Soviet calculations, see Walter Laqueur, *The Soviet Union and the Middle East* (New York, 1959), esp. Chs. 1-2; Pipes, *The Formation*, esp. Ch. VI; E. H. Carr, *The Bolshevik Revolution, 1917-1923* (New York, 1951-1953), Vol. I, esp., Chs. 10-14, and Vol. III, esp. Chs. 26, 32; E. H. Carr, *Socialism in One Country* (New York, 1964), Vol. III, Part II, Chs. 37-38.

[18] See Mikoyan's remarks in *Protokoly Desyatogo S'ezda RKP(b)* (Moscow, 1963), pp. 207-208.

ble, he asked, for "comrades, communists, advanced proletarian elements [to know and care so little about minority nationalities, and even] enter into situations of contradiction and conflict with the toiling masses of [formerly] oppressed people"? He suggested, most probably with tongue in cheek, that this could be understood only if one viewed the behavior of European communists as "completely unconscious."[19]

It is surely ironic that, aside from Lenin, only one man in the party's supreme councils gave more than passing attention to this matter: Joseph Stalin. Indeed, some of Stalin's rivals may have underestimated him partly because he made his way to the top apparently on the strength of his seeming expertise in the "nationality question," especially as it pertained to Central Asia and the Caucasus. His rivals' fatal mistake may have been compounded by their initial tendency to consider Stalin and to tolerate him as a convenient though somewhat crude "representative of Eastern peoples" in Soviet ranks.[20] Aside from its significance in depicting the relationships and the implicit pecking order in the nascent Bolshevik elite, such an attitude was in itself suggestive of the place occupied by "Eastern" problems in the early Soviet value-system and order of priorities. And it may help to explain why, after Lenin was gone, there was hardly anyone in the top ranks—with the exception of Stalin—to claim even a modicum of interest or informed judgment with respect to Russia's Asian traditional societies.

The Specter of Political Reductionism

In part because of the absence of an operational chart, because of the growing bureaucratization of the Soviet apparatus, because of the powerful centripetal pressures exerted from Moscow, and because of so many communists' indifference, the party's attitudes in regard to Russia's Asian societies tended—as Lenin noted with growing unease—towards *shablonizatsiia*. This denoted operational and organizational homogenization, in effect the reduction of all forms of enterprise and association to stereotyped molds conceived in, and ruthlessly enforced from, the "revolutionary center."

In the last years of his political life—between the end of Russia's Civil War and his final incapacitation—Lenin attempted to counter this trend by advocating what amounted to operational pluralism.

[19] See Safarov's speech in *Desiatyi S'ezd RKP(b)*, p. 189.

[20] See, e.g., Isaac Deutscher, *Stalin, a Political Biography* (New York, 1949), esp. pp. 121-22, on Trotsky's initial response to Stalin.

It seems quite a safe inference that such advocacy did not spring so much from a democratic impulse as from the urge to rationalize the process by which the Soviet state should develop. Indeed, he urged a "scientific approach" to issues of social transformation precisely because the road to socialism was without precedents, theories, and models. For Lenin, to recognize this meant to recognize the need to consider and test every plausible idea. It meant to evaluate and compare local proposals, initiatives, and experience— and then generalize those forms and practices that proved to be most advantageous. This clearly presupposed "the full and unhindered development not only of locally peculiar characteristics, but also of local initiative, local innovation, of diversity in the means and approaches . . . toward a common goal." Thus, Lenin almost explicitly sanctioned what later came to be called "different roads to socialism." More than that: he proposed that, in order to find the most appropriate—as well as the "most economical"—of these roads, it was necessary to give free, even "competitive," play to local innovation throughout the Soviet Union's multifaceted communities.[21]

On this basis, it seemed self-evident to Lenin that "democratic centralism" (officially the ground rule of Soviet politics) did not preclude "autonomous" and "federative" forms. As he put it, "Nothing can be more mistaken than the confusion of democratic centralism with bureaucratism and *shablonizatsiia*." Centralism "that is understood in a genuinely democratic sense" could not possibly ignore the "uniqueness" of local conditions, the "peculiarities of local economic systems and modes of life," the "degree of preparedness on the part of the local population." It was important for Moscow's emissaries to understand that the conditions prevalent in the Asian borderlands were especially far removed from those characteristic of European Russia. Hence it was "indispensable that our tactics not be copied [in Soviet Asia]"; that, instead, they be "thoughtfully modified and adapted with differing concrete conditions in mind." Accordingly, it was necessary to "think independently," and to "apply to local conditions not the letter but the spirit, the meaning, the lessons of [Russia's] experience between 1917 and 1921." Transition to socialism in the Asian borderlands

[21] See Lenin's "Iz pervonachal'nogo nabroska statii 'ocherednye zadachi sovetskoi vlasti," dictated March 28, 1918; *Soch.* (4th ed.), Vol. 27, pp. 180-82, as quoted in *Lenin o Natsional'nom i Natsional'no-Kolonial'nom Voprose* (Moscow, 1956), pp. 470-72.

called for "more gentleness, more caution, [a more tractable and] yielding [attitude] with respect to [local social strata]." It was to be expected that here such a transition would have to be "slower, [more gradual], more systematic" than in Russia.[22]

Needless to say, all this was easier said than done, and Lenin found himself shocked by what in fact occurred, particularly in the Asian periphery. He found that his lieutenants could easily take advantage not only of his physical incapacitation but of the contradictory thrust of most of his ideas. While urging careful differentiation between various regions and cultures, he also insisted on "absolute harmony and unification" in the functioning of the Soviet Union's main economic sectors. Though calling, in effect, for a free play of ideas, and for a rational comparison of locally conceived social experiments, he also warned that such "competitive initiatives" must not be permitted to degenerate into mere *original'-nichanie*—that is, originality for its own sake, wild and reckless "idea-mongering." Whereas one of his interpretations of "democratic centralism" allowed for diversity in the development of Soviet Asia, others stipulated the leading role of the "advanced" Russian revolutionary center in ruling and transforming the "ossified" East. Likewise, while some of his exhortations called for gradualism, adaptability, and caution in dealing with Oriental societies, others prescribed the "skipping" of historical stages by these societies, and their movement from medievalism directly to communism.[23]

Thus, the most ambitious and aggressive of Lenin's comrades could proceed with utter disregard of his implicit advocacy of different roads to socialism. Ruthless bureaucratic centralizers could ignore his notions of local autonomy and innovation. In the process, subtlety and forethought were often thrown to the winds. Instead of encouraging local initiative and improvisation, Moscow's agents tended to demand that the center's structures and tactics be copied in every respect. In short—as was apparent from Lenin's last impassioned pleas before his death—the cause of flexible,

[22] This collation of Lenin's arguments is based on two of his pronouncements between 1918 and 1921: "Iz pervonachal'nogo nabroska statii 'ocherednye zadachi sovetskoi vlasti," dictated March 28, 1918, *Soch.* (4th ed.), Vol. 27, pp. 180-82, as quoted in *Lenin o Natsional'nom*, pp. 470-72; "Tovarishcham-kommunistam Azerbaidzhana, Gruzii, Armenii, Dagestana, Gorskoi respubliki," April 14, 1921, *Soch.* (4th ed.), Vol. 32, pp. 295-97, as quoted in *Lenin o Druzhbe*, pp. 318-20.

[23] See the preceding two footnotes.

methodical, carefully tested approaches to social change in Soviet Asia could be easily subverted at the outset; local inventiveness and adaptation could be dismissed in favor of rigid, crudely wrought, reductionist injunctions from above.[24]

The Specter of Economic Exploitation

While Lenin was, of course, quite eager to reclaim all former Tsarist colonial possessions during the Civil War, and was delighted to congratulate his generals when Soviet armies occupied Central Asia, there were signs that he came to share with a handful of his disciples a sharp unease regarding the economic policies of Soviet agencies in the re-conquered region. It seems that, in the name of "the primacy of the revolutionary center," or altogether without bothering to search for an excuse, official representatives of the Soviet regime proceeded to treat the area just as it had been treated in the defunct Russian empire: purely as an economic appendage, as a base of food and raw materials—cotton, wool, oil, metals, cattle, fruit.

Thus, when Frunze's troops broke White resistance and marched into Central Asia in 1919, his triumphant message to Moscow announced that the "road to the cotton of Turkestan" was now open. This prompted Zinoviev's cool proposal to barter Russia's "civilization" for Central Asia's raw materials.[25] At the Tenth Party Congress (1921) Zatonskii gave what was perhaps the classic expression to this attitude (and one that was evidently shared by many of his comrades). As he put it, " . . . even if there had been no military considerations" at stake, the imperatives of ironclad unity and tight economic coordination were bound to determine the relations between the center and the periphery. Moreover, while this center happened to be, "by accident," the home of Great Russians, it was also the crucible of revolution and the locus of industry—and, as such, it played a special role and commanded definite priority. Hence it was both "indispensable" and "completely natural" to fortify this center: if this had to be done at the expense of the borderlands, it would be "correct" to do so; if, for this purpose, it should be necessary to adopt a policy of "plundering the borderlands," this, too, would be correct.[26]

There were obvious dangers in such behavior. Aside from the

[24] See the reference in the preceding note.
[25] See Park, *Bolshevism*, p. 261.
[26] See Zatonskii's remarks in *Desiatyi S'ezd RKP(b)*, p. 203.

48

difficulty to justify it on moral grounds, there was the danger of continuing colonial distortions in the area's economic development. This could not but discourage the evolution of local societies in the Soviet image, make a mockery of the area's progress toward communism, and generate lasting distrust, disillusionment, and disaffection on the part of indigenous populations. Indeed, leading Turkic radicals and communists lost no time to warn Moscow about "[looking at] Eastern republics . . . mainly with 'economic eyes.' "[27] Some of them (including Ikramov, destined to become the First Secretary of the Uzbek Communist Party) did not hesitate to raise the issue of "red colonialism,"[28] and even voiced protests to this effect at the First Congress of the Peoples of the East (in 1920), to the intense embarrassment of Moscow's organizers at the congress.[29] In 1921, Lenin strongly admonished Caucasian (and, by clear implication, Central Asian) communists to insist on balanced development of their societies and economies.[30] In effect, he urged Soviet Asian communists not to tolerate the economic exploitation of their homelands by Bolshevik super-centralizers and Russian chauvinists.

In the same year (at the party's Tenth Congress) Safarov, most probably with Lenin's encouragement, spoke in barely veiled terms about the consequences of permitting traditional Russian contempt and brutality toward Moslems to influence Soviet policies in Central Asia. Such policies could only lead to "unforgivable mistakes" and would completely "block [the Asian borderlands'] revolutionary development."[31]

The Specter of Coercion and Rebellion

Nothing disturbed Lenin so deeply as the spectacle of victorious communists—leaders and rank and file alike—indulging their ambitions and appetite for power at the expense both of each other and of the societies they had conquered. Marxist ideology and the

[27] *ZhN*, 11 (68), April 18, 1920, as quoted in Park, *Bolshevism*, p. 261.

[28] See I. V. Stalin, *Sochineniia* (Moscow, 1946), Vol. v, pp. 306-307.

[29] *Pervyi S'ezd Narodov Vostoka, Baku, 1-8 sent. 1920g. stenogr. otchety* (Petrograd, 1920), pp. 87-89.

[30] See his letter, "Tovarishcham-kommunistam Azerbaidzhana, Gruzii, Armenii, Dagestana, Gorskoi respubliki," as quoted in *Lenin o Druzhbe*, p. 320.

[31] See Safarov's speech, *Desiatyi S'ezd RKP(b)*, pp. 189-201. Cf. Lenin's unease on this account, in his "Zakliuchitel'noe slovo po dokladu o partiinoi programme 19 Marta" (1919), as quoted in *Lenin o Natsional'nom*, p. 484.

moral dimensions of Leninist teachings seemed to play no role at all in the relationship between Russian—or Russified—party functionaries and Asian peoples, including Asian communists.

As Lenin saw it, the ruthless self-assertion of his own lieutenants —such as Stalin, Ordzhonikidze, and Dzerzhinsky—was coming to play a "fatal role" in Soviet politics. They, and their emissaries in minority-milieus (especially in Soviet Asia), seemed to have a cynical disregard for the basic principles that were to guide communist leadership: "self-control," "proletarian solidarity," and "national equality." They were prepared to crush and browbeat anyone opposing their will, even the most dedicated local communists. They, as well as Russian officials, settlers, and workers in colonized provinces (particularly in Asia) treated minority populations with "abuse," "brutality," and "contempt." They behaved like "common scoundrels," and "violators," in effect like Tsarist imperialist *dzerzhimordy*—men with a coarse police mentality (literally, holders-of-the-snout, ugly muzzlers).[32] Given such men and such behavior, it was inevitable that the new native political leadership among Asian minorities—a stratum that was as thin and weak as it was preciously important—would "drown in the sea of Great Russian chauvinist riffraff like a fly in milk."[33]

Thus, it would seem that behind Lenin's references to the need for "independent thinking" in revolutionary initiatives in Soviet Asia, and behind his emphasis on requisite respect for the "uniqueness" and "diversity" of local ways of life, there was an apprehensiveness about the broad implications of Soviet actions. It clearly concerned the possibility that Russian great-power chauvinism, as well as the Bolsheviks' heedless centralizing drive—involving rank repression of any assertion of individuality and autonomy by smaller, particularly Asian, nationalities—might submerge all other considerations in the life of the party and in the operation of the Soviet regime. Behind the pleas for gentleness and caution lay

---

[32] See Lenin's "K voprosu o natsional'nostiakh ili ob 'avtonomizatsii' " (in three parts, dictated December 30-31, 1922), *Kommunist*, No. 9, 1956, as quoted in *Lenin o Natsional'nom*, pp. 546-52. See also the last note Lenin dictated (on March 6, 1923) before suffering his final paralyzing stroke, a note that dealt specifically with the "connivances" of Stalin and his minions; the Trotsky Archive, T-788, as quoted in Pipes, *The Formation*, p. 289. For a full translation and perceptive discussion of all these notes, see Pipes, *The Formation*, pp. 282-93.

[33] K voprosu o natsional'nostiakh . . . ," as quoted in *Lenin o Natsional'nom*, p. 547.

Lenin's fear of arbitrary and generalized coercion, one that might gravely impair the legitimation of Soviet rule even before the communist program could begin to be implemented.[34]

As Lenin visualized it, then, two long-term and equally disastrous consequences might easily ensue. Externally, Soviet actions that smacked of Great Russian imperialism could arouse the suspicions of, and eventually antagonize altogether, the rising peoples of Africa and Asia. And that would happen at precisely the time when—Lenin was becoming increasingly convinced—the colonial and underdeveloped "East" was coming to be a far more promising revolutionary theater than the capitalist-industrial West.[35] Internally, there would be irreparable alienation of the minorities and their leaders from the Soviet cause, distortion or paralysis of local development, a permanent state of tension between Moscow and the borderlands, a break in the recruitment of indigenous cadres, and eventually, as the *basmachi* revolt in Central Asia had proved, rebellion and civil war.[36]

Safarov (again, very likely with Lenin's concurrence) carried these warnings one step farther. As he pointed out at the Tenth Party Congress, it was especially dangerous to compound the injustices and distortions of Soviet socioeconomic policies by tying them to a bureaucratic apparatus that continued to be based in Slavic-controlled cities rather than in the native countryside. Such an arrangement not only compromised the natives' ability to "rule themselves"; it permitted neither the "expression" nor the "defense" of their "class interests," that is, "the interests of human

[34] See "Zapiska v Politburo o bor'be s velikoderzhavnym shovinizmom," Oct. 6, 1922; *Soch.* (4th ed.) Vol. 33, p. 335, quoted in *Lenin o Natsional'nom*, p. 544, and "K voprosu o natsional'nostiakh . . . ," Part III, Dec. 31, 1922, quoted ibid., pp. 551-52.

[35] See "K voprosu o natsional'nostiakh . . . ," Part III, Dec. 31, 1922, quoted in *Lenin o Natsional'nom*, pp. 551-52, and "Luchshe men'she, da luchshe," March 4, 1923 in Lenin's *Soch.* (4th ed.), Vol. 33, pp. 455-58, as quoted ibid., pp. 553-56 (esp. 554). Cf. "Probuzhdenie Azii," May 7, 1913 in Lenin's *Soch.* (4th ed.), Vol. 19, pp. 65-66, as quoted ibid., pp. 75-76; and "Kul'turnye evropeitsy i dikiie aziaty," April 14, 1913, in *Soch.* (4th ed.), Vol. 19, pp. 37-38, as quoted ibid., pp. 73-74. See also "K desiatiletnemu iuvileiu 'Pravdy,'" May 2, 1922; Lenin, *Soch.* (4th ed.), Vol. 33, pp. 312-15, as quoted ibid., esp. p. 542.

[36] For explicit or implicit indications of this concern, see Lenin's "Pis'mo A. A. Yoffe," Sept. 13, 1921, quoted in *Lenin o Druzhbe*, pp. 324-25, and "K voprosu o natsional'nostiakh . . . ," Part III, Dec. 31, 1922, quoted in *Lenin o Natsional'nom*, pp. 551-52.

beings who had [long] been oppressed and enslaved." In fact, this arrangement made it especially clear why, in regions such as central Asia, "the national question" and "class inequality" were so intimately connected. To wit: Slavs (and especially Russians), claiming to be more "advanced," not only continued to hold most of the choice land, industrial jobs, and professional positions, but also maintained a firm grip on the entire administrative apparatus. Thus *national predominance* in crucial economic and administrative sectors constituted *de facto class predominance* as well.

As Safarov saw it, such a situation carried the seeds of grave predicaments. On the one hand, it was absolutely impossible to gain access to a native milieu where Russian-held cities were considered "sources of all police-scorpions"; where the distrust of things Russian in a native was "ingested with his mother's milk"; where a Russian could still be considered "an overlord, a violator, a plunderer"; where Russian colonists were still "hunting down [natives] like wild beasts"; and where native proverbs continued to claim that "if you've got a Russian for a friend, keep a stone on the ready." On the other hand, there could be no point in considering "one or another kind of nationality policy," and no possibility at all of commencing the revolutionary transformation of Central Asian societies, as long as "the dead [held such a grip] . . . upon the living"; as long as "old colonial relationships [continued] under the mask of Soviet forms"; as long as Soviet policies "caused the contradictions between town and country to assume the character of national antagonism."[37]

Thus, Safarov's linkage of national and class oppression implicitly applied to Soviet Central Asia Lenin's earlier arguments about the demise of global imperialism through the collapse of its "weak links" in colonized societies. What this meant was that by permitting its agents to ride roughshod over native sensibilities, Moscow faced in its Asian borderlands not merely a civil war but a war of national liberation.

That is why, in his last impassioned warnings on this account, including his letter, "To the comrades and communists of Turkestan,"[38] Lenin stressed that the establishment of "correct," even "exemplary," relations with Central Asians was, for Russia, of "gigantic, world-historic" significance. All Asia, and the entire

[37] See Safarov's speech in *Desiatyi S'ezd RKP(b)*, pp. 189, 191-98.
[38] Lenin, *Soch.* (4th ed.), Vol. 30, p. 117, as quoted in *Lenin o Druzhbe*, p. 272.

colonial world, would in effect be watching how Russia treated "weak, formerly oppressed . . . peoples." That is why it was "devilishly important for our entire *Weltpolitik* to *win* the natives' trust . . . to win it [again and again] . . . to prove that we are *not* imperialists. . . ."[39] For, after all was said and done,

> . . . there is nothing that delays so much the development and consolidation of proletarian class solidarity as does national injustice, and offended members of minority groups are of all things most sensitive to the feeling of equality and to the violation of that equality by their proletarian comrades, even through [mere] carelessness, even in the form of a joke. That is why in this case it is better to stretch too far in the direction of concessions and gentleness toward the national minorities, rather than too little.[40]

But concessions leading merely to "formal equality" were not enough:

> . . . we, the members of a great [Russian] nation . . . are guilty . . . of an infinite amount of coercion and insults [with respect to the smaller peoples within our borders]. . . . It behooves us [therefore] to *indemnify* [our] minorities . . . in one or another way—in the way we behave and in what we concede—for the mistrust, for the suspicion, for the insults which the ruling "great" nation has brought them in the past.[41]

For Lenin, one of the first such acts of reassurance and indemnity had to be the formulation of a code of political behavior—in effect, a new set of constitutional rules defining the rights and obligations of republics and ethnic groups vis-à-vis the Soviet regime. First and foremost, such a new code (to be drawn up with the help of Russia's minorities themselves) was to guarantee the "full independence" of local administrative organs in all but military and diplomatic matters, and prevent "abuses [of authority]" by Moscow's agents and agencies in their dealings with minorities.[42]

Yet as Stalin (and others) could easily argue, citing copiously Lenin's own pronouncements and actions on different occasions,

---

[39] "Pis'mo A. A. Yoffe," quoted in *Lenin o Druzhbe*, p. 325 (italics in the text).

[40] See "K voprosu o natsional'nostiakh . . . ," Part II, Dec. 31, 1922, quoted in *Lenin o Natsional'nom*, pp. 548-50. Cf. Part III, ibid., pp. 551-52.

[41] Ibid. (italics supplied).   [42] See ibid., Part III, p. 551.

there were definite dangers in "stretching too far" to accommodate the minorities' sensibilities and demands. Opportunities for full-fledged national autonomy could not only vitiate the principles of political unity and economic rationality. They could perpetuate indefinitely the influence of traditional solidarities, cultural identities, and ruling classes. And they could engender particularistic, nationalist, and ultimately separatist tendencies.[43] Indeed, national self-determination that would provide Moslems with strictly proportional representation (i.e., with at least 95 percent of posts in the Soviet apparatus) could mean, in effect, "[the] end of the Bolshevik government" in Central Asia.[44]

In this way, Bolshevik arch-centralizers could always justify a ruthless crackdown on personally or politically inconvenient local leaders as a political necessity, the necessity to root out opponents of "overall coordination" and hence harbingers of "fragmentation." Lenin's admonitions that such allegations might be mere pretexts for coercive self-seeking were to no avail. His warnings that brutal, quasi-imperialist behavior will be far more harmful to the Soviet cause than imperfect coordination and less-than-total institutional unification were, at least initially, for the most part ignored.[45]

Thus, Lenin's final preoccupations before his death reveal just how far post-revolutionary realities had departed from his expectations. Social and economic conditions proved more shocking, ethnocentric tendencies more deeply entrenched, and the importance of both the organizational and the human factor far greater than he had allowed. This in a sense was Lenin's tragedy: that he ran afoul of the deeply authoritarian propensities within his own movement just as he was beginning to fathom the whole range of their implications for the Soviet system, yet when he no longer had the strength to deal with opposition and to enforce his will; and that

[43] See, e.g., Stalin's speech at the Party's Tenth Congress in March, 1921 (*Desiatyi S'ezd RKP(b)*, pp. 700-701), and Stalin's remarks in *Desiatyi Vserosiiskii S'ezd Sovetov . . . 23-27 dekabria 1922 goda* (Moscow, 1923), p. 185. Cf. Lenin, *Soch.* (2nd ed., Moscow, 1926-1932), Vol. XVIII, p. 327; Vol. XXI, pp. 316-17; Vol. XXII, p. 434; and Lenin, *Natsional'nyi Vopros* (Moscow, 1936), esp. p. 64. For a thorough and fully documented discussion of all major issues, see Pipes, *The Formation*, Ch. VI (esp. pp. 269-93).

[44] See F. M. Bailey, *Mission to Tashkent* (London, 1946), pp. 190-91, as cited in Carr, *The Bolshevik Revolution*, Vol. I, p. 334.

[45] See "K voprosu o natsional'nostiakh . . . ," Part III, Dec. 31, 1922, as quoted in *Lenin o Natsional'nom*, pp. 551-52.

he was confronted with such propensities and implications before he had had a chance to address himself to what he considered the crucial, truly creative, yet infinitely complex, task facing a victorious revolutionary party. This task concerned the forging of a strategy of social change for widely varying social systems and developmental circumstances, including barely impaired Moslem and traditional, tribal and communal, as well as agricultural, pastoral, and nomadic milieus in Soviet Central Asia. It was not feasible to approach such a task in a meaningful way while the regime's access to these milieus was severely delimited and its influence evanescent —and while this, in turn, was due not only to primordial situational factors in the area but also to destructive, self-engendered limitations on the part of the Soviet regime.

PROBLEMS OF ACCESS AND INFLUENCE: INITIAL APPROACHES

By the time Lenin died, no overall, coherent plan of action in Soviet Asia had materialized. A handful of party leaders—such as Stalin, and particularly two of the leading Turkic communists, Safarov and Sultan-Galiev—had made a few proposals on this account. But these were not only fragmentary and vague; they were largely eclectic collations of a number of inferences implicit in Marxist and Leninist formulations. They also reflected the imperatives of personal, factional, schismatic, and ethnic struggles within the party rather more than any systematic thought about, and detailed acquaintance with, the realities of Central Asia's societies and cultures.

To be sure, the germs of a number of subsequently implemented ideas were already evident in these proposals, such as those pertaining to the collectivization of agriculture, the formation of mass-organizations for peasants and nomads, and the revolutionization of education. But no significant attempts were apparent to differentiate revolutionary approaches in accordance, specifically, with local socio-cultural conditions. Stalin, Safarov, and Sultan-Galiev (as well as, at one time, Mikoyan) were eager to follow Lenin in calling for Soviet institutions and revolutionary techniques in Asian milieus to be carefully "suited to the local way of life." But even Safarov and Sultan-Galiev, who were passionately concerned with this problem, and were more cognizant of the life-styles of a Turko-Islamic world than most of the party's leaders, in no way indicated just what "fit" and "suitability" might mean, and where they would

55

lead. They seemed just as confounded as Lenin by the dilemma of reconciling "national-cultural self-determination" in a polyethnic milieu with the requirements of a centralized, monolithic, one-party state.

Moreover, Safarov's repeated public indictments of Great Russian chauvinism in the party, and his demands for tangible guarantees of "national-cultural autonomy" in Soviet Asia (including genuine nativization of local party and governmental agencies as well as of cultural and educational enterprises, and the distribution to native peasants of land that had been plundered and settled by Slavic colonists) allowed Stalin to brand him as a "Bundist," i.e., a follower of a Jewish autonomist heresy in Russia's labor movement, and hence one not to be trusted.[46] At the same time, Sultan-Galiev's explicit emphasis on removing Turko-Islamic nationalities altogether from the Russian fold and forming a separate international bloc (in effect, a Colonial International) of non-European, underdeveloped, formerly colonized nations quickly aroused Moscow's suspicions of subversion, thus excluding a dynamic and inventive Turkic leader quite early from the highest councils of the party.[47] Indeed, both Safarov and Sultan-Galiev had barely started formulating some potentially important if piecemeal proposals for mobilizing Moslem societies when they were isolated (in the early 1920's) and then liquidated on Stalin's orders.

It took at least a decade after the October Revolution (until about 1926) for Soviet transformationist action in Central Asia to get into high gear. The emerging picture during the first decade is, on the one hand, one of determined pressure in the consolidation of the formal apparatus of Soviet power, and, on the other hand, one of pronounced ambivalence, indifference, or caution in tackling the indigenous socio-cultural and economic milieu. There can be little

[46] For an excellent indication of Safarov's views, and a sample of his proposals, see his speech at the Tenth Party Congress, in *Desiatyi S'ezd RKP(b)*, pp. 189-201. For Stalin's formal (and competing) "Theses" on the national question, and Safarov's corrections, see ibid., pp. 698-708. For Stalin's speech in support of his theses, see ibid., pp. 181-87. For an indication of the manner in which Stalin managed to browbeat Safarov and his supporters into silence (immediately after Safarov's speech at the congress), see ibid., pp. 210-15.

[47] For a brief but very useful discussion of Sultan-Galiev's role, see Pipes, *The Formation*, pp. 260-62. For a comprehensive treatment, see A. Bennigsen and Ch. Quelquejay, *Les Mouvements nationaux chez les Musulmans de Russie-le "sultan-galievisme" au Tatarstan* (Paris-The Hague, 1960).

doubt that hesitation in these spheres was due at least in part to the battle of wills and views raging within the party's central apparatus on the eve of Stalin's accession to power—a battle that had, in and of itself, little or nothing to do with the tasks pending in Central Asia.

It is thus fair to say that if a rudimentary, relatively specialized action-scheme in the Moslem borderlands did finally evolve, it did so gradually, pragmatically, at times spasmodically, and it was dogged at every step of its evolution by just those dilemmas that haunted the minds of Lenin and a handful of Turkic and Russian revolutionaries. The main spheres of initial Soviet dispositions and attempted action, which might be viewed as indirect approaches to social engineering,[48] may be abstracted in three basic categories: constitutional, environmental, and organizational.[49]

[48] The primary emphasis of this study is on what might be viewed as *direct* approaches to social reconstruction, including what I have called revolutionary legalism, administrative assault, and systematic social engineering (see my Introduction to Part Three). Hence this section of this chapter is provided here largely as background and stage-setting material, and is accordingly schematic and brief. It is drawn from a part of my paper, "The Vulnerability of Islamic Society to Revolutionary Social Engineering," read at the Plenary Session of the Annual Meeting of the Middle East Studies Association, Austin, Texas, November, 1968.

The basic distinctions between *direct* and *indirect* approaches to social engineering may perhaps best be visualized as distinctions between attempts to manipulate, respectively, intimate, spontaneous, and simple relations among people rather than public, standardized, and complex ones; informal networks and sacred realms of human life-styles rather than formal and secular arrangements; consummatory rather than instrumental values; expressive and evaluative as against emotionally neutral areas of activity; covert and private as against overt and public behavior; ascribed rather than achieved roles.

[49] In keeping with stated Soviet aims, it would be equally useful to include a fourth category, cultural engineering, among the indirect approaches to social change. Given the conventional Soviet definitions of the term culture, such an approach may be said to have involved the expectation that the introduction of Soviet educational, medical, sanitary, propaganda, and entertainment media in the traditional milieu, combined with an especially suited linguistic policy, would serve to fundamentally reorient the beliefs and values of young generations, and would thus help to produce citizens with dispositions, loyalties, and skills desirable from the Soviet point of view.

However, for a variety of reasons, very little was done in this respect in Central Asia by the mid-1920's. Moreover, in those areas where outward signs of success were indeed present by 1925-26 (as reflected, e.g., in the

Constitutional Engineering

It is difficult to overemphasize how keenly Lenin and most of his closest lieutenants were aware of the fact that their success in 1917 was due in good measure to their timely and pragmatic utilization of two prime moving forces in Russia's revolutionary upheaval: the long-term national and social grievances, both engendered by Tsarist autocracy and imperialism and triggered by a disastrous world war. Soviet attempts to deal with Russia's minority nationalities immediately after the civil war closely reflected this realization, and involved a deliberate effort to capitalize on the autonomist aspirations on the part of a number of ethnic groups.

In the simplest sense of the term, the process of constitutional engineering involved, *inter alia*, the delimitation of Central Asia in the 1920's into five major component republics (Uzbekistan, Tadzhikistan, Turkmenistan, Kazakhstan, and Kirghiziia), all with at least nominally distinct ethnic populations, languages (or dialects), capitals, flags, governing bodies, and constitutions of their own. It is quite legitimate to view this process primarily in the context of Moscow's moves to impose or augment a system of controls among minority nationalities.[50] But it is also important to see Soviet national delimitation as an instrument of social engineering, pertaining both to directed social change and to polyethnic integration. Thus the establishment of formal ethno-cultural units in the Soviet Union may be visualized as the formation of what might be called *tactical nation-states*, units designed largely exogenously, that is, at

---

quantitative growth of a secular press in the region) the initial results were at best mixed (see Park, *Bolshevism*, Ch. IX). More important, though, was the growing conviction in Soviet ranks that action in the cultural sphere, especially in Central Asia, would be more relevant (and more speedily successful) if cultural systems were viewed as an interlocking of values and beliefs with specific customs, relationships, and roles. In fact, when a number of communist organizers, beginning in the mid-1920's, called for a "cultural revolution" in the Asian borderlands, they had in mind precisely such an interlocking of cognitive and social patterns (as reflected, e.g., in the status of Moslem women). Thus, "cultural revolution" came to denote a *direct* engagement with a traditional social order. Accordingly, I have chosen to deal with it in detail in the chapters that follow which are specifically devoted to the exploration of what I understand to have been direct Soviet approaches to social engineering.

[50] Pipes and Bennigsen, among others, tend to deal with this issue largely in these terms (see their studies—Pipes, esp. Ch. VI; Bennigsen, esp. Ch. 8— cited in Note 1 of Chapter One, above).

the initiative and under the control of outside powers, to serve as temporary and expedient means toward larger ends.[51]

In general terms, the new units were designed to stress at least the formal equality and self-determination of ethnic groups within a constitutionally federal system, to meliorate at least the overt and violent forms of Russian chauvinism, and to make more palatable the underlying realities of a highly centralized Soviet political system. More specifically, they were expected to tap local reservoirs of ethnic pride, and hence elicit the cooperation of local reformist and nationalist elements considered indispensable in managing a particular milieu, thus hopefully neutralizing in the short run the most potent local sources of pressure and unrest. They could, at the same time, serve as models and foci of attraction for nationalist movements coming to the fore in the colonial world abroad.

By emphasizing the relatively smallest and most specific ethnic subdivision as the ordering criterion of societies, these units were also expected, however, to nip in the bud all potential larger-scale solidarities built around racial, national, or religious identities that might threaten the viability of the Soviet state. In Central Asia, the potential solidarities feared most were those based on the ideas of Pan-Turanic or Pan-Islamic union, since such a union could weld into a single bloc a strong array of ethnic groups within the U.S.S.R., and induce the gravitation of this bloc toward the Turkic or larger Moslem world outside Soviet borders. In this sense, tactical nation-states were designed to promote short-term political stability and legitimation, and potential ethnic integration, by way of especially tailored national administrative structures.

But longer-term Soviet expectations clearly concerned the service new republican structures could render in local social transformation. If the new ethno-cultural subdivisions in Central Asia were small in relation to other possible solidarities, they were rather large in relation to existing tribal and village communities. Accordingly, they could be expected to exert an upward pull on communo-centric and kinship-oriented loyalties, thus helping to induce desirable forms of social mobilization and political participation among the minorities, erode parochial orientations, and promote socio-cultural and economic homogenization as well as political integration of the Soviet multi-national state.

[51] I examine this concept and process in some detail in a separate monograph, "Tactical Nation-States: Approaches to Controlled Modernization and Polyethnic Integration in Soviet Central Asia," now in preparation.

It can be said, then, that the new integrative units were cast in a rather unusual role. On the one hand, they were expected to help in releasing human beings from traditional solidarities, to overcome primordial cleavages and absorb local communities in more inclusive units, and to spur the aggregation of loyalties and energies at the supra-communal level. On the other hand, however, they were intended not to consolidate the commitments of newly mobile men at the ethno-cultural level, but to induce them to *transcend* local ethnicity and culture. In effect, they were to mediate between individuals and what was to be in reality a unitary state; they were to be mere way stations between a communo-centric and a trans-national universe. As such, then, they were purely instrumental in character, and were indeed expected to be *self-liquidating* in the shortest possible time.

Small wonder that the dilemma inherent in such expectations affected every facet of Soviet actions. In part, and paradoxically, this was due to what were clearly self-engendered limitations. The regime operated within a realm of specific, sharply conflicting imperatives: to encourage the "nativization" (*korenizatsiia*) of the new republican apparatus, yet preserve the hegemony of Slavs and Bolshevik centralizers in the power structure; to encourage the "flowering" (*raztsvet*) of local cultures, including linguistic and expressive components of a unique ethnic identity, yet extend the influence of Russian language and Soviet Russian culture as a guarantee of the eventual "obliteration" (*stiranie*) of differences between ethnic groups, and of their "rapprochement" (*sblizhenie*) and "amalgamation" (*sliianie*); to exert, through the new republican structures, a nationality-oriented pull on the traditionalist countryside, yet prevent the new secular intelligentsia (the only major exponent of the national idea) from utilizing the new system of social communication for the dissemination of the very idea the new structures were supposed to epitomize; to spur local economic development, yet prevent any and all autarchic tendencies that might affect the requisites of tight economic integration and interdependence within a multi-national state. In short, the basic issue was how to encourage the collaboration of local leadership in nation-building and socio-cultural change yet oblige this leadership to adhere to the official Stalinist formula for the new state units: "Proletarian in Content, National in Form."

Thus, it turned out to be far from a simple matter to use tactical nation-states for reaching the bulk of the population—the rural masses—and for shifting traditional orientations and loyalties from family, religion, village, and clan to distant, impersonal, bureaucratic, urban-based structures. These structures were, after all, built on a criterion—nationality—that was barely familiar in the local cultural and historical context. Also, the new Republican machinery was staffed by secular, modernist strata who were relative newcomers in the local social universe, who were barely known or deeply mistrusted as revolutionaries and infidels in the traditionalist countryside, and who cooperated with the Bolsheviks in excluding from the newly formalized political process—and in persecuting—precisely those men who traditionally commanded respect and authority at the communal grassroots: the Moslem clergy, clan elders, and village and tribal notables. Finally—as a native Moslem could easily surmise through personal confrontations with new settlers on the land, with skilled labor in industry and transportation, and with new power-wielders in towns—ultimate control of the new Republican apparatuses was not only in the hands of local infidels but of aliens as well, aliens who happened to be the kinsmen of those who had occupied the region before them.

These are but a few illustrations of the ways in which the new Republican structures were handicapped from the very beginning as instruments of mass mobilization and socialization. Moreover, if this dimension of Soviet approaches was intended to provide surrogate forms and experience of local self-determination, other concurrent moves tended to dilute or altogether cancel out the effect of this approach. Instead of diminishing, the weight of European, and especially Slavic, personnel in the political and administrative apparatuses (particularly in the most authoritative and security-sensitive positions) of the Central Asian republics inexorably grew. The jurisdiction of Republican agencies was severely delimited, and their dependence on central decision-making bodies was commensurately increased. Local patterns of economic and cultural activity were tied in ever more forcefully with centrally prescribed molds. At the same time, the influx of Slavic settlers to the Central Asian countryside, and of European and especially Russian technical personnel to local cities, was not only permitted to continue as under Tsarist rule but was perceptibly accelerated.

Indeed, the more explicitly formalized became the regime's experiments in constitutional engineering, the greater was its concern with measures to police the new arrangements and the more compulsive were its efforts to ensure that the new structures would not

61

interfere with the requisites of Soviet Russian presence in the borderlands.

Needless to say, such a compulsion tended to provide the makings of a self-fulfilling prophecy. The Bolsheviks, including many of Lenin's closest collaborators, had never regarded the new secular intelligentsia (including indigenous communist leadership) in the Asian republics as particularly trustworthy; in all too many cases, the distrust verged on barely concealed contempt. As the native intelligentsia flocked to staff the freshly provided agencies of development and self-rule in the republics, its expectations necessarily collided with the realities of rigidly centralized political machinery and of what could easily appear as a continuation of Tsarist colonizing policies. In turn, the more vocal were the intelligentsia's grievances and the more self-assertive its posture, the more did this tend to confirm Moscow's suspicions that local secular elites (including communists) invariably harbored nationalist and separatist ambitions, and only waited for a chance to turn tactical into genuinely sovereign nation-states.

Accordingly, Moscow's crackdown on these elites was increasingly ferocious, and that precisely at a time (beginning in the early 1920's) when the imperatives to woo and train local cadres were considered self-evident, and when the risks of alienating the converts from localism and tradition were all too obvious. Thus, even when local leading figures did emerge in the Republican apparatuses—with ideological propensities acceptable to the Soviet regime, and with personal and ethno-cultural qualifications that inspired trust and made them potentially acceptable to the masses of their countrymen—they were not really given the opportunity to use the new structures fully and consistently for the intended purpose. As a result, the new overarching structures could not easily serve in the prescribed roles, both because they were deprived of dynamic leadership and because their assigned functions could not readily provide acceptable substitutes for the deeply valued functions customarily exercised by local kin-groups, informal (including religious) associations, and traditional authority figures. By the same token, the new constitutional arrangements could not quickly and easily acquire the requisite qualities of access, authenticity, and legitimacy to be fully effective in the process of social engineering—as the Soviet regime strove to endow a social and territorial universe with features of a nation-state, yet to make those features selective and impotent enough to forestall the emergence of a real national consciousness and the formation of a real nation.

Environmental Engineering

For a Marxist, it should have been unquestionably most congenial to view radical socio-cultural and political change as a direct function of rapid and radical alterations in a society's material environment. Indeed, no matter which approach to social engineering ultimately came to be emphasized in Soviet ranks, one cardinal assumption had to be formally adhered to: in the long run, a fundamental shift in the relationships, values, and beliefs (i.e., in the "superstructures") of Moslem and other traditional societies would inevitably follow on the heels of fundamental changes in the "base" of those societies. The latter would of course be brought on not only by elimination of private ownership of the means of production and by formal changes in "production relations" but also by resulting economic development itself (subsuming industrialization and new patterns of production and distribution) and by concurrent urbanization and the extension of transport and communications. To be sure, changes in the superstructure might lag to some extent behind those in the base. But the ultimate outcome could not possibly be in doubt.

Yet Soviet authorities in Central Asia were never quite comfortable about this assumption. In part, this was due to the inherently interventionist temper of Leninist ideology, and in part to the realization of how distant the stage of Central Asia's economic development was from that of European Russia, not to speak of that envisioned for a socialist era. What was, however, even more important, environmental engineering, beginning with economic development, turned out to be itself dependent on a number of variables, and to a far greater extent than in European Russia.

Some of these variables came into play as a result of self-engendered limitations. For example, we know that, in the decade following the seizure of power in 1917, Russian chauvinists and Bolshevik centralizers in the Soviet apparatus were none too eager to invest heavily in the economic development of a distinctly underdeveloped periphery. This was not merely a matter of scarce investment-resources (although these were scarce enough). Central Asia tended to be *undervalued*: politically (as a tradition-bound, "backward," "semi-feudal" universe vis-à-vis Russia, the "cradle of the Revolution," the home of an "advanced, victorious prole-

63

tariat," that needed to be built up and preserved at all cost); militarily (in that it was relatively more secure than other regions of the Union in the face of possible outside intervention); and economically (in that funds for industrial development might be most fruitfully committed first in already industrialized, i.e., Central Russian, regions).

Thus, it was natural, at least initially, for the line of least resistance to lead to an emphasis on the region's "specialization" as a source of cash crops (specifically cotton), cattle, and industrial raw materials. In particular, stimuli to local agricultural recovery were admittedly applied in order to free the Soviet Union from dependence on foreign cotton-imports, to activate the idle or damaged textile plants in European Russia, to clothe the masses of labor tending toward Russia's urban and industrial centers, and to acquire an exchange medium (cotton goods) for dealing with Russia's peasantry—a peasantry not interested in exchanging breadgrains for Soviet paper currency. Animal husbandry (providing a large supply-base of wool, meat, and hides) was similarly encouraged. In both cases, material incentives could obviously be justified on the grounds that they ensured large and immediate returns on a relatively modest and short-term investment. In both cases, also, there was the implicit assurance that Central Asia would remain as dependent on bread-imports from Russia as in Tsarist times, and would thus have as little opportunity as ever to develop autarchic, hence potentially separatist, propensities. Commensurately, while the region's output of fibers, food, and minerals by and large recovered to pre-revolutionary levels in less than a decade, only a bare trickle of funds for industrial development was forthcoming at that time, and there were no significant signs of an intent to transfer industry *en masse* to the sources of raw materials in Central Asia.[52]

Other factors limiting the scope of environmental engineering were of course inherent in the milieu itself. Thus, even where some funds for industrial development were available, a pool of requisite native labor was not. Just as the dearth of industrial complexes tended to hold back the recruitment and training of native industrial labor, so did the absence of a significant pool of skilled labor tend to hamper the building and staffing of industrial complexes.

[52] For a comprehensive account of initial Soviet economic policies and achievements in Central Asia, see Park, *Bolshevism*, Chs. VI-VII.

For native labor to be appropriately motivated, mobilized, and trained, indigenous Moslem communities had to be accessible. And this is precisely what they were not. Moreover, while Central Asia's new secular elites (including some leading communists) insisted on balanced, multi-faceted economic development, and openly resented what seemed like a continuation of Tsarist economic policies on the part of Moscow, they showed little enthusiasm for a violent, all-out attack on local social institutions as a prerequisite for rapid, large-scale economic mobilization.

The one realm where the regime apparently found a good measure of positive popular response and cooperation at that time was that of large-scale irrigation. It would seem that these early Soviet ventures in rural locales (which were, for the most part, quite uninhabitable without a reliable irrigation network) were welcome and supported in Moslem traditional communities as enterprises that were palpably life-enhancing, congruent with old communal labor patterns, easily fitting in local group-focused images of change, and deeply valued by both religion and custom.[53] But this developmental sector tended to be compartmentalized in such a way as to minimize the hoped-for social changes. On the one hand, agricultural activities related to irrigation by and large fitted the long established production patterns (as well as social solidarities) in the area, thus providing a modicum of continuity rather than basic change. On the other hand, it would seem that the region's rural masses manifested relatively little drive or interest in grand schemes of industrial development, and not much taste for the unaccustomed rigors of industrial performance, since the latter involved not only rigid and impersonal discipline but also the need to move (often alone) to a distant and alien environment and to work under the command of alien (mostly Slavic) supervisors.[54]

Needless to say, the situation had the makings of a vicious circle, and it was reflected as such in the growing frustration of communist organizers in the field. One way to go around the problem was to import Russian industrial labor and technical personnel, just as the

[53] I will deal with this issue in a separate study, now in preparation: "Systematic Social Engineering in Soviet Central Asia: Tactics, Problems, and Achievements." For responses to equivalent actions in different cultural contexts, see, for example, A. O. Hirschman, *The Strategy of Economic Development* (New Haven, 1958), pp. 11-15.

[54] See the reference to my forthcoming separate study in the preceding footnote.

antecedent Tsarist regime had done. The Soviets did just that. Undoubtedly, this augmented local capacities for industrial growth (and could thus be justified as "fraternal assistance"), and at the same time served the regime's quiet resolve to have a growing Slavic contingent in a Turko-Iranian world. But it also had definite drawbacks. Such a policy could not but indefinitely postpone the formation of a native industrial and professional stratum (an "indigenous proletariat") and sharply limit native labor to agricultural and pastoral pursuits or to otherwise menial tasks. This would surely make a mockery of communist ideological postulates, retard not only economic but also social, political, and psycho-cultural development in the region, and aggravate further Moscow's relations with indigenous modernizers and reformers.

Against this background it was understandable for concerned Soviet communists to cast about for means to achieve a dramatic breakthrough in mobilization and transformation. The Leninist revolutionary heritage, the radical impatience of Bolshevik modernizers, as well as Moscow's growing conviction of the urgency of social engineering (not merely for the sake of modernization and economic development, but also for the sake of optimization of political control in an elusive social milieu) militated against an extended period of passive waiting, certainly against waiting for changes in the physical environment to materialize and have the desired effect. *Ipso facto*, this militated against excessive reliance on environmental engineering as a prime instrument of social change—except, of course, for the very long term.

Organizational Engineering

Early Soviet approaches through constitutional and environmental engineering reflected, respectively, purely situational and orthodox Marxist appraisals of Central Asian realities. Organizational engineering, on the other hand, involved a standard Leninist Bolshevik disposition to believe that problems of social revolution were, first and foremost, organizational problems. The proliferation and consolidation of Communist Party cells, of village soviets and Soviet administrative agencies, as well as of especially tailored trade unions and cooperative forms of agricultural labor, would not only amplify the control-capabilities of the Soviet regime but would also help to revolutionize the attitudes, practices, and relationships of a Moslem traditional milieu. Obviously, such a disposition connoted a powerful emphasis on formal political action (subsuming organization and propaganda) as a relatively autonomous force, as both the maker and the breaker of human beliefs, values, and ties—and a corresponding de-emphasis of social and psycho-cultural elements as determinants of institutional arrangements, human behavior, and social change.

At first, then, we have in Soviet Central Asia a rather simple encounter between revolution and tradition, reflecting the simplicities of early Soviet politics in the large. As I have argued elsewhere,[55] there was a belief that disadvantaged men (and most men in traditional society were "disadvantaged") would readily take to a social transformation carried out by dedicated reformers operating new formal institutions superior to the old. This belief was encouraged by the apparent ease with which the revolutionary takeover was accomplished in Central Asia; by the Marxist-Leninists' erstwhile apocalyptic view of revolution itself, a view of violent revolution as a final and definitive act, a consummation rather than a mere beginning; and by the belief, shared by communists with other children of the Enlightenment, in the great strength of rationally devised social machinery as against the implicit norms and networks of informal expectations of prerational society. There was to be revolutionary machinery, and revolutionary products would issue from it as a matter of course.

The failure of this hopeful approach, perhaps more crushing in Central Asia than anywhere else, was one of the first great traumas of Soviet rule. And, paradoxically, just as in the case of constitutional and environmental approaches, at least some of the causes of this failure could be traced to self-engendered limitations. Among the latter, several became immediately obvious. First, the very formality, impersonality, and bureaucratic rigidity of Soviet organizational units tended to discourage genuine popular participation, especially in a milieu long accustomed to rely on face-to-face relationships. Second, the fact that most of these units were primarily urban-based, were clearly imposed on a community from above, and were blatantly secular, revolutionary, and atheistic in orientation made them suspect in rural locales. Third, it was difficult to hide the fact that, in the mid-1920's, even the most important of Soviet units in Central Asia—the Communist Party—was not only fashioned by strangers, but was overwhelmingly Russian

---

[55] See my article "Law as an Instrument of Revolutionary Change in a Traditional Milieu," *Law and Society Review*, Vol. II, No. 2 (Feb., 1968), pp. 183-84.

or European in active membership and supreme leadership. It was difficult to dissociate the image of such an organization in the popular mind from the image of a foreign invader and occupier.[56]

But what was perhaps most disturbing from the Soviet point of view, was that even where Soviet organizational forms did seem to take hold in the Moslem traditional hinterland in the early 1920's, they appeared to function in ways very different from those that had been anticipated. By 1926, the incongruence between appearance and reality was coming to be perceived with a sense of urgency. As Kuchkin, a veteran Soviet scholar, put it: Soviet "forms" apparently existed in Central Asia, just about everywhere, but "contents," "substance," "authenticity" were missing.[57] This was true for party, soviet, as well as mass (*Koshchi*)[58] peasant organizations freshly established at the grassroots. Most of them seemed to be held in bondage by "tribal ideology," by traditional habits, by kinship ties. Most were found to be subject, directly or indirectly, to the influence of, or to outright domination by, local traditional elites.[59]

The political process at the grassroots, while formally institutionalized in a Soviet framework, revolved around what were in fact paper organizations and enterprises, and had very little to do with Soviet initiatives and goals. Indeed, it tended to reflect the maneuvers of self-assertive kin and communal groups represented by local chieftains, notables, or patriarchal males of a particular extended family pursuing their own interests.[60] For example, what were supposed to be Soviet elections turned out to be largely a game of musical chairs between local kin-groups, or between al-

[56] See, e.g., A. P. Kuchkin, *Sovetizatsiia Kazakhskogo Aula, 1926-1929-gg* (Moscow, 1962), p. 16. Cf. Fat'ianov, *VS*, 19, 1927, p. 18.

[57] See Kuchkin, *SKA*, especially pp. 14-35; while Kuchkin concerns himself primarily with Kazakhstan, he makes it clear that this state of affairs prevailed throughout Central Asia at that time (see, e.g., p. 14). Cf. *Ocherki Istorii Kommunisticheskoi Partii Turkmenistana* (Moscow, 1961), p. 318.

[58] Literally, "The Plowman." For a brief but very useful account of the rise and fall of these rural associations in Central Asia, see Park, *Bolshevism*, pp. 146-54.

[59] Kuchkin, *SKA*, pp. 247-48. Cf. Brullova-Shaskol'skaia, *NV*, 16-17, 1927, p. 301; Vorshev, *RN*, 12(58), 1934, pp. 69-72.

[60] See Kuchkin, *SKA*, p. 248; see also Kuchkin, *VI*, 10, 1946, pp. 5 ff. Cf. M. Pravda, *SS*, 12(41), 1929, pp. 108 ff.; F. Khodzhaev, *SS*, 2, 1926, p. 119, I. S. Kraskin (ed.), *Zemel'no-Vodnaia Reforma v Srednei Azii* (Moscow, 1927), pp. 3-4.

liances of ethnic-regional groups. As Kuchkin has pointed out, local elections in the mid-1920's were found to be marked not by "class struggle" but by "clan struggle." The "poor" tended to support their "rich" kinsmen in such electoral conflicts. Moreover, when the struggle threatened to become too destructive, or when Soviet surveillance was uncomfortably close, patriarchs of competing kin-groups were not above entering *sub rosa* deals whereby representatives of various clans peacefully followed each other in public office in rotation. Under the circumstances, the figures of popular participation in elections, as reported by Soviet functionaries, surely had no basis in reality.[61]

Entire party cells (as well as peasant and trade associations), especially in nomadic and semi-nomadic districts, tended to be organized along lines of kin. Thus, they tended to further the primordial propensities of what Moscow's emissaries referred to as *vozhdism*[62] (literally, "führerism")—or of what might have been better understood as a form of authoritarian personalism characterizing political relationships in tribal, village, as well as family contexts in a Moslem and Turko-Iranian milieu. In practice, then, political attachments in the countryside continued to be focused primarily on local figures who were respected and authoritative in that they possessed personality traits, exercised customary functions, and commanded kinship ties that were traditionally valued and legitimated.[63]

The first Soviet-sponsored attempts at comprehensive land reform (in the mid-1920's) encountered a peculiarly complex response. In some cases, local *mullahs* who seemed inclined to cooperate with the Soviet regime in some aspects of social policy (and were hence considered "red," or "progressive") tended to support the redistribution of land, and even cooperative or collective forms of agriculture, on the ground that such principles were explicitly or implicitly legitimized by Koranic prescriptions.[64] Yet, paradoxically, given its monopolistic political bias, the Soviet regime could

[61] Kuchkin, *SKA*, pp. 16, 27, 37, 129-35. See also Kuchkin, *VI*, 10, 1946, p. 8.

[62] See Vorshev, *RN*, 12(58), 1934, pp. 69-72. Cf. A. Mitrofanov, *RN*, 1, 1930, pp. 29-36; G. Karpov, *SS*, 11(28), 1928, pp. 61-69, and *SS*, 6(35), 1929, pp. 64-68.

[63] I deal with this issue in a separate monograph, "Engineered Delegitimation: The Crisis of Traditional Authority in Soviet Central Asia," now in preparation.

[64] See Park, *Bolshevism*, pp. 340-41, including Note 47.

not permit such analogies between Islam and communism to go too far—and hence could not for long tolerate and use "red *mullahs*" as allies—lest *Islamic* auspices of a reformist movement make *Soviet* auspices in this and other realms appear to be superfluous.[65]

At the same time, for each reported case of positive response to economic reorganization, there were all too many negative ones. Even those who were viewed as the poorest among Moslem peasants or nomads, upon receiving their share of a richer man's land or cattle from a Soviet functionary, often returned the property secretly to the original owner, with apologies. Those who kept their allotted share were often ostracized and subjected to a "black"—or "reactionary"—*mullah*'s curse for enjoying the fruits of an evil deed. In fact, a man designated as a native *kulak* was found to be able to evade the proceedings of a land-reform altogether. He could divide his holdings among sons, kinsmen, or neighbors before a Soviet committee's arrival, and collect them again after its departure. Or he could see to it that the numerous farmhands in his employ, even though *prima facie* evidence of his being a *kulak,* would testify that their work for him was not for money at all, but out of "friendship."[66] In some pastoral locales (for example, in Turkmenistan) where land and water rights were claimed by clans or tribes rather than by individuals, attempts to transfer ownership tended to arouse the wrath of entire communities, and hence blurred rather than sharpened potential class distinctions.[67] Thus, while Moscow had vested much hope in the land reform as a catalyst of class struggle,[68] initial outcomes were far from encouraging; indeed, they tended to underscore native discomfort with the very notion of deliberate class differentiation.[69]

Moreover, one of the immediate repercussions of the attempted land reform carried the threat of widespread inter-ethnic (and inter-racial) struggle. In areas heavily (and forcibly) colonized by Slavic settlers before 1917 (especially in Kazakhstan) a number of native communists supported local demands to allot land first of all to the indigenous population, and primarily at the expense

[65] See Chapter Eight of this study (*passim*).

[66] For a discussion of these manifestations as observed in the 1920's, see, e.g., A. Fominov, *RN*, 6, 1930, pp. 69-79. See also Park, *Bolshevism*, p. 344, including Note 54.

[67] See Park, *Bolshevism*, pp. 348-49.

[68] See ibid., pp. 335ff., 350ff.

[69] See B. Hayit, *Turkestan im XX Jahrhundert* (Darmstadt, 1956), p. 267, including Note 799. Cf. Park, *Bolshevism*, pp. 330, 334.

of Slavic holdings.[70] In effect, in 1925-26 this issue alone seems to have elicited an unusual degree of consensus: communists, nationalists, and traditional leaders alike either viewed land reform as irrelevant and unnecessary or proposed to use it as a vehicle for returning plundered lands to native communities and even for summarily evicting foreign settlers from the native countryside. These pressures reached a climax in late 1926 when reportedly pitched, bloody battles erupted in rural (especially Kazakh) locales, as native nomads and peasants attempted to reclaim their land by force.[71] Moscow's emissaries viewed this denouement as all the more ominous in that the invasions of Russian and Ukrainian farms were for the most part collective rather than individual acts, wherein native traditional communities (villages or large kin-groups) acted in unison, and were either led or inspired by traditional authority figures, while native rural soviets often aided or abetted the raids.[72]

As Moscow was deluged by reports from alarmed Slavic settlers and functionaries (as well as by impassioned statements of native grievances) the party dispatched high-level officials (including Andreev, emerging at that time as one of Stalin's principal troubleshooters) to take matters in hand. It also handed down a number of sharply worded directives categorically prohibiting a redistribution of land that would dispossess European farmers, and calling on local officials to turn Central Asia's masses against their own "ruling classes" rather than their former national oppressors.[73] But, as it turned out, directives from above, in this as in other cases, either never reached the grassroots at all, were incomprehensible if they did arrive, or were often simply ignored.[74] Members of what were presumably Soviet and party units in the native countryside were found not only to oppose or distort the land reform but also to accept bribes, engage in private trade, and maintain connections with what were officially referred to as "socially alien elements."[75]

[70] See, e.g., Safarov's views as stated in *Desiatyi S'ezd RKP(b)*, pp. 193-94.

[71] In some instances (though apparently rather less frequently) the reverse took place, as Russian and Ukrainian peasants tried to take over additional acreage (see the footnote that follows).

[72] See Kuchkin, *SKA*, pp. 166-76.

[73] Ibid.

[74] Ibid., p. 248.

[75] Ibid. Cf. Mitrofanov, *RN*, 1, 1930, pp. 29ff., and *RN*, 2, 1930, pp. 36ff.; I. S. Kraskin (ed.), *Zemel'no-Vodnaia Reforma v Srednei Azii* (Moscow, 1927), p. 118.

Not only were there observant Moslems among them, but entire Islamic sects, especially among sedentary peasantry and mountaineers, managed to constitute themselves into separate party cells.[76] People at the traditionalist grassroots, then, continued to live a life of their own, infiltrating the new organizational framework and using it for their own purposes.

How was one to account for these anomalies? The official party view, as expressed in 1927[77] by two of Stalin's closest collaborators, Molotov[78] and Andreev,[79] arrived at a fairly unorthodox proposition: The persistent strength of Central Asia's traditional elites, unlike that of a Russian *kulak*, did not rest on material wealth alone. The sources of their seemingly pervasive influence in Soviet-sponsored organizations were deeply embedded in kinship ties and in the way of life built around them, making basic social relationships in Central Asia "feudal-patriarchal" in nature. It was precisely this that made a Central Asian *bey*, for example, far more dangerous than a Russian *kulak*. It was also this that made Soviet penetration of the traditionalist countryside extremely difficult.[80]

A number of close communist observers and organizers in the field were quick to amplify this explanation. It was true that all levers of brute force, and all "commanding heights" in the region, were securely in Soviet hands. Yet what the regime demonstrably lacked was genuine *access* to the Moslem traditional milieu. Indeed, questions of *dostup* (access), *vliianie* (influence), and *avtoritet* (authority) came to the forefront of Soviet concerns in Central Asia in the mid-1920's. It seemed increasingly apparent that formal Soviet organizations were quite inadequate to bridge the gulf between the rulers and the ruled. It was not just the area's vast size and formidable terrain that stood in the way, but also historical memories (Tsarist imperial domination), recent military confrontations (with invading Soviet forces), and cultural distance (between a vast Moslem, Turko-Iranian countryside and an ethni-

---

[76] See Kuchkin, *SKA*, p. 248, and Mitrofanov, *RN*, 2, 1930, pp. 36-38.

[77] As we shall see in the chapters that follow, this view, while formally expressed at the highest official level in 1927, was already well crystallized in the mid-1920's.

[78] At the Fifteenth Party Congress in December, 1927, in Moscow.

[79] At the Sixth Party Conference of Kazakhstan in November, 1927.

[80] See *XV S'ezd VKP(b), Stenograficheskii Otchet* (Moscow, 1928), p. 1047, as cited in Kuchkin, *VI*, 10, 1946, p. 4. See also Kuchkin, *SKA*, pp. 20-21, 246-47. Cf. I. Trainin, *SS*, 8(121), 1936, p. 19.

cally and/or ideologically alien and city-based Soviet regime). These problems were further compounded in pastoral milieus, where the nomads' frequent movement, as well as their dispersal, made them a highly elusive body of men with whom even rudimentary administrative contact was far from simple. In any event, even reasonably established village soviets tended to be viewed by the rural population as merely new instruments in the hands of urban tax collectors.[81]

Most important of all—as Soviet analysts saw this—after nearly ten years of Soviet rule Central Asian traditional elites (religious, tribal, and communal) still commanded "respect," "influence," and "authority" among the natives; the Soviet regime did not. Why was it that, instead of gravitating naturally toward the Soviet fold, even the "poorest" among local Moslems tended to submit to traditional leaders unquestioningly, "without a murmur of complaint"? It could not be merely because a few powerful and wealthy men (the purveyors of *vozhdism*, tribal and communal "führerism") held entire communities by the throat, dominating and exploiting them for private gain. Indigenous masses submitted to traditional elites primarily because the latter included genuinely "honored persons." Some of these (especially clan notables) were honored because they literally "personif[ied] the kin group," while the individual personalities of rank-and-file members tended to be "completely obliterate[d]" by the group. But most of these personages—including Moslem clergymen (*mullahs* and *ishans*) and healers (*tabibs*), tribal chieftains, and village elders and clan notables (*aksakals, atkamners, manaps,* and *beys*)—were respected because they "discharged social functions . . . that [made them] indispensable." It was these strata that provided a native's daily "counsellors," "mentors," and "judges" in large matters and small; his "spiritual doctors," dispensers of talismans, supervisors of every ritual connected with marriage, birth, and death; his teachers, agronomists, and physicians, who were consulted in times of crop failure, storm, and drought; his suppliers of potions for children's ailments and female troubles, as well as for cattle's murrain. These men stood, therefore, at the heart of a village-community's everyday human preoccupations. Anyone who intended to establish genuine local con-

[81] See M. Pravda, *SS*, 12(41), 1929, pp. 105 ff.; I. Gelis, *KP*, 6, 1929, p. 35; Kuchkin, VI, 10, 1946, pp. 5-6; I. Ch., *KP*, 2-3, 1928, pp. 254 ff.; Maiorova, *Ka*, 6, 1928, p. 88.

tacts had to keep all this in mind—i.e., that he would eventually have to provide acceptable equivalents of all these functions, as well as acceptable substitutes for those who performed these functions.[82]

It would seem that it was, above all, this realization that served to diminish complacent expectations in Soviet ranks regarding the usefulness of a formal organizational framework in social engineering, even if that framework was anchored in a monopolistic, single-party state. It appeared to be far from adequate to rely on the mere proliferation of units that were built to orthodox Bolshevik specifications, and that mechanically replicated centrally prescribed forms. It was not so much that the new revolutionary machinery was attacked and incapacitated by reactionary strata. Rather it was that the new political institutions, pressed into action essentially "from above," could not even begin to permeate the vast regions of society outside of the urban administrative centers, and that, insofar as they did gain entrance, they tended not to transform accustomed ways but to be themselves "traditionalized."

Thus, Soviet political institutions tended to be adapted to serve specific local needs, to deflect Soviet demands, to preserve elaborate appearances of compliance, and to perpetuate the influence of solidarities based on ethnicity, kinship, custom, and belief. In this sense, they tended to provide merely a new setting in which affairs proceeded much as before. As Marx and Engels might have forewarned the Communist Party, the difficulties of transition from "gentile" to "civilized" social organizations had to do, first and foremost, with problems of access and authority: " . . . the mightiest prince and the greatest statesman or general of civilization might [well] envy the humblest of the gentile chiefs the unforced and unquestioned respect accorded to him." In effect, as in "gentile" communities, Central Asia's traditional elites stood "in the midst of society," in that they continued to command respect and authority at the grassroots. The agents of the Soviet state stood "outside and above" that society.[83]

[82] For summary statements as well as various elements of this argument, see V. Shokhor, *SS*, 8-9(13-14), 1927, pp. 109-10; Pravda, *SS*, 12(41), 1929, pp. 105-14 (*passim*); Kuchkin, *VI*, 10, 1946, pp. 5 ff.; Sev, *Turkmenovedenie*, 3-4(7-8), 1928, pp. 15-19; I. Arkhincheev, *SS*, 2(43), 1930, pp. 98-113; V. Dzasokhov, *RN*, 2-3, 1931, pp. 65-67; A. Vel'tner, *RN*, 12, 1931, p. 29 ff.

[83] See F. Engels, *The Origin of the Family, Private Property, and the State* (New York, 1942), p. 156.

74

THE QUEST FOR LEVERAGE:
THE RELEVANCE OF "ACTION FROM ABOVE"

In some ways, it might have been possible to be content with the rate of progress experienced or envisaged during the first decade of Soviet presence in Central Asia but only if one took a rather spacious view of time: time to enroll more natives in the communist parties despite the many prevailing obstacles; time to achieve a reconstitution of agricultural production and the agricultural labor force; time for education and indoctrination to do their work among an illiterate population accessible only to as yet non-existent face-to-face contacts (and, indeed, a formerly literate population made illiterate by the introduction of a strange—Latin—alphabet).[84]

Indeed, Lenin's New Economic Policy, instituted following the disastrous excesses of War Communism during Russia's civil war, had to some extent implied a willingness to be patient—in socio-cultural and political as well as economic spheres. Needless to say, though, far from all Bolsheviks were content with the gradualism and moderation of the N.E.P. Bolsheviks were not, after all, men of a moderate stamp, and the manifold external and internal problems of the Soviet state could only exacerbate their impatience. While Lenin was alive, his authority sufficed to hold this impatience in check. And for a short time after his death, the struggle for his mantle served to deflect ambitions from transformationist preoccupations to maneuvers for power. Once these hurdles were cleared, radical activism asserted itself again. It could do so all the more potently, of course, because its temper was the temper of the victorious—Stalinist—faction in the party, and because that faction was coming to operate with more singleness of political purpose than at any time during the party's existence. Against this background, the confluence of a fresh sense of urgency (about pending revolutionary tasks) and a sense of disillusionment (concerning the efficacy of initial transformationist attempts) could easily radicalize Soviet initiatives in Central Asia.

There were several possible responses to the perceived slowness or failures in Central Asia's social transformation. One was to use the coercive power of the regime to excise the more manifest ob-

[84] For an account of Soviet actions in these spheres, see, e.g., Park, *Bolshevism*, esp. Chs. IV, VII, and IX.

75

structive elements (especially the traditional elites)[85] and to force the general population into compliance with revolutionary ways, thus accomplishing quickly revolutionary ends. Another was to find a weak link in society, a relatively deprived and hence potentially deviant and subversive stratum susceptible to militant appeal, a *surrogate proletariat* where no proletariat in the real Marxist sense existed. Given such a stratum, it was conceivable that reliable native cadres could be recruited from it and used, first to loosen and disintegrate traditional social relationships, then to rebuild society when its very dissolution compelled reconstitution. Both approaches have a crucial point in common, one that would appear to have wide significance for the deliberate transformation of any and all societies: transforming social institutions that still are going concerns would seem to presuppose a prior weakening, if not utter destruction, of the institutions to be transformed, and hence the discovery of crucial actors whose deliberately engineered separation or alienation from the institutions will cause these to be drained of vitality.

The initial Soviet political reflex in this case was essentially an orthodox one, reverting to a hard, fundamentalist Bolshevik bias: to attack the obstructive elements head-on—from above, as it were—and to excise them from the local body politic. Without waiting for either political or economic development to take its course, the party chose to attack directly the network of traditional authority relationships, and to strike it at a point that could logically be considered its nerve-center and its head. It called upon its cadres to subordinate everything to the requirements of class struggle in the traditionalist countryside, and to concentrate, first of all, on undermining, isolating, and physically removing the traditional elites of Central Asia.

[85] It should be borne in mind that members of these elites had not been invariably considered obstructive. In fact, the very persistence of these elites was due in part to erstwhile Soviet policy to rely to some extent on what were considered to be "respected," "authoritative," and hence "stable" elements in the Moslem countryside, as distinguished from "marginal" and hence "unstable" ones. (See, e.g., F. Niurina, *Ka*, 4, 1925, p. 81. Cf. Vorshev, *RN*, 12(58), 1934, pp. 69-70; E. Shteinberg, *Ocherki Istorii Trukmenii* [Moscow, 1934], pp. 99-100.) However, while such arrangements (in effect, a form of indirect rule) had obviously been considered prudent in the critical years of Civil War, military re-conquest, and national delimitation in Central Asia, they came to be viewed as a dangerous anachronism once the job of overall pacification appeared to be done and the tasks of revolution were perceived with growing urgency.

It would seem that, at first, these moves were to be covert and executed gradually and in stages, to parallel the process of land and water reform initiated in Central Asia in late 1925. (The reform itself was supervised by a special commission of the party's Central Committee; Stalin and Kalinin became members of this commission.) [86] However, there is reason to believe that the assault on local authoritative figures developed a momentum of its own. By the autumn of 1926 the offensive was accelerated by explicit party directives from Moscow. Even though this policy was not implemented simultaneously throughout Central Asia (in some areas the separation of traditional leaders from their followers did not enter a massive stage until the summer of 1928), the pattern of Soviet pressure on traditional elites was already clearly apparent in the closing months of 1926, including moral denigration, political isolation, economic deprivation, selective resettlement, and massive roundup and deportation. [87]

It is little wonder that, in these circumstances, all notions even faintly alluding to social harmony as a special characteristic of Moslem traditional communities were officially declared to be reactionary. This included views held by a number of Central Asian leaders, including native communists, to the effect that "organic bonds" existed between traditional leaders and their followers; that

---

[86] See Park, *Bolshevism*, p. 336.

[87] Moral denigration included inflammatory, widely publicized accusations of moral turpitude and transgressions against kinsmen, kinswomen, and local taboos. Political isolation involved, *inter alia*, prohibition of electoral and other political participation. Economic deprivation involved, first of all, prohibitively high taxes coupled with confiscation of animal herds. It is quite clear that forced resettlement meant removal to Central Asian districts where the dominant tribal units were alien to the deportee's kin group, thus separating the deportee from his natural constituency and sharply reducing his opportunities to influence and lead. It is a safe inference that deportation meant removal beyond the confines of the region, most probably to Siberian settlements and concentration camps.

For explicit or implicit references to this process, see, e.g., Kuchkin, *SKA*, Chs. IV and VI. On some occasions (e.g., pp. 263-64, 428-29) Kuchkin places the most draconic stage in the summer of 1928. But in other instances (e.g., p. 248) his evidence clearly suggests that the process was already well under way (at least in Kazakhstan) in the latter half of 1926. Cf. Shikhmuradov and Rosliakov (eds.), *Ocherki Istorii Kommunisticheskoi Partii Turkmenistana* (Ashkhabad, 1961), pp. 346 ff., and ibid., rev. ed., 1965, pp. 316 ff. and 319 ff. I deal with this and related issues in detail in a separate monograph, "Engineered Delegitimation: The Crisis of Traditional Authority in Soviet Central Asia," now in preparation.

clan-members followed their chieftains with blind devotion; that tribal relationships were inherently, even uniquely, democratic; or that the traditional way of life literally "[incarnated] the ideas of communism," being entirely free of warring classes.[88] All such notions were seen as dangerous propaganda helpful to the social enemy: tribal-patriarchal relationships merely submerged, and masked, class relationships; it was clearly in the interest of traditional elites—the native "exploiting strata"—to perpetuate the myths about equality and harmony in traditional milieus; while "[the exploiters did so] *consciously* . . . , the vast majority of the exploited . . . [lent] their support *unconsciously*"; forceful action against traditional leaders would help to make the exploited conscious of their real interests and thereby prove that the unity of the traditional community was but a myth.[89]

In order to deal effectively with traditional elites, the Soviet regime needed some assistance at the grassroots. It needed "underprivileged" members of a community to point out or reveal the whereabouts of "privileged" men. For this purpose, Moscow's emissaries attempted to enlist the services of the Union of Koshchi, a mass association of Central Asian peasants and nomads organized in the early 1920's. Evidently it was found that this organization was not entirely cooperative and reliable in pursuing this task, and an attempt was made to find collaborators (and hence potential revolutionaries) among four groups considered to be of especially low status in the countryside: *chairiker*, farmhands hiring themselves out for seasonal work on the land or with cattle; *dzhatakchi*, "the motionless," those with too few cattle for extended nomadic movement; *attykchi*, those who stayed behind to sow and tend winter fodder, while their richer kinsmen departed with the herds for summer pastures; and *dzhilangach*, "the naked ones," recently settled, who owned a little land but had to borrow seeds and draught animals from a richer relative or fellow villager, for which they paid up to one half of their harvest.[90]

---

[88] See Kuchkin, *SKA*, pp. 69-70, and *VI*, 10, 1946, p. 4. Cf. Arkhincheev, *SS*, 2(43), 1930, pp. 98-99; Dzasokhov, *RN*, 2-3, 1931, pp. 65 ff.; Vorshev, *RN*, 12(58), 1934, pp. 69-70; O. I. Shatskaia, *SE*, 1, 1936, pp. 51-52.

[89] See Arkhincheev, *SS*, 2(43), 1930, p. 98 (italics in the text).

[90] Only the first of these groups was propertyless and was found in purely sedentary locales. The others belonged primarily to nomadic or semi-nomadic communities, and had some property in cattle or in land, sometimes on a communal basis. Thus, official preoccupation with all four of these groups indicated the regime's awareness of complexity in

While there is no way of telling to what extent these men collaborated with Soviet authorities, it is clear that, beginning in the mid-1920's in the Kazakh steppe, a number of the most conspicuous, formally high-ranking traditional authority figures were arrested and deported or physically liquidated. They included those designated by Moscow as "princelings" (*sultans* and *manaps*); those identified as the "ruling oligarchy" held over from Tsarist times (*beys, aksakals*, and other "honored persons"); petty clan and village notables (especially patriarchs representing influential families); and the upper crust of Moslem clergy.[91]

Some of the assumptions underlying such drastic action were made quite explicit. As two authoritative Soviet analysts explained this, it was expected that the surgical sweep would eliminate strata whose very presence "preserved semi-feudal, patriarchal, and tribal relationships," and thus prevented full-fledged sovietization of the Central Asian village.[92] It would allow the Soviet regime to capture strategic political positions in the countryside, and thus enable it to proceed with social, economic, and cultural reconstruction.[93] It would literally "root out . . . reactionary forms of authoritarianism" in Central Asia,[94] forms that had made local communities especially resistant to outside intervention. And it would ultimately help to sway native masses to the Soviet side, since it would "decisively persuade" them that the regime was fighting on their behalf and that Soviet power was indeed "invincible."[95]

It may be said, then, that the Soviet decision to seek leverage through action from above involved an expectation that the liquidation of traditional elites would amount to a political decapitation of the traditional command system, and that it would thus serve to remove the linchpin from the formal organizational structures of local communities and tribes. As a result, local social structures

---

designating "exploited" strata in the region. It also indicated an awareness that residues of tribal organization were most pronounced (and hence presented the greatest challenge) in pastoral milieus, especially in Kazakhstan, Turkmenistan, and Kirghiziia. See A. Fominov, *RN*, 6, 1930, pp. 69-79. Cf. A. I. Kastelianskii (ed.), *Formy Natsional'nogo Dvizheniia v Sovremennykh Gosudarstvakh* (St. Petersburg, 1910), pp. 579-84; Masal'skii, *Turkestanskii Kray, passim.*

[91] See, e.g., Kuchkin, *SKA*, Ch. VI, esp. pp. 263-64, and pp. 428-29.

[92] Kuchkin, *VI*, 10, 1946, p. 18.　　[93] Kuchkin, *SKA*, pp. 23-24.

[94] Arkhincheev, *SS*, 2(43), 1930, p. 100.

[95] Kuchkin, *VI*, 10, 1946, p. 22.

would presumably collapse, the hold of primary and local groups upon their members would break down, and minds as well as bodies would be released from the previous equilibrium and set adrift, as it were, and be delivered into the Soviet fold.

As it turned out, the rate at which these measures could be put into effect was very uneven.[96] Moreover, in a number of cases, entire clans, when faced with the deportation of their leaders and notables, tended to flee either abroad or to inaccessible desert hideouts.[97] In other cases, popular hostility in regions where confiscation and deportation proceedings were in progress expressed itself in scattered resistance or massive slaughter of cattle.[98]

However, what seemed to disturb the regime above all while the attack was in progress was that the removal of what appeared to be the hard core of traditional elites did not make a community automatically available for Soviet-sponsored mobilization.[99] As perceived by Soviet analysts, the main obstacles continued to group themselves around two basic, and intimately correlated, traditionalist propensities in the dealings of local groups with outsiders: secrecy and solidarity. If anything, intensified Soviet pressures upon tribal and communal leadership seemed, at least in the short run, to strengthen the resolve of communities and groups—or even to activate fresh or previously dormant dispositions—to guard the walls of secrecy and internal solidarity.

Thus, in some Kazakh-Kirghiz locales, Soviet attempts to get what were presumably disadvantaged members of a clan to identify, or to testify in court against, a more privileged kinsman encountered a barrier of silence. Lips were sealed by *bata*, a religio-tribal vow taken collectively by members of a community to say absolutely nothing at Soviet court proceedings against men of the same group.[100] The party's frustration was tersely recorded: "[It] is generally impossible to establish the truth" during attempts to

[96] See, e.g., Shikhmuradov and Rosliakov (eds.), *Ocherki Istorii*, pp. 346 ff.

[97] Ibid.

[98] This was so especially in pastoral milieus where the attack against traditional leaders was coupled with attempts to herd nomads into cooperative farms and settle them on the land. I deal with this problem in a separate study, "Nomadic Tribes and Revolutionary Politics in Soviet Central Asia," now in preparation.

[99] See, e.g., Fominov, *RN*, 6, 1930, pp. 69-79, *passim*; Dzasokhov, *RN*, 2-3, 1931, p. 66.

[100] V. Zasukhin, *VS*, 8, 1931, p. 27. Cf. Kuchkin, *VI*, 10, 1946, p. 11.

penetrate local groups; "[when the interests of the clan demand it,] truthfulness and honesty assume a different character from that implied in the usual meaning of these terms . . . ; the interests of the clan come first, truth comes second."[101]

While, before the revolution, a man who broke *bata* was likely to be murdered, now more circumspect methods were used to deal with him. He was likely to be elaborately framed, with false denunciations heaped against him by members of his clan—denunciations delivered, of course, to *Soviet* authorities. Just to make sure that its case was airtight, the clan supplied as many false witnesses as necessary. In addition, not only a *bata*-breaker but anyone who ventured to collaborate with Soviet authorities at the expense of his group was subjected to subtle forms of persecution and to a comprehensive social boycott, including the clan's refusal to support him in disputes with outsiders, or to pay the *kalym* (bride price) that would enable him to marry. The tightness of the circle of boycott was assured either through bribery or with the covert assistance of the clan's representatives in the Soviet apparatus.[102]

Commensurately, *namyz*, clan pride, was now invoked more strongly than in the recent past. As Soviet investigators saw this, it was the unwillingness, shame, or fear to do anything that would go against *namyz* (and thus cause the clan to lose its good name) that "[made] poor natives go against their [own] class interests. . . ." Poorer and socially disadvantaged kinsmen were thus perfectly willing to hide the identity as well as property of richer and more authoritative relatives. Transgressions against *namyz* provoked the contempt of the entire clan for the culprit, and usually led to the latter's expulsion from the community.[103]

In locales where the sense of *namyz* was apparently not considered potent enough to ensure the group's solidarity and cohesion, new arrangements were devised. Specifically, Tash-Kuran associations—referred to by Soviet investigators as "secret . . . , avowedly counterrevolutionary organizations"—sprang up in the countryside, especially in Kazakh and Kirghiz locales. The associations were formed with the avowed purpose of preserving *narkh*, local values and customs. What the regime found particularly disturbing about them was their strong Islamic emphasis, a paradoxical devel-

[101] Zasukhin, ibid.; P. Kushner, *RV*, 2, 1927, pp. 156-57.

[102] See Zasukhin, ibid.; Shokhor, *SS*, 8-9(13-14), 1927, pp. 109-10; S. M. Abramzon, *SE*, 2, 1932, pp. 95-97.

[103] Zasukhin, ibid.

opment in areas (the nomadic and semi-nomadic hinterland) where Islam had heretofore been but a thin veneer on the body of tribal custom and shamanistic practices. Without a doubt, religion was coming to be increasingly utilized to ritualize and consolidate primordial solidarities. The very name of the associations stemmed from the ritual of a solemn oath taken collectively by kinsmen, an oath to protect the traditional way of life that was pronounced over the Koran. The Koran was covered during the proceedings by a stone (*tash*), the symbol of strength in Central Asia. Hence Tash-Kuran.[104]

Likewise, renewed emphasis was placed by tribal groups on *bitium*, the peaceful reconciliation of hostile individuals or parties by influential personages. Even in cases of murder, every effort was made to arrange for *bitium*—accompanied by payments of *kun* (blood-money in a variety of forms) to the victim's kinsmen—thus keeping intra-group tensions under control, and keeping, as well, disputes, feuds, and litigations within and between groups as far away as possible from Soviet eyes, ears, and courts of law.[105]

[104] See Abramzon, *SE*, 2, 1932, pp. 95-97. Cf. Zasukhin, *RN*, 12(46), 1933, p. 39. Zasukhin seems to be mistaken in referring to *narzh* and *Tash-Kural*, respectively. In any case, *Kuran* is a Russian transliteration of Qur'ān.

Apparently the emergence of *Tash-Kuran* associations was but one sign of growing Islamic penetration of the nomadic steppe. Tribal and village notables seemed more eager than ever to invite *mullahs* to their communities —to collect a religious tax, and even to build mosques—at a rate far greater in 1917-26 than in 1900-17 (see Abramzon, *supra*).

[105] See Zasukhin, *VS*, 8, 1931, p. 27. Cf. N. Fioletov, *SP*, 1(25), 1927, p. 146; Shokhor, *SS*, 8-9(13-14),1927, pp. 109-10; N. Balaban, *VS*, 40-41, 1928, pp. 15-17; Kh. Suleimanova, *SGP*, 3, 1949, p. 67.

To be sure, there was here, as far as the Communist Party was concerned, at least one consolation. One common effect of the superimposition of Soviet political and administrative structures upon local groupings had been exacerbation of ancient local animosities. Faced with new organizational forms, some local kin-groups attempted to gain or retain predominance in their area by infiltrating soviets and party units, and using these as bases for silencing rivals and extending control. In such cases, representatives of one clan were not above informing against kinsmen of another. It was this dimension that was so characteristic of party politics in Central Asia during purges. (See, e.g., Kushner, *RV*, 2, 1927, pp. 156-57; A. Mitrofanov, *RN*, 1, 1930, pp. 29-36, and *RN*, 2, 1930, pp. 35-49.)

Nonetheless, even if such manifestations afforded the Soviet regime some leverage in permeating and undermining a number of local solidarities, the net effect could not have been very gratifying. For one thing, as was pointed

In sum, it would appear that the separation of traditional leaders from their followers, even when successfully carried out—which was not everywhere the case—did not immediately and automatically lead to a community's dissolution. It seems quite a safe inference that this was due, in part, to the fact that in the Central Asian traditional milieu communal structures were essentially segmentary rather than hierarchical in nature. In such structures, elites tended to be quite flexible in composition, and were not highly differentiated in incumbent political roles. Incumbents in such roles could easily be substituted, since the roles themselves persisted, and valued lines of kin could serve as vehicles to fill whatever gaps there were. In effect, it is probable that *any* locally respected and strategically connected patriarch (both in terms of his age, patrilineal descent, and affinal links with related groups) could step in to take the place of lost traditional leaders or figureheads. It is also likely that heads of extended families or their eldest sons were able to form new, informally operating communal councils almost as quickly as members of old ones were removed by Soviet police.

Thus, far from being supplanted by considerations of class, property, and bureaucratic status, the old unities based on kinship, custom, and belief showed signs of persisting even in the absence of traditional figureheads and seemed to present just as great an obstacle to the diffusion of Soviet influence as before.[106]

---

out earlier, cases of cooperation among various groups—including *sub rosa* agreements to rotate in nominally Soviet office, and to keep the Party's investigators and purge officials as far away and as disoriented as possible—would seem to have been at least as numerous as those of inter-communal strife. For another thing, it was far from an unmixed blessing, from the regime's point of view, to have cleavages along *tribal* and *communal* lines crisscrossing *party* and *soviet* organizations. And in the third place, the use of the tribal or communal informer to undermine local unities was ultimately a negative weapon. One could keep groups off balance in this fashion, and one could extirpate the most vocal and authoritative opposition, *but one could not gain genuine adherents.* It would seem that even the informers often denounced a member of a rival clan to the authorities, not because of a sudden conversion to the Soviet cause, but because they were convinced that their action would best serve the interests of their own clan. (For expressions of alarm over the state of Central Asian party and soviet organizations, see, e.g., Kushner, ibid., and Mitrofanov, ibid., in this footnote. Cf. Vel'tner, *RN*, 12, 1931, p. 29.)

[106] If further evidence was needed of the stubborn persistence of old solidarities, such evidence was supplied in the course of the first wave of attempted collectivization of Central Asian agriculture. Reports from far-

THE QUEST FOR LEVERAGE:
THE IMPERATIVES OF "ACTION IN DEPTH"

It could be argued, of course, that the situation did not necessarily need to be viewed as an alarming one. Some advances, for example in the organizational and economic spheres, were unquestionably taking place, and could be counted on to effect significant shifts in traditional attitudes, relationships, and roles—albeit only in the long run.[107] By the same token, the deportation of a number of "semi-feudal lords," designed to undermine the system they dominated, might also have been expected to have significant repercussions in the local networks of traditional authority relationships—though, again, in the long run.

Indeed, some of Moscow's observers in the field proposed that it was merely the "residues" of feudalism in traditional relationships that "perverted" or "masked" class relations—that is, denied the latter free play—so that all that was necessary was to gradually "untangle . . . [and] . . . cleanse" these relationships from the accumulated dead weight of tribalism and patriarchism.[108] Others rationalized observed trends in a similar vein by taking their cue from Lenin, to the effect that, "when the old society dies, it is not feasible to ram its corpse into a [coffin] and deposit it into a grave. [This corpse] is decomposing in our midst, and [as it rots] it infects us all. The socialist revolution cannot be born in any other way."[109]

But such an outlook could not be accepted with equanimity by the radical core of a revolutionary elite that continued to press for what was typically referred to as "the liberation of [Central Asian masses] from the repulsive nightmare of feudal [patriarchal and]

---

flung locales confirmed one another: coercion or threats indeed brought into being what appeared to be the collective farms (*kolkhozes*) demanded by Moscow; but, on closer examination, not only were most of these found to exist largely on paper; even where the collective farms did seem to satisfy some Soviet structural criteria, old allegiances and customs were found to have migrated into the new collectivistic forms. For that matter, entire *kolkhozes*, or labor brigades inside them, were found to be organized along lines of kinship and cultural identity (see, e.g., Zasukhin, *RN*, 12(46), 1933, pp. 38-40).

[107] See, e.g., S. Pisimennyi, *RK*, 10, 1928, pp. 11-20, *passim*. Cf. Zasukhin, *RN*, 12(46), 1933, pp. 38-40.

[108] See Arkhincheev, *SS*, 2(43), 1930, p. 99.

[109] See Zasukhin, *RN*, 12(46), 1933, p. 38.

tribal relationships in the shortest possible time. . . ."[110] What came to be perceived in this context as a crucial desideratum in Central Asian conditions was nothing less than a "cultural revolution."[111]

A cultural revolution denoted here an intense and all encompassing effort to overcome a distinct "[cultural] lag," that is the lag of human relationships, attitudes, and customs behind new organizational forms.[112] As a number of important communist organizers saw it, the blow dealt to tribal-patriarchal elites was but one blow, and possibly not the most crushing and important one. One needed to deliver "a second blow," one that would destroy the residues of "tribal-patriarchal . . . ideology," an ideology that, through persistent loyalties and habits, made it possible for old kin- and custom-based unities to survive even when the old elites were gone.[113] In other words, the surgical excision of traditional elites meant primarily action "from above"; neither the ideology nor the legitimacy of the traditional order had been sufficiently impaired by it. What was needed in addition was a set of approaches that would engage Moslem societies "in depth," approaches that would reliably disengage human beings from the matrix of traditional ties, values, and beliefs; that would both tap potential sources of indigenous support and change traditional orientations and commitments beyond recognition.[114]

Where was one to begin? The answer, as one party analyst saw it, could be as dramatically unorthodox as it was apparently simple: "[The] real battle against harmful . . . tribal-patriarchal residues . . . , [against] the survivals of the old order . . . [blocking the path of Soviet development], must begin from the destruction of the old . . . family—of that primary cell of the conservative [Central Asian] village, [a cell] that refuses to surrender its positions to [the forces of] the new . . . [world]."[115] Moreover (as a number of

---

[110] Ibid., p. 40 (italics supplied).

[111] See K. Tabolov, *RK*, 8, 1928, p. 22; Pisimennyi, *RK*, 10, 1928, p. 11.

[112] See references in preceding note.

[113] See Arkhincheev, *SS*, 2(43), 1930, pp. 99-100; Zasukhin, *RN*, 12(46), 1933, p. 39. For instances of traditional unities continuing to exert their influence through poor and disadvantaged kinsmen whom the party had appointed to responsible posts, see, e.g., Dzasokhov, *RN*, 2-3, 1931, p. 66.

[114] See Arkhincheev, ibid., p. 99. Cf. Pravda, *SS*, 12(41), 1929, pp. 107, 110.

[115] See Dzasokhov, *RN*, 2-3, 1931, pp. 66-67. While the author uses here the example of the Kirghiz family, explicit proposals offered both by him

leading party analysts perceived this) if the key to genuine cultural revolution was in the destruction of traditional family structures, the undermining of the kinship system itself could most speedily be accomplished through the mobilization of those of its members who were the most consistently "humiliated . . . [and] exploited," who were, as a rule, segregated, secluded, and constrained, who were, in effect, "the lowest of the low," "the most enslaved of the enslaved": its women.[116]

Accordingly, while the overall Soviet assault on Central Asia's Moslem traditional societies proceeded on a number of levels, and with widely varying degrees of success, one essential facet of that assault came to be the deliberate attempt to stimulate and manipulate sexual and generational tensions that would help to induce an

---

and by others (cited further in the text), stress the need to effect the breakdown of the Central Asian family unit as such. Also, while Dzasokhov evidently wrote this in 1930-31, he was (as will be seen further in this chapter and in the chapters that follow) merely restating the gist of a variety of proposals presented in 1926-29. I cite his argument here primarily because it formulates the basic issues in a particularly forceful and precise way.

[116] This argument is implicit in Dzasokhov (pp. 65-66); but it was made very explicit by many analysts and organizers cited further in the text. It should be kept in mind, though, that the emphasis on women, in this context, was not the only one in vogue. There were those who felt that native social organizations would collapse the moment they lost, in particular, the young generation, "the marrow of their bones." And that, in turn, would happen when young men turned against their elders, and sons against their fathers, and when Central Asia's youth came over *en masse* to join the *Komsomol* (see, e.g., Fominov, *RN*, 6, 1930, pp. 69-79, *passim*). Hopes for an early denouement in this realm appear to have been dashed, however, when organizational work with Moslem youth (which, in the 1920's, could only have been almost exclusively *male* youth) turned out to be one of the most badly lagging sectors on the entire Central Asian front (some concrete indications of this failure will be found in most of the chapters that follow, esp. in Chapters Seven to Nine). While the reasons for this were necessarily complex, it would appear that at least one of them had to do with the status of young males in Islamic societies. In these societies, while the father's authority was indeed supreme, it was not necessarily arbitrary, overwhelming, and, therefore, resented. Most important, in relation to that authority, sons comprised a stratum that, no matter what its socio-economic background, tended to be the most highly prized and favored one, and hence indulged, in the extended, patriarchal Moslem family. Thus it would seem to have been far from a simple matter to elicit grievances of young Moslem males on these grounds, and to turn them against the kinship system itself.

upheaval in a traditional system of values, customs, relationships, and roles, beginning with the primary cell of that system: the extended, patriarchal Moslem family.

Thus, at least three basic propositions were implicit in the decision to use women to break up Moslem traditional societies. First, that "class struggle," in some societies, did not need to express itself exclusively through social strata conventionally designated on the basis of property and relation to the means of production. Second, that "patriarchism" characterized authority relationships not only in large and complex social organizations in Central Asia but also, and perhaps most strikingly, in the primary cell of the native traditional world, i.e., in the extended family. Third, that in such a milieu, social status, and hence potentially social tensions, could be based as much on sexual as on economic or other roles.

There was at least one congenial ideological precedent for such a view. Engels had written:

> *The first division of labor* is that between man and woman for the propagation of children. . . . *The first class opposition* that appears in history coincides with the development of the antagonism between man and woman in monogamous marriage. . . . *The first class oppression* coincides with that of the female sex by the male. . . . The modern family contains in germ not only slavery (*servitus*) but also serfdom, since from the beginning it is related to agricultural services. It contains *in miniature* all the contradictions which later extend throughout society and its state.[117]

One factor made such an analysis particularly relevant where Central Asia was concerned. Marxist references to female inferiority in a capitalist industrial system were relatively marginal illustrations of the hypocrisy and inequality accompanying the struggle between the classes. In the case of the emergence of the patriarchal family, however, the thrust and imagery of the analysis placed male-female relationships at the center of the class struggle. Moreover, precisely because Central Asian societies were viewed as feudal-patriarchal, backward, primitive, and semi-savage, they could be equated all the more easily with the early stages of social development ("the transitional period between the upper and middle stages of barbarism")[118] that formed the matrix for Marxist

[117] See Engels, *The Origin*, pp. 51, 58 ff. (italics in the text).
[118] Ibid., p. 54.

theoretical propositions about the family. The presence of polygamy here could only compound the relevance and strength of the argument. In fact, Marxist analysis of the Athenian patriarchal family—presented as one of the earliest clearcut models of exploitative male-female relationships, where love was ruled out and where women were viewed as things and could choose only between servitude and prostitution—could be made to apply, almost word for word, to the Moslem traditional family as visualized by many party organizers in Central Asia.[119]

This kind of analysis, as well as the sense of failure while attacking traditional elites head-on, undoubtedly helped to strengthen conclusively the arguments of those Soviet activists who had been insisting all along[120] that there were highly unusual opportunities for revolutionary action in Moslem traditional societies, and that women were the key to those opportunities. Deliberately to proceed on the assumption of a woman's dumb, isolated, subordinated, exploited, depersonalized, will-less, and loveless existence could presumably help the party find more than merely additional social leverage in Central Asia. Deliberate and planned utilization of this issue could prove to be social dynamite *par excellence*. It could attack what might be potentially the weakest link in the solidarities of native kinship systems, and could thus speed up immensely the processes both of social disorganization and of reintegration under Soviet auspices.

In this sense, it seems fruitful to visualize Soviet experience in Central Asia as a complicated search for strategic factors in a revolutionary transformation—for techniques, instrumentalities, and targets that would provide the regime with relatively high leverage in undermining and transforming a Moslem traditional milieu. In other words, it was a quest for a structural weakpoint through which particularly intense conflict could be engendered in society and leverage provided for its disintegration, the recruitment of sympathetic elements from its ranks, and, finally, its reconstitution.

Of course, to the extent that Soviet goals involved the deliberate disruption of an entire milieu, one of the primary problems in such a purposive enterprise was that of control. Soviet experience suggests—to borrow Anatol Rapoport's terms[121] from another context

---

[119] Ibid., pp. 50 ff., 54-59, 68-70, 127, 148.

[120] See the chapters that follow.

[121] See his "Models of Conflict: Cataclysmic and Strategic," in A. de Reuck, *et al.* (eds.), *Conflict in Society* (Boston, 1966), pp. 259-87.

—an attempt to induce a strategic conflict at the nerve-centers of a social order and to avoid a cataclysmic one; commensurately, control of the revolutionary process turned out to be one of the most sharply perceived imperatives in Soviet experiments with social engineering, perhaps more so in Central Asia than in other parts of the Soviet Union.

PART TWO

Justification for Action:
The Potential Use of Women
in Revolutionary Transformation

THREE · *Moslem Women as a Surrogate Proletariat: Soviet Perceptions of Female Inferiority*

Toward a Vision of a Surrogate Proletariat

ONE of the main stimuli for turning to Central Asian women as a potential revolutionary stratum undoubtedly was the growing Soviet awareness of the difficulties involved in applying conventional criteria of "class struggle" in the Moslem traditional milieu. Those designated as underprivileged, exploited, and poor in that milieu seemed, by and large, not conscious of themselves as a class and not to act in ways consonant with such consciousness. This, in turn, held back social differentiation, maintained the influence of traditional elites, preserved traditional solidarities, attitudes, and customs, made a mockery of Soviet organizational forms, and blocked the paths of mass-mobilization.

To turn from conventional categories of class struggle to the role of the family and its members meant to turn from macrocosmic perceptions of social revolution to microcosmic ones; from abstract to intimate and detailed preoccupations in social engineering; from settled notions of social process and action to research, experiment, and improvisation; from class struggle to the novel, and unfamiliar, realms of sexual and generational tension; from a real proletariat to a surrogate for it.

To do so, however, required a plausible vision of a disadvantaged stratum, a vision backed with evidence or at least meaningful illustrations from real life. It called for the exposition in careful detail of every possible reason why a native woman could be considered, and should consider herself, "the lowest of the low," "the most oppressed of the oppressed," "the most enslaved of the enslaved"[1] in her society. This would both justify and make possible an approach to her as a potentially subversive and revolutionizing force in her milieu.

[1] See S. Liubimova, *VPG*, p. 11; A. Nukhrat, *OZV*, p. 36.

93

We know that party activists sent to Central Asia, particularly women activists, in many cases came to make it their business to study local societies and cultures with care before actually confronting them. Particularly closely perused were translated excerpts from the Koran; commentaries on the *shariat* (Moslem religious law); texts of Central Asian and Caucasian *adat* (local customary law); works on Central Asia by Tsarist Russian historians, legal scholars, geographers, ethnographers, and travelers; and memoirs of Tsarist officials and their wives, especially those containing some detailed references to the local way of life.[2] It is on the basis of these early studies, and of accumulating periodic reports from organizers in the field, that there came into being a rather detailed frame of reference concerning Moslem women.

It is safe to assume that, in seeking to make their case as strong as possible, proponents of female mobilization as an important dimension of revolutionary strategy were especially sensitive to the negative elements in a woman's life. And they tried to build these elements, and their darkest inferences, into a comprehensive and internally consistent picture. What follows, then, is a cumulative catalogue of female inferiority in Central Asia as conceived by party analysts and activists during the 1920's.[3] It was not a sys-

[2] E.g., A. Lomakin, *Obychnoe Pravo Turkmen* (n.p., n.d.); Leontovich, *Adaty kavkazskikh gortsev* (St. Petersburg, 1883); Rashid Bek Efendiev, *Mukhtasar Shariat* (n.p., n.d.); Masal'skii, *Turkestanskii Kray*; D. N. Logofet, *Strana bezpraviia* (St. Petersburg, 1909); Ye. P. Kovalevskii, *Stranstvovatel' po sushe i moriam* (St. Petersburg, 1871); Dukhovskaia, *Turkestanskiye Vospominaniia* (1913). These sources are cited in V. Moskalev, *Uzbechka* (Moscow, 1928); *Bezbozhnik* (news.), e.g., 10, 1928, p. 6; A. Nukhrat, *OZV* (Moscow, 1927), pp. 22, 28; S. Liubimova, *VPG* (Moscow, 1958), p. 12; B. Pal'vanova, *DSV* (Moscow, 1961), p. 20; M. V. Vagabov, *Islam i Zhenshchina* (Moscow, 1968).

For an example of rather extensive utilization of pre-revolutionary publications for a specific political purpose, see L. Klimovich, *Islam v Tsarskoi Rossii* (Moscow, 1936).

For notes on the initial helplessness of some Russian emissaries in Central Asia, and their engagement of disaffected Tatar women to explain to them local mores, see, e.g., L. Otmar-Shtein, "V Staroi Bukhare," in *ZVR* p. 345 ff; cf. J. Kunitz, *Dawn Over Samarkand* (New York, 1935), p. 287 ff.

[3] It is important to remember that this catalogue is cumulative in at least two ways: in the sense that it represents Soviet perceptions formulated in a number of contexts over a period of time; and in the sense that it constitutes my own compilation of these perceptions from a variety of Soviet sources. It never appeared *in toto*, and in the order in which it is presented here. Nonetheless, I have made an effort to insure that both the thrust and flavor of the overall Soviet argument be reflected in the text.

94

tematic analysis of native social values concerning female roles. Nor did it necessarily reflect the women's own awareness of their life situation. It may be said that it was a vision engendered partly by reality and partly by necessity—and presented with a special purpose in mind.

While it would be of obvious value to test such a catalogue against more objective data, no attempt is made here to do so, and that for two reasons. First, we have no significant samples of such data from the field. Although some first-hand descriptive accounts have been rendered by anthropologists and historians, they tend to be fragmentary and sketchy, and they date mostly from the nineteenth and early twentieth centuries.[4] Second, while attempts at rigorous investigation in other Islamic milieus tend to confirm some important components of the Soviet catalogue,[5] it is so far a moot point to what extent conclusions regarding the inferior status of Moslem women actually fit those women's self-image. In some circumstances, what an outsider views as *prima facie* proof of inferiority may well be considered locally as an indication merely of difference in sexual roles.[6]

[4] For some informative ethnographic notes, see, e.g., Masal'skii, *Turkestanskii Kray*; Bartol'd, *Istoriia*; Czaplicka, *The Turks of Central Asia*; F. H. Skrine, *The Heart of Asia* (London, 1899); Arminius Vambery, *Western Culture in Eastern Lands* (New York, 1906); V. Nalivkin and M. Nalivkina, *Ocherk Byta Tuzemnoi Zhenshchiny Fergany* (Kazan', 1886); *Mir Islama* (journal, Petrograd, 1912-1913); Klimovich, *Islam*.

For some recent summary accounts in English, see, e.g., L. Krader, *Peoples of Central Asia*, which includes a comprehensive bibliography; Hudson, *Kazakh Social Structure*; Winner, *The Oral Art*; Bacon, *Central Asians under Russian Rule*; Dunn, "Soviet Regime and Native Culture in Central Asia and Kazakhstan," *Current Anthropology*, Vol. 8, No. 3 (June, 1967), pp. 147-208.

[5] For comparative material on the status of Moslem women in other milieus, see, e.g., H. M. Miner and G. De Vos, *Oasis and Casbah: Algerian Culture and Personality in Change* (Ann Arbor, 1960); J. G. Peristiany (ed.), *Honour and Shame: The Values of Mediterranean Society* (London, 1965), esp. essays by Bourdieu and Abou-Zeid. For a very interesting case-study including an excellent bibliography, see David C. Gordon, *Women of Algeria: An Essay on Change* (Harvard, 1968). Cf. W. J. Goode, *World Revolution and Family Patterns* (New York, 1963), esp. Ch. III; J. Berque, *The Arabs: Their History and Future* (New York, 1964), esp. Ch. IX; M. Berger, *The Arab World Today* (New York, 1964), esp. Part One; R. Levy, *The Social Structure of Islam* (Cambridge, 1962), esp. Chs. I-VI.

[6] For some sensitive notes on such a problem of interpretation, see E. E. Evans-Pritchard, *The Position of Women in Primitive Societies and Other Essays in Social Anthropology* (New York, 1965), esp. pp. 37-58.

We are dealing here, then, with dimensions of female inferiority as perceived, for the most part, through the spectacles of revolutionary elites frustrated by the resistance and resilience of traditional society. We are dealing with notions of social deprivation conceived not as dispassionate fact—at least not necessarily so—but as perceptions of a missionary imagination intent upon mass-mobilization and radical social change. It is safe to assume, of course, that some, if not all, aspiring Soviet social engineers believed that their research and interpretations faithfully reflected actuality. There are also ample indications that their versions of reality were not invariably or completely arbitrary; in many cases they were conscious or unconscious exaggerations based on actual facts. But what distinguishes these versions is their systematic bias: their emphasis on elements that would make the case for a woman's inferiority consistent; their attempt to generalize from pre-selected samples and thus continuously to transform possibility into probability or certainty; their failure to draw significant distinctions between the life-styles of various Central Asian ethnic groups, and thus to allow for possible variations in female statuses and roles; their effort to infer or impute motivations and values based largely on Western experience. Nonetheless, while the Soviet catalogue was selective and deliberately slanted for maximum effect, it was complex and responsive enough to include instances and imagery from real life. As such it was unquestionably of great evocative power.

THE CATALOGUE AND IMAGERY OF FEMALE INFERIORITY

"Before the October Revolution, there was, throughout the vast expanse of Russia, no human being more ignorant, more downtrodden and enslaved, than the Eastern woman."[7] So Nukhrat, one of the first Turkic female writers, party propagandists and organizers in the Soviet period, summarized the matter. Together with a number of Soviet analysts and organizers, especially officials and activists of the *Zhenotdel*, the party's Women's Department, she spared no effort in unearthing what she considered to be a Moslem woman's most deeply felt grievances, and bringing them to the attention both of the party's leadership and cadres and of the Central Asian masses themselves. The sense of urgency in defining and stating the case stemmed not only from the compulsion to overturn the exist-

[7] Nukhrat, *OZV*, p. 8.

ing order as quickly and completely as possible, but also from a deeply held conviction that the female masses of an Islamic world were voiceless *par excellence*. They were considered voiceless in the sense of being deliberately deprived of rights and opportunities for self-assertion and self-development in society, as well as in the sense of lacking internal capacities for perceiving and articulating their existential situation, grievances, and needs. Broadly speaking, the indictment of Islamic and local customary rules under which a Central Asian woman had to live concerned four main spheres: education, economic activities, social participation, and family life.

Education

As Nukhrat and other field-organizers saw it, for a Moslem woman, ignorance was inevitable. Although the *shariat* did not prohibit a woman's education, it circumscribed this right to the extent that female literacy—at least functional literacy—was nearly zero. The circumscription was effected quite simply: the *shariat* rules concerning female seclusion cut down drastically a woman's freedom of movement. Second, according to traditional Moslem attitudes and customs a woman had neither the mind nor the need for knowledge. Soviet activists were quick to point to an array of Central Asian proverbs to prove this case: "A woman's hair is long, but her mind is short"; "Forty women have less sense than one cockerel"; and "No matter how much a woman may study, she could never be a *kazi*." Moreover, "A woman must know how to read"—local "rules of life" were cited—"because she must read the holy book of the Koran; but she must not know how to write, for she would then be able to write love letters."[8]

While the party's analysts emphasized this as *prima facie* evidence of hypocritical evasion, they could well have recognized (as they did in other contexts[9]) some additional moving forces in this situation. It seems certain that what was also manifested here was a Moslem family's fear for a girl's chastity, and a Moslem husband's deep unease about his wife's fidelity, manifestations affecting virtually every aspect of social life in Moslem traditional societies. There was surely good reason to assume that a corollary

[8] Ibid., p. 32; B. Pal'vanova, *DSV*, p. 19; N. Lebedev and Ye. Avksentievskaia, *RN*, 90, 1937, p. 52.

[9] See the sections on "Social Participation" and "Family Life" in this chapter, *infra*.

expectation was at work, too, namely that an educated woman would actively and successfully compete with a man in every field —an utterly unacceptable prospect from the male's point of view.[10]

It was not surprising, then—as Soviet cadres repeatedly stressed —that the Central Asian woman had always been condemned to "live in darkness."[11] It was pointed out that there had been only two known female poets in Central Asia's history. Fittingly enough, both came from mercantile families; both grew up in the capital and court of a local khanate; both wrote under pseudonyms (Ziniiat, "the beautification [of life]," and Makhzuna, "the sad one"); and one of them appeared in public only "in man's clothing."[12]

Economic Activities

It was not difficult to draw the appropriate conclusions: almost complete lack of education meant that a woman could not be suitable for any profession requiring systematic knowledge or special skills. Moreover, her childhood commitment to certain rigidly designated tasks insured that she would continue with them during adulthood, and would be unprepared for others. Most work roles outside the household were closed to her because of a father's or husband's fear of her potential contacts with other men.

Niurina and Nukhrat—both engaged in organizational work among Central Asia's women in the 1920's—pointed to a number of corroborating examples of this state of affairs. In some of the region's ethnic groups, especially among nomads and mountaineers, "the woman does everything, the man almost nothing." She worked in the fields, carried water, earth, and manure on her shoulders, wove cloth and rugs, processed wool, cotton, and animal skins, made clothes, tended cattle, prepared cheese and butter for the market, cooked food, and brought up her children. The man's work in the household amounted to plowing up his field, if any (and that, "once and carelessly"), protecting his cattle and harvest, selling the surplus of produce on the market, and buying what was needed by the entire family. In his free time, a man "lounges" at his house or tent, "sleeps, drinks, dances . . . , goes around visiting . . . , sits in [teahouses and] bazaars . . . , orders his wives around in a lordly voice . . . , or cleans his gun." When things get

[10] See Levy, *Social Structure*, pp. 132-33.
[11] Nukhrat, *OZV*, p. 8; Moskalev, *Uzbechka*, pp. 23-24.
[12] Moskalev, *Uzbechka*, pp. 25-26.

"overly boring, and he cannot bear sitting aimlessly," he mounts a horse and "gallops around the steppe." After all, "he is a warrior. He is ashamed to toil in a household. That is something for lower creatures to do—for women."[13]

Shatskaia, a Soviet ethnographer specializing in Central Asia, alluded to this syndrome in the course of analyzing the life style of Turkmen. Her analysis seemed to suggest that there were four basic dimensions in what she referred to as the "circle of perceptions" of traditional Moslem males (especially those closest to a nomadic and pastoral way of life), and that all of these dimensions were characterized by persistent "anticipation [of pleasure]," by interest in "predictions [of the future]," by deeply felt "wishes [and fancies]." These perceptual dimensions included: (1) dreams of abundance, especially of food; (2) fervent hopes to perpetuate the network of kinship and lineage, especially through sons; (3) a militant impulse to dominate, preferably in warrior-roles; and (4) a highly charged, possessive sexuality, often expressed in markedly "libertine" proclivities.[14] Needless to say, there seemed to be little, in such a "circle of a man's perceptions," that concerned achievement through hard work.

Although Shatskaia, Nukhrat, and Niurina did not mention this, it is likely that this picture was complicated by some new factors at play. To wit: while a man might think of himself as a warrior, during the late Tsarist and early Soviet periods he could no longer be one. The result could easily have been a sense of humiliation which may have stiffened his resolve not to engage in labor traditionally belonging to a woman.

The imagery used by cadres in depicting the conditions of women's work was characteristic for its emphasis on the immediate and the personal. A woman's toil was menial, grubby, never done. A woman meant "labor power." She was "always in a hurry"; she had to work "from dawn to dusk," in "merciless heat and cold," "her bones weary," "her lips caked," "her spine bent for hours."

Rug-weaving, for example, among Turkmen women was especially torturous. Working by hand up to sixteen hours a day, a woman spent the years of her youth with little to show for it: she wove perhaps one square meter of a rug in a month, "squatting

---

[13] Niurina, *Ka*, 4, 1925, p. 82; Nukhrat, *OZV*, pp. 13-16; for some statistics on female economic performance in a household, see P. Kalachev, *Ka*, 8, 1927, p. 58.

[14] See O. I. Shatskaia, *SE*, 1, 1936, p. 46. Cf. Nukhrat and Niurina, ibid.

[painfully at all times]," "her head weighted down by her heavy [traditionally prescribed headgear], her eyes flooded with sweat, . . . [her spine burdened by] an infant tied to it . . . ," with "early blindness [as much a certainty as] consumption." A Turkmen saying reminded her that she had no alternative: "If a woman is unable to weave rugs neither shall she eat." At the same time she worked with the most primitive tools possible, or without any tools whatever. While a man's work was light, it was considered more responsible, and hence more valuable and important than a woman's. The latter's toil was despised precisely because it resembled "slave labor" and "penal servitude." Yet "she had to bear her fate without a murmur"; "who would dare to question it?"[15]

It seemed perfectly consistent to relate these circumstances to broader dimensions of economic exploitation. The main thrust of the argument was as follows.

While doing the lion's share of a household's heaviest and most productive labor, a woman received little or no remuneration, and certainly nothing to even approach the extent of her work. Her rights to inheritance were heavily circumscribed, and often remained a mere formality. The purse-strings were held tightly by males—fathers, brothers, husbands, guardians. There was no way in which a woman could use on her own the resources she either earned or inherited. As a rule, she could not sell what she produced —rugs, for instance. Her husband was her ordained middleman. While being, in other words, the household's chief producer, she was treated with scorn, as if she were not only a servant, but an extra mouth to feed. Her "economic dependence," therefore, was "total."[16]

From the Soviet point of view, it was important to show how even the exceptions underscored the rule in the case. It was pointed out as highly significant that there was apparently only one instance in Central Asian history in which a woman was known to have occupied an important post in economic administration before Russian occupation: that of *mirab*, supervisor of a district's irrigation system. Of equal significance, however, was the fact that this wom-

---

[15] Nukhrat, *OZV*, pp. 13-17; cf. S. Shimko, *Ka*, 12, 1925, p. 66; Burlova, *Ka*, 8, 1928, p. 89; Pal'vanova, *DSV*, pp. 30-32; Niurina, *Ka*, 4, 1925, pp. 82-83. For some statistics on the extent of women's work, see G. Ibragimov, *Ka*, 10, 1925, p. 87.

[16] Z. Prishchepchik, *Ka*, 12, 1925, p. 63; Nukhrat, *OZV*, pp. 21-22; Pal'vanova, *DSV*, pp. 30-32; Moskalev, *Uzbechka*, pp. 17, 22-24.

an, Khal'-bibi, working in the first half of the nineteenth century in the district of Namangan (now in Uzbekistan), was herself the widow of a highly authoritative *mirab* of the same district. She assumed the post relatively late in life; had developed, in her husband's company, a high degree of expertise in irrigation; had a "pert, sharp, commanding" personality; had always "delved in men's affairs"; had "donned man's clothing" after her husband's death; and had gained valuable contacts in the local khan's court—which subsequently helped her son to become a district governor.[17] It was difficult to miss the impression of extraordinary parallels between this case and those of Central Asia's few female poets.

Social Participation

The themes of female disability to participate in public life were based as much on local lore as on the cadres' personal observation and interpretation. The picture presented on this account was unrelenting in its grimness. A woman's duties were in the home. Especially in towns and among sedentary peasantry, she was confined to separate female quarters "for life." But even in the nomadic countryside she was expected to remember her place. A Kazakh saying put it quite laconically: "A woman's path is between the house and the well." A Turkmen saying seconded this: "The world is a man's house, while the house is a woman's world." She could not show herself in the streets unless she had specific and legitimate business there, and unless there was no man to discharge these tasks for her. In any case, she could seldom leave the house without a female escort or her husband. In some Central Asian towns, she could not show herself in the main streets at all. That is why Central Asian streets and bazaars were filled primarily with men; women were a rare sight, and they tended to "creep close to the walls," like "quailing, faceless, eyeless shadows."[18] The guide-rule for them was silence and segregation. There could be no question of a woman's freely talking to a strange man in the street. For that matter, when on the street, women "must not speak aloud, or laugh, or turn around to look at passers-by."[19]

Accordingly, virtually any and all public meetings were off limits

[17] Moskalev, *Uzbechka*, pp. 24-25.

[18] Prishchepchik, *Ka*, 12, 1925, p. 63; T. Michurina, *Ka*, 10-11, 1926, p. 81; Nukhrat, *OZV*, pp. 19-20; Moskalev, *Uzbechka*, pp. 17-22; cf. F. Halle, *Women in the Soviet East* (New York, 1938), pp. 78-79, 106.

[19] Nukhrat, *OZV*, p. 20; cf. F. Niurina, *Parandzha* (Moscow, 1928), p. 5.

for women, and certainly most meetings where men were present.[20] Organized female demonstrations in public were out of the question.[21] Both Moslem religion and local custom stood squarely against all such activities outside the home, regarding them in some cases as an outright "sin." If that was not sufficient to discourage a woman's venture into the outside world, she still had to contend with the jealous alertness of fathers, brothers, husbands, and the community at large.[22] The objective was quite specific: to "fence off women from society."[23]

While freedom of movement was somewhat less circumscribed in purely nomadic communities, it was tolerated only for movement from place to place, not for social participation on an equal footing with men. Nor could women address public meetings of any kind,[24] though in some communities rare exceptions were made in the case of wives of religious leaders, or of old women who proved to be especially "wise."[25]

Quite consistently, Soviet analysts related these aspects of inferiority and segregation to what were apparently far broader inequalities in the public realm. Just as public affairs were outside of a woman's preserve, so was politics, and so were all organizational and associational forms in her community. By the same token, specifically female organizations were out of the question. A woman's associational life was supposed to be limited to visits for the exchange of gossip with female relatives and friends, and to occasional collective pilgrimages with other women to places hallowed by Islam or local custom. The reasons were often explicitly stated. Women were not reliable and certainly far less reliable than men, because they were less capable than men. More than that, they were dangerous. If let loose, particularly in the field of politics, not only their stupidity, but their natural proclivity for promiscuity, and for consorting with the devil, would place the entire community in danger. This dichotomy—the sense of both a woman's inherent inferiority and dangerous capability—was clearly expressed in Central Asian proverbs. On the one hand, "It takes ten women to make

[20] Prishchepchik, *Ka*, 12, 1925, p. 63; V.K., *Ka*, 9, 1925, p. 70; cf. Liubimova, *Ka*, 10, 1927, p. 56.

[21] *BSE*, Vol. 25, 1932, p. 255.

[22] T. Shirman, *Ka*, 4, 1927, pp. 73-74.

[23] Nukhrat, *OZV*, p. 20.

[24] Ibid., p. 21.   [25] Nukhrat, *VMV*, pp. 27-28.

one hen; [and yet], if the hen had any sense, how could it be eating dung?" Again, "If a true believer needs counsel, let him ask the mullah; if the mullah is not there, then his father; if not—his elder brother; if not his brother then his uncle; if not—his neighbor; but if nobody is there [to give a true believer counsel], then let him ask his wife and do exactly the opposite of what she says." On the other hand, "A man with head of brass is better than a woman with a head of gold," and "The cunning of a single woman is load enough for forty asses."[26]

In any case, fathers, brothers, and husbands knew best what was good for their families, and were thus fully empowered to represent the family in the community and to defend family interests in the political marketplace. Moreover, politics meant not only a battle of wits but often bloody combat, in defense of "honor," family, and property. And just as combat of any kind was a man's preserve, so were all matters pertaining to "honor," family interests, and the ownership of property. While a woman's physical endurance was sufficient for tending to a household, harvest, and animal-herd, it was not suited to the domain of public affairs. Neither could there be any recognition for a woman in this domain. As stated succinctly by a Kazakh proverb: "At the races, there can never be prizes for mares."[27]

From the Soviet point of view, even the most generous interpretation of such restrictions could not negate the compelling nature of the facts. For one thing, community affairs required time, something a woman certainly did not have.[28] Also, where the lines of kinship and politics were closely meshed, and where households were organized on the patrilineal principle, a woman's direct participation in politics could prove explosive, since she was, as often as not, a stranger in her community, i.e., an arrival from a different village and kinship group.[29] Most important of all, formal participation in politics, and the holding of public office, would auto-

[26] Pal'vanova, *DSV*, p. 22; Nukhrat, *OZV*, pp. 24-25; Michurina, *Ka*, 10-11, 1926, p. 81; cf. Halle, *Women*, pp. 78-79, 106. See also Levy, *Social Structure*, pp. 99, 132-33.

[27] Michurina, *Ka*, 10-11, 1926, p. 81.

[28] See Ibragimov, *Ka*, 10, 1925, p. 87.

[29] While this point was not made explicitly, it was strongly implicit in Soviet accounts of inter-familial and inter-clan relationships, and of the position of a newly married woman in this context. See the section on "Family Life" in this chapter, *infra*.

103

matically place women not only in direct competition with men, but would allow them to be superior to men: *to judge, command, and rule over men.*[30] Such a prospect could scarcely be entertained in a Moslem traditional society.

It was clear to Nukhrat and her co-workers in the communist apparatus that this tended to limit very severely a woman's civil rights. Even where *shariat* provided for such rights, Central Asian *adat* "turned these into dust."[31] This was particularly obvious in the legal realm. No woman could be a judge or any other legal personage. A woman could plead her own case only in courts concerned especially with family matters.[32] Even there, her testimony as a witness equaled, in validity and strength, only half that of a man. This meant that, for every man, literally two women were required to bear witness, if a woman's case was to stand any chance at all.[33] The implication was that a woman is not only ignorant, but particularly prejudiced, and concerned with herself alone.

Just as a woman's inheritance rights were limited in practice in favor of males, so were her rights to divorce. As a rule, it was entirely a man's prerogative to initiate and attain divorce, and that for virtually any reason at all. A woman could do so only in exceptional cases, e.g., when she could prove her husband's impotence. Even so, a husband could complete a divorce merely by declaring three times in front of witnesses that he was divorcing his wife. The latter, however, needed to carry her case to court. More than that: in most cases divorce, especially if initiated formally by the wife, or if brought about *de facto* by her flight from the house, meant a woman's departure not only without property, but without children. A mother had no inherent right to her offspring. For that matter, a husband who wished to get rid of an unwanted wife, and

---

[30] The regime's cadres in the field became aware quite early of the unease of Central Asian males in this respect. This is clear from Soviet accounts and interpretations of the men's ferocious resistance to women's participation in Soviet elections and arrival in authoritative public posts. See, e.g., A. Artiukhina, *Ka*, 5, 1927, p. 4; A.Z., *VS*, 52, 1928, pp. 15-16; Yu. Potekhin, *SS*, 28, 1928, p. 86; V. Tarantaeva, *Ka*, 11, 1928, p. 45; V. Tarantaeva, *VS*, 51, 1927, p. 10.

[31] Nukhrat, *OZV*, p. 21.

[32] Depending on the locale, these were *kadi* or *kazi* (canonical) courts, conducted according to the *shariat* and/or *adat*, and dealing with such matters as divorce and inheritance. See Chapter Five for a discussion of Soviet perceptions and actions in this matter.

[33] Nukhrat, *OZV*, p. 21.

to retain her property and children, needed only to torture her enough to provoke her demand for divorce, or her illegitimate flight.[34]

In short, where women were concerned, the references to *kafaat*, "equality," in Koranic law were "purely formal" in nature. They were consistently negated by a host of supplementary stipulations, exceptions, and limitations, that made it virtually impossible for a female to make a significant move without the consent of a male, be it a father, a brother, a husband, or a guardian.[35] It was no accident that the Arabic term Islam denoted "[humble] submission," and that Moslem religion "consider[ed] submissiveness to be a woman's chief virtue."[36]

Against this background, the Soviet catalogue emphasized perhaps more frequently and insistently than anything else the nature of the world in which a Moslem woman had to live. The woman's world, as depicted by the cadres, was as violent as it was arbitrary. She could be killed outright, with either religious or customary sanction, for, among other things, illegitimate loss of virginity, for adultery, and for undermining the family's honor. She could be beaten as savagely and often as a father, husband, or male guardian deemed right. Though Moslem canonical law enjoined moderation, it explicitly allowed a woman's physical punishment.[37] In cases of her grave mutilation, a man was liable only to a fine.[38] In some Central Asian locales, where custom frowned on heavy beatings, for example, among some Uzbek villagers, certain forms of "retribution" were explicitly sanctioned. Thus, upon catching a runaway wife, a husband was perfectly within his rights to "bite off her nose."[39] Among some Turkmen, on the other hand, even the mere suspicion of a woman's infidelity could legitimately lead to "the branding of her sexual organs with hot iron."[40] No sanctions at all were attached to a man's marital infidelity.[41]

From the point of view of communist organizers who reported cases of this kind from native villages, the fact that canon and cus-

---

[34] Ibid., pp. 22, 30-31. Cf. Sulaimanova, *ISGPU*, Vol. I, pp. 260-61, citing Khidaia, *Kommentarii Musul'manskogo Prava* (ed. N. I. Grodekov, Tashkent, 1892), Vol. I, pp. 200, 221, 435.

[35] Sulaimanova, ibid., pp. 254-56, citing Khidaia, ibid., Vol. I, pp. 151-52, 165-66.

[36] See Pal'vanova, *DSV*, p. 21.   [37] Ibid., p. 31.

[38] Liubimova, *VPG*, p. 11.   [39] Nukhrat, *OZV*, p. 23.

[40] Michurina, *Ka*, 10-11, 1926, p. 81.

[41] Nukhrat, *OZV*, p. 23.

tomary law sanctioned such explicit inequality said much about fundamental Islamic attitudes towards women. Islam had to be an "accomplice in a woman's slavery." It always stood on the side of "oppressors and exploiters . . . on the side of the strong . . . ," i.e., of men. Both *shariat* and *adat* in Central Asia "consolidate, legalize, and sanctify a woman's serfdom and a male's mastery." They "do not recognize a woman as a human being."[42] They "[condemn a woman to] completely arbitrary rule [and] humiliation."[43] Bartol'd—one of the great Russian Turkologists, whose career spanned the late Tsarist and early Soviet periods—summed up this matter somewhat differently, though without contradicting the main thrust of this argument. As he put it: "The Koran treats a woman's identity almost exclusively from the point of view of a jealous husband."[44]

The communist indictment of Islam, on this account, was replete with corroborative evidence. Thus, both religious and customary laws were cited as preventing women from becoming religious leaders.[45] (While the corollaries of such a restriction were not explicitly delineated in this context, it is obvious that they were clearly understood: because all education was in the hands of the Moslem clergy, and was primarily religious in character, no woman could be a teacher. For largely the same reasons, she could not be a healer either, except when she served exclusively women, i.e., in the role of midwife and, sometimes, fortune-teller. Of course, her lack of formal education would have disqualified her in any case.)

A woman could not lead a community in prayer, and could officiate at religious festivals only in the role of a witch. Thus, even on those holiest occasions which involved the entire community, women could be only spectators. They were required to stand to one side, and in the background.[46] For that matter, neither Moslem religion nor Central Asian traditions had any place at all for festivals devoted to women nor did they provide them with any equal, meaningful opportunities for participation and celebration. Consistently enough, in a world where dramatic entertainment was intimately related to religious or religio-customary rituals, women

[42] Ibid., p. 17; cf. Pal'vanova, *DSV*, pp. 21-28.

[43] Liubimova, *VPG*, p. 11.

[44] V. V. Bartol'd, *Islam* (Petrograd, 1918), p. 36, as quoted in Vagabov, *Islam i Zhenshchina*, p. 19.

[45] Nukhrat, *OZV*, p. 21.

[46] See, e.g., Liubimova, *VPG*, pp. 21-22.

could not, as a rule, play actor-roles in public, not even in roles calling for female performers.[47]

The mosque was primarily for men. Women were segregated in it, and were not expected to attend its rituals as frequently and consistently as men. With rare exceptions, they could neither ascend to sainthood nor command respect in the religious realm.[48] Neither was it expected that they would pray, fast, and perform ablutions as often as required of a man. The reason for this was that they were considered religiously "impure"[49] far more often than a man; menstruation and childbearing, among other things, made them so. Also, the very frequency and intensity of women's illnesses made them often too weak to fast even in the holy month of Ramadan. The convergence of all these factors could not but reinforce the vicious circle of female inferiority, for a Moslem's standing in God's accounts, and his fate after death, were directly dependent on the number of good deeds he accumulated in a lifetime. Since good deeds began with prayer, fasting, and ablutions, a woman could hardly compete on this account, and hence her inferiority was inevitably compounded.[50]

[47] See Pal'vanova, *DSV*, pp. 66, 91; Liubimova, *VPG*, p. 43. For some exceptions to this rule—in the form of exclusively female celebrations constituting survivals of the matriarchate among the nomads—see, e.g., Nukhrat, *VMV*, pp. 23-31.

[48] If a woman was a descendant of the Prophet, a *sharifa*—something which was in any case very difficult to prove—she could claim a measure of respect; the rare cases of female saints almost invariably pertained to magic feats on their part; see Levy, *Social Structure*, pp. 130 ff. Quite understandably, this part of the overall Soviet argument was merely implicit in the public utterances of the regime's agents (see the preceding two paragraphs). It would have been awkward, for an avowedly atheistic movement, to dwell too insistently on this type of inequality in the religious realm. All the same, circumstantial evidence suggests that points to this effect were indeed made in private confrontations with native women (see the sources cited in this section, esp. Nukhrat, and in that on "Family Life").

[49] See Nukhrat, *OZV*, p. 24.

[50] The last paragraph owes much to my discussions with Mohammed Guessous, a Moroccan sociologist. Of the themes noted here, only segregation in the mosque and female impurity have been explicitly and systematically dealt with in Soviet sources—at least in those which have been available to me so far. For obvious reasons, neither sainthood nor good deeds sanctioned by Islam could be fittingly discussed by revolutionaries looking towards a communist society. Nevertheless, Bolshevik awareness of these matters, too, is clearly mirrored in the tailoring of notes on death and paradise (see *infra.*, in the text); cf. Levy, *Social Structure*, pp. 131-32.

Where it concerned the theme of discrimination—in the mosque or in the constellation of saints—the Soviet indictment was generally restricted to allusions or tersely factual references, and its tone was by and large restrained.[51] No such restraint was apparent in the handling of logically related themes that directly concerned a woman's existential situation. Here, the exhortations and illustrations were emotionally charged to the point of being inflammatory. The thrust of the argument was as follows. The prevalence of women's and children's diseases ensured that women would need the ministrations of Moslem healers and shamans more frequently than men. A woman, moreover, was dependent on childbearing, and especially the bearing of sons, as a source of any modicum of status and respect. Hence the high incidence of female visits to the local mullah or healer, and to Islamic "holy places," in search of physical and emotional help as well as miracles.[52] Given the general state of feminine ignorance, this reliance could only work to deepen superstition among women, and make them especially vulnerable to "spiritual imprisonment" by religious personages. More than that: spiritual dependence meant not only economic exploitation— since repeated payments and offerings were involved—it also meant repeated opportunity for sexual exploitation, both of mothers and daughters, on the part of Moslem clergymen and healers, often attained by force and under the guise of special "ablutions."[53]

Even the thought of death among Central Asian Moslems—the argument went on—was marked by clear-cut sexual discrimination. In addition to debarring women from taking part in funerals, it involved obvious contempt for a woman's life. As a proverb put it: "If anything is fated to spill, let it be whey; if anyone is fated to die, let it be a woman." Not inconsistently, a Moslem woman's inferiority and humiliation persisted after her death. Her grave was dug deeper than a man's, for "her remains cannot be on the same level" as those of a man. Even the "eternal bliss" of paradise, promised to all Moslems after death, was not open to a woman as an equal. She could get there "only if her husband took her with him." And

[51] For some of the reasons for this, see the last footnote cited in the preceding paragraph.

[52] See, e.g., Liubimova, *VPG*, p. 17; *Bezb* (ill.) 11-12, 1931, pp. 12-13.

[53] See Shirman, *Ka*, 4, 1927, p. 74; *Bezb* (news.) 4, 1927, p. 5; *Bezb* (news.) 31, 1928, p. 7; *Bezb* (ill.) 11-12, 1931, pp. 12-13; *Bezb* (ill.) 5, 1936, pp. 4-6.

what if he did not? Or if a woman was without a husband? Then "the female soul would lie, without a perch, at the threshold of paradise, like dust at the feet of the loyal servants of Allah."[54]

Just as hell (*doudakh*) was visualized in Central Asian lore (as elsewhere in Islam) as a place belching fire, crawling with scorpions, and cursed with the sight of constantly disappearing water, so paradise (*dzhennet*) was distinguished for its particular solicitude to a male's comforts and taste: pleasant, well-watered coolness, limitless amounts of *pilau*[55] and tea—and a limitless availability of women, especially virgins. Just as husbands could choose to partake of their former wives—the latter "visiting" them in paradise—so single men, including those who had been too poor on earth to afford the bride price (*kalym*) and marry, would be provided a "large choice" of women in accordance with each man's desire.[56]

Family Life

Soviet arguments and illustrations concerning a woman's life in the family testified to the cadres' prodigious industry in perusing available documents and finding corroborative material in personal interviews with native women. The treatment of intimate details in this case was as comprehensive as it was dramatic. Even more consistently than in the case of her social participation, the nuances of a woman's existence in the web of familial relationships were brought to light from every conceivable angle, and pursued literally from the cradle to the grave. What follows is but a small sample of this treatment.

When a woman became pregnant, her family hoped for a boy. A girl's birth was greeted with undisguised disappointment, and her mother was likely to hear: "You had better given birth to a stone; at least it would have been useful to repair the wall"; and "A son means treasure—a daughter, a heavy burden." Often, a girl was named with "reproach and irony," e.g., Doidyk ("We have had enough"), Oguldursyn ("May there be a son"), and Ogulgerek

---

[54] Pal'vanova, *DSV*, pp. 21-22; Ye. Ross, "K Svetu i Znaniiam," in *ZVR*, p. 356.

[55] A rice-and-meat dish preferred for festive occasions throughout the Middle East.

[56] See Brullova-Shaskol'skaia, *NV*, 16-17, 1927, p. 302; while this particular source is largely concerned with Turkmen, the imagery seems to have applied to Central Asia as a whole.

("We need a son").[57] Of a man in whose home a daughter was born, soothsayers were likely to say that he had been skimping on his religious offerings.[58]

As she grew up, a girl was treated as a second-class member of the family. While her brother would be indulged, and encouraged to play, she was tied down early to heavy work in the household.[59] Equally early, she was made aware of her sex as a potential source of shame and danger to herself and of dishonor to her family. She was obliged to be self-effacing and furtive. She had to hold her tongue and guard her impulses. She was taught that hers would be the role of *arvat*—a creature marked especially for its "nakedness"[60]—and that as such it was her duty always to protect that nakedness. A woman was something to be "hidden," for she represented a man's "honor." She was, in other words, evidence of both his sexual prowess and his social and economic achievement. For a man, for one or another reason, to lose his woman meant to lose his honor and his standing in the community. In such a context, for a woman to be referred to as *arvat* was to be called "by the most humiliating name in the entire [history of] mankind."[61]

(Reuben Levy explains this from a broader Islamic perspective[62] as a phenomenon wherein the wife's honor was "entirely in the keeping of her husband," whose business it thus was to see that this honor was not violated. If a violation occurred, it was not to the woman that the stigma was in fact attached but to him; it was his failure to do his duty of guarding and prevention. In other words, a *woman's* lapse of conduct was a *man's* disgrace.)

Accordingly, as soon as she entered early adolescence—and often when she was only eight or nine years old—a girl was obliged to don heavy cotton gear (*parandzha*) that covered her from head to toe, as well as a black veil made of horsehair (*chachvan*) which could never be taken off in public, nor even at home in the presence of men who were not the family's close relations. Even where the veil was not habitually worn—among Turkmen, for example—the

[57] Pal'vanova, *DSV*, p. 22. [58] Shatskaia, *SE*, 1, 1936, p. 46.

[59] See Kalachev, *Ka*, 8, 1927, pp. 59-60; for a comparison of early roles of boys and girls, see Halle, *Women*, pp. 80-82.

[60] See Moskalev, *Uzbechka*, pp. 33-34. This term, as used in Soviet sources, probably derives from the Arabic *'irwah*, nakedness; *arvat* is referred to as one of the most frequently used "general" and "official" terms applied in Central Asia to women before the October Revolution.

[61] Ibid. [62] See his *Social Structure*, p. 94.

mouth had still to be covered, especially when strangers were around, as a "sign of silence." Among the sedentary and semi-nomadic peoples only prostitutes were assumed to appear in public without a veil.[63]

A girl was constantly reminded that she was but a transient in her own home, for she was bound to leave early to live with another man's family. As Central Asian proverbs put it: "Girls are fed for strangers"; whatever is spent on a girl is like a "coin down a bottomless well."[64]

A daughter's relations with her father were marked by distance. When direct dealings did materialize, they only served to confirm the father's despotic rule.[65] A father could kill his daughter if she was discovered to have lost her virginity in an illicit relationship. For just as she was considered potentially the weakest link in the chain of her family's honor, so it was drummed into her, from the very first, that the years she spent with her family must be exclusively devoted to preparation for marriage, and the sooner the better. She was likely to be reminded that "a woman without a husband is like a horse without a bridle." She could have no other purpose in life.[66]

When she reached marriageable age, it was, of course, her father who decided whom and when she would marry. She had no will of her own. As a Turkmen saying had it, "Just as a cow does not choose the water [she drinks] so does a woman not choose her husband." She had to marry a man whom she had never seen, and whom she might even despise. There could be no question at all of friendship much less of love. If she married her beloved against her father's wishes, her father could kill her. Her marriage was, to all intents and purposes, a forced marriage.[67] A girl, no matter how young, was mercilessly torn from her mother's bosom and transplanted to the alien world of her future husband.[68]

Although bred for marriage, when the time came she was the object, not the subject, of the contract. Even as an infant she might have been promised by her father to a particular man and trans-

---

[63] See, e.g., Nukhrat, *OZV*, pp. 19-20; Nukhrat, *RN*, 3, 1933, p. 47.

[64] As quoted in Halle, *Women*, p. 78 ff.

[65] Nukhrat, *OZV*, p. 36.

[66] See ibid., as well as the preceding two footnotes.

[67] Nukhrat, *OZV*, pp. 22, 36; cf. Liubimova, *VPG*, p. 11; Michurina, *Ka*, 10-11, 1926, p. 81; Halle, *Women*, pp. 78-79, 106.

[68] Pal'vanova, *DSV*, p. 24.

ferred to that man's family at the age of seven or eight. In any case, in accordance with the *shariat*, she was considered marriageable by the time she was nine years old, or sometimes even earlier, which might or might not have been the time of her puberty. (A boy, however, was assumed to have reached maturity only at the age of twelve.[69]) No one asked her whether she was physically or psychologically ready for the event. More often than not she was a mere child-bride. As the Turkmen were fond of saying: "Hit a girl with your fur cap; if it does not knock her off her feet, it means she is ready for marriage."[70]

Her father's choice of a husband was part and parcel of an undisguised business transaction. The choice depended on the importance of the groom's kin-group, and on the amount of money and goods the groom bid for the bride. The haggling was open and fierce, and a father might carry on negotiations with a number of suitors or their families before deciding on the most advantageous match. Even where two fathers avoided the burdens of *kalym* on behalf of their sons by simply exchanging daughters, the latter still remained exactly that: the means of exchange. *Kalym* itself figured so prominently because a girl's marriage meant a loss of labor power to her family.[71]

Accordingly, a girl was bought and sold like a commodity. She was an object of speculation. She was her father's means of exchange. As *adat* said: "A girl is a sack of nuts: she can be bought and sold." A Central Asian going to the bazaar was just as likely to inquire about the price of women that day as about the price of grapes or camels.[72] Prices for orphans, widows, and divorcées were as a rule lower than in other cases for they were less desirable, and should, in any case, have considered themselves lucky to be "owned" by a man at all. Since bride-prices tended to be quite

---

[69] See Sulaimanova, *ISGPU*, I, p. 256, where this assertion is based on a Russian edition of Moslem canon law: Khidaia, *Kommentarii Musul' manskogo Prava*, I, p. 165. While Sulaimanova's analysis was published in the 1960's, it seems certain that it was based on sources also used by communist organizers in the 1920's. For that matter, the thrust of her argument often (and admittedly) reflects almost exclusively the sensibilities and approaches of Nukhrat, Liubimova, Michurina, and other Soviet activists in Central Asia during the first decade of Soviet rule.

[70] Nukhrat, *OZV*, p. 29; Pal'vanova, *DSV*, p. 25.

[71] Nukhrat, ibid., p. 18.

[72] Ibid., pp. 25-26; Pal'vanova, *DSV*, p. 23.

high,[73] they might be prorated, in the case of infant-marriages, for instance. Refusal of either side to consummate the marriage at the appointed time had to be followed by the return of paid-up *kalym*, and in any case could easily lead to blood-vengeance.[74]

A poor man clearly was at a distinct disadvantage. While a rich man might be able to afford a number of wives, beginning when he was young, a poor one might have to wait till he was fairly old, and had accumulated enough property, to afford even one wife. Or he might indenture himself to his father-in-law, paying with years of labor a prorated *kalym* before he could call his wife his own. Since polygamy by the rich inflated the price of marriageable girls, in many cases men's poverty made it impossible for them to marry at all. Hence the high rate of homosexuality, particularly with *bacha*, small boy-dancers in Central Asian teahouses.[75]

The case of the poor father could, of course, be no less compelling. A poor peasant or nomad, with daughters on his hands, if already debt-ridden and hit hard by a failure of crops or pestilence among his cattle, might find himself in double jeopardy. On the one hand, he would see the price of *kalym* fall together with the price of cotton and sheep, in a bad year. On the other hand, he would be forced to sell his daughters to the first comer—often only for a sack of rice—for girls might be the only acceptable commodity of exchange left to him.[76]

In any case, a nine- or ten-year-old girl was more than likely to be sold to an old man of sixty, and into a polygamous household, if the bid was high enough—just as she could be sold or forcibly delivered to the harems of emirs or khans.[77] It was here that a girl's terror and tragedy were greatest: bought perhaps by an old syphi-

---

[73] For samples, see Nukhrat, *OZV*, p. 25; and Pal'vanova, *DSV*, p. 23.

[74] Nukhrat, ibid., pp. 25, 28-29.

[75] Nukhrat, ibid., p. 26; I. I. Kryl'tsov, *SP*, 5(29), 1927, p. 133. Cf. Masal'skii, *Turkestanskii Kray*, p. 389; Czaplicka, *The Turks of Central Asia*, p. 34.

[76] Pal'vanova, *DSV*, pp. 17, 19-20; cf. "Osvobozhdennaia Gairam," *Bezb* (ill.), 2-3, 1940, p. 12. As in the case of Sulaimanova, Pal'vanova's work is recent (1950's). Yet even a cursory perusal of her book shows how closely she follows the arguments of Soviet organizers in the 1920's. Thus, in both cases it seems quite safe to use the arguments and illustrations as reflecting views held in the earlier period, especially when they help to fill gaps in the materials available outside the U.S.S.R.

[77] Pal'vanova, ibid.; *Bezb* (ill.), ibid., p. 12.

litic, a "wrinkled old snake," she was "like a little flower that had no chance to bloom," a flower that was "crushed under a coarse boot." By the time she reached twenty-five, she was a dried up old woman.[78]

The fact that *kalym* in Central Asia was very high led to marriage-by-abduction. Especially among nomads and mountaineers, a girl might be "stolen just like cattle." She was seized by force by a band of strangers, taken to a distant hideout, and became the wife of the one who raped her on the way. Fear and shame would prevent her leaving her new husband, or even complaining about her abduction. In any case she knew full well that, having lost her virginity in this fashion, she could expect to find no place for herself in her own community. What this meant, then, was that a woman's life and will were subject at any time to arbitrariness and brute force. It was not surprising that in many such cases of abduction, particularly of girls ten or twelve years old, the victims fell ill soon thereafter, or became insane.[79]

It made little difference that, in many cases, abduction had come to be only a symbolic act, involving a symbolic struggle between the bridegroom's clansmen and the family of the bride, or an organized ceremonial hunt by bands of young horsemen after a number of small girls assembled by their own parents in the steppe. The terror of being chased by unknown grown men, and captured, thrown across the saddle, and raped without further ado remained just as real and just as destructive.[80]

More normal wedding rites differed from this only in the circumstances and degree of a girl's humiliation. At a Turkmen wedding, for instance, the bridegroom was given a whip, as a symbol of manhood and power to be exercised in the household. And he was reminded: "If your wife is foolish, let your whip be thick"; and "Beat your wife three times a day, and if you have not the strength to do so, then at least beat the earth on which she sat."[81]

During the first night with a husband she had never seen before, a girl's first experience of conjugal relations was likely to be sud-

[78] Niurina, *Parandzha*, p. 6; Nukhrat, *OZV*, p. 29; *Bezb* (ill.), 2-3, 1940, pp. 12-13; cf. Pal'vanova, *DSV*, p. 25.

[79] Nukhrat, ibid., pp. 27-28.

[80] See Brullova-Shaskol'skaia, *NV*, 16-17, 1927, pp. 302-303; cf. Nukhrat, *OZV*, pp. 27-28.

[81] As quoted in Halle, *Women*, p. 100; cf. Michurina, *Ka*, 10-11, 1926, p. 81.

114

den and violent. Just as it was the groom's expectation to exercise his rights of ownership, and to prove his manhood to relatives and friends assembled and waiting close outside, so it was the bride's duty to submit without question. It was not for her to expect pleasure. She learned at once that she was there to be used, that she could be but "a submissive tool of a man's lust."[82] If she was still a child, and not developed enough for conjugal relations, she might be sent back for "the most terrible operations" to be performed on her sexual organs.[83]

Once inducted into her husband's family-household, a woman was likely to find herself in deeply alien territory. Much time would pass before she would be fully accepted in the new village, where she was, of course, an intruder in a new social system, and often in a locale far away from her parental domicile. Besides, more than one master expected her in her new home. Her mother-in-law, in particular, was likely to distrust or hate her, and to exploit every ounce of her strength for heavy labor. If the bride was very much older than the groom—the latter, depending on when his father paid *kalym*, might still be a boy playing with toys—the father-in-law might attempt to exploit her sexually. If the family was polygamous, she would find there all the more vicious competition and tension, and older wives might persecute and beat her.[84] If the young bride happened to be an orphan she was likely to be treated like an animal by one and all, for she could not even hope for her kinsmen's intervention.[85]

The husband would, in any case, be the lord; the wife, his slave. There was no ambiguity in Central Asian folk cultures on this account: "There is only one God in this world; [but] for a woman there are two: God and her husband." Her relation to her husband was like that of "a serf to a freeman." If her husband was a Kirghiz, he might exchange her for a friend's wife for a night or two. A husband was "the owner not only of her body and her labor, but of her life, too." As Central Asian *adat* explained: "Just as the shepherd may cut the throat of any of his herd's sheep, so is the husband entitled to dispose of his wife's life." And further, "To kill a man is

[82] Nukhrat, *OZV*, p. 23; cf. *Bezb* (ill.), 2-3, 1940, p. 13.

[83] Niurina, *Parandzha*, p. 6.

[84] See Ye. Mukhitdinova, *Ka*, 9, 1929, p. 39; A. Nukhrat, *Stepnoi Skaz* (Moscow, 1928), esp. pp. 10-24, 30 ff.; and Pal'vanova, *DSV*, pp. 26-27.

[85] See Pal'vanova, ibid., pp. 82-83; cf. Lebedev and Avksentievskaia, *RN*, 90, 1937, pp. 52-53.

a grave sin, even if he be a criminal; to kill a neighbor's woman is punishable as if you kill your neighbor's cattle; but if you kill your own wife, that is your own business." If a man claimed his wife's infidelity, he was not liable at all. If the murder was "unmotivated," all he was liable for was half the prescribed amount of *kun*—money and goods in lieu of blood—that was usually paid in other cases of blood vengeance to a wife's kinsmen.[86]

Economic exploitation followed as a matter of course, and that in the most menial tasks.[87] A wife learned, furthermore, that, while she was expected to be monogamous, her husband was entitled to four wives at a time and could manipulate Moslem law to have ten or more.[88] She also learned that only slavish obedience or "wild antagonism and scheming competition for influence over the husband" would keep her alive in the new world. She might live in perpetual humiliation and terror, as her husband's whims permitted him to shift his favors from one to another wife or concubine, while treating the others with ostentatious brutality or contempt. Yet, despite the jealousies and enmities, and the vicious infighting, a façade of harmony and solidarity had to be presented to the outer world.[89]

Most important, a wife learned that she was never outside of her husband's suspicions. "As mountains are never free from mist, so is a woman never free from suspicion," a Central Asian proverb maintained. Since both Islam and Central Asian customs held her to be inherently crafty and promiscuous,[90] she was surrounded by a number of taboos. These included not only the veil and seclusion in female quarters,[91] but also detailed rules for behavior at home

[86] Niurina, *Ka*, 5-6, 1929, p. 22; Michurina, *Ka*, 10-11, 1926, p. 81; Nukhrat, *OZV*, pp. 17, 23; Pal'vanova, ibid., p. 25; cf. G. Borodin, *Cradle of Splendor* (London, 1945), p. 185.

[87] See the section on "Economic Activities," *supra*, in this chapter.

[88] See Pal'vanova, *DSV*, pp. 26-27.

[89] See Mukhitdinova, *Ka*, 9, 1929, p. 39, and Nukhrat, *Stepnoi Skaz*, *passim*.

[90] See Michurina, *Ka*, 10-11, 1926, p. 81; Halle, *Women*, pp. 78-79, 106. Arabic folk-culture views a woman's sexual desire as being ninety-nine times stronger than that of a man. Hence the need to guard her against herself—and to protect her husband and kinsmen, of course, from dishonor. (I owe this observation to Mohammed Guessous of the University of Rabat, Morocco.)

[91] Both practiced more vigorously among sedentary than nomadic peoples; see Nukhrat, *OZV*, pp. 19-20.

and in public. These rules were especially stringent when strange males were present, inside or outside the house. In sedentary communities, no part of a woman's body might be bared except her hands. In all communities, when men were present, women had to be absent. If they happened to be around, they could not betray any sort of familiarity with a strange man, either in movement, words, or laughter. The slightest transgression of these rules, or the slightest sign of recognition from a strange man, might arouse the husband's suspicions at once. The result: merciless beatings, imprisonment in the house under lock and key, or banishment from the household altogether.[92]

Not only were women "beaten more than donkeys"; as a rule, a man could not really converse with a woman, and "it is out of the question to shake a woman's hand."[93] Commensurately, just as man and wife were strangers to each other when they married, so they remained strangers for years after the wedding. Two people living side by side remained "two separate worlds . . . each on his own." They "do not entrust their thoughts" to each other. They "go to sleep in silence."[94]

When husband and wife were outside of the house together, he either rode or walked in front; she always walked behind, at a respectful distance. It was she who carried a load, if any, even when her husband was riding.[95] At mealtimes, especially when guests were in the house, the wife did not eat together with her husband, but served him food until he had had enough. In some locales, among the nomadic peoples especially, she sat by the door of her house or tent and watched him eat, while he "scornfully throws her bones, as though to a dog." Among the same peoples a wife slept "at her husband's feet, until called by a kick, like a dog, to satisfy his [conjugal appetite]."[96]

When a woman was pregnant she usually was called upon to do her work all the same. This often resulted in her giving birth in the open field, or in a trench by the road. In any case, a woman was considered unclean during the period of childbearing. Accordingly, if she happened to be at home she was often dispatched to a cattle-

---

[92] Ibid., pp. 23-24, 30-31. Cf. Michurina, *Ka*, 10-11, 1926, pp. 81-82.

[93] Shirman, *Ka*, 4, 1927, p. 74.

[94] See Nukhrat, *Stepnoi Skaz*, pp. 23-24; cf. Krupskaia, regarding all traditional marriages, in *ORSZ* (Moscow, 1926), pp. 82-83.

[95] Niurina, *Parandzha*, p. 4; cf. Liubimova, *VPG*, pp. 16-16.

[96] Nukhrat, *OZV*, p. 24; Liubimova, ibid., pp. 22-23.

shed to have her child. If she was helped during delivery, such help was marked by practices in which filth as well as the cruelty of men were ever present. Among most Central Asians a woman had to deliver standing upright or crouching, often over a hole filled with ashes. If birth was slow, women were given "awful things" to drink, including "extracts of boiled flies"; they were strung up high and shaken; their abdomen was subjected to heavy blows; they were dragged through a narrowly sewed up sheepskin, so as to squeeze out the baby; they were dropped into icy water; they were forbidden to rest. Especially in nomadic areas, a slow birth was likely to be public. The huskiest young men of the village, as well as the local *tabib*,[97] sat in a circle around the woman in labor, watched her twisting in agony, and all the while, produced "the most soul-rending sounds": they uttered terrible cries, pounded utensils or drums, cracked whips or fired guns—all presumably, to guard against *dzhinns* (evil spirits). If this did not make the baby come, the strongest among them would "grab the woman from behind, just under the breasts, and squeeze with all their might. . . ." It is no wonder that this often caused not only the baby, but the uterus, too, to be expelled. It explained the extremely high rate of gynecological illnesses as well as of infant mortality, the latter approaching 80 percent in some places. It also explained why, after a few such deliveries, the lower part of a mother's body often became paralyzed—if, that is, both mother and child did not die in the first place.[98]

Just as motherhood tended to "maim a [Central Asian] woman physically and morally," so did childrearing practices either kill or disfigure the baby. Not only filth did so; the Central Asian cradle, in which children were tied down until several years old, was nothing but a "medieval instrument of torture."[99]

With the arrival of children, the iron constriction of a woman's life was completed. To be sure, as a mother, and especially a mother of boys, she enjoyed somewhat more respect as a person, both in her husband's and in the community's eyes. But because heavy work did not cease, and because diseases, aches, and pains assailed her and her children with growing frequency, she became

[97] Depending on the area, this could be a Moslem *mullah* and healer, a local shaman, a wiseman, a sorcerer, a quack.

[98] Brullova-Shaskol'skaia, *NV*, 16-17, 1927, pp. 299 ff; cf. Nukhrat, *OZV*, pp. 33-34; Sulaimanova, *ISGPU*, I, p. 274.

[99] For details, see Niurina, *Parandzha*, pp. 4-5; Nukhrat, *OZV*, pp. 34-35.

118

more than ever sensitized to the perils of her world, more than ever secretive and superstitious. With children on her hands, she found open revolt yet more difficult. In a world of ruthless competition for her husband's favor, and of "oppression of the weak by the strong," she easily turned into a "blind tool of her own subjugation"; she "helped to forge her own chains."[100]

If her husband's cruelty towards her continued, she might try divorce. But her husband was in a much better position to wield divorce as a weapon. He could do so if she bore no children, and especially no sons; if she was too weak to work; if she was not sufficiently obedient; or if she was no longer sexually attractive. When initiated by her, divorce was rarely consummated. Even when it was, she had to leave the house without her children, and with but her clothing on her back. Only an infant-in-arms might go with her, and he, too, had to be returned to the father when breast-feeding was no longer required. Moreover, for a woman divorce meant renewed dependence on her old family—not always an attractive prospect. It also meant that her status in the community would be drastically lower, that her new marriage might be even worse than the old one (since, as a divorcée, she was less desirable as a marital partner), or that there might be no marriage at all.[101]

If she tried to run away without a divorce, her fate was even less enviable. It was the duty of her kinsmen, beginning with her parents, to return her to her husband, or return the *kalym* he had paid with interest—a difficult choice. Thus, not only her husband might beat or kill her, if he caught her, but her kinsmen too were likely to be ambivalent or hostile.[102] A runaway woman could not easily find a place for herself in her natal community. To be sure, her parents might try to take advantage of the situation by selling her again to someone else. But the threatened revenge of her husband's kinsmen made this a risky business for all concerned.[103]

Even when her husband died, she was the last to have any say as to her and her children's fate. The custom of levirate, especially among Central Asia's nomads, ensured that she would be passed

[100] Pal'vanova, *DSV*, pp. 27-28.

[101] See Nukhrat, *OZV*, pp. 30-31. Cf. Liubimova, *VPG*, p. 11; Michurina, *Ka*, 10-11, 1926, p. 81. Cf. Sulaimanova, *ISGPU*, Vol. I, pp. 260-61.

[102] Nukhrat, *OZV*, pp. 25, 30-31.

[103] See, e.g., Liubimova, *VPG*, p. 47 (for the case of a woman's inability to free herself from persecution by her husband and his kinsmen when the latter demanded that the *kalym* be returned).

on to her husband's brother or uncle.[104] The resulting tensions might be especially trying. For, although levirate provided a widow and her children with a home, it also united her with a man in whose eyes she was among the least desirable of women. She was tolerated simply because no additional *kalym* needed to be paid for her by males in her husband's family. Worst of all, however, her new husband might turn out to be a mere baby, "younger than her own children." It was then "her cruel fate to bring up her husband together with her children." By the time he grew into a young man, she was an old woman, and then obliged to "find him a wife."[105] In either case—whether she spent her life with a child-husband, or managed to live on her own or with her old family as a widow— she was the object of gossip and maltreatment in her village, and considered fair game by her community's males. Only the poorest and least prestigious men would want to marry her.

In other words, what a woman found, in a moment of despair, was that hardly any alternatives were open to her, and certainly no alternative born of her own will. Never having left the grooves of her traditional habitat, she knew nothing of the outer world, and could only be terrified by it. To assert herself actively, and choose a radically different way of life, was beyond both her imagination and her strength. The authority of kinship, custom, and religion, as conceived and enforced by men, had her completely in its power; for as the Koran itself had said, women were but fields to be plowed by their male owners.[106]

The Consequences

What was the meaning of such a life for a Moslem woman? What impact did it have on her over the long term? In summing up their case against a system that apparently held in store for women nothing but segregation, subordination, and exploitation, communist cadres cast their indictment in metaphors of outrage and tragedy.

Anna Nukhrat seemed to set the tone in this respect when she declared: "The human tongue is too weak to depict fully the fate of an Eastern woman."[107] Niurina, Zavarian, Shirman, and Shimko

---

[104] Nukhrat, *OZV*, p. 22. [105] Pal'vanova, *DSV*, p. 24.

[106] Salim, "Musul'manskaia Religiia i Zhenshchina," *Bezb* (news.) 10, 1928, p. 6, citing the Koran, Chapter 2, § 223.

[107] Nukhrat, *OZV*, p. 35. It should be kept in mind that the term "Eastern" usually referred to all Asian women, including those in Siberia and the Caucasus as well as in Central Asia. However, since Georgian,

—to mention but a few of her co-workers in the party's agencies concerned with the mobilization of Central Asian women—also did much to draw the appropriate conclusions in terms that were as incriminating as they were bitter.

Unlike a man—the indictment charged—a Moslem woman had, in effect, "five masters": God, the emir, the landowner, the mullah, and her husband. None of these considered her a person, or valued her "more than a dog." They made her "keep her gaze down all her life." They made sure that she was "chained by the laws of *shariat*" just as she was "bound by the *parandzha* and *chachvan*." Having transformed a woman into a commodity, and a man's chattel, they made her "into the most contemptible thing alive."[108] Thus, she had to live by rules that were, in effect, "in the heads and hands of . . . her clan's elders." These rules were debated and interpreted by "pompous, polygamous graybeards and gluttonous [clergymen]." They were "written in holy books, and in well-decorated Arabic letters . . . ," but "in every letter there are a woman's tears and blood," and "on every page there is a sea of suffering and sorrow."[109]

"From [cradle] to grave, a Moslem woman was taught silence and obedience"; and her "total obedience" was set against her husband's "unlimited and arbitrary power." What else was there for her "but to be submissive"? An Eastern woman's life was one of "deepest tragedy." She was a "prisoner of gloomy *ichkari*," the female quarters, where she was "walled in." She was "a man's accessory," a "resigned tool of a man's lust," a "voiceless slave," a "beast of burden," without a shred of self-esteem, without even a "conscious sense of being alive." She had "never experienced

---

Armenian, and even some Azerbaidzhani (all in the Caucasian region) women demonstrably exercised not inconsiderable influence in their societies, and since other Asian women (in the Caucasus as well as in the Urals and Siberia) belonged to numerically and politically insignificant groups, there was a tendency to use the term "Eastern" especially frequently in connection with Central Asia. Perhaps it is most accurate to say that in the Soviet view the life of Central Asian women exemplified most consistently what were depicted as the horrors of the "feudal" and "medieval" Orient.

[108] Akhun-Babaev (the President of Uzbekistan), *SS*, 12, 1937, pp. 89-90, quoting the public testimony by Moslem women at various Central Asian congresses in the 1930's.

[109] Nukhrat, *OZV*, p. 35.

[a man's] sympathy and consideration." "For ages, her path [had been] a bloody one. . . ."[110]

"Every mud wall" in Central Asia—"seemingly so peaceful on the outside"—"every . . . stone . . . around women's quarters . . . can tell thousands of terrible stories, stories that can make the hair of the most well-tried person stand on end." The history of Moslem women was a history of those who have been "buried alive," "thrown into precipices," "stabbed with stilettos," "poisoned," not only by husbands but by their own fathers and kinsmen. It was a history of wives "committing suicide by setting themselves on fire" —for, a Moslem "religious specialist" argued, this kind of suicide was "sinless," and a woman could thus "enter paradise." It was a history, also, of wives who, "unable to withstand the horror of a husband's depredations, kill him."[111]

Commensurately, both the death-rate and suicide-rate for girls and women was far higher than for men. For that matter, just as the combination of heavy labor, child-marriages, a girl's forced sexual cohabitation before puberty, early motherhood, and prevailing unsanitary conditions led to grave illnesses or sterility, and inflated female death-rates, so did the destructive moral conditions ensure that it was virtually *women alone* who committed suicide.[112] Taken together, it helped to account for there being only about 45 women for every 55 men in Central Asia.[113] Also, it could not but lead to "degeneracy" among the region's peoples.[114]

And what of those who survived? When one saw them in the street one could not even determine "their sex or age." When one saw them without their "stifling cover that [kept] out light, air, and sun" for years, one saw women from whom "youthful, girlish beauty has been sucked out" by greedy men; women "who have gotten old far before their time"; women "with a sad little smile"; "child-women." When one gave them toys for their children, "their eyes [lit] up with a child's wonder." Why? Often only fourteen

[110] Niurina, *Ka*, 4, 1925, p. 80; N. Zavarian, *Ka*, 6, 1926, p. 70, Nukhrat, *OZV*, pp. 23-24, 30, 39.

[111] Niurina, *Parandzha*, p. 6; Pal'vanova, *DSV*, p. 27; Nukhrat, *OZV*, p. 36.

[112] Brullova-Shaskol'skaia, *NV*, 16-17, 1927, pp. 299 ff; Moskalev, *Uzbechka*, p. 23; Pal'vanova, *DSV*, citing research by M. S. Andreev, in his *Tadzhiki Doliny Khuf*, p. 182.

[113] See Pal'vanova, ibid., pp. 32-33; cf. P. Kalachev, *Ka*, 8, 1927, pp. 57-58.

[114] Ye. Butuzova, *Ka*, 9, 1927, p. 62.

years old when turned into mothers, they "had never had a chance to taste the sweetness of a toy." They had never known youth and girlhood at all.[115] Could there be any wonder that, when desperate, a Moslem woman cried out, "May the day be cursed when I was born a woman!!!"[116]

The Implications

It is, of course, impossible to say precisely to what extent the picture drawn by Soviet analysts was distorted. As was pointed out earlier,[117] there were two basic strands in the Soviet mode of building the argument. We know, on the one hand, that in a number of cases Soviet inferences and illustrations indeed derived from real life. On the other hand, it is clear that the argument as a whole was placed in the service of revolutionary politics; it reflected an attempt to generalize from pre-selected samples so as to make the case for women's inferiority consistent. Even where we have evidence that some of the cited attitudes and manifestations were definitely an operative part of the traditional social order, we do not know how prevalent these were in Central Asia at the time of the initial revolutionary moves. Nor do we really know to what extent the specific prescriptions of religion and custom concerning sexual inequality were actually followed. And we know least of all about the ways in which the women themselves perceived and responded to their life-situations.

Still, it is important to keep in mind some of the more obvious omissions in the Soviet case. The party's cadres did not really try to resolve the logical contradictions between various elements of the argument. For example, they did nothing to account for the contradiction between a woman's high valuation as a repository of a man's and family's honor, and her extremely low status. Similarly, they did not attempt to explain how men could actually divorce women on a moment's whim, invariably mistreat them, and even subject them to continuous, arbitrary violence. Were not these women a scarce and precious commodity in a world of high rates of female mortality, high bride-prices, and polygamous practices of the rich? Would not a husband's arbitrary maiming or killing of his wife mean harming a member of another kin-group, thus pro-

[115] Niurina, *Parandzha*, pp. 3, 7; Shirman, *Ka*, 4, 1927, p. 74; cf. Shimko, *Ka*, 12, 1925, p. 66; Moskalev, *Uzbechka*, pp. 22-23; Pal'vanova, *DSV*, p. 19.
[116] Nukhrat, *OZV*, p. 36.
[117] See the "Introduction" to this chapter.

voking a potentially disastrous blood-feud? Likewise, no attempt was made to explore possible avenues for a woman's self-assertion and self-defense: as a mother of her children, and as a link in a far-flung and sensitive network of blood-relatives, could she not exercise, even if only informally, far more influence than was attributed to her? By the same token, the horrors associated with local child-bearing practices might have been viewed in a different perspective: as a manifestation of a primordial life style, operating within given confines of knowledge, belief, and available resources, and not as deliberate cruelty inflicted by men on passive and defense-less women.

Needless to say, without some consideration of issues such as these it was unlikely that Soviet cadres could move toward a realis-tic, comprehensive view of the values and relationships character-izing local traditional societies. However, this—it is important to remember—was not the cadres' prime purpose. Theirs was not a quest for balanced, long-term evaluation. Rather, it was an impa-tient quest for loci of actual or latent antagonism and tension, and hence of possible revolutionary leverage, in an unfamiliar milieu. Under the circumstances, the crucial questions were: How relevant were Soviet insights concerning the possible sources of resentment and conflict in a Moslem traditional milieu? How and to what ex-tent could the manipulation of sexual and generational tensions facilitate rapid revolutionary change in this milieu?

Clearly, the answers to such questions hinged, at least in part, on the degree and consistency of differentiation between social roles on the basis of sex, and on the manner in which such differ-entiation was enforced. Here, the record—fragmentary as it is—is unquestionably persuasive. Judging from all accounts, the differ-ences between male and female roles in Central Asia were pro-found. Indeed, sexual roles were sharply polarized. What is even more important, these differences allowed—where women were concerned—very little leeway for crossing boundaries defined by custom and religion and guarded by taboos. They left women with scarcely any meaningful alternatives to traditionally prescribed po-sitions—at least none in the sense of *overt* departure from the norm, or departure with public franchise. And they could indeed be enforced with a severity that sometimes went even beyond local-ly tolerated limits.

If these differences were not already deeply resented at the time of the Soviet arrival, the incoming revolutionary elites could well

124

argue, with some justification, that resentment could be elicited through appropriate actions. If, for example, polygamy, levirate, forced marriage, marriage by abduction, and marriage of young girls to old men—as well as draconic repressions of female deviance from set norms—were not as widespread as alleged by the regime, women's *residual awareness* of such manifestations had to be present, and could be heightened and tapped by appropriate means. Given the frame of mind of communist elites, they could indeed be tempted to evaluate their chances of success in terms of the Thomas theorem: "If men define situations as real, they are real in their consequences"; human perceptions and behavior are determined not only by the objective features of a situation, but also, at times primarily, by the meaning assigned to this situation.[118] From the Soviet point of view, if Moslem women could not spontaneously ascribe appropriate meanings to their life-situations they could be *led* to do so—as individuals who had sufficient grounds at least to be susceptible to manipulation. Marx had, after all, no compunctions about stating the need for revolutionaries to relate spontaneous and deliberately induced class-consciousness:

> It is necessary to make the actual pressure even more pressing by adding to it the consciousness of pressure; the shame even more shameful by making it public. . . . We have to make the ossified conditions dance by singing them their own melody! We have to cause the people to be *frightened* by their own image, in order to give them *courage*.[119]

To accomplish this in the Central Asian context it was necessary, from a Marxist point of view, that the designated revolutionary stratum have not only manipulable grievances but also a modicum of group identity and solidarity. It is precisely this theme that received considerable and early attention from some Soviet activists. Simply put, the argument stated that the consequences of inferiority, segregation, and humiliation, of deliberate separation from society, politics, and the economic marketplace, manifested themselves in a unique and peculiarly suggestive disposition among Central Asian women. Moskalev, one of the first communist publicists to attempt a summary account of the life style of Uzbek

[118] For a discussion of the Thomas theorem and its implications, see R. K. Merton, *Social Theory and Social Structure* (Glencoe, Ill., 1957), pp. 421 ff.

[119] Quoted in Meyer, *Leninism*, p. 19.

125

women, explained this as follows. "As a reaction" to her profound-ly negative life-situation, the "[Moslem woman's] character . . . has developed a [propensity towards a] very high degree of sociability with other women." "Even when utter strangers to each other," these women, after being together "not more than an hour or two . . . feel and act as if they had known each other for a long time." There was "an immediate sense of mutual sympathy" among them. "After only one encounter," they readily called each other either *ortak*, "friend and comrade," or *apa*, "sister." After all, "associa-tion with other women has been the only ray of light in a [Moslem woman's] life, the only entertainment and diversion. It stands to reason that this persistent disposition to sociability . . . [should prove] far from unimportant [for women's success] in building a new life."[120]

It is safe to assume that such references to the unusual solidarity-potential of Moslem women were closely related to the views of those who maintained that, in Central Asia, women had a greater revolutionary potential than men—that they were, in effect, a *sui generis* proletariat in a society where a conventionally defined pro-letariat was not readily available. Indeed, as we shall see,[121] an im-portant segment of the communist apparatus proposed to act precisely on this assumption.

The Soviet call to a new life was also couched in terms that clear-ly echoed the Marxist dictum about the makings of revolutionary class-consciousness: it was necessary not only to cause people to be frightened by their own image but also to give them courage. Nukhrat, Niurina, Zavarian, and Moskalev were but some of many communist analysts and organizers who showed themselves to be sensitive to this need. Their appeals to Moslem women to rise and join the Soviet fold, while often stressing different facets of the struggle, shared this basic theme: what was must not be and will not endure, for "the past is rotten."[122] There was nothing inevitable about the old customs, and there was no magical strength in them. "Powerful subterranean shocks [have already shaken] the old strata that had been solidly entrenched for a thousand years. The deep waters of the revolution have washed away the ground, and the strata [of the old order] are settling, rocking, losing their primordial stability. . . . [This, in turn,] spreads terror and confusion among

[120] Moskalev, *Uzbechka*, p. 24.   [121] See the following chapter.
[122] Nukhrat, *OZV*, pp. 37, 84; Niurina, *Parandzha*, p. 7.

126

the savage fanatics, the custodians of medievalism."[123] The old world would end when a woman would see her past life as "non-existence"; would get the taste of "joyous [social] labor" and of "an independent life"; would acquire a "sense of personal dignity" and become "conscious of herself as a human being"; would realize what her rights are and "sense her will, [initiative], and strength"; would, when still a girl, tear off the "dark prison" of the veil, and show the world her "luxuriant, desirable . . . rose-like beauty"; would be able "to abandon a husband she does not love and get herself another man"; would perceive the new world as "a world of limitless possibility."[124]

It may be said that such appeals to a new life were intended to induce—to use Julian Huxley's terms—not just new dimensions in an ancient struggle for existence and survival, but an unprecedented struggle for fulfillment: "the realization of inherent capacities . . . and of new possibilities . . . by the individual; the satisfaction of needs, spiritual as well as material; the emergence of new qualities of experience to be enjoyed; the building of personalities."[125] But such appeals also reflected cold instrumental considerations: to induce, through female mobilization, an upheaval in an Islamic traditional system of values, customs, relationships, and roles, and to reintegrate the shattered social order under the auspices of the Soviet regime. For this purpose, it was not enough to proclaim the inherent disadvantages of a woman's status, and to catalogue her deprivations; it was necessary to relate them to specific revolutionary needs and opportunities. Likewise, from the Soviet point of view it was not enough to call Moslem women to a new life; it was necessary to show how their activation as a surrogate proletariat would serve real revolutionary ends in society as a whole. As we shall see, this was exactly what a number of the party's organizers in Central Asia set out to do.

[123] Niurina, *Parandzha*, p. 7.

[124] See Moskalev, *Uzbechka*, p. 48; Zavarian, *Ka*, 6, 1926, p. 70; Niurina, *Ka*, 4, 1925, p. 79; Nukhrat, *VMV*, pp. 28-31; cf. *Bezb* (ill.), 2-3, 1940, pp. 13, 15.

[125] J. S. Huxley, *Evolution in Action* (New York, 1953), pp. 162-63.

FOUR · *Female Inferiority and Radical Social Change: Soviet Perceptions of the Revolutionary Potential of Women*[1]

REVOLUTIONARY ACTION AS ACTIVATION OF A SURROGATE PROLETARIAT: SOME IMPLICIT SOVIET ASSUMPTIONS

CLEARLY, the catalogue of female inferiority in Central Asia, as conceived by Soviet revolutionary elites, was predicated on some very specific assumptions:

(1) To begin with, there was the underlying assumption, stemming from the very heart of Marxism, that there could be no such thing as a society without antagonisms, and without accompanying cleavages. Every society had to be, by definition, in a permanent state of change and flux, the latter simultaneously brought on by, and giving birth to, ever new and antagonistic social forces. This dialectical process—a veritable *perpetuum mobile* of social tensions—would be terminated only in the last, communist, stage of social evolution.

(2) Any lack of clearcut manifestations of social struggle—as in Central Asia—could have at least two reasons. For one thing, the process of struggle could be masked, as it were, by veils of harmony and solidarity spun over many generations. An experienced social analyst and revolutionary could penetrate the elaborate screens of decency and recognize the battling forces for what they were. For another thing, even if, for some reason, the named and identified parties to the proceedings failed to behave in the expected manner—and if they failed to respond with adequate intensity to the stimuli administered by a revolutionary elite—there was still no reason to relinquish one's basic expectations. Given the stage of Central Asia's socio-economic development, and given the peculiarities of established ties of kinship, custom, and religion, it was perhaps too much to hope for social fragmentation to pro-

[1] This chapter develops in detail some notions stated in my article in *Law and Society Review*, pp. 188-93.

128

ceed at the required rate and through conventional channels. There could be—there *had* to be—other ways of approaching the main tasks of the revolution.

(3) The very nature of Moslem traditional societies offered unique targets for revolutionary engagement. While these targets were not strictly conventional in terms of grand revolutionary strategy, they could be quite helpful not only in bringing about or accelerating more "advanced" forms of social strife, but also in revolutionizing and transforming the entire milieu more speedily and thoroughly than it would have otherwise been possible. Women could be such targets and could play such a role. This could be assumed, on the one hand, on the basis of first-hand study and observation. On the other hand, Marxism itself offered legitimate grounds for expecting just that, especially in a milieu where the patriarchal family was still intact.

(4) Even a cursory examination of the conditions of a local woman's life, and of the folk culture in accordance with whose precepts she had to live, warranted the assumption that this woman could not but seethe with resentment against the old order. Only naked force could have been holding her at bay—restraining her, that is, from overt and concerted action against her community's authority-relationships, customs, and beliefs. Just to neutralize the traditional foci of power would do much to lift the perpetual pall of violence hanging over a woman's life, and thus precipitate the latter into resolute action on her own behalf.

(5) Even if the mass of Moslem women were generally "unprepared," continued to cling to their accustomed grooves, did not comprehend the meaning of the events around them, and might fail to act accordingly,[2] there was no cause for abandoning the struggle. There were, after all, some good reasons to account for this: lack of significant revolutionary experience among Moslem women; relatively late arrival and consolidation of Soviet rule in Central Asia; the strength of kinship, customary, and religious ties.[3] Thus, female resentment and discontent, far from being absent, had to be at least *latent*. The same circumstances that endowed Central Asian women with their peculiar status and thus made them *objectively* into a potential revolutionary force—with a combustion-potential

[2] See A. Nukhrat, *OZV*, pp. 37, 42-43, 46-47; cf. Pal'vanova, *DSV*, pp. 41, 56.

[3] See references in preceding note.

possibly higher than that of men[4]—could be responsible for keeping them submerged, as it were, in a state of mind just as conservative as, or even more conservative than, that of their men folk. Women in a traditional society might indeed be relatively more committed to established patterns of authority; relatively more socialized into the non-rational, including the magical and folk-religious components of their culture; relatively more withdrawn into the narrow concerns of their domestic world; relatively less disposed to view themselves as a coherent group or class.[5] All the same, the vicious circles of traditional female attitudes and behavior could be short-circuited, and a "breach in the primordial wall" could be made—as Lenin had suggested—by "waking up" a woman's consciousness and will:[6] by making her aware of the world of fresh alternatives within her reach, by providing her with opportunities to exercise the novel options, by giving her an unprecedented sense of individual potency and organized collective strength.[7]

In other words, Soviet revolutionary elites gave every evidence of assuming that the peculiar lack of desirable forms of "class struggle" in the traditional countryside was but a passing phenomenon. The age-old variants of communal, affinal, and consanguinal peace depended on factors which were themselves susceptible to manipulation and change. Such peace was not only deceptive; it was itself based on ingrained fear and primordial habit, and could last only as long as a truly excruciating challenge to tradition was absent from the scene, i.e., a challenge to the traditional assumptions in which sexual and generational roles were grounded.

Where a Moslem woman was concerned, party activists could reason—certainly not without some psychological justification—that under the seeming bedrock of her traditional entrapment there seethed deep currents of humiliation, frustration, and hatred; and

[4] For strong hints of such an expectation, see A. Safadri, *Ka*, 11, 1928, p. 31; cf. Tarantaeva, *Ka*, 11, 1928, pp. 46-47.

[5] For a suggestive variant of this argument—concerning women as a whole, but obviously more applicable to Moslem than to Russian women—see Krupskaia, *ORSZ*, pp. 50-55.

[6] Pal'vanova, *DSV*, pp. 41, 55; cf. Lenin, *Soch.*, Vol. 32, p. 277, as cited in Liubimova, *VPG*, pp. 6-7.

[7] See, e.g., Liubimova, *VPG*, pp. 7-10, 64-65; N. K. Krupskaia, *Zhenshchina v Strane Sotsializma* (Moscow, 1938), p. 45; Nukhrat, *OZV*, pp. 83-84; Pal'vanova, *DSV*, pp. 7-14, 51-52, 81-83.

that these currents could be shaped into elements not just combustible in the short term but inherently and fundamentally subversive to the entire spectrum of traditional behavior, relationships, and norms. It was not of decisive significance whether a woman's fate was, in her own perception, as bleak as the party saw it, or wished it to be seen. More relevant: there was a possibility that the very terms of contact with unprecedented concepts of human existence would hold up an extraordinary mirror to a woman's eyes, letting her see herself as she had never seen herself before; that they would activate currents of unaccustomed restlessness, agitating minds and feelings into a search for ways to establish the newly perceived identity, to realize a novel sense of human worth and potentialities; that they would, in effect, raise to a conscious level the sense of outrage on account of an existence that could not fail but be perceived as being, relative to men, dramatically inferior. A woman might endure perpetual inferiority, degradation, and segregation, but only as long as she lacked the capacity to visualize, and the opportunity to grasp, alternative possibilities. As soon as the psychological and organizational barriers were breached—as soon as the past and future were perceived in a radically new light—a dramatic turnabout could not fail to take place.

THE ACTION-SCHEME: SOVIET PERCEPTIONS OF OPERATIONAL IMPERATIVES AND OPPORTUNITIES

The party's tasks were thus twofold. To maximize female revolutionary potential, it was necessary to maximize female discontent, and to minimize the obstacles in the way of a woman's perceiving, articulating, and acting upon that discontent. Along with this, it was the party's task to find the right keys to the latent revolutionary currents, and the right molds for harnessing the unleashed forces and channeling them in desirable directions—i.e., to find optimal social controls for unleashed social energies. This would require careful engineering: as good an estimate as possible of the linkages, in every conceivable sphere, between female mobilization and broader social transformation, of the specific advantages and forms of utilizing female revolutionary energy, and of the ways in which the latter could contribute to, or endanger, the stabilization, legitimation, and development of the revolutionary regime itself.

Given such requisites, what were Soviet expectations regarding

131

the actual operational opportunities and potentials?[8] How could women be used to help in the revolutionary transformation of a traditional society, and what impact could such use be expected to have?

To the extent that we can speak of a Soviet plan of action,[9] it should be emphasized that such a plan crystallized only gradually, that it was by no means consistent and continuous, and that it constituted a loosely linked set of beliefs about ways in which female mobilization in a Moslem milieu should or would contribute to the revolutionary modernization of that milieu. Moreover, in a number of cases, some of these beliefs were overtly expressed by some party or government officials, but not by others, making it difficult to determine to what extent particular assumptions and conclusions were shared by the regime's decision-making bodies.[10] Thus, we are dealing here, of necessity, with a composite and cumulative picture of inputs in the Soviet perceptual matrix (inputs reflecting more than a decade of revolutionary experience) rather than with a rigorously articulated and summarily adopted operational code. We are dealing here, also, with a set of actual or inferred programmatic doctrines, proposals, and commitments (which were themselves a reflection of the debate on revolutionary tasks in Central Asia evolving in Soviet ranks in the course of the 1920's), but not necessarily with the specific strategies and tactics that could translate belief into practice.[11]

In this sense, the Soviet plan of action may, perhaps, best be visualized in a series of operational themes stated in propositional form[12]—themes that constitute a brief and selective projection of

---

[8] In the set of themes charted in the pages that follow, references to specific Soviet perceptions are made only when such perceptions were manifestly apparent or clearly implied. Even then, of course, it is not always easy to distinguish between *a priori* Soviet expectations and conclusions derived from experience with specific moves.

[9] Strong circumstantial evidence that the party's Secretariat in Moscow was beginning, in 1923, to devise what it considered "plans" and to allocate special funds for approaching Central Asia's women may be found in Liubimova, *VPG*, pp. 26-27.

[10] By the same token, we do not know enough to be able to distinguish clearly between particular political factions clustering around particular points of view.

[11] The chapters that follow are devoted specifically to an examination of some of the actual strategies and tactics employed by the regime.

[12] It should be emphasized that these themes were never articulated by Soviet organizers rigorously enough to be considered formal propositions;

the dominant imperatives and premises underlying the Soviet action-scheme, that relate immediate means to ultimate ends, that are interdependent, and that fluctuate in emphasis within a spectrum from moral to instrumental considerations, from revolutionary idealism to cold political pragmatism. It seems most useful to present these themes in the form of more or less explicit Soviet expectations concerning the payoffs of female mobilization in a number of related realms.

Libertarian and Humanitarian Implications

The emancipation of women—and, with women, of the young generation—from "slavery in the feudal-patriarchal order" of kinship, custom, and religion means, first and foremost, their emancipation as individuals.[13]

As a corollary, the emphasis on personal liberation on purely moral grounds, in fulfilling the egalitarian strictures of Marxism with respect to the family, contributes to the legitimation of the communist movement as well as engages the humanitarian and reformist impulses of important segments of the emerging male and female elites in Russia and Central Asia.[14]

Such an attitude was shared by a large number of Soviet activists, especially women, although only a few were able to uphold it consistently in public. Among the latter, some tried especially hard to keep these considerations from becoming totally submerged by broader Bolshevik concerns with utility and power. To mention some of them (all women), especially those who emerged on the scene in the early 1920's: Krupskaia, Lenin's wife and a revolutionary in her own right, deeply preoccupied with issues of communist education as well as women's liberation, including, particularly after Lenin's death, the emancipation of women among Russia's Asian minorities; Anna Nukhrat, a talented Chuvash teacher and

---

nor were they merely random, accidental, and unconnected reflections of particular political campaigns to be viewed merely as propaganda themes, pure and simple, unrelated to social action. Needless to add, the form in which they are stated is not a precise rendition of Soviet beliefs; it is intended as a reconstruction and representation of the logic and intent of these beliefs in as accurate a manner as is warranted by available evidence.

[13] See Nukhrat, *OZV*, pp. 46-47.

[14] For some samples of the feelings of Russian female activists, in this respect, see Liubimova, *VPG*, p. 14, cf. Butuzova, *Ka*, 9, 1927, p. 62; L. Otmar-Shtein, "V Staroi Bukhare," in *ZVR*, pp. 345-49.

writer, raised first in a Moslem and then in a Russian milieu of Bashkiriia, passionately committed to the cause of secular revolution in Russia's traditional societies, and devoting all of her energies to organizational and propaganda work among Central Asian women; Anna Aksentovich—referred to as "Central Asia's Clara Tsetkin"—one of the first communist organizers sent by the central Zhenotdel (the Central Committee's Department for Work among Women) to head female mobilization in the Ferghana region; Yevstaliia Ross and Lidia Otmar-Shtein, both political commissars in the Red Army during the civil war, both participants in the battles on the Turkestan front, and both commandeered by the Revvoyensovet (Revolutionary-Military Council) of their army-unit in Central Asia to organize Moslem women under Zhenotdel auspices in Turkmeniia and Bukhara, respectively; Serafima Liubimova and Nadezhda Kleiman, both dispatched from responsible communist posts in central Russia to head Zhenotdel work in Sredazburo (Central Asian Bureau of the party's Central Committee); Zinaida Prishchepchik and Yelizaveta Popova, both shifted from important party assignments in Moscow to head the Uzbek and Kazakh Zhenotdel, respectively.[15]

Thus, while a handful of native Central Asian women did emerge as important actors in the campaign in the early 1920's (for example, Kulieva in Turkmenistan, Gaibdzhanova in Uzbekistan, Yesova in Kazakhstan), leadership was almost exclusively in the hands of outsiders. Characteristically, most of the latter were Russian, Armenian, or Jewish, most joined the party before or during the Russian revolution and civil war, and most were single and in their mid-twenties when commandeered to Central Asia. It is not surprising, therefore, that they brought with them not only Bolshevik political experience and toughness but also youthful revolutionary fervor and a sense of moral outrage characteristic of European radicals exposed to feminist as well as socialist ideology. Completely unprepared for Central Asian realities, they were appalled by what they encountered.[16] It would seem that what revolted them had to do not so much with primitive sanitary and living conditions, or with poverty, illiteracy, and disease (Russia was not totally different in this respect), as with the prevalent symbols of rank female inferiority and with what seemed like monstrous, openly humiliat-

---

[15] See *ZVR*, pp. 337-79, for details.
[16] See, for example, *ZVR*, ibid.; Liubimova, *VPG*, pp. 14 ff.

ing customs emphasizing this inferiority at every turn. It is this sense of shock and missionary zeal on the part of arriving female communist organizers that initially informed the style and substance of official Soviet perceptions and commitments.

It is safe to say that the emotional underpinnings for just such perceptions had been established immediately after the conclusion of the civil war, at the first large-scale confrontation of Russian and European female communists with Central Asian women, the latter constituting the first major contingent of Moslem female delegates to arrive in Moscow at the party's invitation. The occasion was the Second International Conference of Communist Women in June, 1921. It took place under the leadership of such veteran revolutionaries as N. K. Krupskaia, A. M. Kollontay, S. N. Smidovich, K. I. Nikolaeva, V. P. Golubeva, and L. N. Stal'. It was presided over by Inessa Armand, Lenin's confidante, Bolshevik organizer, and radical feminist. It also boasted the presence of Clara Tsetkin, Lenin's old friend and a European Marxist with a worldwide reputation, especially among Western feminist movements. By most accounts, what constituted the most impressive and memorable moment at the conference was the arrival of Russia's Asian women in the hall and on the podium. Most of them came veiled, and some removed their veils briefly in order to address the assembly—in languages hardly anyone understood, but with a passion that was unmistakable. Their presence packed such power not only because it was unprecedented, but because—as one eyewitness put it—it was so "purely symbolic" in nature: an international meeting of revolutionary leaders was being addressed by those who "[might have been] harem girls" only yesterday, who were "pioneers" in the literal sense of the term, emerging from "grim, barbarian slavery" and from a land "as distant as a fairy tale." It would seem that many in the audience who, either by training or inclination, could have been expected to have little use for sentiment, were "deeply moved," "stunned," "reduced to tears" on this occasion.[17] When they vowed, in impassioned speeches, to liberate Russia's Asian women, they were obviously responding to the imagery carried by human beings who were chattels far more literally than anyone else with whom they could have ever come in contact. What Central Asian women may have projected so intimately, to mature and

---

[17] See Liubimova, *VPG*, pp. 7-10; Pal'vanova, *DSV*, pp. 7-14, citing *Ka*, 14-15, 1921, pp. 16-17.

135

battle-hardened female activists and apparatchiks, was not merely an illustration for yet another stylized and abstract slogan, but the *reality* of human bondage.[18]

Against this background, it is not surprising that one dimension of stated Soviet concerns in Central Asia stressed primarily personalistic values in female emancipation. Thus, the abolition of *kalym* was seen as a woman's liberation from entrapment by an institution that "constrained her will, [violated] her feelings, [rendered her] dumb." The effect of *kalym* had been not merely to deprive a Central Asian woman of her "personal freedom"; it constituted "an act of the crudest, most outrageous violation" of that freedom, by "making her into an object of purchase and sale," that is, into someone not very different from a slave.[19]

The effect of polygamy on a Moslem woman's personality and style of life was seen to be as destructive as that wrought by *kalym*. Accordingly, to eradicate polygamy meant to free a woman from the yoke of an institution that perpetuated her role as an object of purchase and sale; that delivered her, more often than not, into the hands of an old, depraved, and cruel man; that "outraged her personality and dignity" by throwing her together with other women into the snakepit of a household marked by constant competition for a husband's favor, and hence by constant recriminations, hatreds, tension, and violence.[20] Parallel concerns were voiced in regard to two other customary institutions that were mutually reinforcing as well as interconnected with polygamy and bride-price. In this perspective, forced marriage (arranged and contracted solely by a father or male guardian) served to reinforce in a girl's mind the sense that, for her, there could be no freedom of choice, that she could have no will of her own, that only the will of her parents and kinsmen was the touchstone of her life.[21] The marriage of a girl when she was still a child, on the other hand, made the assertion of parental authority all the more easy, and thus made forced marriage virtually automatic. Often taking place before a girl's puberty, and leading to very early pregnancy, child-marriages had a pre-

[18] It appears that Lenin, too, was deeply moved when the Central Asian visitors stopped by to see him in the Kremlin, and "one of them threw her arms around him." See Krupskaia, *Zhenshchina*, p. 45.

[19] See Pal'vanova, *DSV*, p. 38; S. Akopov, *RN*, 4-5, 1930, p. 62; "V Tsentral'nykh . . . ," *SS* (5), 1926, p. 159.

[20] Akopov, *RN*, 4-5, 1930, p. 62; Mukhitdinova, *Ka*, 9, 1929, p. 39.

[21] S. Mokrinskii, *SP*, 3(27), 1927, pp. 111-12.

dictably debilitating effect: they spelled the "[physical] ruination" of both the young mother and her offspring.[22]

In this sense, then, the imperatives of female emancipation were focused on freedom of the will as well as on respect for human sensibilities. Nukhrat summarized this attitude when she insisted: "*Kalym* must go—a woman cannot be sold like cattle. . . . Child-marriages must be abolished—a woman is maimed by them. Polygamy must be rooted out—it humiliates a woman. . . . Forced marriages . . . must cease—a woman is not a thing to be shunted by a master's will from hand to hand."[23] And Krupskaia carried this notion even farther when she maintained that the entire pattern of marital relations had to be destroyed, for it "ignores [what must be] the very essence of a conjugal marriage"—"the mutual pull of one human being towards another, mutual trust, mutual [love and] understanding . . . "; it even "[ignores] the natural change in human sympathies," and "the humanized sexual instinct" itself.[24]

Soviet imagery concerning the manifestations of female seclusion in Central Asia was marked by a similar moral strain. A Moslem woman's separation in female quarters (*ichkari*) of her own home, and her partial or total exclusion from public sectors open to men, was seen as deliberate and coercive physical segregation based on sex. Such institutionalized apartheid amounted to a "nail" holding a woman's life down in its customary groove.[25] It emphasized and reinforced her role as a "tool [of a man's lust]," as "the master's toy," and, at the same time, as a creature that was "unclean" and "dishonorable."[26] Therefore, to break the chains of sexual apartheid and to liberate Moslem women from the walls of *ichkari* would mean to free them from being "buried alive," "deaf and dumb," "fenced off" from the outer world, and hence from varied, enriching, fulfilling human contacts.[27] It would mean to remove the barriers from women's minds as well as bodies, by making it possible for them at last to "move," "laugh," and "talk" in the open, and

[22] I. I. Kryl'tsov, *SP*, 5(29), 1927, p. 137.

[23] Nukhrat, *Stepnoi Skaz*, p. 71.

[24] See Krupskaia, *ORSZ*, p. 82. While Krupskaia spoke of the pre-socialist marital systems as a whole, without ethno-cultural differentiations, she made it clear in other contexts that she found the Moslem family to be an especially vivid example of what she had in mind. See also Pal'vanova, *DSV*, p. 36.

[25] Nukhrat, *Ka*, 6, 1928, p. 78.

[26] Nukhrat, *OZV*, pp. 18, 24.

[27] Pal'vanova, *DSV*, pp. 28-29.

to develop freely as human beings.[28] The same was true for veiling. Aside from strengthening the bonds tying her to hearth and home,[29] a woman's *parandzha* and *chachvan*[30] made up a "hot," "dank," "dark" prison that prevented her "[enjoyment of] air and sun," and that, at the same time, did irreparable harm to her and her infant's health.[31] However, the implications of freeing a Moslem woman from her veil were far more dramatic than the mere reversal of a physically undesirable condition. It would mean, in effect: to liberate her eyes—"to enable [her] to look at the world with clear eyes," and not just with unobstructed vision;[32] to liberate her voice, a voice "deadened" by a heavy, shroud-like cover;[33] to rescue her from a condition of perpetual "depersonalization," a condition in which neither her sex, nor age, nor distinct individuality was apparent;[34] to free her from a symbol of perpetual "degradation," a "symbol of . . . silence . . . timidity . . . submissiveness . . . humiliation."[35] Of course, to let her see the world meant also to let the world see, and admire, *her*—her "youth . . . and . . . beauty [unencumbered by the veil's] bag of slavery . . . moveable prison . . . black cloud . . . "—and to let her mix freely in the new world with men as well as women, be they friends, or mates, or "wise and learned people."[36]

It followed, from this perspective, that the case for an inclusive social-service network serving women's needs had to, and could,

[28] Niurina, *Parandzha*, p. 5; Nukhrat, *OZV*, pp. 19-20.

[29] G. A. Limanovskii, *Sov. Khlopok*, 11-12, 1937, pp. 91 ff.

[30] A combination of a heavy cloak enveloping the entire body, including the arms, and a stiff veil made of horsehair and attached to the cloak.

[31] See Moskalev, *Uzbechka*, p. 23; Nukhrat, *OZV*, pp. 19-20, 86; *Bezb* (ill.), 12, 1938, p. 7; *Bezb* (ill.), 2-3, 1940, pp. 14-16; cf. Halle, *Women*, p. 168 (of course, this had to pertain primarily to women and children in orthodox Moslem milieus, such as Uzbekistan, Tadzhikistan, and parts of Turkmenistan—where women were, as a rule, heavily veiled—and less so to those in Kazakhstan and Kirghiziia).

[32] S. Yesova, "Protiv Parandzhi," in *ZVR*, p. 374.

[33] Pal'vanova, *DSV*, p. 63.

[34] Osman Dzhuma Zade, *Ka*, 7, 1929, p. 48; Niurina, *Parandzha*, p. 3; Nukhrat, *OZV*, p. 20.

[35] Liubimova, *VPG*, p. 69; Nukhrat, *OZV*, p. 20; Shatskaia, *SE*, 1, 1936, p. 53.

[36] Bil'shai, *RZVS* (Moscow, 1959), p. 192 (citing Khamza's revolutionary poetry); Pal'vanova, *DSV*, pp. 10, 19, 28-29; Liubimova, *VPG*, p. 68; Niurina, *Parandzha*, p. 15.

also be perceived and presented in moral terms, as could the case for a broad spectrum of roles and opportunities to be accessible to Moslem women. Thus, the organization of hygiene circles, and the building of hospitals, mother-and-child centers, and crèches serving especially the needs of women and their children was justified on the grounds that, in a Moslem society, females and infants were particularly vulnerable to sickness and debility, were especially badly neglected, and were totally dependent on *mullahs*, healers, and shamans. Similarly, it was seen to be imperative to build literacy centers and schools, and encourage girls and women to attend these, because their education had been traditionally neglected, leaving them perpetually without socially valued skills and capabilities, and hence an easy prey to superstition and the community's contempt.[37]

Commensurately, to draw Moslem women into clubs and associations projected especially for them, and to attract them to theaters and films, meant to enable them to do something unprecedented in their lives as individuals: to break out from the enforced, mentally and physically debilitating isolation of the home's female quarters, to gather and to establish social contacts freely, to enjoy themselves in groups of their choosing, to acquire a sense of the world around them.[38]

The same had to be true for providing women with fresh opportunities in the economic sphere. Thus, to draw them into handicraft, agricultural, and consumers' cooperatives, to attract them to factory labor, to enable them to become nurses, doctors, teachers, or tractor drivers—all this denoted their economic independence and hence self-reliance; it promised to bring them a sense of accomplishment and self-respect; and it could be counted on to stimulate the respect of men. The latter could not but see their equals in those who were able to discharge even the most complex tasks,

[37] See, e.g., Liubimova, *Ka*, 11, 1927, pp. 73-74; Kasparova, *Ka*, 7, 1925, pp. 88-89; Moskalev, *Uzbechka*, pp. 39-44; Kolychev, *RN*, 4-5, 1930, p. 119; Krupskaia, *Ka*, 12, 1928, pp. 9-10; *Bezb* (news.), 34, 1929, p. 2; Smirnova, *Ka*, 8, 1929, p. 27. Cf. Pal'vanova, *DSV*, pp. 41, 55, 97.

[38] See, e.g., Krupskaia, *Ka*, 12, 1928, pp. 5-12; and "Rabotnitsa i Religiia" in *ORSZ*, pp. 50-55; Nukhrat, *VMV*, pp. 7-37 (*passim*); *OZV*, pp. 18-20, 24; *Ka*, 7, 1927, p. 36; *Ka*, 8, 1927, p. 20; and *Ka*, 6, 1928, p. 78; Niurina, *Ka*, 4, 1925, p. 80; Prishchepchik, *Ka*, 9, 1926, p. 76; Zavarian, *Ka*, 12, 1925, p. 28; V.K., *Ka*, 9, 1925, pp. 68-70; Liubimova, *Ka*, 7, 1926, p. 70; Shirman, *Ka*, 4, 1927, p. 76; cf. Pal'vanova, *DSV*, pp. 28-29.

who brought secular enlightenment and medical help to their communities, and who produced most of life's material necessities.[39]

Parallel implications were envisaged in the political sphere, too. Moslem women—beginning with "[the lowliest] shepherds' daughters"—who were assured the opportunity to vote, to attend mass meetings, to represent their sisters in national conferences and congresses, to have access to all social and political organizations, to play judicial roles, and to manage their community's and republic's affairs would not thereby merely acquire access to vehicles of formal political participation. They would, as a direct consequence, acquire a sense of themselves as human beings who can be as effective, self-confident, and authoritative as men.[40]

Nukhrat expressed a sense of the overall thrust of the moral imperative when she asked: "Who told you that . . . the Moslem woman . . . had [ever] been considered human?" It was the October Revolution that brought her not just "political and social rights," but "life itself—the right to be a human being."[41] Commensurately, "Among a free people in a free country there can be no female slavery."[42] A woman's life must cease to flow in accordance with laws residing "in the heads of old men." "Light," "knowledge," "a better lot" must take care of that.[43] For "a woman is the mother of a people, and she deserves respect and every consideration. . . . A woman is a person, she must have her own will, and not just submit to the will of her husband. . . . She must be able to choose for herself the kind of life she wants . . . ; to study, live, and work independently . . . ; to own land and have control over her property and children. . . ."[44] She must be able "to participate consciously and actively in social life."[45]

Given such a context, it is not surprising that many Soviet activ-

[39] See, e.g., Butuzova, *Ka*, 9, 1927, pp. 62-67; Liubimova, *Ka*, 7, 1926, pp. 70-72; Tunik, *Ka*, 5, 1927, pp. 56-58; Shirman, *KP*, 4, 1927, pp. 75-77; Nukhrat, *VMV*, pp. 28-29; *OZV*, pp. 76-78; Zavarian, *Ka*, 6, 1926, p. 70; Niurina, *Ka*, 4, 1925, p. 79; Kasparova, *Ka*, 7, 1925, pp. 87-88. Cf. Pal'vanova, *DSV*, pp. 11, 66, 91, 107-12; Liubimova, *VPG*, p. 43.

[40] See, e.g., Nukhrat, *Ka*, 12, 1927, p. 44. Cf. Liubimova, *VPG*, pp. 7-10, 64-65; Krupskaia, *Zhenshchina*, p. 45; Nukhrat, *OZV*, pp. 76-78, 83-84; Pal'-vanova, *DSV*, pp. 7-14, 51-52, 81-83.

[41] Nukhrat, *OZV*, p. 4.

[42] Nukhrat, *OZV*, pp. 4, 7, 38; Nukhrat, *Stepnoi Skaz*, p. 71.

[43] Niurina, *Parandzha*, p. 7; Nukhrat, *OZV*, p. 35.

[44] Nukhrat, *Stepnoi Skaz*, pp. 70-71.

[45] Niurina, *Ka*, 4, 1925, p. 83.

ists in this realm—from Anna Nukhrat to Maxim Gorky—viewed the tasks of female mobilization among Moslems primarily in individualistic and libertarian terms. Thus, it was expected that to free women from the influence and ministrations of the Moslem clergy, of soothsayers, and of tribal shamans would mark these women's emergence as "new persons . . . free from the survivals of serfdom, of religious fanaticism and superstition."[46] It would signify, in the deepest sense, their "spiritual independence."[47] By the same token, to free them from a "tribal-patriarchal order" would mean to liberate them from the chains of an order marked by the "despotic power of husbands, families, and clans" by a deeply "reactionary form of authoritarianism."[48] It would mean that "all that was alive and fit for life [would be] . . . emancipated from hated fetters."[49]

It is safe to assume that this overall set of themes served twin purposes. It provided the moral underpinnings for rallying European and indigenous cadres for work among Moslem women. And it constituted the core of Soviet mobilizational appeals to the mass of women themselves, in the course of their individual and institutional contacts with agents of the new order. But at no point were Soviet activists permitted to forget that the struggle for women's liberation could not be an end in itself.[50] As we shall see, the development of female roles in revolutionizing Moslem societies was viewed at the apex of the party as requiring an emphasis on instrumental, coldly pragmatic considerations. As a result, moral, humanitarian, and generally romantic notions were repeatedly pushed into the background.

Implications for Traditional Authority Relations

To emancipate women from the traditional fold is to undermine the prevailing patterns of traditional authority—the "reactionary forms of authoritarianism"[51]—based on lineage, kinship, conquest, custom, religion, and age, as well as on the absolute superiority of

---

[46] Pal'vanova, *DSV*, p. 97.

[47] M. Gorky, in a letter to R. Rolland, *Soch.*, Vol. 30, p. 16, as cited in Pal'vanova, *DSV*, p. 96.

[48] Pal'vanova, *DSV*, pp. 77-78; Vorshev, *RN*, 12(58) 1934, p. 72; Nukhrat, *OZV*, pp. 46-47.

[49] Bil'shai, *RZVS*, p. 105.

[50] See, e.g., M. Amosov, "Shire . . . ," *Ka*, 14, 1929, p. 26.

[51] See, e.g., the views of Arkhincheev, in *SS*, 2(43), 1930, p. 100.

men. Specifically, to endow women with unprecedented socio-political roles, and to back these roles with an organizational framework, with educational and material opportunities, and with the legal and police-power of the new state, is to render untenable the entire antecedent role-network on which the concepts of authority depend. By the same token, it means to undermine the backbone of a traditional community's political cohesion, and ease as well as hasten, thereby, the grafting and assimilation of new Soviet authority patterns at the grassroots.[52]

As a corollary, to politicize the latent or actual grievances of the most disadvantaged females is to make them especially disposed to burn their bridges to the old world altogether, to enter the Soviet fold, and actively to seek vengeance. This helps the regime to gain, in effect, a political fifth column in the Moslem traditional milieu. By being disposed to act in such a role, women should be uniquely suitable elements in depriving native kinship units and village communities of their salient traditional advantages in dealing with outsiders: their secrecy and solidarity.

Soviet expectations to this effect were quite readily apparent, for example, in the case of female suffrage and its political concomitants. Arguing on the basis of observed or inferred trends in Central Asia, party activists like Nukhrat, Karimova, and Karpov saw at least one conclusion as inescapable: to provide women with unconditional access to suffrage, and to all elective or appointive, as well as legislative and administrative, offices in the land, would not just challenge the traditional male monopoly of the political arena; it would immediately and decisively undermine the position of traditional political elites—tribal chieftains, village elders, and notables.[53] Implicitly or explicitly, it was expected that such a move, if consistently followed through, could not but revolutionize two major assumptions governing traditional political culture, and thereby disrupt a crucial nexus of traditional political relationships and practices. For one thing, women's political participation had to mean direct competition for positions of power and prestige with men, and with previously authoritative male figures. Quite obviously, this had to pose an unprecedented challenge to traditional

[52] See Niurina, *Ka*, 4, 1925, pp. 79, 82-83, on the relationship between female emancipation, the revolutionization of Central Asian societies, and the consolidation of Soviet rule in the region.

[53] See Karimova, *Ka*, 3, 1929, p. 43; cf. Karpov, *SS*, 11(28), 1928, pp. 61-69, and *SS*, 6(35), 1929, pp. 64-68; Nukhrat, *OZV*, p. 82.

142

rules of the game in the political marketplace, rules established for and by men. For another thing, the presence of women in the apparatus of control had to mean a woman's potential power not only over other women but over men as well. The political arrangements of a Moslem traditional community would not be able to endure very long under such extraordinary circumstances.[54]

Such reasoning found especially dramatic expression in Soviet attempts to redefine the requisites of class-struggle in Central Asia. As we have seen,[55] the initial Soviet reflex in stimulating such a struggle here (in the mid-1920's) had been to designate local traditional elites as the ruling class, and to attack this stratum head-on —through isolation, deportation, or outright shooting. While a number of the party's analysts came to express dissatisfaction with the results (in the latter half of the 1920's), no one linked proposed solutions with the role of Moslem women as clearly as Karpov and Arkhincheev.[56]

In this view, the attack on traditional elites had indeed been a "crushing blow" to the entire traditional system. But it had to be considered merely as a "first step," a bare beginning, creating only the "elementary preconditions" for the "real sovietization" of the Soviet East. The "second blow" was still pending. This was the complex and difficult task of "liberating, untangling, and cleansing . . . social [i.e., class] relationships . . . from feudal and patriarchal survivals that perverted those relationships." While the first blow had been directed at the apex of traditional systems—at the clergy, large landowners, and tribal-patriarchal nobility—the second one needed to be directed in a special way downwards, toward the society's grassroots. This meant an assault on those conditions which permitted the survival in Central Asia of the phenomenon of *vozhdism,* a form of tribal-patriarchal "führerism." The latter involved "arbitrary rule of the strong" as well as subtly wrought and very intimate ties between traditional leaders and their kinsmen, ties rooted in complex mutual obligations and frequently accompanied by a group's veneration and blind following of its leader-

---

[54] See, e.g., Nukhrat, *OZV,* pp. 76-78.

[55] In Chapter Two.

[56] Very little is known about these men's background and position in the hierarchy. It would seem that both were on special assignments in Central Asia in the 1920's, probably on behalf of the Department for Nationalities in the All-Union Central Executive Committee. Both appear to have been especially interested in modes of adapting formal Soviet political institutions and practices to Central Asia's socio-cultural milieu.

ship. These conditions made two things possible: the capacity of traditional elites consciously to manipulate their milieu; and the propensity of traditionalist masses to support unconsciously the predominance of those elites, as well as to acquiesce in, and adhere to, traditional mores, beliefs, and ties without question, even when the elites were removed from the scene. Quite obviously, such commitments tended to dilute the potentialities for the crystallization of distinct social classes. However, the political mobilization of women in such a milieu could serve to galvanize some of the potentially most reliable male strata. While it had indeed proved very difficult to arouse the "class consciousness" of underprivileged Central Asian males by way of orthodox Bolshevik tactics, it might be possible to do so by sponsoring an unprecedented tactical political alliance—beginning with local electoral campaigns—among native farmhands, poor peasants, and women. In such a context, one could count on the emergence of a new social stratum with clearly shared grievances, and with a political core characterized by a truly revolutionary consciousness as well as pro-Soviet orientations. The heretofore united traditionalist front could not possibly withstand the subversive impact of such an alliance.[57] It is in this sense that the political mobilization of women would be of immediate and specific help in forcing a shift in traditional Moslem societies from "tribal patriarchal" to "class" relationships.[58]

For such a perspective to be especially persuasive it had to incorporate some notion of women's political potentialities in a Moslem milieu as being especially explosive, perhaps more potent than those of men. We find precisely such a notion materializing on a number of occasions. The most clear-cut expectation to this effect was voiced by those Soviet analysts and organizers who attempted to go beyond the notion of female inferiority *per se* as a potential revolutionary catalyst in an Islamic community. For them, the questions of immediate significance concerned not so much the female stratum as a whole as the most disadvantaged elements within that stratum. These came to be identified without hesitation: orphans exploited and tormented by a hierarchy of guardians, and ready to run away; girls separated from lovers by elders' authority and force; girls feeling themselves deprived and stifled under parental authority; child-brides married to old men; young women

[57] See Karpov, *SS*, 11(28), 1928, pp. 61-69, and *SS*, 6(35), 1929, pp. 64-68; cf. Arkhincheev, *SS*, 2(43), 1930, pp. 98-100, 103.

[58] See Amosov, *Ka*, 14, 1929, pp. 23-24; cf. Krupskaia, *Ka*, 12, 1928, p. 7.

144

married to unloved and cruel men; as well as widows and divorcées. It is *their* grievances that were seen as unquestionably the most bitter and explosive in traditional Central Asian societies. Accordingly, their alienation from tradition, if properly engineered under alert revolutionary auspices and telescoped in space and time, was expected to be especially intense. Hence the conclusion: such intensity of alienation would tend to politicize their accumulated private resentments and despair, and do so far more powerfully than in the case of men. In effect, their revolutionary élan itself could be relied upon to be both purer and stronger, and their capacity for daring political action greater, than that of Moslem men.[59]

Nukhrat offered an especially suggestive reason why these girls and women could be expected to develop a highly emotional commitment to the new regime, and to be particularly prone to burn completely their bridges to the old order: the moment they acted publicly on their grievances—for example, by joining the Communist Party—there would be no other place for them to go. They would become outcasts in their own society. As she put it, for a Central Asian woman to enter the party meant

> . . . to throw down the gauntlet to all and everything: to terrible Allah himself; to his servants—the sharp-clawed, grasping, greedy mullahs and ishans; to the family's elders; to all kinsmen; to the entire surrounding primordial style of life. . . . The Eastern woman who enters the party breaks with the past forever; once she has thus crossed the threshold of a new life, there can be, for her, no way back.[60]

Given such an evaluation of the roots of female resentment and likely new commitments, it is not surprising that communist organizers came to view Moslem women as not just disposed to abandon the old world but as ripe and ready to seek vengeance.

The case of Salomat Dzhakhongirova, a Tadzhik woman living in Bukhara when the Soviets arrived in 1920, may serve as but one of many striking illustrations of the way Soviet perceptions could materialize on this account. An orphan almost from birth, Salomat had apparently been shunted from one guardian's household to an-

[59] See, e.g., Karpov, *SS*, 11(28), 1928, p. 66, and *SS*, 6(35), 1929, p. 67; Safadri, *Ka*, 11, 1928, p. 31, cf. Tarantaeva, *Ka*, 11, 1928, pp. 46-47; Nukhrat, *OZV*, pp. 51, 82; Mitrofanov, *RN*, 2 (June), 1930, p. 46.
[60] Nukhrat, *OZV*, p. 82; cf. Liubimova, *VPG*, pp. 40-41.

other, mostly in the role of a maid-servant doing the most menial and backbreaking jobs in the ménage of rich relatives' wives. It would seem that, throughout this time, her sense of degradation and humiliation was only matched by the extent of her physical suffering: in the course of one particularly furious beating, she was severely injured and lost all of her teeth. Probably viewed as undesirable for any other purpose after the last beating, she was given in marriage to a farm-laborer. The two spent the initial period of their married life working as hired hands in a variety of peasant households. At the time of the Soviet conquest of Bukhara Salomat found herself in one of the lowliest of traditional occupations: one of the five female watercarriers in the palace of the Emir of Bukhara.

With the Red Army in control of the city, a group of Russian soldiers was apparently assigned to share quarters with Salomat and other watercarriers. As Salomat recalled later, the girls cooked the soldiers' food and washed their clothes. By 1921, Salomat's promise as a rebel and activist was evidently sufficiently recognized by the party; she was dispatched as Bukhara's representative to one of the first women's congresses in Moscow, where she was introduced to Lenin. In 1924, she was invited to the First Congress of Soviets of the Uzbek republic, and was honored with a seat in the congress' presidium. There, she happened to find herself side by side with M. I. Kalinin. Probably taken aback at the sight of a relatively young and yet quite toothless woman, the President asked her for the reasons. In response, Salomat told him the story of her life. The President of the Soviet Union counselled vengeance.[61]

Salomat's subsequent political career was not unlike that of a number of young women of her background. In 1925, she became a member of the Commission for the Improvement of Conditions of Women's Lives, at Bukhara's Soviet Executive Committee. In this capacity she traveled far and wide throughout the hinterland, organizing women in special clubs, enlisting them for schooling, and pressing for the abolition of the veil—as well as leading the assault against traditional elites. In 1930, she became a member of the Central Committee of the Communist Party of Tadzhikstan, and for a number of years headed the Central Committee's Wom-

---

[61] See Pal'vanova, *DSV*, pp. 88-89; cf. S. Dzhakhongirova, "Dvazhdy Rozhdënnaia," in *Uchastnitsy Velikogo Sozidaniia* (Moscow, 1962), pp. 90-92 (notes on Dzhakhongirova's life story as recorded by M. D. Khansuvarova).

en's Department.[62] Other women of her generation became equally devoted agents of the new regime, especially in the role of public prosecutors or judges.[63]

It is safe to assume that it is on the basis of their early experience with Salomat and others like her that communist organizers came to this conclusion: Moslem women could become, in effect, the regime's political fifth column in their own society.[64] They could— as Salomat herself did when the Red Army arrived—point out to Soviet secret police the hiding places of important officials of the Bukharan emirate, after their master had fled to Afghanistan.[65] They seemed prepared to procure intelligence on locally active guerrillas and bandits.[66] They appeared to be especially disposed— seemingly more so than men—to unmask "class enemies": members of traditional elites who had not been detected, or who were returning secretly from places of deportation or imprisonment.[67]

It is on such grounds that the basic argument could be built re-

[62] See Pal'vanova, *DSV*, p. 89. For the background, probable motivations, and careers of other early female converts to the Soviet cause, see ibid., pp. 81-83.

[63] See, e.g., Nukhrat, *OZV*, pp. 78-79; Pal'vanova, *DSV*, pp. 81-83; cf. Halle, *Women*, pp. 297-314, 339-40; Ivetova, *Ka*, 8, 1925, pp. 64-65. The rise of a female political elite will be considered, along with other dimensions of the modernization process in Central Asia, in a separate study (see Note 19, Chapter Six).

[64] One of the earliest public hints of such expectations on the part of the Soviet regime is to be found in Kalinin's observation, during a visit to Central Asia in 1925, that "the whole truth" about local conditions would never be known to the party without the establishment of firm contacts with women (see Liubimova, *VPG*, p. 66). In 1928 the first note appeared that Moslem male officials refused to accept representatives of newly established Councils of Women's Delegates as special apprentices, regarding them as "spies." See Nukhrat, *Ka*, 7, 1928, p. 58.

[65] See Dzhakhongirova in *Uchastnitsy*, p. 91.

[66] Frunze, commanding the Red Army on the Central Asian front during the civil war, alluded to precisely such expectations; Pal'vanova, *DSV*, p. 46. For notes on a famous counter-guerrilla agent, see Halle, *Women*, pp. 123-25.

[67] For a forceful argument that Moslem women were both well placed and particularly well disposed to recognize "class enemies," see Nukhrat, *Ka*, 1, 1928, p. 54. For notes on women's ability and readiness to unearth *lishentsy* (those deprived of the vote, and often of their property, on account of undesirable social background), beys, and anti-Soviet bandits "masquerading as common peasants," see Prishchepchik, *Ka*, 7, 1927, pp. 77-78; *PV*, 2.11, 1930, p. 2; cf. Karpov, *SS*, 6(35), 1929, pp. 66-67; Amosov, *Ka*, 14, 1929, p. 27.

garding female mobilization in Central Asia: Moslem women were uniquely suitable for depriving native communities of their greatest traditional advantages in dealing with outsiders, secrecy and solidarity.

It was perfectly logical for such a view to be also applied to the operation of Moscow's most important vehicles of power and sovietization in the region, the local branches of the Communist Party. Throughout the 1920's these branches had been viewed, with increasing concern, as extremely unreliable, as all too obviously pervaded by tribal, parochial, religious, traditionalist, or nationalist orientations. Accordingly, ever more insistent demands were voiced that these units be "bolshevized" as quickly as possible. At the same time, even some of the party's highest leaders—including Stalin's closest collaborators in dealing with Asian minorities, such as Manzhara, Zelenskii, and Yaroslavsky—showed that they were prepared to believe that Moslem women could indeed be quite useful in such a process of "bolshevization." In this view, the advent of female political converts, activists, and cadres in Central Asia, and their participation in party-politics on all levels, could accomplish two important things. It could help to "liberate [indigenous communists] . . . from [their main] weakness . . . : from [the residues of a tribal-patriarchal] ideology that is alien to and hostile toward the party."[68] And it could augment the regime's capacity to conduct a thoroughgoing purge of the local political and administrative apparatuses, including the party itself—because local female communists could be expected to have a particularly strong "revolutionary consciousness," were especially "pure" and "incorruptible," "utterly selfless and devoted," and could thus recognize enemies inside and outside the party with dispatch.[69]

In this sense, then, female political mobilization meant not just the destruction of traditional authority relations and, with them, of the role of traditional elites. It also meant the liberation of all men from their age-old role as authoritarian kingpins in a traditionally male-controlled world. It meant, as well, the development

[68] Manzhara, representing the Central Control Commission, in a speech to Central Asian communists, in the spring of 1927; see A. Nikolaeva, *Ka*, 8, 1927, p. 52. Cf. Zelenskii's and Yaroslavsky's speeches in Yaroslavsky, *Ka*, 1, 1929, p. 31.

[69] See Vel'tner, *RN*, 12, 1931, p. 29; Nukhrat, *Ka*, 1, 1928, p. 54; Nukhrat, *OZV*, p. 82; Mitrofanov, *RN*, 2, 1930, p. 46.

of an additional dimension of checkup and surveillance over the loyalties and performance of native male cadres in the local communist apparatuses.

It is no wonder, therefore, that many Soviet organizers came to see women's political recruitment as a task vital for the release and disciplined engagement of political energies in a Moslem traditional milieu, energies considered to be essentially untapped from the Soviet point of view. That is why such a task came to be referred to as relatively the most important political and social undertaking in Central Asia,[70] as vital for the region's "socialist development," and for "hasten[ing] the victory of communism" there.[71] At the very least, and as a first step in this direction, the task was seen as a crucial component of a larger strategy: to redefine female roles—considered critically important in the interdependence of traditional beliefs, values, and ties—to such an extent as to undermine the very backbone of a traditional community's political cohesion.[72] Abidova, one of the first authoritative native females in the party, visualized this quite imaginatively. As she put it, to establish purposive political links with Moslem women meant to "find that link in a chain which, when [grasped and] pulled, would enable [the party] to pull out the entire chain" holding the traditional system together.[73]

Effects on Kinship and Community

Female mobilization in a Moslem traditional milieu leads to the disruption of the kinship system and the village community. Specifically, to endow women with unprecedented social and economic roles, to encourage and sponsor divorces initiated by women, and to involve them in massive and dramatic violations of traditional taboos is to undermine local traditional solidarities revolving around clan-loyalties and ties of family and custom.

As a corollary, revolutionary actions impinging upon kin-oriented solidarities compound the power of attraction upon male as well as female youth, by stressing a new accessibility of the sexes

---

[70] Shirman, *Ka*, 4, 1927, p. 73.

[71] For the earliest expressions of this belief, see the decisions of the Fifth Congress of the Communist Party of Turkestan (1920), as cited in Pal'vanova, *DSV*, pp. 47-48. Cf. Tarantaeva, *Ka*, 11, 1928, p. 43.

[72] See, e.g., Zavarian, *Ka*, 6, 1926, p. 70.

[73] Abidova, *RN*, 3(73), 1936, p. 47; cf. Zakharian, *Ka*, 3, 1926, p. 42.

149

to each other: an accessibility based on free choice and no longer
dependent on customary and religious rules, or on tribal, com-
munal, or paternal authority; an accessibility involving unprece-
dented dimensions of contact, courtship, and romantic love. By the
same token, such actions help either to subvert the traditional
realms and hierarchies of loyalty and socialization, and thus re-
lease women and/or youth into Soviet socializing media, or gain
inside those realms exceedingly important allies in bringing up the
young generation—present or future mothers.

Two things seemed increasingly obvious to Soviet organizers in
the course of the 1920's: first, that the survival of traditional communities depended to a large extent on the perpetuation of human
relationships institutionalized in the kinship system and consecrated by prevailing customs; and second, that the viability of traditional kinship and customary patterns was itself significantly contingent on traditional female roles and status in society. As we have
seen,[74] Dzasokhov was but one of many communist analysts of
Central Asian affairs to recognize the implications of this reciprocity, albeit one who presented his conclusions more bluntly
than others. He summed up nearly a decade of observation and experience when he proposed that "the real battle against . . . tribal-
patriarchal residues . . . , [against] the survivals of the old order
. . . , must begin from the destruction of the old . . . family—of that
primary cell of the conservative [Central Asian] village. . . ."[75]

He did not hesitate to admit that the extended patriarchal Moslem family was among the institutions that are least susceptible to
manipulation, constituting "[a cell] that refuses to surrender its
positions to [the forces of] the new [order]."[76] But it seemed
equally clear to him that the trappings of equality in a traditional
solidarity-unit—trappings especially apparent in a tribal milieu—
were but a façade; that this façade masked long-established patterns of harsh stratification and humiliation; and that women were
the lowest of the low in such a system of "thinly veiled . . . slave
relationships."[77] While Dzasokhov did not find it necessary, in this
instance, to carry this argument to its logical conclusion, others did
it for him, both earlier and later. It became well-nigh axiomatic that

[74] See the concluding section of Chapter Two.
[75] Dzasokhov, *RN*, 2-3, 1931, pp. 66-67.
[76] Ibid.
[77] Ibid., pp. 65-66. Cf. Mokrinskii, *SP*, 3(27) 1927, pp. 115-16.

150

female mobilization, accompanied by deliberate manipulation of sexual and generational tensions, would be enormously helpful in exploding the traditional family—and, with it, the social bases of traditional authority and community—from within.[78]

Which dimensions of such mobilization might be especially important for this purpose? Soviet views on this account did not spring fullblown, nor were they fixed and homogeneous. Nevertheless, both official and unofficial expectations seem to have shared this element of certainty: each act of female self-assertion, each significant redefinition of female roles, constitutes a violation of Moslem traditional taboos. As such, it detracts immediately and quite tangibly from the authority of men and from the potency of institutions holding traditional solidarities together. To endow women with unprecedented roles is to drain former customs, values, and beliefs of their meaning, and thus to deprive traditional units of essential cement. If such acts are clearcut and massive enough, and if they persist in their challenge to tradition while the old order is unable to generate sufficient forces of retaliation and repression (something the Soviet state must, of course, help to insure), the revolutionary momentum becomes irreversible.

Within the framework of this general assumption, specific expectations were spelled out with varying emphases. Broadly speaking, these tended to tackle the basic issue from the vantage point of three major perspectives: how new conditions of social mobility would affect, alternatively, the women themselves, the dominant males, and the kinship system as a whole.

New opportunities for self-assertion and mobility were seen as changing a woman's self-perception beyond recognition. Niurina and Aksentovich, for example, were certain that the emergence of women from enforced centuries-old confinement, isolation, and segregation, and their arrival en masse in the streets and in all public places heretofore reserved exclusively for men—especially if accompanied by women's public and dramatic renunciation of the veil—would mark both a psychological and a physical breakthrough in the traditional milieu. Such a direct and sudden breakdown of the walls of sexual apartheid would have what would amount to a cathartic effect on female actors and on male and female witnesses, revolutionizing women's aspirations as well as pre-

---

[78] See, e.g., Vorshev, *RN*, 12(58), 1934, p. 72.

paring society at large for new female roles in all spheres of life.[79] Similarly, Nukhrat, Liubimova, and Sokolova were agreed that the mere fact of women's capacity to be involved in newly engineered social situations outside the home—be it in sexually segregated or mixed company, in mass-associations or public events—would powerfully enhance their sense of personal significance and collective strength.[80] This would be especially so if the legal and police power of the Soviet state could guarantee the safety of such new ventures, and if, correspondingly, the traditionalist enemies of women's mobility and full-fledged social participation should prove to be impotent to interfere.[81] *Ipso facto*, the impotence of men in general and of traditional elites in particular to stop and reverse this process was expected to compound women's self-assurance and alienation from tradition, for these women would have "tasted the sweetness of struggle and victory."[82]

There was equally broad agreement that women would gain a new sense of self-worth, achievement, discipline, toughness, and daring in some other circumstances which were unprecedented in the local traditional milieu: when endowed with new skills and roles in the economy; when encouraged to sue for divorce or to exercise their own will in choosing a mate;[83] when enabled to play female dramatic roles on stage;[84] when permitted to compete openly with males in sports events, or when persuaded to assume martial

[79] See Niurina, *Parandzha*, pp. 7-10; for observations by Aksentovich— one of the party's leading female representatives in Central Asia—see Halle, *Women*, pp. 171-72. See also Chapter Six of this study.

[80] See Nukhrat, *VMV*; Liubimova, *Ka*, 2, 1928, pp. 83-86; Sokolova, *Ka*, 2-3, 1930, pp. 40-42. For other examples of such reasoning—in the context of evaluating the progress made by women's clubs—see, e.g., Prishchepchik, *Ka*, 12, 1925, pp. 63-64 and *Ka*, 9, 1926, pp. 76-78; Zavarian, *Ka*, 6, 1926, pp. 68-69 and *Ka*, 12, 1925, pp. 27-28; Nukhrat, *Ka*, 8, 1927, pp. 19-22; Niurina, *Ka*, 4, 1925, pp. 80-81; Anisimova, *KP*, 1, 1927, pp. 75-77.

[81] For a plea to *make sure* that this was the case, see Liubimova, *Ka*, 8, 1928, p. 75.

[82] See A. Ar-na, *Ka*, 1, 1928, p. 63.

[83] For Soviet views concerning these capacities and roles, see the *first* set of themes in this chapter, *supra*. See also Chapter Five.

[84] See, e.g., Pal'vanova, *DSV*, pp. 66, 91. For notes on Soviet interpretations of the impact of the first films designed with Moslem women in mind, see Liubimova, *VPG*, p. 43. For views of parallel effects of especially tailored plays and staged weddings and family dramas, see Moskalev, *Uzbechka*, p. 44.

152

roles in paramilitary formations, including the operation of air-planes, the use of parachutes, and the handling of guns.[85]

Such reasoning, of course, emphasized the expected effects on the women themselves. Yet the major stress came to be on the anticipated consequences among Moslem men, and on the likely impact upon the kinship system as a whole. The cause-and-effect relationship came to be expressed in very simple terms: a radical change in a woman's self-image, capacities, and roles necessarily implied an equivalent change in her standing in the eyes of a father, kinsman, suitor, or husband. But the opportunity was also taken to explain the expected metamorphosis in ways that would be concrete and attractive enough from a woman's point of view. The reasoning was suggestive: in turning from mere objects of sexual and socio-economic calculation into prime subjects of action, with the prerogatives of independence, initiative, decision, and choice, women would, in effect, deprive men of the monopoly of "heroism."[86]

This meant not only the loss of a monopoly in martial and related roles. It meant, specifically, that some of the authoritative males' most important sources of control and prestige would dry up. Such sources included the custodianship of ancient customs and taboos; the guardianship of family honor; the choice of marital mates; the manipulation of the bride-price, the claim of being a family's sole breadwinner; the allocation of work; and the distribution of rewards. Under the circumstances, the traditional pattern of kin-relations, including the hierarchies of authority and loyalty, was bound to be gravely affected.[87]

The net effect of such a denouement was expected to manifest

---

[85] For some observations on women's role in sports and paramilitary organizations, see Leontiev, *RN*, 2(84) 1937, especially pp. 53-64; *Bezb* (ill.), 2, 1938, p. 7; Kharchenko, *RN*, 7(77) 1936, pp. 58-60; "Postanovlenie . . . Ts.I.K.," *RN*, 10(80) 1936, pp. 95-96. Cf. Pal'vanova, *DSV*, p. 11, and *PV*, 9.18.1938, p. 4. While most of these reports and interpretations date from the mid-1930's, they convey the impression that this particular matter had been under consideration for some time (at least since the mid-1920's). The chapters comprising Part Four of this study should make it clear why much time elapsed before the regime was willing to test some of the proposals advanced by its representatives in Central Asia.

[86] See Pal'vanova, *DSV*, p. 11; cf. Nukhrat, *VMV*, pp. 28-29.

[87] For an example of such reasoning—and for notes on some phenomena that had obviously inspired such reasoning—see Liubimova, *VPG*, p. 42.

itself in at least three ways. First, it seemed logical that, by declining vis-à-vis women, the functions and status of authoritative men would also decline vis-à-vis a community's relatively underprivileged males, and a family's sons. In part, this had to be due to new conditions of accessibility of the sexes to each other. After all, such accessibility would no longer be dependent on traditional rules, or on tribal, communal, or paternal authority.[88] Involving, as it did, the principle of free choice—of "will . . . and . . . strength"—on both sides, it was bound to involve unprecedented dimensions of contact, courtship, and romantic love.[89] Thus, female mobilization could not but compound the Soviet power of attraction upon male as well as female youth, and play a direct role in mobilizing the entire young generation.

Second, as the party's high command was quick to recognize and emphasize, the mobilization of women could be expected to subvert traditional patterns of socialization, by gaining inside this realm exceedingly important allies in bringing up the young generation: present and future mothers. Stalin visualized this quite clearly, though with the Soviet Union as a whole in mind: "Women are the mothers who bring up our youth—the future of our country. They can either cripple a child's soul, or give us a youth that is healthy in spirit and capable of moving our country forward. . . . [Whether one or the other happens] would depend on whether the woman-mother sympathizes with the Soviet regime or, instead, drags herself behind the priest, the kulak, or the bourgeoisie. . . ."[90] Bil'shai, a noted Soviet analyst of female emancipation, echoed this conclusion in somewhat different terms, still from a Union-wide perspective: "[a capitalist] needs a woman's enslavement and cultural backwardness for the attainment of [bigger] surplus-profits by way of intensive exploitation of female labor. . . . [But he also needs her for another reason;] a downtrodden and backward woman serves as a [distinctly] conservative power in the family and in society, [a power that] constitutes a brake on the development of class-con-

---

[88] This reasoning is clearly implicit in Nukhrat's observations on the phenomenon of poor native males turning to the party's Women's Department for help in getting a wife. See Nukhrat, *OZV*, p. 70.

[89] See, e.g., the songs and poetry promoted by the regime, as quoted in Nukhrat, *VMV*, pp. 30-31. Cf. Sannikov, *RN*, 8(54), 1934, pp. 45-46; Lakhuti, *RN*, 9(55), 1934, pp. 70-71.

[90] "Rabota sredi rabotnits i krestianok" (1925), as quoted in *BSE*, vol. 25, 1932, p. 240.

sciousness not only in the toiling woman herself but, to a significant extent, in her kin."[91] Kalinin, however, in a speech to the First Congress of the Uzbek Communist Party in 1925, and during his subsequent tour of Central Asia, advanced this proposition in simple declarative terms, emphasizing its special significance in revolutionizing a Moslem society: "It is especially among women that [cultural development] must be promoted, for women exert a far greater influence on their children than men."[92]

Finally, it seemed to be accepted as a matter of course that the cumulative effect of the expected shifts would be a change in size and nature of what had been an extended, patriarchal Moslem family. There were a number of nuances of explicit or implicit arguments to this effect. Some suggested that the endowment even of the least desirable, and hence traditionally the cheapest, women in the community (daughters of socially disadvantaged males, as well as orphans, widows, and divorcées) with equal rights and opportunities for social mobility would tend to remove the most likely source of wives for, and thus directly undermine, the polygamous family.[93] Others anticipated that greater awareness of new opportunities on the part of women would lead to a growing disequilibrium of the traditional family, and to speedy emergence of nuclear family units. For example, it seemed logical to expect that, in response to Soviet appeals and to a shift in roles of men in community and family, girls would feel emboldened to leave their natal families, just as orphan-girls would feel disposed to abandon natal communities and guardians, and seek protection, support, and a completely fresh start in Soviet ranks. Similarly wives, beginning with young brides recently married on parental command to old or unloved men, might feel all the more encouraged to break unilaterally an unhappy union through Soviet-sponsored divorce, and to seek a mate of their own choice.[94] In short, with such new social

---

[91] Bil'shai, *RZVS*, p. 26.

[92] *Pervyi S'yezd Komm. Partii (bolshevikov) Uzbekistana. Steno. Otchet* (Tashkent, 1925), p. 28, as cited in Liubimova, *VPG*, pp. 65-66.

[93] This expectation is implied, for example, in Pal'vanova's account of the removal of orphans from households of relatives into special Soviet institutions. See Pal'vanova, *DSV*, p. 60.

[94] For some early Soviet perceptions on this account see Zakharian, *Ka*, 3, 1926, pp. 42-44; Michurina, *Ka*, 10-11, 1926, p. 83. Cf. Nukhrat, *VMV*, pp. 30-31; Sannikov, *RN*, 8(54), 1934, pp. 45-46; Lakhuti, *RN*, 9(55), 1934, pp. 70-71.

155

and psychological factors coming into play, prevalent traditional patterns of interdependence, mutual obligation, and automatic solidarity rooted in extended kinship could not possibly be maintained.

In sum, there appeared to be a growing consensus in Soviet ranks in the 1920's that the manipulation of female roles had to be a key tactic in disrupting and transforming the traditional kinship system in Central Asia. Such a belief carried an important implication: to disrupt primary social groups meant to undercut the mainstays of traditional community; in turn, to induce strain and fragmentation in family, clan, and village-community meant to make individuals more accessible to the regime, and thus to make society at large more susceptible to permeation, mobilization, and control.

Effects on Religion and Custom

To revolutionize the status of Moslem women is to significantly weaken some crucial moorings of Islam in a traditional society. In particular, to endow women with unprecedented cultural roles and civil rights, to back those rights with a new and especially tailored judicial system, and to staff that system, in part, with women is to undermine immediately the codified religious laws of the shariat, *and the main repository of local customary laws, the* adat.[95]

As a corollary, to impair the viability and relevance of sacred institutions governing the minutiae of daily life is to undermine the status, authority, as well as livelihood of the traditional custodians of these institutions: the local religious, tribal, and communal elites.

Those Soviet analysts who saw important linkages between female roles and the viability of Central Asia's religio-customary systems, and called for the mobilization of women precisely for this reason, based themselves on at least one cardinal proposition. As they saw it, it was in traditional family-life, and especially in the everyday life of a Moslem woman, that Islamic and Islamicized customary laws, prescriptions, practices, and rituals had exercised a profoundly "circumscribing" and "highly detailed" influence.[96] Given this assumption, it was not illogical to expect that the attainment by Moslem women of "spiritual independence from Islam"

[95] For some indications of such expectations, see Kobetskii, *RN*, 5(63), 1935, p. 74.

[96] See *BSE*, Vol. 29, 1935, p. 395; cf. Sev, *Turkmenovedenie*, 3-4, 1928, pp. 5-20.

156

(as Gorky envisaged it in a letter to Romain Rolland)[97] would help to make Islam itself into an empty husk where society at large was concerned.

What had kept Moslem women especially dependent on sacred • institutions and their custodians? Soviet analysts identified the reasons without hesitation: illiteracy, ignorance, superstition, as well as generalized inferiority in cultural and judicial roles. To revolutionize the latter condition would irreversibly alter the former one. Thus, female literacy and women's emergence in the roles of nurses, doctors, teachers, scholars, and artists would pose a directly competitive (and symbolically crushing) challenge to older cultural institutions and to the traditional elites that staffed them.[98] Similarly, the emergence of women in the roles of people's assessors, prosecutors, and judges would make the antecedent judicial system utterly incoherent. After all, a social stratum that had been specifically excluded from exercising legal functions, and even whose value as witness in court had been held to be specifically inferior to that of males, would suddenly have the capacity to make, interpret, and administer the law, with respect to men as well as women.[99]

In turn, the availability of new institutions of health, education, and welfare staffed, as a matter of high priority, by native women, and the opportunity to redress grievances in similarly staffed courts, would have an electric effect on female masses. As a general principle, both the demonstrable superiority of the new network and its sexually and ethnically akin staff could be expected to establish a relationship of trust between the regime and native women. This would help to legitimize the new political order as much as to neutralize the appeals of local elites to traditionalist or nationalist loyalties.[100]

[97] M. Gorkii, *Sochineniia*, Vol. 30, p. 16, as cited in Pal'vanova, *DSV*, p. 96.

[98] See, e.g., *Bezb* (news.), 10, 1928, p. 5; cf. Sev, *Turkmenovedenie*, 3-4, 1928, pp. 5-20 (*passim*), and Smirnova, *Ka*, 8, 1929, p. 27.

[99] See, e.g., Nukhrat, *OZV*, pp. 63-67, 78-79; Pal'vanova, *DSV*, pp. 56-57; Liubimova, *VPG*, pp. 48-49; Balaban, *VS*, 40-41, 1928, pp. 15-17; Akopov, *RN*, 4-5, 1930, pp. 68-69; Kasparova, *Ka*, 7, 1925, pp. 91-92; Zavarian, *Ka*, 6, 1926, p. 66. Cf. Kobetskii, *RN*, 5(63), 1935, p. 74.

[100] For commentaries on the entire spectrum of this argument, see, e.g., Pravda, *SS*, 12(41), 1929, pp. 111-12; *Bezb* (news.) 4, 1927, p. 6; Fioletov, *SP*, 1(25), 1927, p. 144; Liubimova, *Ka*, 9, 1926, pp. 74-75; Liubimova,

But the pull on Moslem women was bound to have more specific and immediate effects, too. "Rational medical assistance" and "sensible counsel"—for example, with respect to childlessness or to other intimate, personally distressing matters that habitually sent women in search of "saintly" help—would serve to woo women away from the influence of Moslem "teachers," village "wise men" and "holy men," and tribal shamans. It was of incalculable importance that the latter would, in one blow, be deprived of what had been traditionally their most frequent and submissive clients.[101]

There were at least two dimensions of Soviet expectations in this case which concerned specifically the likely response of native males. Both sought to neutralize the constraining influence of men upon women in the latter's exercise of new options. Both relied on negative incentives to attain the goal. One of them emphasized, often quite frankly, erotic factors. The other stressed political endurance and power.

On the one hand, those most closely associated with the tactics of "militant atheism" in the battle with Islam seemed to expect that attitudes of traditional males towards local sacred elites would be revolutionized when sexual jealousy came into play. Specifically, they championed attempts suggesting, among other things, that a *mullah*'s presumed spiritual guidance of a man's wives and daughters could easily go hand in hand with sexual exploitation.[102] It could have appeared logical that such insinuations—especially if accompanied by sufficiently "realistic" and lurid details—would arouse the suspicions, jealousy, and protectiveness of fathers, brothers, and husbands, gravely compromise locally revered figures, and irreparably damage their influence at the grassroots.

On the other hand, those specifically in charge of organizing women seemed to shy away from such initiatives as potentially too

---

VPG, pp. 49-50; Nikolaeva, *Ka*, 8, 1927, p. 53; Zavarian, *Ka*, 12, 1925, p. 25; Nukhrat, *Ka*, 12, 1927, p. 44; Akopov, *RN*, 4-5, 1930, p. 66; *BSE*, Vol. 29, 1935, p. 396; cf. Berin and Yoshpe, *RN*, 3(85), 1937, pp. 67-70 (esp. p. 69); cf. also Smirnova, *Ka*, 8, 1929, p. 27; Kliuchnikov, *KP*, 5, 1929, pp. 60-61; Kliuchnikov, *KP*, 12, 1929, pp. 64-68; Dimanshtein, *Ka*, 5-6, 1929, pp. 49-51; Pismennyi, *RK*, 10, 1928, pp. 11-20 (*passim*).

[101] For implicit as well as explicit Soviet expectations on this account see, e.g., Moskalev, *Uzbechka*, pp. 39-44; Kolychev, *RN*, 4-5, 1930, p. 119; Krupskaia, *Ka*, 12, 1928, pp. 9-10; *Bezb* (news.), 34, 1929, p. 2; Smirnova, *Ka*, 8, 1929, p. 27.

[102] See, e.g., *Bezb* (news.), 31, 1928, p. 7; *Bezb* (ill.), 11-12, 1931, pp. 12-13; *Bezb* (ill.), 23, 1931, pp. 10-11; *Bezb* (ill.), 5, 1936, pp. 4-6.

explosive. Instead, they called for reliance on meticulously planned supportive structures as a guarantee of real victory in this case. The reasoning went approximately as follows: If women departing from the ministrations of old sacred elites actually find tangible organizational, material, and psychological support within the Soviet framework, the custodians of tradition will be put in a politically embarrassing and precarious position. The latter would, in effect, be exposed as *helpless*: helpless to keep or win back their female clients, to invoke their previously unquestioned authority, to exercise their primordial functions. Such a manifestation of helplessness was bound to be especially dramatic in that it would involve a sharp shift in the relationship between traditional elites and women —that is, between those who had been, respectively, the strongest and the weakest political actors in a traditional community. The impact of such a spectacle on the sensibilities of the mass of traditional males was bound to be tremendous. It would help to persuade them that resistance to change was futile, that acquiescence or a modicum of cooperation with the revolutionary regime, in all spheres of life, was mandatory. As Artiukhina and Nukhrat[103] visualized this, it is primarily in this fashion that "the myth of [the Islamic system's] durability . . . and invincibility" would be smashed,[104] and "the old East . . . and [its] laws . . . would die."[105]

Ultimately, it seems, even when proposed tactics differed, official perceptions of the crucial task to be accomplished in this case remained the same. The task (and expected effect of Soviet moves) was to break the monopoly of knowledge, and of political, adjudicative, intellectual, educational, spirtual, and consecrative functions, held by males in general and by traditional elites—religious, tribal, and communal—in particular. To accomplish this would mean to undermine the status and livelihood of these elites, as well as the cultural bases of their legitimacy and authority.[106] It would also mean to subvert not only the claims of religion and custom upon human beliefs, values, commitments, and ties, but also the hold of religious and customary institutions upon the hierarchies

---

[103] Artiukhina headed the party's Women's Department in Moscow at that time. Nukhrat was emerging as a leading ideologist and organizer of women's emancipation among Russia's Asian minorities.

[104] See Ar-na, *Ka*, 1, 1928, p. 63.

[105] See Nukhrat, *OZV*, pp. 84-88 (especially p. 88 for quote).

[106] See, e.g., Griaznov, *RN*, 7(40), 1933, p. 77; Sev, *Turkmenovedenie*, 3-4, 1928, pp. 15-20 (*passim*).

of society and family, the administration of justice, the system of education, property relations, and the overall pattern of daily life. As one party analyst put it: "That is why the struggle for the emancipation of Eastern women is so intimately connected with the struggle against Islamic influence . . . "; a breakthrough in the former would have immediate repercussions in the latter.[107] A political organizer in Uzbekistan, focusing on but one element of the envisioned struggle, expressed the same view with stark simplicity: "When a [Moslem woman's] veil falls, so will [her] religion."[108]

Implications for Property Relations

To endow women with opportunities for choice in personal matters and with equal rights in the economic domain is to disorient and weaken prevailing concepts of property in a traditional Islamic system. A revolutionary regime can bring about such weakness and disorientation by bringing into question the woman's role as (in the Bolshevik interpretation) her father's means of exchange, and her husband's beast of burden, chattel, and property in marriage; and by forcefully stressing and challenging the entire range of her legal and customary inferiority, particularly with respect to her control and inheritance of property, including land. As a corollary, engineered incoherence in concepts and relations concerning property compounds the power of the regime's pull upon poor and socially disadvantaged males. It has this effect because it affords the opportunity to stress a new availability of brides that is no longer dependent on the social status of a man and his family or clan, or on the requirements of property in the form of the traditional bride-price (kalym).

In terms of the broad requirements of both ideology and power, it would hardly have been relevant for the regime to pursue linkages between female status and concepts of property. After all, the nationalization of all means of production, including land, was a postulate from which the Bolsheviks never retreated. In the final analysis, it could not matter very much whether and to what extent relations between the sexes impinged on property relations, and

---

[107] See *Bezb* (news.), 10, 1928, p. 5, for a review of female inferiority as the fulfillment of Islamic dicta, and, at the same time, as the linchpin of Islam's stability as a system of beliefs, values, and customs. Cf. Dimanshtein, *Ka*, 5-6, 1929, pp. 49-51.

[108] See Liubimova, *VPG*, p. 70.

vice versa. In the end, all such issues were bound to dissolve in the larger perspective of a socialist economic system.

But in Central Asia of the 1920's the Bolsheviks were dealing with a milieu where economic patterns were proving to be just as resistant to speedy permeation and transformation as local societies and cultures—certainly less familiar and more resistant than in Russia. Even land reform (as yet without a hint of collectivization) encountered delays and problems largely unknown in European Russia. It is safe to assume that these peculiarities spurred official Soviet interest in views that sought at least some explanations and solutions, in the context of traditional Islamic society, in those patterns of social stratification which were based on sex. The main thrust of these views was based on two assumptions: first, that social, cultural, and economic roles and relationships in Central Asia were far more intimately interrelated and interdependent than in Russia; and second, that, in a number of cases, the characteristic forms and strength of this interaction depended quite heavily on traditional definitions of the role and status of women. It followed that, at least in the transitional period, some special dimensions of female mobilization could make important contributions to the attainment of broader economic and political objectives.

What seemed most obvious to Soviet organizers in the field concerned the overall impact of the campaign: a woman occupied a crucial place in a traditional household's productive activities, and was the most exploited of its members; hence her economic mobilization would help to undermine the traditional pattern of economic pursuits and would radically alter the traditional division of labor.[109] While this may have been an obvious outcome to expect, it was also too general and distant to be reassuring—especially to impatient Bolshevik elites bent upon quick, concrete, dramatic results. It is not surprising, therefore, to find communist analysts, in the 1920's, attempting to draw ever more specific inferences from developments in the field.

Kasparova, a Russian organizer among Moslem women, was among the first to stress heavily the strategic relationship between some Central Asian customs (polygamy, child-marriage, arranged and forced marriage, bride-price) and what she saw as "the institution of property." In her view, it was of paramount importance to understand that a calculated approach to female emancipation

---

[109] This argument is clearly implicit in Niurina, *Ka*, 4, 1925, p. 82.

161

would make prevailing concepts of property simply untenable. Among other things, that calculated approach would undermine the status and customs of the region's largest property holders, since it was presumably they who were in a position to take the greatest advantage of prevailing customs, and to profit from them most.[110] Such an approach would also disrupt in a special way some traditional production relations in extended kin-groups: orphaned or poor girls cared for by richer kinsmen (and working in their household) could be encouraged to consider their relatives not as guardians but as employers and exploiters, and to enter into negotiated contractual agreements with them.[111]

Other leading analysts and organizers including Liubimova, Michurina, Zakharian, and Zavarian, developed in depth a number of nuances of this argument. In most cases, the expected payoffs were seen as optimizing the conditions for a successful land and water reform. Female roles tended to reinforce traditional property relations in that Moslem women were cast in the role of a father's means of exchange, and a husband's chattel and property in marriage, while their rights to control and inherit property were severely circumscribed and made dependent on the authority of men. The more consistent and concrete the emphasis on bringing into question this dependent and inferior role, the more susceptible would Central Asian societies be to a revolution in property relations. This susceptibility would be all the more pronounced if land- and water-rights were allocated not to households as a whole, but to individuals, including women; if traditionally the most disadvantaged females in the realm of property ownership—orphans, widows, and divorcées—were, as a matter of high priority, specifically encouraged to claim their share in the general redistribution; if women were placed in authoritative positions on official committees conducting land reform.[112]

It was logical to expect that such dramatic shifts would, as a matter of course, guarantee a woman's economic independence and

[110] See Kasparova, *Ka*, 7, 1925, p. 88.

[111] Ibid., p. 91.

[112] For views and reports on the special role assigned to women in Central Asia's land-reform, see Kryl'tsov, *SP*, 5(29), 1927, pp. 134-35; Liubimova, *VPG*, pp. 54-58; Pal'vanova, *DSV*, pp. 92-95; Moskalev, *Uzbechka*, pp. 36-37; Zakharian, *Ka*, 3, 1926, pp. 43-44; Liubimova, *Ka*, 4, 1926, pp. 56-57; Zavarian, *Ka*, 6, 1926, p. 67; Michurina, *Ka*, 10-11, 1926, p. 83.

162

thus lead her to support Soviet initiatives.[113] But field-organizers in Central Asia came to place even greater emphasis on the ways in which these shifts would maximize the opportunities for attracting poor and socially disadvantaged males to the Soviet regime.

For example, a poor bachelor would suddenly be able to surmount at least two salient disadvantages. For one thing, most variants of local customary law—as interpreted by the party's specialists in the matter—gave a man access to land- and water-rights only if and when he married. Moreover, his share could often rise in direct proportion to the number of wives he managed to acquire, which tended to reinforce the institution of polygamy just as it subjected a poorer man to a specific kind of discrimination. It followed, in the Soviet view, that a radical shift in the criteria of property-ownership would bring to the fore a stratum of men who had been perennially disadvantaged.[114] For another thing, it appeared that men unable to pay the bride-price were often fated to postpone marriage for a long time, often in humiliating circumstances—for example, as indentured servants of a prospective father-in-law. Many could never marry at all. Here too, then, very important payoffs could be expected by the regime through a concerted assault on the institution of *kalym*, as one dimension in the campaign for women's liberation.[115]

In addition, there appeared to be some opportunities for exploiting possible tensions in families where prospective grooms and brides were mere infants or children, and hence where the entire burden of *kalym* payments had to be borne by the father. Thus, some Soviet analysts considered it important to emphasize the constant threat of bankruptcy faced (and resentment experienced) by poor families with many sons to wed and hence with overwhelming bride-price obligations to discharge.[116] Others seemed convinced that one could anticipate (or induce) a sense of deprivation and

[113] See references in preceding note.

[114] See, e.g., Michurina, *Ka*, 10-11, 1926, p. 83.

[115] For some indications of such a view, see Kasparova, *Ka*, 7, 1925, p. 88; cf. Petukhov, *RN*, 2(48), 1934, pp. 41-42. For an example of a letter written by a poor peasant party member to the party's Women's Department, requesting a wife, see Halle, *Women*, p. 134; it is safe to assume that those who obtained this letter, and publicized it, used it as evidence that confirmed their original expectations. See also Kryl'tsov, *SP*, 5(29), 1927, pp. 136, 138; Akopov, *RN*, 4-5, 1930, p. 62.

[116] See, e.g., Mokrinskii, *SP*, 3(27), 1927, pp. 111-12.

humiliation in poor men who had daughters and were obliged, particularly in economically bad years, to sell them against their will, for a price dictated by a rich and prestigious patriarch.[117]

In sum, it seemed quite reasonable, from the Soviet point of view, to expect that in societies where the availability of women was sharply curtailed by relatively high female mortality, by high bride-prices, and by polygamous practices of relatively rich and privileged males—and where, therefore, the percentage of unmarried adult males had to be high—the conflict over women could assume highly emotional overtones. In such a context, one of the effects of engineered female mobilization presumably would be to endow the poorer males' sense of sexual deprivation with overtones of social, economic, and political deprivation, making the conflict over women into a potential fulcrum for a sharpening class-conflict.[118]

Implications for Recruitment of Labor and Technical Cadres

To mobilize Moslem women is to gain, in heretofore secluded female masses, a large and reliable labor pool, and a potentially important reservoir of technical cadres. Tapping the new source of labor supply serves, in the short run, to maximize the scope and tempo of economic development and, over the longer term, to release the productive and creative potentials of a traditional society.

As a corollary, the emergence of female masses as an autonomous producing force in the marketplace compounds the emotional pressures upon the whole male population, by exposing it, in every role, enterprise, and sphere of life, to unprecedented competition from women. At a minimum, this exposure deprives men of the traditional haven of unquestioned acceptance and superiority in the family and in public life, making it necessary for men to seek new criteria of self-assertion, self-esteem, competence, and accomplish-

---

[117] Clearly implied in a poem in *Bezb* (ill.), 2-3, 1940, pp. 12-13. While this particular reference is to an item published in 1940, there is circumstantial evidence that some party analysts proposed to act on this assumption at the height of the emancipation campaign in the 1920's. See the footnote that follows.

[118] For explicit and implicit indications of such reasoning, see Akopov, *RN*, 4-5, 1930, p. 62; Krupskaia, *Ka*, 12, 1928, p. 7; Kasparova, *Ka*, 7, 1925, p. 88; Pal'vanova, *DSV*, pp. 38, 92-93; Kryl'tsov, *SP*, 5(29), 1927, pp. 136, 138; Liubimova, *VPG*, p. 55; Liubimova, *Ka*, 10, 1927, p. 60; cf. Halle, *Women*, pp. 133-34.

164

*ment, and hence stimulating their economic performance and po-
litical cooperation.*

In the themes concerning labor recruitment as a concomitant of
female emancipation, Soviet considerations were perhaps more
overtly and coldly instrumental than in other cases. To be sure,
there is some circumstantial evidence that some Soviet activists,
with a deep personal commitment to women's liberation on moral
grounds, emphasized the labor-payoffs merely as an obvious incentive for the regime to commit itself (and its resources) to the emancipation of Moslem women. But it is safe to assume that, as a rule,
official interest and actions in the 1920's in this sphere expressed
an intense (and distinctly growing) preoccupation with Moslem
women primarily as an under-utilized source of human energy. In
some cases, this preoccupation showed itself to be strong to the
point of being exclusive, and certainly strong enough to move other
considerations into the background.

Nukhrat tried, when discussing the requisites of labor recruitment, to balance moral and instrumental considerations. The Soviet
regime was seeking to eradicate the traditional way of life, she suggested, because the latter was characterized by "inertia" and "stagnation." As such, it was "an obstacle to the cultural and economic
development" of the concerned nationalities. At the same time, it
made it impossible "to enlist Eastern women in the overall creative
work of the Soviet state. Millions of female [working] hands are
kept under lock and key: the laws of seclusion are a hindrance to
the utilization [of those hands] in socially significant work. [The
same laws] do not permit women to attain full emancipation."[119]
Maksimova, in a slightly different vein, called for the state's tangible investment in "raising the cultural level" of Russia's oriental
women, and in "the eradication of poverty" in their milieu. The
payoffs were bound to be important to all: "only thus shall we obtain the new productive energy [required] in the reconstruction of
agriculture and in the economic growth of the country as a
whole."[120] Zakharian, too, stressed the direct correlation between
female emancipation (including new roles in the work force) and
economic development. As she put it, "the deep contradictions
[between Soviet economic imperatives and the] customary and legal

---

[119] Nukhrat, *OZV*, pp. 38-39.
[120] Maksimova, *Ka*, 6, 1928, p. 95; cf. Aitakov, *SS* (10-11), 1927, p. 76.

norms . . . of a feudal-patriarchal system" were intolerable; female emancipation could be counted on to "untie the bonds" holding that system together, and to remove the shackles "holding back [Central Asia's] economic and cultural development. . . ."[121]

Other Soviet views, however, were more narrowly focused, and made no bones about the specificity of the expected benefits. To solve the problem of access to Moslem women, it was argued, would make them immediately available for mass-recruitment into Soviet-sponsored enterprises, beginning with specialized agricultural and industrial labor.[122] Stalin was, of course, quite explicit about this at the outset of the collectivization campaign, when he declared it to be "criminal" not to mobilize for collective labor that fifty percent of the population which was female.[123] But already in the early 1920's, Frunze—at that time, a pivotal figure in Central Asia's military and political administration—had expressed a keen interest in Moslem women as a potentially large labor pool, and demands to this effect were intensified as time went on.[124] These demands did not merely recapitulate the general argument for enhancing the country's "productive power," as stated by Alexandra Kollontay, one of Russia's leading communist feminists;[125] they were quite specific about the projected use of Central Asian women as the *primary* reservoir of labor in particular realms: the growing of cotton, the production of silk, and the expansion of textile, clothing, and food industries.[126]

The expected emergence of a female labor pool in Central Asia carried with it what were, from the Soviet point of view, at least three important concomitants. First, it was considered obvious that the recruitment of women *en masse* into novel forms of economic, and especially industrial, activity, and their training for unprece-

---

[121] Zakharian, *Ka*, 3, 1926, p. 42.

[122] See, e.g., Anisimova, *Ka*, 8, 1927, pp. 54-56; cf. Limanovskii, *Sov. Khlopok*, 11-12, 1937, pp. 91-95.

[123] See Nukhrat, *RN*, 3(36), 1933, p. 53.

[124] See Pal'vanova, *DSV*, p. 46. Cf. ibid., pp. 11-12; Brutser, *KP*, 4-5, 1930, pp. 91-93; Nuflhrat, *RN*, 3(36), 1933, pp. 46, 51.

[125] See R. Schlesinger, *Changing Attitudes in Soviet Russia—The Family in the USSR* (London, 1949), pp. 48, 52.

[126] See, e.g., Sakhudri, *Ka*, 4, 1928, p. 70; Butuzova, *Ka*, 9, 1927, p. 62; Moskalev, *Uzbechka*, p. 46; Nukhrat, *RN*, 3(36), 1933, p. 54; Sazonova and Chernova, *RN*(49), 1934, p. 53; Vorshev, *RN*, 12(58), p. 72; Pal'-vanova, *DSV*, p. 112; P. A. Pavlenko, *Puteschestvie v Turkmenistan* (Moscow, 1935), pp. 190-91.

dented and gainful roles in these spheres, would create optimum conditions for their economic independence—and "moral independence" as well—from elders, fathers, and husbands, and hence from the patriarchal family.[127] By the same token, a woman's newly autonomous status in the economy would also mean a new status for widows, divorcées, and orphans. Thus, even the most disadvantaged women would be able to make choices—for example, concerning marriage or remarriage—that were utterly unthinkable in a traditional context.[128] It was to be expected, furthermore, that a woman's rising economic skills and capabilities, going hand in hand with an independent income, would demonstrate dramatically to society at large her "equal usefulness and worth," and her "equal contribution to national economic development." The new perception of a woman's capacities was bound to alter radically her status in the family.[129] It followed that the woman's arrival in the factory and the producers' cooperative could be counted on to weaken all the more surely such traditional arrangements as bride-price, polygamy, and levirate,[130] all of which were presumably predicated on economic need as well as lack of choice. The woman's arrival in the industrial marketplace could also be counted on to lead all the more relentlessly to the decline and dissolution of the extended Moslem family, and to the decline of patriarchal authority in it.[131]

Second, it was proposed that a woman's new economic capabilities and roles would help, perhaps more directly and permanently than anything else, to alter her self-image and her image of the surrounding world. This change was seen not merely as an alteration

[127] For some forceful references to the theme of independence, see, e.g., Kasparova, *Ka*, 7, 1925, pp. 87-88; Pal'vanova, *DSV*, pp. 111-12; Niurina, *Ka*, 4, 1925, p. 79; Zavarian, *Ka*, 6, 1926, p. 70; Prishchepchik, *Ka*, 12, 1925, p. 63.

[128] See, e.g., Moskalev, *Uzbechka*, pp. 36-37.

[129] See Kasparova, *Ka*, 7, 1925, pp. 87-88.

[130] See Kasparova, *Ka*, 7, 1925, p. 88; Mukhitdinova, *Ka*, 9, 1929, p. 39; Zavarian, *Ka*, 6, 1926, p. 67; Michurina, *Ka*, 10-11, 1926, p. 83; cf. Kryl'tsov, *SP*, 5(29), 1927, pp. 134-35.

[131] Soviet observers were particularly quick to note the unease in the traditional milieu over the woman's projected role in industrial labor. As one mother-in-law's warnings to her son were quoted: Don't let [your young wife] go to work in the factory; once she leaves her home, she will leave you, too." See Limanovskii, *Sov. Khlopok*, 11-12, 1937, pp. 91-95. This particular source is cited because of the clarity of its argument. While it is dated in the 1930's, it leaves one with the strong impression that its evidence and arguments were under consideration in the 1920's.

in her attitudes with respect to her inherent worth and potentialities. A woman's sojourn in the collectivistic milieu of a factory or handicraft cooperative—specifically, her habituation in operating a machine—was expected to motivate and enable her to move in several directions at once: to neglect or abandon traditional practices (such as veiling) that hampered the optimum fulfillment of complex tasks; to rely less on religious personages and traditional authority figures for spiritual and material support, and more on her own resources and the assistance of her labor collective sponsored by the state; to develop an interest in social and political issues, and in Soviet-sponsored associations, transcending her immediate surroundings. In short, as Moskalev saw it in a widely publicized pamphlet, to teach Moslem women to operate modern machinery as part of a production team would mean enabling them to "bridge the gulf" between traditional orientations and presently required commitments and habits.[132] Pal'vanova has presented the essence of such expectations in strikingly suggestive terms: beginning in the mid-1920's, industrial establishments were counted on to become a Moslem woman's "university," her chief "mooring," the "fortress" of her independence.[133]

It is not surprising that such views gained currency very quickly in the Soviet context. In accepting those views, Soviet elites could, of course, draw on important elements in Marxist reasoning, concerning especially the relationship between modes of production and human sensibilities and beliefs. But, perhaps more important, they could rely on Lenin's own vision of the consequences of industrial recruitment among women as a whole. Quite justifiably, they could perceive this vision as especially relevant to Moslem women, so sensitively were Lenin's terms tuned to what could seem the equivalent of an Islamic traditional environment. For Lenin, the enlistment of traditionalist women in industrial work promised to "pulverize [the chains of] their patriarchal seclusion"; to serve as a powerful mobilizing tool with respect to "those who had never before stepped outside the narrow circle of home and family relationships"; to "attract them toward direct participation in social production"; to "push forward their [humane] development . . . and

---

[132] Moskalev, *Uzbechka*, pp. 38-39, 46. Cf. Seifi, *Ka*, 9, 1925, pp. 74, 76-79. See also Kasparova, *Ka*, 10, 1925, pp. 84-86; Zavarian, *Ka*, 6, 1926, p. 68; Zavarian, *Ka*, 12, 1925, p. 29; Ross, *Ka*, 3, 1926, pp. 73-75; Liubimova, *Ka*, 5, 1927, pp. 51-53; Bol'shakov, *Ka*, 5, 1927, pp. 53-56.

[133] Pal'vanova, *DSV,* pp. 111-12.

168

independence"; in effect, to create conditions of life that would decisively transcend "the patriarchal immobility of pre-capitalist relationships."[134]

If the preceding two sets of themes could hark back to more or less familiar ideological postulates, a third one might have been viewed as a somewhat esoteric, even romantic, improvisation, though possibly of great interest and promise in the specific conditions of Central Asia. It was expressed perhaps most dramatically by Pavlenko, a Russian journalist, essayist, and propagandist. It seems likely that, in doing so, he took his cue from those organizers in Central Asia who saw Moslem women as potentially more loyal, cooperative, and reliable converts to the Soviet revolutionary cause than their menfolk.[135]

Pavlenko's argument was that Central Asian women (beginning with Turkmen women)[136] might, if given a chance, be expected to abandon the primitive, inefficient local cottage industries and to form an industrial labor pool, before native men did so. In this process, their dispositions would be importantly influenced by a lifetime of characteristic experience: by their traditionally heavy representation in local handicrafts; by the need to be engaged (unlike their menfolk) in heavy work—in effect, to be veritable "amazons of labor"—all their lives; and by their traditional status as the most oppressed of the oppressed in their societies. As a result, these women could be expected not merely to join with special ease a newly structured labor pool, but to be psychologically prepared to form Central Asia's industrial working class, its first genuine proletariat, before men.[137]

It would seem that all of these themes played a role in solidifying a central, widespread conviction in Soviet ranks, a corollary to all other expectations voiced on this account: the recruitment of Moslem women *en masse* into novel forms of economic activity, and

[134] Lenin, *Soch.*, Vol. 3, pp. 480-81, as cited in Bil'shai, *RZVS*, p. 24; cf. Karl Marx, *Capital, A Critique of Political Economy* (Modern Library, n.d.), p. 536, and Kollontay, *Trud Zhenshchiny v Evolutsii Khoziaistva* (Moscow, 1921, 2nd ed.), pp. 161-62, as quoted by T. Anderson, in *Masters of Russian Marxism* (N.Y., 1963), p. 165.

[135] See the *second* in the series of operational themes developed in this chapter.

[136] Pavlenko's observations were apparently based on an extended trip to Turkmenistan in the 1920's, although his argument seems to have been intended to apply to Central Asia as a whole.

[137] See Pavlenko, *Puteshestvie*, pp. 210-11.

169

their capacity to play unprecedented roles in this sphere, would re-move the traditional "middlemen"—fathers, brothers, and hus-bands—standing between women and the economic market-place.[138] The removal of "middlemen" would not merely create favorable conditions for the women's economic independence from husbands, families, and clans, and for their commensurate attrac-tion to, and socialization in, the Soviet system. It would, perhaps more tangibly than anything else, expose traditional Moslem men, in every task and enterprise, to unprecedented competition from women.

The negative concomitants of such competition were obvious: the male's role-monopolies, and hence his status and authority, both in the household and in society, would be conclusively broken.[139] But the positive concomitants, while less apparent, could be equally if not more important. New female roles would deprive men of the traditional haven of unquestioned acceptance and su-periority, thus goading them, through a sense of shame or threat, to keep pace with female achievements, in labor performance, in the acquisition of new skills, or in the elimination of illiteracy.[140] It is indicative of the extent of Soviet expectations that, at some point, hopes were entertained in the communist command structure that Moslem women might help to insure their menfolk's loyal ser-vice in the Red Army: girls would impress young men with their self-sacrifice and courage, and with their readiness to serve as equals in defending the country; mothers would refuse to hide and coddle malingering sons and would encourage them to join the army; wives would expose and divorce draft-dodgers.[141]

[138] For some sharply argued cases, see Shirman, *KP*, 4, 1927, pp. 73-80; cf. Nukhrat, *OZV*, pp. 71-74; Liubimova, *VPG*, pp. 51-53; Pal'vanova, *DSV*, p. 92; Michurina, *Ka*, 10-11, 1926, p. 83.

[139] See especially Shirman, *KP*, 4, 1927, pp. 75-77.

[140] See especially Nukhrat, *RN*, 3(36), 1933, esp. p. 54; cf. V. N. Petrova, *Bor'ba za Khlopok*, 1-2, 1934, pp. 34-37; and Liubimova, *VPG*, p. 71. For specific examples of such expectations concerning other spheres of action, based on first-hand observation in Turkmenistan, see Karpov, *SS*, 11(28), 1928, pp. 61-69 (esp. p. 66), and *SS*, 6(35), 1929, pp. 64-68 (esp. p. 67); Karimova, *Ka*, 3, 1929, p. 43; Liubimova, *Ka*, 10, 1927, pp. 56-57; Krylov, *SS*, 5(70), 1932, pp. 113, 115; Gladovskii, *SS*, 5(34), 1929, pp. 166-69; Amosov, *Ka*, 14, 1929, pp. 26-27.

[141] See, e.g., *PV*, 7.25.1931, p. 1; *PV*, 7.15.1931, pp. 1, 3; cf. *PV*, 9.2.1931, p. 3. While these illustrations are from the early 1930's (involving appeals to Moslem women during the first large-scale military recruitment

In this sense, women's large-scale arrival as competitors in society and economy was expected to compound the emotional pressures upon the whole male population, making it necessary for men to seek new—that is, Soviet—criteria of self-assertion, self-esteem, competence, and achievement, and hence stimulating their overall performance in the Soviet system. It is safe to assume that there was a tie-in between these expectations and the growing impatience, on the part of Russian communists, with the level of cooperation and performance of Moslem males. Earlier evaluations of these men's attitudes to work had, after all, been scathing: in the judgment of Soviet (especially female) organizers, Central Asian males (particularly those with recent ties to the nomadic way of life) were more partial to the dream-life of sensualists and warriors than to the exertions of heavy labor.[142]

As Moscow's demands for sweeping economic mobilization of the entire country hardened, the sense of irritation and impatience concerning the performance of Moslem men, an attitude verging on contempt, came into the open. "The Soviet Union is a land of tempo! . . . " declared *Pravda Vostoka*, the party's main Russian-language newspaper in the region. "An end must be put [in Central Asia] to the inveterate Eastern sloth, to the [natives'] interminable scratching and groaning. . . ."[143] It would seem that Moslem women were expected to help in moving things in the right direction.

Implications for Recruitment of Political and Politically Relevant Cadres

The attraction of Moslem women to the Soviet fold permits, and is in turn predicated on, the recruitment among them of political, administrative, and professional cadres. These cadres can be of immediate help in reliably staffing and expanding the network of Soviet influence and control, including the new system of communications, health, education, and welfare. They also dramatize the new relations of the sexes, and can serve directly as sharp political tools, assisting deliberately and actively in the fragmentation of tradition. Thus, Moslem women can be unique agents as well as

---

campaign in Central Asia), there is reason to suppose that such hopes were entertained in the mid-1920's; see, e.g., Nukhrat, *Stepnoi Skaz*, pp. 76-79, where some of these themes are apparent.

[142] See the section on "Economic Activities" in Chapter Three.

[143] L. Lench in *PV*, 2.14.1930, p. 3.

catalysts[144] *in the overall revolution of modernization, and in the shaping of new foci of socio-political integration under the auspices of a revolutionary regime.*

As a corollary, the endowment of Moslem women with unprecedented rights and roles in all spheres of social action may be expected to elicit their exceptional gratitude and cooperation. The reason for this is that such endowment would take place entirely under Soviet auspices, and women's training, organization, and socialization could thus be substantially de novo. *This should allow the revolutionary regime exceptionally broad leeway in the allocation of values, skills, resources, and manpower, in the implantation of new organizational forms in society and economy, and in the overall coordination of initiatives called for by both modernization and control.*

At first glance, it might seem all too self-evident to emphasize this set of expectations as a distinct and separate dimension of Soviet views. Also, it might appear to add little to the desiderata expressed by Soviet elites in other contexts. There is reason to suppose, however, that such a formulation of attitudes, even though overlapping with others to some extent, did play an important role in the evolution of official beliefs and programs in Central Asia. It did so primarily in connection with a distinct organizational dilemma, a dilemma perceived here by the regime rather more sharply than in other parts of the Soviet Union.

We know that the notion of cadres as the fulcrum of mobilization, revolution, and control was central in the Soviet belief-system. But it is precisely the quest for reliable cadres that turned out to be extremely problematical in Central Asia—far more so than in

---

[144] Gerald Sumida, a colleague at the Center of International Studies at Princeton University, has expressed some reservations on this account. As he sees it, the concurrent use of the terms "agent" and "catalyst" in this context may involve some contradictions. For example, if commonly accepted definitions of these terms are adhered to, agents of change are themselves transformed either before or during the overall process of transformation, whereas catalysts of change remain unchanged while inducing the transformation of a particular environment. This is unquestionably so. But in using both terms here, I wish to emphasize the dichotomy in Soviet expectations concerning precisely this issue. As we shall see, some Bolshevik (especially female) organizers were genuinely interested in changing the status of Moslem women in the course of transforming the entire Islamic milieu. Others (particularly men) were not averse to using Moslem women merely as catalysts of an especially delimited revolutionary process, wherein the tasks of female emancipation were distinctly subordinate to the imperatives of power and control.

172

Slavic regions, of course; but more so even than in such other pre-dominantly traditional milieus as Georgia, Armenia, and Azer-baidzhan. Unlike in these locales, the revolutionary process in Central Asia antedating the Soviet arrival failed to generate a stratum of cadres whose size, quality of commitment, and degree of prior interaction with Bolshevik revolutionaries was significant enough to provide the new regime with immediate political anchorage. Here, then, social factors coalesced with those of ethnicity and culture to make the problem of cadres especially acute. Here, cadres were scarce not only as cutting edges of the new order but even as elements to adorn the elaborately conceived façades of local autonomy, façades considered to be imperative by Moscow in the overall system of rule. In short, cadres were scarce (and in some areas nonexistent) for purposes of revolution as well as of what came to be referred to as nativization (*korenizatsiia*): the process of staffing the new apparatuses of modernization and control with natives to an extent sufficient to make the new order more comprehensible, acceptable, and hence legitimate at the grassroots, but not great enough to endanger the mainstays of centralized rule. It was in this context that some Soviet organizers (including rather influential ones) came to envision the role of Moslem women as especially promising.

Soviet arguments to this effect evolved on several levels. One of them concerned the need for conduits to the female masses as such. Just about without exception, responsible officials of the party's Women's Department, in Moscow and in Central Asia, agreed: only specifically female cadres could contact and mobilize the bulk of the region's women; to be at all persuasive at the grassroots, these cadres had to be not only female but also native or otherwise acceptable on ethnic or cultural grounds; without such an activist core, it was foolhardy to expect that any of the projected enterprises concerning women's role in revolutionary change would ever get off the ground. The terms used to express this need were quite suggestive. As a number of the regime's high-echelon female emissaries in Central Asia—including Liubimova, Shimko, Niurina, Smirnova, and Nukhrat—saw it, the Soviet state had to place a high priority on the development of specifically female cadres here because only such cadres could serve as the regime's "tongue" at the grassroots, as its "mouthpieces" and "conductors."[145]

[145] See Liubimova, *Ka*, 10, 1927, pp. 55-56; Shimko, *Ka*, 12, 1925, p. 67; Smirnova, *Ka*, 10, 1928, pp. 81-82; Nukhrat, *Ka*, 10, 1928, pp. 75-78, and

Specifically, a modest investment in training Moslem women—
who, together with local farmhands and poor peasants, were regarded as potentially the most reliable stratum—could be expected
to yield a harvest of cadres serving at least in twin capacities. For
example, needed specialists in the rural hinterland (agronomists
and veterinarians as well as teachers and nurses) might be expected, because of their former status and new capabilities, to double as "social activists,"[146] as the regime's first real "scouts" in the
countryside.[147]

Native professionals and activists could do so not only because
they knew the native milieu best, but also because they were especially motivated: having been trained outside their home grounds,
they would yearn to return to help their people with new skills.
Moreover, as Arkhincheev[148] put it, for such an activist—"one who
had gotten used from diapers on to the poverty and deprivations"
of the traditionalist hinterland, and one who would be received with
pride and joy by kinsmen and friends—neither work nor life would
be "especially difficult . . . in just about any out-of-the-way, god-
forsaken corner of the native land."[149] By the same token, Russians
and other Europeans could hardly be useful in such a milieu, in
that they were aliens here in more ways than one. Thus, the training of indigenous activists would carry an added benefit: it would
make it less necessary to "import" large non-native contingents of
unsuitable, unwilling, and, in any case, sparse cadres to the Central
Asian hinterland.[150]

The notion of cadres as conduits—as elements whose development had to precede rather than merely accompany or follow social
mobilization, and without whom general mobilization was itself unthinkable—was related, in the Soviet view, to the notion of cadres

---

Ka, 19, 1929, pp. 34-38; Niurina, *Ka*, 4, 1925, pp. 79-80; Niurina, *Ka*, 5-6,
1929, pp. 22-25.

[146] See Arkhincheev, *SS*, 2(43), 1930, pp. 105, 107, 11.

[147] *Bezb* (news.), 10, 1928, p. 5.

[148] Unfortunately, without access to party archives, it is not feasible at
this time to reliably determine Arkhincheev's status and background. His
contributions to party journals in the 1920's show him as a serious, able,
quite inventive, and apparently authoritative analyst of ethnic politics in
the U.S.S.R.

[149] Arkhincheev, *SS*, 2(43), 1930, p. 111.

[150] Cf. Kozlovskii, *SS*, 11(64), 1931, pp. 94-98 (especially p. 94).

174

as models. This seemed especially important with respect to Moslem women, whose ordained status made it extremely difficult for them to visualize themselves as full-scale participants and prime actors in public life. In these circumstances, the recruitment of female cadres was important not just for the fulfillment of specific operational tasks but, perhaps more significantly at the outset, for setting an example, for dramatizing the new relations of the sexes as well as the new roles a woman could play. For field-organizers of the party's Women's Department in Central Asia, female cadres had to project to female masses a new sense of authority, creativity, and dignity as well as of maximum exertion, disciplined service, and practical accomplishment. Only native women could do this, and only if they were trained for and placed in genuinely creative and authoritative positions.[151]

By implication, it seemed impossible to conceive of female mobilization except in stages. The first and crucial task had to be the investment of time and resources in training carefully selected native women for multi-purpose functions: as representatives and agents of the new state, as interpreters of its objectives at the grassroots, as conscious catalysts of required change, and as professional cadres staffing the new institutional framework, thus helping to shape new foci of socio-political integration under Soviet auspices.[152]

This set of arguments intersected at many points with another one, impinging on the entire issue of *korenizatsiia*,[153] the nativization of the Soviet apparatus among ethnic minorities. This was not merely a matter of solving the problems of revolutionary access and leverage in a traditional milieu by finding suitable agents and catalysts for this purpose. Perhaps more important, it had to do with the problem of implementing a program of ethnic balancing in the

---

[151] For references to the themes of potency, creativity, and dignity, see, e.g., Zavarian, *Ka*, 6, 1926, p. 70; Niurina, *Ka*, 4, 1925, p. 79. For comments on specific positions of authority and accomplishment see Mostovaia, *Ka*, 2, 1929, p. 35, and Nukhrat, *RN*, 3(36), 1933, p. 55. For arguments on the need for women to portray female roles on stage and in selected social situations, see Pal'vanova, *DSV*, pp. 66, 91; Moskalev, *Uzbechka*, p. 44; Liubimova, *VPG*, p. 43.

[152] For explicit or implicit indications of such reasoning, see the preceding five footnotes as well as Seifi, *Ka*, 4, 1925, p. 73; Zavarian, *Ka*, 12, 1925, p. 31; Vinogradov, *RN*, 4-5, 1930, p. 136; Nukhrat, *Ka*, 3, 1927, pp. 50-54.

[153] From the Russian term *koren'*, root.

Soviet Union. Such a program, including at least the symbols of federalism, ethno-cultural pluralism, and proportional representation, had to be both effective and safe. It had to be effective in the sense of sufficiently appealing to at least some politically relevant segments of the local population, thus furthering the legitimation of the Soviet regime; and safe in the sense of precluding the evolution of local institutions into agencies of genuine ethnic bargaining, self-determination, and self-rule. Moscow was in no mood to permit experiments that would in any way jeopardize the Bolshevik principle of rigidly centralized authority and, concomitantly, threaten Russian presence in Asian borderlands.

It should be useful to reconstruct here the basic thrust of Soviet reasoning, as it pertained both to the problem as a whole and to the potential role of Moslem women in dealing with some of the attendant issues. That *korenizatsiia*, in some form, would be imperative was beyond question.[154] What was at issue concerned the manner and tempo of introducing native personnel in Central Asia's political and administrative framework, and the criteria for selecting and assigning natives at various levels of command. Two basic (and antithetical) proposals were considered in the 1920's. One called for "proportional nativization" of the apparatus; the other, for "functional nativization."

It would seem that, from the point of view of the party's high command, both proposals involved considerable risks. On the one hand, the heedless pursuit of "proportional nativization," in which the percentage of native personnel would correspond to the weight of a locale's native population, could have at least two consequences. It could result in the wholesale eviction of qualified executive and technical personnel—most of it Russian, of course—from the Soviet apparatus, and its replacement by a semi-literate or totally illiterate staff. It could also bring to the levers of power those natives who, because of their former monopoly of knowledge, were technically qualified but politically untrustworthy: those of an inadmissible social background (including the traditional elites) and those with nationalist, and hence potentially separatist, propensities. Concomitantly, proportional nativization would, of course, mean the wholesale eviction from positions of power and influence of politically tested revolutionary elements that had been dispatched to Central Asia from Moscow. The repercussions both for

154 See, e.g., Arkhincheev, *SS*, 2(43), 1930, pp. 98-113; cf. T. Ryskulov. *Kiafiztan* (Moscow, 1935), pp. 134-35; Seifi, *Ka*, 4, 1925, pp. 73-78.

modernization and for control under Soviet auspices could be disastrous.[155]

On the other hand, a rigid adherence to "functional nativization" could be equally dangerous. For function-oriented criteria of personnel-selection would emphasize with cold objectivity the requisites of, and qualifications for, a particular job. Under the circumstances, hardly any natives at all would stand a chance of being admitted to the apparatus for the foreseeable future. As a result, the predominance of "European" elements in the organs of Soviet rule—and the continued overlordship of Great Russian chauvinists —would be institutionalized.[156] It was not difficult to visualize the effect of such a policy both on native sensibilities at home and on the perceptions of colonized peoples abroad. Neither was it difficult to guess that this policy would vitiate altogether Soviet attempts to gain access to the traditional milieu.

In retrospect, it is obvious that Arkhincheev was indicating the outlines of an officially favored compromise solution when he suggested what a proper "scheme of organizational methods" should be like. In brief, such a scheme had to recognize, among other things, the need for a decisive shift from a "national" towards a "social" principle for nativization. Not just natives but only those of a desirable social background were to be attracted to the apparatus. Who would, in this respect, be most suitable, given the nature of Central Asian societies? Arkhincheev's answer clearly took its cue from other current proposals concerning the role of Moslem women in revolutionizing their traditional milieu. He suggested that the most desirable native social strata were farmhands, poor peasants, and women.[157]

What of the fact that it was precisely these social segments that had had least exposure to literacy, social participation, and political involvement? Would this lack of previous exposure not make them, obviously, least prepared for political, administrative, and

---

[155] For a clear-cut example of such reasoning see Arkhincheev, *SS*, 2 (43), 1930, pp. 101-102.

[156] Ibid., especially pp. 103-104.

[157] Ibid., pp. 105-107. The bracketing of women with farmhands and poor peasants seemed to draw its inspiration not only from the inferior social status which all presumably shared but also from the reasoning of many of the party's organizers in the field: especially tailored initiatives concerning Moslem women were bound, for a number of reasons, to attract young and poor native males to the Soviet fold (see the *third* and *fifth* set of themes developed in this chapter).

177

managerial positions? The answer was twofold. For one thing, because they lacked preparedness, these segments had to be mobilized and trained for appropriate roles gradually, and had, in effect, to be apprenticed to Russians in positions of leadership or special skill. In turn, given the length of time such a process required, it was both necessary and just to retain the bulk of Russian cadres (leading, executive, and technical) for an unspecified period in all crucial spheres, certainly in all commanding positions.[158]

It seems certain that the assumptions underlying this conclusion were closely related to those held by communist organizers in other contexts of revolutionary strategy in Central Asia. The unstated (as against official) reasoning was apparently this: farmhands, poor peasants, and especially women were traditionally the most disadvantaged social strata in the region; their social inferiority not only made them politically acceptable to the Communist Party but also insured that they would be especially grateful to the Soviet regime for providing them with unprecedented rights and opportunities; in turn, gratitude and inexperience would make them all the more disposed to accept any, including distinctly subordinate or purely symbolic, posts, and all the less willing and able to question the authority of their Russian elder brothers; they were likely to understand better than others that the Russians were extending not merely a "leading" but a "helping" hand.[159]

Such an approach, then, appeared to be the best way to break out of what came to be perceived as a "vicious circle" of conflicting imperatives in Central Asia. Niurina, Smirnova, and Nukhrat[160] saw this in very concrete terms. For them, staffing low-echelon posts operationally closest to the grassroots with natives, and posts dealing directly with local female masses with native women, promised to be the first significant step in the legitimation of the Soviet regime: it would cut the ground from under malicious anti-Soviet whispering campaigns apparently rife throughout the region, break through the natives' sullen refusal to establish contacts with "aliens" and "infidels," and at last begin to instill trust towards the agencies of the new order.[161] Kalinin, too, had this in mind, and

[158] Arkhincheev, *SS*, 2(43), 1930, especially pp. 110-11.

[159] For strong hints of such a line of argument, see ibid., pp. 98-113; cf. Vel'tner, *RN*, 12, 1931, pp. 29 ff.

[160] All of them were highly-placed officials in the party's Women's Department active in Central Asia.

[161] Niurina, *Ka*, 5-6, 1929, p. 23; cf. Smirnova, *Ka*, 8, 1929, p. 27; Nukhrat, *Ka*, 3, 1927, pp. 50-54 (esp. p. 52).

178

counseled Moscow accordingly. After visiting Central Asian villages in 1925, the *de facto* President of the U.S.S.R. was apparently deeply concerned about the elusiveness of the traditional countryside to Soviet manipulation, about the gap that existed between Soviet structures and local communities—as well as between the natives' public declarations (for the benefit of visiting dignitaries) and private behavior. For him, as for many others in the Soviet apparatus, there was a direct correlation between the extent of female political mobilization and the consolidation of the communist control system. As he put it: "Our rule [in Central Asia] will never be solid if [the local] women will not participate in it. . . ."[162]

Apparently, all these proposals and expectations were based at least in part on a central assumption concerning the response of Moslem women to Soviet initiatives. While political expediency must have argued against the explicit statement of this assumption in public, it was more or less obviously implicit in most of the arguments about female roles in revolutionary strategy.

In reconstructed form, those arguments ran thus: in all respects, the mobilization of Moslem women involved their movement from typically marginal and dependent to central and responsible positions in society, from typically non-participatory to participatory roles in public arenas. Their gratitude to the sponsor of such a dramatic shift was but one of the responses to be expected. The other had to do with the concrete circumstances of the process of female mobilization. Virtually every dimension of this process—be it the elimination of illiteracy, acquisition of technical and managerial skills, participation in new voluntary associations, or political recruitment at high levels of command—had to involve training and socialization that was literally *de novo*, and that would take place entirely under the auspices of the Soviet regime. It was to be expected that, under these circumstances, the revolutionary agent would be in close control of the inputs in a client's new world, and that the client would be correspondingly receptive to both the forms and contents of these inputs. In short, Moslem women were bound to be especially receptive to new values and beliefs as much as to new economic tasks and organizational arrangements. This would make the recruitment of female cadres in Central Asia an

---

[162] M. I. Kalinin, *Statii i Rechi*, Book II, pp. 14-16, as cited in Pal'vanova, *DSV*, p. 144; cf. Liubimova, *VPG*, pp. 65-67; and Prishchepchik, *Ka*, 12, 1925, p. 65.

extremely valuable component of the regime's overall designs. It would, at the very least, allow the new state rather broad leeway in experimenting with various approaches to social engineering, and in coordinating the initiatives pertaining to the process of modernization as well as to the system of control. This line of reasoning indeed appeared to be strongly implicit in specific arguments concerning a number of spheres where Central Asian women were due to actively participate: in the formation of producers' and consumers' cooperatives;[163] in the collectivization of agriculture;[164] in the expansion of cotton crops;[165] in the new educational process;[166] in Soviet-sponsored voluntary associations;[167] and in politics.[168] What all these arguments assumed, then, was that crucial organizational and developmental tasks in Central Asia would benefit greatly from tapping what was seen as the unique revolutionary potential of Moslem women: their likely disposition to identify strongly with the Soviet system, to perceive it as both powerful and liberating in nature, to be responsive to its appeals and designs, and to support it staunchly and uncritically.

Implications for Revolutionary Potentials Abroad

To revolutionize the status and redefine the roles and opportunities of women among Russia's Moslems is to compound the power of attraction of the Soviet system upon other traditional societies—and societies sharing ethnic identity or cultural and his-

---

[163] See, e.g., Nukhrat, *Ka*, 1, 1928, especially pp. 55-56.

[164] For implicit as well as explicit expectations in this respect, see Amosov, *Ka*, 14, 1929, p. 26; Burshtina, *RN*, 75(5), 1936, p. 34; Moskalev, *Uzbechka*, pp. 38-39; Nukhrat, *Ka*, 1, 1928, pp. 53-56; Maksimova, *Ka*, 6, 1928, pp. 93-95. For a case in which an appeal to women was expected to be of help in the nationalization of water wells, see Pavlenko, *Puteshestvie*, pp. 120-37.

[165] See, e.g., Nukhrat, *RN*, 3(36), 1933, pp. 53-54. Cf. the decision of the Ekonomsektor of Sredazburo Ts.K. *VKP(b)* "On measures to increase female labor in cotton-growing," as cited in Khronika, "Ob uvelichenii zhenskogo truda v khlopkovom khoziaistve," *Khlop. Delo*, 9, 1930, pp. 1125-26. Cf. also Nukhrat, *VS*, 6, 1933, pp. 8-9; and Bauman's speech, echoing Stalin's earlier dicta, at the 17th Party Congress in *Semnadtsatyi S'ezd, Zasedanie chetvertoe*, p. 107.

[166] See, e.g., Pismennyi, *RK*, 10, 1928, pp. 11-20.

[167] Such as women's clubs. See Prishchepchik, *Ka*, 12, 1925, pp. 63-64 and *Ka*, 9, 1926, pp. 76-78; Zavarian, *Ka*, 6, 1926, pp. 68-69 and *Ka*, 12, 1925, pp. 27-28; Nukhrat, *Ka*, 8, 1927, pp. 19-22; Niurina, *Ka*, 4, 1925, pp. 80-81; Anisimova, *KP*, 1, 1927, pp. 75-77.

[168] See Nukhrat, *OZV*, p. 82.

torical experience with Central Asia's peoples—outside Soviet borders. The buildup of egalitarian and high-achievement imagery in the realms of youth and sex spurs revolutionary ferment in the colonial and semicolonial world, and opens up, thereby, unprecedented potentials for the formation, in that world, of a revolutionary and modernizing elite and élan.

In some ways, it was perhaps most congenial for proponents of female emancipation in Central Asia to couch their argument in approximately these terms. Both Lenin and Stalin had indicated in no uncertain terms their intention to make Central Asia into a showcase of Soviet achievements for the entire East. They had made clear their conviction that the example of the Moslem borderlands would help to spark or accelerate revolutionary processes as well as wars of national liberation in traditional and colonial milieus.[169] The Bolsheviks' burgeoning hopes on this account clearly derived from at least two sources: the failure of communist revolutions in the capitalist-industrial West, and the expected shift of the global revolutionary struggle to what was presumably a more propitious locale, the colonized, underdeveloped East, the "weak link" in the West's imperial structure.

Thus, viewed in general terms by an authoritative Soviet analyst, female roles in Central Asia's developmental pattern promised to underscore the latter's distinctive feature: its intended service as a "model for the realization of the theoretical [propositions formulated] by Marx, Engels, and Lenin and [incorporated] in the program of the Comintern. . . ." These propositions, Vel'tner suggested, had anticipated "the possibility of noncapitalist development of lands where the transition from feudalism to capitalism was not completed, where tribal survivals were still strong, and where class-differentiation was as yet at a low level [of development]." But the very nature of such a milieu also required the recognition of two interlocking needs in revolutionary strategy. On the one hand, "the historical peculiarities of [the current stage of Central Asia's] cultural and economic development [had perforce left] their imprint on the development of mass organizations" in that region: they necessitated flexible, especially tailored means in furthering the overall organizational revolution. On the other hand, the mo-

---

[169] For Stalin's hopes on this account, where Central Asian development as a whole was concerned, see his letter to Tadzhik communists of March 15, 1925, in Lenin and Stalin, *Statii i Rechi o Srednei Azii i Uzbekistane* (Tashkent, 1940), p. 223. Lenin's notions are briefly commented on in Chapters One and Two.

bilization and political recruitment of Moslem women was of "particular importance" precisely because of its promise in fashioning the new means, thus making the Soviet developmental model in Central Asia not only workable at home but applicable in traditional societies abroad.[170]

Niurina was rather more specific and direct in this respect. She seemed to express the judgment of many of her comrades in the party's Women's Department when she said, on the eve of a major turn of the campaign for female mobilization in the region:

> Our work in the [Soviet] East is assuming now [in 1925], in the present international situation, an extraordinarily important role. It is not by sheer accident that the Eastern question is now at the center of world politics. It is no longer subject to any doubt that the [present trends] in the colonial and semi-colonial countries make them into virtually the weakest and most vulnerable points of the [Western] imperial system. It can, by the same token, no longer be doubted that the example of the Soviet Eastern Republics is playing a far from unimportant role in fashioning the revolutionary climate in the non-Soviet East. . . . Our Eastern Republics are bordering directly on a number of [such] Eastern lands (Persia, Afghanistan, and others). Every veil that is torn away [from our women's faces], every Uzbek or Turkmen woman who is drawn into a soviet, or recruited into the party or the komsomol, or even into a school, becomes a revolutionizing factor in those foreign lands.[171]

*   *   *

The eight sets of themes developed here constitute the spectrum of insights, proposals, and commitments apparent in Soviet ranks in the 1920's. They unquestionably showed a high degree of awareness of reciprocity between female mobilization and virtually all other aspects of revolutionary modernization in a Moslem traditional society. But, as we shall see, they were not uniformly realistic, and not necessarily consistent with each other. Nor could they be implemented immediately and to best advantage. Perceptions of revolutionary needs and opportunities could not be automatically translated into coherent revolutionary strategies.

[170] The direct quotes are from Vel'tner, *RN*, 12, 1931, p. 29. The line of reasoning as it concerns specifically Moslem women is strongly implicit in Vel'tner's overall argument.

[171] Niurina, *Ka*, 4, 1925, pp. 78-79, 83; cf. Ishkova, *Ka*, 11, 1928, p. 62.

PART THREE
Early Soviet Actions, 1924–1927

INTRODUCTION

Toward a Strategy of Engineered Revolution

REVOLUTIONARY ACTION AS INSURGENCY BY AN INCUMBENT

THE multifaceted justifications for work with Moslem women were, of course, designed to secure the party's acquiescence in ideologically unorthodox initiatives, as well as its maximum support with cadres and funds. But, if the party's high command came to see the promise of such action, and accordingly proceeded to set in motion a number of initiatives on this account, it also came to perceive sharply the dangers implicit in such an undertaking. To attempt a sudden and full-fledged mobilization and emancipation of Moslem women, to stage an all-out, undifferentiated assault on the realities and symbols of sexual apartheid and female inferiority in a traditional Islamic world, was to initiate what was perhaps the most overtly illegitimate action in that world.

The perception of, and responses to, this dilemma undoubtedly played a crucial role in the evolution of Soviet approaches to female mobilization in Central Asia. Concerned ever more concretely with the extension of Soviet influence from urban hubs to a vast countryside, with the creation of reliable access routes to the grassroots of Central Asia's societies, with the subversion of established native solidarities, and, simultaneously, with laying a groundwork for an efficient mobilization system, the Soviet regime found itself in need to strike a balance among a host of conflicting imperatives. While these were subject to repeated questioning and revision, and were affected not only by the Central Asian milieu but also by the ferocious struggle of wills and views inside the party, *the action-scheme that evolved in the process was analogous to insurgency— albeit insurgency generated and controlled by the incumbent and, therefore, governed both by the requirements of social revolution and by the imperatives of incumbency itself.*

As such, insurgency by an incumbent could not but entail some inherent paradoxes. In Soviet Central Asia it was designed to set in motion a course of tensions, conflicts, and selective violence, and

185

hence an upheaval in the traditional system of values, customs, relationships, and roles within the existing structures of society. In effect fundamentally reversing the essential order of Marxist expectations, it marked an incumbent's calculated effort to induce insurgent attitudes, an effort calculated to induce a pervasive sense of alienation from traditional commitments, orientations, and modes of life, and a commensurate attraction to radically new ones: those furthered by victorious revolutionaries. Basically, then, this process had twin purposes: to induce a psychological and organizational revolution at the nerve-centers of a relatively intact social order, and to consolidate and legitimize the incumbent's power. It turned out to be of fundamental importance that the imperatives of insurgency could not be reconciled with the imperatives of incumbency, since both sets of imperatives were generated, and needed to be weighed, by one and the same party: the incumbent revolutionary Soviet regime.

Alternatives for a Strategy of Engineered Revolution: Revolutionary Legalism, Administrative Assault, and Systematic Social Engineering

Not all of the relevant implications of this dilemma were anticipated by the party's organizers, and some were anticipated with greater sensitivity than others. Moreover, some of the consequences, while anticipated quite perceptively by a number of the party's field-workers in Central Asia, were either under-estimated or deliberately ignored by leading echelons on ideological grounds, and were acted upon only after precipitous political initiatives revealed just how disastrous the consequences could be. Nonetheless, Soviet initiatives tended to order themselves into a definite pattern. Soviet experience suggests three paths to making a revolution beyond the mere winning of political incumbency, which may be viewed as direct approaches to social engineering.[1] These are "revolutionary legalism," "administrative assault," and "systematic social engineering." While this typology involves a rather high level of abstraction, it reflects quite closely the predilections, commitments, and actions entertained in Soviet ranks in the early experimental stages of revolutionary transformation. The three strategies

[1] For a discussion of what I consider to have been indirect approaches to social engineering, see the second section ("Problems of Access and Influence: Initial Approaches") in Chapter Two.

of planned social change may be conceived as three main steps in a learning process on the part of Soviet revolutionary elites, a process with what were at first rudimentary though by no means negligible feedback mechanisms. This process led, over a relatively short period of time, to repeated assessments of costs and payoffs of a particular strategy, and to a periodic quest for courses of action that would combine optimal fulfillment of Soviet goals with minimal risk, given the resources available to the regime.

Although these approaches were at no time considered or pursued exclusively, in neat separation from each other, and *in toto* by Soviet elites, and the substantive, logical, and chronological overlapping between them was very extensive, the three courses of action came to represent three identifiable nuances of Soviet points of view. Each of these emphasized a different mix of perceived imperatives and ordained moves. Needless to stress, we are dealing here with ideal types and analytical constructs, and not with rigorously delimited historical stages. Our terms for them derive very closely from Soviet terminology in this and related contexts, involving, respectively, *revoliutsionnaia zakonnost'* (literally, revolutionary legality), *administrativnyi naskok* (literally, head-on assault by administrative fiat), and *sistematicheskaia rabota* (literally, systematic work).

The three approaches may be distinguished from each other on the basis of the following criteria: a) time perspective; b) basic operational objectives; c) means of implementation. The typology of these approaches is presented schematically in a summary table on the following page.

The course of revolutionary legalism tended to rely primarily on the superimposition of a new judicial system for the routinization of revolutionary norms in a traditional society.[2] By competing with, and ultimately supplanting, traditional adjudicative institutions, and by championing and systematically applying the principle of

---

[2] Useful accounts of Soviet perceptions, action, and experience in the legal sphere in Central Asia may be found in Kryl'tsov, *SP*, 5(29), 1927, pp. 130-38; Mokrinskii, *SP*, 3(27), 1927, esp. pp. 103-17; Fioletov, *SP*, 1 (25), 1927, pp. 132-46, and *NV*, 23-24, 1928, pp. 204-17; Akopov, *RN*, 4-5, 1930, pp. 58-69; Shokhor, *SS*, 8-9(13-14), 1927, pp. 94-114; Suleimanova, *SGP*, 3, 1949, pp. 61-69; and 10, 1948, pp. 65-69; Dosov, *Ka*, 5, 1928, pp. 29-32; K., *VS*, 46, 1928, pp. 19-20; Bil'shai, *RZVS*, pp. 110 ff.; *BSE*, Vol. 25, 1932, pp. 252-55. A general historical account in English is provided in Park, *Bolshevism,* pp. 221-37.

CRITERIA	Revolutionary Legalism	Administrative Assault	Systematic Social Engineering
A *Time perspective*	intermediate	short-term	long-term
B *Basic operational objective*	retention of power and incremental change	cataclysmic revolutionary overturn	institutionalized social revolution
C *Means of implementation*			
Primary emphasis on the selection of means	avoidance of risks	payoffs irrespective of risks	balancing payoffs and risks
Primary emphasis on the justification of action	normative	dogmatic	instrumental
Primary focus of action	provision of legal rights	violation of traditional taboos	redefinition of roles and opportunities
Primary emphasis on initiating social mobilization	legislation	command and conscription	involvement
Expected basis for mass-response	adherence to rules	outrage and obedience	self-interest and achievement
Primary emphasis on the consolidation of commitment	prescription	conversion	socialization
Expected mode of breakdown of the old order	reform	destruction	subversion and atrophy

equality of the sexes before the law, the new judicial system was expected to set in motion a fullfledged revolutionary process—without, at the same time, affecting the stability of Soviet rule.[3] Such a process was seen as developing, at a certain point, a momentum of its own, one that would ultimately help to change traditional beliefs, values, customs, and ties beyond recognition. In this sense,

[3] See, e.g., Suleimanova, *SGP*, 10 (Oct.), 1948, pp. 68-69.

female emancipation was viewed primarily as a juridical problem to be solved by a stress on strict legalistic consistency.[4]

The course of administrative assault reflected a radical impatience with the potentially slow, long-term implantation and routinization of new behavioral norms by way of legal and other mediating institutions. It also reflected a suspicion that these institutions might be relatively autonomous and not easily manipulable.[5] Thus, it involved a preference to engage traditional society head-on, to "storm" it. It called for reliance on administratively inspired mass action, i.e., direct action in response to direct command from above, reflecting a revolution's "heroic" as against "economic" ethic.[6] Such action, involving primarily massive, public, and dramatic violations of traditional taboos pertaining especially to women (beginning with induced mass-unveiling and enforced sexual desegregation on the streets), was expected to have a shock-effect on traditional mores and institutions. In the process of such a widespread and simultaneous combustion on political cue, prevailing "feudal-patriarchal" attitudes, customs, and relationships were expected to be short-circuited, ushering in a "cultural revolution" and causing the walls of tradition to crumble virtually overnight.

The course of systematic social engineering reflected a realistic appreciation both of the narrowness and limitations of revolutionary legalism, and of the pitfalls and illusions implicit in administrative assault.[7] It called for systematic evaluation, exploitation, and coordination of diverse courses of action: legal, associational, cultural, and economic.[8] It involved an aggressive search for, on the one hand, means to optimize the conditions of insurgency, modernization, and development, and, on the other hand, ways to min-

---

[4] Clearly implicit in Krupskaia's *rejection* of such a position; see Krupskaia, *Ka,* 12, 1928, p. 7, as well as pp. 5-12, *passim.*

[5] See, e.g., Liubimova, *VPG,* pp. 72-73; Nukhrat, *OZV,* pp. 84-85, 88.

[6] The terms "heroic" and "economic" are Kenneth Boulding's. Even though he uses them in a slightly different context, they seem appropriate here. See his *The Impact of the Social Sciences,* p. 68.

[7] For one of the earliest, as well as most comprehensive and authoritative, Soviet discussions of the imperatives of "systematic work" in Central Asia, see Ar-na, *Ka,* 1, 1928, pp. 57-63; cf. Krupskaia, *Ka,* 12, 1928, pp. 5-12.

[8] See, e.g., the resolution of the *Orgburo Ts.K.,* June 5, 1927, as cited in Pal'vanova, *DSV,* p. 103; cf. decision of Ts.K. *VKP(b).* "O Rabote Partorganizatsii Uzbekistana," (May 25, 1929) as cited in Amosov, *Ka,* 14, 1929, p. 23.

imize the dangers implicit in this process for the incumbent regime. It thus engendered a pragmatic commitment to relatively patient and systematic social action, wherein at least as much time and effort would be devoted to the building of bridges to traditional society, and to the creation of an infra-structure of alternative institutions and opportunities for the meaningful exercise of rights and roles, as to actual and direct confrontation with the traditional system.[9]

In retrospect, the evolution of Soviet policy in Central Asia may be said to have involved a trial-and-error progression from one approach to another: from the first (about 1924-1928), to the second (about 1927-1929), to the third (about 1928-). At first glance, the periodization of these distinct emphases in the commitments of Soviet elites might appear to be misplaced. It is possible to argue, for example, that exactly the opposite was true. Formally, the call for "systematic work," and for avoidance of head-on collision with traditional institutions in Central Asia, was issued by both Lenin and Stalin and was repeatedly endorsed by their lieutenants in the early 1920's. Formally, the order to commence an all-out assault on traditional Moslem beliefs and practices, especially as they pertained to women—the order to set in motion a full-fledged "cultural revolution" in Central Asia—was issued in late 1926, and first implemented on a large scale in March, 1927. Again, formally, a new network of courts and a new and exhaustive code of laws replaced the antecedent Moslem judicial system in September, 1927, and April, 1928, respectively. Further to confuse the issue, some variants of administrative assault not only cropped up in the area both before and after the decreed attempt at cultural revolution, but may be said to have merely foreshadowed the far larger and more inclusive attack on the old order throughout the Soviet Union, an assault that commenced under Stalin's command precisely at the time, i.e., in 1929, when we suggest a rather different operational emphasis was coming to the fore in Central Asia.

A closer look at the record, however, will reveal a considerable disparity between official pronouncements and what we consider to have been the dominant operational commitments in Central Asia. No matter what ambitions Moscow may have had for a cataclysmic revolutionary upheaval in the Moslem borderlands, and for

[9] For some examples of such reasoning, see *BSE*, Vol. 29, 1935, p. 395. For a brief discussion of this approach, see Chapter Nine of this study.

an absolutely homogeneous action-scheme throughout the Soviet Union, a variety of factors vitiated such ambitions. Unanticipated imperatives and problems between 1924 and 1929, pertaining especially to female mobilization, came to assert themselves quite strongly, calling for continuous redefinition of required action. To be sure, these redefinitions were made grudgingly, and were accompanied by a ferocious (though not always publicized) struggle of wills and views in communist ranks. Nonetheless, as we shall see, the reassessments in the latter half of the 1920's came to reflect a goodly measure of recognition, on the part of the Soviet elites, of the limits of both revolutionary legalism and administrative assault in Central Asia, and included significant if quiet concessions to some of the salient propositions immanent in systematic social engineering.

FIVE · *Toward Radical Judicial Reform: The Pattern of Revolutionary Legalism*

DETERMINANTS AND OBJECTIVES

THE drive to supplant the system of Moslem traditional adjudication, including its structures and norms, derived its impetus from a number of sources. Most obviously, the early Soviet emphasis on attaining complete homogeneity of the state's legal and administrative underpinnings throughout the land could not but mean the elimination of any and all deviant and competitive subunits. By definition, local Islamic and customary legal institutions, as part and parcel of the prerevolutionary system of justice, could no more than others be exempted from this process. If anything, the very nature of these institutions made them especially dangerous from the Soviet point of view, since they tended to regulate all too many aspects of human relationships in the area. In this perspective, as pointed out by Park, such institutions were not only "unsuited to the requirements of Soviet policy relating to the administration of justice"; they were seen as "weapon[s] utilized by the Moslem ruling classes to oppress and exploit the native poor and to preserve the remnants of the crumbling feudal-patriarchal mode of life." As such, then, they were indeed "a barrier separating the Soviet authority from the Moslem masses and hindering the execution of Bolshevik social objectives." By the same token, they were "an obstacle to the establishment of the unified people's court as the judicial organ of the proletarian dictatorship . . . [and] as a frank agent of class warfare. . . ."[1]

There was here, however, as least one subtle variation of emphasis, one that tended to distinguish the functions of the overall Soviet judicial model from those envisaged specifically for Central Asia,[2]

---

[1] Park, *Bolshevism*, p. 223.

[2] It is regrettable that not a single major Western work on Soviet legal institutions has appraised their functions and operation outside of the Russian (or "generally" Soviet) context, thus blurring some significant distinctions between different milieus.

For some representative general studies of the role of law in the U.S.S.R., see H. J. Berman, *Justice in the U.S.S.R.* (New York, 1963); J. N. Hazard,

and it was apparent especially in the case of family law. As I have pointed out elsewhere,[3] early Soviet legislation concerning family relations, while embodying a number of Marxian postulates, was designed within, and by and large for, European Russia. Most important, in many spheres (such as cohabitation and divorce, as well as female and generational roles and rights in the familial and societal context) Soviet family law was designed to formalize and legitimize at least as much as to encourage a normative and behavioral revolution that was *already* well underway in the Russian milieu. In the case of Soviet Central Asia, however, it became apparent in fairly short order that socio-cultural realities (beginning with the kinship system and interpersonal relations) differed profoundly and called for special ways of approaching the problem of revolutionary transformation. This was not merely a question of devising different laws for a different milieu. It meant, above all, the endowment of Soviet judicial institutions in Central Asia with functions that were rather more specialized than in Russia, functions that were far broader in scope, more significant and autonomous in expected impact, and more sharply focused toward social destruction and reconstruction. In other words, to the extent that the antecedent judicial system was to be uprooted, and Soviet law deliberately used as an instrument of revolutionary change, this process assumed far greater intrinsic significance in Central Asia than in Russia. In Russia, the manipulation and politicization of the judicial realm was designed, by and large, to accelerate and consolidate a revolution in society and culture; in Central Asia, it was expected to help in *inducing* such a revolution in the first place.

In this context, the extirpation of traditional authority relationships and behavioral norms, as well as the emancipation of women and youth, was viewed as primarily a juridical problem, to be solved by a stress on strict legalistic consistency. Obversely, the desired shift in female status was expected to occur primarily as a

---

Law and Social Change in the U.S.S.R. (London, 1953); G. C. Guins, *Soviet Law and Soviet Society* (The Hague, 1954); K. Grzybowski, *Soviet Legal Institutions* (Ann Arbor, 1962). Cf. H. K. Geiger, *The Family in Soviet Russia* (Cambridge, Mass., 1968), *passim*; and A. Kassof (ed.), *Prospects for Soviet Society* (N.Y., 1968), esp. Ch. 5, 14.

[3] See my paper, "Family Law and Social Mobilization in Soviet Central Asia: Some Comparisons with Communist China," read at the Annual Meeting of the Association for Asian Studies, Boston, Mass., March 1969, pp. 4-5.

result of the regime's emphasis upon, and of popular acceptance in Central Asia of, the new legal norms and institutions simply because they were legal. It is in this sense that revolutionary legalism may be characterized, to paraphrase Judith Shklar,[4] as an ethical and political attitude that holds moral and politically requisite conduct to be a matter of rule-following, and moral as well as instrumental relationships to consist of duties and rights determined by rules that are imposed and enforced by revolutionary elites. Specifically, this meant that in Central Asia the revolutionization of rules pertaining to personal status and family relationships, and particularly the legal emancipation of women, was expected to have *sui generis* and highly significant repercussions in virtually all realms of social life. Concurrently, there was to be a dynamic interaction, as well as mutual and cumulative reinforcement, between judicial and societal upheavals. Thus, the institutionalization of unprecedented female rights was seen not just as a powerful boost to female mobilization but as a catalyst undermining both the traditional kinship system and the Islamic-customary legal system itself. In turn, the weakening of traditional adjudication—a highly important element in the cement binding Moslem communities, families, and clans—was expected to unravel still further the social fabric, and to make the existing pattern of authority and roles untenable.

In 1925, the First Congress of the Uzbek Communist Party formally concluded that legal emancipation of Moslem women was an especially urgent task because it was "[intimately] interwoven" with the fundamental requirements of political, cultural, and economic development in the region.[5] In 1926, Zakharian, an astute party organizer among Asian women, carried forward this theme of functional reciprocity, and summed up the characteristic arguments quite precisely. On the one hand, as she saw it, emphasis on new legal rules was crucial in the cause of "the defense of women's interests." On the other hand, however, in Central Asia, unlike in Russia, it was not enough merely to "keep proclaiming sexual equality" in general terms. Here, the peculiarities of economy, society, and way of life both called for and were especially susceptible to a strong drive for legal emancipation of women. In such a milieu, the concrete and deliberate adaptation of new legal rules

[4] See J. Shklar, *Legalism* (Cambridge, Mass., 1964), p. 1.
[5] See Prishchepchik, *Ka*, 12, 1925, p. 63.

194

to actual or potential female grievances was so important (and hence potentially so fruitful) because female rights and roles were critically interdependent[6] with so many realms of the traditional life-style.

Thus, for example, customary land- and water-rights were intimately tied in with traditionally sanctioned marital unions and were, as well, biased in favor of men; the same rights were also, to a large extent, predicated on the institution of *kalym*—the payment of a bride-price as a *condition of forming a family*; rights of inheritance and succession were specifically geared to female inferiority; in part, patterns of marriage and, therefore, of economic activity and interdependence rested heavily on the traditional obligation of widows to marry a husband's brother or relative, and on the obligation of female hired hands to marry their employer if he so desired. Michurina, Akopov, and Kryl'tsov, three of the most important Soviet proponents and analysts of the judicial revolution in Central Asia, saw additional dimensions of such interdependence. For example, customary and religious prescriptions concerning *kalym* both legitimized and made possible a great variety of other traditional relationships, such as patriarchal rule, the preeminence of parental and gerontocratic authority in all decision-making (affecting not only women but youth as a whole), polygamy, and early marriages (including contracted marriages of infants). Similarly, the custom of *kun*—blood vengeance—and its management by aggrieved tribal units under Soviet rule permitted traditional communities to conduct their affairs apart from the Soviet system: conflict-resolution could be secret and private, and could bypass Soviet institutions; the issue of a man's murder by a member of another kin group could be resolved not by retributive killing, but by appropriate payments in money and cattle or by the transfer of a woman to the aggrieved clan, to serve as concubine or wife to the nearest relative of the victim.[7] These arrangements merely underscored the broader dimensions of interdependence between the entire spectrum of customary behavior and the informal traditional pattern of conciliation and adjudication.

Thus, as Zakharian saw it, there were, in this milieu, "deep contradictions between a developing economy and customary and legal

[6] This particular formulation is my own, but it is clearly implicit in Zakharian's overall argument.

[7] See Zakharian, *Ka*, 3, 1926, pp. 42-43; Michurina, *Ka*, 10-11, 1926, p. 81; Kryl'tsov, *SP*, 5(29), 1927, pp. 136, 138; Arkopov, *RN*, 4-5, 1930, p. 62.

norms that are still rooted in a feudal-patriarchal household." It was, consequently, especially important to realize that "the problems of legal emancipation of Eastern women are all the more urgent because they are connected with the entire economic and socio-cultural structure of eastern nationalities; hence, the solution of these problems [will] *ipso facto* serve to untie the bonds that hamper the economic and cultural development of these peoples."[8]

THE DRIVE AGAINST TRADITIONAL LEGAL STRUCTURES

Soviet approaches to revolutionary change through law proceeded on two planes: (1) the decreed abolition of traditional court structures, including religious and customary tribunals, and their replacement by a secular, uniform, centralized, bureaucratic, and hierarchical system of Soviet courts; (2) the decreed abolition of religious and customary law, applying (for the purposes of this study) to personal status and family matters, and their replacement by a secular, egalitarian, uniform, and written code of statutory laws.

In the period between 1918 and 1927 traditional courts were subjected to gradually increasing pressure which included (a) growing competition from a parallel Soviet court structure, (b) separation from sources of material support, (c) infiltration of judicial personnel, and (d) delimitation and successive amputation of jurisdictional realms. In September, 1927, traditional courts were formally proscribed and abolished as legal tribunals.

At first sight, it might seem surprising that a radical, authoritarian regime needed fully ten years to complete its formal moves against traditional courts. The party was, after all, well aware of the crucial role played by these courts in sustaining traditional solidarities and way of life, and in perpetuating the influence of (as well as providing a livelihood for) traditional elites, such as the Moslem clergy and a variety of tribal and village notables.[9] It was fully in keeping with this awareness that draconic moves against Islam and its judicial institutions had been initiated almost immediately after the October Revolution. Yet these initiatives had been

---

[8] Zakharian, *Ka*, 3, 1926, pp. 42-43. Cf. Akopov, *RN*, 4-5, 1930, p. 62; Kryl'tsov, *SP*, 5(29), 1927, pp. 136, 138.

[9] See, e.g., Fioletov, *SP*, 1(25), 1927, pp. 132-40; Sev, *Turkmenovedenie*, 3-4, 1928, pp. 5-20.

196

rescinded in fairly short order, in favor of graduated, carefully phased, and at least initially circumspect pressure.

Among the reasons which led to the deliberate delay, one was clearly paramount. It had much to do with the way the fledgling Soviet regime assessed its capacity for taking risks in a complex, ethnically and culturally alien, and incipiently hostile milieu. Thus, it was found to be grossly imprudent to inflame the sensibilities of the local population by precipitate moves while the Red Army was still in the process of occupying the region, and while the new regime was seeking bases for its own legitimation. The consequences of such imprudence became especially apparent during what came to be known as the *basmachi* revolt in Central Asia (about 1918-1922). Riding on a wave of pent-up popular resentment, *basmachi* leadership (a mixed and unstable array of princely-theocratic, clerical, and tribal elements) could all too easily win a hearing in the countryside by depicting the Soviet regime not just as a foreign occupier but as a despoiler of Islam and of primordial institutions and sentiments.[10] While the armed units of the *basmachi* were ultimately crushed by superior Soviet forces, Moscow was quick to realize that its own timely concessions to traditionalist sensibilities had much to do with the collapse of the revolt in Central Asia and with the general pacification of the countryside.[11]

In the mid-1920's contra-traditional pressures were markedly accelerated, as Moscow manifested a hardening determination to move towards avowed goals. A confluence of factors accounted for that acceleration. The Civil War in Russia was over, and the Soviet Union's international position was relatively secure. The revolt in Central Asia was under control. Central Asia's delimitation into constituent republics was successfully accomplished (in 1924), providing better access through centrally controlled regional apparatuses. With Lenin out of the picture, and his restraining influence on the wane, Stalinist elements were in the ascendancy within the party, while their competitors were in disarray. At the same time, the imperatives of economic development and fundamental

---

[10] See, e.g., Suleimanova, *SGP*, 3, 1949, p. 67; Shokhor, *SS*, 8-9(13-14), 1927, p. 108; Fioletov, *SP*, 1(25), 1927, pp. 141-42; Sulaimanova, *ISGPU*, Vol. I, pp. 501-503.

[11] Useful historical accounts of the *basmachi* revolt may be found in Pipes, *The Formation*, pp. 176-83, 255-60; and in Park, *Bolshevism*, pp. 34-58. Cf. Fainsod, *How Russia Is Ruled*, p. 97.

socio-cultural change were perceived with a fresh sense of urgency, just as the potential role of Moslem women in furthering revolutionary transformation in Central Asia was seen in a new light.

In these circumstances, moves against the traditional court-structures followed each other in rapid succession.[12] While Soviet decrees in 1922 specifically recognized the legal personality and autonomy of traditional courts, thus confirming the existence of a dual legal system in Central Asia, a series of steps in 1923, 1924, and 1926 increasingly subordinated these courts to the parallel apparatus of people's courts which had been initially brought into being at the end of 1917. The subordination became most readily apparent in the allocation of powers of cassation and general supervision, successively, to the region's Council of People's Courts and Soviet Commissariat of Justice.

People's courts gained a further competitive edge when they were subdivided into units serving separately the European and Moslem population. The Moslem units not only conducted their affairs in the native tongue, and were staffed to a large extent with natives, but were explicitly permitted to refer in some cases to the *shariat*, especially if this reference would not clearly contradict the norms of "revolutionary consciousness" or Soviet legislation. To augment this competitive impact, Commissariats of Justice of Central Asian republics created a number of model courts that would show the advantages of the Soviet legal system, and established special bureaus dealing, respectively, with law-related agitation and propaganda and with legal aid.

The position of traditional courts was directly undermined when they were formally denied all material support by the state in late 1923 and early 1924; Moslems who chose to rely on the services of these courts were obliged to finance their operation.

Whereas the local election of *mullahs* and *alims* as *kadis* (judges) in these courts was guaranteed in 1922, a number of successive provisos in 1923 and 1924 opened Moslem judicial personnel to intensifying manipulation and infiltration. First, the *kadi-*

---

[12] For a detailed, excellent account of these moves in English, and one on which I rely in this section, see Park, *Bolshevism*, pp. 221-37. For comprehensive Soviet accounts, see especially Sulaimanova, *ISGPU*, Vol. I, pp. 468-508, and Vol. II, pp. 186-96; Fioletov, *SP*, 1(25), 1927, pp. 132-46, and *NV*, 23-24, 1928, pp. 204-17; Shokhor, *SS*, 8-9(13-14), 1927, pp. 94-114; Suleimanova, *SGP*, 10, 1948, pp. 65-69, and *SGP*, 3, 1949, pp. 61-69.

elections themselves came under the supervision of executive committees of local soviets; both the lists of qualified voters and the *kadi*-candidacies became liable to the committee's scrutiny (to prevent electoral participation by individuals and social strata declared to be ineligible by Soviet decrees); the same committees were empowered to nominate their own candidates (preferably "progressive" or "red" *mullahs*), to choose for the judgeship one of the two popularly elected *kadis*, and to remove a judge from office for political or criminal transgressions, or for professional unsuitability. Moreover, elected *kadis* were provided by the state with two appointed assistants (usually nominees of the local communist apparatus) as people's assessors.

If this series of steps was intended to curtail severely the autonomy of Moslem courts, other moves were designed to delimit drastically the jurisdiction and competence of these courts. Even while far-reaching concessions were made to customary-religious tribunals in the early 1920's, the pattern of jurisdictional demarcation was already taking shape. By and large, *kadi*-courts were to concern themselves with the realm of family law, including marriage, divorce, and succession, and with some aspects of civil law found to be relevant to adjudication on the basis of the *shariat* and *adat*. Offenses deemed by the regime to be "political" in nature were altogether outside the domain of these courts, being assigned successively to local soviets, to special counter-revolutionary tribunals, and to people's courts. Furthermore, whatever the jurisdiction of a traditional tribunal, it could not go beyond specified (rather low) ceilings imposed on the value of claims and fines, and on the period of imprisonment for a criminal offense, in a particular case.

In 1923, the *kadi*-courts could no longer levy fines in criminal cases, or deal with civil cases involving the inheritance of land. In February, 1924, these courts lost all jurisdiction in criminal cases, and the ceiling on the value of civil claims they could handle was drastically cut (to 25 rubles). The October, 1924, supplement to the criminal code of the R.S.F.S.R. (made applicable in Central Asia) formally invalidated some of the most important prescriptions of the *shariat* and *adat* which conflicted with revolutionary norms, namely *kalym*, polygamy, and the forced marriage of women. Since all three had figured prominently in the legal realm traditionally administered by native courts, and since both marriage and divorce had in any case been the subject of blanket Soviet decrees

199

and proclamations from the first days of the October Revolution, the cumulative impact on the jurisdiction and competence of religious-customary tribunals had to be unusually great.

In concurrent steps that unquestionably compounded this impact, the authority of a *kadi*'s verdict was deliberately undermined. It was made mandatory that all sides to a litigation had to agree on using the traditional court before a case could be presented to a *kadi*. Moreover, a *kadi*'s verdict was declared to be automatically null and void if any one of the litigants expressed dissatisfaction with it and demanded a retrial in a Soviet people's court. This principle was extended still farther in 1926, when all customary religious courts in Central Asia were declared to be but "voluntary" judicial organs, the implication being not only that the verdicts of these courts were in no case legally binding, but also that the legal personality of these courts was altogether questionable.

On September 21, 1927, the Central Executive Committee of the U.S.S.R. formally disposed of the entire issue in a decree "On Shariat and Adat Courts." Essentially, the decree divested still functioning traditional courts of all vestiges of legal personality, and proscribed the creation of new ones. Their verdicts could no longer carry legal force, or be recognized and enforced by organs of the state. With this act, to put it in Alexander Park's words, the Soviet government "delivered the coup de grâce . . . ; for practical purposes, [it] put an end to the customary court."[13] The government's figures could not but bear this out; by official count, the number of traditional courts in Central Asia fell sharply from some hundreds in the early 1920's to barely two dozen in 1927, with all of the latter reportedly on the verge of collapse.

THE DRIVE AGAINST TRADITIONAL LEGAL NORMS

The phased acceleration of pressure against traditional courts was also reflected in Soviet approaches to religious and customary law. In the course of the post-1917 decade, and especially after the national delimitation of Central Asia in 1924, successive legislative enactments gradually extended the list of proscribed customary relationships and conduct.

Early Soviet legislation pertaining to personal status and the family in the Union as a whole involved a number of radical de-

[13] Park, *Bolshevism*, p. 237.

200

partures from antecedent norms.[14] A series of decrees between November, 1917, and November, 1920, explicitly spelled out the terms of the new revolutionary morality. Marriage could be contracted only by voluntary mutual consent; it became effective upon simple registration at Z.A.G.S. (Soviet civil registry) and without religious consecration; it could be terminated by a simple unilateral declaration on the part of one of the spouses. Children born out of wedlock were to have the same rights as legitimate children. Abortions were legalized. The marital age was fixed at eighteen for males and sixteen for females. Bigamy was proscribed. Concurrently, together with the equal right to effect a divorce, women were guaranteed the right to equal pay for equal work, and the right to vote and to be elected to all organs of the Soviet state.

By implication, the legislation enacted by the Bolshevik regime was applicable in all areas under Soviet rule. Yet, probably in part because of the protracted hostilities in Central Asia, the relationship between centrally proclaimed norms and actual practices in Moslem societies was allowed for some time to remain ambivalent. As a rule, Moscow's decrees were merely reprinted in Central Asian newspapers.[15] Only with respect to civil registry of natives was an attempt made (in November, 1919) to assume a tangible supervisory role: in conjunction with a command to establish Z.A.G.S. offices in Central Asia, Moslem religious authorities were ordered to surrender all registry books (pertaining to births, deaths, marriages, divorces, etc.) in their possession to local soviets "for safekeeping."[16]

The pattern of action began to take shape in 1920. It was predicated on a modicum of differentiation between European and non-European parts of the Soviet Union, and hence between widely differing socio-cultural milieus. In the Moslem borderlands of Central Asia (as well as, e.g., among the Moslems of the Caucasus

[14] No attempt is made here to provide a detailed account of these early legislative moves for the Union as a whole. Surveys and bibliographies may be found in Schlesinger, *The Family*, esp. pp. 30 ff., 280 ff.; V. Gsovski, "Marriage and Divorce in Soviet Law," *Georgetown Law Journal*, xxxv, No. 1 (Jan., 1947), pp. 209-23; V. Gsovski, "Family and Inheritance in Soviet Law," *The Russian Review*, 7 (1947). See also works cited in Note 2 of this chapter.

[15] See, e.g., Sulaimanova, *ISGPU*, Vol. i, pp. 257-58.

[16] Sulaimanova, *ISGPU*, Vol. i, pp. 262-63. There is no evidence to what extent this order was obeyed.

and the Buddhists of Siberia) transgressions against the new norms were to be treated as "crimes based on custom," *bytovye prestupleniia*. Such a category of criminal acts—variously referred to as "rooted in a former way of life," "based on survivals of religion and tradition," and "representing the relics of a tribal order" —clearly carried the implication of a double standard, and of conflicting premises and desires. On the one hand, the new category reflected an attempt to visualize traditional rules and practices as dangerous manifestations of a competing way of life, as clear and simple violations of the new revolutionary order, and hence punishable to the fullest extent of the universalistic code. On the other hand, though, there was, in this case, an implicit proviso: "crime" was based on differing motivations, and hence carried very different connotations, in Central Asia and Russia respectively; Central Asian "custom" in some ways both explained and justified certain forms of local behavior; local transgressions against revolutionary norms could not be measured—and punished—in accordance with a universal yardstick.

Soviet moves against "crimes based on custom" in Moslem societies between 1920 and 1924 generally reflected this ambivalence. Thus, on the one hand, in intermittent orders issued by Soviet organs of justice and internal affairs in Moscow and Tashkent, the 1918 legal code of the R.S.F.S.R. (subsuming most of the early radical legislation on family and personal status) was declared to be applicable in Central Asia. On the other hand, two interrelated initiatives materialized in some of the larger local cities. In 1920, the Turkestan Commissariat of Justice called into being a commission of Moslem legal experts—evidently including "red" *mullahs*— to ascertain the possibility of "reconciling" Koranic and socialist norms, and to draft a legal code for Central Asian Moslems that would reflect this reconciliation.[17] In 1921, a number of commissions were created and attached to regional units of Soviet judicial administration (beginning in Samarkand), with the express purpose of "adapting" the 1918 R.S.F.S.R. code to the specific sociocultural conditions of Central Asia. Among the proposals made by the commissions were that: Moslems should be given greater leeway than allowed by the 1918 code in the registry of births and deaths, so as to establish a greater correspondence with existing mores and religious prescriptions; Moslem girls should be exempt

[17] Suleimanova, *SGP*, 3, 1949, p. 67.

from the requirement for both bride and groom to appear at the registration of a marriage (which, of course, carried the connotation that Soviet stipulations regarding voluntary and personal consent of bride and groom, and minimum marital age, could not really be tested and applied); on account both of earlier sexual maturation of native children, and of prevailing beliefs and practices, the marital age for Moslems should be lowered to fifteen, or less, if necessary; in order to effect a compromise between Soviet and Moslem norms on polygamy (the former insisting on strict monogamy, and the latter permitting four wives) Moslem males should be allowed to have two wives, and, in case one of them was sick, three.

These and other proposals were discussed at joint regional conferences of department heads of judicial administration, chiefs of militia, and managers of Soviet registry offices. They were also considered in 1923 and 1924 by the Central Executive Committee and the Council of People's Commissars of R.S.F.S.R. Needless to say, when the latter two supreme state bodies announced on September 15, 1924, a special dispensation concerning Central Asian Moslems—"On Supplementing the [R.S.F.S.R. Civil] Code of laws . . . in accordance with local socio-cultural conditions in the republic of Turkestan"—only the milder of the proposed changes (such as the registration of births and deaths) were implemented. All of the other proposals were summarily rejected. And, by the end of 1924, all local commissions on reconciling Koranic and socialist norms, and adapting Soviet legislation in a Moslem milieu, were abolished.[18]

Soviet hesitation on these issues between 1920 and 1924 was also reflected in the specific contra-traditional decrees promulgated at that time in Moslem republics. Apparently without a great deal of interrelation and coordination, a series of decrees, decisions, and proclamations materialized under a variety of auspices, such as that of the Central Executive Committee of the Russian republic (V.Ts.I.K., R.S.F.S.R.), and of supreme Soviet executive organs in Bashkiriia, Azerbaidzhan, Kirghiziia, and Turkestan. While all dealt with offenses against women's rights, they seemed to stress revolutionary exhortation rather than consistent and unified action. Thus, some decrees, in some locales, were directed in particular against marriage by abduction; some attacked *kalym*, polygamy,

18 Sulaimanova, *ISGPU*, Vol. I, pp. 263-67.

and child-marriage; some forbade blood feuds, rape in the course of abduction, and the forced marriage of women.[19] Moreover, in most cases, they merely "named the crime and mentioned that it is subject to punishment, but made no specific references concerning the nature and extent of punishment."[20]

It seems safe to assume that the locally issued decrees constituted primarily verbal revolutionary exercises designed to satisfy the intermittent pressures emanating from Moscow. Even when specific custom-based acts were clearly proscribed, and the applicability of R.S.F.S.R.'s Family Code of 1918 and Criminal Code of 1922 was forcefully stressed, the reference tended to be exclusively to Turkestan. The Bukharan and Khivan republics—that had been semi-autonomous under princely-theocratic rule while Central Asia was under Tsarist rule, and that had retained a modicum of autonomy under the Soviets, particularly the autonomy of religious-customary courts—were explicitly exempted from Soviet criminal law and legislation concerning family and personal status. There, the laws of *shariat* and *adat* were allowed to stand largely unchallenged well into the mid-1920's.[21] Characteristically, even when the Central Committee of the Communist Party of Turkestan demanded in 1923 and early 1924 the immediate implementation of Soviet laws in Central Asia ("On Putting into Practice Turk.Ts.I.K.'s Statute on Family Law for the Indigenous Population [of Turkestan]"), the practical emphasis was, first of all, on obliging native communists and komsomolites to adhere to the new norms.[22]

But beginning in late 1924, Soviet initiatives showed signs of growing premeditation and coordination. In October, 1924, a supplement to the criminal code of the R.S.F.S.R. (made almost immediately applicable in Central Asia) unequivocally outlawed polygamy and forced marriage, as well as the payment of *kalym* and of *diya* (indemnity paid to the victim of a hostile act or to his kin).[23] As a result, it became mandatory, first of all in Uzbeki-

---

[19] For the chronology, origin, and details of these moves, see Sulaimanova, *ISGPU*,Vol. I, pp. 272-73; *BSE*, Vol. 25, 1932, pp. 252-55; *BSE*, Vol. 29, 1935, pp. 395-96; Pal'vanova, *DSV*, pp. 37-39; Schlesinger, pp. 188-223.

[20] Suleimanova, *SGP*, 10 (Oct.), 1948, p. 69; cf. Sulaimanova, *ISGPU*, Vol. I, pp. 257-58.

[21] See, e.g., Sulaimanova, *ISGPU*, Vol. II, pp. 86-88; Vol. I, pp. 404-408.

[22] Pal'vanova, *DSV*, p. 58.

[23] See text in Lozovskii and Bibin, *Sovetskaia Politika za 10 let po natsional'nomu voprosu v RSFSR . . .*, pp. 316-18, cited in Park, *Bolshevism*,

stan (in 1925), for Z.A.G.S. agencies registering a Moslem marriage to demand that the couple present, first, evidence of their identity, age, and personal status, and, second, a certificate (from the administrative authorities of their municipal or rural district) attesting to the fact that the marriage was indeed based on voluntary consent of both sides and that the groom had not paid *kalym* to the bride's parents.[24]

In October, 1926, a new code on domestic relations was promulgated in the R.S.F.S.R. It finally invalidated all religious authority in marriage, stressed that acts of marriage and divorce are matters of private concern, and declared that unregistered (*de facto*) marriage entailed the same rights and obligations as a registered one: the established fact of sexual cohabitation and a joint household constituting sufficient evidence of a marital union. While this code was not made explicitly applicable in Central Asia, it marked the next to last stage in Moscow's drive for a secular, uniform code of statutory laws, in family, personal status, and criminal matters, that would be both congruent with general revolutionary norms and applicable to specific manifestations of "crimes based on custom" in Central Asia. Debate before its promulgation served to accelerate the passage of contra-traditional legislation in Central Asia in mid-1926, even if this legislation was still disparate and piecemeal.[25] Thus, for example, the criminal code issued in Uzbekistan in July, 1926, formally included *kalym*, polygamy, and forced marriage among proscribed acts involving stiff penalties.[26] At just about the same time, however, Turkmen authorities, while listing *kalym* as an offense, merely granted *kalym*-payers the right to sue payees for return of the bride-price.[27] In November, 1927, the Uzbek code

---

pp. 234-35. See also Akopov, *RN*, 4-5, 1930, p. 59; Sulaimanova, *ISGPU*, Vol. I, p. 273.

[24] The certificate was to be supplied by *mahallah* commissions, administrative units of the lowest echelon in Central Asia (the equivalent of borough or ward units in local government). Sulaimanova, *ISGPU*, Vol. II, pp. 219-21.

[25] See, e.g., the legislation passed by the Turkmen Central Executive Committee, as discussed in Kryl'tsov, *SP*, 5(29), 1927, pp. 137-38, and in Akopov, *RN*, 4-5, 1930, p. 61; Uzbek legislation is reviewed in Sulaimanova, *ISGPU*, Vol. II, pp. 219-21.

[26] Sulaimanova, *ISGPU*, Vol. II, p. 231.

[27] Kryl'tsov, *SP*, 5(29), 1927, p. 138; cf. "V Tsentral'nykh . . . ," *SS* (5), 1926, p. 159.

added the marriage of minors to the list of criminal offenses.[28] In Turkmenistan, however, there was still a tendency merely to recognize "the right of [young people] who reach marital age to refuse a marriage that had been arranged for them by parents or relatives in accordance with local custom when they were still children."[29]

But, most important, the passage of the 1926 R.S.F.S.R. family code marked the intensification of a concerted effort initiated in October, 1925, to assess—with the cooperation of legal specialists, political activists, and experts on the U.S.S.R.'s oriental minorities—the relevance and impact of antecedent Soviet laws in Moslem traditional societies,[30] to draft proposals for a comprehensive, unified new code, and to circulate them for initial reactions in Central Asia. It would seem that the airing of these proposals (for a period of close to two years) before actual promulgation was considerable in scope, and was designed to maximize discussion and a sense of participation by indigenous Soviet cadres, as well as to elicit, where possible, spontaneous or engineered popular assent in the Moslem borderlands.[31]

In April, 1928, Moscow was ready to formalize its campaign in this sector. At that time, a virtually exhaustive, unified code of laws, *On Crimes Constituting the Relics of the Tribal Order*, was enacted by the Russian republic (for the non-European minorities in its territory) as a special supplement (Ch. X) to the R.S.F.S.R. Criminal Code. Within a few months, its statutory standards came to be reflected, with only minor variations, in the legal systems of all Central Asian republics. In addition to proscribing a number of customary forms of inter-tribal and inter-clan relations (such as blood-vengeance and blood-money for claimed loss, damage, or dishonor) the new code addressed itself virtually to the entire range of manifestations denoting the inferior status of women. The catalogue of proscribed acts included bride-price (carrying sanctions against both giver and receiver of payment), child-marriage, forced marriage (involving either physical or psychological coercion), marriage by abduction, rape (with or without intent to marry),

---

[28] Sulaimanova, *ISGPU*, Vol. II, p. 231.

[29] "V Tsentral'nykh . . . ," *SS* (5), 1926, p. 158.

[30] For references to various investigative steps, see Fioletov, *SP*, 1(25), 1927, pp. 145-46, and Mokrinskii, *SP*, 3(27), 1927, pp. 103-104.

[31] See, e.g., Pal'vanova, *DSV*, pp. 38-39; Mokrinskii, *SP*, 3(27), 1927, pp. 103-108, 111-15; Sulaimanova, *ISGPU*, Vol. II, pp. 222-24.

polygamy, levirate, and in effect all customary acts of compulsion involving females. The sanctions ranged from a year of hard labor for polygamy, and a year in jail for payment and receipt of *kalym*, to up to two years of jail for forcing (or abducting) a woman into marriage or marrying a person under statutory marital age, five years for rape (including rape in the course of marriage by abduction), and eight years for marrying (or inducing to marry, or forcibly cohabitating with) a person before puberty.[32]

In conjunction with the new criminal code, Central Asian laws were allowed, in some cases, to depart from the R.S.F.S.R. model, in partial recognition of local conditions. While the Russian family code set the marital age for both men and women at eighteen, the Uzbek code, e.g., set it at eighteen for men and sixteen for women. *De facto* (unregistered) marriages, permitted in Russia, were explicitly forbidden in Central Asia. The reason given was understandable under the circumstances: without a formal requirement to register a marriage in a Soviet agency, Moslems could easily use the guise of a *de facto* union to perpetuate polygamy, levirate, and religiously consecrated marriages.[33] In parts of Uzbekistan that had been within the frontiers of the former Turkestan republic, only those religiously consecrated marriages were declared legal that had been contracted before December 20, 1917. However, in the territories of the former Bukharan and Khivan khanates (divided in 1924 in part between the Uzbek and Turkmen republics), the date of legal validity in this case was made coincidental with the date of the new code's formal promulgation in Central Asia, i.e., June, 1928. The reason was obvious: Moscow had permitted Bukharan and Khivan Moslem clergy, unlike their colleagues in the rest of Central Asia, to retain a monopoly in administering family law in accordance with the *shariat* until late in 1924, and religious marriages were recognized as legally valid here for at least a year after the national delimitation.[34]

[32] For details, see *Ugolovnyi Kodeks R.S.F.S.R.* (Moscow, 1957), pp. 100-103. For concurrent Soviet interpretations, see Sulaimanova, *ISGPU*, Vol. II, pp. 224-31; Moskalev, *Uzbechka*, pp. 47-48; Dosov, *Ka*, 5, 1928, pp. 29-32; Mokrinskii, *SP*, 3(27), 1927, pp. 11-12.

[33] Sulaimanova, *ISGPU*, Vol. II, pp. 225-26. Note that while the most reliable and comprehensive data available at this point are from Uzbekistan, it is safe to assume that the equivalent legislation in other Central Asian republics coincided with Uzbek models in form, substance, and timing.

[34] Sulaimanova, *ISGPU*, Vol. II, p. 226.

207

Adjustments were also made in some cases involving proscribed marital unions. If several women were married to a man who, at some point, was found out and became subject to prosecution for polygamy or marriage to a minor, all these wives were entitled to a share in the property of the dissolving household, as if all of the man's marriages in question had been legal. This was clearly intended to place all the blame for a proscribed marriage on the man, to provide some assurance that an illegally acquired wife would not become destitute overnight, and to make it both legally dangerous and materially unattractive for a man to enter more than one union.[35]

A separate series of decrees and constitutional guarantees were promulgated in Central Asia with the express purpose of ensuring the absolute equality of the sexes. Thus, on the one hand, marriages newly concluded under traditional-religious auspices were declared to be invalid; only registration in appropriate Soviet state agencies (Z.A.G.S.), accompanied by proper evidence regarding age, health, and mutual consent of the marital partners, could make the unions legal. On the other hand, a number of women's rights were spelled out, contravening the very core of religious and customary prescriptions regarding sexual apartheid and female inferiority: the right to initiate divorce (as against a Moslem male's prevailing right to unilateral divorce action through simple repudiation); the right to equal succession (as against religious or customary provisions for female inequality in the inheritance of property); the right to equal witness in court (as against specific Islamic stipulations that the testimony of two female witnesses be required in contesting the testimony of one man); as well as the right to full-fledged participation in public life, including general education, professional training, and participation in all socio-cultural, economic, and political pursuits, services, and organizations on equal terms with men. The latter denoted not only voting but also service in all, including the highest, elective and appointive public offices in the land, with early and special emphasis given to service in judicial roles in the new Soviet court system. In recognition of the obvious possibility that overt acceptance of women's legal rights might go hand in hand with covert denial of real opportunities to exercise these rights, Central Asian republican constitutions incorporated

[35] Dosov, *Ka*, 5, 1928, p. 31; cf. Mokrinskii, *SP*, 3(27), 1927, pp. 116-17.

explicit provisions for sanctions in cases of resistance by anyone and in any form to the actual emancipation of women.[36]

Also, in recognition óf the initial practical difficulties a Moslem woman might encounter in taking advantage, first of all, of her new marital rights, cadres of the party's Zhenotdel were assigned to the task of directly assisting women in the legal sphere. This included widely publicizing the new legislation; personally informing native women of their rights, partly through the medium of legal aid bureaus proposed especially for this purpose; encouraging them to sue for divorce from enforced, cruel, old, unloved, polygamous, or otherwise unacceptable husbands; personally supervising and assisting them towards this end in court; and formally serving (without remuneration) as their legal advisers and public defenders.[37]

A formal beginning in institutionalizing this procedure was made in March, 1924, when, by special order of the Turkestan Commissariat of Justice, *kadi*-courts could not examine cases involving women's property-rights unless Zhenotdel representatives were present.[38] A second order of the Commissariat at the end of 1924 obliged all people's courts in Turkestan to consider all marital and property litigations initiated by Moslem women as matters of urgent priority, to be expedited immediately and without regard to other pending cases.[39]

As some of the widely circulated official reports saw it at the time (particularly in the period between 1924 and late 1926, when piecemeal implementation of Soviet family laws was becoming a reality in Central Asia), there was good reason to believe that these moves were slowly but surely accomplishing their purpose. Not only was there an apparently marked shift of the native population away from *kadi*-courts, but women appeared to be among the first and most frequent users of the new Soviet legal network. Moslem women were reportedly turning to the people's courts directly or

[36] See, e.g., Kryl'tsov, *SP*, 5(29), 1927, p. 133; Sulaimanova, *ISGPU*, Vol. II, pp. 120-21, 176-77, 195-96, 224-31; Bil'shai, *RZVS*, pp. 105-98 (*passim*).

[37] See, e.g., Pal'vanova, *DSV*, pp. 56-57; Mukhitdinova, *Ka*, 9, 1929, p. 41; Dosov, *Ka*, 5, 1928, p. 31; Liubimova, *VPG*, p. 45; Kasparova, *Ka*, 7, 1925, pp. 88-89, 91; Sulaimanova, *ISGPU*, Vol. II, p. 219. For notes on the formation and initial purposes of Zhenotdel units in 1920 in Central Asia, see Sulaimanova, *ISGPU*, Vol. I, pp. 275-76.

[38] Sulaimanova, *ISGPU*, Vol. I, p. 271.

[39] Ibid., p. 272.

209

to appeal the verdicts of *kadis*, especially in cases of marital and property litigation,[40] and the pace of female-initiated divorce proceedings was rising.[41] Guided by Zhenotdel officials, women seemed to be increasingly successful in 1925-26, not only in abrogating undesirable marriages, but also in a number of other realms: in winning, in conjunction with an evolving land reform, individual assignations of land (especially in the case of widows);[42] in forming handicraft cooperatives; and in joining Councils of Women's Delegates especially created to help women in gaining access to public arenas, and to train them in rudimentary forms of political participation. In the process, instances of illegal polygamous unions, forced marriages, marriages of minors, and *kalym* payments were being exposed and brought to court, which promised to hasten the erosion of ancient patriarchal family and authority patterns.[43]

In this sense, the developments seemed to bear out the premises underlying the emphasis on revolutionary legalism. At least three mutually reinforcing causal relationships were seen as coming into play here, all of them of prime relevance to the Soviet revolutionary effort, and all of them underscoring the payoffs of consistent and radical judicial reform. First, and most obviously, there was the anticipated direct relationship between Soviet legal action and female emancipation in Central Asia. The Party's Organizational Bureau and the Plenum of the Central Committee saw this in their decisions in late 1924 and 1925 ("The Immediate Tasks of the Party in its Work with the Female . . . Toilers of the East"),[44] and the Presidium of the Central Executive Committee reaffirmed it early in 1925 ("To the Peoples of the Soviet East . . . ")[45]: the Eastern woman's "actual emancipation" was contingent upon "full

---

[40] See, e.g., ibid., p. 506, and Vol. II, pp. 218-19; cf. Michurina, *Ka*, 10-11, 1926, p. 83.

[41] See Michurina, *Ka*, 10-11, 1926, p. 83.

[42] Shimko, *Ka*, 12, 1925, p. 67; Kryl'tsov, *SP*, 5(29), 1927, pp. 134-35; Liubimova, *VPG*, pp. 54-58.

[43] See, e.g., Shikhmuradov and Rosliakov, *Ocherki Istorii*, pp. 290-91.

[44] See "Postanovlenie Plenuma Ts.K. RKP(b) . . . ," in *Ka*, 2, 1925, p. 45; cf. Bil'shai, *RZVS*, pp. 185-86.

[45] See "K narodnostiam Sovetskogo Vostoka," in *Ka*, 3, 1925, pp. 3-5; cf. Liubimova, *VPG*, pp. 45-46; *BSE*, Vol. 29, 1935, pp. 395-96. See also the earlier decision of the Turkestan Ts.K. and Ts.I.K. (April 18, 1923), regarding the implementation of emancipatory legislation, in Pal'vanova, *DSV*, p. 58.

and exact implementation" of Soviet laws pertaining to women's rights in the realms of family, marriage, and property.

Second, there was the perceived relationship between divorce and revolutionary consciousness. Specifically, it was seen that by far the greatest promise of legal action lay in a particularly strong emphasis on female-initiated divorces. The growing number of such divorces testified to the "rise in self-awareness" in Moslem women, to their maturing aspiration to "free themselves from forcibly imposed, [inherently] unequal marriages that had been their lot by virtue of old mores and laws," to "free themselves from bonds that [humiliated them], deprived them of human dignity."[46] Or, as the Uzbek government put it in 1926, in a circular affirming the emphasis on revolutionary law and the significance of divorces, "the rise in instances of divorce should be looked upon . . . as [a reflection of] the development of a woman's law-consciousness, as her protest against economic dependence on [her] husband and against the old order."[47] Accordingly, the Uzbek Commissariat of Justice was among the first in Central Asia to insist (in March, 1926) that female-initiated divorces be processed in Soviet courts as a matter of high priority, and that they be approved "without fail" and "irrespective of the reasons that moved [a native woman] to sue for divorce."[48]

In a broader context, of course, from the point of view of strict interpreters of revolutionary legalism, this implied a productive intensification of class-struggle in a Moslem milieu. In the words of one official report, with "poor [natives] and women" constituting by far the greater part of the initial clientele of Soviet courts, "one can say with certainty that Moslem [people's] courts are [becoming a significant] factor in accelerating the awakening of class-consciousness in the masses, and will play a very important role . . . in attracting [these masses] to the [principles and] aims pursued by the Soviet regime."[49]

Then there was, thirdly, the perceived relationship between female emancipation—beginning with divorce—and radical socio-cultural change. In successfully asserting her new legal rights—a number of communist organizers concluded—a Moslem woman was fundamentally transforming not only herself and the conditions

[46] Sulaimanova, *ISGPU*, Vol. II, p. 216.
[47] Quoted ibid., p. 218.
[48] Ibid., p. 217.
[49] Quoted in Sulaimanova, *ISGPU*, Vol. I, p. 391.

of her life, but also the entire system and way of life of which she was a part. As visualized with increasing frequency by Central Asian party leaders and political analysts between mid-1924 and 1928, legal emancipation of Moslem women was of crucial importance for the success of all other Soviet policies in an Islamic milieu. It was to be viewed as the main front in the attack against "dangerous residues of a traditional way of life . . . that hamper the . . . development of backward [societies] . . . "; it constituted a "fundamental issue" of overall social reconstruction under Soviet auspices; it was "one of the most important prerequisites" for success in solving the problems of economic development and cultural change.[50]

[50] See Liubimova, *VPG*, p. 69; Pal'vanova, *DSV*, pp. 76-78; Dosov, *Ka*, 5, 1928, pp. 29-30.

SIX · *Toward Cultural Revolution by Decree: The Pattern of Administrative Assault*

DETERMINANTS AND OBJECTIVES

WHEN the party's top leadership was finally beginning to see female emancipation in Moslem societies as a matter of potentially great political significance, it showed itself perfectly cognizant of the fact that such emancipation could not be expected to follow the mere mechanical imposition of a host of statutes and a network of courts. Thus, while prompting Central Asian party units to concentrate on emancipation as a matter of urgent priority—and to do so by way of legal action, and the development of local Zhenotdel units to help in such action—a special resolution of the party's Thirteenth Congress (May, 1924) specifically accompanied this directive with two provisos. First, it urged that the legal offensive be conducted "with careful attention to local conditions and possibilities." In this, it obviously harked back to Lenin's repeated calls for special caution in the Moslem borderlands, and his warnings about the dangers of impinging on local sensibilities through mechanical, haphazard application of Soviet structures and norms. Second, this resolution (as well as other directives that followed shortly) stressed that the process of legal emancipation be correlated with systematic efforts to create for Moslem women a special network of associational, vocational, and social-service units (such as "Assemblies of Women's Delegates"; "Down with *Kalym* and Polygamy" associations; clubs; producers' and consumers' cooperatives; literacy and hygiene circles; and medical dispensaries) designed to spur their cultural reorientation, political indoctrination, economic participation, and recruitment into the party.

Towards this end, administrative agencies were directed to make the first significant allocation of funds, to be drawn from central as well as local budgets.[1]

Yet, just as the Thirteenth Congress coincided with the intensification of the power struggle in Moscow (and hence with drastic

---

[1] See *KPSS v resoliutsiiakh* . . . , Part I, pp. 895-96 (7th edition, M. 1953); cf. Shikhmuradov and Rosliakov, *Ocherki Istorii*, pp. 290-91.

213

shifts in the party's top echelons), it also coincided with a growing polarization of views in Central Asia as to the best means of managing the emancipation of women as part of the assault upon Moslem traditional societies. Inevitably, the intense political ferment throughout the apparatus played havoc with whatever balanced, rationally conceived plans might have been taking shape at that time, and with their consistent execution. While lip-service was indeed beginning to be paid at that time to the requirements of building a new social infrastructure for Moslem women, and while some modest steps in this direction were beginning to be made in 1924 and 1925 (mostly on the personal initiative of a handful of Zhenotdel activists), the attention of responsible Soviet cadres was clearly concentrating elsewhere.

The Promise of Head-on Assault

Along with a decided upswing in law-oriented activity, there came a growing emphasis on female-initiated divorces, as the most desirable (and dramatic) manifestation of change. And it is precisely these divorces that came to be the pivotal issue of debate.[2] On the one hand, as we shall see (in the following two chapters), the very success of this enterprise, at least as reflected in its rising tempo, was beginning to cause unease in many quarters and for varying reasons. Along with signs of social ferment there came also indications of deep resentment in the traditional countryside, and indications as well that locally recruited Soviet cadres were increasingly unhappy with the turn of events. Accordingly, searching questions were asked both in Moscow and in Central Asian capitals, and proposals were quietly made to tone down the legalistic emphasis—in effect, to apply brakes to divorce-centered enterprises as "demoralizing" to all concerned,[3] as deeply threatening not only to local sensibilities but also to the stability of the Soviet regime.

On the other hand, though, there were those who arrived at a very different assessment of the matter, and who offered conclusions and proposals for action that were diametrically opposed to the preceding ones. Paradoxically, they saw the developments as extremely encouraging. For them, female-initiated divorces, and the accompanying social ferment, were signs *par excellence* of fun-

[2] See, e.g., Sulaimanova, *ISGPU*, Vol. II, p. 216.

[3] Sulaimanova, ibid. For a detailed account of the events and perceptions in question, see the chapters that follow (Seven and Eight).

damental change, of surging revolutionary awareness. Traditionalist resentment only confirmed that female mobilization was on the
proper track, that it hurt badly, that it was intensifying the class
struggle.[4] For that matter, the signs of success in divorce proceedings—a result of unprecedented self-assertion by Moslem women
—as well as the progress made in land-reform, wherein widowed
and divorced women in particular were emerging as individual
owners of land, justified the conclusion that a real revolutionary
breakthrough was at hand, that the traditional world was tottering,
that the ground was "ready for communist sowing," for "uncompromising and consistent struggle," for an "intensified . . . decisive
. . . attack."[5] Hence, far from calling for greater caution, the situation seemed to be offering opportunities for consistent Leninist tele-
scoping action. It called, if anything, for an *acceleration* of Soviet
pressures. It called for immediate, all-out assault, on "feudal . . .
and tribal-patriarchal residues," on "everything that was old and
obsolete," on "all that stood in direct contradiction to . . . and impeded socialist construction."[6]

It was symptomatic of such militancy that it could, simultaneously, reflect an upsurge of revolutionary self-confidence, enthusiasm,
and zeal as well as of radical impatience born of pessimism and
frustration. The former had its roots, of course, in optimistic interpretations and romantic projections of some observed trends. The
latter drew on disillusionment and anger in activist ranks, especially
on account of the interminable delays, complexities, evasions, or
sabotage accompanying the implementation of new norms through
legal or other mediating institutions.[7]

Thus, side by side with moves gradually evolving in the legal
sphere, we have an upswing of an extreme activist mood in Soviet

[4] See Sulaimanova, *ISGPU*, Vol. II, pp. 216 and 218, and Vol. I, p. 391.

[5] See Liubimova, *VPG*, pp. 72-73; Niurina, *Ka*, 4, 1925, p. 83; Z.P.,
Ka, 6, 1928, p. 84; Ar-na, *Ka*, 1, 1928, pp. 57-58; Nukhrat, *OZV*, pp. 85, 88;
Pal'vanova, *DSV*, pp. 95-97.

[6] For various expressions of the need to dispose at last of the "brakes"
on socialist development and on the consolidation of Soviet rule in Central
Asia, see, e.g., Z.P., *Ka*, 6, 1928, p. 84; Liubimova, *VPG*, p. 73; Pal'vanova,
DSV, pp. 95-96; Nukhrat, *Ka*, 6, 1928, p. 78.

[7] For examples of frustration with the tempos of legal action, see
Kasparova, *Ka*, 7, 1925, pp. 88-89; Kalachev, *Ka*, 8, 1927, p. 60; Mostovaia,
VS, 9, 1928, pp. 7-8. For a detailed account of various dimensions of
popular response and institutional performance in this respect, see the
following chapters.

215

ranks in 1925 and 1926, a burgeoning impatience with long-term legal and organizational approaches, and a commensurate attraction to shortcuts that held out the promise of a sweeping advance. But just as the overall pattern of legal action had generated a growing concentration on the relatively narrow issue of divorce, so did the activist extra-legal dispositions reveal a determined, ever-narrowing emphasis on a single issue: female seclusion and veiling.[8]

Beginning with cut-and-dried proposals to *outlaw* the veil, activist pressures escalated to a demand to *destroy* it forthwith, through administered mass action in the streets. Legalistic concentration on divorce had been expected to undermine the traditional family, and thus affect Islamic society indirectly. However, an extra-legal as well as legal attack on the institution of veiling, as well as forcefully administered sexual desegration in public, was expected to engage —and shatter—the entire socio-cultural system directly, head-on. Thus, the ultimate goals remained the same, but the operational and time perspectives showed a marked change. It is this particular junction of the debate that revealed most clearly the potential affinity between legal action and administrative assault. It is in this sense that revolutionary legalism may be said to have harbored within it the seeds of dogmatism, and of totalitarian extremism. An increasingly strident emphasis on the implementation of revolutionary norms tended to grow quite easily into an insistence that the entire spectrum of undesirable mores and customs be subject to proscription by decree, and that the new norms be observed immediately and unconditionally in daily life.[9]

While some of the immediate causes of a growing predilection to "storm" a Moslem society were rooted in optimistic assessments of divorce trends, some were part and parcel of a very different set of orientations. For one thing, the Leninist heritage itself could, of course, serve as a source of mutually contradictory counsels. Just as one could find in it justifications for gradualism, persuasion, patient experimentation, and consummate caution as requisites of social action, one could easily deduce (from theory, exhortations,

[8] See, e.g., Sulaimanova, *ISGPU*, Vol. II, p. 327.

[9] For an example of such insistence, see, Liubimova, *Ka*, 8, 1928, pp. 73-75; for examples of protests against this insistence, see, "Nuzhno li izdat' dekret', zapreshchaiushchii noshenie chadry," *Ka*, 8, 1928, pp. 79-81; cf. Krupskaia's indictment of such pressures as an example of dogmatism, and her implicit likening of revolutionary legalism—in its most radical phases—with administrative assault, in *Ka*, 12, 1928, pp. 5-12.

and actions alike) arguments for all-out attacks against an enemy, for maximum concentration on a "weak link," for ruthless suppression of all deviant behavior—in short, for what came to be a dictum of Stalinist politics: *nazhim*, forceful and relentless pressure.

Likewise, the decision to strike could be predicated on "objective conditions," on a society's reaching an appropriate stage of socio-economic development, as reflected in the readiness of the masses to follow the party's call to action. But it could also be based on the communists' correct assessment of a special opportunity. In the latter case, instead of waiting for the masses to develop a proper momentum for revolutionary action, the party had a responsibility to engineer such action, in the full expectation that the masses could not only be made to follow, but would also learn best about a revolution in the process of experiencing and making one. Mass action, then, could be both a cause and a consequence of revolutionary initiatives, a pre-condition for purposive communist moves as well as a teaching and conditioning experience under communist auspices.

Accordingly, proponents of all-out assault in Central Asia were quick to point to the promise of engineered mass-action as both kindling revolutionary enthusiasm and a final break from tradition in direct participants, and inducing acceptance or surrender in others.[10] In other words, they envisaged large payoffs over the short term—a relatively "painless" act of social surgery, wherein the risks were minimal or could be ignored—if only "sufficient energy" were invested in the operation.[11]

They rejected arguments to the effect that, as a rule, head-on collisions ought to be avoided, to allow legal action to take its course, and to permit the investment of cadres and resources in new institution-building, the kind of building that would develop in women new skills, commitments, and a general state of "enlightenment" over the long term. Instead, they stressed sweep and boldness in attacking tradition. They obviously felt that one could and needed to circumvent the frustratingly complex, drawn-out maneuvers on the road to re-socialization, and that such maneuvers did not need to be prerequisites for real emancipation. One could avoid

[10] See, Anisimova, *Ka*, 8, 1927, p. 56; cf. Liubimova, *Ka*, 8, 1928, pp. 73-75; Ishkova, *Ka*, 11, 1928, pp. 59-62; Bogacheva, *Ka*, 11, 1928, p. 66.
[11] Compare the judgments in Ar-na, *Ka*, 1, 1928, pp. 57-58; Ishkova, *Ka*, 11, 1928, p. 60; Mokrinskii, *SP*, 3(27), 1927, pp. 106-107. See also Lenin's *indictment* of this position in *Lenin o Natsional'nom*, pp. 470-72.

217

the drudgery of trying to attract Moslem women to Soviet schools and other enterprises in the face of a myriad of barriers. *Mass unveiling itself* would induce directly the desired psychological revolution, constitute emancipation *par excellence*, and serve to deliver women naturally and quickly to Soviet enterprises and the Soviet fold. Massive, public, and dramatic violations of veiling and seclusion as pervasive traditional taboos could be expected to have a shock-effect on the attitudes and relationships of all concerned. In the process, direct access-routes to local communities would open up, and the walls of tradition would crumble everywhere and in short order. Those who doubted such an outcome, and attempted to dissuade the party from all-out assault, were but irritants and pessimists.[12]

The Danger of Competitive Models

Most of the preceding arguments may be considered to have been, from the Soviet standpoint, positive reasons for the proposed offensive. It would seem that at least two sets of negative reasons were also offered in the course of the debate. Both had to do with the perceived consequences of inaction, or alternative actions, at that time. Both seem to have reflected fear on the part of many communists of actual or potential competition in conjunction with the revolutionary process.

One of the issues concerned what was perceived to be external competition. Obviously, it would have been unusual for a self-conscious revolutionary regime to give the impression that, in initiating particular revolutionary moves, it was merely following someone else's models or responding to someone else's initiative. It was clearly of crucial importance for the party's self-view, and for its self-legitimation, to maintain the image of its rule as that of the first

---

[12] For examples of such reasoning, see Anisimova, *Ka*, 8, 1927, p. 55, and Niurina, *Parandzha*, pp. 10-11; cf. Liubimova, *Ka*, 8, 1928, pp. 73-75, and Z.P., *Ka*, 6, 1928, p. 84.

For expressions of Soviet frustration on account of the inaccessibility of the Central Asian milieu, beginning with its women, see, e.g., Prishchepchik, *Ka*, 12, 1925, p. 63; Otmar-Shtein, in *ZVR*, pp. 345-49; Nukhrat, *OZV*, pp. 48-49, 50-51, 59; Pal'vanova, *DSV*, pp. 49-50, 54, 80, Liubimova, *VPG*, pp. 16-17, 22, 32, and in *Ka*, 7, 1926, p. 70.

For instances of early intoxication with the possibilities of assault, see Anisimova, *Ka*, 8, 1927, pp. 54-56; Nikolaeva, *Ka*, 8, 1927, p. 52; Rigin, *Ka*, 5-6, 1929, pp. 58-59; Liubimova, *Ka*, 10, 1927, p. 61; Nukhrat, *Ka*, 6, 1928, p. 78.

and only communist revolutionary regime in history. Accordingly, references which would leave a contrary impression could hardly be expected to appear in public, certainly not in print. It is, therefore, of particular interest that one of the rare slips should have occurred in connection with the emancipation of Moslem women. Even though the evidence is fragmentary, it is beyond doubt that one of the impulses behind growing Soviet disposition to attack Central Asia's traditional world head-on was the perceived competition from Turkey. Atatürk's own assault against the mainstays of custom and Islam in Turkey reached its highest intensity between 1925 and 1927. And the major thrust of his attempted secular revolution concerned (at least for a time) the emancipation of women, beginning with a massive effort to induce their unveiling, to break their customary seclusion, and to speed their arrival in schools, industry, the professions, and even politics.

There is every reason to assume that Atatürk's initiatives became the subject of fierce debates in Soviet ranks in 1925 and 1926, in Moscow as well as in Central Asia. Fears that Turkish competition would reinforce nationalist propaganda in Central Asia could seem especially justified when what was viewed as a potentially subversive organization was discovered in the Old City of Tashkent in mid-1926. The association ("Young Forces") had been formed by native female teachers who claimed to be interested in studying the works of the Turkish female writer, Khalide-Khanum. They were also interested in the Turkish feminist movement and found much to their liking in Atatürk's reformist program. For that matter, even Afghan legislation abolishing polygamy and lowering the amount of *kalym* seemed of interest to some of them. It is a measure of official unease in Central Asia that, when reporting all this to Moscow, local Zhenotdel functionaries urgently demanded detailed information on Turkish and Afghan reforms as well as clear guidelines for further action.[13]

Under any circumstances, it could have been argued that to be left behind by other regimes in initiating sweeping emancipatory moves might mean, at best, to lose face, and, at worst, to lose political initiative to those regimes both abroad and at home. But Turkey posed an especially delicate problem. Here was a regime presiding over a society that was geographically close and ethnically, culturally, and historically related to the Moslem societies of

---

[13] See Liubimova, *Ka*, 9, 1926, pp. 74-75.

the Caucasus and Soviet Central Asia. As it happened, the fledgling secular intelligentsia of both the latter regions had come into their own—had taken on the rudiments of a national and reformist identity—at least in part under direct or indirect Turkish tutelage. Not surprisingly, Moscow had worked hard from the first days of the 1917 revolution to cut this incipient link. Now it could easily be argued that, if left unmatched, Atatürk's dramatic initiatives in 1925-1927 could have the effect of stealing the communist thunder in the Islamic world, of disillusioning the more impatient and radical elements within the Soviet apparatus, and of further encouraging the incipient nationalist movements in Central Asia and in the Caucasus to seek their cues in all matters of reform and development in Ankara. In such a context, it is not difficult to understand Moscow's sensitivity when the first warnings were sounded (by proponents of assault and of legal prohibition of the veil) in Central Asia that the Soviet regime dared not "drag [itself] behind Turkey" in contra-traditional legislation and action, and especially in female emancipation.[14]

The Danger of Subversive Superstructures

The other major issue, far broader in its implications, and far more intimately enmeshed in the dynamics of Soviet politics, concerned precisely the approach the rudiments of which were present in the directives of the party's Thirteenth Congress in May, 1924. These directives involved, of course, building a new social infrastructure especially to serve women's needs, as an important contribution both to female emancipation and to long-term socio-cultural transformation. It was not merely the costs of such an enterprise—in time, cadres, and resources—that worried those who opted for direct assault. Their unease stemmed from a fundamental distrust of all specialized mediating networks standing between the population and the Party-State. It stemmed from a suspicion that the growth of such mediating institutions might, for a variety of rea-

---

[14] For expressions of unease regarding the possible takeover of revolutionary activity by a nationalist movement (one that might find an association with Turkish reformism more congenial than with Soviet Russian leadership) see, e.g., Liubimova, *VPG*, pp. 42-43. For perceptions of the potential impulse generated by Turkish emancipatory politics—including unveiling—see "Nuzhno li izdat' dekret', zapreshchaiushchii nosheniie chadry," *Ka*, 8, 1928, pp. 79-81; and "Mestnye Rabotniki—ob Izdanii Dekreta," in *Ka*, 1, 1929, p. 32 ff.

sons, become spontaneous and uncontrolled, thus posing a clear competitive challenge, and a potentially serious threat, to the unitary structure, value system, and power monopoly of the Soviet apparatus. In the highly suggestive terms of one communist analyst who preferred to remain anonymous at that time, the proliferation of women's special-purpose organizations might lead to a set of potentially autonomous, separatist, and hence "[subversive] superstructures" within the Soviet system.[15]

This line of argument rested on a set of related assumptions. The first and most critical of these assumptions was that, in promoting the development of an auxiliary service-network for women, Soviet cadres might deliberately or unwittingly encourage the emergence of what would be in effect "voluntary associations"—units with organizational propensities, interests, and values fundamentally alien to the Soviet regime. Given the evident weakness of the party's apparatus in Central Asia, "spontaneous generation and growth" of such units at the grassroots would make adequate party influence, supervision, and control in this context well nigh impossible. Under the circumstances, the resulting vacuum in ideology and leadership might all too readily be filled by local nationalist elements that were waiting for just such a chance.[16]

A second assumption followed logically from the first. Given the

[15] For this view, see V.K., *Ka*, 9, 1925, pp. 70-72; cf. Zhukova, *Ka*, 10, 1928, pp. 79-80. (On the basis of other contributions to the debate, one can venture a guess that V.K. stood for V. Kasparova, a leading member of the Zhenotdel in Central Asia who seems to have been accused of Trotskyism later in the 1920's, and who disappeared from the scene shortly thereafter. V. Karpych, a Soviet analyst of Eastern affairs, is another, though more remote, possibility as the author of the cited article.)

It is important to keep in mind here that it is not yet possible, on the basis of available documents, to establish a direct connection between this argument and the arguments of those who called for an assault in Central Asia. Most of those who argued against multiple superstructures did not openly declare themselves in favor of assault. Most of those who openly called for direct mass action had comparatively little to say about superstructures. Yet a close contextual analysis of the material leaves very little doubt that there was indeed a very strong affinity between these two orientations, not only a logical affinity but also an intellectual one. The extensive overlap of these views in a number of cases leads one to regard them as components of a single general orientation characterizing a single, though variegated, group. Of course, available data do not permit us to identify such a group precisely and to place it as a clear-cut unit in a factional lineup within the Soviet regime.

[16] See Zavarian, *Ka*, 7, 1926, p. 37; cf. Pal'vanova, *DSV*, pp. 41-43.

221

overly exclusive preoccupation on the part of a female-oriented network with "specifically female problems," such a network could spur the development of a "women's movement" on distinctly Western and bourgeois lines, i.e., it could lead to "feminism." In turn, a feminist orientation in organizational and institutional development would distort and detract from the overall Bolshevik thrust, would dilute the participants' revolutionary concerns, and would altogether sidetrack women into purely feminist pursuits. Specifically, it would take Moslem women out of the political and economic marketplace and concentrate their attention and efforts on comforts and achievements close to home.[17]

Third, since a self-generating associational network, especially in the form of "voluntary associations," would tend to approach and attract women *qua* women, irrespective of their social background, the organizational bias would be towards "mass" rather than "class." As a result of such "unprincipled [and completely undifferentiated] classlessness," both the notion and the management and process of a hoped-for "class struggle" in Central Asia under Soviet auspices would be compromised and undermined.[18] In stating her argument in this fashion, Zhukova, a high party official in Central Asia, not only reaffirmed her Bolshevik orthodoxy, she also used the issue as a forum for developing a seriously damaging case against a number of communists (largely unnamed) who presumably argued in party councils in favor of a flexible, experimental, and fairly permissive approach to women's organizations. Of course, the threat of a grave political indictment implicit in Zhukova's terms, one that could obviously be used in a general purge, only helped to show how vulnerable the entire concept of work with women was to Bolshevik ideological subversion. It is not surprising, therefore, that not a single voice arose in public in direct response to the argument. It also helps to explain why, especially after Stalin's rise to power in the late 1920's, Soviet discussions of female mobilization had to be increasingly couched, like other politically sensitive discussions, in the stylized terms of esoteric communication.

A fourth, and related, assumption was extrapolated from tendencies observed, or merely presented as observed, in Central Asia in the wake of the party's call to female-oriented institution building

[17] See Butuzova, *Ka*, 9, 1927, pp. 66-67; V. K., *Ka*, 9, 1925, pp. 70-72; Nukhrat, *RN*, 3(36), 1933, p. 49; Liubimova, *VPG*, p. 28.
[18] See Zhukova, *Ka*, 10, 1928, pp. 79-80.

in the mid-1920's. It also followed logically from earlier warning concerning subversive superstructures. Essentially, this argument implied that the imperatives of female mobilization had been erroneously perceived in the first place, and thus were erroneously presumed to call for a multi-faceted and well-integrated approach to the female masses. Should female-oriented enterprises be permitted to develop as unduly complex, integrated units there was the distinct danger of persistent functional imperialism on the part of these units. What were supposed to be merely auxiliary foci for the "political enlightenment" of women would "absorb" and "usurp" agitational as well as educational, legal, and economic functions, and integrate these functions under one institutional umbrella. In warning about such prospects, Brutser, a Soviet analyst not clearly identified at that time, was obviously alluding to views that were widely shared in the ranks of the Central Asian Zhenotdel in the second half of the 1920's. Those views, and attempts to implement them, concerned the role and structure of Women's Clubs in a Moslem milieu. It seemed axiomatic to a great many Zhenotdel organizers that, in such a milieu, clubs could play their assigned role best if allowed to become multi-purpose agencies, with "red corners," literacy circles, legal aid units, health units, vocational training courses, gardening, handicraft, and consumers' cooperatives, industrial production units, and even savings banks, assembled under one roof and centralized direction—preferably, of course, under the Zhenotdel's direction.[19] To Brutser, and to those for whom he spoke, this was impermissible. No matter what the alleged promise of such an arrangement in mobilizing and organizing the women of a Moslem traditional milieu, it could by no means justify the very real danger of operational autonomy and self-sufficiency, and even of organizational separatism and "independence," on the part of the new institutional network.[20]

---

[19] This point of view, and the approach it characterized, was championed by proponents of what came to be called "systematic work." A comprehensive review and analysis of this approach will be found in a separate study, *Systematic Social Engineering in Soviet Central Asia*, now in preparation.

[20] See Brutser, *KP*, 4-5, 1930, pp. 91-93. The fact that this article was written in 1930, and hence *after* the original debates concerning administrative assault in Central Asia, in no way invalidates its relevance here. Brutser merely expressed publicly, clearly, and unequivocally what was implied or circumspectly stated in print on many occasions a few years earlier. In this context, then, the article's argument becomes especially

It stands to reason that, from such a point of view, not even the party's own Women's Department could be above suspicion. When related to all other assumptions about the dangers of feminism and of organizational autonomy in the Soviet system, suspicions about the Zhenotdel's attempts to centralize all work with women under its aegis inevitably led to demands that its operations, too, be circumscribed, dispersed among a number of agencies, or dispensed with altogether.[21]

A final group of assumptions pertained to a very closely related issue: allocation of revolutionary energy. As Zhukova put it, those who insisted on careful and patient experimentation with new forms in the party's work with Moslem women, including "voluntary associations," failed to realize that to do so meant " . . . to divide [and scatter] the attention and forces of . . . [communist] cadres among [ever] new superstructures, to divert the party from organic leadership . . . in [female] emancipation, and to demagnetize on this account other social organizations which had barely started to operate. . . ." As a result, "[both the interests of the state and] the cause of female emancipation would be harmed."[22]

In saying this (in 1928), Zhukova clearly harked back to views propounded anonymously in 1925. To permit over-elaborate and incipiently autonomous superstructures to develop, it was argued then, would mean to promote structures that were "artificial," "withdrawn and closed-in," "divorced . . . from party and soviet work, . . . [and hence] from life."[23] It would mean to promote *the forced acceleration . . .* of a women's movement [of the wrong kind, at a time] when *a certain slowdown* [in this type of mobilization was definitely called for]."[24] Thus, even if it should be necessary to build a separate auxiliary institutional network for Moslem women, its structure and functions would have to conform to strictly enforced criteria. For one thing, voluntary associations—*whatever* the purpose behind them—were out of the question. For another thing, if some functionally specialized and sexually segregated

---

valuable as the quintessence of a point of view that was crystallizing at a time crucial in our analysis, but could obviously be expressed only in the privacy of the party's inner councils.

[21] An account of the Zhenotdel's formation, structure, operations, and problems will be found in a subsequent study (see Note 19).

[22] Zhukova, *Ka*, 10, 1928, pp. 79-80.

[23] V. K., *Ka*, 9, 1925, pp. 70-72; cf. Brutser, *KP*, 4-5, 1930, pp. 91-93.

[24] V. K., ibid., pp. 71-72 (italics added).

units should be allowed to exist, they could function only if they were the party's "supplementary organs" and useful "transmission belts," and if they served the regime's basic need: the conscription of a female labor army for agriculture and industry.[25]

All these reasons, positive as well as negative, for attacking a society and culture head-on, for inducing a full-fledged "cultural revolution" in Central Asia, and thus dispensing with protracted mobilizational efforts requiring complex instrumentalities and time, were based on several closely related Bolshevik perceptions. They grew out of a sense of impatience with substantive and procedural matters connected with the law, particularly when the most dramatic immediate results of legal action, such as female-initiated divorces, seemed to hold out the promise of far greater gains if the legal stage were skipped. They grew, likewise, out of a sense of impatience with, and fundamental suspicion of, unorthodox organizational arrangements connected with building a new social infrastructure concerned exclusively with women.

The obverse of such an orientation was the desire to gain direct as well as immediate access to female and male strata. It was a desire to obviate or minimize the need for specialized and potentially unreliable institutions, and to induce the kind of social mobilization that would permit direct and massive recruitment of human beings into enterprises whose structure and functions were familiar to Bolshevik organizers, relatively homogeneous, undisputably relevant to long-term Soviet aims, and securely centralized under the party's aegis. Fundamentally, then, overly complex, elaborate, and specialized involvement in work with women was seen as bearing the threat of heterogeneity, autonomy, and pluralism within an avowedly unitary, monolithic system. In this sense, all-out assault on the mainstays of tradition, far from being intended merely to liberate Moslem women from particular shackles, reflected a desire to use women more speedily, massively, and efficiently as pivotal actors in the destruction of traditional society as a whole. Far from being intended to free women for self-selected pursuits *qua* women or individuals, the attempted cultural revolution in 1926-1928 in Central Asia was ideally expected to produce quickly an army of citizens and workers whose roles and functions were carefully co-

[25] V. K., ibid., pp. 70-72, and Brutser, *KP*, 4-5, 1930, pp. 91-93; cf. Nukhrat, *Ka*, 1, 1928, p. 55, and *VMV*, p. 18; Karpov, *Ka*, 9, 1928, pp. 82-84; Safadri, *Ka*, 11, 1928, p. 34.

ordinated and graded on a single scale, whose talents were developed and fully devoted to the building of socialism as envisioned by Moscow, whose status depended on their usefulness to the new system, and whose commitments and loyalties, violently wrenched from ancient solidarities, were securely focused on the Party-State. As Amosov, a leading party analyst of Central Asian affairs, saw it, there could be no question of "the struggle against female enslavement [becoming] an end in itself."[26]

Under the circumstances, it is not surprising that the actions envisaged by the proponents of *khudzhum* were to rely chiefly on extra-judicial mechanisms and pressures, just as the mass-realization of new norms was to take place outside of formal judicial and organizational channels. In such a contest, fragmentation and re-integration were, in effect, expected to be a coterminous process, with the energies released by one transferred automatically into the organizational and motivational framework of the other. In this sense, the assault-period in Central Asia may be said to have reflected an unbridled Bolshevik political imperative, a militant proclivity to seek violent shortcuts, to bypass the details, complexities, and rigors of institutionalization and legitimation, to dispose of all constraints and disabilities at one stroke. We may visualize this (in Kenneth Boulding's terms) as an assertion of a revolution's "heroic" as against "economic" ethic, or (in Max Weber's terms) the assertion of the "ethic of ultimate ends" as against the "ethic of responsibility."

KHUDZHUM: HEAD-ON ASSAULT ON CUSTOMS AND TABOOS

As far as it is possible to reconstruct the events preceding the main stage of the decreed offensive, it would seem that the first signal of an impending new move was contained in a Central Committee resolution of June 18, 1926, "On the Work of Central Asian Party Organizations among Working- and Peasant-Women." The resolution was obviously addressed to Sredazburo, the Central Committee's Central Asian Bureau in Tashkent, the party's main political coordinative agency for the entire region. The intent of the directive was unmistakable. On the one hand, it was a workmanlike response to a full-scale report on the state of female mobilization in Central Asia, delivered to the party's Secretariat in Moscow by

[26] Amosov, "Shire . . . ," *Ka*, 14, 1929, p. 26.

226

Liubimova, a top official of the Central Asian Zhenotdel (formally, the Women's Department of the Sredazburo). The resolution marked a continuation of the trend in central directives in 1924 and 1925, and showed a fairly consistent and logical attempt to extend and exploit precisely those gains that were perceived to have been made in the course of legal action and of initial, if rudimentary, moves in building a supportive social infrastructure for Moslem women. It called, among other things, for "experimental" political schools for newly recruited native female communists, special courses for training female organizers in Central Asia, a strengthened network of legal aid units in women's clubs, and speedier action in training and promotion of female judicial personnel. It also recommended especially strong efforts in the political recruitment of female handicraft workers and of peasant women who received land in the course of the land reform. It was subtle enough to note "the special significance" that communist Pioneer units of young Moslem girls could have in the struggle against the old order, and, accordingly, ordered the allocation of funds in the 1926/27 budget for the creation of such separate units.

But, at the same time, the resolution called in no uncertain terms for an "intensification" of the struggle against residues of feudal-patriarchal attitudes towards women. "Greater firmness" in this matter was to be adopted, first of all, within the party apparatus itself. Central Asian communists were to prove, by personal example, and without further ado, that they had implemented Soviet legislation concerning female emancipation.[27]

Preparations for the Campaign

The party's orders were discussed and augmented in late 1926 (First Central Asian Party Conference) and in early 1927 (Twelfth Plenum of Sredazburo; Regional Conference of Zhenotdel Workers among Eastern Women; Third Congress of the Uzbek Communist Party). On all these occasions, two men, Zelenskii and Manzhara, played an especially active, clearly supervisory and coordinative role.[28]

The choice of these men as the party's main troubleshooters in the campaign tells us something about the regime's view of the

[27] Liubimova, *VPG*, pp. 72-73; Z. P., *Ka*, 6, 1928, p. 84; Nukhrat, *Ka*, 6, 1928, p. 79; Bil'shai, *RZVS*, p. 191; Shikhmuradov and Rosliakov, *Ocherki Istorii*, p. 290.
[28] See Nikolaeva, *Ka*, 8, 1927, p. 52; Anisimova, *Ka*, 8, 1927, p. 54.

tasks ahead and its assessment of the reliability of native Soviet leadership in this connection. Both men were Russian or Russified communists on assignment in Central Asia from Moscow. One of them (Manzhara) had played a crucial role in the seizure of power in Central Asia (1917-1919), and both had been leading members of the regime's supreme Soviet ruling bodies in the early 1920's. Both had been deliberately installed in commanding positions as counterweights to native leaders coopted into top party and government echelons in the region. Both had a record of primary loyalty to central authorities and of ruthless implementation of Moscow's orders. And both seem to have had a reputation of distrust bordering on contempt for indigenous male personnel in the Soviet apparatus, to an extent where both could be counted among those who had been uneasily referred to by Lenin as Great Russian chauvinists.[29] It is surely also of special significance that, while Zelenskii (as General Secretary of Sredazburo) acted at that time in the capacity of chief political executive for the entire region, Manzhara's role was that of representative of the party's Central Control Commission, a clear indication that Moscow intended to use the decreed operation not just for the officially announced purpose, but also as a means for detailed inspection of Central Asia's party-units and screening of their membership. Thus, Manzhara's involvement only confirmed what was already implicit in the Central Committee resolution of June 18, 1926, ordering Central Asian communists to prove by personal example that they had shed traditional attitudes and customs, beginning with those regarding their women. The campaign shaping up in late 1926 unmistakably carried the threat of a general purge—what would be, in effect, the

[29] See Hayit, *Turkestan im XX Jahrhundert*, pp. 48n., 57n., 100n., 108, 242, 246n., 247, 267n. Zelenskii, while arriving in Central Asia much later than Manzhara, seems to have had his own special reasons for executing and even anticipating Moscow's will with particular alacrity. Having headed Moscow's party organization, and having come under suspicion as an associate of Kamenev, he was sent by Stalin to Central Asia in 1924. He may have needed all the more to prove his loyalty to Stalin at a time (in 1926-27) when Kamenev and other members of the opposition were being systematically destroyed by Stalin's political machine. See Schapiro, *The Communist Party of the Soviet Union*, p. 285. For a systematic analysis of the phenomenon of Great Russian chauvinism in Soviet politics, see Barghoorn, *Soviet Russian Nationalism*, especially Chapter II ("The Doctrine of Russian Leadership"). Cf. Aspaturian, "The Non-Russian Nationalities," in Kassof, *Prospects for Soviet Society*, pp. 143-98.

228

first comprehensive purge of communist organizations in the region.[30] Indigenous Soviet cadres could not have missed the point, then, that in this fashion their own political survival was being made dependent on what many of them surely regarded as a secondary issue or a purely personal matter: the successful elimination of traditional behavioral patterns in society at large and in their own kin-groups.

What emerged from the series of meetings under Zelenskii's and Manzhara's guidance was a demand potentially vast in scope. It was an order to commence decisive moves against the institution of female seclusion (*zatvornichestvo*) in Central Asia. The term officially selected as a rallying cry for the campaign—*khudzhum*—was striking in its implications. It denoted, especially in the military sense, "all-out attack," "sweeping advance," "assault," "storm" in all three main languages of Central Asia's cultural heritage: Turkic, Arabic, and Persian.[31]

Zatvornichestvo—the Russian term for female seclusion among Moslems—could of course refer to a broad spectrum of Central Asian practices and norms. If interpreted literally and in all of its possible meanings, it could not but subsume all of the following: physical segregation and seclusion of Moslem women in special female quarters in the home (in Uzbekistan, *ichkari*), which of course had its larger-scale counterpart in the harem; a female's ritualized inferiority in her husband's, or other related male's, company in and out of the home; ritualized female inferiority, including in most cases injunctions against female presence, in the company of male guests; traditional injunctions against the departure of females from the house without explicit permission of the dominant male, or without the company of other males or females trusted by

---

[30] For some of the earliest hints to this effect, see Nikolaeva, *Ka*, 8, 1927, p. 52. The impression that an attempt was being readied to combine a general assault on tradition with a drastic shakeup of party units is further reinforced by the fact that, while the Stalinist machine first became solidly entrenched in the apparatus in early 1926, it was between the party's Fifteenth Conference (October/November 1926) and Fifteenth Congress (December, 1927) that Stalin finally crushed the intra-party opposition led by Trotsky, Zinoviev, and Kamenev, and moved to remake the party in his image. See Fainsod, *How Russia Is Ruled*, pp. 189 ff.

[31] The Turkic term *hücum* derives from the Arabic *hujūm*. The guttural *kh* in the term is, of course, a Russian adaptation of the soft Arabic *h*. I am indebted to Professor R. Bayly Winder of New York University for his help in tracing these connections.

the kin-group; absolute proscription of a female's dealings with male strangers outside the home, as well as of her presence in public places frequented by or especially reserved for males; severe customary restraints on female participation in most realms of public life, including schooling, most professions, buying and selling in a public market, a number of religious activities and folk festivals, social organizations, and politics; and, of course, veiling (in Uzbekistan and Tadzhikistan, *parandzha* or *chachvan*, veils covering not only the face but the entire body from head to toe; in Turkmenistan, *yashmak*, covering only the mouth).

Not surprisingly, then, Soviet references to *zatvornichestvo* tended to relate to a Moslem woman's being not just "secluded," but "shut in," "shut off," "covered up and locked away"; leading a "barred," "shuttered," "isolated," "solitary" life. The image of a woman's seclusion was linked with that of her partial or total exclusion from the public sectors of social life. Perceived as the incarnation of institutionalized inferiority and apartheid based on sex, *zatvornichestvo* was now seen as the system primarily responsible for a host of sins: perpetuating old preconceptions and superstitions regarding human roles, relationships, and potentialities; encouraging "inertia" and "stagnation"; keeping millions of female working hands "under lock and key," and hence away from "socially significant work"; obstructing the development of the productive forces of the country; hampering fundamental social and cultural transformation, beginning with the formation of a new (nuclear and monogamous) Soviet family; inhibiting the full mobilization and political participation of the masses; hindering the communist upbringing of the young generation; and even delaying "the bolshevization and consolidation of the Party itself" in Central Asia.[32] In effect, *zatvornichestvo* was the "nail," not only holding a Moslem woman's life down in its customary groove, but actually holding the whole traditional system intact.[33] By implication, with the nail gone, the system had to fall apart.

While the argument was not illogical, the implications for action were obviously staggering. To build a political campaign around a move to eliminate *all* possible manifestations of seclusion, while ideally desirable, must have struck a number of party officials as

[32] See Z. P., *Ka*, 6, 1928, p. 84; cf. Nukhrat, *Ka*, 6, 1928, p. 78, and Nukhrat, *OZV*, pp. 38-39; Pal'vanova, *DSV*, pp. 95-97.

[33] See Nukhrat, *Ka*, 6, 1928, p. 78; cf. Nukhrat, *OZV*, pp. 18-24; Pal'vanova, *DSV*, pp. 28-29; Niurina, *Parandzha*, p. 5.

physically impossible and tactically unwise. Indeed, even though formal preparations for *khudzhum* continued to call for destruction of seclusion as a whole, and throughout Central Asia, there were signs in late 1926 of significant delimitations in the party's plans. Just as the primary emphasis in legal action had shifted from over-all legal emancipation to the specific issue of divorce, so did the main thrust of extra-legal moves shift from seclusion as a whole to veiling in particular,[34] and from Central Asia in its entirety to Uzbekistan as the initial testing ground for the offensive.[35]

A good case could be made for concentrating the massive assault especially on the veil. Most obviously, the Leninist disposition to concentrate the heaviest fire on a weak but crucial link could

[34] See, e.g., Liubimova, *VPG*, p. 73, 69-71.

[35] It made sense, from the Soviet standpoint, to limit initial action to Uzbekistan. Tashkent, the Uzbek republican capital, served as the head-quarters for all Soviet apparatuses—political, economic, and military—of overall regional administration in Central Asia, and was, by the same token, the most important single link between Moscow and the Moslem borderlands. Uzbekistan (excluding the areas of the former Bukharan emirate, of course) was among Central Asian areas that had been relatively long under both Tsarist and Soviet rule, and that were therefore relatively most secularized and industrialized, at least in urban locales. Uzbekistan had the largest, most widely distributed, consistently sedentary, and most diversely skilled population (in modern terms), and was unquestionably developing the most numerous and dynamic secular intelligentsia in the region. Uzbekistan was also the principal locus of one of the Soviet Union's most valuable cash-crops: cotton. At the same time, though, it could be said that Uzbekistan, especially from the vantage point of its rural hinterlands and such old seats of Islamic orthodoxy as Bukhara, was precisely the place where the traditional structures, practices, and norms singled out for attack by Moscow were most overtly in evidence and most heavily concentrated. This does not mean that other Central Asian republics were completely exempted from *khudzhum*. While veiling, e.g., was not, or not as con-sistently, practiced in some of the other areas (Kazakh and Kirghiz) as in Uzbekistan, most other norms and practices associated with female seclusion and general status-inferiority were clearly present everywhere. Accordingly, pressures to implement the party's decisions were in varying degree evident in all of the region's republics in 1926-28, but a full-scale, dramatic assault in these republics seems to have been made contingent on prior success in Uzbekistan. It would seem, then, that the latter was coming to be viewed by the regime as the pivotal component in Central Asia's regional arrange-ment, and as a potential model for other Central Asian republics in the execution of revolutionary and developmental policies. Cf. the view on the re-emergence of the Uzbeks, under Soviet tutelage, as Central Asia's "ruling nationality," in Aspaturian, "The Non-Russian Nationalities," in Kassof, *The Prospects for Soviet Society*, especially pp. 151-52, 185-86.

be readily applied here. The veil could be seen not only as the most tangible, publicly perceived embodiment of physical and symbolic apartheid, but as the very linchpin of seclusion itself. If women could be moved to unveil massively and in public, their act would, in and of itself, constitute a challenge to all other manifestations of seclusion. If the former would succeed, the latter could not possibly endure for long. The black veil was clearly the most dramatic public indication of female status; conversely, unveiling could be expected to be the most dramatic public act in violation of traditional taboos and of the entire primordial status-structure. Unveiling would revolutionize women's imagination as well as the attitudes of the world around them, would open up for women an entirely new world of social contacts, roles, and functions, and would thus directly undermine the entire traditional pattern of human relationships and ties. In the stringent terms of one Soviet analyst, the removal of a Moslem woman's veil would altogether "remove a bond binding her to hearth and home."[36]

There were also more immediate and practical considerations. Economic development, and particularly industrialization and the formation of a native proletariat, would immediately benefit from unveiling. In Uzbekistan alone there were at that time, by Soviet estimate, at least two million female working-hands, and they were "tied down by the veil."[37] As this was expressed rather more explicitly later, " . . . how can a veiled, heavily clad [Moslem] woman serve as a tractor- or combine-driver? How can she operate cotton gins, [and] textile machines, . . . when she is trammelled by a veil from head to foot . . . , when even in broad daylight, in the street, she can hardly see where to put her foot down?"[38]

Finally, there were quite precise political considerations. While unveiling was expected to serve as a particularly efficient lever in

[36] Limanovskii, *Sov. Khlopok*, 11-12, 1937, pp. 91 ff. While this happened to be said in 1937, it was merely the most precisely worded expression of a conviction that came to be widely shared in Soviet ranks in the 1920's. See, e.g., Yesova, in *ZVR*, p. 374; Pal'vanova, *DSV*, pp. 10, 19, 28-29, 63; Osman Dzhuma Zade, *Ka*, 7, 1929, p. 48; Niurina, *Parandzha*, pp. 3, 15; Nukhrat, *OZV*, p. 20; Bil'shai, *RZVS*, p. 192; Liubimova, *VPG*, p. 68.

[37] See Liubimova, *VPG*, p. 69.

[38] Limanovskii, *Sov. Khlopok*, 11-12, 1937, pp. 91 ff. While these words happened to be written in 1937, they, again, merely expressed most precisely what was clearly on the mind of most Soviet officials in the 1920's. See, e.g., Liubimova, *VPG*, p. 69; Nukhrat, *OZV*, pp. 38-39; Maksimova, *Ka*, 6, 1928, p. 95; Aitakov, *SS* (10-11), 1927, p. 76.

232

psychological reorientation, and in social, cultural, and economic reconstruction, it seems to have been also perceived as an especially simple and unambiguous gauge of compliance, first of all on the part of the native male personnel of the Soviet apparatus.[39] Presumably there could be no two ways here about a local communist's implementation of the party's order: either he unveiled his mother, wife, sisters, or daughter, or he did not. If he did, he would clearly reaffirm his loyalty to the regime and his break from tradition; he could be expected to serve as a model to his kinsmen and to the population as a whole; and he could be entrusted with further political responsibility, beginning with the management of *khudzhum* itself. If he did not, he could not possibly hide this fact.

Of course, a highly important by-product was to be gained here at once. It was logical to expect that a communist's family would constitute the most accessible and best sensitized source of female converts to the new ideology and recruits to the Soviet apparatus.[40] Whether or not a male communist fulfilled the new demands with dispatch, the chances were good that women in his family would now be more easily contacted from outside, or that they would themselves be willing and able to exert far greater pressure from inside the family for their own emancipation.

The First Phase

During the first phase[41] of *khudzhum*, operations seem to have been by and large limited to communist, official, urban, and relatively most secularized strata of the population. In December, 1926, and in January and February, 1927, under the supervision of Sredazburo emissaries and of the specially formed "[Uzbek] Republican Commission for *Khudzhum*,"[42] meetings of the communist *aktiv*[43] were called in all major cities of Uzbekistan, beginning with those considered "most advanced" and hence "best prepared" for the occasion: Tashkent, Ferghana, Samarkand, and Zerafshan.[44] Such meetings were extended downward to the province and district levels of the apparatus as special Party-State com-

---

[39] One does not need to read too closely between the lines to arrive at this conclusion. See, e.g., Liubimova, *VPG*, pp. 69-71.

[40] For strong hints of such expectations, see Bil'shai, *RZVS*, p. 191.

[41] For a Soviet view of these phases, see Z. P., *Ka*, 6, 1928, p. 84.

[42] Anisimova, *Ka*, 8, 1927, p. 54.

[43] Leading cadres, responsible officials, and activists involved in running the Soviet apparatus and official campaigns.

[44] Pal'vanova, *DSV*, p. 98.

missions for managing *khudzhum* were formed at these levels under the general supervision of local party committees. As a rule, the *khudzhum* commissions were to include local party secretaries, Zhenotdel chiefs, and representatives of the Komsomol, trade unions, and of commissariats of labor, justice, and education.[45] Significantly, orders for the *aktiv* meetings stipulated that the latter be followed in short order, and repeatedly, by meetings of the entire party and Komsomol membership at all levels of the apparatus—including, however, not only communists but also their wives.[46]

A single theme dominated the main addresses at the meetings of the *aktiv*. It found its most succinct expression in speeches by Manzhara and Zelenskii. As the former put it, "It is indispensable to begin a more decisive struggle with anti-party acts based on residues of local custom . . . , [practices] that impede the liberation [of native communists] from an ideology that is alien to, and hostile towards, the party, as well as [detrimental] to the development of party and soviet organizations and to economic development."[47] The ominous link in Manzhara's terms between a communist's attitudes to female emancipation and the degree of his fidelity to what was obviously a "feudal-patriarchal" (and hence subversive) ideology was even more explicitly established by Zelenskii. The latter referred to traditional attitudes as a decided "weakness" in the makeup of a native communist. And he declared:

> We will have no clear-cut results in the struggle for [female] emancipation until we get rid of this weakness in [Central Asian] communists, until we confront every communist holding a responsible post with more decisive, stern demands, until we say to our communists, to the high-placed executives, who lay claim, on the basis of their [membership in the] party, to leading positions in the party and in the Soviet apparatus [:] if, as a communist, you claim a place [in the leading echelons], then, if you don't mind, be good enough to follow the precepts of communist ideology, of the communist program [;] but if you are unable to conform to [these precepts], if you have not yet fully gotten rid of bourgeois ideology, if beys, mullahs, and ishans are still holding you tight in their clutches, then, if you please, lay no claims on the party's leadership and the leadership of the Soviet apparatus.[48]

[45] Ibid.   [46] Nikolaeva, *Ka*, 8, 1927, p. 52.

[47] Ibid.

[48] As quoted in Yaroslavsky, *Ka*, 1, 1929, p. 31.

234

At the Third Congress of the Uzbek Communist Party in early Spring, 1927, these allusions were taken one step farther. Party members were called upon to carry out the new directive immediately and without reservations; they were to insure the unveiling not only of women in their immediate family but also of all of their female relatives; most important, the practice of veiling and of seclusion in general in a communist's family was declared to be incompatible with his continued membership in party ranks.[49] At the same time, in a somewhat softer vein, female communists were asked to "undertake the obligation" not to wear the veil.[50]

The demand was now clear-cut, and the threat was there for all to see. Attainment or retention of power, perquisites, and status in the new system was being made contingent upon sudden and drastic alterations in personal orientations and lives. According to all reliable accounts, the consternation in native Soviet ranks was immediate and profound. The sense of unease and disbelief deepened when male communists were obliged to come to party meetings with their wives. In the words of one participant, "no one quite knew what to do after the official part was over"—that is, the part wherein the imperatives of *khudzhum* were formally outlined, and Manzhara's and Zelenskii's warnings officially presented; "no one felt quite well."[51] It would seem that most of the communists' wives came to the party meetings fully veiled, and many—perhaps in order to gain some courage, perhaps to hold on to something familiar from homelife, perhaps in response to a husband's explicit orders—brought their infants with them. In some cases, the initial unease at the meetings was reportedly dispelled only after harassed chairmen turned them into the equivalent of christening parties—of course, in their communist version, *oktiabrienie*.[52]

As Nikolaeva (a senior official of the Central Asian Zhenotdel) noted at the time, even at the Central Asian Regional Conference of Zhenotdel Workers among Eastern Women, i.e., a conference attended primarily by women, including most of the region's cadres and activists, which Zelenskii personally addressed, "not all comrades had an adequately clear notion just what Zelenskii's slogan of 'assault' on behalf of female emancipation really meant." Only repeated meetings of the *aktiv*, and of entire party cells, apparently succeeded in "clarifying" the aims of *khudzhum* to the party's rank-and-file.[53]

---

[49] See Bil'shai, *RZVS*, p. 191; cf. Nukhrat, *OZV*, p. 84.
[50] Nukhrat, *RN*, 3, 1933, p. 46. [51] Nikolaeva, *Ka*, 8, 1927, p. 52.
[52] Ibid. [53] Ibid.

Thus, if it had been felt that tangible signs of female emancipation in a communist's kin-group must precede a mass-offensive in society as a whole, the events in early 1927 could not but bear out this judgment. Not only were palpable models needed for general emulation, but a large-scale campaign was manifestly impossible unless it was led and staffed at the grassroots by the native—that is, predominantly male—personnel of the Soviet apparatus. Yet, in order to be able to do this, native cadres had to be able—and willing —to confront not just their ethnic brethren, but also their kinsmen, their women, and, of course, themselves. The interaction between perceptions of this inherent dilemma on the part of the prime actors and the growing sense of urgency and pressure conveyed by Sredazburo was most dramatically apparent in the course of closed meetings of leading party cadres, i.e., at meetings where the latter were both obliged and able to speak more frankly than elsewhere. What is probably the only stenographic report of such a meeting available outside the Soviet Union makes this quite clear. The meeting was that of the party *aktiv* of Tashkent's Old City,[54] and the notes were taken by none other than Liubimova, at that time a leading official of Central Asia's Zhenotdel apparatus, obviously taking the pulse of the proceedings on Moscow's orders.[55] While some of the participants are not readily identifiable, it is clear that all held responsible or leading posts in the Uzbek apparatus, i.e., in the most important republic in the region, and of the region's largest and most populous city, a city long exposed to Russian and Soviet influence and, at the same time, serving as the central locus of Soviet power for the entire area. Since it is certain that the stenographic report was duly sent to Moscow, we can be sure that the party had a chance to take a full measure of what transpired here and else-

[54] The older and predominantly native section of the city, as distinguished from the New City—built under Tsarist rule, populated mostly by Europeans, and housing the Tsarist, and then the Soviet, administrative apparatuses.

[55] Serafima Liubimova—a Russian, and an old member of the party— was dispatched from Moscow in 1923 to head the Zhenotdel of what was then the Turkestan republic. While, on one level, her immediate superiors were in the Secretariat of Sredazburo, she was also at the end of another line of command leading directly to the head of the central Zhenotdel in Moscow (A. V. Artiukhina, Russian, with important links to the Central Committee Secretariat and Politburo, and apparently on Stalin's side in the crucial stages of the factional battles in Moscow in the 1920's) and hence to the party's top leadership.

236

where. Here is a shortened rendition of one of the exchanges that took place at the meeting in Tashkent:[56]

> *Yakubov*: You are not a communist if you are not a revolutionary; and you are not a revolutionary if you do not actively fight for female emancipation. While we have been cautious until now, it is necessary at this time to openly raise the question of unveiling. As I see it, we must talk first of all about the wives of responsible officials.

> *Unidentified voice*: Is your own wife unveiled?

> *Yakubov*: And how about the Chief of Agitprop[57]—is his wife unveiled?

> *Kadyrov*: Our communists have a poor comprehension [of these matters], not only with respect to work among women, but also regarding the larger issues [that are involved here]. Even old party members cannot get rid of the old habits. We have communists in every *mahallah*,[58] but the *ishans*[59] are organizing the elders against us [making it difficult for a communist to act in his own family in accordance with the party's demands regarding female emancipation and unveiling].[60] We must start this campaign in the *mahallahs* [that is, at the grassroots, not at the top]. [By the way,] my own family is unveiled.

> *Tursun Khodzhaev*: You are lying, [no one in your family] is unveiled. To begin with, we must raise the question, not of unveiling, but of educational work [of general enlightenment]. If we managed to carry out the land reform, and we did not falter, [surely] we can carry out this assignment, too. Why do you think Tatar women are unveiled? After all, they too had been veiled at one time. [The answer is:] life itself compelled them. [Thus, we must first] carefully prepare ourselves [and pave the way], and begin not in one place but in a hundred places simultaneously.

---

[56] See Liubimova, *VPG*, pp. 69-71.

[57] Department for Agitation and Propaganda in the Party's Secretariat.

[58] City ward.   [59] Moslem religious personages.

[60] The speaker seems to have referred here either to particularly respected elders in the local community or to the parents of local communists—or to both.

Rasulov: The wives of those [communists] who moved to the New City [of Tashkent] have unveiled, but whenever they come to the Old City they put on the veil again. [The lesson is:] at first, we must conduct educational work, and the veil will fall by itself.

Khodzhaev [probably *Faizulla*]: Everybody talked a lot, but nobody really did anything. [Here you are:] "Communists do not object to unveiling their wives, but there is this or that trouble in the *mahallah!*" While it is timely for the Zhenotdel to have raised the question of the veil, one cannot limit oneself [to this issue]: "What is required is general enlightenment work amidst the people." [Look:] I have been agitating for five years in my own family, trying to persuade my wife to throw away her veil, but, while she is unveiled in the New City, she veils herself again the moment she returns to the Old one. She tells me: "Fine, I will take off the veil, but what about the neighbors? Let them do it, too."

Tairov: The veil is a dark curtain of religion. If a party-member [really] does not want to follow [the old] religion, he must unveil his wife. When the veil falls, religion will fall, too. Some people say that if you take the veil away, wives will leave their husbands. This is not true. European women are not veiled, and yet they are being abandoned by their husbands more frequently [than ours]. [What is really the matter here is this:] there are people among us who [deliberately] try to undermine the authority [and besmirch the reputation] of women who take off the veil.

This exchange speaks for itself. It is a measure of the discomfort that affected even the highest echelons of the Uzbek apparatus, the moment the new orders became known. It is a vivid illustration of the range of responses materializing among veteran native communists in the first blush of *khudzhum*: from self-justification to barely veiled anger and rank dissimulation; from attempts to attribute all difficulties to the clergy's machinations, patriarchal disapproval, or overall community pressure, to self-exculpations laying the blame at the door of the women themselves; from vague proposals to wait for objective conditions to change human behavior to demands for an immediate crackdown on all and everything that stood in the way.

238

It would seem that whatever the doubts that might have been engendered in the minds of Sredazburo's or Moscow's leadership by reports such as this, they were not allowed to influence the course of the campaign. Meetings of the political *aktiv*, and of entire party cells, were followed by mass meetings of urban trade union members and artisans,[61] where the aims of *khudzhum* were explained by communist emissaries. As a follow-up to these meetings, trade unions, beginning with the Uzbek union of metalworkers, were ordered to arrange quickly and as frequently as possible intimate "family evenings" (preferably with dinner or tea) of native workers with their wives. Among the young male workers, married Komsomol members were to set an early example. The purpose of getting together small groups of married working-class couples in private homes was to ensure an atmosphere wherein men would feel inclined to accept the presence of women in their company, and might be persuaded to permit the unveiling of their wives in the course of the evening.[62]

The Second Phase

If the first phase of *khudzhum* was deliberately selective in its emphasis and targets, and was clearly intended to secure models of right conduct among strata judged to be most amenable to the new norms, the second phase was marked by a massive effort to engage the population as a whole, and to focus the attention of the entire Soviet apparatus toward this end.[63] Beginning in early spring of 1927, an attempt was made to set a number of interrelated processes in motion. The mass media were flooded with appeals for general unveiling.[64] A doctors' conference was especially convened to attest to the grave harm done to Moslem mothers and infants by the veil—not only depriving them of sun and air but directly causing skin and other diseases—and the findings of the conference were widely publicized.[65] Native artists were mobilized to compose and publicly recite poems and to stage plays designed to stir a female audience and to induce in it, through passionate representa-

[61] Z. P., *Ka*, 6, 1928, p. 84.

[62] Nikolaeva, *Ka*, 8, 1927, p. 54; cf. Pal'vanova, *DSV*, p. 100; Liubimova, *VPG*, p. 71; Niurina, *Parandzha*, p. 13.

[63] See Nikolaeva, *Ka*, 8, 1927, p. 52.

[64] See Vagabov, *Islam i Zhenshchina*, pp. 109-10; Nukhrat, *OZV*, pp. 88-89.

[65] Nukhrat, *OZV*, p. 86.

tions of female degradation in Islam, the courage to challenge traditional institutions, i.e., first and foremost, the courage to break out of seclusion and to unveil.[66] The titles of some of these creations speak for themselves: "The Secrets of the Veil," "The Traitors of Khudzhum," "The Tragedy of the Mobilized," "The Old Intrigues," "The Woman's Voice," "The Song of Free Women." All of these served as indictments of "reactionary Moslem . . . and feudal-patriarchal morality," "religious fanaticism," and "male despotism," and all dealt with veiling and related rituals as "survivals of barbarism and savagery in relation to women" and as expressions of "female humiliation and slavery" in the Islamic world.[67] The party singled out for special commendation and wide dissemination plays whose dramatic contents were observed to be powerful enough to move Moslem women to tear their veils off then and there in acts of collective catharsis.[68] Apparently "The Moslem Woman," a film produced in Bukhara under the auspices of the Central Asian Zhenotdel and one in which most of the actors were native female activists, was singled out for the most widespread and simultaneous screening in the region. It was the first product of the mass media deliberately designed to show "what a Moslem woman's life was really like." It reportedly made "a stunning impression" on local female audiences.[69] Turkic dramatists and poets judged to be particularly sympathetic to the cause were dispatched to the traditionalist countryside as propagandists of female emancipation. Characteristically, at least some of them (e.g., Hamza Hakim Zada Niyaziy, a prolific writer, early Uzbek communist, and militant atheist, with distinctly pro-Russian and pro-Soviet commitments[70]) were expected to combine public appeals for the liberation of women with anti-religious agitation in villages containing some of Central Asia's holiest Islamic shrines.[71]

"Cultural offensives" (*kul'tpokhod*) were initiated in villages and towns. These involved not only propaganda on the evils of illiteracy, particularly among women, but also mock trials especially staged for native women by Zhenotdel activists in city and village

---

[66] For some examples, see Pal'vanova, *DSV*, pp. 51-52; Vagabov, *Islam i Zhenshchina*, pp. 106-108. Cf. Allworth, *Uzbek Literary Politics*, pp. 217-18, 222; Halle, *Women*, pp. 137-38.

[67] See Vagabov, ibid., pp. 107-108; Bil'shai, *RZVS*, pp. 190-91.

[68] Vagabov, ibid., p. 108.

[69] Liubimova, *VPG*, p. 43.

[70] See Allworth, *Uzbek Literary Politics*, pp. 63, 122, 216, 218, 257-58.

[71] See Sulaimanova, *ISGPU*, Vol. II, p. 318.

squares, in which the "accused" were ancient rituals, harmful and demeaning customs, as well as disease and dirt.[72]

At the same time, widespread public demands were elicited, especially on the part of already unveiled Moslem women, to ban female veiling altogether.[73] These demands were floated as trial balloons in all mass media, and party meetings were convened to determine the feasibility of a legal prohibition of the veil.[74] Where veiling was not as characteristic a feature of female attire as in Uzbek and Tadzhik areas (for example, in Turkmenistan and Kirghiziia) the issue of legal prohibition was raised in regard to other traditional articles of female, and even male, attire, including fur hats.[75]

On the eve of March 8, 1927, female members of the Uzbek Communist Party, and what appears to have been the entire male *aktiv* of the Uzbek apparatus together with their wives and other female relatives, were ordered to appear at special convocations marking Soviet Woman's Day. Female communist sympathizers and other non-party women were invited to separate gatherings under the aegis of the Zhenotdel. The meetings were reportedly held in all major cities and towns of the republic, including provincial and district centers. At these convocations, addressed by leading functionaries of the regime, *khudzhum* was declared to be entering a mass action phase, and all women present were called upon to unveil that very evening. Male officials in particular were reminded that this was the time to lead in the proceedings by setting a personal example in unveiling their female relatives in front of the assembly. According to widely publicized reports, the party's call was heeded everywhere, and in many cases the ceremonies were marked by tempestuous female demonstrations.[76]

[72] See, e.g., Nukhrat, *Ka*, 9, 1929, pp. 32-35; Byzov, *Za Sots. Turk.*, 12, 1928, pp. 57-61; Pal'vanova, *DSV*, pp. 70-72.

[73] See, e.g., Rigin, *Ka*, 5-6, 1929, p. 59.

[74] Nukhrat, *Ka*, 6, 1928, p. 78; Liubimova, *Ka*, 8, 1928, pp. 73-75; Bogacheva, *Ka*, 11, 1928, p. 66; Ishkova, *Ka*, 11, 1928, pp. 59-62; Osman Dzhuma Zade, *Ka*, 7, 1929, pp. 48-49; "Nuzhno li izdat' dekret' . . . ," *Ka*, 8, 1928, pp. 79-81; Safudri, *Ka*, 13, 1929, pp. 42-44.

[75] Nukhrat, *Ka*, 9, 1929, p. 32; Pal'vanova, *DSV*, pp. 104-105. Note that even though most of the formal demands for such legal prohibition were discussed in print in 1928 and 1929, they convey a strong impression that their actual testing in the field commenced on a large scale in early 1927.

[76] *PV*, March 10, 1927, as cited in Bil'shai, *RZVS*, p. 192. See also, Nukhrat, *RN*, 3, 1933, p. 46; Nukhrat, *OZV*, pp. 84-86; Pal'vanova, *DSV*, p. 98. Cf. Halle, *Women*, p. 173.

March 8 editions of major Central Asian newpapers were outfitted with special *khudzhum* supplements.[77] In these, the most dramatic appeals to Moslem women were carried in the form of revolutionary poetry, with striking imagery of liberation from the veil.
The poems were clearly intended for recitation to mass audiences
during the day. One of these, in the form of a mother's lullaby to
a baby girl,[78] was a song of maternal protectiveness as well as of
joy, encouragement, and vengeance on the eve of battle with the
old order. Some of its lines are amply suggestive of the motivations
they were intended to reinforce:

> . . . I shall no longer hide you under the veil's dark lid. Let the
> *ishan* shed his tears for us. . . . After all, it is he who has been
> saying that it is a sin to uncover our face, that disgrace [and
> shame] will fall upon the head that dares. We have lifted with
> our own hands the heavy load of "thou shalt not," we dared to
> look directly into life's turbulent eyes. Today is spring's best day,
> one that's been awaited for such a long, long time. [In one day,]
> we have stepped over [the barrier of many] years. . . . Do not try
> to frighten us in the dark night, cruel devil-wind. . . . You don't
> know, my baby daughter, about Anna Dzhamal and Enne
> Kulieva,[79] whose cheerful laughter was stifled [by enemies of our
> freedom], whose souls were lost for the sake of better days. . . .
> Sleep well, you're safe, we shall get through. . . . Like a sharp-
> clawed bird of prey, vengeance guards our roads. With a strong
> beat of the drum, with a strong and precise beat of a [host of
> marching] feet, we shall [reach the highest places and] from
> there we shall look across the precipices of the past. Let the
> [cleric] keep in custody our cruel [customs of] *adat*; as for our
> life, it will be much easier without the *shariat*. . . . Sweet dreams,
> my child, have no fear: [we shall not let] the veil torture your
> body with its grey fetters, . . . with its thorny bonds. . . .

[77] While direct references to such supplements mention specifically *Pravda
Vostoka*—Central Asia's most important Russian-language daily published
in Tashkent—it is reasonable to assume that the contents of the latter included translations of materials carried by other native-language publications. See Nukhrat, *OZV*, pp. 88-89.

[78] See Nukhrat, *OZV*, pp. 88-89. No attempt is made here to present the
original linear and rhythmic structure or to render a precise translation of
this and the other poems that follow.

[79] Two Turkmen female communists and leaders in the struggle for
emancipation, killed (reportedly lynched) by Central Asian counterrevolutionaries in the mid-1920's.

242

Another typical, widely disseminated poem, "Away with the Veil,"[80] contained some striking exhortations, replete with symbols of strong-willed action:

> . . . A tempest . . . tears the sombre clouds of the accursed *chachvan*. . . . Lift up your eyes! . . . [The veil is but] a curtain of blind and crazy error [which is now torn down], . . . [just as] the shameful laws of the dead past [that had] for eons cast a net over you [are now destroyed]. . . . [Until now, your life was confined to] mouldering . . . cramped and low-roofed huts . . . to boggy fields. . . . [Now, over these huts and fields] the dawn is red. [Lift up your eyes, and] one will shall . . . flash in the East . . . from the burning eyes of a million souls. . . . You brown-skinned women, haste to work: unveiled you weave the dawn's red glow!

A third characteristic piece—a poem, "To Uzbek Women," by Hamza Niyaziy[81]—carried an appeal that was frankly sensual and that, at the same time, freely adapted some of the hymnal lines of the *Internationale* to the cause and audience at hand, linking the promise of new personal worth and beauty with the splendor of the world to come:

> . . . Take off your [black pall, your coverall], open your face, be beautiful for all! Split and crush your chains to pieces, get rid of them, be free! Thrust the dagger of [light and] knowledge deep into the heart of ignorance [and darkness]. Reach out for wisdom, for worldly knowledge. . . . Give your face grown pale in darkness a chance to blossom out with joy; [go on to] beautify the feats of scholars and of wisemen, be a fine red rose! . . . Let the rays of learning play upon your eyes, and not the lead-gray covers of antimony. . . . Go on, enter the palaces of art and science, be beautiful for all!

On the morning of March 8, a massive outpouring of crowds of Moslem women was organized in major Uzbek cities. Led by Zhenotdel activists, and protected by police cordons, they marched in procession to especially designated city squares. Some of the latter were located in European sections, and were dominated by newly erected statues of Lenin. Others (such as the Registan in Samarkand) were the traditional meeting places of native quarters,

---

[80] See translation in Halle, *Women*, pp. 169-70.
[81] See Bil'shai, *RZVS*, p. 191.

bordering on former princely palace grounds and Moslem religious shrines. In all cases, the squares were reportedly outfitted with large daises, and decorated with flowers, oriental carpets, red banners, and placards with revolutionary slogans concerning the liberation of women. Military bands and native orchestras were provided to greet the female processions upon their arrival in the squares. In the course of the morning, the assemblies were addressed not only by party and state dignitaries, but by a variety of female speakers mustered by the party's Women's Department for this occasion: native and Russian Zhenotdel leaders; native activists freshly unveiled only the evening before, with red kerchiefs on their heads; Tatar and other female communists especially invited from European Russia; and Turkic actresses and musical performers from Central Asia's urban centers and from elsewhere in the Soviet Union—all of them, of course, unveiled.

In formal speeches, and in what were reported to be fiery recitations of revolutionary poetry—featuring especially the poems of Hamza Niyaziy—the themes of female liberation were carried to the assembled multitudes. Vehement indictments of the old order were coupled with passionate calls to a new life under the aegis of the Soviet regime. The prime emphasis in speeches, poems, and songs was on unveiling, as a woman's most important and promising step towards self-assertion and self-realization. It would seem that in most cases formal and dramatic presentations were brought to a head when small groups of veiled native women (probably held in reserve and coached by the Zhenotdel) stepped up to the podium and, in full view of the crowds, ostentatiously tore the veils from their faces, threw them into prepared bonfires, and exhorted others to do the same. According to official and eyewitness reports, the cumulative effect on the assembled Moslem women was profound: thousands were moved into collective, simultaneous, and tumultuous burning of their veils, and then surged through city streets unveiled, chanting challenges to the old order.[82]

Initial reports from the field immediately following the events of March 8, 1927, indicated what appeared to be extraordinary success, not only in Uzbekistan but also (though to a lesser extent) in adjoining areas inhabited by Uzbeks, including Tadzhikistan, at

[82] See Bil'shai, *RZVS*, pp. 191-92; Liubimova, *VPG*, pp. 68 ff.; Nukhrat, *OZV*, pp. 84-88; Niurina, *Parandzha*, pp. 7-10, 15; Z. P., *Ka*, 6, 1928, p. 84; Nikolaeva, *Ka*, 8, 1927, p. 52. Cf. Halle, *Women*, pp. 169-70, 172-73; Borodin, *Cradle of Splendor*, pp. 186-87.

that time a component part of the Uzbek republic. In July, 1927, representatives of the Sredazburo and of the Uzbek republican leadership solemnly (and apparently personally) reported to the Organizational Bureau (Orgburo) of the party's Central Committee in Moscow the results of the campaign. It appeared that on the morning of March 8 alone about 10,000 women burned their veils in Uzbek city squares. By the beginning of April, about 70,000 veils had been disposed of. Sometime in May, the official count for Uzbekistan alone reached 90,000.[83]

It is easy to understand the sense of triumph with which these reports were delivered in Moscow and communicated through Central Asian mass media. The spring events of 1927 were seen as a dramatic breakthrough, and a confirmation of all the party's expectations of *khudzhum*. They were cited as evidence of a genuine "revolutionary wave" generated throughout the region, wherein female liberation from ancient bonds was "progressing with a grandiose sweep," one that had "colossal," "historic" implications.[84]

Not only in the Uzbek countryside, but throughout the Central Asian hinterland, the echoes of *khudzhum* were seen as having an unprecedented effect. Enthusiastic analysts felt that already in mid-1927, they could detect a trend among Central Asia's women: those who had been veiled as well as those who had never been veiled before (Kazakh and Kirghiz women) seemed to show *en masse* a disposition to attend Soviet schools, to join Soviet enterprises and organizations, to run for elected posts in local soviets, and to vote.[85] Even men were reported to be responding with unusual alacrity. As Anisimova, a Zhenotdel analyst, itemized this,

---

[83] Ar-na, *Ka*, 1, 1928, p. 57; Liubimova, *Ka*, 10, 1927, p. 61; Nukhrat, *OZV*, p. 87; Nukhrat, *Ka*, 6, 1928, p. 78; Bil'shai, *RZVS*, p. 192; Zaitsev, *VS*, 4, 1928, p. 9. While some of the above sources cite July 6, 1927, as the date of the report to the Orgburo, Pal'vanova (*DSV*, p. 105) gives the impression that the report was made on June 5 of that year. While it makes little difference, in the context of this analysis, just what was the exact date of the report (although it seems certain that it was July 6) it should assume greater significance at some point in the future, when Central Asian archives might be opened for scholarly perusal, and appraisals of the interaction between lower and higher echelons in Soviet politics might become possible.

[84] Anisimova, *Ka*, 8, 1927, pp. 54-56.

[85] Anisimova, *Ka*, 8, 1927, p. 55; Nikolaeva, *Ka*, 8, 1927, p. 52; Rigin, *Ka*, 5-6, 1929, pp. 58-59; Kuchkin, *SKA*, p. 238.

roving government representatives were transmitting to Tashkent what appeared to be formal requests by entire Uzbek villages for central authorities to send unveiling commissions to them, too, so that the "[great] popular celebrations" that took place in the cities on March 8 could also be enacted in the countryside. Moreover, even in remote villages a sense of the impending demise of the old order seemed to be affecting the old, traditionalist generation: "[Uzbek fathers] no longer believe that it is possible to save the veil, and are in a rush to marry off their underage daughters, so as to [get rid of the spiritual responsibility for unveiling them] and to transfer that responsibility to the girls' new husbands."[86] What did all this mean? In Anisimova's words, it meant that "a decisive rebuff has been administered to those who kept saying that one must first enlighten [and educate a Moslem woman], and only then unveil her." Such defeatist talk could now be dismissed: "The [unveiled and therefore] emancipated woman will be [perfectly] capable of enlightening herself."[87] Liubimova, Moscow's emissary at the helm of the Central Asian Zhenotdel, concurred: "the results of the enormous work carried out by the party in the Soviet East" were there for all to see; the "assault on the survivals of the old order, the merciless struggle with the remnants of the slavish past" were at last on the threshold of success. "[The course of] *khudzhum* is the best possible proof that [we are done and] finished with that . . . [slavish] past. The female laboring masses of all Eastern peoples have risen from bondage to [the rudders of power] in the land—[the same women] of whom comrade Lenin had, in his own time, said: 'There are rising here to a fully conscious life the most oppressed of the oppressed. Now the victory of the toilers is secure.' "[88]

The events of spring, 1927, were but the first act in an intensive and far-flung campaign. In the months that followed, *khudzhum*, both on its own momentum and in interaction with responses of the affected milieu, was to evolve into a harsh general crackdown on all deviants from superimposed rules. It was to take the course of massive enforcement and repression wherein legalism and direct assault, both as dispositions and as actions, coalesced into an all-out offensive that was expected to shake the traditional world to its foundations.

[86] Anisimova, *Ka*, 8, 1927, pp. 55-56.
[87] Ibid., p. 55.   [88] Liubimova, *Ka*, 10, 1927, p. 61.

PART FOUR

Responses and Outcomes, 1925–1929

INTRODUCTION

Heretical Models and the Management of Induced Tensions

REVOLUTIONARY ACTION AS A TENSION-MANAGEMENT SYSTEM[1]

THE use of revolutionary legalism and administrative assault as the Communist Party's strategic approaches to radical social change may be said to have involved the introduction of *a specialized tension-management system* into a traditional milieu, a system combining tension-inducing and tension-controlling purposes. Specifically, the strategic objectives came to be: to induce (positive) tensions that would fundamentally undermine the traditional order (the target system), and, at the same time, to control those (negative) consequences of induced tensions that threatened to affect the stability of the Soviet regime (the sponsor system) and the safety of its developmental objectives. In other words, a new system of norms and rules had both to encourage and to maintain a delicate balance between disequilibrium and stabilization, fragmentation and integration, social revolution and orderly development. Moreover, it had to take into account not one homogeneous universe of clients, but, as we shall see, many—and overlapping—social interests and groups.

LEGALISM AND ASSAULT AS HERETICAL MODELS

As we have seen, Soviet views both of legal and of administrative action were, from the very beginning, frankly instrumental. As perceived by the regime, these actions were designed for four basic purposes: to destroy the antecedent social order; to ensure the discipline of a population mobilized to create a new industrial and political system; to ensure the security of the Party-State that gen-

---

[1] W. Moore and A. Feldman have proposed to view society itself as a tension-management system. See their "Society as a Tension-Management System," in G. Baker and L. S. Cottrell (eds.), *Behavioral Science and Civil Defense Disaster Research Group*, 16, 1962, pp. 93-105.

erated and administered this system; and to serve as a means in building what was conceived to be a communist society.

However, fragmentation and destruction necessarily had to precede reconstruction and re-integration. Paradoxically, perhaps, the success of revolutionary rules in controlling tension was bound up with their capacity to induce appropriate tensions in the first place, tensions that would challenge the *status quo* and prepare the ground for sweeping transformation. In fact, in their norms, forms, procedures, and personnel, and in their massive and detailed concentration on sexual equality, Soviet initiatives in Central Asia were meant to pose a fundamental challenge to the structure and life style of local communities. Indeed, they constituted powerful *heretical models.*

They were heretical in that (a) in and of themselves, they constituted deliberate and absolutely autonomous action by secular authority in any and all, including the most sacred, realms of life—something that Islamic orthodoxy has long regarded as by definition not only heretical and illegal but a contradiction in terms, given the avowedly revealed, comprehensive, and perfect nature of Moslem law and of the customary social order; (b) rather than merely questioning the interpretation of one or another belief, they called into question the basic assumptions underlying the prevailing belief and value systems, and thus invited radical skepticism about the moral basis of society; (c) rather than merely calling for some adjustment in one or another dimension of social esteem, they threatened a *total* abrogation of the primordial status system, beginning with the structure and hierarchy of sexual and generational roles; (d) by assigning drastically new meanings to authority and domination, and to religious, communal, and affinal obligations, they negated ancient paradigms of solidarity and trust, sanctioned the abrogation of traditional social controls, and cast grave doubt on the justice, utility, and hence legitimacy of the entire social order; (e) in addition to engendering a revolutionary interpretation of the present and the past, they formulated radically new goals for the future, thus engendering unprecedented aspirations with respect not only to rights but also to roles, possibilities, and opportunities, and hence encouraging individual concerns deeply at variance with and apart from those of the local group; (f) in making tabooed issues a matter of open concern, they threatened, in effect, to make many latent conflicts manifest.

While, in this sense, the new initiatives were profoundly heretical, they could also serve as tangible models in that (a) rather than involving merely the sporadic propagation of whispered or printed doubts on the part of deviant men or groups of men, they were a negation of the social order embodied in a system of laws, courts, and administrative commands forcefully grafted and backed by the overwhelming power of a state; (b) in marking not only a departure from particular precedents but a complete abolition of all antecedent judicial channels and procedures, as well as customary arrangements and taboos, they claimed a monopoly of the legal, customary, and moral universe; (c) in turn, no matter what their intrinsic merits in the eyes of the population, they were visible and available, calling for immediate utilization, decreeing massive confrontation, and thus serving as constant catalysts and exerting constant leverage; (d) insofar as Moslem women, for example, pioneered in using the services of the new legal system and the opportunities offered by administrative assault—in enacting the new precepts and, most important, in joining the ranks of revolutionary personnel—Soviet initiatives provided palpable standards, consistent alternatives, for comparison and choice.

Implicit in such operation of heretical models were aspects that were both defensive and offensive, therapeutic and punitive, integrative and disruptive, purposes that involved both learning and unlearning. Hence, in a deliberately induced revolutionary situation, the new legal and administrative arrangements might have been expected to function, at one and the same time, in a number of ways: (a) as repositories of new ideal norms; (b) as parental surrogates, indicating do's and don'ts as well as right and wrong; (c) as foci of accumulated grievances; (d) as instruments of mobilization; (e) as arenas of participation and recruitment; (f) as instruments of class struggle; (g) as instruments to extirpate the antecedent legal and customary systems; (h) as tripwires, or warning systems, signalling to enemies the limits of tampering with the new order; (i) as protective shields for revolutionary agents and converts.

Furthermore, from the Soviet point of view there might have been expected to be at least four basic categories of clients affected in diverse ways by the function of the two sets of Soviet initiatives as heretical models. If short-term Soviet operational objectives—based at least in part on female mobilization and emancipation—involved the productive intensification of class struggle in the traditional milieu and the resultant unraveling of the traditional social fabric, the attitudes and responses of these four client categories had to be taken into account. (1) *A principal beneficiary client group*, including of course primarily women. (2) *A secondary beneficiary client group*, including primarily unmarried young and poor men, owning neither land nor flocks, i.e., men socialized in traditional values and solidarities, but lacking authoritative standing both in private and in public realms, lacking significant access to material and spiritual goods, and lacking significant access to women as well, such access having been traditionally delimited by ritual, hereditary, authoritarian, and financial considerations. (3) *A secondary adversary client group*, including primarily married (monogamous) men, either poor or moderately well off, i.e., men with a large but limited stake in the traditional order in the sense of having access to women and commanding patriarchal authority in the kin-group, but having relatively little authoritative influence at the suprafamilial level of community or society, and relatively narrow access to material and spiritual goods. (4) *A principal adversary client group*, including primarily polygamous, well-to-do, or socially esteemed patriarchs, and the surviving authoritative traditional elites (religious, tribal, and communal), i.e., men with a very high stake in the traditional order in the sense of having relatively broad access to, or actually controlling the allocation of, a community's social and political statuses as well as material, spiritual, and sexual objects.

On purely rational grounds, the Soviet regime could expect to find in the first group not only natural followers and friends but also enthusiastically devoted agents. In turn, the successful mobilization of the first group might have been expected to intensify the adherence and participation of the second group, and its delivery of what could be viewed as the regime's natural allies. While the third group had relatively greater cause than the first two to be repelled by Soviet initiatives and goals, it might have been expected to have commensurately little incentive to stake its life on the defense of the *status quo*; it could be expected to remain at least cautiously neutral and tacitly accommodationist to Soviet revolutionary moves. For obvious reasons, the fourth group could certainly be expected to muster the regime's staunchest and natural enemies. Yet, given its originally small size, the thinning of its ranks through Soviet-sponsored deportations and executions, a measure of internal division (e.g., into red/progressive and black/reactionary *mullahs*), the shattering impact of large-scale defections from tra-

dition on the part of kinswomen, kinsmen, parishioners, and countrymen, as well as the ever growing threat of draconic Soviet sanctions, it might have been confidently expected that the fourth group
would find itself increasingly isolated and shorn of influence, and
that it could in any case do very little damage.

The cumulative effect could thus be assumed to be obvious: a
marked acceleration of a shift in the psycho-cultural and political
orientations of virtually *all* clients. As we have seen, nuances of
precisely such expectations were advanced by many communist
field-organizers in justifying Soviet revolutionary initiatives. The
concurrence of the highest echelons of the party was indeed reflected, in part, in official proposals that the revolution in Central
Asia be spearheaded by a political alliance of landless farmhands,
poor peasants or nomads, and women.

Yet, as we shall see, even this relatively subtle turn of political
judgment ran afoul of social reality.

RESPONSES AND OUTCOMES: PROBLEMS OF ASSESSMENT

An assessment of the outcomes of Soviet moves in Central Asia
is subject to considerable constraints, perhaps more so than in
other contexts of communist action. For one thing, data tend to be
especially fragmentary and difficult to interpret because they relate
to intimate details of social and political behavior. For another
thing, an assessment of successes and failures of a set of policies—a
complex task under any circumstances—is particularly problematic
when these policies are intended to set in motion an all-encompassing process of social change, and when the results are judged in the
perspective of only a few years.

Yet, even though we must rely on inference as much as on evidence, there are grounds to suppose that the evaluation of a vast
social experiment over the short term is both feasible and legitimate. Paradoxically, it is warranted, in part, because the assessment *itself* became a prime datum of Soviet politics in Central Asia.
As might have been expected, communist elites, both as power-
technicians and as revolutionaries and modernizers, were far from
content to initiate a particular action and then wait, with folded
arms, for long-term payoffs. If anything, their radical impatience
at that time (as well as the relentless pressure of factional battles
within the party) compelled them to anticipate outcomes even before the actions themselves were fully under way: not only to seek

immediate results, but to reassess their relevance and implications without delay (even though the conclusions on this basis might be premature), and to act at least in partial accordance with this reassessment.

Perhaps in few cases was this Bolshevik proclivity to anticipate quick and unambiguous results as apparent as in the process of female mobilization in Soviet Central Asia. For that matter, it may be said that the attempts at soul-searching and rational analysis in this case were probably among the most subtle and elaborate to be undertaken overtly in the course of Soviet history before Stalin's death.

What follows, then, does not pretend to be (and cannot yet be, at this point) a full-scale assessment of the experiment. Rather, it is a preliminary examination, often in bare outline, of the outcomes of communist policies in two perspectives: in the light of the regime's expectations, as well as in the light of its own judgment of the utility or inutility of its major undertakings between 1925 and 1929.

One more caveat is required. While it is both necessary and (to some extent) possible to differentiate the *inputs* in the case under review—as they concern particular Soviet orientations and strategies—it is not yet possible, given the state of our knowledge, to deal similarly with the *outcomes*. Specifically, while we can distinguish reasonably well Soviet commitments and actions concerning revolutionary legalism and administrative assault, we have no reliable means for rigorously separating popular and organizational responses to official initiatives. It is not merely the general scarcity of data that is at fault. In principle, the historical experience of deliberate or spontaneous social change does not yet permit us to distinguish clearly the effects of particular policies—for example, in the sphere of law and administrative command—from those of other concurrent stimuli and moves. In the first place, it is difficult to isolate the consequences of a set of actions over the long term (and thus construct a truly "pure" case) because we know very little about the influence of law, for example, on attitudinal and behavioral patterns, as compared with the impact of other social forces and political instruments. If this is true for relatively open societies, it should certainly be true for the Soviet case, where the difficulty of direct access compounds the problem of broad generalizations in this matter. Moreover, there was much overlapping among Soviet approaches to social engineering. And, as we have seen, the main thrust of administrative assault materialized while actions in the legal sphere were still growing in intensity and scope, and while a broad spectrum of other policies—and hence other stimuli—in the political, economic, and cultural realms was simultaneously taking shape.

Therefore, we shall examine the responses to revolutionary legalism and administrative assault not separately but jointly. Whenever feasible, we shall demarcate these reactions in the course of the analysis, but it must be understood that cases of such demarcation can be considered only as exceptions to the rule, and that the choice of these exceptions is a matter both of specific indications in Soviet (hence official) sources and of personal judgment.

SEVEN · *Patterns of Popular Response: Implications of Tension-Inducing Action*[1]

As was suggested earlier,[2] actions called for by revolutionary legalism and administrative assault involved the introduction of a specialized tension-management system into a Moslem traditional milieu. At the risk of oversimplification, we can say that such a system combined tension-inducing and tension-controlling purposes. In their role as heretical models, Soviet initiatives were designed to induce tensions that would undermine the traditional order. In their role as regulative mechanisms, they were expected to control the negative consequences of induced tensions that might affect the stability of the Soviet regime.

Thus, it seems analytically most useful to group the outcomes in two major parts:[3] the implications, respectively, of tension-inducing and tension-controlling action. In turn, each of these may be subdivided into two distinct categories, involving, respectively, popular responses as they related to females and to males; and the responses and performance of the Soviet administrative apparatus as they pertained to its native and non-native personnel (or to its local and central agencies).[4]

---

[1] Chapters Seven and Eight develop in some detail the analytical scheme suggested in my article in *Law and Society Review*, pp. 202-19.

[2] See the "Introduction," Part Four, *supra*.

[3] These are structured here as Chapters Seven and Eight, respectively.

[4] It should be kept in mind that not even a rough quantitative distribution of modes of response on the part of the relevant actors can be attempted at this point. This goes as much for the attitudes and actions of the popular masses—male and female—as for those of the relevant cadres—native and non-native, local and central, leading and rank-and-file—of the Soviet apparatus. Similarly, we have no reliable indications of the regional distribution of local responses to Soviet moves. For example, there is reason to suppose that both the thrust of official policies and the reaction of the local milieu in this case were more pronounced in Uzbekistan than in Tadzhikistan and Kirghiziia. But we do not know enough to differentiate clearly the types and intensity of response characterizing particular locales and ethnic groups. Accessible Soviet sources have so far given no meaningful clues on this account, and sample attitude-surveys have, of course, been out of the question. When Soviet Central Asian archives are opened to

PATTERNS OF POPULAR RESPONSE: FEMALES

The response of indigenous Moslem women to the norms and thrust of Soviet legal and administrative moves was varied in the extreme. It tended, at least at first, to be dependent on the attitudes and actions of males in general and the tug-of-war between traditionalist and Soviet forces in particular. Broadly speaking, female response may be said to have ranged from what might be characterized as avoidance and selective participation to militant self-assertion and uncontrolled involvement.

Avoidance

During the initial period of Soviet emancipatory initiatives in Central Asia in legal and extra-legal fields (1924-1926), what appears to have been the majority of Moslem women showed few if any signs of being interested in, or affected by, the unprecedented developments. They did not unveil; they failed to vote or otherwise assert their newly proffered rights; they avoided contact with Soviet agents and institutions; and, most important, they failed to bring their grievances to Soviet courts.[5]

In attempting to explain this peculiar lack of response, communist field-organizers came to the following conclusions:

Moslem women in the traditional hinterland were not really aware of the new Soviet legislation and of the rights and opportunities it promised. In most cases the only people who could inform them about their civil rights, and urge them to utilize these rights, were native (i.e., male) Soviet officials, and they in particular were not going out of their way to do so. Thus, the disadvan-

---

scholarly perusal, some rough estimates might become feasible.

Needless to say, the fourfold categorization of outcomes is necessarily imprecise. For example, there certainly were cases where the attitudes of local and central cadres and of native and non-native personnel of the Soviet apparatus tended to coincide. Likewise, there were individual cases where the attitudes and actions of males and females in the traditional milieu tended to coincide, and where, on the other hand, the behavior of traditional men and traditional male elites was not invariably the same. Thus, for the grouping to be fully revealing of actual dispositions in the real world, the distinctions would need to be much finer than they are here. Unfortunately, available data permit only a fairly crude dichotomization, and the one suggested here seems to be reasonably useful at this point.

[5] See, e.g., Michurina, *Ka*, 10-11, 1926, pp. 81-82.

taged either did not know about it, or did not know how to take advantage of, the new world embodied in the new law.[6]

The psychic world in which a Moslem woman lived constituted a "primordial wall" which one needed to break through. This wall was made up of "primordial habits and religious fanaticism," of "wild customs and superstitions," and it stood guard over a "slough of darkness and culturelessness." That world had made the woman "passive," engendering the feeling that "her slavelike position in the family and her isolation from society were predetermined from above [were decreed in heaven], were external and inviolable."[7]

Precisely because—without "long-term preparatory enlightenment work" by the party—these women were "not fully aware of their own slavelike existence," they considered all contacts with strangers as a "[mortal] sin." This was compounded by their living in perpetual fear of their fathers, husbands, brothers, or guardians, and of condemnation by the community as a whole for breaking the solidarity and violating the mores of the group.[8]

In certain situations a woman had especially pressing, concrete reasons not to bring her grievances to a Soviet, or any other court, especially in cases of human interaction in intimate situations. Thus, if a young widow or orphan, for example, was pressed to enter into a polygamous union, even as a third or fourth wife, she could hardly afford to refuse or to protest in public. Given her very low status and minimal access to personal property, her prospects for finding a secure social niche of her own choosing were quite slim.[9]

By the same token, if a girl was compelled by her family to marry a man she did not know or want, and such a forced marriage was accompanied by payment of *kalym*, she had to think twice before informing the authorities. To do so meant to denounce her own as well as her husband's parents or even entire clan. Similarly, if a woman was abducted with intent to marry, and raped on the way, she either had to marry her abductor or risk becoming an out-

[6] See, e.g., Nikiforov, *Ka*, 15, 1929, p. 45.

[7] Pal'vanova, *DSV*, p. 41, 55; cf. Liubimova, *Ka*, 11, 1927, pp. 73-74; Kasparova, *Ka*, 7, 1925, pp. 88-89; Dosov, *Ka*, 5, 1928, p. 32.

[8] See Zasukhin, *VS*, 8, 1931, p. 27; Zasukhin, *RN*, 12(46), 1933, p. 39; Balaban, *VS*, 40-41, 1928, pp. 15-17; Shokhor, *SS*, 8-9(13-14), 1927, pp. 109-10; Guber, *RV*, 8, 1930, pp. 276-77; Abramzon, *SE*, 2, 1932, pp. 95-97. Cf. Kalachev, *Ka*, 8, 1927, p. 60; Akopov, *RN*, 4-5, 1930, pp. 60-61; Mokrinskii, *SP*, 3(27), 1927, pp. 104-105.

[9] Mukhitdinova, *Ka*, 9, 1929, p. 39.

cast in her own community, since she had no other place to go and hardly any chance to marry someone else. Under these circumstances, she was not likely to report the violation in a Soviet court lest she burn all her bridges behind her.[10]

Selective Participation

Under certain circumstances, and in certain locales (especially in urban locales and those nearby), women did show signs of willingness to assert, albeit selectively, their new rights. If contacted by a woman (especially by a kinswoman or a woman of the same ethnic and cultural background) and in circumstances considered natural and harmless by the dominant male in the family, they were disposed to bring up relatively frankly their grievances, needs, and hopes.[11]

If provided with segregated electoral districts, they appeared, even if hesitantly at first, at the polls. The same was true for any meetings held outside the home. In all such cases, though, they responded with greater assurance if invited to attend through special official summonses delivered personally to each woman. Apparently both they and their husbands regarded such individual summonses, issued in the government's name, as sufficiently important to constitute what religious and customary law considered "valid reasons" or "extenuating circumstances" permitting a woman to leave her home.[12]

If provided with tangibly practical incentives (such as scarce consumers' goods, vocational and household counsel, medical assistance for themselves and their children, a chance to earn extra income, or merely a chance to enjoy and participate in collective

[10] See Mokrinskii, *SP*, 3(27), 1927, pp. 114-15, 119; Akopov, *RN*, 4-5, 1930, pp. 58-61; Michurina, *Ka*, 10-11, 1926, p. 81 (also footnote); Dosov, *Ka*, 5, 1928, p. 31.

[11] See, e.g., Liubimova, *Ka*, 10, 1927, pp. 55-56; Shimko, *Ka*, 12, 1925, p. 67; Smirnova, *Ka,* 10, 1928, pp. 81-82; Nukhrat, *Ka*, 10, 1928, pp. 75-78, and *Ka*, 19, 1929, pp. 34-38; Niurina, *Ka*, 4, 1925, pp. 79-80; Nasurullin, *NKK*, 11-12, 1928, p. 273; Butuzova, *Ka*, 9, 1927, p. 62; Minina, *KP*, 1, 1931, p. 46; Nukhrat, *OZV*, pp. 58-60.

[12] See, e.g., Liubimova, *VPG*, pp. 60-61. Cf., for early voting figures, Sulaimanova, *ISGPU*, Vol. II, p. 120. See also Karpov, *SS*, 11(28), 1928, pp. 61-69 (esp. p. 66), and *SS*, 6(35), 1929, pp. 64-68 (esp. p. 67); Karimova, *Ka*, 3, 1929, p. 43; Liubimova, *Ka*, 10, 1927, pp. 56-57; Krylov, *SS*, 5(70), 1932, pp. 113, 115; Gladovskii, *SS*, 5(34), 1929, pp. 166-69; Amosov, *Ka*, 14, 1929, pp. 26-27.

entertainment), and if assured of a secluded (i.e., segregated) situation, they showed an interest in joining a Soviet-sponsored club, a handicraft or consumers' cooperative, or a literacy circle in close proximity to their homes.[13]

But in most cases they tended to retain their veils—at least on the way to and from the new milieu, to remain completely within the confines of their traditional community, and to shun communication, commitments, and actions that would in any way violate traditional taboos and provoke opprobrium or wrath from the community or kin-group.

Militant Self-Assertion

In relatively urbanized locales, in especially engineered emotional situations, and under close personal guidance by congenial leaders, some women (especially maltreated wives, wives of polygamous men, recent child brides, menial employees in well-to-do households, orphans, widows, and divorcées)[14] showed themselves willing to exercise their rights and challenge the traditional *status quo* through massive, public, and dramatic violation of traditional taboos.

Encouraged and trained in the relative isolation of the first women's clubs, some indigenous women were persuaded to take (unveiled) female roles in the theater, and to give concerts and to dance in public. Especially recruited by female agents of the Communist Party's Zhenotdel, some Moslem women volunteered to run

---

[13] See, e.g., Nukhrat, *Ka*, 7, 1927, p. 36, *Ka*, 1, 1928, pp. 53-56, *RN*, 3(36), 1933, pp. 51-53, *Ka*, 11, 1928, pp. 57-59, and *VMV*, pp. 7-19 (esp. p. 18); Abidova, *RN*, 3(73), 1936, pp. 46-50; Ibragimova, *Ka*, 10, 1925, p. 88; Davydova, *Ka*, 11, 1928, p. 68; Smirnova, *Ka*, 8, 1929, p. 27; Seifi, *Ka*, 4, 1925, p. 78, and *Ka*, 9, 1925, p. 76; Safadri, *Ka*, 11, 1928, pp. 31-32; M. S-i, *Ka*, 9, 1925, p. 28; Akopov, *RN*, 4-5, 1930, pp. 67-68; V. K., *Ka*, 9, 1925, pp. 68-70; Shirman, *Ka*, 4, 1927, pp. 73-76; *BSE*, Vol. 25, 1932, p. 255; Ross, *Ka*, 8, 1926, pp. 57-58; Liubimova, *Ka*, 7, 1926, p. 70; Zavarian, *Ka*, 12, 1925, p. 28, *Ka*, 6, 1926, pp. 69-70; Prishchepchik, *Ka*, 9, 1926, p. 76; Niurina, *Ka*, 4, 1925, p. 80; Kasparova, *Ka*, 10, 1925, pp. 85-86.

[14] For some examples of the social background and motivations of early female recruits, see Pal'vanova, *DSV*, pp. 81-83; S. Dzhakhongirova, "Dvazhdy Rozhdennaia," in A. Artiukhina (*et al.*, eds.), *Uchastnitsy Velikogo Sozidaniia* (Moscow, 1962), pp. 90-97; Nukhrat, *OZV*, p. 51; Liubimova, *VPG*, pp. 40-42; Ross, *Ka*, 8, 1926, pp. 57-58; Sulaimanova, *ISGPU*, Vol. II, p. 328. Cf. Halle, *Women*, pp. 297-314; and Kunitz, *Dawn Over Samarkand*, Ch. xv.

on the party's ticket and to be elected to public posts in "Assemblies of Women's Delegates," in soviets, and in the administrative and judicial apparatuses. Some, albeit relatively few, joined the party.[15]

Befriended, supported, and coached by Zhenotdel representatives, a rapidly growing number of women abandoned marital litigations in Moslem canonical courts and initiated divorce proceedings in Soviet courts, accompanied by demands for equitable division of property and assignment of children. By mid-1926 communist organizers reported a veritable "divorce wave" in some Central Asian districts, especially in Uzbekistan and Turkmenistan,[16] or simply "massive . . . epidemic [abandonment]" of husbands by their wives, especially by child brides and by second and third wives.[17] Reports reaching the central committees of the Turk-

---

[15] See references in preceding note as well as Nukhrat, *OZV*, pp. 78-79; Ivetova, *Ka*, 8, 1925, pp. 64-65. No attempt is made here to evaluate statistical information on female membership in mass-associations, public office, and party units in the 1920's. Information of this kind is highly fragmentary or quite unreliable. In any case, Moscow's own investigations of this matter in the 1930's revealed that in many instances such statistics were fictitious. At the same time, as we shall see, even where specific figures did reflect female participation in particular units, there was a wide disparity between actual female roles and functions in such units and those implied in formal membership reports. (See the section on "Sabotage," under Soviet Administrative Apparatus: Native Personnel Behavior, *infra*, in Chapter Eight.) The role of women in native political elites rising under Soviet auspices in the 1930's will be discussed in a separate study (See Note 19, Chapter Six).

[16] It is possible that such appearances of regional distribution are due simply to the fact that available illustrations are primarily from Uzbek, Turkmen, and to a lesser extent Kazakh locales. It is more likely, though, that available evidence indeed reflected local realities. For one thing, the main hubs of Soviet power in Central Asia were located in Uzbekistan, Turkmenistan, and Kazakhstan, both in terms of Sovietized urban strongholds and in terms of long-established pockets of Slavic population. This meant greater availability of revolutionary cadres as well as greater proximity between foci and targets of pressure. For another thing, for a variety of reasons Uzbek and Turkmen women seemed more susceptible to emancipatory appeals than their sisters in other parts of Central Asia. Moreover, Kirghiz, Tadzhik, and in some cases Kazakh traditional communities were initially more elusive to manipulation: they were more dispersed and less accessible than others in the region.

[17] See Zakharian, *Ka*, 3, 1926, pp. 42-43. Cf. Kryl'tsov, *SP*, 5(29), 1927, p. 138; Sulaimanova, *SGP*, 3, 1949, pp. 68-69, and *ISGPU*, Vol. 2, pp. 217-18. Nukhrat (*Ka*, 8, 1925, p. 65) provides an example of the Zhenotdel's role in inducing the divorce wave; while her example is drawn

men and Uzbek Communist Parties at that time—beginning with an extraordinarily candid report from the Zhenotdel in Khorezm—spoke of this trend as approaching the magnitude of an "elemental . . . widespread . . . collapse of family units."[18]

At the same time, some women proceeded to sue retroactively for a part of the family's property, even in cases where divorce had taken place long before the passage of Soviet emancipatory legislation.[19] In some instances, women who had been denied a divorce on acceptable terms, and had been persecuted by their menfolk for initiating it, were reported to have killed their husbands in revenge.[20]

In March, 1927, the party succeeded in organizing in Central Asia, principally in Uzbekistan,[21] the first great marches of female crowds in public. Exhorted by fiery recitations, revolutionary songs and music, and agitators' calls for immediate female liberation and sexual desegregation, great crowds of women not only entered into public quarters traditionally reserved for men, but also marched into locales sanctified for special religious purposes. There, as already noted, thousands burned their veils *en masse* and moved unveiled through the streets in a dramatic challenge to the old order.[22]

Throughout 1926, 1927, and early 1928, groups of women ap-

---

from Dagestan, it is safe to assume that the proceedings in Central Asia were conducted in roughly the same fashion.

[18] See references in preceding note.

[19] See Sulaimanova, *ISGPU*, Vol. 2, p. 218.

[20] See Kasparova, *Ka*, 7, 1925, p. 89.

[21] Some of the reasons for this are self-evident. Uzbek women were more consistently veiled—and hence were more obvious targets—than others in Central Asia, and were concentrated in sedentary communities that were relatively accessible to Soviet mobilization agencies. While Tadzhik women were, as a rule, also veiled, they were initially not involved to the same extent: first, because Tadzhik communities, some of them high in the Pamir range, were not easily accessible; and second, because the territory of Tadzhikistan happened to be, during the 1920's, a hotbed of *basmachi* rebel activity, making Soviet authorities more hesitant to initiate provocative, taboo-breaking actions. There is also circumstantial evidence that Tadzhik cadres were less cooperative, in this respect, than those in Uzbekistan, and Soviet policies concerning female mobilization were thus not as readily translated into practice.

[22] For accounts of actual proceedings, see Nukhrat, *OZV*, pp. 86-89; Niurina, *Parandzha*, pp. 7-10; *PV*, 3.10.1927, as cited in Bil'shai, *RZVS*, p. 191, and in Halle, *Women*, pp 172-73.

peared at labor exchanges in Central Asia's major cities demanding jobs and equal employment opportunities.[23] At the same time, a growing number of village-women, principally widows and divorcées in the Uzbek, Turkmen, and Kirghiz countryside, came forward to claim land- and water-rights.[24]

Beginning in early 1927 (especially in Uzbekistan), groups of women from poorer native quarters, led by communist Zhenotdel officials and accompanied by Soviet militiamen, roamed village and city streets, tearing veils off richer women (especially at weddings and religious festivities), hunting for caches of food and cotton hidden by peasants and traders, and hunting as well for members of traditional elites subject to arrest and deportation. Some denounced to the police traditionally authoritative males discharging proscribed functions in secret or simply hiding from the law, as well as patriarchs contracting polygamous marriages, and fathers and kinsmen contracting the payment of a bride-price and forcibly arranging the marriages of girls. Some reported on such manifestations of deviance as "parasitism," opium smoking, homosexuality, and corruption. Others reported to the Red Army and the secret police (beginning already in the early 1920's) the hideouts of former emirate and khanate officials and of remaining local guerrillas.[25]

Even in some isolated outposts in the hinterland, party officials reported cases of especially aggressive Moslem women arriving in local party headquarters, offering their services as village organizers, and only asking for "guns, secretaries [and bodyguards]" to settle old accounts in the countryside. They needed the guns, they said, "because otherwise the men are not afraid."[26]

Throughout the entire period, 1925-1928, field reports con-

---

[23] See, e.g., Nukhrat, *RN*, 3(36), 1933, pp. 51, 57-58; cf. Nukhrat, *Ka*, 1, 1929, pp. 25-27.

[24] See, e.g., Shimko, *Ka*, 12, 1925, p. 67; Liubimova, *Ka*, 4, 1926, pp. 56-59, and *Ka*, 10, 1927, p. 60; Zavarian, *Ka*, 6, 1926, p. 67; Liubimova, *VPG*, pp. 54-58; Pal'vanova, *DSV*, pp. 91-95. Cf. Halle, *Women*, p. 191.

[25] See Dzhakhongirova, "Dvazhdy Rozhdennaia" (Note 14 in this chapter); Nukhrat, *OZV*, pp. 62-65; *Ka*, 1, 1928, p. 54, and *Ka*, 7, 1928, p. 58; Pal'vanova, *DSV*, pp. 46, 93; Prishchepchik, *Ka*, 7, 1927, pp. 77-78; *PV*, 2.11.1930, p. 2; Karpov, *SS*, 6(35), 1929, pp. 64-68, and *SS*, 11(28), 1928, pp. 65-66; Smirnova, *Ka*, 10, 1928, pp. 81-82; Amosov, *Ka*, 14, 1929, p. 27; Liubimova, *Ka*, 10, 1927, pp. 56-57; Mitrofanov, *RN*, 2, 1930, p. 46. Cf. Halle, *Women*, pp. 123-25, 171-72.

[26] See Nukhrat, *Ka*, 10-11, 1926, pp. 78-79.

sistently emphasized a growing trend that seemed to be shared by virtually all sections of Central Asia. Zhenotdel units in urban and rural locales were emerging as important foci for airing female grievances. At an accelerating pace, girls and women were arriving in offices of the party's Women's Department to ask for advice and support on a vast number of issues. Zhenotdel officials found these requests both moving and perplexing: "I was sold for *kalym*; I am now eighteen years old; my future husband is twelve; what shall I do?" "My husband has just died, and his older brother has taken away all of our property. What can be done?" "I don't want to live with my husband. I want to leave him. But he has given all of my property to the older wife. How can I get my part?"[27]

Mothers came with their teen-age daughters, bringing gruesome tales of abuse and oppression: of young girls from starving families hired for a pittance as servants and nannies by richer peasants, and then terrorized and sexually exploited by their employers; of young women driven to insanity by a husband's ferocious beatings; of wives rejected by their husbands as no longer desirable, replaced by other women in the household, and thrown out into the street with no means to survive; of runaway child-brides hiding in their mothers' homes to escape exploitation and brutality, and in need of official protection from a man's vengeance.[28] With what appeared to be growing frequency, young women—especially orphans, runaway child-brides, disaffected wives, as well as homeless widows and divorcées—made their way alone to the Zhenotdel. Many came angry, frightened, starving, sometimes with infants in their arms, often bleeding from wounds inflicted at home, asking for help, bread, a roof over their head, and some arrangements for the future. In effect, they seemed ready to make the most difficult and dangerous step for someone of their background: to burn their bridges to the traditional community, and to make an agency of the Communist Party into their home.[29]

[27] Fominov, *RN*, 6, 1930, pp. 69-79.

[28] See Liubimova, *VPG*, pp. 17-18.

[29] See, e.g., Balaban, *VS*, 40-41, 1928, pp. 15-17; Kasparova, *Ka*, 7, 1925, pp. 88-89; Mukhitdinova, *Ka*, 9, 1929, p. 41; Burlova, *Ka*, 8, 1928, p. 89; Zakharian, *Ka*, 3, 1926, p. 43; Nukhrat, *OZV*, p. 70, and *VMV*, pp. 16-17; Liubimova, *VPG*, pp. 17-18, 46-48; Fominov, *RN*, 6, 1930, pp. 69-79; Mitrofanov, *RN*, 2, 1930, p. 38. Cf. Halle, *Women*, pp. 133-34, 136; Kunitz, *Dawn Over Samarkand*, pp. 278 ff.

264

Uncontrolled Involvement

By 1928 communist officials in Central Asia reported with increasing frequency and unease that in locales where divorce proceedings, public unveiling, and overall female mobilization had gone farthest, conditions were "verging on [mass] prostitution."[30]

They offered two basic reasons for such an unprecedented turn of events: economic and psycho-cultural. For one thing, women abandoning—or being obliged to leave—their communities and kin-groups, with or without a divorce, had neither the means and skills nor the requisite attitudes and opportunities to support themselves.[31]

For another thing, women emerging suddenly from a Moslem traditional milieu, and coming into unrestricted contact with men in a variety of social situations, were emotionally unprepared for the occasion. As one Tadzhik party organizer put it, speaking about herself as well as her peer group:

It is generally the adventurous, daring, and, naturally enough, rather good-looking woman who flings aside her *parandzha* [veil]. . . . As a reaction to her previous enforced meekness, she now tends to become more self-assertive and unrestrained than is good for her . . . [for] . . . in her relations with the opposite sex she is helpless. Not having been trained since childhood to meet men, she has not built up the particular defenses which a woman needs if she is to meet men freely, on an equal basis. In her work she mingles among men without being emotionally prepared to ward off their equivocal remarks and persistent advances. Whenever she is in a mixed group, the atmosphere becomes charged —passion, jealousy, fear—much more so than you probably find among European men and women. The woman here needs a good deal of discipline and balance, particularly when her habitual defenses have been surrendered and no new ones have as yet been erected. . . . In my own case this resulted in tragedy. Meeting men was to me a novel and thrilling experience. A compliment or an embrace was a grand experience. I lost my head.[32]

[30] For one of the earliest such reports, see Zakharian, *Ka*, 3, 1926, pp. 42-43.

[31] See Nukhrat, *VMV*, pp. 16-17.

[32] See the interview with Khoziat Markulanova referred to in Kunitz, *Dawn Over Samarkand*, pp. 298-300.

265

If, then, suddenly emancipated Moslem women appeared to be acting like harlots it was because "this new freedom was too much [for them]"; they were "doomed to burn their wings in their heedless dash for freedom."[33]

PATTERNS OF POPULAR RESPONSE: MALES

The pattern of male response within the traditional milieu may be said to have ranged from evasion and selective accommodation to limited retribution and massive backlash.

Evasion

Moslem males, in both traditionally authoritative and non-authoritative roles, were found as a rule to evade the newly imposed rules and to avoid entanglement with the new judicial institutions.[34]

The reasons were manifold. First, it is safe to assume that, as in Islamic contexts elsewhere, the cultural reflex of Central Asian men was to pay, overtly, elaborate and even reverent obeisance to formal requisites imposed by a predominant outside power, but, at the same time, covertly, to expend inordinate energies on evading the law, including even the laws of the *shariat*—whenever the latter conflicted with locally valued mores and customs or with the perceived self-interest of individuals, local communities, and groups.

Second, the rules, procedures, and structures of the new Soviet legal system—not to speak of those implicit in administrative assault—could be viewed, especially where they concerned women, as directly antithetical to legitimate institutions. In addition to being, on general grounds, profoundly heretical and fundamentally subversive in traditional Moslem and customary tribal contexts, the new system embodied several specific features making it especially repellent. Its institutions were rigidly formal, bureaucratic, and impersonal, hence lacking the familiar, flexible, sacred, or charismatic attributes of mediation and control long considered requisite

---

[33] Ibid.

[34] See Nukhrat, *Ka*, 9, 1929, p. 32, and *OZV*, pp. 46-47; Mostovaia, *VS*, 9, 1928, pp. 7-8; Balaban, *VS*, 40-41, 1928, pp. 15-17; Zasukhin, *RN*, 12 (46), 1933, pp. 38-40; Mokrinskii, *SP*, 3(27), 1927, p. 105 (footnote); Mukhitdinova, *Ka*, 9, 1929, p. 40; Kasparova, *Ka*, 7, 1925, p. 88; Anisimova, *Ka*, 8, 1927, p. 56; Ibragimov, *Ka*, 10, 1925, p. 87; Liubimova, *Ka*, 2, 1927, pp. 50-51, and *Ka*, 11, 1927, pp. 73-74.

and legitimate in local communities. It was sponsored and staffed by aliens and infidels—Russians, communists, and native reformers. And its emphasis on sexual equality was tantamount to subversion and regulation of the most deeply embedded, sensitive, intimate, and sacred aspects of private life.

Thus, as Soviet court officials reported uneasily from various Central Asian locales, native males not only regarded the new laws as "sinful," and hence evaded them, but when apprehended and indicted for "crimes based on custom"—"crimes constituting survivals of a tribal way of life"—they "[experienced] no sense of guilt . . . [and] . . . could not understand why they were being punished."[35] Even when indicted for killing their wives, some men readily admitted this, but denied any wrongdoing: "My wife, for whom I paid *kalym*, went to a [Communist Party] school against my will. While in school, she talked to [other] men; she lost her sense of shame; she forgot [the prescriptions of] *adat*. . . . [Our] customs tell me to kill such a wife [while our religion does not consider this a crime and] a *kadi* will not try me for it. . . . Therefore I killed her."[36]

In some instances, to follow the new rules meant to incriminate oneself immediately and automatically. For example, two fathers (representing two extended families or clans) planning the marital union of their children and arriving in a Soviet agency to register the union, could at once be liable to imprisonment and fine if, as was customary, a bride-price was involved, if the explicit consent of both marital partners was not secured, or if the boy's, or more usually the girl's, age was under the legal limit. Further, a male planning to acquire a second or third wife and who agreed to register his new marriage in a Soviet agency would likewise be subject to prosecution.

Under such circumstances, Moslem men tended not to utilize the legal auspices of formal Soviet institutions, not even to report the birth of a child, lest its age be thus incontrovertibly established. They continued, instead, to use the services of a *mullah* in traditionally sanctioned, private ceremonies.[37]

[35] See, e.g., *Uch. S'ezd Kaz. ASSR*, p. 31; Kasparova, *Ka*, 7, 1925, pp. 88-89; Dosov, *Ka*, 5, 1928, p. 32; Ross, "K svetu i znaniiam," in *ZVR*, p. 353; Shirman, *Ka*, 4, 1927, pp. 73-74; Dosov, *Ka*, 5, 1928, p. 32.

[36] See Vagabov, *Islam i Zhenshchina*, p. 102.

[37] See, e.g., Mukhitdinova, *Ka*, 9, 1929, pp. 39-40. Cf. Sulaimanova, *ISGPU*, Vol. II, p. 219.

Polygamous unions continued to be consummated, in various ways, though under suitable camouflage. In some cases, men simply registered in Z.A.G.S. (Soviet bureau of civil registry) one of their wives, while acquiring others in separate religious ceremonies performed in accordance with the *shariat*.[38] In other cases, men accumulated wives while claiming that they were hired farmhands. Even when these women bore children Soviet law could not do much in the matter, as long as the marriages were not formally registered and as long as the women refused to file a complaint. When a man, tired of the old "farmhand," threw her out of the household and replaced her with another, there still was very little that could be done about it. A variant of this device was employed by men who wished to take a second wife but were too close to the regime's ears and eyes to risk doing so too obviously. Their solution was to arrange a formal divorce in Z.A.G.S. with the first wife, and legally marry the other. At the same time, though, they did not follow up the formal divorce with one in accordance with the *shariat*. This allowed them to continue living with both wives, as long as neither complained. Even if the first one wished to leave, her chances of finding someone else in the community to marry her were slim, since without a religious divorce she was still considered a married woman.[39]

If it was impossible to hide the fact of a traditional marriage involving the payment of *kalym*, and if pressed to register it under the law, male heads of families and clans simply invented new modes of negotiations for a bride-price that evaded official detection. In cases where the traditional transfer of cattle or commodities in lieu of *kalym* could be easily traced, many prospective husbands and fathers-in-law were found to be switching to cash. Since formerly ritualized pre-marital negotiations—involving much mutual visiting, as well as protracted haggling in the presence of many witnesses—were unduly open to scrutiny, the traditional parleys were often shifted to more suitable locales. Thus, the regime's agents reported throughout the latter 1920's that much of the sharp bargaining observed in the pandemonium of Central Asia's bazaars —ostensibly concerning sheep, camels, and cows—actually pertained to child-brides come of age. In other reported cases, payments of *kalym* were made under the guise of elaborate wedding

[38] Ibragimov, *Ka*, 10, 1925, p. 87.

[39] Nukhrat, *OZV*, p. 46; Mostovaia, *VS*, 9, 1928, pp. 7-8; Mukhitdinova, *Ka*, 9, 1929, p. 39.

gifts from the bridegroom's kinsmen, and were just as readily accepted in the form of the groom's labor benefiting his in-laws' household. Families obliged, for one or another reason, to forgo such payments, were found to be simply exchanging sons for daughters (often mere infants) to ensure the availability of marital partners and hence the perpetuation of the family line. Moreover, in some instances Soviet investigators encountered large organizations of middlemen ready to supply both sides with sons and daughters to order.[40]

When pressed to supply witnesses to verify the facts in a particular case (for example, concerning the age of marital partners), families and clans supplied as many false witnesses as needed, including false grooms and brides, in order to legalize a traditional union in a Soviet institution.[41] Often, in order to facilitate the marriage of a child-bride, the girl's older sister or even her own mother was sent in her place.[42]

Selective Accommodation

Under some circumstances, and in some realms, males in general and traditional elites in particular showed signs of interest in responding to the challenge of female emancipation through selective accommodation.

On one level, the response seemed to be essentially competitive in nature. In some districts where women turned out in significant numbers to vote, men, too, reportedly showed up in unprecedented numbers at the polls. Some Soviet political analysts and voting officials saw the reasons for this as twofold: native males were made uneasy by the implications of leaving the field to possible female majorities or female candidates; and young and less privileged males, in particular, confronted with examples of women's fearless self-assertion at the polls against formerly authoritative men, were goaded or encouraged to do the same.[43]

[40] See Balaban, *VS*, 40-41, 1928, pp. 15-17; Ibragimov, *Ka*, 10, 1925, p. 87; Mokrinskii, *SP*, 3(27), 1927, p. 105 (footnote); Sulaimanova, *ISGPU*, Vol. ii, pp. 330-31; Brullova-Shaskol'skaia, *NV*, 16-17, 1927, pp. 290-303, *passim*. Cf. Halle, *Women*, pp. 133 ff.

[41] See Anisimova, *Ka*, 8, 1927, pp. 54-56. Cf. Akopov, *RN*, 4-5, 1930, pp. 66-67.

[42] Anisimova, ibid., p. 56.

[43] For examples of such interpretations, based on first-hand observation in Turkmenistan, see: Karpov, *SS*, 11(28), 1928, pp. 61-69 (esp. p. 66), and *SS*, 6(35), 1929, pp. 64-68 (esp. p. 67); Karimova, *Ka*, 3, 1929, p.

But other interpretations of apparently the same facts saw this matter in a rather different light. According to a number of official reports, especially from the nomadic and semi-nomadic hinterland, women's rising electoral participation was not a cause but a consequence of certain changes in male commitments. It appeared that Soviet adjustments in electoral laws and procedures in Central Asia in the mid-1920's—designed, in part, to "isolate the tribal aristocracy" and destroy its influence in the countryside, by constraining and discrediting it, and by depriving it of the right to vote—had spurred surviving clan leaders and village notables (or those who took their place) to cast about for help from every available source. Two things were at stake: to gain for communities and kin-groups at least some form of representation in local governing bodies; and to ensure the competitive advantage of one kin-group vis-à-vis another in a given locale. With this in mind, heads of large and important families proceeded to mobilize every voter the kinship system could deliver. In the process, some felt obliged to do the unprecedented: they pressed their wives and all available female relatives into service, and delivered them to the polls *en masse*.[44]

Similarly, aroused by the visible and potential consequences of Soviet-sponsored mobilization among women, some Moslem clergymen and village and clan notables launched what was in effect the first conscious organizational effort in local cultural history directed along tribal and religious lines to "win back" women and youth. This effort included the following components: (1) recruitment of *mullahs'* and notables' wives and female relatives, or of locally respected older women, as initial cadres in establishing regularized contacts with female masses; (2) tribal and village sponsorship of "women's meetings" and elaborate feasts and celebrations— *toy* and *ash*[45]—prominently involving women, and often scheduled

---

43; Liubimova, *Ka*, 10, 1927, pp. 56-57; Krylov, *SS*, 5(70), 1932, pp. 113, 115; Gladovskii, *SS*, 5(34), 1929, pp. 166-69; Amosov, *Ka*, 14, 1929, pp. 26-27.

[44] For especially dramatic examples of this trend, based on observation in Kazakhstan, see Kuchkin, *SKA*, pp. 238 and 225. For background information, see ibid., pp. 220 ff., and 263 ff. The observations cited in this and preceding footnotes refer to local elections held between 1926 and 1928.

[45] *Toy*—a general term for traditional feasting, often of several days' duration, often involving not only eating, drinking, and socializing, but

to coincide (and hence compete) with Soviet official gatherings and holidays; (3) clerical and kin-group sponsorship of festivals in honor of unveiled women resuming the veil; (4) intensification of almsgiving and gift-allotment to needy women and children, especially widows and orphans, in conjunction with important Moslem holidays; (5) material help in furthering cooperative arrangements for women in the community—including, for example, simple machinery for the manufacture of dairy products; (6) the formation under clerical auspices of Moslem youth groups, for girls as well as boys, to rival the Komsomol; (7) the recognition of at least some form of women's education as imperative and the establishment, both overtly and covertly, of special girls' schools for "religious enlightenment," lest women, and the young in their charge, "lose their faith in Islam . . . , their honor . . . , and their respect for [others]," and thus proceed to "live like animals"; (8) the attraction of women into the mosque, ". . . lest they go to the Zhenotdel instead"; (9) the recognition of women, at least by some religious leaders, as fit to hold spiritual office, and the recruitment in some Central Asian districts of female *murids*, literally, "seekers"—in effect, grassroots activists among the faithful in conjunction with religious holidays and pilgrimages, and especially in conjunction with the association of believers in religious orders; (10) the denial, at least in some cases, that the *shariat* necessarily ordained the veiling of women and their inequality in marriage, divorce, inheritance, and court proceedings; (11) the insistence, at least by some Moslem scholars ("red" or "progressive" *mullahs* and *ulema*), that there were no significant differences between socialism and Islam, and that communist egalitarian aims, concerning women as well as men, had been fully anticipated in Mohammed's teachings; (12) the establishment, in what were projected as centers of Moslem religious administration, of special "Women's Departments" under a female *kadi*, to rival the party's Zhenotdel, accompanied by a widespread rumor campaign labeling the latter as *dzhinnotdel*, "the department of evil spirits."[46]

---

also horseracing and fighting contests; *ash*—a celebration usually marking a year after a kinsman's death and the conclusion of the period his wife was obliged to wait before marrying again.

[46] For evidence and commentaries on the entire spectrum of traditional response in these realms, see Shimko, *Ka*, 12, 1925, pp. 67-68; *Bezb* (news.), 4, 1927, p. 7; Shirman, *Ka*, 4, 1927, p. 76; Akopov, *RN*, 4-5, 1930, p. 66; Krupskaia, *Ka*, 12, 1928, p. 6; Nikolaeva, *Ka*, 8, 1927, p. 53; Rigin, *Ka*,

From the Soviet point of view these efforts were important enough to constitute an actual or potential danger, or at least a challenge to Soviet political creativity. Krupskaia and Nikolaeva, for example, leaned towards the latter view. As they saw it, while the extraordinary about-face on the part of communal leaders indeed denoted the "surrender [by the traditionalist enemy of some] fundamental positions," it also constituted a significant competitive response. Such attempts to "[turn] the woman-hating dogmas [of Islam upside down]," and thus, in effect, to "revise . . . the Koran," were reflections of weakness and panic. But they could also be signs of pragmatic capacity, in traditional Islamic ranks, to "adapt Moslem religion to modernity," and hence pose a significant challenge to the innovative and developmental capabilities of the Soviet regime.[47] Others, while agreeing with the premise, saw the implications and the dangers in a harsher, conspiratorial light. For them, even the claims of seemingly "progressive" Moslem leaders were to be regarded as highly, perhaps especially, suspect. As they argued, these claims, "equating Islam and socialism [just as easily as] religion and nation," and thus "playing upon the sensibilities of believers [with the deceptive imagery of human] brotherhood and unity under the banner of Islam," were real, full-blown "counter-revolutionary attempts" to adapt Islam more easily to the new exigencies of class-struggle, and thereby deflect and disrupt revolutionary initiatives, as well as incite Moslem nationalities against Soviet rule and entice them away from the Soviet fold.[48]

While it is not feasible to determine the real scope and intensity of these adjustments in the traditional community, it is perhaps more realistic to view them as a series of awkward, isolated, small-scale attempts, in self-defense, to formulate a response to the challenge of a secularist revolution under communist auspices. It was, by and large, a series of uncoordinated, half-hearted, and often mutually contradictory and short-lived endeavors to introduce some flexibility into the customary and Islamic view of social rela-

---

5-6, 1929, pp. 58-59; *BSE*, Vol. 29, 1935, pp. 394-96; Fioletov, *SP*, 1 (25), 1927, p. 44; Nukhrat, *Ka*, 12, 1927, p. 44, *Ka*, 8, 1927, p. 20, and *VMV*, pp. 7-17; Vagabov, *Islam i Zhenshchina*, p. 86; Bil'shai, *RZVS*, p. 193; Liubimova, *Ka*, 9, 1926, p. 74, and *VPG*, pp. 49-50; *ZVR*, pp. 416-17. Cf. Halle, *Women*, p. 197.

[47] See Krupskaia, *Ka*, 12, 1928, p. 6; Nikolaeva, *Ka*, 8, 1927, p. 53; Bil'shai, *RZVS*, p. 193.

[48] See *BSE*, Vol. 29, 1935, p. 396. Cf. Liubimova, *VPG*, pp. 49-50.

tions and roles, and to provide some alternatives to the rights proffered and the opportunities promised by the Soviet regime.

In all these spheres, the attempts at adaptation by and large reflected collective and communal concerns. On another level, though, the response of young, poor, and single males, in particular, reflected rather special notions of self-interest. In the second half of the 1920's, party organizers reported an apparently growing number of these men coming to regard the regime as a potential supplier of women at a reasonable price or at no cost at all. To the extent that Zhenotdel units were becoming the refuge of orphaned girls, runaway child-brides, and disaffected widows and divorcées, some men turned to the Zhenotdel for help in procuring a wife.[49]

Others took a different route. In a number of cases, men who found themselves working, in lieu of *kalym*, in a prospective father-in-law's household, and were or felt cheated in the course of the waiting period, proceeded to petition Soviet courts on this account. Men who worked for years in this fashion, only to see their promised bride given to someone else, sued for back wages and financial compensation. Others who had made a downpayment on *kalym*, and now thought it opportune to get out of the remaining payments, denounced their in-laws to the authorities as rich *beys*[50] conspiring to commit "crimes based on custom."[51]

At the same time, some enterprising families, especially in Turkmenistan, Kazakhstan, and Uzbekistan, were found to take special advantage of the new divorce laws by engaging in what was officially referred to as "speculation in women." Between 1926 and 1928, Soviet reports from the field pointed with concern to a rapidly growing number of cases where families deliberately induced their married daughters to leave their husbands (since divorce could be easy and, sometimes, automatic) and then arranged their marriage

---

[49] See Zakharian, *Ka*, 3, 1926, p. 43; Nukhrat, *OZV*, p. 70; Fominov, *RN*, 6, 1930, pp. 69-79; Mitrofanov, *RN*, 2, 1930, p. 38; Liubimova, *VPG*, pp. 16-18, 46-48. Cf. Halle, *Women*, pp. 133-34, 136.

[50] In Soviet terminology, the Central Asian equivalent of a Russian *kulak*, a rich peasant exploiting the labor of others.

[51] See, e.g., Akopov, *RN*, 4-5, 1930, p. 62; Kasparova, *Ka*, 7, 1925, p. 88; Petukhov, *RN*, 2(48), 1934, pp. 41-42; Krupskaia, *Ka*, 12, 1928, p. 7; Kryl'tsov, *SP*, 5(29), 1927, pp. 136, 138; Liubimova, *Ka*, 10, 1927, p. 60, and *VPG*, p. 55; Pal'vanova, *DSV*, pp. 38, 92-93. For a very suggestive example of a poor peasant's petition to the court, see Halle, *Women*, pp. 133-34.

to another man, thus immediately collecting more *kalym*. In some districts, this practice reportedly reached a point of "[repeated] selling and reselling" of girls by their fathers or male guardians.[52]

Limited Retribution

When faced with growing female self-assertion and participation, or pressure to participate, in the public realm, males responded—albeit largely as individuals, and largely in private—by applying proscriptive counterpressures. Their motives were explicitly reported by Soviet organizers. They were, primarily, the fear of female economic and political competition; the fear of the effect that social participation would have on the attitudes, morality, and fidelity of daughters and wives (and hence the fear of other men's sexual competition); and the fear, ultimately, of the loss of authoritative male dominance over females.

In widely scattered locales, especially in the countryside, girls and women were persuaded, sometimes forcefully, to keep away from schools and voting booths. Heads of families tended to permit a modest degree of such participation, as in women's producers' cooperatives and clubs, only when enticed by the promise of extra income and assured of complete sexual segregation and absence of "corruption" and "debauchery" in these realms, or when confronted, as on voting days, by police and the Red Army.[53]

While some husbands and fathers were tempted by the promise of extra income, they were reported to have deep misgivings about their females' going to work in a factory. Here the degree of the community's supervision over its members was bound to be much lower, and the chances of unrestricted contact with other men much higher than usual. In parallel fashion, while unmarried and relatively poor males showed signs of welcoming greater access to females, they were reported to feel deeply threatened by women's arrival in the economic market-place in general and in factories in particular.[54]

[52] See, e.g., Kryl'tsov, *SP*, 5(29), 1927, p. 138; Nukhrat, *Ka*, 9, 1929, p. 32.

[53] See, e.g., Artiukhina, *Ka*, 5, 1927, p. 4; A. Z., *VS*, 52, 1928, pp. 15-16; Potekhin, *SS*, 28, 1928, p. 86; Tarantaeva, *Ka*, 11, 1928, p. 45, and *VS*, 51, 1927, p. 10; Nasrullin, *NKK*, 11-12, 1928, p. 273; Butuzova, *Ka*, 9, 1927, p. 62; Minina, *KP*, 1, 1931, p. 46; Nukhrat, *OZV*, pp. 58-60.

[54] See, e.g., Nukhrat, *RN*, 3(36), 1933, pp. 51, 57-58; cf. Nukhrat, *Ka*, 1, 1929, pp. 25-27, and Limanovskii, *Sov. Khlopok*, 11-12, 1937, pp. 91-95.

When faced with divorce proceedings initiated by women, and with the first acts of female unveiling, Moslem husbands and kinsmen responded with privately administered beatings and, to a growing extent, with the expulsion of these women from home. What seemed particularly ominous in the eyes of Soviet officials was the fact that, with or without a divorce, women were being unceremoniously thrown out into the streets, and were left without property and children that legally belonged to them, as well as "without a roof over their heads, and without a piece of bread . . . [to keep body and soul together]."[55]

Likewise, when apprehended and pressed to dissolve a polygamous marriage, native males tended simply "to throw the [extra] wife [or wives]—in most cases the old ones and the cold ones—out the door, denying them even the least bit of property." It appeared, then, that by pressing the issue the regime was likely to wind up with a vast throng of old, lonely, and destitute women on its hands.[56]

Massive Backlash

When faced with a mounting wave of divorces and organized public unveiling (1926-28), and with the concomitants of women's spatial and social mobility, including widespread desegregation, political denunciations, and prostitution, Moslem men responded with an explosion of hostility and violence apparently unequaled in scope and intensity until then on any other grounds.[57]

Two sets of mutually reinforcing perceptions seem to have been set in motion here. First, under the umbrella of Soviet rule a native male's opportunities for martial, acquisitive, and hegemonic self-

---

[55] Ishkova, *Ka*, 11, 1928, pp. 60-61; cf. "Nuzhno li izdat' . . . ," *Ka*, 8, 1928, p. 81; Burlova, *Ka*, 8, 1928, p. 89; and Sulaimanova, *ISGPU*, Vol. ii, p. 230.

[56] See Mukhitdinova, *Ka*, 9, 1929, pp. 39-40. Cf. Nukhrat, *VMV*, pp. 16-17.

[57] Of course, this does not include the period of civil war and *basmachi* revolt in Central Asia (primarily 1918-22). But even at that time, popular violence expressed itself primarily in large or small guerrilla attacks, organized along dynastic or clan lines, in relatively isolated and geographically delimited locales. *Per contra*, the violence generated in the course of *khudzhum*, while, as a rule, not involving head-on attacks on Soviet troops, tended to be widespread and pervasive, and involved individual as well as collective acts of terror against a great variety of targets. It seems to have touched personally far more people, expressing a deep malaise at all levels of local communities.

assertion had been severely circumscribed. This meant that the act of asserting himself vis-à-vis a woman was one of the very few realms, if not the last one, left to him for the assertion of authority and virility. Under these circumstances, *khudzhum*, the "cultural revolution" launched through legal as well as extra-legal channels, by suddenly and powerfully intensifying men's apprehensions and anxiety stemming from the threat of impotence, apparently precipitated a crisis in the male's self-esteem. Moreover, the sudden threat to the nexus of authority relationships in the most intimate circle of a man's life—the sense of being *dispossessed* in sexual and generational realms—served to provide the vehicle that fused men's unease and resentment stemming from the entire spectrum of Soviet-inspired actions in the traditional milieu. By the same token, despondency, hatred, and violence heretofore devoid of clearly identifiable objects for blame could suddenly focus upon the sponsors of *khudzhum*: female defectors from tradition, male communists, infidels, and aliens. It is safe to assume that at least some Soviet organizers were becoming aware of this chain reaction when they reported ruefully from the hinterland that some native males viewed the Soviet regime solely in terms of "a power that takes away women and divorces them from their husbands."[58]

Second, both the Islamic and customary components of Central Asian folkways had always carried expectations that unrestricted female mobility and unveiling would inevitably lead to widespread social disorganization, demoralization, promiscuity, and harlotry. Some aspects of female mobilization seemed to confirm these traditional expectations, thus providing the makings of a self-fulfilling prophecy.[59] Not surprisingly, this, too, was linked in men's minds with the role of the Soviet regime in the matter. One of the most widely shared grievances in Central Asia was expressed in starkly direct terms: Bolsheviks were dishonoring Moslem women and turning them into harlots.[60]

[58] See *1-2 Sessii Ts.I.K. Turk.S.S.R.*, p. 59. The reports were based in this case on contacts in Turkmen villages. Cf. Nukhrat's argument about the implications of the Moslem male's loss of his "overlordship" over women, in *OZV*, pp. 46-47.

[59] See the section "Uncontrolled Involvement" in the pattern of female response in this chapter, *supra*. For a highly suggestive illustration of this phenomenon, see Kunitz, *Dawn Over Samarkand*, pp. 298-99.

[60] See Kunitz, *Dawn Over Samarkand*, pp. 231-32. Kunitz refers to this point as the first on the list of grievances circulated by Ibrahim Bek, a Tadzhik guerrilla leader, during the last major *basmachi* raid into Central

276

The resulting backlash, beginning in sporadic bloody riots in Turkmenistan in 1925-26[61] and on a large scale in the spring of 1927 (i.e., immediately after the first organized public unveilings) in Uzbekistan and elsewhere,[62] marked the massive consummation of two interrelated trends: the radicalization of male attitudes to women and the radicalization of native male attitudes toward the Soviet regime.

The backlash patterns included the following manifestations which in turn constituted stages following each other in rapid succession and reaching their most violent forms within weeks of the pattern's inception:

(1) An insidious rumor campaign was launched by *mullahs*, associating Soviet-sponsored emancipatory and related activities with whatever actual or potential calamities might befall individuals or entire communities of believers. Destructive earthquakes which took place in some Central Asian locales (especially in Namangan) in 1927 were interpreted as Allah's punishment for female unveiling. It was prophesied that the minarets of mosques would collapse upon the heads of those who transgressed against custom and religion. It was also prophesied that women participating in Soviet enterprises would be unveiled by their new patrons by force, and that unveiled girls would, "in accordance with a special decree issued in the cities," be forced by communists into public baths with men, where they would be deflowered. In some instances, the faithful were warned that female unveiling was but the first step in a process leading to the desecration and destruction of all holy places, including Moslem cemeteries, which would be plowed under and turned into fields and orchards. In the event that women persisted in their actions, Moslems were told to expect *kiyemat*—the end of the world.[63]

Asia in 1931. While, on the face of it, the guerrilla "manifesto" formally articulated this grievance several years after the commencement of *khudzhum*, it was obviously designed to tap a sense of resentment that was deeply felt, widely shared, and frequently expressed in the course of *khudzhum*, as we shall see in the section that follows immediately.

[61] See, e.g., *1-2 Sessii Ts.I.K. Turk.S.S.R.*, p. 59; Nukhrat, *OZV*, p. 48; Liubimova, *VPG*, p. 48; Zavarian, *Ka*, 12, 1925, pp. 25-26; Kryl'tsov, *SP*, 5 (29), 1927, p. 138; Pal'vanova, *DSV*, p. 79; Kasparova, *Ka*, 7, 1925, pp. 89-90.

[62] See references in preceding note, and the footnotes which follow.

[63] For these and related manifestations, see Artiukhina, *Ka*, 1, 1928, p. 62; *Bezb* (news.), 6, 1928, p. 4; Nikolaeva, *Ka*, 8, 1927, p. 53; Akopov, *RN*,

Growing tensions between England and Russia, culminating in severance of diplomatic relations, were ascribed to the world's revulsion against *khudzhum*, and were cited as a prelude to British invasion of the Soviet Union (probably through Afghanistan) to save the faith.[64]

A particularly interesting and revealing example of such warnings is provided by a document which was apparently circulated and quoted in Central Asia in 1927 and 1928, although it was said to have originated in Bashkiriia, in largely Moslem rural districts due north of Kazakhstan. It was referred to as "Mohammed's Last Will [and Prophecy],"[65] and the insights it affords concerning Moslem fears and sensibilities in a time of grave revolutionary challenge are readily apparent and obviously of great value.

Produced in the form of a letter to the Moslem community, the document proclaimed the regime's policies of female emancipation and class-struggle as "horrible and foul," yet also "God's punishment for apostasy and non-observance of religious prescriptions." It called on believers to resume support of religious institutions and to hide all grain from state collectors. It urged all Moslems to repent on the eve of the day of doom. It set down, year by year and step by step, the stages of destruction. As a document purportedly bequeathed sometime in the past, it referred to all events in the future tense:

> At the end of 1922, I shall withhold from the earth all abundance and bliss;[66] in 1923, wives will cease to obey their husbands;[67] at the end of 1930, there will be terrible hunger, followed by strong rains and earthquakes, in which all of the

---

4-5, 1930, p. 66; Vagabov, *Islam i Zhenshchina*, p. 109; Liubimova, *Ka*, 10, 1927, p. 61, and *VPG*, p. 73; Sulaimanova, *ISGPU*, Vol. II, pp. 319-20, 327.

[64] See Akopov, *RN*, 4-5, 1930, p. 66.

[65] See Shokhor, "Zaveshchanie Magometa," *Bezb* (news.), 20, 1929, p. 1. (Cf. ibid., 4, 1927, p. 6.) The Russian translation (under the auspices of the Association of Militant Atheists) provides only selected excerpts. Those who had allegedly composed the document (several *mullahs* or people with religious training domiciled in Bashkiriia) were arrested in June, 1928, tried in September of that year by the Supreme Court of Bashkiriia, and sentenced to several years in prison.

[66] This apparently refers to the time when armed Moslem resistance in Russia was decisively crushed by the Red Army.

[67] This seems to refer to the first important attempts to apply among Moslems laws concerning female emancipation.

earth's living creatures will die; in 1933, monstrous thunder and lightning will afflict the world, but this time beneficial rains will not follow; after 1937, [Dajjāl, the Enemy of God][68] will come to rule the earth.[69] I shall be gracious unto those who will carry this [will and prophecy] of mine from village to village, from city to city, from one mosque to another. Those who, having heard this [word], will fail to pass it on to others, shall be banished from the sight of God, and their countenance will darken. I asked the Archangel Gabriel how many times he will descend to earth after my death. [His reply was:] "I shall come down ten times. During my first descent, I will take the bliss away from [man's] daily bread. The second time, I shall deprive women of their respect for men. . . . The third time, I shall take away [all] joy, contentment, [and delight]. The fourth, I shall cause women to lose their patience [and self-control]. The fifth, I will deprive poor men of forbearance and love [for their richer kin]. . . . The sixth time, I will cause people to lose their goodness and cordiality. The seventh, I shall take away man's kindness to his kin and friends. The eighth, I shall deprive the rich of generosity. The ninth, I shall take away God's Koran. And when the tenth time comes, believers will lose their faith in God." Of all the things that are listed here, eight have already come to pass, and only two remain: the withholding of the holy Koran and the loss of belief in God. If this, too, should come true, the end of the world will be upon you. . . .

(2) Men who acquiesced in their womenfolk's participation in public unveiling and related activities were threatened with casting out (amounting to excommunication) from the community of believers. Religious leaders declared women's attendance at Soviet schools and clubs, and their membership in Soviet associations, as "crimes according to *shariat*." At the same time, husbands, broth-

---

[68] The Russian translation refers to "Antichrist." It is probably safe to assume that the original text (apparently written in Arabic) dealt with the equivalent of Antichrist in Islam, whose name in Arabic is Dajjāl. I owe this deduction to Mohammed Guessous, a Moroccan sociologist.

[69] It is interesting to speculate what Russia's Moslems (and Russians) thought of this prophecy at its appointed time: in 1930, when forced collectivization led to widespread destruction of people, livestock, and grain; in 1933, when hunger, partly as an aftermath of total collectivization, decimated the Soviet population, especially in the countryside; and in 1937-38, when Stalin's great purge culminated in grizzly show-trials, persecutions, and deportations, in which millions perished.

279

ers, and kinsmen were charged with full responsibility in this matter, and told that they were "duty-bound before God to chastise such women with utmost severity."[70]

(3) In response to the spate of rumors, warnings, and admonitions, some communities made preparations for the end of the world by slaughtering their herds and abandoning all care for their households. In others, crowds of outraged men appeared in the streets, demanding an immediate end to unveiling, and the return of women to female quarters in the home. At the same time, public pressure was brought to bear in districts as far apart as northern Kazakhstan and southern Uzbekistan and Turkmenistan against marriages of Moslem girls to members of the Komsomol, and against the Komsomolites' continued sojourn in native villages (implying that members of the Soviet youth organization were to be regarded as outcasts). In the same locales, still other demands were voiced in public: to elect only "honest Moslems," not communists, to local soviets; to prevent the formation of agricultural collectives; to remove the officially imposed age-limit concerning children studying in religious schools; to return all mosques, as well as religious and secular schools and orphans' homes, to the care of local communities; to return all books of civil registry to local mosques; to reinstate the *mullahs'* civil rights and free them from taxes; to prohibit all oral and written anti-religious propaganda; to resume the teaching of religion in Soviet schools.[71]

According to Soviet reports, some of the immediate by-products of this growing wave of agitation, becoming especially apparent in 1927, were a very substantial rise in the attendance of prayers and meetings in mosques; widespread withdrawal of Moslem children, especially girls, from Soviet schools; and a rise in resignations on the part of native youth from the Komsomol.[72]

(4) The worsening climate of fear, hostility, and vengeance generated two successive waves of violence. In 1925-26, Turkmen villages were swept by bloody disturbances which continued well into the late 1920's. According to all available reports, these were connected primarily with the mounting divorce wave in Turk-

[70] See *Bezb* (news.), 4, 1927, p. 6; Liubimova, *VPG*, p. 73; Sulaimanova, *ISGPU*, Vol. II, pp. 319-20, 332.

[71] See Vagabov, *Islam i Zhenshchina*, p. 109; *Bezb* (news.), 4, 1927, pp. 6-7.

[72] See, e.g., "Zaveshchanie Magometa," *Bezb* (news.), 20, 1929, p. 1.

menistan, and involved both collective riots and individual cases of murder, particularly the murder by husbands of wives suing for divorce.[73]

On the other hand, immediately following the first mass unveilings in March, 1927, in Tashkent, Samarkand, Bukhara, and elsewhere, unveiled women were subjected to growing harassment and shaming in the streets. This was especially so in what had been Central Asia's most orthodox Islamic milieus, including Uzbekistan and adjacent Turkmen and Tadzhik districts inhabited by Uzbeks. As some eyewitness reports described this, crowds of men followed unveiled women around, "jeering," "laughing at them," attributing "all kinds of shameful, ignominious things to them." In public places they were spat upon, and "slops were poured over them."[74] "Now we can do without Russian women," the word was passed around; "now we have our own prostitutes."[75]

All reports from the field agree that within days this harassment took an ominous turn. In some cities and villages, unveiled women were seized in the streets and raped by bands of youths. With growing frequency, these women were killed, not only by roving gangs but by their own kinsmen at home, as traitors to tradition and prostitutes. Young men reportedly murdered their sisters after swearing on the Koran to do so in defense of the family's honor; the religious oath-taking ceremonies were apparently arranged by their own fathers in consultation with local *mullahs*. Some killings were perpetrated with extraordinary ferocity: pregnant women were murdered, and then disemboweled, after having been violated by scores of men.[76]

(5) The rising wave of violence did not remain confined to women who had merely discarded the veil and sought a divorce. By mid-1928, the backlash pattern emerged full-blown, including the vilification, persecution, and murder of female activists and their families, and of anyone even distantly connected with the "cultural revolution," male as well as female.

Official expressions of alarm spoke of a veritable "wave of ter-

[73] See esp. Kasparova, *Ka*, 7, 1925, p. 89; Akopov, *RN*, 4-5, 1930, pp. 65-66; Kryl'tsov, *SP*, 5(29), 1927, p. 138; Zavarian, *Ka*, 12, 1925, pp. 25-26.

[74] See Nukhrat, *RN*, 3, 1933, p. 47; *Bezb* (news.), 22, 1930, pp. 3-4.

[75] Halle, *Women*, p. 175.

[76] See Nikolaeva, *Ka*, 8, 1927, p. 53; Nukhrat, *OZV*, p. 87, *Ka*, 6, 1928, p. 78, and *RN*, 3, 1933, p. 47; Amosov, *Ka*, 14, 1929, p. 25; Sulaimanova, *ISGPU*, Vol. II, p. 328.

281

ror," wherein attacks were bolder, more desperate, better planned, and less discriminating in their targets as time went on. They involved night assaults on families marked for elimination; kangaroo courts in isolated communities; burning of homes belonging to communists; ambush of suspects in back-alleys and on deserted roads; and single assassinations as well as lynchings attended by large groups of men. They were directed against native actresses who performed on stage unveiled, organizers and high officials of the Zhenotdel, leading members of local soviets, functionaries of local executive committees, and secretaries of party-cells, including their families, especially if they played an important role in the process of *khudzhum*, or if they presented an opportunity to settle an old feud.[77]

In the period between March, 1927, and December, 1928, alone, about eight hundred women reportedly perished.[78] Yet by late 1928, only forty-five percent of those murdered were reported to be women.[79] The number of wounded was never released. The number of unsuccessful attacks with intent to kill was likewise never made known. At the same time, Soviet officials in the field were well aware that available figures referred only to cases actually brought to court,[80] and that far from all violent attacks were actually reported to the authorities, given the secretiveness of traditional communities, and the fear of local functionaries for their lives. On this basis, it seems safe to conclude that altogether thousands of men and women were killed or wounded in 1927 and 1928 in connection with *khudzhum*. Such an order of magnitude is very significant indeed, considering that widespread killings connected with women's emancipation reportedly continued (at an even more feverish pace)[81] well into 1929. It assumes all the greater importance when it is judged in terms of the lives it represents: by all counts, the overwhelming proportion of men and women

[77] See esp. Nukhrat, *Ka*, 6, 1928, p. 78, and *RN*, 3, 1933, p. 47; Nikolaeva, *Ka*, 8, 1927, p. 53; Khodzhaev, *SS* (35), 1929, p. 59; Akopov, *RN*, 4-5, 1930, pp. 65-66; Liubimova, *VPG*, pp. 19-20, 48, 73; Bil'shai, *RZVS*, pp. 192-96; Sulaimanova, *ISGPU*, Vol. II, pp. 318-32, *passim*.

[78] This tentative estimate is based on fragmentary data in Amosov, *Ka*, 14, 1929, pp. 24-25; Yaroslavsky, *Ka*, 1, 1929, pp. 28-30; Polianskaia, *RN*, 3, 1930, pp. 93-94; Akopov, *RN*, 4-5, 1930, pp. 65-66; Sulaimanova, *ISGPU*, Vol. II, p. 329; Bil'shai, *RZVS*, pp. 193-94.

[79] See Amosov, *Ka*, 14, 1929, pp. 24-25.

[80] See, e.g., Akopov, *RN*, 4-5, 1930, p. 66; cf. *BSE*, Vol. 29, 1935, p. 395.

[81] See, e.g., Polianskaia, *RN*, 3, 1930, pp. 93-94.

caught up in the wave of violence was made up of activists, field-organizers, and low- or middle-echelon officials staffing various agencies of the fledgling Soviet apparatus at the grassroots. There can be little doubt that, for such an apparatus, comprising an extremely thin layer of trusted and experienced cadres, the losses were enormous.

As the wave of violence connected with female emancipation rolled on in the late 1920's (continuing at a varied pace into the early 1930's),[82] it engulfed a number of women and men whose role in the revolution transcended a particular locale. Those who lost their lives included Anna Dzhamal and Enne Kulieva, who had been among the first native high officials of the Central Asian Zhenotdel; Tursunoi, Mekhrikhanum, and Nurkhon, the first three of a handful of native actresses who ventured on stage; and Hamza Hakim Zada Niyaziy, a leading Uzbek writer, dramatist, and militant atheist with pro-Russian and pro-Soviet commitments, who played a leading role in the course of *khudzhum*.[83] Among those attacked and badly wounded was the wife of Bauman, the highest official of Sredazburo, the Central Asian Bureau of the Central Committee of the Communist Party, responsible for the political administration of the entire region.[84]

As Soviet organizers reported from the field, both the causes and the process of the backlash tended to lead to the closing of traditionalist ranks and to the hardening of traditionalist attitudes. The specter of massive and dramatic emancipatory activities in public seemed to drive traditionalist males—"poor" as well as "rich"— and the sacred Moslem intelligentsia and clan notables closer together, for all of them felt challenged as Moslems, as heads of kin-groups, and as males.[85] Artiukhina (the head of the central

---

[82] See, e.g., Nukhrat, *RN*, 3(36), 1933, p. 58; Sulaimanova, *ISGPU*, Vol. II, p. 441.

[83] See Sulaimanova, *ISGPU*, Vol. II, pp. 318, 328-29; Pal'vanova, *DSV*, pp. 84, 100-101, 159.

[84] See *Izvestiia*, August 29, 1962. It is a measure of the intensity of the attacks that Bauman's wife was wounded in their home in Tashkent.

[85] See, e.g., Nukhrat, *RN*, 3, 1933, p. 48; Zasukhin, *RN*, 12(46), 1933, p. 39; Abramzon, *SE*, 2, 1932, pp. 95-97; Balaban, *VS*, 40-41, 1928, pp. 15-17; *Bezb* (news.), 4, 1927, p. 6; Artiukhina, *Ka*, 5, 1927, p. 4; Pal'vanova, *DSV*, p. 50; Bil'shai, *RZVS*, pp. 191-93; Liubimova, *VPG*, p. 48. Cf. Zakharian, *Ka*, 3, 1926, pp. 42-43; Michurina, *Ka*, 10-11, 1926, p. 83; Kryl'tsov, *SP*, 5(29), 1927, p. 138; Khodzhaev, *SS*, 1(42), 1930, p. 23; Karpov, *SS*, 6(35), 1929, pp. 65-66; Salim, *Bezb* (news.), 10, 1928, p. 6.

Zhenotdel in Moscow) and Nukhrat (a leading organizer of women in Central Asia) were among the first to point to this denouement: even those poor peasants and nomads who had responded favorably to some Soviet policies—concerning, e.g., redistribution of property and sovietization and nativization of the administrative apparatus—and had actively struggled against richer kinsmen and traditional elites, seemed inclined to rejoin the traditional fold and to turn against the regime the moment female emancipation entered a mass-stage. "[The threat of losing] their unlimited dominion over women" seemed to supersede all other considerations.[86]

Thus, male strata that might have been expected to be increasingly divided by Soviet moves into self-perceiving beneficiaries and adversaries of female mobilization—with beneficiaries surely in the majority—showed signs of shared and growing hostility to the entire enterprise as well as to its communist sponsors. This meant that, instead of sharpening the class struggle, as the communists had hoped, precipitate Soviet initiatives tended to mitigate that struggle. Instead of leading to the alienation of substantial segments of society from the traditional way of life, sudden and massive female mobilization tended to lead to widespread and intense alienation from the Soviet system and its works, accompanied by cleavages running along primarily sexual and ethnic lines. Instead of helping to induce conflicts that would be socially, culturally, politically, and economically productive from the Soviet point of view, precipitate female mobilization was activating conflicts that were highly destructive.

[86] See Artiukhina, *Ka*, 5, 1927, p. 4; Nukhrat, *OZV*, pp. 46-47. For a hint by the Prime Minister of Uzbekistan that "class struggle" and "struggle against the emancipation of women" could mean one and the same thing, and could be directed against the Soviet regime, see Khodzhaev, *SS*, 1(42), 1930, p. 23.

EIGHT · *Patterns of Institutional Performance: Implications of Tension-Controlling Action*

FACED with the unanticipated consequences of its actions, the Soviet regime had to weigh carefully the implications of taking particular countermeasures. The problem of enforcing superimposed rules and repressing deviant behavior comprised two broad sets of issues: (1) To what extent and in what realms could exogenous rule-making and application negate the locally established moral order without generating undesirable and unmanageable tensions? How could new rules (as regulative mechanisms) control the accumulating revolutionary tensions while continuing (as heretical models) to induce these tensions as before? How could Soviet authority successfully legitimate itself while it was destroying and transforming the social bases on which legitimacy had to rest? (2) If countermeasures were called for, against whom could the sanctions best be invoked—against all *de facto* transgressors, or only against some selected individuals or strata? How strongly and consistently might the sanctions be applied—massively or selectively, draconically or with restraint?

There were no easy answers to these questions, not even for a radical, determined, authoritarian regime commanding an absolute monopoly of brute force. This was due not only to the elusiveness, tardiness of compliance, and ferocious resistance of the traditional milieu, but also to the fact that the very instrument entrusted with application and adjudication of the new rules—the new Soviet apparatus in Central Asia—could by no means be taken for granted.

As was to be expected, the quality and thrust of the Soviet apparatus turned out to be heavily dependent on the motivations and commitments of the human element that staffed it. The task of managing female mobilization and emancipation had to be performed at the grassroots by cadres composed largely of native males, which made for extraordinary complexities. The pattern of institutional performance was influenced at least as much by the response of the law-administering and commanding personnel to the new norms as by the pressures for compliance emanating from the Bolshevik (and largely Russian) core of the political machine.

285

SOVIET ADMINISTRATIVE APPARATUS: NATIVE PERSONNEL BEHAVIOR

The response of native political and administrative personnel may be said to have ranged from circumlocution and selective co-operation to sabotage and uncontrolled self-indulgence.

Circumlocution

Since public violation of traditional taboos was the *sine qua non* of the "cultural revolution," local native officials were obviously put on the spot.[1] It was they who were obliged, as a first step, to set a personal, dramatic example by bringing their own female relatives to mass meetings and by unveiling, and thus symbolically liberating, their wives, sisters, mothers, or daughters in public.[2] As the experiment got underway on a large scale in the spring of 1927, it became apparent that, while engaging in spirited public exhortations on behalf of female equality, native officials made every artful effort to dodge the issue in private, shocking Moscow's inspectors.[3]

Native communist functionaries either forced their womenfolk back under the veil immediately after the *khudzhum* meetings—the "storming" exercises of the "cultural revolution"—or never sent them in the first place. Instead they engaged in *maskara*, the traditional mode of dissimulation. First, they hired "substitutes" to be publicly unveiled, the substitutes often being Tatar or Kirghiz women who were not habitually veiled anyway. Second, they dispatched these women from meeting to meeting to be "officially" unveiled a number of times, thus inflating the figures for the record, and documenting their own organizational success.[4]

---

[1] For an excellent example of the consternation in Central Asian party ranks, see the debate among Uzbek communists on the eve of the "storming" campaign, as recorded by Liubimova, *VPG*, pp. 69-71; for other instances of such consternation, see Nikolaeva, *Ka*, 8, 1927, p. 52.

[2] See, e.g., Z. P., *Ka*, 6, 1928, p. 84; Nukhrat, *OZV*, pp. 84-86; Pal'vanova, *DSV*, p. 98; Nikolaeva, *Ka*, 8, 1927, p. 52; Bil'shai, *RZVS*, pp. 191-92. For the Central Committee's call on Central Asian communists to "set a personal example," see Nukhrat, *Ka*, 6, 1928, p. 79.

[3] See, e.g., Michurina, *Ka*, 10-11, 1926, p. 82; Nikolaeva, *Ka*, 8, 1927, pp. 52-54; Nukhrat, *Ka*, 12, 1927, p. 44, and 6, 1928, pp. 77-80; Yaroslavsky, *Ka*, 1, 1929, pp. 28-31; Nikiforov, *Ka*, 15, 1929, p. 45; Perimova, *Ka*, 9, 1929, pp. 37-38; Liubimova, *VPG*, pp. 59-61; Ar-na, *Ka*, 1, 1928, p. 61; Pal'vanova, *DSV*, p. 98.

[4] Ar-na, *Ka*, 1, 1928, p. 61; Nikolaeva, *Ka*, 8, 1927, p. 53. Parallel behavior was observed in the course of successive purges in Central Asia;

As Moscow's purge-commission in Central Asia (led by Manzhara) revealed in 1929, such disparities between public posture and private behavior persisted in virtually all spheres involving traditional practices and female roles. Native officials, including even some judges and prosecutors freshly appointed to the Soviet judicial structure, while delivering speeches about women's rights at public parades and celebrations, continued to keep their own women in segregated quarters and in seclusion, continued to keep them out of school and away from Soviet meetings, enterprises, and associations, and continued to pay and receive the bride-price and to arrange traditional marriages for their children. A good number continued surreptitiously to practice polygamy and to observe the requisites of levirate.[5]

In a number of cases, native communists named their newborn children, both boys and girls, *Khudzhum*, to signify their enthusiasm for the cultural revolution. They did the same when there was an opportunity to rename some Uzbek and Tadzhik factories in their charge.[6] While some of them may have been sincere in doing this,[7] there is reason to suppose that most of them seemed inclined to use such a device as yet another way to assume self-protecting coloration. Although the complete results of the party's investigation of its Central Asian membership in the late 1920's were never made public, it is clear from fragmentary official reports that circumlocution was widespread. For example, it was discovered that in the Andizhan region of Uzbekistan, one of the most important cotton-producing areas of Central Asia, and one that had been easily accessible to the Soviet control apparatus from the very beginning, fifty percent of local communists kept their wives veiled and completely secluded. Yet even this unusually high figure turned out to be quite unreliable. It came to light that at the onset of the purge (in 1929), when confronting Moscow's control commissions, native party members ordered their wives to remove the veil; when

---

see, e.g., Perimova, *Ka*, 9, 1929, pp. 37-38. Cf. *PV*, 1.30.1930, p. 4, and *PV*, 1.17.1935, pp. 2-3.

[5] See Manzhara, *PV*, 1.24.1930, p. 2. Cf. Zavarian, *Ka*, 6, 1926, p. 66; Liubimova, *Ka*, 2, 1927, p. 50; *PV*, 1.30.1930, p. 4; Mitrofanov, *RN*, 1, 1930, pp. 29-36 (*passim*); and *RN*, 2, 1930, pp. 35-49 (*passim*). For similar reports in the mid-1930's, see, e.g., *PV*, 1.17.1935, pp. 2-3.

[6] Pal'vanova, *DSV*, p. 100.

[7] This was probably most likely in the case of husbands of female communists.

the purge was over, the women were obliged to don the veil again.[8] Similarly, while loudly extolling the virtues of *khudzhum* at formal party meetings, many native officials shamed and compromised unveiled women in private, condemning them as prostitutes at informal community gatherings.[9]

When cases of polygamy were uncovered among native communists, some of them were reported to be perfectly at ease about this. One statement in self-defense was reported to be typical: "The Party Rules say nothing about the emancipation of women: quite to the contrary, we have been told that the time will come when communists will have five to eight wives."[10]

As Moscow's inspectors noted with concern, the obvious disparities between the functionaries' public exhortations and private practices made them the laughing stock of their communities.[11] Knowing full well about their new leaders' adherence to customary norms, local peasants and nomads could indeed tell Soviet emissaries with complete equanimity: "If a communist can take four wives, they won't forbid the rest of us to [do the same], for Allah himself commanded it."[12]

Yaroslavsky—emerging in the late 1920's as the regime's leading "specialist" in the battle against religion and custom, as well as Stalin's henchman and the party's chief purger—emphasized the gravity with which Moscow viewed this situation. Addressing the Fourth All-Union Conference of Party Workers among Eastern Women in December, 1928, he cited the quickly accumulating evidence of evasion and circumlocution on the part of Central Asian communists—including ranking officials of district and regional party committees—and warned that the party could not afford to tolerate such anomalies for long. They made a mockery of Soviet initiatives in all spheres, affected adversely the organizational performance of entire party cells, and, at the same time, reinforced the traditionalist propensities of the native masses. For that matter, it was apparently becoming impossible even to persuade Moslem males to allow their wives to participate in ordinary Soviet-spon-

---

[8] See Mitrofanov, *RN*, 2, 1930, p. 39. Cf. Perimova, *Ka*, 9, 1929, pp. 37-38; *PV*, 1.30.1930, p. 4.

[9] Manzhara, *PV*, 1.24.1930, p. 2.

[10] Mitrofanov, *RN*, 2, 1930, pp. 37-38.

[11] See, e.g., Nikolaeva, *Ka*, 8, 1927, pp. 52-53; Yaroslavsky, *Ka*, 1, 1929, pp. 29-30.

[12] Halle, *Women*, p. 139.

288

sored meetings, since these men could now safely say: "When the communists permit *their* wives to attend meetings, we shall let ours do the same."[13]

Needless to say, all this not only called into question the wisdom of the regime's policies; at the very least, as far as the central authorities were concerned, it made all local official reports about the progress and achievements of *khudzhum* immediately suspect.

Selective Cooperation

Without necessarily meaning to willfully disregard Soviet laws, some native officials felt it necessary to bend them locally on the grounds that their consistent enforcement would be difficult, unrealistic, and dangerous in local cultural conditions.

When faced with divorce cases initiated by women—and backed by party activists—some native judges in the Soviet apparatus attempted to transfer the suit to a *kadi*'s (canonical) court, if one was still available in the area, as a traditionally more legitimate medium for dealing with marital problems. Others went through the official motions while privately urging the women to withdraw from public litigation, reach some understanding with their husbands, and go home. They even took it upon themselves—again, in private, and parallel to their formal judicial functions—to serve in many kinds of cases in the role of traditional mediators between aggrieved parties, often for a fee.[14]

In instances where informal mediation bore no fruit—as in cases of divorce actively pressed by the Zhenotdel—local judicial officials were inclined to legalize a divorce sought by a woman but did so by and large on traditionally prescribed terms. In practice, this meant that, even if successful, female litigants were assigned little or no property in the settlement, while those who won control over their children were also obliged to support them.[15]

On other occasions, attempts were made to reconcile Soviet and customary rules in special ways. Soviet legislation had explicitly proscribed *kaitarma*—the paying of *kalym* in installments—in accordance with which the bride's parents had been entitled to withhold her from the groom, even after marriage, until the bride-price was paid in full. Under the new law, a married woman's parents

[13] Yaroslavsky, *Ka*, 1, 1929, p. 29 (italics supplied).

[14] See, e.g., Fioletov, *SP*, 1(25), 1927, p. 146; Sulaimanova, *ISGPU*, Vol. II, pp. 230-31, 217.

[15] See Sulaimanova, *ISGPU*, Vol. II, pp. 229-30, 216-18.

could not hold her against her will. Many local courts proceeded to apply this rule, but with a shift in emphasis: a woman was ordered to be delivered to her husband even if she herself wished to remain in her natal home. Similarly, Soviet legislation had made it mandatory for courts to grant divorces initiated by women, except when there was evidence that such litigation was instigated by the woman's kinsmen with the purpose of reselling her to another man for additional *kalym*. The courts had but one responsibility: to determine whether an act of coercion had indeed taken place. In many cases, native court officials chose to apply this injunction literally, but in a very different context, and in ways consonant with local custom. Divorce suits initiated by women on grounds of maltreatment by their husbands were summarily denied if the plaintiff could show no evidence of bruises or other signs of maltreatment or coercion.[16]

When faced with obviously false testimony in civil registry agencies or in court (e.g., pertaining to bride-price, marital age, or polygamous status), some native functionaries went along with such testimony, conscious of the fact that not to do so would only drive the clients away from Soviet institutions and auspices in other cases as well.[17]

Others did more than that. Native officials had been conscious of the fact that Moslem couples stayed away from Soviet registry agencies and preferred marriage under religious auspices, in part because Soviet regulations called for medical certification of the partners' ages based on a physical examination. Moslems found it especially abhorrent to have their womenfolk examined by strangers, possibly men. With this in mind, the Uzbek government had exempted Moslem marriages (in January, 1927) from the rule. Natives still needed to bring proof of legal age, mutual consent, and absence of *kalym* agreements, but such a certificate could now be obtained from the soviet of the local community. Almost immediately it became apparent that local soviet officials were prepared (with or without a bribe) to supply any and all certificates which would permit members of their community to evade the law.[18]

It also became apparent that in the crucial years of legalism and *khudzhum* (1926-1928) Central Asian Z.A.G.S. agencies (Soviet

---

[16] See Perimova, *Ka*, 9, 1929, p. 38.

[17] See, e.g., Zakharian, *Ka*, 3, 1926, p. 44; cf. Dosov, *Ka*, 5, 1928, p. 30.

[18] See esp. Sulaimanova, *ISGPU*, Vol. II, pp. 219-20; Balaban, *VS*, 40-41, 1928, pp. 15-17 (*passim*); Amosov, *Ka*, 14, 1929, p. 25; Mitrofanov, *RN*, 2, 1930, p. 38.

offices of civil registry) made quiet allowances for what amounted to polygamy by consent. In effect, a man could legally register a second marriage if he produced his first wife's written consent. Some of the highest echelons of republican administration—e.g., some departments of the Uzbek Commissariat of Justice—not only knew about it but supported it, without making the matter public.[19]

In instances when such polygamy by consent was uncovered by outside inspectors or denounced by one of the wives, and could not very well be publicly explained and defended, local people's courts were likely to react by applying the law quite literally, as if proving to all concerned (including Moscow's emissaries) the folly of attempting to disrupt established relationships. They tended to indict not only the man but his women, too. First wives who had granted their consent to a husband's polygamous union, but later complained about it, were indicted for "consenting to proscribed acts." Second or third wives who sued to leave such a union, and take some property with them, were indicted for "entering a polygamous relationship while knowing that Soviet laws forbade it." In most of these cases, the women were ordered to leave the household at once, and without property.[20]

While cooperating in the apprehension of robbers and wanton killers, for example, native policemen were often particularly careful to avoid embarrassing entanglement in cases involving women. For example, as was illustrated in a great number of instances, if a local policeman saw a woman being beaten by her husband (at home or in the street, and no matter how savagely), he took good care, as tradition demanded, not to intervene. This was true even when wives were being murdered in broad daylight. When pressed by the victim's friends to do something about it, policemen insisted on the need for "neutrality" in the matter. A typical reply was reported to be: "This is a private affair between husband and wife; no one must interfere." Moreover, if notified by a local family that a wife or daughter had run away from home (e.g., to avoid an arranged marriage, escape maltreatment, etc.), policemen often collaborated in apprehending the woman and delivering her to her household. If anything, they seemed far more eager and efficient in executing these tasks than in pursuing other lines of duty.[21]

An especially flagrant case of such behavior was reported from

[19] See Sulaimanova, *ISGPU*, Vol. II, pp. 230-31.

[20] Mukhitdinova, *Ka*, 9, 1929, pp. 39-40.

[21] See Michurina, *Ka*, 10-11, 1926, p. 82. Cf. Nikiforov, *Ka*, 15, 1929, p. 46.

Kazakhstan, with the implication that it represented a typical illustration of the dilemmas encountered by Soviet authorities in dealing with native personnel. Sometime in early 1928 a half-starved Kazakh woman appeared in the camp of a Russian oil-exploration team, begging for help. She had apparently been "sold" by her father to a rich clansman for a large bride-price. With her husband dead soon afterward, she returned to her home and then fled to the house of a man she loved but who had no intention of paying *kalym* for her. Almost immediately, her former brother-in-law, exercising the customary rights of levirate, claimed her as his "inheritance," and an armed band from his clan kidnapped her and delivered her to him. Against great odds, she succeeded in escaping from her new master. Now she feared for her life, and needed asylum and assistance. As it turned out, not a single Russian in the camp dared to do anything for her, even if only to hide her until her father's arrival. The secretary of the local party cell also refused to commit himself. As he put it: "You aren't going to stir up trouble on account of a woman, are you?" Within a short time, Kazakh militiamen arrived in the camp to claim her as "subject to the laws of her native district [where she must answer for her] crime"—i.e., for willfully abandoning a household where she belonged. When informed that there appeared to be no such crime under Soviet law, the Kazakhs shrugged: "That's impossible; it is a crime in our district." They escorted the woman out of the camp without further challenge. Upon one man's proposal to send Russian police in pursuit, the response of the local Russian official in command was decidedly negative: "We cannot use *our* militiamen to go to *their* districts . . . [certainly not] in such a case." After some time, the Kazakh police unit filed what was apparently a routine report in such cases: the detail of two armed militiamen had been "overtaken" by a band of ten men (unarmed) who "kidnapped" the woman and rejoined their clan. When prodded by a Soviet investigator to explain why such things were permitted to happen, the Kazakh officer in charge was perfectly candid: "Do you realize what would happen if all women suddenly felt free to leave their husbands?"[22]

Official investigations conducted throughout Central Asia in 1929 revealed extensive collusion between criminal, judicial, and administrative local organs in delimiting or blunting the effects of emancipatory legislation. In hundreds of documented cases in each

[22] Balaban, *VS*, 40-41, 1928, pp. 15-17.

republic, official action on reported "customary crimes" of all kinds was delayed for up to three years. In many such cases, the delays permitted local organs to grant the accused amnesty shortly after conviction or even before they could be tried. Appeals for clemency, acquittal, or dismissal of a case due to extenuating circumstances seemed to be accepted and approved far more efficaciously than demands for criminal prosecution and indictment. And in all cases involving women native functionaries seemed especially disposed to bend over backwards not to offend traditional sensibilities, taking local customs into account far more consistently than Soviet legislation. Even when confronted with *prima facie* evidence of murder of female activists by traditionalist males, they showed little enthusiasm for rounding up the culprits and prosecuting them with the full severity of the law.[23]

When pressed to explain why the cooperation of local governmental agencies was so selective, and why so much of Moscow's emancipatory legislation was permitted to remain on paper, even the most highly placed native communists pleaded for understanding and restraint. Some of them soft-pedaled the matter by invoking a fundamental Marxist tenet: there was no cause for alarm; customs were nothing but a superstructure, one that would change in and of itself when the economic base changed.[24] Others cited primordial native concerns about procreation and continuation of the family line as special extenuating circumstances. They maintained, for example, that it made no sense to prosecute each and every polygamous male. There were poor men among them as well as rich. A man might try to acquire an additional wife not in order to exploit her but to fill a void created by the first wife's illness, or barrenness, or inability to produce sons.[25]

Still others risked being considered counter-revolutionaries in the course of defending their countrymen's conduct. At the height of *khudzhum*, Kasym Khodzhaev, the Deputy Chairman of Uzbekistan's Central Executive Committee, publicly defended a group of men on trial for killing a woman. He apparently justified

---

[23] See, e.g., Nikiforov, *Ka*, 15, 1929, pp. 45-46; Amosov, *Ka*, 14, 1929, p. 25; Perimova, *Ka*, 9, 1929, pp. 37-38; Mukhitdinova, *Ka*, 9, 1929, p. 40; *PV*, 2.3.1930, p. 1. Cf. Michurina, *Ka*, 10-11, 1926, p. 82; Kasparova, *Ka*, 7, 1925, p. 91; Shimko, *Ka*, 12, 1925, p. 67; Ibragimov, *Ka*, 10, 1925, p. 88; Mostovaia, *VS*, 9, 1928, pp. 7-8.

[24] See Perimova, *Ka*, 9, 1929, p. 38.

[25] This is implied in Mostovaia, *VS*, 9, 1928, pp. 7-8. Cf. Halle, *Women*, pp. 139-40.

their act on "cultural" grounds: one had to understand the sensibilities of people outraged by violations of their customs and
taboos. (Moscow's immediate response was to relieve Khodzhaev
of his duties. It is not clear what followed.)[26]

Attitudes such as these were apparently responsible for what the
party's investigators referred to as a peculiarly "conciliatory" spirit,
a "spirit of compromise [and] benevolence," characterizing the
conduct of leading native communists. In 1928 and 1929, while
serving on local control commissions in preparation for the first
major purge in Central Asia, these men tended simply to ignore the
record of their subordinates' private life. They did so especially if
the record involved continued adherence to customary norms concerning women. As a result, the pre-purge investigation apparently
"had none of the expected effect."[27]

Many local communists, some of them in authoritative positions,
were prepared to defend both their own and their comrades' conduct as beneficial from the viewpoint of political tactics. Some had
been found to play an active role in their religious community, had
joined *mullahs* in 1927 and 1928 in attributing the region's natural
disasters (especially earthquakes) to mass unveiling, and had
helped to organize special prayers and sacrificial offerings on this
account; some had ordered their wives and kinswomen to don the
veil immediately after public unveiling, and helped to circulate
rumors that unveiled women were prostitutes; some had merely
collaborated in supplying themselves and their kinsmen with all
kinds of official certificates—concerning bride-price, marital age,
etc.—helpful in evading the law. In many of these cases, their justification in self-defense was extraordinarily simple: they were doing all this out of sound political considerations; they felt obliged
to maneuver in, and adapt to, a backward and hostile environment; they tried to "avoid the censure of people who were not
members of the party."[28]

It goes without saying that, when confronted with such attitudes

[26] For the evidence in Khodzhaev's case, and for hints about his motives,
see Amosov, *Ka*, 14, 1929, p. 25. For implicit indications that there were
other leading native functionaries who shared his views, see Yaroslavsky,
Ka, 1, 1929, p. 29.

[27] Perimova, *Ka*, 9, 1929, p. 37. Cf. Amosov, *Ka*, 14, 1929, p. 30;
Yaroslavsky, *Ka*, 1, 1929, pp. 28-31.

[28] See Mitrofanov, *RN*, 2, 1930, pp. 35-38; Yaroslavsky, *Ka*, 1, 1929,
p. 30 (and pp. 28-31 *passim*); Manzhara, *PV*, 1.24.1930, p. 2, and Pal'-
vanova, *DSV*, p. 98.

294

and conduct on the part of local personnel, central authorities could not always be sure how to view them. They could be manifestations of loyal service and shrewd Leninist improvisation. They could also reflect intellectual confusion, professional incompetence, rank hypocrisy, or outright sabotage.

Sabotage

If there were some native officials who refused to go along with some aspects of female emancipation because they believed them to be either impracticable or unwise, there were others who felt strongly enough about the matter to denounce and sabotage the entire operation.

Some simply indicted Moscow's initiatives because they felt they were reckless and insulting in that they failed to take account of the feelings and judgment of Central Asia's rising secular intelligentsia —a relatively moderate reformist stratum that was supposed to enjoy the Bolsheviks' friendly partnership in modernization and not to have to buckle under Moscow's unilateral decisions. Some warnings to this effect were sounded in the early 1920's, i.e., before emancipatory initiatives were shifted into high gear. In 1921, Otmar-Shtein, a female political commissar of the Red Army on the Central Asian front, was dispatched by Frunze and Kuibyshev (the party's highest plenipotentiaries in charge of the re-conquest of the region) to organize Bukharan women. She encountered unusual difficulties. Merely to contact local women she was obliged, with the party's special dispensation, to don a veil. Even so, she was accused of violating local taboos, and was arrested and expelled on orders of the Bukharan Communist Party, a party composed of men who had, after all, helped the Red Army to crush the Bukharan Emir's resistance to Soviet occupation. With Otmar-Shtein's forced departure, the Women's Department she had freshly established in the local Central Committee was summarily liquidated. Liubimova, arriving from Moscow in 1923 to re-establish the special unit, was unceremoniously ordered by Bukhara's authorities to desist. The leadership of the Bukharan Central Committee refused even to introduce her to their wives.[29] (Several years later, at the height of legal and administrative assault, a number of Central Asian communists were found to have acquired vicious dogs to guard female quarters in their homes, preventing all out-

[29] Liubimova, *VPG*, p. 22; Otmar-Shtein, "V Staroi Bukhare," in *ZVR*, pp. 345-49.

siders from visiting their wives or inviting them to public meetings.)[30]

By 1924, even the most useful and trusted Turkic Bolsheviks—for example, Tiurakulov[31]—were made uneasy enough by the developing Soviet legal drive to indict the latter as, in effect, harebrained abolitionism. Said Tiurakulov: "Those profoundly learned in Marxist literature, [who know] nothing about our practical situation . . . [simply] come with [official] prescriptions to people who have not yet left the diapers of a clan-system. . . . [They come] with (n + 1) . . . calculations and order: 'Peoples of the East! All is ready! Go ahead with the Latin alphabet, with the women's question, with the Allah-question, with the [question of] permeation by the Soviet regime!' . . ." What did these "prescriptions" have to offer, in dealing with deeply entrenched Islamic customs? Coming as they did "from the laboratory of some Marx institute," they proposed that traditional institutions and customs simply be "abolished." "All we want," Tiurakulov openly insisted, "is that such problems be left to us who come from the minority groups of the U.S.S.R.; we shall ourselves solve these problems in a way that we shall deem to be both convenient and correct. . . ."[32]

In 1926, other highly placed Turkic communists, including the communist leadership of at least two Central Asian republics (Turkmenistan and, apparently, Kazakhstan), went farther. When faced with the divorce wave in Central Asia, they not only tried to halt it secretly; they were embittered enough to demand formally that the divorce wave be stopped forthwith, as "ill-advised" and "[prohibitively] massive," and that Zhenotdel activists be immediately enjoined by Moscow from agitating and inciting Moslem women. The main reason cited by native communist officials to Moscow's investigators was as stark in form as it was dramatic in implications: "Every divorce initiated by a woman—no matter what the reason—amounts to the moral murder of her husband."[33]

[30] See Mitrofanov, *RN*, 2, 1930, p. 37.

[31] One of Moscow's prime trouble-shooters in handling broadly Islamic affairs, not only in Central Asia, but as an emissary in Mecca as well. See Hayit, *Turkestan im XX Jahrhundert*, pp. 184, 227, 306, 314-15.

[32] Tiurakulov, *ZhN*, 1(6), 1924, pp. 38-40.

[33] Liubimova, *VPG*, p. 48; Zakharian, *Ka*, 3, 1926, pp. 42-43; Michurina, *Ka*, 10-11, 1926, pp. 82-83; Kryl'tsov, *SP*, 5(29), 1927, p. 138. While available Soviet sources of the late 1920's explicitly mentioned Turkmen

While Turkmen, Kazakh, Uzbek, and other native communists also argued that the divorce wave was undermining established households, fragmenting fields under cultivation, harming agricultural production, and thus intensifying hunger and chaos,[34] they were emphatic in identifying the main source of evil: divorces initiated by native women were profoundly "demoralizing" in nature, in that they led to the "corruption [and disintegration] of the moral bases of the family." This led Moscow's emissaries to conclude, with a mixture of derision and unease, that it was not only *traditionalist* males who could entertain such "a peculiar notion of [masculine] honor with respect to women."[35]

In October, 1926, in what was apparently a defiant move,[36] the Turkmen Executive Committee (Third Session), obviously reflecting the judgment of the Central Committee of the Turkmen Communist Party, formally called for a radical curtailment of divorce proceedings among natives. The reasons given included not only "the immediate destruction of households as economic units," but also the "groundlessness" of all too many divorce litigations initiated by women. The latter were declared groundless primarily due to the women's "intellectual darkness and rank ignorance" which was easily exploited by people with ulterior motives.

The Executive Committee ruled that, unlike in European Russia, Turkmen divorce litigations should be handled exclusively through formal court proceedings rather than through offices of civil registry. It imposed a sanction of three years in jail on all those who, for reasons of their own, "forced [or incited]" a Moslem woman to demand a divorce. Among the possible instigators of such action the

---

leaders in this connection, they merely hinted about the involvement of others, notably Kazakhs and Uzbeks, in this fashion. In 1933, Nukhrat's review of these events included Kirghiz communists as well (see *RN*, 3(36), 1933, p. 49).

[34] See Nukhrat, *RN*, 3(36), 1933, p. 49. Cf. Kasparova, *Ka*, 7, 1925, p. 89.

[35] See ibid., and Sulaimanova, *ISGPU*, Vol. II, p. 216. For earlier manifestations of such an attitude, see Sulaimanova, ibid., Vol. I, p. 269.

[36] The formal justifications and demands in this case were virtually identical with those cited (and assailed) by Soviet investigators in 1925 and 1926. Thus, at least in some respects, this move by Turkmen leadership deliberately ignored pressures emanating from Moscow as well as the more compliant anti-traditional legislation enacted by Uzbeks. Compare the wording in Michurina, *Ka*, 10-11, 1926, p. 83 and in "V Tsentral'nykh . . . ," *SS* (5), 1926, pp. 158-59.

committee listed parents, relatives, and "outsiders"—an obvious allusion to the Zhenotdel.[37]

At the same time, the Executive Committee went on record as opposed to criminal prosecution of recipients of *kalym*. Instead, it proposed that payers be merely given the right to sue payees for return of the bride price.[38]

Such dispositions on the part of leading local personnel found a clear expression in its performance in the course of *khudzhum*. While some native court officials attempted merely to blunt the edge of criminal prosecutions for traditional offenses, others were found to be inclined to go much farther. According to reports from all parts of Central Asia, indictments for offenses connected with female emancipation were deliberately sidetracked, shelved, and withheld from scrutiny by central authorities. In what were apparently hundreds of cases, native functionaries (including Communist Party members) refused altogether to investigate reported offenses and to press charges against transgressors, even against killers of female activists.[39]

Most important, using the passing of personal status and civil rights laws as an excuse, and the decrees of the "cultural revolution" as a screen, what appears to have been the bulk of native officialdom deliberately refrained from any other action on this account. Thus, in the heat of the social upheaval in 1927 and 1928, they refused to provide what actual and potential female defectors from tradition needed most: moral, organizational, educational, and economic support.

In a number of cases this failure was accompanied by open expressions of contempt for female-oriented enterprises as "irrelevant, worthless, trivial," and by a systematic withholding of funds.[40]

[37] See "V Tsentral'nykh . . . ," *SS* (5), 1926, pp. 158-59; cf. Zakharian, *Ka*, 3, 1926, pp. 42-44, and Kryl'tsov, *SP*, 5(29), 1927, p. 138.

[38] "V Tsentral'nykh . . . ," *SS* (5), 1926, p. 159.

[39] See, e.g., Akopov, *RN*, 4-5, 1930, pp. 63-64; Liubimova, *Ka*, 2, 1927, pp. 50-51, and *VPG*, pp. 22, 24, 48; Amosov, *Ka*, 14, 1929, p. 25; Perimova, *Ka*, 9, 1929, p. 38.

[40] See, e.g., Nukhrat, *Ka*, 1, 1928, p. 55, and *Ka*, 4, 1928, pp. 68-69; Burlova, *Ka*, 8, 1928, pp. 88-90; A. N., *Ka*, 9, 1926, pp. 34-36; Khodzhaev, *SS* (35), 1929, p. 59. For notes on the earliest manifestations of this trend, see Liubimova, *VPG*, p. 24. For some data on Central Asian communists purged in 1929 for such sabotage in the course of *khudzhum*, see Manzhara, *PV*, 1.24.1930, p. 2.

In other cases, responsible party officials reportedly sabotaged female mobilization by ignoring the entire matter, on the grounds that they "could not quite comprehend" why Moscow would want them to "intensify" a struggle that was already causing dangerous dislocations.[41] The dominant attitude among these functionaries was reported to be one of cold disdain: it was the job of the Zhenotdel to work with women; if the female activists of the party's Women's Department wanted to intensify the drive, that was their business.[42]

Thus, women (especially activists and widows) who had succeeded, with the Zhenotdel's help, in obtaining individual land-allotments in the course of the land reform, were confronted with insurmountable obstacles. In what was apparently a consistent pattern, local officials tended to withhold credit, seeds, and agricultural implements from such households, and to deny them assistance during plowing, sowing, and harvesting. As a result, by the end of 1928 most of the new female-led households were reportedly ruined, and women, unable to tend the fields on their own, were found to be renting out, disposing of, or altogether abandoning their freshly won parcels of land.[43]

Discrimination against women in schools also proceeded apace. Girls and women won over to attend literacy courses were, in most cases, provided with neither quarters, teachers, books, or paper to do any significant work. Girls enrolled for the first time in Soviet Central Asian schools were intimidated or ignored, and their number—pitifully small in the first place—was allowed to drop drastically, and this precisely at the time (in 1927) of the decreed "head-on assault." In this way, in the educational sphere, official sabotage compounded the effects of popular resentment and backlash. In effect, it aggravated what was already a volatile situation, wherein Moslem parents were inclined to withdraw their children (especially girls) from school, or to forbid their attendance in the first place. As a result, by the end of 1928, after several years of dutifully reported "victories on the educational front," the literacy rate for Uzbekistan as a whole—i.e., for what was declared to be Cen-

---

[41] See Nikolaeva, *Ka*, 8, 1927, pp. 52-54; Nukhrat, *Ka*, 6, 1928, pp. 77-80.

[42] Yaroslavsky, *Ka*, 1, 1929, pp. 28-31. Cf. Amosov, *Ka*, 14, 1929, p. 30.

[43] See Liubimova, *Ka*, 4, 1926, p. 57, *Ka*, 11, 1927, p. 76, and *VPG*, pp. 54-58; Nukhrat, *Ka*, 6, 1928, p. 80; Pal'vanova, *DSV*, p. 94.

tral Asia's "most advanced" republic—was found to be below four percent, while that for Uzbek women was only one percent.[44]

Similarly, a goodly number of reportedly established women's clubs turned out to exist only on paper, and this at the height of *khudzhum*. Most of those that did exist were found to be ghost-institutions, with no people in them, just "dreary . . . [little places] . . . encased in dust and spiderwebs."[45] The situation in regard to the fledgling network of special stores and "red corners" which were supposed to have been established for Moslem women was found equally incongruous. As *khudzhum* wore on, existing stores were, more often than not, liquidated rather than expanded, and that by order of local authorities. When exposed and pressed for an explanation, these officials tended to justify their decision on the ground that, with "mass unveiling" taking place, there was no need to bother with such expensive and unorthodox enterprises as special associational forms for native women. At the same time, auxiliary units that were supposed to serve as women's "red corners"—places designed to disseminate, on an elementary level, communist propaganda—were found to be shut down or turned into "[facilities] for storing refuse."[46]

Recruitment of women into industry was sidetracked wherever possible. Those courageous or desperate enough to report for factory work were assigned primarily to enterprises—such as silk-weaving plants—for which no other suitable workers could be found. Those native women who did obtain jobs in industry through forceful party pressure were relegated to menial tasks, deprived of advanced training, and cut off from supervisory positions. Their pay was at the low end of the wage structure. They were consistently ignored by the political and cultural cadres of their enterprises, as well as by local trade unions and Commissariats of Labor. In extreme cases, they were discriminated against or openly insulted by their co-workers, including Russian and other European women, and by the male management, both native and Russian. Even when installed by administrative order in a supervisory capacity, their executive role tended to be purely *pro forma*. Thus, no one bothered to tell them what they were supposed to do, and how, which made it easy for management to "prove" their ignorance and failure, and to demote or fire them without further

[44] Amosov, *Ka*, 14, 1929, pp. 23-24, 28; Ar-na, *Ka*, 1, 1928, p. 59; Nukhrat, *Ka*, 6, 1928, p. 80.

[45] Ar-na, ibid., pp. 59-60; Amosov, *Ka*, 14, 1929, p. 27.

[46] Ar-na, ibid., pp. 60-61; cf. Prishchepchik, *Ka*, 9, 1926, p. 76.

ado. In any case, those native women who continued to be tolerated in formally responsible posts were treated as inconvenient fixtures and were unceremoniously shunted aside by those who were supposed to be their "deputies," including native males and Russian women.[47]

In early 1928, Artiukhina (the head of the central Zhenotdel) summed up the matter with a mixture of bewilderment and anger: the first contingent of native women (several thousand strong) recruited for industrial work in Central Asia had been expected to serve as the proletarian core, "the party's . . . fulcrum," in the course of *khudzhum*; by the same token, hundreds of women newly recruited as people's assessors in courts, as members of handicraft and agricultural cooperatives, and as students in literacy circles and courses for teachers and midwives were supposed to have been organized in a political network and especially cared for by local officials, so as to strengthen the impetus of the regime's offensive and to allow it to consolidate its gains; nothing came of these expectations.[48]

Official reports concerning female political participation were found to be quite misleading. In some instances, male functionaries managed to show female membership in a local soviet by handpicking some older, illiterate women, bribing them with a few rubles, and carrying their names on the books.[49] When pressed to accept female activists of Delegatskie Sobraniia, newly founded "Assemblies of Women's Delegates," as special apprentices in administrative agencies, Moslem officials found countless excuses to refuse. As it turned out, many of them regarded the proposed apprentices as "spies" who would report on local doings to higher authorities.[50]

The handful of women who, after years of pressure, were finally elected or appointed to seemingly responsible positions in the party apparatus, and in courts and soviets, were found to lead (in 1927-28) a decidedly shadowy political existence. They tended to be collectively ignored, leading Zhenotdel investigators to conclude that female political roles were, as a rule, a "mere formality" or a

---

[47] See Sulaimanova, *ISGPU*, Vol. II, p. 442; Ar-na, *Ka*, 1, 1928, p. 58; Nukhrat, *Ka*, 6, 1928, p. 79; Amosov, *Ka*, 14, 1929, p. 30. For comprehensive reviews of the spectrum of problems encountered in recruiting Moslem women for industrial work, see Sakhudri, *Ka*, 4, 1928, pp. 70-73; Ibragimov, *Ka*, 9, 1928, pp. 88-90; Krupnikova, *Ka*, 10, 1928, p. 85; Davydova, *Ka*, 11, 1928, pp. 67-68; Nukhrat, *Ka*, 1, 1929, pp. 24-27.

[48] Ar-na, *Ka*, 1, 1928, pp. 58-61. Cf. Nikolaeva, *Ka*, 8, 1927, p. 53; Amosov, Ka, 14, 1929, pp. 27, 30.

[49] See Halle, *Women*, p. 198.   [50] See Nukhrat, *Ka*, 7, 1928, p. 58.

"[disgusting] mockery." They were not invited to (and not even notified about) official meetings; they were neither taught nor guided in their new roles—and were then accused by male officials of being "utterly [irresponsible], incapable of discharging their duties"; instead of being assigned to responsible practical tasks, many were relegated to cleaning the premises and washing the floors; in some cases, they were simply "[shunted into] back rooms where no one could see them," while what were supposed to be their male "secretaries" not only conducted their business for them, but blocked their contact with the outside world.[51]

In sum, while legal and related enterprises tended to encourage the *mobilization* of growing contingents of women, native male functionaries were found to be willing and able to sabotage the means of tangible female *participation* in the promised new world.

Uncontrolled Self-Indulgence

In 1927 and 1928, far from merely sitting on their hands or engaging in open or clandestine sabotage of the "cultural revolution," at least some native functionaries, both party and non-party personnel, especially in the middle and lower echelons of the Soviet apparatus, showed that they were capable of what Zhenotdel activists called "[other forms of] conservatism,"[52] as well.

There was what one native female communist characterized as a "[peculiar] psychological aberration" in the attitude of native male communists toward women who had unveiled themselves[53] and joined the party. This attitude prevailed even among "the most devoted and brilliant comrades in our party . . . [among] our best, most sincere, intellectually most emancipated and principled communists. . . ." Their behavior was thought to be determined by their cultural background:

> The ancient Moslem attitude toward women, the feeling instilled in everyone since childhood that a woman who uncovers her face in the presence of strange men is a harlot, has so conditioned man's psychology in Central Asia as to make it impossible

---

[51] Ar-na, *Ka*, 1, 1928, p. 61; Tarantaeva, *VS*, 51, 1927, p. 10, and *Ka*, 11, 1928, p. 45; Nukhrat, *Ka*, 12, 1927, p. 44; Liubimova, *VPG*, pp. 59-60; Pal'vanova, *DSV*, p. 144; Vagabov, *Islam i Zhenshchina*, p. 96.

[52] Nukhrat, *Ka*, 12, 1927, p. 44.

[53] Of course, this was more relevant in the case of Uzbeks, Tadzhiks, and Turkmens than of Kazakhs and Kirghiz. Among the latter, veiling was, as a rule, not practiced.

for him to react to an unveiled woman in a manner that you Europeans would consider normal. . . . [Hence communists, too, even in the highest echelons were unable] . . . to suppress a reaction which in its immediacy is tantamount to a conditioned reflex; even they, although unconsciously, tend to assume that peculiar freedom of manner which men allow themselves in the presence of women of "questionable character."[54]

There was also what party inspectors found to be "scandalous" behavior toward unveiled peasant women on the part of communist officials at the village level. They made advances to such women, and when rebuffed, either lured them into well-protected quarters (including local party headquarters) or simply ordered their arrest, after which the women were raped by large companies of "communist and responsible officials," sometimes "by the entire party cell headed by the ranking functionary."[55] It would seem that on some such occasions the men tried to insure themselves against possible complications by obliging a violated woman to sign a statement to the effect that she had given herself voluntarily.[56]

Russian as well as native female activists sent by the party for organizational work in the hinterland reportedly experienced such propensities first hand. Their initial reception by individual leaders of local party cells and soviets, even though deliberately evasive and vague, was generally courteous. But the moment the news of their arrival spread, they apparently had to sit up nights in their tents with guns at the ready in order to ward off groups of native Soviet functionaries bent upon rape.[57]

[54] Kunitz, *Dawn Over Samarkand*, p. 298.

[55] Ar-na, *Ka*, 1, 1928, pp. 61-62; *PV*, 1.24.1930, p. 2; Mitrofanov, *RN*, 2, 1930, pp. 37-38.

For evidence of the persistence of such practices in the 1930's, particularly with regard to unveiled and divorced women (ostensibly because they "disgraced" the community and its women, and therefore deserved retribution), see, e.g., *PV*, 1.17.1935, pp. 2-3; Dimanshtein, *RN*, 12(58), 1934, p. 35. Note that some of the women violated in this fashion came to be used by the party as "public accusers" during the purges in Central Asia; see, e.g., *PV*, 1.17.1935, pp. 2-3.

[56] While such an instance was reported several years after the period under review (see Dimanshtein, *RN*, 12(58), 1934, p. 35) this report as well as other circumstantial evidence leave one with a strong impression that such bureaucratic self-insurance stratagems first came to light during the "cultural revolution."

[57] See Nukhrat, *OZV*, pp. 48 ff. Cf. Pal'vanova, *DSV*, p. 80.

Bizarre variants of such intense preoccupations came to light in Uzbekistan. Here, the party's agencies, by becoming the refuge of orphaned girls, runaway child-brides, and disaffected widows and divorcées, tended to inflame the expectations of local communists. The latter considered it as both their opportunity and their right to look for female companionship among the party's new wards. Apparently the demand in such a context was so great that a number of local party officials, including even some native female communists, made it their business to supply their comrades with women for a fee.[58] Those city-based party members who momentarily lacked access to women not only flocked to prostitutes but, in some cases, when out of cash, left their party membership cards with the girls "as security for payment." This became known when some prostitutes, having waited for payment in vain, came to one of the party's district committees "to lodge a complaint."[59]

Rather more alarmingly, not only unattached women were involved. In some cases, communists sent as teachers to newly organized literacy courses for married women were found to spend more time in erotic pursuit of their students than in teaching. Infuriated husbands promptly withdrew their wives from school, contributing to the collapse of the literacy campaign among women.[60] In other reported cases, whether or not with marital plans in mind, at least some local soviet officials seemed self-confident enough to "forcibly take over" unveiled married women who caught their fancy, including "wives of farmhands and poor peasants."[61] This went so far that in some locales (e.g., in villages around Bukhara) Central Asian peasants openly refused to unveil their wives or let them participate in public functions on the grounds that they were "afraid lest [their women] catch the eye of [communist] functionaries."[62]

SOVIET ADMINISTRATIVE APPARATUS: NON-NATIVE PERSONNEL BEHAVIOR

Given the pattern of popular response to the new norms and the dispositions of much of its personnel, the Soviet administrative and judicial apparatus was obviously in no position to perform strictly on Moscow's cues. Moreover, neither the supreme leadership in Moscow nor the local communist machine was of one mind as to the proper course to be pursued under the circumstances. The per-

[58] See Mitrofanov, *RN*, 2, 1930, p. 38.
[59] *PV*, 9.25.1931, p. 3.
[60] Mitrofanov, *RN*, 2, 1930, p. 38.
[61] Ibid.
[62] Ibid.

formance of the apparatus charged with the enforcement and adjudication of the new rules was uneven, inconsistent, and veered from one extreme to the other. The performance-pattern may be said to have ranged from dissonant improvisation and selective enforcement to limited retaliation and massive repression.

Dissonant Improvisation

The burdens of the Soviet legal drive were particularly great because the decreed legal revolution had to be wrought through new, unprecedented, still to be legitimated judicial structures enforcing prescriptions that constituted, literally, a normative revolution. Confusion and disarray verging on paralysis, especially in cases involving women and personal status laws, ensued throughout the 1920's. The specific problems accounting for the normative and administrative dissonance were manifold, and the problems themselves were merely encapsulated or (often) aggravated by disparate Soviet attempts to improvise local solutions.

(a) Given the rather sudden shift to a judicial system embodying values and presupposing administrative qualifications largely unprecedented in the Central Asian milieu, the requisite native judicial cadres were simply not available to build, manage, and routinize the new network of institutions everywhere and at once.[63] Moreover, to replace the old with new judicial personnel was not a mere matter of switching civil servants. In most of Central Asia's communities—both sedentary and nomadic, both orthodox Moslem and shamano-Moslem in character—the role of local administrators of justice (whether *mullahs, kadis,* clan elders, tribal leaders, village notables, or other men commanding what the party described as "respect," "prestige," and "authority" in a given locale) was not that of an impersonal servant of a bureaucratic machine applying rigid laws and relying on a police system to enforce them. It tended to be, as Bolshevik organizers came to realize, rather the role of a largely informal "guide," "arbitrator," "mediator," "conciliator," just as popular adherence to the decreed compromise tended to be "voluntary" and "automatic."[64] To dispose of such

---

[63] See, e.g., Michurina, *Ka*, 10-11, 1926, p. 82; Nikiforov, *Ka*, 15, 1929, p. 45; Mukhitdinova, *Ka*, 9, 1929, p. 40; Zavarian, *Ka*, 6, 1926, p. 66; Digurov, *SS*, 2(19), 1928, pp. 56-60. Cf. Sulaimanova, *ISGPU*, Vol. ii, pp. 636-37 (for attempts in the early 1930's to remedy this situation).

[64] See, e.g., Fioletov, *SP*, 1(25), 1927, p. 146; Kryl'tsov, *SP*, 5(29), 1927, p. 137. Cf. Shatskaia, *SE*, 1, 1936, pp. 52-53; Michurina, *Ka*, 10-11, 1926, p. 80; Pravda, *SS*, 12(41), 1929, p. 108; Shokhor, *SS*, 8-9 (13-14),

personnel, while simultaneously trying to find, train, and legitimize an entirely different kind of public servant, was far from a simple matter.

Under the circumstances, former personnel, including even Moslem *kadis*, frequently found it easy to slip back into the role of judge in a new Soviet court. This happened at times because local Soviet officials, desperate to report the establishment of a new court, were either not especially careful about whom they appointed, or knowingly (and secretly) hired the man they preferred. For traditional figures to administer Soviet laws was a prescription for chaos.[65]

The alternative was hardly more attractive. Trying to fill the institutional vacuum with partly trained and politically reliable people, central Bolshevik authorities all too often pressed Russian communists into local service. This frequently led to complete paralysis. Native officials, eager to disavow responsibility for handling a potentially embarrassing case, all too willingly dropped the case into a Russian's lap. In turn, knowing neither the language nor the mores of the locale, and unable to orient himself in the maze of claims and counterclaims, the Russian official either referred the case upward through the apparatus or simply shelved the matter.[66]

(b) Given the region's enormous size, the inaccessibility of many of its locales, and the nomadic habits of a good part of its population, it was a foregone conclusion that the Soviet legal system would have difficulty in establishing a physical presence here. Moreover, the role of local customary law (*adat*) in Central Asia tended to be, especially in nomadic and semi-nomadic locales, far more pervasive than that of *shariat*, while customary adjudication was relatively independent of formal structures and specialized personnel. This meant that throughout great stretches of the hinterland, adjudicative procedures were far more elusive to bureaucratic

---

1927, p. 110; Sev, *Turkmenovedenie*, 3-4, 1928, pp. 5-20; O. A. Sukhareva, *Islam v Uzbekistane* (Tashkent, 1960), pp. 79-80.

[65] For implicit and explicit indications of the presence of traditional figures in the Soviet political, administrative, and judicial apparatuses in the late 1920's, see Mitrofanov, *RN*, 2, 1930, pp. 35-49, and *RN*, 1, 1930, pp. 29-36. For a discussion of the origins of this problem in the early 1920's, when canonical courts were supplemented with two tiers of people's courts (one for Europeans and one for Moslems), see Suleimanova, *SGP*, 10 (Oct.), 1948, pp. 66-68, and *SGP*, 3 (March), 1949, pp. 63-67.

[66] See, e.g., Michurina, *Ka*, 10-11, 1926, p. 82.

suppression than canonical courts manned by Moslem legal experts.[67] Thus, even a speedy destruction of the formal Islamic judicial structures did not necessarily lead to an immediate breakup of the traditional adjudicative network. The smashing of *kadi* or *kazi* courts in Central Asia, far from marking the end of the battle against the system of customary adjudication, marked only its beginning.[68]

A measure of the problem—and of Soviet awareness in this matter—is that some communist officials proposed, in the late 1920's, forming "mobile," nomadic, court units to service the hinterland, as well as experimental "Reconciliation Commissions" in local soviets (particularly in tribal milieus) that were especially far removed from cities, and hence from the reach of the regular Soviet people's courts.[69] The former were to bring special sessions of the Soviet court from the city to the nomadic range. The latter were obviously intended to adapt the Soviet court structure to local customary forms of adjudication, emphasizing mediation rather than criminal sanctions in selected cases, so as to compete more successfully with traditional institutions, such as customary arbitration courts. Both of these improvisations (apparently implemented piecemeal and on a small scale in some locales, beginning with Kazakhstan, in the late 1920's) constituted imaginative attempts to deal with an elusive and diverse milieu. But they were not an unmixed blessing: they were not readily susceptible to consistent implementation, supervision, and coordination, precisely because they

[67] See Note 64 in this chapter, *supra*. For some suggestive examples of Soviet ambivalence as to exactly what was responsible for the failure of the new legal system to take root quickly in Central Asia, see Kasparova, *Ka*, 7, 1925, pp. 88-89; Liubimova, *Ka*, 11, 1927, pp. 73-74; Digurov, *SS*, 2(19), 1928, pp. 56-60; Balaban, *VS*, 40-41, 1928, pp. 15-17. Cf. Sukhareva, *Islam v Uzbekistane*, pp. 79-80.

[68] This should emphasize the difference between my own judgment and that of Alexander Park, who seems to suggest (in *Bolshevism*, p. 237) that the formal substitution of Moslem courts and laws by the Soviet legal system in Central Asia marked the end of the traditional adjudicative network.

[69] See, e.g., K., *VS*, 46, 1928, pp. 19-20, for a review of Moscow's attempts at that time to "bring Soviet courts closer to the native population" of the Kazakh hinterland (exemplified by the decision by V.Ts.I.K. and S.N.K. R.S.F.S.R. of October 8, 1928, "Ob ustanovlenii osobogo poriadka osushchestvleniia sudebnykh funktsii v aulakh, kishlakakh, i poselkakh Kaz. A.S.S.R." Cf. Shokhor, *SS*, 8-9(13-14), 1927, p. 110; "V Tsentral'nykh . . . ," *SS*, 4(33), 1929, p. 154.

stressed mobility and adaptation to local custom, and because the required material and human resources were simply not available; at the same time, and by their very nature, they contributed to the general dissonance of legal norms and arrangements in Central Asia.

As a result, during the crucial time of the "cultural revolution" in Central Asia (1926-1928), the region comprised a deeply variegated and multi-layered universe of laws, courts, judgments, and judges. In practice such legal patchwork meant inordinate delays, continuous questioning and cancellation of lower court decisions by central authorities in the cities (a tug-of-war in which local officials were disinclined or fearful to make decisions at all), enormous turnover of personnel, and exceedingly limited effectiveness in inducing and managing the revolution through law.[70] The situation was such that a man unable to consummate legally a polygamous marriage in one locale could do so simply by going to another.[71]

Selective Enforcement

Because of the persistence of solidarity and secrecy in local groups, because of the dilemmas confronting an outcast who had violated the mores of the group, and because of the characteristically private and intimate nature of the situations subject to the new legal rules, the very *detection* of "crimes based on custom" turned out to be a delicate and highly complex problem. Moreover, the fact that a native male, even when apprehended, felt no sense of guilt for his transgression made it extremely risky to apply consistently all rules in the face of a community's outrage and hostility.[72]

[70] For some early Soviet perceptions of this situation, see Liubimova, *Ka*, 2, 1927, pp. 50-51; Kryl'tsov, *SP*, 5(29), 1927, pp. 130-38; Fioletov, *SP*, 1(25), 1927, p. 144; Zavarian, *Ka*, 6, 1926, p. 66; Akopov, *RN*, 4-5, 1930, p. 65; Mostovaia, *VS*, 9, 1928, pp. 7-8; Brullova-Shaskol'skaia, *NV*, 16-17, 1927, pp. 300-301; Mukhitdinova, *Ka*, 9, 1929, p. 40. Cf. Sulaimanova, *ISGPU*, Vol. I, pp. 270-71, Vol. II, pp. 216-18, 229-30.

[71] See, e.g., Zakharian, *Ka*, 3, 1926, pp. 44-45; Liubimova, *Ka*, 2, 1927, pp. 50-51.

[72] For some Soviet perceptions of the problems of detection and of the accompanying risks, see Kalachev, *Ka*, 8, 1927, p. 60; Akopov, *RN*, 4-5, 1930, pp. 60-61; Mokrinskii, *SP*, 3(27), 1927, pp. 104-105; Zasukhin, *VS*, 8, 1931, p. 27; Zasukhin, *RN*, 12(46), 1933, p. 39; Balaban, *VS*, 40-41, 1928, pp. 15-17; Shokhor, *SS*, 8-9(13-14), 1927, pp. 109-10; Guber, *RV*, 8, 1930, pp. 276-77; Abramzon, *SE*, 2, 1932, pp. 95-97.

Accordingly, some local officials obtained, in a number of cases, the tacit or explicit agreement of central Bolshevik authorities to be cautiously selective and to refrain from precipitous action. This was true in instances where to enforce existing laws with complete consistency (e.g., in cases of divorce initiated by a woman) meant to accelerate the breakup of households as economic units, undermine the self-sufficiency of local economies, provoke bloody disturbances, as well as condemn a growing number of women to homelessness and indigence.[73] It was also true in circumstances where there might be some doubt as to the nature of a particular "crime based on custom" (e.g., in cases where *kalym* was found to be spent on the wedding itself and on the bride's trousseau).[74] It was especially evident in situations where to indict every person guilty of a particular legal transgression (e.g., in cases of marriages of minors sponsored and bride-price paid by an entire clan) called, in effect, for the arrest and indictment of an entire local community.[75]

It would seem that, in some of the latter instances, central authorities were sometimes inclined to disregard what amounted to collective transgressions by parents and kinsmen, ordering, instead, that an attempt be made to remove a child-bride, if possible, from her "harmful environment" and to deliver her to a Soviet institution for children.[76]

There were still other indications, in the late 1920's, that Moscow's Commissariat of Justice was willing to go a long way in tolerating exceptions to the rule. Thus, some Central Asian offices of civil registry seem to have been quietly encouraged to register native marriages (except in blatantly offensive cases) even if they involved minors and the payment of *kalym*. The intent was, quite obviously, to provide Moslems with some alternatives to traditional auspices and institutions.[77] At the same time, some of the regime's legal specialists urged that polygamous marriages antedating the

---

[73] See, e.g., Zakharian, *Ka*, 3, 1926, pp. 43-44; "V Tsentral'nykh . . . ," *SS*(5), 1926, pp. 158-59; Kryl'tsov, *SP*, 5(29), 1927, p. 138.

[74] See, e.g., Mokrinskii, *SP*, 3(27), 1927, p. 113.

[75] See ibid. For an opposing hard-line view, demanding that *all* those involved in a proscribed arrangement be prosecuted, see Dosov, *Ka*, 5, 1928, p. 30.

[76] See Halle, *Women*, p. 138.

[77] See Dosov, *Ka*, 5, 1928, p. 30; Zakharian, *Ka*, 3, 1926, p. 44; Halle, *Women*, pp. 132 ff.

publication of the 1928 Legal Code be altogether exempted from prosecution.[78]

Limited Retaliation[79]

In considering countermeasures in the face of open and defiant disregard of the new rules and of massive backlash by traditionalist strata, as well as of sabotage and bacchanalian self-indulgence by native officials, the Bolshevik core of the political machine found itself divided from the very beginning.

A number of communist officials (both in Moscow and in Central Asian administrative centers), particularly those active in the law-administering function, counseled moderation and purposive discrimination in applying countermeasures. Specifically, they urged that reprisals be directed only against the surviving traditional elites and those in the highest echelons of the local Soviet apparatus. They urged, also—and were apparently listened to, in some cases—that the sanctions not be applied with unvarying severity, lest they exacerbate what was already an ugly mood in traditionalist ranks and in the ranks of native Soviet cadres.[80]

Their argument was primarily tactical in nature. For example, fragmentary data seemed to indicate that in some Moslem locales more than half of those indicted for polygamy (in 1927 and 1928) were poor or middle peasants. Thus, to press an indiscriminate attack against polygamy meant to be put in a position of applying harshly punitive measures not only against rich peasants and village notables but also against socially and economically disadvantaged rural strata—who, together with women, were assumed to be the regime's potentially most useful allies.[81]

[78] Dosov, *Ka*, 5, 1928, p. 31; Mokrinskii, *SP*, 3(27), 1927, p. 116. Cf. Mukhitdinova, *Ka*, 9, 1929, pp. 39-40.

[79] As in the case of "Selective Enforcement," this section provides only a brief indication of Soviet attitudes and actions that are relevant here. While arguments to this effect were seriously considered in the mid-1920's, they tended to be largely ignored at the height of *khudzhum*-oriented massive repression (see the section that follows). They were officially accepted and developed only when the disastrous implications of massive repression became apparent in 1928-29. Accordingly, they are presented in some detail in the concluding chapters (Nine and Ten) of this study.

[80] See especially Akopov, *RN*, 4-5, 1930, pp. 58, 60; Dosov, *Ka*, 5, 1928, p. 32; Mukhitdinova, *Ka*, 9, 1929, pp. 40-41; Mokrinskii, *SP*, 3(27), 1927, pp. 106-107. Cf. Pal'vanova, *DSV*, pp. 84-85.

[81] See Mukhitdinova, *Ka*, 9, 1929, p. 39.

Massive Repression

Unquestionably the dominant mood in Bolshevik ranks, at least one that was most vociferously expressed at the height of the "cultural revolution" in 1927 and 1928, was that of head-on assault, strict enforcement, draconic repression. Not to apply the law everywhere, consistently, and at once—so the argument went—and not to punish any and all offenders to the utmost limits of the law would not only blunt the edge of the "cultural revolution" and paralyze the mobilization of women, but make a mockery of Soviet norms and institutions, constitute a loss of face, and be a dangerous sign of weakness. Hesitation and retreat would merely embolden the traditionalist enemy, as well as cause victimized women to lose all faith in the regime. A regime that had the power to declare the law could not seem timid or impotent to enforce it.[82]

Dosov, the head of the Department for Nationalities of the All-Union Central Executive Committee (V.Ts.I.K.), seemed to speak for important sectors in the government when he called, in mid-1928, for an acceleration of the tempo of criminal prosecution in cases involving "crimes based on custom."[83] Nikoforov and Amosov, also apparently authoritative figures in the central apparatus,[84] echoed this view some months later, spelling out the dangers of inaction. First and foremost, to tolerate the delays, evasion, and vacillation on the part of the native personnel meant to "create the impression [in Central Asia] that women who unveil are [completely] defenseless, while men who [assault or] kill them can do so with impunity. Such a situation [cannot but immediately] affect the entire process of female emancipation."[85] Moslem women who had broken with tradition and had been victimized in the course of *khudzhum* could not be expected to hold out for long unless they were persuaded, by a decisive crackdown, that "the Soviet regime —and *only* this regime—really protects [their] interests and rights."[86] Moreover, even those native males who were potentially

[82] For explicit or implicit arguments to this effect see Michurina, *Ka*, 10-11, 1926, p. 82; Aitakov, *SS* (35), 1929, p. 63; Dosov, *Ka*, 5, 1928, p. 32; Amosov, *Ka*, 14, 1929, p. 25; Akopov, *RN*, 4-5, 1930, pp. 68-69; Mukhitdinova, *Ka*, 9, 1929, p. 40.

[83] Dosov, *Ka*, 5, 1928, p. 32.

[84] Their specific responsibilities and positon in the hierarchy were not made clear at the time.

[85] Amosov, *Ka*, 14, 1929, p. 25.

[86] Mukhitdinova, *Ka*, 9, 1929, p. 40. Cf. Perimova, *Ka*, 9, 1929, p. 38.

311

well-disposed towards the regime might have second thoughts
about their commitment. As Nikiforov warned:

> It should come to no one as a surprise that even those [of our
> Central Asian] citizens who are sympathetic to the soviets are
> [increasingly cautious and] silent: they see the weakness of our
> struggle against crimes based on custom, and they are [becom-
> ing] fearful lest, by reporting such crimes, they will draw upon
> themselves the wrath of the criminals whom they unmask. . . .
> It is this which accounts for the social passivity [in Central Asia
> in the face of crimes against women] . . . ; it is this [which is
> ultimately responsible for] the absence of broad [public partici-
> pation and] social control to back up [our attempts to] imple-
> ment Soviet legislation in the all-important realm—the struggle
> for the emancipation of women. . . . There are, in this, grave
> dangers. . . .[87]

Accordingly, the two years of all-out assault witnessed a
crescendo of demands for uncompromising pressure. The demands
impinged upon the entire spectrum of issues involved in female
mobilization.

Thus, proponents of accelerated divorce proceedings indicted
as fraud and pretense all arguments about the deleterious effects
of a divorce wave in a Moslem traditional milieu. In this view, beginning with that of Michurina[88] and including unnamed but clearly
authoritative officials cited by Nukhrat, arguments about female-
initiated divorces being responsible for the fragmentation of
households as economic units, and for the disruption of agricultural
production in Central Asia, were merely excuses on the part of
native functionaries. The latter were seen as having but one thing
in mind: the threat posed to their manhood and status by rapid
female emancipation. Accordingly, it was considered imperative
that delays and impediments in divorce proceedings be viewed as
willful evasion and sabotage.[89]

Likewise, hard-line proposals emanating from the central apparatus in mid-1928 (as reported by Dosov) rejected the principle
of selective enforcement. They insisted that, whenever marriages

[87] Nikiforov, *Ka*, 15, 1929, p. 46.

[88] Apparently an emissary of Moscow's Commissariat of Justice in Central Asia in the mid-1920's.

[89] See Michurina, *Ka*, 10-11, 1926, p. 83. Cf. Nukhrat, *RN*, 3(36),
1933, p. 49.

of minors (especially girls) or *kalym*-payments were uncovered, *all* those in any way involved be punished with utmost severity, even if this action called for the prosecution of the groom, two sets of parents, guardians, and kinsmen, as well as a number of inter-mediaries. *All* were to be dealt with as accomplices, and direct ac-cessories to the crime. The Presidium of the All-Union Central Executive Committee was asked to consider, as well, that the same "measures of social defense" be applied in cases where members of an extended family prevented a girl of marital age from marrying the man of her choice. These demands also proposed to "take into consideration the psychology of the backward nationalities" in meting out punishment: since traditionalist males seemed unim-pressed by Soviet legislation, and were apparently not cowed by imprisonment, it was important to accompany all jail sentences with heavy fines, preferably involving the defendants' personal property.[90]

The same uncompromising attitude became increasingly appar-ent towards the end of 1928 in pressures for official "intervention" even when a girl or woman failed or refused to report a crime wherein she was herself the victim. For example, it had been argued that a woman's silence (such as in cases of polygamy, un-derage marriage, abduction, and rape) was understandable and might best be temporarily respected; such a woman might be too "backward," or too deeply compromised in the eyes of her com-munity (and aware of the lack of viable alternatives), or too afraid to subject her entire kinship network to criminal prosecution, or too fearful for her own life to lodge a complaint with Soviet au-thorities. Such arguments were now summarily rejected. Demands aired by officials of the central apparatus (such as Dosov and Niki-forov) implied that whatever might be a woman's motives in such cases, they were to be ignored. Criminal charges were to be pressed automatically, in spite of a woman's wishes if necessary. This im-plied a proposition of seminal importance: *anyone* could initiate criminal proceedings, not just the victim. It was both the right and the duty of rank-and-file citizens as well as prosecutors, Zhenotdel agencies, and voluntary associations to unearth and bring to court "crimes based on custom." Accordingly, village soviets, rural teachers, local Zhenotdel units, trade unions, and Komsomol or-ganizations were asked, in effect, to staff a new network of inform-

90 See, e.g., Dosov, *Ka*, 5, 1928, p. 30, and *VS*, 16-17, 1928, pp. 31-32. Cf. Sulaimanova, *ISGPU*, Vol. II, p. 330.

ers at the grassroots. They were made responsible for making up lists of those suspected of traditional offenses, and for periodic delivery of these lists to organs of criminal investigation for immediate action. At the same time, cassational courts (located in the region's major cities) and ranking prosecutors were given the right to take over at any time from lower people's courts any case they deemed to be "of particularly great complexity and of particular significance to society and to the state." Such pressures to "intervene" at all levels of society were accompanied by increasingly open demands for mass indictments and show-trials.[91]

Funerals of female activists killed in the course of *khudzhum*— "martyrs fallen on the front of women's liberation"—were surrounded with elaborate public rituals. These included martial processions and oath-taking ceremonies wherein other women swore in graveside orations to take the place of their fallen comrades, to avenge their death, to denounce fearlessly all enemies of the Soviet regime, and to serve the Communist Party in every way.[92] Every medium was used to circulate what were purported to be the "last words" of faith and defiance uttered by female revolutionaries before their execution by traditionalist lynch-mobs.[93] At the same time, widely publicized governmental decisions made it clear that the state would allot pensions to the families of murdered female activists, and would undertake the upbringing and education of their orphaned children in special institutions.[94] In order to protect unveiled women from attacks in the streets, Central Asian (especially Uzbek) Komsomol organizations were ordered to supply teams of male bodyguards. They were to accompany their charges (beginning with native actresses) wherever they went.[95]

[91] See Dosov, *Ka*, 5, 1928, pp. 31-32; and Nikiforov, *Ka*, 15, 1929, p. 45. Cf. Mukhitdinova, *Ka*, 9, 1929, p. 41, and Sulaimanova, *ISGPU*, Vol. II, p. 195.

[92] The funeral of Anna Dzhamal (one of the first female communists in Central Asia) in 1925 apparently served as the prototype of such arrangements in 1927-29. See, e.g., Nukhrat, *OZV*, p. 90; Pal'vanova, *DSV*, p. 84; Sulaimanova, *ISGPU*, Vol. II, pp. 328-29.

[93] See Bil'shai, *RZVS*, p. 195.

[94] Polianskaia, *RN*, 3, 1930, pp. 93-94; Pal'vanova, *DSV*, pp. 79, 84.

[95] Nukhrat, *Ka*, 1, 1929, pp. 24-25, and *RN*, 3, 1933, p. 48; Pal'vanova, *DSV*, p. 103. Nukhrat had argued (*Ka*, 1, 1929, ibid.) that it was impossible to rely on police alone for protection; all members of local Soviet organizations—political and professional—had a responsibility in this matter. This argument, calling also on Russian male and female workers

314

The period between 1927 and 1929 also witnessed a crescendo of progressively sterner sanctions for molesting and killing unveiled and politically active women. In the process, the very meaning of such acts was drastically redefined. On March 7, 1927 (the first day of the decreed mass-phase of *khudzhum*), the Central Executive Committee of Uzbek Soviets, obviously prodded by the Sredazburo (the Central Asian Bureau of the Central Committee of the All-Union Communist Party), issued the first comprehensive warning concerning interference with the unveiling campaign. Complaints about insult, molestation, or coercion lodged by women in the course of unveiling were to be handled by investigators, prosecutors, and courts immediately and as a matter of highest priority —ahead of any other criminal cases that might be on the calendar. The appropriate judicial organs were to adhere in all such cases to two fundamental guidelines: native women (preferably the victims themselves) were to serve as Public Accusers in court, side by side with official prosecutors; as a rule, all public proceedings were to be structured as show-trials.[96]

On April 27 of the same year, the Sredazburo itself, clearly alarmed by the swiftly rising level of violence in response to *khudzhum*, ordered all local party organizations to devise emergency measures for the protection of unveiled women, and to ensure that "the most severe measures of revolutionary legality" would be applied to the enemies of *khudzhum*.[97]

By December, 1928, the escalation of officially sanctioned repression reached a qualitatively different stage. In a special appeal to Central Asian communists, Komsomolites, workers, and peasants, calling on all to help the party meet the deepening crisis, the Sredazburo referred to militant opponents of *khudzhum* not as "backward," confused, tradition-bound natives responding blindly to a cultural threat, but as "class enemies" pure and simple.[98] Simultaneously, Yaroslavsky (Stalin's henchman and leading troubleshooter in the struggle against manifestations of traditional culture, as well as against political deviants and Stalin's competitors inside the party) carried the redefinition of "crimes based on custom" one step farther. In an address to the Fourth All-Union Con-

---

to participate in guarding unveiled women, left the impression that the party hesitated to involve non-natives directly in this struggle.

[96] Sulaimanova, *ISGPU*, Vol. II, p. 195. Cf. Bal'shai, *RZVS*, p. 194.

[97] Pal'vanova, *DSV*, pp. 102-103.

[98] *PV*, 12.21.1928, as quoted in Bil'shai, *RZVS*, pp. 194-95.

ference of Party Workers among Eastern Women in Moscow, he painted a grim picture of the situation in Central Asia. In losing hundreds of female activists on the battlefronts of *khudzhum*, he said, the party was losing its precious revolutionary cadres, its "most advanced detachments" in the attack against tradition. Under the circumstances, it was no longer acceptable for Soviet legislation to "view [such violent acts] as ordinary crimes based on social custom. . . . It is necessary to say it loud and clear that these crimes constitute counterrevolutionary acts, and must be dealt with accordingly."[99]

What Yaroslavsky meant by this redefinition became clear on April 23, 1929. At that time, the Uzbek and Turkmen Central Executive Committees, following the lead of the All-Union Ts.I.K., introduced significant changes in the criminal codes of their republics. First, it became a criminal offense to hinder in any way women's attendance of schools, clubs, and other cultural institutions, and their participation in social enterprises, politics, and public service. Second, the penalty for "any and all infringement on a woman's person or dignity in connection with her emancipation" was raised from three years in jail to five years "in strict isolation," i.e., in all likelihood in a concentration camp. Third, and most important, all attempts on the life of female activists were classified as terrorist and counterrevolutionary acts, punishable by death.[100] On February 16, 1930, the Presidium of the All-Union Central Executive Committee in effect abolished the distinction between activist and non-activist women implicit in the preceding formulation. Attempts on *any* woman's life, if in any way connected with her emancipation, were now classified as crimes against the state, i.e., distinctly political, counterrevolutionary crimes, carrying the obligatory sentence of death by shooting.[101]

As both Khodzhaev and Aitakov (two of the highest-ranking native communist leaders in Uzbekistan and Turkmenistan, respectively) found it necessary to acknowledge at the time, the new watchwords had to be: "punitive politics"; "ironhanded implementation"; "intensified repression."[102]

[99] Yaroslavsky, *Ka*, 1, 1929, pp. 28-29.
[100] See Sulaimanova, *ISGPU*, Vol. ii, pp. 331-32.
[101] See Akopov, *RN*, 4-5, 1930, p. 65; and Sulaimanova, *ISGPU*, Vol. ii, pp. 441-42.
[102] See Khodzhaev, *SS* (35), 1929, p. 59, and Aitakov, *SS* (35), 1929, p. 63, reporting on the proceedings of the Third Congress of Uzbek and Turkmen Soviets, respectively.

The crackdown became widespread in 1928-1929. While the action took place mainly in urbanized locales (i.e., in places within relatively easy reach of central authorities), and while it tended to occur spasmodically rather than at a steady pace, it had all the earmarks of an attempt to break through everywhere and at once. Mass trials of traditionalist offenders followed each other in rapid succession. Some of the reported trials concerned the murder not only of women but also of native male communists active in *khudzhum*. In all cases, the show-trials were accompanied by attempts to bring in as many people as possible from the surrounding countryside to witness and be involved in the proceedings. Multiple, well-publicized death verdicts became the order of the day, and pressure was apparently exerted on local communities to discuss these verdicts in special meetings and to manifest approval by mass acclamation.[103]

The ferocity of repression became increasingly apparent in cases involving traditional elites as well as native communist officials. By 1929, accusations against surviving *mullahs* and village elders for their alleged conspiratorial role in the traditionalist backlash were not only accompanied by death sentences; they were coupled with demands for the closure of mosques and for public repudiation of traditional leadership and practices. A revealing case of local attempts to respond to such pressures was reported by Mitrofanov, one of the party's most meticulous analysts of revolutionary politics in Central Asia. Both the context and tone of the report suggest that this case was by no means an isolated one. In a village of the region of Bukhara the secretary of the party cell circulated among the inhabitants two lists for personal signature: one for closing the local mosque, the other against it. The collection of signatures was accompanied by threats to the effect that all those against closure would be deported. Faced with such a threat, all, including the former village elder (*aksakal*), declared themselves for closure. Probably in order to prove his good faith—and to impress the community with the extent of the party's victory—the *aksakal* was promptly forced to climb to the top of the mosque's minaret (whence the *muezzin* usually calls the faithful to prayer) and was obliged to urinate from there while prayers were in progress.[104]

[103] See, e.g., Nikolaeva, *Ka*, 8, 1927, pp. 53-54; Nukhrat, *RN*, 3(36), 1933, p. 58; Polianskaia, *RN*, 3, 1930, pp. 93-94; *PV*, 2.10.1930, p. 3; Yakubovskaia, *IZ*, 48, 1954, p. 189; Pal'vanova, *DSV*, pp. 102-103; Sulaimanova, *ISGPU*, Vol. II, pp. 328-29.

[104] Mitrofanov, *RN*, 2, 1930, p. 37.

While the assault on surviving traditional elites had gathered momentum ever since the proclamation of *khudzhum* in the spring of 1927, the humiliation and repression of native Soviet personnel took on the most virulent forms in 1928-1929, when the first major purge of Central Asian communists was formally inaugurated. The fact that it was Yaroslavsky, the party's chief "theoretician" of the purge,[105] who had been most forceful and specific in promising such reprisals in December, 1928,[106] makes it likely that the reckoning in Central Asia owed much of its impetus to him. While the purge of party ranks at that time ultimately affected the Soviet Union as a whole, its process in Central Asia proved to be intimately correlated with the most intense (and last) phase of *khudzhum*.

The linkage between the projected purge and the "administrative assault" in Central Asia was made explicit as early as February, 1928. At that time, the Sredazburo ordered a checkup of native communist cadres, focused on the extent to which they were themselves carrying out, in official capacities and in their own households, the party's directives concerning female emancipation. In order to insure "full objectivity" in this matter, the specially-formed communist investigative commissions were obliged to scrutinize party cells other than their own.[107] Shortly thereafter (in mid-1928), as the resistance and elusiveness of local party units to such a review became more clearly evident, new orders showed a shift in emphasis. The instructions were to " . . . turn [the investigation decreed in February] into a full-fledged check-up of [all] members of [Central Asian] party units," for the purpose of determining each man's real ideological commitments and actual conduct in executing the party's tasks.[108] Thus, the inauguration of the purge on an All-Union basis (at the Sixteenth Party Conference, in late April, 1929) merely formalized a process that had already been underway in Central Asia for many months. Moreover, in the Moslem borderlands a crucial criterion for judging a communist's record was already established: his performance in the course of *khudzhum*.[109]

[105] See Z. Brzezinski, *The Permanent Purge* (Cambridge, Mass., 1956), p. 38.

[106] At the Fourth All-Union Conference of Party Workers among Eastern Women in Moscow. See Yaroslavsky, *Ka*, 1, 1929, pp. 28-31.

[107] See Pal'vanova, *DSV*, pp. 98-99.

[108] Amosov, *Ka*, 14, 1929, pp. 29-30.

[109] See Ar-na, *Ka*, 1, 1928, pp. 57-63; Nukhrat, *Ka*, 6, 1928, pp. 77-80; Yaroslavsky, *Ka*, 1, 1929, pp. 28-31; Amosov, ibid.

In turning the thrust of political repression against its native personnel in Central Asia, the Soviet regime applied a line of argument that paralleled its rationalizations in another realm, the realm of criminal responsibility in hampering female emancipation. Artiukhina (the head of the central Zhenotdel, a candidate member of the party's Secretariat, and a member, together with Yaroslavsky, of the Central Control Commission) set the stage for this argument in early 1928. As she put it, the process of *khudzhum,* in addition to accelerating female emancipation, was to make possible the "sifting, screening, [and elimination]" of male communists who were politically unreliable, who "showed no inclination to break their ties with *mullahs* and *ishans,*" and who "turned out to be under the influence of an ideology alien to the party."[110] In mid-1929, the new party line brought this reasoning to its logical conclusion. It was enunciated most clearly by Perimova, a leading official of the Turkmen Zhenotdel and a hard-line proponent of repression. Her argument was simple. The "offensive" of local traditional elites against the Soviet system was most pronounced in the realm of female emancipation. What was the enemy's ultimate objective in rallying the masses against women's rights? "Restoration of [feudal-patriarchal and] capitalist relationships." It followed that resistance to emancipation was *prima facie* an act of "counterrevolution." Since it was obvious that the enemy was pinning his hopes on this issue as a means of perpetuating tradition and overthrowing the Soviet regime, all native communists who urged a "conciliatory" approach in this matter—who, by commission or omission, impeded the mobilization of women—were, in effect, allies of traditionalist forces, right-wing deviationists, and accomplices of counterrevolution.[111]

The inescapable conclusion was that even those native communists who were merely passive or negligent in implementing the tasks of revolutionary legalism and administrative assault could not be merely expelled from the party in the course of the purge. At the very least, they were subject to prosecution for grave malfeasance in office and a criminal breach of trust.[112] On the other hand, the purge of those who were in any way actively engaged in opposing female mobilization was to be accompanied by their indictment for

[110] Ar-na, *Ka,* 1, 1928, pp. 62-63. Cf. Yaroslavsky, *Ka,* 1, 1929, pp. 30-31.
[111] Perimova, *Ka,* 9, 1929, pp. 37-38.
[112] See Akopov, *RN,* 4-5, 1930, pp. 68-69.

sabotaging the party line and collaborating with enemies of the revolution.[113]

This approach indeed became the norm, and was applied with growing severity, between early 1928 and late 1929. In the process, an apparently large (though never clearly specified) number of responsible native functionaries, at all levels of command, in and out of the judicial apparatus, were arrested, publicly disgraced in spectacular show-trials, and sentenced to prison, deportation, or death.[114] There are grounds to assume that, in some cases, alleged anti-*khudzhum* activity (or private violation of the Soviet code concerning women) was used as a pretext for eliminating politically undesirable personnel or for settling accounts in personal and factional battles. Available figures suggest that, in 1929, party organizations in predominantly native and rural Central Asian milieus were among the most heavily purged units in the U.S.S.R. (with membership losses approaching twenty-five percent, as against about ten percent for the Union as a whole). They also suggest that nearly one-quarter of those purged were found guilty of "crimes based on custom," of counteracting the *khudzhum* offensive, and of sabotaging female unveiling and emancipation, while another quarter consisted entirely of "hostile elements," i.e., members of socially alien classes (including traditional elites) as well as political deviationists and nationalists.[115]

Significantly, the ferocity of the impetus implicit in repression tended to spill over into the realm of female mobilization itself, and it manifested itself there in highly unusual forms. Demands were voiced in party and governmental organs in Turkmenistan and Uzbekistan, clearly inspired by Moscow's emissaries, to outlaw by decree not only the veil but all other kinds of traditional native dress as well, and the first scattered attempts were made in 1928-1929 to exclude veiled women altogether from schools, literacy

[113] Implicit in Perimova (Note 111) and Akopov (Note 112) as well as in Nikiforov, *Ka*, 15, 1929, pp. 45-46; Amosov, *Ka*, 14, 1929, pp. 29-30; Yaroslavsky, *Ka*, 1, 1929, pp. 30-31.

[114] See Nikolaeva, *Ka*, 8, 1927, pp. 52-53; Niurina, *Ka*, 5-6, 1929, p. 24; Aitakov, *SS* (35), 1929, p. 63; Nukhrat, *Ka*, 6, 1928, p. 79.

[115] These estimates are based on fragmentary data, much of it from Uzbekistan, in Mitrofanov, *RN*, 2, 1930, pp. 37, 46-47, and Manzhara, *PV*, 1.24.1930, p. 2. For a broad review of these and related offenses in Central Asian party units, see also Mitrofanov, *RN*, 1, 1930, pp. 29-36; *PV*, 1.30.-1930, p. 4; *PV*, 2.7.1930, p. 2; *PV*, 2.11.1930, p. 3; *PV*, 9:25.1931, p. 3. For a follow-up report several years later, see Dimanshtein, *RN*, 12 (58), 1934, pp. 21-35.

circles, theaters, and even women's clubs.[116] At the same time, with official demands for such proscriptive laws multiplying, yet with the laws themselves still not on the books, communist teams dispatched to organize massive female demonstrations and public burnings of the veil did more than that. Where women seemed disinclined to cooperate—out of disinterest, shame, or fear—forced-draft tactics were used. In some cases, party officials attempted to fine all women who failed to show up at the mass unveiling meetings, and to fire from jobs and expel from trade unions local professionals (such as teachers) who failed to cooperate in conducting the operation. Rather more frequently, strict orders were issued setting a day-and-hour deadline for particular locales to complete the process of unveiling. When the deadline was not met, entire villages and native city-quarters were rounded up, and women were unveiled at gunpoint by communists, Komsomolites, and policemen.[117]

It goes without saying that, in such an atmosphere, the distinctions between legal and administrative action became increasingly blurred. The most radical dispositions immanent in legalism and direct assault tended to coalesce, with a preponderant emphasis placed on extirpating deviant attitudes and behavior everywhere and at once. Considerations of punitive politics drowned out and superseded all concerns about maintaining a balance between the imperatives of inducing revolutionary tensions and of controlling the negative consequences of these tensions.

---

[116] On this account, Central Asian communists were apparently urged to follow the example set by some officials in Azerbaidzhan, a Soviet republic in the Caucasus inhabited mainly by Moslems, and neighboring Central Asia across the Caspian Sea. See Nukhrat, *Ka*, 6, 1928, p. 78, *Ka*, 9, 1929, p. 32, and *RN*, 3, 1933, p. 46; Rigin, *Ka*, 5-6, 1929, p. 59. Cf. Pal'vanova, *DSV*, pp. 101-102.

[117] See especially Anisimova, *Ka*, 8, 1927, p. 56; *Bezb* (news.), 6, 1928, p. 4; Mitrofanov, *RN*, 2, 1930, p. 38; *Bezb* (ill.), 22, 1930, pp. 3-4; Nukhrat, *Ka*, 6, 1928, p. 78 and *RN*, 3, 1933, pp. 46-47. Cf. Pal'vanova, *DSV*, pp. 101-102.

It is not clear to what extent these moves were specifically prescribed and personally spearheaded by non-native functionaries and Moscow's *apparatchiks*. Nor is it clear which of these initiatives were devised as emergency measures by jittery native officials in response to Moscow's growing pressures for tangible results. But one thing is certain: the tone and content of party and governmental resolutions emanating from (or inspired by) Moscow carried the unmistakable expectation that in female unveiling, as in the production of economic goods, there could be only one criterion of compliance and achievement: the implementation of decreed actions immediately and *in toto*.

321

NINE · *Reassessment and Retrenchment:* *From Legalism and Assault* *to Systematic Social Engineering*

REASSESSMENT: IMPLICATIONS OF MASSIVE ENFORCEMENT AND REPRESSION

EVEN as repression proceeded, doubts in communist ranks, including the highest echelons, multiplied. As reports from the field poured in, a number of specific problems came to be perceived with varying degrees of clarity, and their ramifications were given due weight.

1. In a revolutionary and developmental period, indiscriminate and draconic repressions tended to have a decidedly negative effect on the scarcest political commodity at the regime's disposal: native cadres. (a) The greater were the pressures to enforce the new contra-traditional code among the native Soviet cadres, the greater was the tendency among them toward local mutual-protection associations, often in alliance with surviving local traditional elites. Moreover, the harsher were the regime's reprisals against the cadres' circumlocution and deviance, and their sabotage of the "cultural revolution" and female emancipation, the more likely was antagonism and the disposition toward evasion and sabotage to spill over into other realms of official performance, and otherwise useful and loyal political servants tended thereby to become irretrievably alienated. Mitrofanov and Peters—the former an important party analyst, the latter a high-ranking supervisor of early purges in Central Asia— confirmed this negative effect indirectly, and made clear that it served to complicate immensely the problems of detection, not only of the cadres' but also of the masses' transgressions, as well as to compound the overall weaknesses of fledgling Soviet institutions.[1]

---

[1] See Mitrofanov, *RN*, 2, 1930, p. 43; Peters, *PV*, 5.24.1934, pp. 1-2; *PV*, 1.17.1935, pp. 2-3. While the latter two references are dated in the mid-1930's (having to do primarily with the purge of 1934), they clearly hark back to the findings of the late 1920's, both confirming and elaborating on these manifestations. Cf. section on "Native Personnel Behavior" (esp. "Sabotage") in Chapter Eight, *supra*.

322

(b) The more consistent and widespread were the regime's attempts (especially if successful) to apply the new rules to native cadres, the stronger was the imperative, and the greater the risk, of precipitous and wholesale purges of those cadres (involving both the loss of actual and the repulsion of potential personnel). These risks were obviously justified, from Moscow's point of view, if they involved primarily the detection and elimination of avowed enemies of the regime itself or of Stalin as its emerging leader. It was far less certain that such risks were acceptable if they involved the repression of native personnel primarily for transgressions against women and their newly proffered rights. This ambivalence (and double standard) became especially evident when the party's central organs quietly ordered the "rehabilitation" of Central Asian communists purged merely for amorous pursuit and "takeover" of married women, on the grounds that these communists might have been deliberately framed by "class enemies" to cast aspersion on the party as a whole.[2]

2. Even when cadre compliance in the course of the "cultural revolution" was not specifically at issue, uncompromising emphasis on "storming" exercises in legal and extra-legal realms—exercises geared to attain at one great stroke legal rigor and behavioral purity —tended to have a negative effect on the allocation of revolutionary and developmental energies. (a) The greater was the regime's emphasis on "storming," the greater was its need for those cadres whose ethno-cultural and linguistic background could have the requisite emotional impact in face-to-face relationships with the indigenous population, i.e., precisely for those cadres that were in the shortest supply. Similarly, the greater was the disposition to "storm," the stronger were the requisites of a massive switch of these cadres to "storming campaigns," with disruptive or paralyzing effects in all other realms of Soviet enterprise.[3]

[2] See Mitrofanov, *RN*, 2, 1930, p. 46; cf. *PV*, 1.14.1934, p. 3. Even though this particular report of an order to rehabilitate and reinstate a party member comes to the surface in January, 1934, there are good reasons to believe that the order merely formalized what was coming to be standard practice in the preceding several years, probably since late 1929 (this may be inferred from the evidence developed in this section of the chapter, *infra*).

[3] See Nikolaeva, *Ka*, 8, 1927, p. 52; Nukhrat, *Ka*, 1, 1929, p. 25. Cf. Pal'vanova, *DSV*, pp. 98, 102. The way local authorities tried to solve this problem was, of course, itself suggestive both of their attitudes to the task and of the reasons for the campaign's failure: a full-scale switch

(b) The greater was the regime's emphasis on the enforcement of legal rules, and on public, massive, and dramatic violations of traditional taboos, the greater tended to be its personnel's disposition to *limit* social action to legalistic and taboo-breaking enterprises (to a quest for shortcuts to "telescope" social transformation) and the less the personnel's interest and investment in systematic organizational and developmental work. Moreover, the greater was the regime's emphasis on action by decree, the greater tended to be the likelihood for careerist, incompetent, or disaffected elements in the apparatus to use the issuance of decrees as a *substitute* for serious, calculated management of the developmental process, or as an excuse and screen for harebrained scheming, irresponsibility, sabotage, or neglect—neglect especially of a painstaking, systematic build-up of institutions and arrangements necessary to reinforce advances in the legal sphere. Artiukhina, Amosov, and Nukhrat—all of them intimately involved in Moscow's decreed offensive—were quick to recognize this danger. They voiced their concern in no uncertain terms: undue reliance on decreed assault as a means of revolutionary action tended to encourage in local personnel "cynical," "circumlocutory," "mechanical," "slogan-mongering" behavior; such behavior was accompanied by "[complete] indifference" to changing imperatives and new lessons, by utter disregard of the need "to adapt . . . and coordinate . . . [social action] in accordance with freshly materializing tasks [and opportunities]," by a disposition to "sit on laurels . . . and abandon all [systematic] work . . . to drift."[4] As Yaroslavsky himself found it necessary to stress, with such attitudes on the part of Central Asia's Soviet leadership not even "the very best decrees . . . and resolutions" handed down from above "could move the cause of actual female emancipation [a single inch] forward."[5]

3. In dealing with traditionalist males, massive enforcement and repression geared to the objectives of the "cultural revolution" tended to negate some of the regime's other crucial commitments. (a) The greater was the regime's emphasis on absolute compliance in the realm of female emancipation, the stronger tended to be

---

of cadres was permitted to take place, but only for a day or two at a time. See Ar-na, *Ka*, 1, 1928, p. 62.

[4] See Ar-na, *Ka*, 1, 1928, pp. 58, 61; Amosov, *Ka*, 14, 1929, p. 29; Nukhrat, *RN*, 3, 1933, p. 47.

[5] Yaroslavsky, *Ka*, 1, 1929, p. 28.

the traditionalist males' determination to resist, and disposition to turn to violence, and the less their cooperation and participation in vital Soviet enterprises in all other spheres. As Nukhrat and other party analysts warned: *khudzhum*, as *coerced* acceleration of emancipatory activities from above, could only "bring harm" to the regime's multiple causes; the "[stupid,] heavy-handed bungling" generated in the atmosphere of urgent commands "played straight into the hands of class-enemies," and provided them with a god-sent opportunity "to intensify their terror."[6]

(b) At the same time, the more uncompromising was the re-gime's disposition to contain and repress traditionalist outbreaks, and to extirpate all deviant behavior in one vast surgical operation, the greater tended to be its need to counter mass malaise with mass terror. Yet, as Anisimova observed at the height of *khudzhum*—most probably speaking on behalf of important sectors in the party's Women's Department—there was something very wrong and incongruous about "conducting [a] persuasion [campaign] with a gun."[7] The logical concomitants of generalized violence in Central Asia were civil war (as explicitly acknowledged by Arkhincheev,[8] an authoritative party analyst) and, given Soviet military capabilities, mass extermination of Central Asia's in-digenous population. Commensurately, at a certain point of cost-benefit calculations, the imperatives of extermination were bound to threaten or irretrievably subvert the Communist Party's implicit and explicit commitments to (and expectations of) conversion and assimilation.

4. Paradoxically, even the regime's successes in female mobili-zation entailed decidedly dysfunctional effects both for the women involved and for the regime. *The implications were dysfunctional because the successes were, so to speak, unidimensional.*

(a) The shorter was the time-limit set by Soviet authorities for female mobilization, and the more massive and dramatic were fe-male demonstrations, unveilings, and veil-burnings in public, the more intensive and generalized became male hostility, violence and terror against those women. Yet, while this made the need to pro-tect women from retribution commensurately greater, calling forth urgent official orders for police and Komsomolites to accompany

[6] Nukhrat, *RN*, 3, 1933, p. 47; cf. *Bezb* (news.), 6, 1928, p. 4, and *Bezb* (ill.), 22, 1930, pp. 3-4.

[7] Anisimova, *Ka*, 8, 1927, p. 56.

[8] See Arkhincheev, *SS*, 2 (43), 1930, p. 99.

these women in public,[9] the regime's capacity to provide such protection proved to be utterly unequal to the need. For that matter, it seems safe to say that the greater the need, the smaller was the relative capacity to meet it, and the more problematic and dysfunctional the implications of meeting it.

As was evident throughout the entire course of *khudzhum*, it proved utterly impossible to protect each and every "liberated" woman from insult, intimidation, and lynching: first, because such acts could take place at any time, in any public or private situation (including acts of retribution by fathers or husbands); second, because consistent protection required the commitment and dispersal of enormous contingents of scarce (and not necessarily reliable) cadres to a myriad of possible loci of retribution, including even the women's homes; third, because even if such cadre-assignment had been feasible it threatened not only to denude other crucial enterprises of personnel, but also systematically to expose the tiny nucleus of Soviet political activists (male and female, native and Russian) to traditionalist wrath, ambush, and assassination. While no communist official could explicitly admit this in public, it seems obvious that no payoffs could justify such risks.

(b) The greater was the rate of female-initiated divorces in court, the rate of impulsive unveiling and of spontaneous abandonment by girls and women of households and husbands, and the rate of retaliatory outcasting of women by men from home, the greater tended to be those women's dependence on the regime's support, and the less the regime's relative capacity to extend such support. As it turned out, *no significant tie-in existed between legal action conferring legal rights and extra-legal initiatives permitting the utilization of these rights in real roles and situations.* Similarly, *no real tie-in existed between massive taboo-breaking exercises and initiatives permitting the maintenance of taboo-violators in secure*

[9] See Nukhrat, *Ka*, 1, 1929, pp. 24-25, and *RN*, 3, 1933, p. 48; Pal'vanova, *DSV*, p. 103; Bil'shai, *RZVS*, pp. 194-95. Nukhrat (ibid.) made it clear that even if the police were to be cooperative in this matter, real protection of unveiled women was impossible unless literally all individuals in any way associated with Soviet organizations—including party members, Komsomolites, Pioneers, members of soviets and trade unions, men as well as women, Russians as well as natives—were induced to join in this task (and form "special surveillance brigades" for duty in specifically assigned enterprises, public buildings, and residential blocks). As Nukhrat must have realized when she spoke of this need, it was not even remotely possible to provide such arrangements.

326

and productive spheres of life. No significant buildup of supportive structures and arrangements (in social, economic, cultural, and political spheres) had taken place in the course of Central Asia's "cultural revolution," and certainly no buildup commensurate with the volume and rate of unidimensional female emancipation. Way-stations for converts from tradition, institutions where new identities, relationships, capabilities, and skills would enable women to make a fresh start in life, were largely lacking. Laws and courts, as well as mass demonstrations and confrontations, encouraged in women iconoclastic dispositions, unprecedented expectations, and some (even if crude) forms of mass participation. But hardly any tangible channels had been prepared to reinforce their new attitudes, to usefully harness their involvement, and to fulfill their expectations. Mobilization had not been accompanied by absorption, organization, and genuine participation in a suitable institutional framework.

Towards the end of the 1920's, responsible communist field-organizers, especially those connected with the party's Zhenotdel, appeared to be nearly unanimous in arriving at this conclusion. They were also quite resolute in warning that the greater was the Moslem woman's dependence on new support, and the less the regime's willingness or capacity to extend it, the heavier would be the regime's burden in shouldering the responsibility for masses of destitute women, some with infant children and no place to go but the street.[10]

(c) The greater was the volume and rate of unidimensional female emancipation, and the more dramatic the context of proffered rights, the more sharply was felt the absence of requisite roles and opportunities to assert these rights. Commensurately, the less the likelihood of women's physical protection and moral, organizational, and material support by the regime, the less also was their incentive to join in risky Soviet enterprises in the first place, and the greater the mobilized women's disposition (out of disillusionment, destitution, disorientation, loneliness, fear, or shame) either to turn to prostitution in the cities, or to slide back into the traditional fold, or even to turn militantly against the regime itself.

---

[10] For explicit or implicit examples of such views, see Michurina, *Ka*, 10-11, 1926, pp. 81-82; Nikolaeva, *Ka*, 8, 1927, pp. 53-54; Ar-na, *Ka*, 1, 1928, pp. 58-61; Burlova, *Ka*, 8, 1928, p. 89; Ishkova, *Ka*, 11, 1928, pp. 60-61; Mukhitdinova, *Ka*, 9, 1929, pp. 39, 41; Nukhrat, *VMV*, pp. 16-17; Amosov, *Ka*, 14, 1929, pp. 27, 30; Akopov, *RN*, 4-5, 1930, pp. 67-69.

Perhaps no other elements in the party's reassessment of its offensive were as difficult to bring to light and to confront as these.
For, in doing so, communist activists had to deal with and explain,
as well as propose solutions for, problems that were not only due
to official commission or omission, but that had all the earmarks
of disaster and defeat. Anna Nukhrat was one of the few party organizers who tried to pursue the matter openly, long after others
fell silent under the pressure of a maturing totalitarian system. She
made her case with stark simplicity: Official policies inducing the
breakup of traditional families, yet unaccompanied by significant
supportive arrangements for women, were indirectly responsible for
an unprecedented rise in female unemployment, homelessness, and
destitution in Central Asia. If this responsibility remained unacknowledged, and unless the Soviet government was prepared to
step in with requisite assistance immediately and on a large scale,
a growing number of Moslem women were bound to "go down a
slippery road."[11]

As was apparent from other concurrent warnings and expressions of alarm, by Nukhrat and some of her comrades in the party,
a slippery road could mean not only vice and prostitution but also
militant self-assertion against the regime itself. In the winter of
1928-1929, the first large-scale hunger riots were reported in Central Asia. The participants were mainly destitute Moslem women
demanding bread and work. Nukhrat's reference to these violent
demonstrations as "women's riots"[12] was obviously a pointed reminder of the accumulating resentments, danger signals which the
regime could ignore only at its own peril.

Another source of strain materialized in the context of Delegatskiie Sobraniia, the newly instituted Assemblies of Women's
Delegates. Here, some of the women elected to what were declared
to be authoritative posts perceived with growing bitterness the disparity between the ceremonial and substantive aspects of their political participation and roles, and apparently registered their disappointment in no uncertain terms.[13]

Even more ominously, women's hostile assertiveness against
Soviet authority became evident within the Communist Party itself.
In late 1928 and early 1929, what appeared to be growing num-

[11] Nukhrat, *VMV*, pp. 16-17.

[12] Nukhrat, *Ka*, 17-18, 1929, p. 17.

[13] See Sevast'ianova, *Ka*, 1, 1928, pp. 63-64; cf. Nukhrat, *Ka*, 17-18,
1929, p. 18.

bers of native female party members openly asserted their right to quit the party altogether. They insisted that, after their unveiling at the height of *khudzhum*, they had been forcibly inducted into party ranks and obliged, against their will, to accept membership cards. Now they refused to obey party orders, turned down all political assignments, and insisted on their right to consider themselves "non-party persons."[14]

Moreover, in some cases, even high-ranking female communists, with a record of active service in revolutionary causes, seemed inclined to challenge the party's right to run their life. The case of Kinzhebaeva is especially revealing in this connection, and the manner and context in which it was reported suggest that it was not an isolated phenomenon. Kinzhebaeva's credentials were, for a Central Asian woman in the late 1920's, quite impressive: she was a party member of relatively long standing, a leading participant in the struggle for female emancipation, and the head of the party's Zhenotdel in Andizhan, one of Central Asia's largest cities, and an administrative and commercial center of the region's crucially important cotton belt. Sometime in early 1929, she was ordered to appear before one of the party's roving control commissions for a prepurge membership checkup and exchange of membership cards. She arrived veiled. When challenged about this, she responded in terms considered incredible from the party's point of view: "I feel like it; it's none of your business." She also disclaimed, in front of the assembled membership, all further involvement in agitational work among women.[15]

Even if the regime was tempted to dismiss such acts of individual defiance as relatively isolated and inconsequential, it could not very well ignore what appeared to be a far more widespread, indeed snowballing, phenomenon: Moslem women already mobilized into the Soviet fold showed a growing inclination to withdraw into traditional grooves, while those who had not yet committed themselves were becoming doubly cautious about affiliation in Soviet enterprises.[16] This was expressed most dramatically in what seemed like a sudden and massive shift in female orientations towards traditional solidarities and the veil itself. The worst fears of a number of party organizers appeared to be borne out, as former female con-

---

[14] See Mitrofanov, *RN*, 2, 1930, p. 38.

[15] Needless to say, she was immediately purged. See Mitrofanov, *RN*, 2, 1930, p. 38.

[16] See Nukhrat, *RN*, 3, 1933, p. 47.

verts from tradition showed signs of renewed acceptance of religious, communal, and patriarchal authority,[17] as girls and women proceeded to withdraw *en masse* from Soviet associations and activities to their secluded but apparently safer and more predictable existence at home,[18] and as the bulk of unveiled women—previously counted, it would appear, in the hundreds of thousands—turned out to have donned the veil again within hours, days, or weeks of having discarded it.[19]

What was especially alarming, the investigation ordered in the summer of 1927 by the party's Orgburo (Organizational Bureau of the Central Committee) revealed that the situation was just as bad in easily accessible and well-controlled districts as in remote and insular ones. For example, in Margelan, a sizable town and important trading center of the Ferghana Valley and cotton belt, three thousand women had reportedly unveiled themselves in the spring of 1927; by mid-summer, only four hundred remained unveiled. In Pskent, a large village only fifty miles from Tashkent, with a regular bus-connection to that city, with an established Soviet club and Zhenotdel, and, most important, with a party *raikom* (district committee) *in situ*, of one and a half thousand women unveiled in the spring, all but thirty were found to be veiled again in mid-summer.[20]

In seeking to explain this extraordinary turnabout, and to utilize the explanations for the purpose of modifying official policy, Soviet analysts showed considerable intellectual sensitivity as well as a

[17] See Nukhrat, *RN*, 3, 1933, p. 48, and *VMV*, pp. 7-17 (*passim*); Ar-na, *Ka*, 1, 1928, p. 62.

[18] For strong hints to this effect, see Niurina, *Parandzha*, pp. 10-14 (*passim*); Nukhrat, *RN*, 3, 1933, p. 48. Cf. the section, "Patterns of Popular Response: Males" (esp. "Massive Backlash") in Chapter Seven, *passim*, and the section, "Native Personnel Behavior" (esp. "Sabotage") in Chapter Eight, *passim*.

[19] See Niurina, *Parandzha*, p. 14; Ar-na, *Ka*, 1, 1928, p. 57; Mitrofanov, *RN*, 2, 1930, p. 38; Nukhrat, *RN*, 3, 1933, p. 48. Cf. Pal'vanova, *DSV*, pp. 100-101. The most reliable of these sources agree on a gross figure of ninety thousand for those who had first unveiled and then (for the most part) veiled themselves again. However, this figure apparently refers only to those who discarded the veil in the spring and early summer of 1927, i.e., at the outset of *khudzhum*. Subsequent references to continuing acts of mass-unveiling leave a strong impression that, by official count, several hundreds of thousands of women were considered to have unveiled themselves and to have donned the veil again at one or another point in the course of *khudzhum*.

[20] See Ar-na, *Ka*, 1, 1928, p. 57.

willingness to come to grips with unvarnished—hence politically unpalatable—realities. As we have seen, Nukhrat, Niurina, and Artiukhina, to mention but three of the most committed and authoritative proponents of official reassessment, dwelt at length, and necessarily, on the failure of material and organizational under-pinnings (as manifested, for example, in destitution and lack of adequate physical protection for emancipated women) as the root causes of the debacle. But they did not hesitate to probe as well for other, and perhaps more subtle, inferences and meanings. While never explicitly suggesting this in public, they repeatedly alluded to what seemed to them a crucial dimension of female response that the regime had failed to take into consideration: the psycho-cultural dimension. As they saw it, this was not merely a matter of women's fear in the face of their kinsmen's hostility and violence, although it was agreed that fear indeed played a very important role in this context.[21] Moslem girls and women who had broken some of their communities' most sacred taboos had immediately jeopardized their affiliation in traditional solidarities. Because they could not easily find under Soviet auspices an equivalent realm of affiliation, recognition, and support, they felt not only threatened and defenseless but also bewildered and lost.

To begin with, as reported by Nukhrat, unveiled women felt virtually naked in public:

> An Uzbek woman [, for example,] who for the first time in her life, [or at least] since childhood, ventures [outside her home] with an open face, feels as a European woman would feel if she found herself totally nude in the middle of a crowded [street]. She feels insulted and abused by every astonished stare, she walks with her head hung low, . . . at once excited, terrified, and ashamed, and anxiety never ceases to gnaw at her: what awaits her at home? how will her family react to the news, to "this disgrace"?[22]

As it turned out, what faced a Moslem woman under these circumstances was not only a pervasive sense of shame, due as much to her uncovered face and untrammelled body as to her community's

[21] See, e.g., Nukhrat, *RN*, 3, 1933, p. 47, and *OZV*, p. 85.

[22] Nukhrat, *OZV*, p. 85. Cf. Pal'vanova, *DSV*, pp. 100-101; Halle, *Women*, p. 173. When Nukhrat wrote these lines (in 1927) she was herself grati-fied and excited by the first wave of unveiling in Uzbekistan at the outset of *khudzhum*. There are reasons to suppose that, under the impact of events in the months that followed, she changed her mind and urged greater cau-tion precisely on the grounds made clear in this quotation.

immediate conclusion that she was a seducer and a harlot. Once released from the emotional mesh of great, taboo-breaking crowds at the outset of *khudzhum*, once out of and away from the perimeter of Soviet force guarding the unprecedented proceedings, the unveiled woman was on her own in more than one sense. In facing the specter of her community's outrage and, at the same time, of physical and emotional separation from accustomed unities and groups—clans, families, and friends—she faced the specter of loneliness.[23]

Moreover, to the extent that she failed to find in the Soviet fold the supportive atmosphere, protective arrangements, equal rights, and genuinely respected and authoritative roles promised by the regime, she had to suffer the consequences of disorientation as well as disillusionment.[24] For in addition to being treated as an outcast by her own people, she was held in contempt by many native male communists. As one female party member in a rural district explained in her testimony before an investigative commission:

> Everybody acts as though he is busily engaged in agitating for female emancipation. [Everybody is shouting,] down with the veil! But go ahead and try to unveil: immediately everyone, including village communists, regards you as a fallen woman. This is exactly what happened to me: at one time I discarded the veil, and everyone persecuted me for this. The communists not only failed to defend me; quite the contrary, they let it be known that I was a prostitute. That's why I donned the veil again, and now people treat me with greater respect.[25]

In such an atmosphere, a Moslem woman was, of course, all the more susceptible to expressions of solicitude and offers of help on

[23] See Niurina, *Parandzha*, pp. 10-13 (*passim*). Cf. Pal'vanova, *DSV*, pp. 100-101.

[24] Needless to say, no Soviet official could openly raise the issue of disillusionment *per se*. It would have impinged too obviously on the legitimacy of the regime itself. However, Soviet accounts and interpretations leave little doubt that this was indeed the case. See, e.g., Mitrofanov, *RN*, 2, 1930, p. 38 (including the pointed reference to the case of Kenzhibaeva, and to mass resignations from the party, cited earlier in this section). See also Sevast'ianova, *Ka*, 1, 1928, pp. 63-64, and Nukhrat, *Ka*, 17-18, 1929, p. 18 (alluding to disillusionment among women elected to nominally authoritative posts in Soviet-sponsored associations). Cf. Nukhrat, *Ka*, 6, 1928, p. 78; Amosov, *Ka*, 14, 1929, p. 25; and Nikiforov, *Ka*, 15, 1929, p. 46 (including references to growing disillusionment and caution due to the regime's inability to support and protect the very people it claimed to be liberating).

[25] Mitrofanov, *RN*, 2, 1930, pp. 37-38.

332

the part of traditional figures, at the price of her rejoining the ancestral order.[26]

This meant that, as Niurina suggestively put it, the regime's policies had "[aroused in Moslem women] a mass nervous energy," but, in effect, failed to provide them with "efficacious [means] for the discharge of the accumulating energy." It was one thing to induce an emotional explosion in the "holiday" atmosphere of mass-unveiling; it was a very different thing to know how to "consolidate" these gains. The creation of the requisite means for this purpose turned out to be a painfully slow process, "[far] slower than [the situation] demands." Without such means, women were unable to make a clean break with the past; they could not possibly make the leap from "yesterday's bondage to today's freedom," and were indeed condemned to slide back into the traditional fold. It was necessary to face this simple truth: "The holiday is over. It is Monday morning."[27]

As Nukhrat pointed out elsewhere, it was precisely because of the failure to face these realities that the decreed "storm" in female mobilization and "cultural revolution" was followed with astonishing swiftness by an "ebb . . . in Central Asia's mass [revolutionary] movement."[28]

Other proponents of reassessment and retrenchment in Central Asia—including most notably Krupskaia (Lenin's widow), as well as some of the party's legal specialists in the battle with tradition, such as Mokrinskii, Akopov, and Kryl'tsov—were quite specific in questioning the assumptions underlying revolutionary legalism and administrative assault. As they noted in a variety of contexts, it was "naive to think that, merely by issuing [a few] laws, we shall be in a position to change prevailing relationships immediately and totally."[29] For that matter, some customary practices—and certainly veiling—could not be expected to yield to, and thus be subject to, decrees at all.[30] In such a context it made little sense "to

[26] Ar-na, *Ka*, 1, 1928, p. 62. Cf. Shirman, *Ka*, 4, 1927, p. 76; Nikolaeva, *Ka*, 8, 1927, p. 53; Nukhrat, *VMV*, pp. 7-17 (*passim*), *Ka*, 12, 1927, p. 44, and *Ka*, 8, 1927, p. 20; Krupskaia, *Ka*, 12, 1928, p. 6; Rigin, *Ka*, 5-6, 1929, pp. 58-59; Akopov, *RN*, 4-5, 1930, p. 66; Bil'shai, *RZVS*, p. 193; *BSE* Vol. 29, 1935, p. 396.

[27] Niurina used the term *budni*, denoting prosaic weekdays. See her *Parandzha*, pp. 12-14.

[28] Nukhrat, *Ka*, 6, 1928, p. 78.

[29] Kryl'tsov, *SP*, 5 (29), 1927, p. 138.

[30] See, e.g., "Nuzhno li izdat' dekret, zapreshchaiushchii nosheniie chadry," *Ka*, 8, 1928, pp. 79 ff. Cf. Krupskaia, *Ka*, 12, 1928, pp. 11-12.

approach the question of female emancipation as if it were . . . a purely juridical problem."[31] It made even less sense—and was, indeed, dangerous—to maintain (as the proponents of *khudzhum* did) that all that was needed for success was to "pursue the matter with sufficient energy," and with sufficiently "draconic measures of social defense." For "a way of life retreats but slowly and involuntarily before the verdicts of a court of law." "Crimes [based on custom] decline in number not so much because the perpetrators begin to take into account the juridical consequences of their acts, as because they come to be less and less impelled towards such acts by the social group that stands behind them." Thus, the struggle against "crimes based on custom" had to be considered "not so much a struggle against a [particular] crime as against the way of life giving birth to such a crime." Otherwise, "the measures of criminal repression [utilized] by a legislator and a court" were bound to strike out merely at "the symptoms . . . of an unfavorable social situation," at "the particular manifestations" of social inequality, while the "roots," the "conditions themselves," remained untouched.[32]

In this view, then, it was imperative to rein in the compulsion of a Soviet legislator to concentrate on finding the means and fixing rigid sanctions for immediate and total suppression of traditional behavior patterns. His aim had to be, instead, to determine "the [optimum] parameters of [traditionalist] conduct . . . in the conditions of a proletarian dictatorship," i.e., the extent to which customary practices really constituted a clear and present "social danger" to Soviet rule and thus needed to be punished.[33] What needed to be the legislator's watchwords, particularly where the masses as a whole were concerned, was above all else "caution," "circumvention." In the realm of sexual desegregation, only those actions were to be considered which promised to be "as painless as possible."[34]

---

[31] Krupskaia, ibid., p. 7. Note that Krupskaia said this in December, 1928 (at the 4th All-Union Conference of Party Organizers among Eastern Women), i.e., after the decreed abolition of Moslem courts in Central Asia (September, 1927), after the promulgation of a comprehensive new legal code outlawing most traditional practices pertaining to women (April, 1928), and during an increasingly bitter assault upon traditional elites in Central Asia, an assault accompanied by show trials and multiple death sentences.

[32] Mokrinskii, *SP*, 7 (27), 1927, p. 106; Akopov, *RN*, 4-5, 1930, p. 58. Cf. Nukhrat, *RN*, 3 (36), 1933, p. 47; Krupskaia, *Ka*, 12, 1928, pp. 8-12.

[33] See Akopov, *RN*, 4-5, 1930, p. 60.

[34] Nukhrat, *RN*, 3(36), 1933, p. 47. Cf. Pal'vanova, *DSV*, pp. 41, 87.

Hence, merely to "promulgate laws" was irrelevant; "legal equality [is meaningless without opportunities for] actual equality in life." What needed to be stressed were measures affecting tangibly and directly the stability and cohesiveness of traditional societies, i.e., not so much laws as new economic, educational, social-service, associational, and organizational forms and opportunities for women as well as men: "Only profound social and political shifts [attained by way of such a painstaking approach], and prophylactic measures undertaken on the basis of [these shifts], are capable of influencing the social roots from which crimes [based on custom] draw their sustenance." Precisely because "the confidence of a given social group in its laws and rightness [comes to] waver only gradually"—because "the strength of historical inertia, and of the spirit of conservatism that characterizes [traditionalist] masses, [is so great]"—"quick and decisive successes" were not to be expected. It would take a "very long time [for the] conditions underlying customary crimes to atrophy." What lay in store, therefore, for those bent upon the fundamental transformation of the Soviet East was "sustained," "protracted," subtly attuned, multifaceted labor. Without such labor in preparation of the ground Soviet laws were likely either "to remain on paper" or to bring on repeated explosions of "[popular] fanaticism"—of passionate and violent expressions of hostility predicated on religion and custom— at the grassroots of a traditional milieu.[35]

RETRENCHMENT: TOWARD SYSTEMATIC SOCIAL ENGINEERING

Faced with the full panoply of implications of massive enforcement and repression, the Soviet regime had the following options: to continue inducing revolutionary tensions as before, to contain them by selective rather than indiscriminate enforcement, to deflect them by retaliating primarily against selected targets, to suppress them at all cost and with all the means at its disposal, or to reduce them at the source. While predispositions to all these choices continued to assert themselves in Soviet ranks, the regime's chief reaction was to attempt mitigating the tensions at their source,

[35] See Mokrinskii, *SP,* 3(27), 1927, pp. 106-107; Akopov, *RN,* 4-5, 1930, pp. 58-59; Kryl'tsov, *SP,* 5(29), 1927, p. 138; Krupskaia, *Ka,* 12, 1928, pp. 10-11. Cf. Tiurakulov, *ZhN,* 1(6), 1924, pp. 38-40; Seifi, *Ka,* 9, 1925, p. 74; Zakharian, *Ka,* 3, 1926, p. 42; Nukhrat, *OZV,* pp. 42-43, and *VMV,* pp. 20-21; Pal'vanova, *DSV,* pp. 41, 106-107.

through a deliberate reduction of legalistic and administrative pressures and a calculated attempt to construct a complex infrastructure of social-service, educational, associational, expressive, and economic facilities that would serve as an underpinning for an alternative way of life.

The Pattern of Retrenchment

By early 1929, only two and one half years after the inception of the "cultural revolution" in Central Asia, the Communist Party felt obliged to bring the "storming" activities on behalf of female emancipation and the massive and overt forms of the cultural revolution itself to an abrupt halt. The retrenchment pattern included the following components: (1) Scaling down some sanctions of the new legal code, and tailoring some of its provisions to bring them into closer accord with local mores, as well as exempting some Central Asian provinces altogether from the application of the new norms. (2) Directing reprisals, by and large, not against all *de facto* transgressors but primarily against selected individuals and strata, especially traditional elites and native Soviet officials. (3) Withdrawal of official encouragement from female-initiated divorces, designed to halt the divorce wave altogether. (4) Prohibition of massive and dramatic violations of traditional taboos, and especially of administered female unveiling in public, as well as shelving, indefinitely, all official proposals for outlawing female veiling and seclusion. (5) Delimiting the organizational and revolutionary role of the Zhenotdel and of affiliated women's associations. (6) Planning of a new social infrastructure to compete with and supplant traditional institutions, concentrating on actually felt needs rather than on political agitation; stressing specialized and selective cadre formation rather than general social mobilization; emphasizing gradual, comprehensive, and coordinated social reconstruction ("systematic work") rather than sudden and violent social revolution; and preserving, where necessary, segregated facilities for Moslem women.

SANCTIONS

The scaling-down of contra-traditional sanctions was reflected first and foremost in the abandonment of their retroactive application in most cases involving "crimes based on custom." Thus, polygamous marriages antedating the new legal code were formally

336

exempted from prosecution.[36] There is reason to assume that local authorities were quietly instructed to approach even freshly contracted polygamous unions in a cautious, prudent, carefully differentiated manner, with a good deal of "political perspective," i.e., keeping in mind the political costs of an undifferentiated crackdown.[37] The rationale behind such self-restraint was spelled out quite frankly. (a) Merely to track down all polygamous marriages, not to speak of dissolving them, required an enormous investment of energy, resources, and cadres. (b) Crude attempts to dissolve such marriages constituted a particularly grave irritation of traditional sensibilities in a milieu where emotional investment in the preservation of lineage was very great, especially in cases where polygamous unions were stabilized and cohesive, where there were pregnant women or women with infants at the breast, or where the presence in a household of more than one wife could be explained by what had been primordially a most important factor in a Moslem traditional milieu, namely a woman's childlessness. (c) Consistent pressure to abolish polygamy placed an insupportable burden both on the women themselves and on their revolutionary patrons, as native polygamous males tended to respond to prosecution by throwing the older and less desirable wives out the door, thus shifting the responsibility for supporting masses of destitute women to the Soviet regime.[38]

Similarly, there are grounds to assume that, in spite of loud and vehement official denunciations of *kalym*, and in spite of mandatory penalties for adherence to this custom, Central Asian judicial organs were encouraged or permitted to refrain from rigid enforcement of the law. The justifications were basically twofold: (a) in a number of unearthed cases marriage seemed to have the bride's assent, and the bride-price, rather than serving as a source of "personal enrichment," appeared to be spent *in toto* on the wedding itself and on the bride's trousseau; (b) even if this was not the case, consistent prosecution of both givers and recipients of *kalym* could easily lead to the mandatory indictment of parents and kinsmen of both bride and groom, thus involving in criminal proceedings a vast

[36] For a discussion, see "V Tsentral'nykh . . . (Turk. S.S.R.)," *SS*, 5, 1926, p. 158. Cf. Mokrinskii, *SP*, 3 (27), 1927, p. 116; Dosov, *Ka*, 5, 1928, p. 31.

[37] See, e.g., Mokrinskii, *SP*, 3(27), 1927, p. 113. Cf. Mukhitdinova, *Ka*, 9, 1929, pp. 39-40.

[38] See, e.g., Mukhitdinova, *Ka*, 9, 1929, pp. 39-40.

number of people, perhaps even—as in marriages of orphans sponsored by the community—an entire clan. On both counts, an uncompromising assault was judged to be "politically unacceptable."[39]

Marriage by abduction accompanied by rape, as well as other forms of forced marriage, were specifically forbidden and subject to harsh penalties. But a number of semi-official commentaries accompanying and following the enactment of the new code indicated that the central government was increasingly ambivalent on this score, and was prepared, under some circumstances, to overlook deviations from the norm (a) if the abductor proved his honorable intentions by actually marrying the girl; (b) if the abducted and violated girl refused, out of shame or lack of viable marital alternatives, to lodge a complaint in court; and (c) if a girl forced into marriage by her parents and kinsmen refused, out of loyalty to kinfolk and custom, to testify against them.[40]

While the Family Code of the U.S.S.R. clearly stipulated a minimum marital age of eighteen for both boys and girls, and while the Criminal Code carried stiff penalties for marrying a minor (especially a girl), a tacit agreement appears to have been reached to lower the legal age requirement in Central Asia. The marital age of Moslem girls was formally fixed at sixteen,[41] and even this seems to have been left open to informal adjustments to suit local conditions and particular cases. (As one authoritative Soviet official put it, the sanctions in this case were designed primarily to "discourage marriages with ten- or twelve-year-old girls," thus implying that even cases involving thirteen-year-olds might be ignored by the regime.)[42] The explicitly or implicitly stated reasons for this were these: (a) While Soviet anthropologists and medical authorities were by no means unanimous in this respect, there seemed to be a predisposition to believe that, by and large, Central Asian girls reached sexual (though perhaps not emotional) maturity earlier than girls in European Russia, and thus might be legitimately considered ready for marriage at a lower age. (b) In many officially reported cases, native adults as well as young people were simply unaware of their own age. (c) Blanket refusal on the part

[39] See Mokrinskii, *SP*, 3(27), 1927, p. 113.

[40] For an excellent example of a semi-official commentary hinting at such concessions, see Mokrinskii, *SP*, 3(27), 1927, pp. 107-108, 114-15, 119.

[41] See, e.g., "V Tsentral'nykh . . . ," *SS*, 5, 1926, pp. 156, 158.

[42] See Dosov, *Ka*, 5, 1928, p. 30.

of Z.A.G.S. agencies (Soviet bureaus of civil registry) to sponsor any but the most minutely documented and legally acceptable marital unions, as well as draconic prosecution of persons arranging under-age marriages, tended to drive most such marriages underground. This merely reinforced the monopoly of consecrative functions held by local religious personages, and encouraged traditionalist masses to "circumvent" all Soviet legislation as well as to stay away from Soviet institutional sponsorship in this and other matters. Thus, some relaxation of demands in this realm promised to enhance the role of Soviet administrative machinery in the traditional community, and even endow the Soviet system itself with a measure of "[legitimate] authority" at the grassroots.[43]

All these adjustments at the operational level, in most cases effected quietly and informally, were clearly predicated on several important assumptions that were gaining currency in Soviet ranks: (a) for some time to come, no strict and mandatory correlation needed to exist between positing a law and enforcing it; (b) the arsenal of sanctions might best be held in reserve rather than imposed at every hint of non-conformity; (c) contra-traditional legislation might best be more rather than less lenient; (d) the application of new norms and sanctions might best be selective and graduated, even if this meant leaving large pockets of traditional behavior and relationships temporarily undisturbed. As the All-Union Central Executive Committee put it, in its comments on the new code enacted in April, 1928, "widespread and sustained enlightenment-work with the masses" was to command definite precedence over, and indeed had to precede, the application of "punitive measures" enacted into law.[44] It was a salient indication of the importance attached to these premises that some of the sanctions of the criminal code enacted in April, 1928, for traditional societies were actually much milder than had been previously envisaged (for example, in the first comprehensive governmental resolution on this account, adopted in October, 1924) even though this fact remained largely unacknowledged until some time later.[45]

[43] See Zakharian, *Ka*, 3, 1926, p. 44; Dosov, *Ka*, 5, 1928, pp. 30-31; Guber, *RV*, 8, 1930, pp. 276-77; Sulaimanova, *ISGPU*, Vol. ii, p. 225.

[44] See Pal'vanova, *DSV*, pp. 106-107.

[45] For a collation of explicit and implicit acknowledgments to this effect, and for some samples of the underlying arguments, see Akopov, *RN*, 4-5, 1930, pp. 59-60; Digurov, *SS*, 2(19), 1928, p. 59. Cf. Mokrinskii, *SP*, 3 (27), 1927, p. 107; Liubimova, *Ka*, 2, 1927, pp. 50-51; Dosov, *Ka*, 5, 1928, p. 32; Guber, *RV*, 8, 1930, pp. 276-77; Pal'vanova, *DSV*, pp. 106-107.

This disposition expressed itself even more dramatically in an unheralded decision early in 1928 to exempt (albeit temporarily) some especially sensitive Central Asian provinces, notably Tadzhikistan, altogether from the implementation of *khudzhum* and from the application of the new family and criminal codes.[46] Officially, this had to do with the psychological unpreparedness of the Tadzhik population, and with the absence of requisite Soviet institutions in the area or their inability to manage the decreed cultural revolution. It is safe to assume, though, that yet another factor played a role here. Ever since the Civil War and the *basmachi* revolt in the region in the early 1920's, Moscow apparently considered the Tadzhik districts bordering on Afghanistan as least accessible, most susceptible to tribal and traditionalist appeals, most volatile in response to revolutionary manipulation, and thus potentially most vulnerable to political subversion by anti-Soviet elements.

REPRISALS

While Soviet reprisals in the face of massive disregard of new rules, and of violent backlash by traditionalist elements, were increasingly severe in late 1928 and early 1929, concurrent official policies showed a growing inclination to apply counter-measures in a purposively discriminating manner. It would seem that, at some point in late 1928, a high-level decision was reached to direct reprisals, by and large, not against all *de facto* transgressors but primarily against selected individuals and strata, especially the surviving traditional elites and high-echelon native officials in the Soviet apparatus. This clearly denoted a resolve to intensify the assault against actual or potential native leadership while, simultaneously, relaxing the pressure on the masses and on rank-and-file cadres.

Although this position was not clearly articulated from the beginning, it assumed a distinctive shape by mid-1929. In essence, it divided actual and potential transgressors in two major categories, based on the offender's purported class-origin and socio-political status rather than on the nature and gravity of the offense. The first category included religious personages (*mullahs, imams, ishans*) as well as surviving tribal and communal leaders (*beys, manaps,* and other traditional village notables). It was apparently made mandatory to prosecute these men for crimes related to custom in their habitat (including the murder of unveiled women and female

[46] See Pal'vanova, *DSV*, pp. 86-88.

340

activists) when the slightest connection could be established between them and the actual perpetrators, even if there was no evidence of their personal participation in such crimes. They were to be singled out as "accomplices," "inspirers," and "spiritual instigators" of criminal offenses based on custom, as the "ideologists" of all traditionalist agitation, as "conscious saboteurs" of female emancipation and other Soviet enterprises. On the other hand, the masses of men included in the second category, primarily poor peasants and nomads, were classified as "backward," "unconscious," and "irresponsible," as "blind followers" of religious and communal leaders, as ignorant pawns who were merely used, urged on, and incited to fanatical acts by class-enemies of the Soviet regime. (Such a manner of apportioning essential characteristics and blame may thus be said to have been analogous to attacking the traffickers rather than the users of drugs in a society facing widespread use of narcotics.) Accordingly, show-trials were held consistently to emphasize this basic dichotomy. At the same time, "the harshest measures of social defense," including confiscation of property, deportation, and death, were to be reserved for the elites. *Per contra*, ordinary—and especially poor—peasants and nomads found guilty of crimes relates to custom were to be treated circumspectly, and subjected to penalties that were politically prudent and primarily "educative" in nature.[47] It was important thus to reassure the Moslem masses that "the Communist Party . . . has no intention to crudely violate their primordial customs, to crush their way of life. . . ."[48]

As Akopov, an authoritative party analyst, pointed out, to act otherwise was to act like a "[legalistic] jurist"[49] who only wants to know whether a crime actually took place, who committed it, and what sanctions were called for by the criminal code. To act on such

[47] See Dosov, *Ka*, 5, 1928, p. 32; *Bezb* (news.), 6, 1928, p. 4; Mukhitdinova, *Ka*, 9, 1929, pp. 40-41; Aitakov, *SS* (35), 1929, p. 63; Akopov, *RN*, 4-5, 1930, pp. 58, 60, 68; "V Tsentral'nykh . . . ," *SS*, 12(53), 1930, p. 144; Nukhrat, *RN*, 3, 1933, p. 48; Pal'vanova, *DSV*, pp. 84-85; *PV*, 2.11.1929, as cited in Bil'shai, *RZVS*, pp. 194-96. Cf. *BSE*, Vol. 29, 1935, p. 395; Sulaimanova, *ISGPU*, Vol. ɪɪ, p. 328; and Yakubovskaia, *IZ*, 48, 1954, p. 189.

[48] Ishkova, *Ka*, 11, 1928, pp. 60-61. To offer such reassurance was apparently all the more urgent in view of the continuing flight of entire rural communities to Afghanistan (see Kolychev, *RN*, 4-5, 1930, pp. 118-19).

[49] Akopov used the Russian term *zakonnik* (practitioner of law), ironically, in quotation marks.

a basis was to engage in "formalistic thinking," one that was "alien to the proletarian worldview," and that would lead one to "slur over [and forget] . . . the class-character" of traditionalist offenses as well as "the political significance" of the regime's struggle against crimes based on custom.[50] On May 21, 1929, the Plenary Session of the Supreme Court of R.S.F.S.R. formally reaffirmed the validity of the new approach. It emphasized the need to deal with each case separately and on its own merits, rather than on the basis of fixed rules; the criteria of indictment and the severity of punishment were to be determined, first and foremost, by the suspect's social class and property ownership.[51]

Four days later, the Central Committee of the All-Union Communist Party reinforced this judgment in a special resolution concerning the performance of party organizations in Uzbekistan. The resolution called for a halt to "highhanded pressure" as a "perversion" of revolutionary tactics, clearly implying that such pressure was decidedly counterproductive in dealing with Central Asian masses. The fire of reprisals for transgressions impinging on female emancipation was to be directed primarily at leading traditionalist elements. In an important new departure, the Central Committee resolution referred to such elements not only as *beys* but also as *basmachi*, a term officially reserved for Central Asian bandits and counterrevolutionaries.[52] In thus linking traditionally influential strata with *basmachi*, the resolution harked back to the days of the Civil War in Central Asia, when the only significant armed resistance to Soviet military penetration was offered by *basmachi* rebels, marauding units of Tadzhiks, Uzbeks, and Turkmen loosely organized on the basis of tribal, communal, and religious solidarity, and fighting primarily for the preservation of traditional values and authority in their rural habitats. It is safe to assume that the party's high command was proposing to re-enact what had been a successful twofold tactic in coping with outraged native sensibilities less than a decade earlier: a merciless crackdown on active and leading

[50] Akopov, *RN*, 4-5, 1930, pp. 58-60.

[51] The Supreme Court decision, "On Judicial Procedures in Cases involving Crimes based on Custom," is quoted in Akopov, *RN*, 4-5, 1930, p. 58. It is safe to assume that, as in other cases of high-level judicial decisions concerning crimes based on custom, the Central Asian republics took their cue from the R.S.F.S.R.

[52] The Central Committee resolution is quoted in Amosov, *Ka*, 14, 1929, p. 23.

exponents of traditionalism combined with far-reaching concessions to the masses. Such an approach was clearly intended to continue the process of neutralizing or destroying traditionally authoritative strata—now designated as "the main enemy" of female
emancipation and social change[53]—while at the same time alleviat-
ing popular grievances and allaying widespread anxieties.

Such purposive differentiation in apportioning blame and directing reprisals was also applied to native officialdom in the Soviet
apparatus, beginning with local communist parties. As Yaroslavsky
put it in December, 1928, a man's refusal to acquiesce in the emancipation of females in his family could not be considered compati-
ble with his membership in the party. But "we [expect and] demand
more of responsible officials," in this respect.[54] Even though Yaroslavsky's retreat from blanket application of new norms was grudging and qualified, it signaled a significant shift in official expectations and commitments. Artiukhina, the head of the central
Zhenotdel, had alluded to the need for such a shift as early as January, 1928, when the dimensions of the disaster in Central Asia
were first becoming apparent.[55] The need for selectivity in retaliating against native Soviet functionaries was finally acknowledged
(obliquely but unmistakably) at the highest levels of command on
May 25, 1929, when the Central Committee of the Communist
Party formally reordered its priorities in Central Asia.[56]

The pattern emerging in the course of this time suggests a twofold intent: (a) to single out for adherence to customary norms—
and to purge, relieve of all posts, and indict in massive show trials
—not so much the rank-and-file cadres as the party's *aktiv*, its activist core and high-echelon, responsible executive personnel; and
(b) to link these officials' traditionalist propensities with the likely
influence of "class enemies" (traditional elites) and "alien class
ideologies" upon them.[57] The gravity of the crime (and punish-

---

[53] See "Proekt programmy . . . ," *Ka*, 10, 1929, p. 62.

[54] Yaroslavsky, *Ka*, 1, 1929, pp. 30-31.

[55] See Ar-na [Artiukhina], *Ka*, 1, 1928, pp. 62-63. Cf. Pal'vanova, *DSV*,
pp. 98-99.

[56] See Amosov, *Ka*, 14, 1929, p. 23, citing the Central Committee's resolution on the performance of Uzbek communist organizations. This resolution had also singled out *beys* and *basmachi*, rather than the masses as a
whole, as the real enemies of female emancipation.

[57] See, e.g., Niurina, *Ka*, 5-6, 1929, p. 24; Perimova, *Ka*, 9, 1929, p. 37.
Cf. Yaroslavsky, *Ka*, 1, 1929, pp. 30-31; Amosov, *Ka*, 14, 1929, p. 23; Ar-na,
Ka, 1, 1928, pp. 62-63.

ment) implicit in such a linkage was presumably intended to serve not only as a possible deterrent to undesirable behavior but also as a perennially useful justification for purging authoritative native personnel under any and all circumstances.[58] Thus, in this case, too, repression tended to be contained (and tension mitigated) in the sense that its focus was narrowed to include primarily the most visible superordinate elements, whose punishment could have an important demonstration effect without simultaneously antagonizing young rank-and-file cadres and the population as a whole.

DIVORCE

Even though female-initiated divorces had been among the most important—and most consistently pursued—objectives of revolutionary legalism in 1925-1927, serious questions were raised in this respect almost from the very beginning. As already noted,[59] in October, 1926, the Turkmen Central Executive Committee formally announced its opposition to widespread divorces.[60] On June 5, 1927, the Central Committee of the All-Union Communist Party cautiously registered its concern with this matter by calling for "a serious study of the processes [especially divorce, and the accompanying problems of property allocation and female unemployment] connected with the disintegration of old family-structures [in Central Asia]."[61] As a consequence of government decisions reached sometime between the autumn of 1927 and the spring of 1929, official encouragement for female-initiated divorces was unequivocally withdrawn throughout Central Asia.[62]

While the reasons for this marked shift were never clearly and openly articulated in official communications, it is reasonably easy to reconstruct these reasons on the basis of field-reports and proposals made by communist analysts and organizers. It would seem that the following factors played an important role in the regime's decision: (a) the intensity of popular malaise, accompanied by widespread hostility and bloodshed in the traditionalist country-

[58] "Secret collaboration with *beys, mullahs,* and *basmachi*" as well as "nationalism and separatism" became the most prevalent accusations against native Soviet elites in the purges of 1929-30, 1933-34, and 1936-38.

[59] See Chapter Eight, section on "Native Personnel Behavior" in the framework of the Soviet administrative apparatus.

[60] See, e.g., "V Tsentral'nykh . . . ," *SS,* 5, 1926, pp. 156-59.

[61] See Pal'vanova, *DSV,* pp. 104-106.

[62] See, e.g., Nukhrat, *Ka,* 9, 1929, p. 32.

side; (b) the extent of official sabotage within the Soviet institutional framework in Central Asia, accompanied by strong and open pressures on the part of the native communist leadership in most of the region's republics to stem the tide of divorce proceedings; (c) the tendency on the part of some parents and guardians to exploit Soviet sponsorship of female-initiated divorces for private gain, by inciting young women to leave their husbands and then collecting repeated payments of *kalym* with each successive remarriage; (d) the tendency for divorce to cause at least as much emotional and material hardship among "poor" as among "rich" males, thus undermining what the regime considered a potential base of "class allies"; (e) the disintegration of families and fragmentation of households as economic units, and the commensurate disruption of agricultural production in the region; (f) the massive arrival of divorced and destitute women in the streets, swelling the ranks of prostitutes and unemployed, and leading to disillusionment and hostility among the women themselves.[63]

Under these circumstances, the Soviet regime not only withdrew from active sponsorship of divorces among natives but approved (albeit temporarily) several far-reaching proscriptive measures initiated by Turkmen authorities in late 1926.[64] These measures introduced a number of procedural obstacles sharply delimiting the natives' right to divorce, and making it especially difficult for Moslem women to sue for legal dissolution of a marriage. First, unlike in European Russia, divorce could now be obtained in Central Asia only in court, rather than through a simple declaration of intent in Z.A.G.S. (Soviet agency for civil registry). Second, native women suing for divorce were obliged to prove in court that they had not been induced to do so for their own or someone else's private gain, in connection with collecting additional *kalym* upon remarriage. (Needless to say, there could have been no illusions about a woman's ability to prove this, since a bride-price payment was likely to be involved in a subsequent marriage whether or not *kalym*-manip-

[63] For the entire spectrum of these arguments, consult Chapter Seven (the section on female responses to Soviet moves), and Chapter Eight (the section "Native Personnel Behavior"). See especially Kasparova, *Ka*, 7, 1925, p. 89; Zakharian, *Ka*, 3, 1926, pp. 42-44; "V Tsentral'nykh . . . ," *SS*, 5, 1926, pp. 158-59; Kryl'tsov, *SP*, 5(29), 1927, p. 138; Pal'vanova, *DSV*, pp. 104-106.

[64] While Soviet reports mention primarily Turkmen initiatives, they leave the distinct impression that these measures were made applicable to other Central Asian provinces as well (see, e.g., Pal'vanova, *DSV*, pp. 104-106).

ulation was actually intended.) Finally, "inducement to divorce" (by a woman's parents or kinsmen, or by intermediaries and other "outsiders") was declared to be a criminal offense subject to severe punishment.[65] (It quickly became apparent that the government meant exactly what it said: in Turkmenistan, for example, the number of cases prosecuted on these grounds in 1928 rose so swiftly that it approached one-third of all cases of "crimes based on custom" dealt with in the course of that year; for that matter, official reports proceeded to include "inducement to divorce" itself in the category of custom-based crimes.[66] Thus, to all intents and purposes, less than three years after helping to set in motion a divorce wave in Central Asia, the Soviet regime proceeded to halt this wave altogether by legal and administrative means.

UNVEILING

The entire concept (and major thrust) of *khudzhum*—the call to "assault" and "storm" in Central Asia—had been predicated on the swift destruction of female segregation and seclusion through administered and massive unveiling of women in public, as well as through decreed proscription of the veil. Yet already in June, 1927, the Organizational Bureau of the party's Central Committee showed itself to be alert to some of the developing problems. While expressing approval of the overall campaign conducted by Sredaz-buro (the Central Asian Bureau of the Central Committee), it registered unease over some of the methods employed so far. Most important, it warned against turning the campaign into the equivalent of a purely military enterprise, devoid of political, economic, legal, and cultural corollaries, and thus unfit to "consolidate [its own] successes."[67] In the fall of 1927, a regional Zhenotdel conference of party organizers among Eastern women discussed the Central Committee's warnings, and apparently brought up for review not only the "rich positive experience [and achievements]" of *khudzhum* but also its "blunders" and "mistakes."[68] In January, 1928, Artiukhina, the head of the central Zhenotdel, took the extraordinary step of publicly dissociating the party's high command

[65] See Zakharian, *Ka*, 3, 1926, pp. 42-44; Kryl'tsov, *SP*, 5(29), 1927, p. 138; Nukhrat, *Ka*, 9, 1929, p. 32; Akopov, *RN*, 4-5, 1930, p. 63; Pal'vanova, *DSV*, pp. 105-106. Cf. "V Tsentral'nykh . . . ," *SS*, 5, 1926, pp. 158-59.

[66] See Akopov, *RN*, 4-5, 1930, p. 63.

[67] Pal'vanova, *DSV*, p. 103.

[68] See Pal'vanova, *DSV*, p. 104.

from any and all responsibility for the Central Asian campaign. Her detailed and scathing indictment of the disastrous miscalculations and failures of *khudzhum* was accompanied by a terse (and demonstrably misleading[69]) observation that "the so-called 'assault' [had been] initiated . . . by the party organizations of Central Asia."[70] Given Artiukhina's high position in the party—membership, together with Stalin, in the Central Committee's Organizational Bureau and Secretariat[71]—it was unmistakably clear that the entire "storming" approach had come under a cloud of official opprobrium.

Yet even this unquestionably authoritative interdiction failed to usher in a decisive change in Central Asian policies. Perhaps the most obvious reason lay in the structure of Artiukhina's own argument. While dissociating Moscow from *khudzhum*, she did not proceed to draw the logical conclusion, namely, that the idea of *khudzhum* itself was at fault. Quite to the contrary, she explicitly defended the original objectives and even the timing of the campaign, reaffirming the "ripeness" of the local milieu for a decisive thrust in late 1926. She explained the accumulating failures as due not only to sabotage but also to gross mismanagement and bungling on the part of local Soviet personnel, and to the latter's unwillingness or inability to secure the gains of *khudzhum* through "systematic work."[72] Understandably, this tended to leave the entire matter up in the air. It could mean that the central leadership was either ambivalent and/or divided on this issue.[73] It could also imply

[69] See Chapter Six of this study; the evidence cited there makes it abundantly clear that the campaign had been ordered by Sredazburo, the Central Committee's chief political organ in Central Asia.

[70] See Ar-na, *Ka*, 1, 1928, p. 57. Of course, the fact that the term assault was in quotation marks was itself an indication of important changes in the regime's attitude.

[71] She was also a member of the Central Control Commission. Her status in the secretariat was that of an alternate member. See her obituary in *Pravda* and *Izvestiia*, April 10, 1969, p. 3. Cf. Avtorkhanov, *Stalin and the Soviet Communist Party*, pp. 96 and 101. Even though Avtorkhanov describes her as a former associate of Tomsky (an early member of the Politburo, and associate in the "right-wing faction" of Bukharin and Rykov, who committed suicide in 1936) and a "neutral" during Stalin's struggle for power, her relations with Stalinists in the party must have been quite good; she survived all purges following Stalin's victory in the 1920's.

[72] See Ar-na, *Ka*, 1, 1928, pp. 57-63, *passim*.

[73] In any case, the struggle for Lenin's mantle was at that time in its crucial and most delicate stage, probably making it all the more difficult

that what was expected was not abandonment but more subtle and consistent prosecution of the campaign. Accordingly, spasmodic attempts to press on with the assault continued throughout 1928. They involved not only administered unveiling but also an accelerated drive to consolidate opinion in the central apparatus as well as engineer local consent in favor of proscribing the veil (and other traditionally ordained articles of female attire) by decree.[74]

Liubimova and Bogacheva, leading Russian Zhenotdel officials in the Central Asian and Turkmen apparatuses respectively, were among the most adamant proponents of action by decree, though it is not clear to what extent they spoke for other high-echelon functionaries in the party's central and local units. We do know, however, that the Orgburo of the party's Central Committee had expressed a guarded interest in reviewing proposals for the decree in its resolution of December 10, 1928.[75] We also know that at just about the same time Khodzhaev, the head of the Uzbek government, felt obliged to call publicly for the abolition of the veil "in the immediate future."[76] Pressures for such action seem to have been anchored by and large in four sets of arguments.[77]

(a) If the government found it possible to pass legislation against *kalym*, and even against *shakhsei-vakhsei* (the custom of self-infliction of wounds in public during religious holidays in some Asian republics), it ought to be possible—indeed, it was surely easier—to legislate against veiling. It was naive to maintain that state intervention in religion- and custom-regulated spheres was especially prone to go too far and turn into "rule by injunction" and pure coercion. In the course of managing a revolution, administrative "distortions" were always present and were bound to occur from time to time. This was no reason for shying away from

---

for the central leadership to take an unequivocal stand on a bafflingly complex confrontation taking place in a distant Asian periphery.

[74] See, e.g., "Nuzhno li izdat' . . . ," *Ka*, 8, 1928, pp. 79-81; Liubimova, *Ka*, 8, 1928, pp. 73-75; Ishkova, *Ka*, 11, 1928, pp. 59-62; Bogacheva, *Ka*, 11, 1928, p. 66; "Mestnye rabotniki . . . ," *Ka*, 1, 1929, pp. 32-35; Zade (Osman Dzhuma), *Ka*, 7, 1929, pp. 48-49; Safudri, *Ka*, 13, 1929, pp. 42-44; Nukhrat, *RN*, 3(36), 1933, pp. 46-47.

[75] See Nukhrat, *Ka*, 1, 1929, p. 24.

[76] See Khodzhaev, *VS*, 52, 1928, pp. 9-12.

[77] In most cases, the arguments had to be reconstructed here; due to the fragmentary nature of the materials, only some aspects could be directly quoted or paraphrased.

forceful action. No realm of life was so "intimate" or "sacred" as to preclude administrative intervention.[78]

(b) It made no sense to leave the decision on unveiling and se-clusion up to everyone's "[personal] desire" and "good will." Such "voluntarism" was merely exploited by *mullahs* and other custo-dians of tradition. It permitted them to continue to maintain their psychological hold on the masses, through threats of excommunica-tion and of "torture in hell." These men knew full well that Mos-lems could not break the precepts of Islamic religion and custom except for a "valid reason." By making the rule against veiling offi-cial, universal, and compulsory, a decree would provide religious believers with precisely the "valid reason" they needed—which, in this case, would be based on a "[clearcut] order of the state." At the same time, it would "disarm" the enemies of social change, by depriving them of a potent psychological weapon and thus "make it easier for the toiling masses to get on with the struggle for wom-en's liberation."[79]

(c) Officially organized large-scale unveiling had encouraged many women to discard the veil. However, public opinion in Mos-lem traditional communities was fickle as well as powerful. The mo-ment some of these women, for whatever reason but especially out of fear of traditionalist retribution, donned the veil again, *all* un-veiled females of the community would feel obliged to do the same.[80] Under these circumstances, only an unequivocal decree could prevent such a denouement. By the same token, it would be a suitable device for "consolidating" the achievements of *khud-zhum*. It would create a "supportive atmosphere" for those women who would otherwise be unable to withstand the pressure, or who would not dare to make a move toward self-emancipation in the first place. Thus, it would "earn their gratitude" as well as "strengthen their awareness that they were not alone [in this strug-gle]." At the same time, an official decree would serve as a "warn-

[78] See Liubimova, *Ka*, 8, 1928, p. 75; "Nuzhno li izdat' . . . ," *Ka*, 8, 1928, p. 81; Bogacheva, *Ka*, 11, 1928, p. 66.

[79] See Liubimova, *Ka*, 8, 1928, pp. 73-75; Ishkova, *Ka*, 11, 1928, p. 60; "Mestnye rabotniki . . . ," *Ka*, 1, 1929, pp. 32-33.

[80] It would seem that this argument was rather more complex as well as contrived than suggested here. Those who advanced it—primarily Liubimova and Bogacheva—were surely aware that many of the initially unveiled women had *already* donned the veil again. Thus, it is a safe guess that the intent was to justify, *ex post facto*, what had happened (or was happening) and propose a new device to undo the damage.

ing to the enemies [of revolution] . . . that they were facing a mass movement [to be reckoned with]," that the new limits were clear and firm, and that the penalties for transgression were swift and strict.[81]

(d) A state decree was not to be viewed merely as a "declarative document . . . inspired from above." For one thing, it would be clearly related to, and would thus simply make manifest and ratify, the realities of the situation: the process of "rot" and "collapse" already affecting all traditional institutions. For another thing, and even more important, the female masses themselves demanded (publicly or privately) such a decree, making it both legitimate and imperative to proceed without further ado.[82]

In spite of these seemingly potent arguments in favor of decreed unveiling, the Soviet high command obviously found it impossible to reach an unambiguous decision in this matter in 1927 and 1928. But it showed no further hesitation in the spring of 1929. By that time, Stalin's victory over his competitors in the party was complete, and their accelerated purge from the ranks was accompanied by a crackdown on all deviant, dissident, and equivocal views.

By January, 1929, it was clear that all proposals for outlawing the veil were to be shelved indefinitely.[83] It is noteworthy that three very different political actors were encouraged or permitted to be among the main spokesmen for this curtailment: Akhun-Babaev, a native of Central Asia and President of Uzbekistan; Krupskaia, Lenin's widow, a leading official of the All-Union Politprosvet (the regime's main agency for "political enlightenment" of the masses),

---

[81] See Liubimova, *Ka*, 8, 1928, pp. 74-75; Bogacheva, *Ka*, 11, 1928, p. 66.

[82] See Liubimova, *Ka*, 8, 1928, p. 74; "Nuzhno li izdat' . . . ," *Ka*, 8, 1928, p. 80; Ishkova, *Ka*, 11, 1928, p. 61; Bogacheva, *Ka*, 11, 1928, p. 66; "Mestnye rabotniki . . . ," *Ka*, 1, 1929, p. 33.

[83] See the speeches of Akhun-Babaev (President of Uzbekistan) and Zhukova at the Fourth All-Union Zhenotdel Conference of Party Organizers among Eastern Women (Dec., 1928, Moscow), in "Mestnye rabotniki . . . ," *Ka*, 1, 1929, pp. 32-35. Cf. Nukhrat, *RN*, 3(36), 1933, p. 47. It is important to remember that even after the bloodbath of the purges in the latter 1930's, Moscow resisted the temptation to outlaw the veil. See, e.g., *PV*, 6.30.1936, p. 2; *PV*, 1.5.1937, p. 3; and especially *Pravda*, 1.15.1940, p. 3, containing an impassioned plea by a Central Asian female communist (Mastura Auezova) to proscribe the veil by decree. While airing such demands in Soviet mass media clearly implied recurrent official interest in the matter, the demands themselves remained ignored.

and a long-time activist in the struggle for women's rights throughout the Soviet Union; and Zhukova, a female Russian official in Central Asia with seemingly very important (though not clearly specified) connections with the central Zhenotdel, with the Commissariat of Justice, and with the party's Central Committee. All three addressed themselves to the issue of decreed unveiling at the Fourth All-Union Zhenotdel Conference of Party Organizers among Eastern Women in December, 1928, in Moscow. It is safe to assume that they were expected to utilize the very different dimensions of their status in the communist movement for the purpose of legitimizing the new policy of retrenchment in Russia's Asian republics.

Their arguments, demonstrably reflecting the views of many other communist organizers, may be reconstructed as follows: (a) It was foolhardy to expect that deeply embedded customs, relationships, and "religious superstitions" could be ruled out of existence by command and decree, that "the most intimate aspects of a [Moslem] way of life"—such as physical and symbolic apartheid based on sex—could be "[reordered] by administrative fiat."[84] As Krupskaia put it, it was both senseless and dangerous to approach such sensitive realms of a life style ". . . from an abstract, moralistic point of view, [without regard for] what [was] and [was not] immediately possible. . . . Of course, one might wish [to say,] to hell with the cloak and veil—but we cannot always get what we want just by issuing a decree."[85]

(b) One of the regime's primary objectives was to attract local women to Soviet schools, clubs, factories, and associations. Formal prohibition of the veil would hinder rather than facilitate this process, because it would compound the anxieties of men as well as sharpen the women's own dilemmas. It was precisely in this realm that it was important to prove to the Moslem masses that "the Communist Party . . . does not intend to crudely violate their primordial customs, to crush their way of life . . . ," that the Soviet regime merely wishes to offer them "literacy, culture, free and fruitful labor." Given such reassurance, traditional men would feel

---

[84] See "Nuzhno li izdat' . . . ," *Ka*, 8, 1928, pp. 79-81; Liubimova, *Ka*, 8, 1928, p. 75. While Liubimova was at that time against this line of reasoning, her article helps to reconstruct the views of Krupskaia and others of her persuasion.

[85] See Krupskaia, *Ka*, 12, 1928, pp. 10-12.

351

more relaxed about letting the females of their household participate in Soviet enterprises.[86]

(c) A Moslem woman's economic security was bound up with her observance of customs and taboos, beginning with veiling. To outlaw the latter meant to impinge immediately on the former. Unless and until the Soviet regime was able to provide for the material support of unveiling women, decreed prohibition of the custom was out of the question.[87]

(d) In and of itself, the veil was not especially important. It was, in effect, one aspect of a cultural superstructure that would disappear when the underlying conditions changed. Thus, to issue decrees in this sphere was to attack the wrong target.[88]

(e) Decreed proscription of the veil might be of some use if it came in response to the demands of the women themselves and of the masses as a whole. However, demands of this kind had been largely manufactured by others. As Akhun-Babaev felt obliged to explain, the demands had been voiced primarily by party, Komsomol, and professional organizations.[89] Zhukova's explanation was less charitable as well as more ominous in its implications. As she put it, only the remnants of the "petty bourgeoisie," members of the "[old] intelligentsia," and some "unstable elements within the party" had raised the issue of a decree. In asking for it, these communists were merely asking for a crutch, for something to "shield" them in a deed for which they felt but little enthusiasm, or which they were too faint-hearted to carry out on their own. To confront the "elemental force" of local custom, beginning with his own kin group, a real communist needed "revolutionary courage" rather than decrees.[90] Only those who lacked such courage could possibly wish to embroil the party in "administrative hit-and-run attacks" on sensitive social spheres, and to issue "[demagogic] resolutions with an [impressively] revolutionary sound [to them]." Such

[86] See Ishkova, *Ka*, 11, 1928, pp. 60-61.

[87] "Nuzhno li izdat' . . . ," *Ka*, 8, 1928, pp. 80, 82; Ishkova, *Ka*, 11, 1928, p. 61; Zade (Osman Dzhuma), *Ka*, 7, 1929, p. 49.

[88] See "Nuzhno li izdat' . . . ," *Ka*, 8, 1928, p. 81.

[89] See Akhun-Babaev's remarks in "Mestnye rabotniki . . . ," *Ka*, 1, 1929, p. 32.

[90] See Zhukova's remarks in "Mestnye rabotniki . . . ," *Ka*, 1, 1929, p. 35. The logic of such a proposition was, of course, dubious. This argument appears to have been advanced primarily as a hortatory and face-saving device.

352

people were clearly infected with the disease of "leftism," long adjudged to be an infantile disorder.[91]

Of course, it was common knowledge in communist ranks that the issuance of a decree against veiling had been seriously considered, not just by some "bourgeois" and "unstable" political elements, but by the Orgburo of the Central Committee of the Communist Party and by the All-Union Commissariat of Justice.[92] Yet the very terms in which these tortuous, *ex post facto* rationalizations were cast in late 1928 and early 1929 must have served as an all the more dramatic indication of a change in the party line, as well as an explicit reminder to those who did not heed the warning.

On May 25, 1929, Moscow was prepared to go farther. In its resolution on the performance of Uzbek party units, the Central Committee of the party categorically indicted the "distortions" accompanying the attack on female seclusion and veiling in Central Asia, and altogether prohibited "administrative coercion" in attaining Soviet objectives in this realm. It proposed to concentrate, instead, on carefully correlated cultural and economic enterprises, intensified propaganda and enlightenment, and long-term political recruitment as the most important and fruitful tasks.[93] In doing this, it placed itself squarely—though somewhat belatedly—behind Artiukhina's suggestive slogan of January, 1928, calling for a shift from "assault" to "systematic work" in Central Asia.[94] While the Central Committee was not very explicit on this subject in its public document, it obviously made a number of things clear by other means, apparently several months before adopting the formal resolution. First, official encouragement of female unveiling was to be withdrawn, except in cases of high-echelon communist, administrative, and professional personnel who were to set a personal example by emancipating the female members of their own households.[95]

91 See Nukhrat, *RN*, 3, 1933, pp. 46-47. This dimension of the argument clearly harked back to Lenin's notions about certain aspects of political leftism as "infantile disorders."

92 See, e.g., "Nuzhno li izdat' . . . ," *Ka*, 8, 1928, p. 79; "Mestnye rabotniki . . . ," *Ka*, 1, 1929, p. 34; Nukhrat, *Ka*, 1, 1928, p. 24.

93 See Amosov, *Ka*, 14, 1929, p. 23.

94 Indeed, Artiukhina's article was entitled, "From 'assault' to systematic work" ("Ot 'nastupleniia' k sistematicheskoi rabote"). See Ar-na, *Ka*, 1, 1928, p. 57.

95 See Amosov, *Ka*, 14, 1929, p. 23. Cf. "Nuzhno li izdat' . . . ," *Ka*, 8, 1928, p. 81; Ishkova, *Ka*, 11, 1928, pp. 61-62; "Mestnye rabotniki . . . ," *Ka*, 1, 1929, pp. 33-35; Zade (Osman Dzhuma), *Ka*, 7, 1929, p. 49;

353

Second, administered massive unveiling in public was to be stopped altogether as an overly crude and dangerous violation of local customs.[96] Finally (and perhaps most remarkably) even women who *wished* to dispose of their veils were to be scrutinized in terms of the impact their act was likely to have on themselves and their environment. As one native female communist explained later,

> Often the first woman in a village to unveil determines the whole course of woman's emancipation in that locality. If she is too weak, she compromises the whole ideal of unveiling. For in the eyes of the village, she is a loose woman, a slut. She compromises, not only the idea of woman's emancipation, but also every other social or economic or educational reform sponsored by the communists. She plays into the hands of the counter-revolutionary elements who generalize her individual failing into an inevitable consequence of yielding to Bolshevik influence. "The Bolsheviki are turning our women into harlots," the enemies whisper. Thus hasty unveilings work at times irreparable harm to our cause. Small wonder we have learned to watch our step. . . . We try to put a brake on impetuous decisions. This is particularly so in localities where the number of unveiled women is still small. . . . Unless we are absolutely sure that the woman has enough character and intelligence to assume the responsibilities of a pioneer, we actually go to the length of discouraging her.[97]

Nukhrat, *RN*, 3(36), 1933, pp. 46-47. Note that Ishkova refers to such instructions from the Central Committee in late 1928.

[96] See "Proekt programmy . . . ," *Ka*, 10, 1929, p. 53; Nukhrat, *RN*, 3(36), 1933, pp. 46-48. Cf. Pal'vanova, *DSV*, pp. 101-102. Even those insisting on continued assault on the institution of veiling no longer mentioned mass-unveiling in public (see, e.g., Karimova, *Ka*, 3, 1929, pp. 43-45). It would seem that, under the pressure of the new party decisions, local functionaries fell into line so quickly that, by late 1929 and early 1930, official commitments to female emancipation in Central Asia tended to be expressed primarily in hortatory declarations during important Soviet holidays, such as March 8 (Woman's Day) and November 7 (anniversary of the October Revolution). This is apparent, for example, from Nikiforov's complaints about the unseemly, "bureaucratic" handling of this matter by Soviet personnel in Moslem republics (see Nikiforov, *Ka*, 15, 1929, p. 45).

[97] Khoziat Markulanova, a Tadzhik female party organizer, quoted by Kunitz in *Dawn Over Samarkand*, p. 300.

ROLE OF THE ZHENOTDEL AND RELATED ASSOCIATIONS

From the very beginning of female mobilization in Central Asia, the Zhenotdel, one of the prime component parts of the Central Committee Secretariat, had been assigned a crucial role in initiating and supervising all aspects of the campaign. It played (or tried to play) this role vigorously at all levels of command: in implementing revolutionary legalism as well as *khudzhum*, in sponsoring divorces and general unveiling, in promoting political recruitment as well as cultural re-orientation and economic mobilization among women, in engineering overall consent and ferreting out resistance to Soviet policies.[98] The Zhenotdel did this in conjunction with several specialized voluntary associations. The first scattered units of these associations in the Central Asian countryside apparently owed their formation and much of their initial impetus between 1926 and 1929 to Zhenotdel pressure, and were clearly within the sphere of its responsibility if not clear-cut jurisdiction. The associations included Delegatskiie Sobraniia (Assemblies of Women's Delegates, designed to provide elementary forms of grassroots political participation); Za Novyi Byt (For a New Way of Life, intended to disseminate new values, skills, and habits); and Doloi Kalym i Mnogozhenstvo (literally, Down with Kalym and Polygamy, a militant association meant to mobilize grassroots opinion in the struggle with local customs).[99] Thus, it is fair to say that the scope and intensity of the Zhenotdel's activities in Central Asia were far greater than in European Russia, in recognition of the special situation created and special political opportunities offered by the status of Moslem women.

By mid-1929, the convergence of profound changes in the system as a whole and of important policy-shifts in Central Asia in

[98] For some accounts of the role of the Zhenotdel, see Kasparova, *Ka*, 7, 1925, p. 90; Ivetova, *Ka*, 8, 1925, p. 65; Zavarian, *Ka*, 12, 1925, pp. 25-27; *BSE*, Vol. 16, 1952, p. 62; Bil'shai, *RZVS*, pp. 186-93. A detailed examination of the Zhenotdel's structure and functions will be found in a separate study, now in preparation (see Note 19, Chapter Six).

[99] Rather little is known about the genesis, composition, structure, and functions of these associations. Some helpful details may be gleaned from Z. P., *Ka*, 6, 1928, pp. 84-85; Arykova, *Ka*, 6, 1928, pp. 81-83; Liubimova, *Ka*, 8, 1928, pp. 75-78; "Proekt programmy . . . ," *Ka*, 10, 1929, pp. 54-55. Additional information is available in summary accounts of the performance of other state agencies; see, e.g., Nukhrat, *OZV*, pp. 67-71; Dosov, *VS*, 38, 1929, p. 13; Popova, *RN*, 3(36), 1933, pp. 60-64.

particular was bound to call into question the role of the Zhenotdel and of affiliated organizations. (a) It goes without saying that the regime's changing attitudes toward divorce and unveiling as well as toward sanctions and reprisals (as related to female mobilization and general social change in Central Asia) placed specialized female-oriented units in an anomalous situation. Faced with the full panoply of implications of unrestrained "cultural revolution" and of massive enforcement and repression, the Soviet regime had clearly opted for a strategic retreat. This involved, first and foremost, a disposition to mitigate revolutionary tensions at their source, through a deliberate reduction of legalistic and administrative pressures. Obviously, such a reduction of tensions was unthinkable without a redefinition of the functions of organizations primarily concerned with inducing revolutionary tensions in society.

(b) From the outset of *khudzhum*, and throughout its course, it was apparent that a strong faction within the Soviet apparatus was uneasy about some aspects of female mobilization in Central Asia. As we have seen,[100] this unease stemmed from a fundamental distrust of all specialized mediating networks standing between the population and the Party-State, especially if those networks were not totally subject to central surveillance, manipulation, and control. In this context, not only such women's organizations as Za Novyi Byt and Doloi Kalym i Mnogozhenstvo but even the Zhenotdel itself came under repeated (albeit not always open) attack as carriers of potentially dangerous propensities.[101] In the view of a number of party organizers, the growth of an exclusively female-oriented organizational network could easily turn into a spontaneous and uncontrolled process; the proliferation of such special-purpose units could lead to the consolidation of genuinely voluntary associations, and hence of potentially autonomous, separatist, and even subversive superstructures within the Soviet system; and an overly narrow and specific preoccupation with the problems of women could encourage the emergence of a full-blown feminist movement, which would, from a Bolshevik perspective, be a malignant bourgeois perversion of revolutionary aims.

It was perhaps a significant indication of the new mood that Zhukova, who proved to be the most vociferous opponent of de-

---

[100] See the introductory sections (esp. "The Danger of Subversive Superstructures") in Chapter Six of this study.

[101] For a detailed discussion and specific references, see ibid.

creed unveiling,[102] was also among the most determined public exponents of the principle of radical organizational delimitation and synchronization in Central Asia.[103] Needless to say, the mood she expressed was in many respects that of the victorious Stalinist faction within the party: a ruthless determination to suppress all spontaneous and heterogeneous and hence potentially autonomous and pluralistic social forces, as intrinsically intolerable in an avowedly monolithic, tightly centralized, organizationally and culturally homogeneous Party-State.

At some point between mid-1929 and early 1930 the new Stalinist leadership made up its mind in this matter. Its decision was perhaps especially important at that time in that it failed to go along with extremist proposals on either side. It involved a distinct compromise between conflicting views on the aims and means of female mobilization in predominantly Moslem milieus, and it differentiated clearly between Central Asia and the rest of the Soviet Union. In mid-1930, the Zhenotdel was liquidated as a distinct component of the Secretariat of the Central Committee of the Communist Party, in conjunction with the reorganization of the party's supreme executive organs at that time. Work with women throughout the U.S.S.R. was designated as merely one of many (and relatively minor) responsibilities of the Secretariat's newly constituted Department for Agitation and Mass Campaigns.[104] It would seem that shortly thereafter Zhenotdel units at all levels of command, including all republican apparatuses, were similarly disbanded. But Central Asia was specifically (albeit quietly) exempted from the liquidation order.[105] Likewise, while Central Asia's women-oriented voluntary associations were dissolved, permission was granted in effect to replace them by strengthening two recently established organizational structures concerned primarily with women: Bytovye Sektsii (Sections for [Dealing with the Local] Way of Life), attached to local soviets; and Komissii po Uluchshenii Truda i Byta Zhenshchiny, or K.U.T.B. (Commissions for Improvement of Women's Labor [Conditions] and Way of Life), attached to

[102] See the preceding section (esp. "Unveiling").

[103] See her article in *Ka*, 10, 1928, pp. 79-80.

[104] See Fainsod, *How Russia Is Ruled*, pp. 190-93.

[105] That Central Asia came to be exempted from the liquidation order is factually noted in *BSE*, Vol. 16, 1952, p. 62. That there was considerable hesitation in formalizing such an exemption is attested to by the fact that the exemption is not even mentioned in *BSE*, Vol. 25, 1932, pp. 139, 237-58, dealing with the Zhenotdel.

357

Central Executive Committees of republican supreme soviets (Ts.I.K.), and to provincial and city executive committees (*ispolkoms*).[106]

To be sure, in both cases the net effect was to circumscribe sharply the scope of operations and the revolutionary role of female-oriented institutions. The Central Asian Zhenotdel was renamed Zhensektor, literally Women's Sector, which was clearly a demotion in the hierarchy of the Soviet apparatus. The leadership of the region's central Zhensektor (attached to Sredazburo, the Central Asian Bureau of the party's Central Committee) passed to Anna Aksentovich,[107] formerly an important Zhenotdel official but one without Artiukhina's strategic connections in the party's highest supervisory bodies (the Secretariat, the Organizational Bureau, and the Central Control Commission). The Zhenotdel's formerly active sponsorship of divorces and unveiling was, in effect, cut short, and many of its other responsibilities were dispersed among various commissariats and other state agencies (such as those concerned with health, education, labor, justice, social security, and political enlightenment). Likewise, the fairly abrupt designation of soviets rather than party units as "the main organizers of female masses,"[108] and the transfer of many day-to-day concerns for women's welfare to K.U.T.B. and Bytovye Sektsii, meant that these concerns were being relegated to what was politically a distinctly inferior domain, given the soviets' largely ceremonial functions and increasingly evident subordination to the party in all matters.[109] In turn, the downgrading and diffusion of institutional responsibilities in this realm meant that the entire enterprise of female emancipation and mobilization in Central Asia was being

---

[106] For some details on the formation and functions of Bytovye Sektsii, see Zaitsev, *VS*, 4, 1928, pp. 9-10; Safadri, *Ka*, 11, 1928, p. 34; "V Tsentral'nykh . . . ," *SS*, 3(44), 1930, p. 138. For accounts concerning K.U.T.B., see Zavarian, *Ka*, 12, 1925, p. 30; Golubeva, *Ka*, 3, 1927, pp. 35-37; "V. Tsentral'nykh . . . ," *SS*, 12(17), 1927, pp. 150-53; Uspenskaia, *Ka*, 1, 1928, p. 67; Ar-na, *Ka*, 3, 1928, pp. 18-24; Liubimova, *Ka*, 3, 1928, pp. 58-61; Nukhrat, *Ka*, 4, 1928, pp. 68-69; Polianskaia, *RN*, 3, 1930, pp. 91-96; "Obzor . . . ," *RN*, 4-5, 1930, pp. 136-37; Akopov, *RN*, 5, 1930, p. 69.

[107] See Nukhrat, *RN*, 3, 1933, p. 54.

[108] See "Proekt programmy . . . ," *Ka*, 10, 1929, p. 54.

[109] An account of the operations and of the jurisdictional struggles involving the Zhenotdel and Zhensektor, K.U.T.B., Bytovye Sektsii, and other state agencies, will be found in a separate study, now in preparation (see Note 19, Chapter Six).

358

reduced to relatively low-priority and low-key activities, and removed to a secondary political plane.[110]

All the same, the mode of retrenchment in this field still differed significantly from concurrent actions in other fields. The fate of two special-purpose, though otherwise unrelated, organizational networks may serve as an illustration of this dichotomy. Both Koshchi (Central Asia's rural trade union, encompassing native peasants, nomads, and agricultural workers) and Evsektsiia (Jewish Sections of the Communist Party) had been formed in the 1920's, as was the case with the Central Asian Zhenotdel and affiliated associations, for the express purpose of facilitating the class struggle, weakening customs and traditional solidarities, and revolutionizing the entire cultural and political milieu of their respective communities. By 1929, Koshchi was reduced to a paper organization,[111] while Evsektsiia was summarily liquidated in mid-1930.[112] A similar fate befell (at just about the same time) all other associations—such as those of writers and scientists—whose structure and internal life were deemed to be insufficiently politicized, and insufficiently susceptible to ideological and organizational regulation from above, for the purposes of a fully unitary state. The fact that especially structured work with Central Asian women was permitted to go on (albeit on a reduced scale) under organizationally distinct and specifically suited auspices made it clear that the Soviet regime still considered it important to respond to the need for "special forms and methods of work"[113] generated by the role and status of women in Moslem traditional societies.

NEW SOCIAL INFRASTRUCTURE AND "SYSTEMATIC WORK"

The regime's growing disenchantment with legalism and assault in Central Asia in 1928-1929 went hand in hand with a quest for optimal components of what came to be referred to as "systematic work." It would seem that, ideally, systematic work denoted gradual, comprehensive, carefully coordinated social reconstruction as

[110] Nukhrat used the terms "pushed into the background . . . as a secondary issue," even though she felt obliged to give rather implausible reasons for this shift. See her article in *RN*, 3(36), 1933, p. 50.

[111] See Park, *Bolshevism*, pp. 146-53.

[112] See Zvi Gitelman, *Jewish Nationality and Soviet Politics: The Jewish Sections of the C.P.S.U., 1917-1930* (Princeton, 1972), esp. the concluding chapter.

[113] See "Proekt programmy . . . ," *Ka*, 10, 1929, p. 53.

359

against sudden and violent social revolution. It was viewed as a task that called for systematic evaluation, exploitation, and orchestration of diverse courses of action—associational, cultural, legal, and economic—as against a compulsive, heavily politicized drive for a breakthrough on a narrow sector of social life. It implied the need to recognize the facts and imperatives of dynamic reciprocity between all realms of social mobilization, and to recognize as well that there was no way around the investment of time, resources, and painstakingly tailored effort in undertaking the complex task of comprehensive social change. It engendered a pragmatic commitment to cautious and patient social experimentation, wherein at least as much time and effort would be devoted to the building of bridges to traditional society—to the planning of an infrastructure of alternative institutions and opportunities for the meaningful exercise of rights and roles—as to actual, direct confrontation with the traditional system. And it entailed a decided preference for specialized and selective cadre formation (one that was directly relevant to the regime's immediate tasks as well as reasonably well suited to local needs), as distinguished from general social mobilization.

As has already been pointed out, these were but ideal notions of the requisites of systematic social engineering. Moreover, some of them were explicitly stated; some were merely hinted at; most were articulated in a fragmentary and often obscure way; most referred primarily to women rather than to society at large. But it is important to remember that they came to be aired in Central Asia at a time (between early 1928 and early 1930) when very different sensibilities were asserting themselves in communist ranks. Stalin's successful drive for power was accompanied not only by growing regimentation and repression, but also by a growing predilection for what Naum Jasny has aptly characterized as "bacchanalian planning." This meant, among other things, that in the hub of Soviet political command the U.S.S.R. as a whole tended to be envisioned as a vast battleground. On this field of battle, a determined revolutionary vanguard was expected to sweep aside all obstacles, ignoring socio-cultural and economic complexities as well as local conditions and peculiarities. The dominant mood was one of radical impatience, pressing for a maximalist solution to the problems of development and control.

It is all the more remarkable that, under these circumstances, some highly placed communist organizers had the courage of their convictions to call for caution and restraint in Central Asia, and to propose significantly different approaches to the problems of social transformation. It is equally remarkable that, in the heat of the developing battle, the Stalinist leadership was not averse to listening to such proposals. Available evidence suggests that the first unequivocal case (at least in public) for abandoning *khudzhum* and turning to systematic work in Central Asia was made early in 1928 by Alexandra Artiukhina, the head of the central Zhenotdel. As we have seen, both the title and tone of her article ("From 'assault' to systematic work . . .") in *Kommunistka*, the main journal of the Women's Department, signaled a hard-headed preference—which must have been shared by at least some of Artiukhina's colleagues in the party's Secretariat and Orgburo—for cutting losses by admitting defeat, studying its causes, and retreating to more modest though also safer and more productive tasks.[114]

However, this argument was notable more for its forceful hortatory quality than for the specificity of proposed alternatives. It presented in a forthright manner and in vivid detail an anatomy of failure in Central Asia.[115] It implied that the foremost value of the experiment with assault in the area lay in teaching the party how *not* to do battle in a Moslem traditional milieu. It left the impression that to turn to systematic work meant, first of all, to learn as much as possible about the practical implications of revolutionary tasks in concrete social situations. It meant to learn how to involve female masses in Soviet enterprises in personally meaningful and locally acceptable ways; how to conduct "[step-by-step] consolidation of attained gains"; how to structure "long-term [commitments]" to social rebuilding in place of the "[spasmodic,] one-day [attacks]" that characterized *khudzhum*. But this was just about as far as the proposals went.

It was Nadezhda Krupskaia who gave expression, some months later, to what was probably the most original and far-reaching argument for systematic work at that time. She did so in a keynote address to the Fourth All-Union (Zhenotdel) Conference of Party Organizers among Eastern Women, on December 10, 1928, in Moscow.[116] She rejected administrative assault as a revolutionary

[114] See Ar-na, *Ka*, 1, 1928, pp. 57-63.

[115] Artiukhina's argument is discussed (together with parallel views) in the introductory section ("Implications of Massive Enforcement and Repression") of this chapter.

[116] See Krupskaia, *Ka*, 12, 1928, pp. 5-12.

361

strategy in terms very much akin to those used by Lenin almost a decade earlier.[117] She saw assault as an expression of rigid and heedless political reductionism (*shablonnost'*), as a desire to cast all life as quickly as possible in a single mold, leading to the mechanical (and coercive) transplantation of stereotyped operational patterns from one region to another, in this case, from central Russia to the Soviet East. As she put it, "One cannot [and must not] impose a dead level on everyone. One cannot apply a single measure to all [people, societies, and cultures, and judge them by it]. . . . [One cannot approach the reconstruction of human lives] from an abstract, moralistic point of view. . . . [We] cannot always get what we want just by issuing a decree."[118] The methods implicit in such a drive—the methods of "attack," "assault," "storm"—belonged to military strategy of an "earlier [and rather] primitive" kind. The circumstances of engaging unfamiliar and resilient socio-cultural systems demanded, first of all, the recognition of "complexity." While the principles of a military offensive were indeed applicable to the tasks of female emancipation—and, concurrently, of disrupting a primordial way of life—the complexity of religious, tribal, and communal factors tied in with female statuses and roles in Central Asia required a "[more modern] military approach" than that adopted in *khudzhum*. Enduring victory would come from "step-by-step . . . penetration of . . . the enemy's positions," from "systematic pressure." Such pressure had to be preceded and accompanied by painstaking ideological, organizational, and economic groundwork. It required a sense of appropriate nuances and "sequences," and a serious concern for "work in depth," i.e., a concern for discerning "[actual human] needs," and thus recognizing and influencing the "roots" of a social organization's vitality and cohesiveness, and not merely surface manifestations.[119]

Thus, while Krupskaia's address was for the most part cautiously worded, and was replete with vaguely assenting references to the current party line, its crucial segments bore all the marks of an intellectual and moral crisis. Lenin's widow in effect rejected some of the most important premises underlying the notion of a revolution from above. She rejected a revolution by administrative command, especially when it involved a sweeping, dogmatic, and ruthless assault on human communities and sensibilities. Hers was,

[117] See Chapter Two of this study.
[118] Krupskaia, *Ka*, 12, 1928, pp. 8, 10-12.
[119] Ibid., p. 12.

quite obviously, a plea for gradualism, and for toleration of a modicum of social and cultural pluralism. It was an urgent plea for respect for, and sensitive adaptation to, local conditions and peculiarities. It appears to have been an argument for an essentially non-violent approach to traditional institutions and taboos.

The tone and substance of Krupskaia's address assume especially great significance when viewed against the background of the attendant circumstances. It would seem that Krupskaia was not only restating Lenin's earlier warnings against the tactics of military communism and Russian chauvinism.[120] She was giving expression to views and sensibilities that could have been easily shared by Nikolai Bukharin, her late husband's, and Stalin's, erstwhile comrade-in-arms. She was doing this after Bukharin's plea (on September 30, 1928) for gradual rather than forced-draft socialist development—one that was "balanced," "systematic," "[mindful of] limits," "carefully thought out"—had been summarily rejected.[121] She was also doing this shortly after Bukharin himself had been assailed (and humiliatingly defeated) as the leader of "right-wing deviationism," and as Stalin's arch-enemy.

At the same time, she could have had few illusions about her own future in the party: ever since the days of Lenin's final illness, she had had to live with the memory of brutal treatment at Stalin's hands, and with the memory as well of her husband's secret (and futile) warnings about the consequences of permitting Stalin to consolidate his hold on the machinery of power in the party. Thus, with a keen and no doubt bitter awareness of the political repressions accelerating in the wake of Stalin's rise to power, and with Stalin's henchmen[122] prominently represented in her audience, Krupskaia in all likelihood attempted to do more than offer some comments on the emancipation of Asian women. She may have tried to use this occasion as one of the few (and last) opportunities available to her for a public (albeit veiled) indictment of the extremist, totalitarian propensities asserting themselves under Stalin's aegis in every facet of Soviet life. Needless to say, where the direc-

---

[120] See, e.g., Lenin's letter to Caucasian communists (regarding the need for "caution," "circumspect" action, "systematic" approaches to socialism), in *Lenin o Druzhbe*, pp. 318-20.

[121] See Bukharin's "Notes of an Economist" (Sept. 30, 1928), translated by B. D. Wolfe, cited in R. V. Daniels, *A Documentary History of Communism* (New York, 1960), Vol. I, pp. 313 ff.

[122] For example, Yaroslavsky, who also addressed the Conference.

tion of the system as a whole was concerned, she was quite power-less to intervene in any other way.

Krupskaia's address in December, 1928, was unusual not only for its courage but also for its analytical style, given the time and place in which it was delivered. Much of it was couched in terms which, it is safe to assume, very few (if any) Soviet communists could have dared to use under the circumstances. It may be said that, for the most part, her argument was concerned with a problem central to revolutionary politics in a relatively intact traditional milieu: how, and to what extent, political power may be deliberate-ly used in destroying customary societal linkages, in undermining traditional solidarities, and in transferring human loyalties to the revolutionary regime. However, unlike most of the Bolshevik lead-ership, Krupskaia posed this problem not in terms of what and who needed to be attacked (and with how much force) but in terms of what the regime could and had to offer to the target population in order to attract it to the Soviet fold. Thus, she emphasized not the deliberate destruction of traditional unities but the provision of ac-ceptable substitutes for these unities that would cause their ultimate dissolution. In other words, instead of concentrating on the tactical aspects of short-term coercion and control, she proposed to con-centrate on root-causes of traditional behavior and on fundamental long-term solutions. Accordingly, her discussion of the issues at stake was singularly free of stereotyped ideological references to class conflict, or to counterrevolutionaries, deviationists, saboteurs, and other alleged enemies of the people.

Krupskaia's argument may be reconstructed as follows. It was senseless to view traditional communities based on kinship and re-ligion merely as expressions of a plot on the part of upper classes to enslave, exploit, and stupefy the masses. These communities "maintain such a solid hold [upon human beings] because [they] . . . serve certain [human] needs [material as well as emotional]." They served these needs because they provided even the lowliest among their members—including women—with what was, in ef-fect, an all-encompassing "social security" system.[123] In such a sys-

[123] Krupskaia did not hesitate to use, in this connection, the official Soviet term, *sobes* (*sotsial'noe obespechenie*), which referred to the entire spectrum of governmental arrangements concerning social security and welfare. Nor did she hesitate to argue her case primarily on the basis of her personal experience—partly in exile with Lenin—in Roman Catholic and Russian

tem, an individual could find "moral support" in times of general calamity and personal grief; "social protection of labor," by way of frequent and elaborately staged days of rest and religious holidays; a form of "health insurance," provided for by customs circumscribing unduly harmful modes of social interaction; as well as satisfying "aesthetic outlets for emotional experience." The emotional outlets (found, for example, in communal performance of religious rites), in combination with other dimensions of collective experience and mutual support, helped to reinforce a traditional community's "organizing principle," that is, its internal cohesion. These, then, were the real "roots" of traditional social solidarity: at least some of the salient functions performed by traditional institutions reflected and responded to deeply felt human needs, and were valued as such in a traditional milieu. In such circumstances, women as well as men could be mobilized and their loyalties and cooperation ultimately won only if and when the Soviet system learned to appeal to their innermost "self-interest," by offering them irresistible functional substitutes for the ties, perquisites, and certainties they clung to in the traditional fold.[124]

Of course, such a definition of the important issues was a far cry from the increasingly dogmatic and demonological perceptions characterizing official discourse at that time. In arguing for systematic work, Krupskaia argued, above all else, for conscientious study and sympathetic understanding of local life-styles as a prerequisite for informed and rational action. In urging painstaking groundwork—psychological as well as material—before each decisive leap, and in insisting on careful planning and testing of important departures and on patient collation of experience, Krupskaia was stressing the need for policies and institutions that were able to perform locally valued functions, that were not grossly offensive to local sensibilities, and that were informed by an awareness of the limits of political action. There can be little doubt that, in taking such a position, she was stressing the importance of adhering to and translating into practice some of Lenin's relatively moderate (albeit fragmentary) notions on this score.[125] She was

---

Orthodox milieus. She seemed to have little use for dogmatic Marxist or Bolshevik formulations in this matter.

[124] See Krupskaia, *Ka*, 12, 1928, pp. 8-11.

[125] See Chapter Two of this study.

also re-emphasizing a need (for investing on a large scale in an especially suited infrastructure) that had been specifically recognized by the Thirteenth Congress of the Communist Party in May, 1924,[126] but had been largely neglected in the intervening years.

How the Stalinist leadership reacted to Krupskaia's appeal we do not know. We do know that she was increasingly isolated in the years that followed, and that she was removed from all but purely ceremonial tasks where her affinal tie with Lenin could be appropriately exploited for the purposes of the regime's legitimation. But we also know that, in the months preceding and following her address, a number of responsible communist analysts and field-organizers showed that they shared her concerns in many ways, although, as we shall see, none of them had the will and capacity to justify their proposals in terms as blunt as hers.[127]

Moreover, on May 25, 1929, there came what was apparently the most important indication of high-echelon official attitudes in this matter. In its resolution on the performance of communist organizations in Uzbekistan at that time, the Central Committee of the party not only proposed to put an end to the most extreme manifestations of *khudzhum* in Central Asia.[128] It indicated, albeit in general terms, a decided preference for an approach—careful correlation of cultural, economic, and political initiatives at the grassroots,

---

[126] See the introductory section in Chapter Six of this study.

[127] For some explicit or implicit reminders of the need to study carefully—"scientifically"—every aspect of life in Russia's Asian borderlands, see, e.g., Kalachev, *Ka*, 8, 1927, pp. 56-57; Amosov, *Ka*, 14, 1929, p. 23; Dimanshtein, *RN*, 1, 1930, p. 19; Karpych, *RN*, 1, 1930, pp. 101-105; Nukhrat, *RN*, 3, 1933, p. 48.

For parallel reminders to keep specific local conditions in mind, see Nukhrat, *Ka*, 1, 1928, pp. 53-56, and *Ka*, 19, 1929, pp. 34-38; Maksimova, *Ka*, 6, 1928, p. 95; Liubimova, *Ka*, 9, 1928, pp. 78-82; Khodzhaev, *SS* (35), 1929, p. 59; Niurina, *Parandzha*, pp. 10-13. Cf. Pal'vanova, *DSV*, p. 103.

For some perceptions of the requisites of planned, carefully attuned mobilizational work, see Nukhrat, *Ka*, 6, 1928, p. 78, *RN*, 3, 1933, pp. 46-48, and *VMV*, pp. 36-37; Ar-na, *Ka*, 1, 1928, pp. 57-63; Amosov, *Ka*, 14, 1929, p. 26; Akopov, *RN*, 4-5, 1930, pp. 67-68; *Bezb* (ill.), 22, 1930, p. 4. Cf. Pal'vanova, *DSV*, pp. 41, 101-102.

Some of these perceptions expressed themselves in demands that the work with women of the Soviet East be included in the five-year plan, since only in this fashion could such work receive proper attention and systematic treatment. See Brutser, *KP*, 4-5, 1930, pp. 91-93; Dimanshtein, *RN*, 1, 1930, p. 18.

[128] See the concluding part of an earlier section (esp. "Unveiling") in this chapter.

especially where Moslem women were concerned—that Krupskaia and others had associated with systematic work. While the formal resolution made no mention of concrete alternative means and institutions for this purpose, there can be little doubt that it was either preceded or accompanied by detailed directives to republican organs. To be sure, the efforts initiated at that time fell far short of those urged by proponents of genuinely innovative and sensitively attuned actions in Central Asia. But even the watered-down compromise solutions supported by the party's leadership involved significant if quiet concessions to some of the salient propositions immanent in Krupskaia's and Artiukhina's arguments. Most important, they involved a serious high-level commitment to a specialized and reasonably coherent and coordinated program of action. This program was specifically devoted to planning a new social infrastructure, one that was attuned to the needs of Moslem women and that could draw on significant budgetary allocations by the state.[129]

The multifaceted effort materializing in Central Asia in the late 1920's may be said to have reflected the regime's recognition that, in some cases, specialized mediating institutions were an inescapable necessity. Such institutions must have seemed necessary even if they introduced unwelcome elements of diversity and potential autonomy in an avowedly unitary state, and even if they violated the principle of the state's direct access to and total permeation of society, by intervening to some extent between the individual and the state. They must have seemed necessary because the state could not attain its goals of transformation, development, and control without some intimate, influential, and productive contacts with the population, and because such desirable linkages between the revolutionary center and the traditional periphery could not materialize automatically once old formal (legal and other) structures were destroyed—could not come *ex nihilo*, as it were. Most obviously, suitable mediating realms were recognized as essential because of their potentially important role in absorbing and channeling the mass of human energies released from traditional grooves in the process of social mobilization.

It would seem that precisely these premises were reflected in the shift from revolution by decree (hence from above) to systematic social engineering. Such engineering clearly involved a commitment

[129] One of the first hints of firm and significant budgetary appropriations may be found in Khodzhaev's report on the Third Congress of Soviets of Uzbekistan. See Khodzhaev, *SS* (35), 1929, p. 59.

to patient, circumspect, and largely pragmatic management of social change, primarily through persuasion and through provision of tangible and attractive alternatives to the traditional way of life, including a diversified, locally adapted network of auxiliary institutions sponsored by the regime. This network came to incorporate, in the course of its intensive buildup between late 1928 and early 1930, a series of associational, vocational, and social-service units designed especially for Moslem women. The structure and functions of the new auxiliary infrastructure reflected to a considerable extent the operational criteria that had been considered desirable by proponents of systematic work in the latter part of the 1920's. This meant that, in the broadest terms, the new institutional network was to serve the cause of deliberately graduated political mobilization and socialization, of purposively adapted economic participation and cultural tutelage, and of selective recruitment. That these criteria were taken seriously by communist organizers, and were often consistently and even imaginatively applied, may be seen from a brief summary of official proposals and actions leading to the formation of the special female-oriented network in Central Asia.[130]

The criterion of voluntarism. It followed from the party's accelerated drive, in the late 1920's, against all spontaneous and hence potentially autonomous and pluralistic social forces (including its decision to delimit the role of the Zhenotdel and of voluntary associations)[131] that the new infrastructure in Central Asia would not be permitted to develop the undesirable characteristics of such forces. Yet repeated representations by communist organizers in Central Asia apparently persuaded the party's leadership to allow for some exceptions to the rule.

The following reasoning seems to have served as a basis for an emerging consensus on this score. In Moslem traditional milieus, the very conditions of access to women were infinitely complicated by local custom, by male jealousy, and by a sense of fear as well as sin on the part of the women themselves. Hence the need for creating conditions that would not "frighten girls [and women] away" from the new institutions in the first place. Hence also the need for

---

[130] A detailed description and analysis of the operation of this network will be found in a separate study, now in preparation (see Note 19, Chapter Six).

[131] See the section on "Role of the Zhenotdel" *supra*, in this chapter.

368

forms and methods of approach that would assure "personal . . . contact," that would not stand "in sharp contradiction to local [mores]," that would be sensitively attuned to the Moslem woman's "language, psyche, and way of life," and that could thus "earn her respect and trust." Accordingly, it was important for the new network to contain at least some dimensions of participation that resembled those of voluntary associations. In practice, this meant that the new infrastructure was to offer an arena of participation where Moslem women would not be subject to the demands and discipline of the regime's main organizational framework (such as the party, soviets, and Komsomol). The auxiliary network was to be one where women could come and go, veiled or unveiled, as they pleased; where they could bring their children with them if they wished; where their activities could be improvised as well as organized; in short, where they could have a sense of free and easy fellowship, a community of purpose, as well as an opportunity to air personal grievances and obtain counsel.[132]

The criterion of "mass" versus "class." As we have seen, the regime's growing emphasis on class struggle in the course of *khudzhum* inevitably led to demands that work with Moslem women, too, be class oriented, i.e., that women who participated in Soviet enterprises be screened, and included or excluded, on the basis of their social background.[133] It would seem that in actuality official policy taking shape in the late 1920's reflected a compromise, and found expression in the following terms. While a "classless" approach to mass-work was indeed ideologically and politically inadmissible, it was a contradiction in terms to insist on a class-approach to Central Asian women. Whether in a rich or in a poor household, girls and women were "equally enslaved" by clans, fathers, and husbands.[134] Moreover, in Central Asia the party confronted a milieu in which "the authoritarian principle is very

[132] For various nuances of this reasoning, see V. K., *Ka*, 9, 1925, p. 70; Ross, *Ka*, 8, 1926, pp. 57-58; Shirman, *Ka*, 4, 1927, pp. 73-74; Sudakov, *Ka*, 8, 1927, p. 26; Arykova, *Ka*, 6, 1928, pp. 81-83; Z. P., *Ka*, 6, 1928, pp. 84-85; Liubimova, *Ka*, 8, 1928, pp. 75-78; Nukhrat, *VS*, 1, 1929, pp. 5-7; *BSE*, Vol. 25, 1935, p. 255. Cf. Pal'vanova, *DSV*, p. 49.

[133] See the introductory sections (esp. "The Danger of Subversive Superstructures") in Chapter Six of this study. In particular, see Zhukova, *Ka*, 10, 1928, pp. 79-80.

[134] See Mokrinskii, *SP*, 3(27), 1927, pp. 115-16. Cf. Vorshev, *RN*, 12 (58), 1934, p. 72.

369

strongly developed [and entrenched]" and where, therefore, "the example . . . of those who are trusted and respected . . . plays an [exceptionally] great role" in inducing the mass to follow suit. Hence, from a purely instrumental point of view, an attempt to apply a consistent class orientation to native women would deprive the party of influential political allies and agents, since it would oblige it to rely solely on "unstable" and "marginal" elements among women, on those who had, for one or another reason, been "thrown out of the grooves of life."[135] Therefore, on the one hand, political "purification" of female ranks in the Soviet fold was to be delimited primarily to leading echelons, permitting the regime to weed out potential "class-enemies" from responsible positions in the main apparatus and in the auxiliary network, and to train for such posts only those women who came from a reliable "class." On the other hand, it was important for the new Soviet institutions at the grassroots to be able, in day-to-day operation, to approach and attract women *qua* women, i.e., as a "mass," a stratum with the lowest status in a Moslem traditional society.[136]

The criterion of functional diversity and integration. As was suggested earlier,[137] the buildup of a special female-oriented institutional network was viewed with misgivings by the more militant party cadres for several interrelated reasons. These had to do, in part, with the possibility that the network might perpetuate overly spontaneous participation-patterns, lead to the consolidation of potentially autonomous and hence subversive superstructures, and encourage the emergence of a feminist movement. Suspicions of this kind were aroused especially when some of the new structures showed signs of developing into complex, multi-functional, well integrated, and internally coordinated institutions. (This was true, for example, in cases where what was originally a women's club also came to include under one roof services pertaining to legal and medical aid, labor recruitment, literacy, and welfare, all of them coordinated by the local Zhenotdel.) Tendencies of this kind were

---

[135] In all likelihood, this referred primarily to widows, orphans, and divorcées, as well as to homeless, unhappy, or otherwise maladjusted girls and women. See Niurina, *Ka*, 4, 1925, p. 81. Cf. Arykova, *Ka*, 6, 1928, pp. 81 ff.; Z. P., *Ka*, 6, 1928, pp. 84 ff.

[136] See Nukhrat, *Ka*, 11, 1928, pp. 57-58.

[137] See the introductory sections (esp. "The Danger of Subversive Superstructures") of Chapter Six, *supra*, as well as the section on "Role of Zhenotdel" in this chapter, *supra*.

denounced as manifestations of a pernicious functional imperialism, leading to self-sufficient organizational frameworks that competed with, and impinged on the jurisdictional realms of, various state organs and restricted the latter's control in important domains.

Given its growing sensitivity on this issue, it is noteworthy that the party resisted the temptation to respond consistently, i.e., to fragment the new structures altogether. We know that one of the party's responses on this score was to delimit the role of the Zhenotdel (and then Zhensektor) in Central Asia, and to disperse some of its responsibilities among local soviets as well as among various commissariats and other state agencies. Thus, a number of functional units serving girls and women came under the jurisdiction of commissariats of health, education, and social security, among others, which was bound to make integration and centralized administration of the infrastructure difficult.

But this was just about as far as the party was apparently willing to go. Available evidence shows that female-oriented structures forming in Central Asia in the late 1920's often came to combine under one roof a great variety of auxiliary units, ranging from women's clubs, literacy, drama, and hygiene circles, and medical dispensaries to women's stores, handicraft cooperatives, legal aid units, and savings banks. It would seem that this structural integration of diverse functions went hand in hand with a modicum of internal coordination, at least in the sense of correlating the policies and operations of relevant units. While the lines of coordinative authority were necessarily blurred, the Zhenotdel/Zhensektor seems to have retained a measure of overall (if only *ad hoc* and informal) guidance and supervision, apparently shared in some cases (though to an unspecified extent) with local Bytovye Sektsii and K.U.T.B. units.[138]

It is a safe assumption that the party's Women's Department could continue to play a broadly coordinative role, and could even repeatedly exert pressure for strengthening this role (in spite of explicit administrative delimitation by the party) for two basic reasons: first, because of the distinct vacuum in supervisory authority created by the dispersal of administrative responsibilities among various agencies; and second, because the Zhenotdel/Zhensektor

[138] Details on the operation and supervision of the entire auxiliary network will be found in a separate study, now in preparation (see Note 19, Chapter Six).

371

had had a decade (1919-1929) of specialization and institutional-ization, commanded a network of highly motivated female organ-izers reaching all the way down to the primary party cell in villages and towns, and had the party's authority and resources behind it.

Such a compromise arrangement tended to be justified on the following grounds. The utilization by girls and women of newly created institutions presented the regime with unique opportunities for recruiting and organizing potential cultural and political con-verts. But the degree to which these opportunities actually material-ized, permitting the regime to consolidate its gains, depended on the extent of well-diversified preparation on the part of the party-state.[139] The nature and diversity of functions performed by Soviet institutions had to respond to actual female needs in local milieus. The most pressing of these needs concerned medical care relevant to mothers and their children, basic consumer goods, basic and locally relevant skills (including immediate opportunities to use them), elementary reading skills, instruction in hygiene, and oppor-tunities for entertainment and companionship. In short (to quote several communist officials) Moslem women needed not only the party's "sensitive and tactful [attention]," but also its "concrete . . . rational . . . yet sympathetic assistance," "sensible counsel," "moral support."[140]

Yet even with the best of intentions, plans for concretely re-sponsive structures were found to come to naught without taking into account the scarcity of resources and suitable personnel, the nature of the milieu, as well as the special difficulty of attracting local women to Soviet enterprises in the first place. These factors definitely militated against the fragmentation of grassroots enter-prises. If anything, they made it imperative that such enterprises be multi-faceted and complex to the point of self-sufficiency, and that their component units be physically contiguous. Diversity and mutual proximity was bound to optimize the utilization of person-nel, especially in Central Asia's vast and rugged terrain, with its

[139] See the reasoning in Nukhrat, *Ka*, 6, 1928, p. 78. Cf. Ar-na, *Ka*, 1, 1928, pp. 57-58; Krupskaia, *Ka*, 12, 1928, pp. 5 ff.; Vagabov, *Islam i Zhenshchina*, pp. 103-105.

[140] See Seifi, *Ka*, 4, 1925, p. 78; S-i, *Ka*, 9, 1925, p. 28; Safadri, *Ka*, 11, 1928, pp. 31-32; Davydova, *Ka*, 11, 1928, p. 68; Smirnova, *Ka*, 8, 1929, p. 27; Pal'vanova, *DSV*, pp. 101, 103-104.

Cf. Ibragimova, *Ka*, 10, 1925, p. 88; Nukhrat, *Ka*, 1, 1928, pp. 53-56, *RN*, 3(36), 1933, pp. 52-53, *VMV*, pp. 7-19 (*passim*); Abidova, *RN*, 3(73), 1936, p. 48.

widely scattered and partly mobile population. In nomadic locales, for example, one multi-functional unit (a mobile "red yurta," or tent, dispensing medical, educational, juridical, and vocational assistance to women) could easily roam the steppe together with the clans it was designed to serve. But most important, native women attracted to (or permitted by their family to accept) one kind of service (for example, medical) could at the same time be induced to utilize other services—and hence be exposed to other cultural and political influences—if these were readily available on the premises.[141]

The criterion of practicality and relevance. This criterion was, of course, implicit in most if not all Soviet considerations concerning work with Moslem women. But beginning in the late 1920's, the emphasis on practicality as well as psycho-cultural relevance seems to have gained strong official backing as a distinct and important desideratum. This clearly underscored the close affinity between Krupskaia's arguments and official thinking in this matter. One of the lessons of *khudzhum* the party leadership proposed to consider seriously was that some practical modes of female mobilization could not be dismissed merely because they smacked of "feminism." Instrumental grounds alone required that the initial organizational approaches be sensibly adjusted to the imagery and level of expectations of local inhabitants.

It was now assumed that, given the Moslem woman's deep involvement in the mores and taboos of the traditional system, and her many-sided dependence on that system, the new Soviet infrastructure could be successfully rooted only if it was inherently attractive and useful to a native woman. It had to be attractive in its fulfillment of deeply felt aesthetic and emotional needs, and useful in its primary emphasis on everyday material concerns and necessities, on the familiar and the practical—in short, on what was to be viewed as a Moslem woman's "sum of life." "Abstractions," including political abstractions, and "abstract problems that are [intellectually unmanageable] and quite distant from a woman's private life," were to be avoided. Soviet-sponsored enterprises at the grassroots were to concentrate on improving a woman's aware-

---

[141] See, e.g., Seifi, *Ka*, 9, 1925, p. 76. Cf. Akopov, *RN*, 5, 1930, pp. 67-68: Vagabov, *Islam i Zhenschina*, pp. 103-105. For arguments concerning the role of "red yurtas" in the nomadic countryside, see Khairova, *Ka*, 1, 1928, pp. 68-70; Burlova, *Ka*, 8, 1928, p. 90; I. Ch., *KP*, 2-3, 1928, pp. 254-62; Gelis, *KP*, 6, 1929, pp. 35-36.

ness and capabilities in such mundane matters as upbringing of children, health and hygiene, nutrition and food, gardening and animal husbandry. To approach a woman "through [a cake of] soap" was more sensible than bombarding her with political slogans, just as assistance with childbirth and trachoma was more relevant at this stage than administered desegregation and unveiling. At the same time, it was the responsibility of a specialized network to provide a native woman with the chance to satisfy her hunger for companionship in communities marked by female isolation and loneliness. In a Soviet-sponsored milieu, a woman was to be able to confront and subdue her fears and superstitions and thus gradually to overcome and be done with traditional taboos. She had to have an opportunity to find some joy and luster—in surroundings made "artistically attractive . . . impressive . . . breathtaking . . . bright" by Soviet communications media—that would bring relief from the grayness of her life and that would, at the same time, provide emotional engagement powerful enough to compete with that offered by religious and tribal-communal rituals.[142]

As Anna Nukhrat characteristically perceived this, clearly implying that responsible officialdom shared her views:

> [It is out of the question] to stuff [the head] of a backward native woman, [even if she was elevated to the position of a Women's Delegate], with problems of world significance. . . . It is imperative . . . to remember that she is used to think in [simple and concrete] images; having never seen a city or a factory, she may not understand at all the meaning . . . of proletarian dictatorship and class struggle. . . . Hence, [first of all] each and every issue of the [Soviet mobilizational] program must be endowed with a [sharply] practical bias . . . [and illustrated with the simplest possible posters that a native woman could immediately comprehend]. . . . Thus, one needs to teach her to become cognizant of her situation, of her enslavement, of her cultural backwardness, [teach her to comprehend the meaning] of dirt, illiteracy . . . child mortality . . . contagious diseases. One needs to habituate her in the perception that, beyond the limits of her

---

[142] See Nukhrat, *Ka*, 8, 1927, p. 20; Krupskaia, *Ka*, 12, 1928, pp. 5-12, and "Rabotnitsa i Religiia," in *O Rabote Sredi Zhenshchin*, pp. 50-55 (which seems to have provided an early model for arguments and proposals in 1928 and 1929. Cf. Niurina, *Ka*, 4, 1925, p. 80; V. K., *Ka*, 9, 1925, pp. 68-70; Zavarian, *Ka*, 12, 1925, p. 28; Liubimova, *Ka*, 7, 1926, p. 70; Prishchepchik, *Ka*, 9, 1926, p. 76; Shirman, *Ka*, 4, 1927, p. 76; Nukhrat, *Ka*, 7, 1927, p. 36, and *VMV*, pp. 7-37 (*passim*).

aul [village] and of the particular mountain [-chain] or steppe she knows, there is another world, there are other people, that she lives in a proletarian state upon whose life her own private life depends. . . . Only then, [basing oneself firmly on such an approach], tying in every question with a [Moslem] woman's private [everyday] life, with the life of her native village, [would it be possible] to lead her—and that cautiously, as if holding her by the hand—towards the affairs of state.[143]

Practicality and relevance carried other implications as well, and these were explicitly considered by communist analysts. Integrated structures, permitting the efficient correlation of material and cultural approaches, could be responsive to female needs while, at the same time, also serving the most pressing needs of the regime.

First, Moslem women could be induced to attend club-meetings (without arousing the suspicions and hostility of their menfolk) if given the opportunity to learn (for example, in affiliated homemakers' circles) about more efficient, and especially more profitable, ways to manage their own households, and thus supplement the income of their menfolk. Once attracted by such tangible material incentives, they could be apprised of the advantages of cooperation, and inducted into garden, handicraft, and consumers' cooperatives attuned to local resources and to the state's needs. Membership in such cooperatives would enable women to buy, produce, and sell products (such as various food products, silk and cotton goods, and rugs) without male mediation, and thus prepare them technically and psychologically for entrance into collective farms as well as into socialized industry and commerce.[144] At the same time, cooperative production units, if tied in with congenially maintained clubs, would facilitate the process of instilling in their members relevant "production habits," and thus speed their arrival in the industrial labor force. Such habits could not be fostered by agitation alone; they could materialize—as Marx had postulated— "on the basis of the woman's new production roles in the overall [system of] production."[145]

Second, an institutional network combining not only clubs and

[143] Nukhrat, *Ka*, 7, 1927, p. 36.

[144] See Nukhrat, *Ka*, 1, 1928, pp. 53-56, and *RN*, 3(36), 1933, pp. 46, 51; Moskalev, *Uzbechka*, pp. 38-43. Cf. Liubimova, *VPG*, pp. 29-35, 44; Pal'vanova, *DSV*, p. 86.

[145] See Akopov, *RN*, 4-5, 1930, pp. 67-68; Nukhrat, *RN*, 3(36), 1933, p. 51; Pal'vanova, *DSV*, p. 104. Cf. Karl Marx, *Capital: A Critique of Political Economy* (New York, Modern Library, n.d.), p. 536.

375

cooperatives but also hygiene circles, mother-and-child clinics, and crèches or day-care centers could have far-reaching effects in several related realms. Women who might otherwise hesitate to come to a Soviet institution would feel encouraged to do so (and would more easily obtain the consent of husbands, fathers, and kinsmen) if the institution held out the prospect of tangible care for children. (While highly prized in Moslem communities, children were also extremely vulnerable to locally prevalent diseases; hence the responsiveness even in the traditional hinterland to child-oriented care.) Treating women together with children in mother-and-child clinics would help to effect a break in the chain of Central Asia's most widespread and destructive diseases, such as malaria, trachoma, tuberculosis, and syphilis, which, in turn, would cut infant and female mortality, provide for population growth, and contribute to the emergence of a hardier and larger labor force, both male and female.[146]

Likewise, exposing native girls and women to instruction in hygiene while they worked in local food cooperatives carried important benefits beyond the confines of the local community. With Central Asia slated to become the Soviet Union's major food- as well as fiber-supplier, sanitary habits acquired voluntarily in a club-like atmosphere carried the promise of purer milk, butter, and meat, and of cleaner fruits and vegetables, for the Soviet Union as a whole.[147]

Moreover, it was to be expected that children's crèches and mother-and-child clinics would not only release more women for work in fields, cooperatives, and factories,[148] as in European Russia. In Central Asian conditions, these components of an integrated network could play a unique role. As visualized by a number of Soviet analysts, both women and children frequenting day-care centers and clinics could be expected to "carry back" to their homes new sanitary habits as well as new attitudes to their social environment. In particular, they were likely sooner or later to cease relying on traditional sources of medical help and moral support,

---

[146] See Kasparova, *Ka*, 7, 1925, p. 90; Nukhrat, *Ka*, 10-11, 1926, p. 79; Butuzova, *Ka*, 9, 1927. Cf. Berin and Yoshpe, *RN*, 3(85), 1937, pp. 67-70.

[147] See Kasparova, *Ka*, 7, 1925, p. 90; Shirman, *Ka*, 4, 1927, pp. 74, 76, 78; Dzasokhov, *RN*, 2-3, 1931, pp. 69-70.

[148] See, e.g., Kolychev, *SS*, 9(50), 1930, pp. 126-27; Sazonova and Chernova, *RN* (49), 1934, p. 53. Cf. "V Presid. Ts.I.K. Turkm. S.S.R." *SS* (91), 1934, p. 109.

thus weakening the influence of *mullahs*, healers, and soothsayers, and ridding native communities of "wild superstitions" and "barbarian customs." Such shifts were bound to have long-term consequences not only for cultural patterns but also for politics in the area.[149]

The criterion of political utility. Emphasizing practical concerns rather than political sloganeering did not mean abandoning basic political objectives. Anna Nukhrat made this clear in interpreting Molotov's dicta at the Fifteenth Congress of the Communist Party (December, 1927): female-oriented structures formed a network of new and indispensable "cultural foci" in Central Asia; there was an "intimate relationship" between the functions of such foci and the requisites of political as well as economic transformation under Soviet auspices.[150]

Specifically, the process of political socialization and ideological change required—as was repeatedly pointed out by responsible officials in the field—"regularity [of access]" to female masses. It also required conditions of contact that elicited the women's initiative and commitment and inspired gratitude and trust. Systematic, regularized, and trust-inspiring contacts could be assured, precisely, by institutions concerned with health, self-help, literacy, and entertainment, things that native women obviously valued most. By the same token, services demonstrating the regime's humanitarian concern, and providing an atmosphere of companionship as well as healing, were also those best suited to expose women to the tenets of Soviet political culture, and to make them especially receptive to the new norms. Thus, women could be best apprised of their new legal rights and social obligations (and of specific opportunities open to them in the new system) while receiving doctors' or nurses' care in a mother-and-child clinic. Similarly, girls and women enjoying their sojourn in clubs, tearooms, drama and literacy circles, and consumers' cooperatives designed especially for them could be sensitized to new political beliefs, and exposed to Soviet political recruitment, far more easily and subtly than under any other circumstances. That is why a diversified and integrated auxiliary network was, as one party analyst put it, of "definite [political] utility" in organizing female masses in Central Asia. This

[149] See Zavarian, *Ka*, 6, 1926, p. 68; Smirnova, *Ka*, 8, 1929, p. 27; Sazonova and Chernova, *RN* (49), 1934, pp. 53-54.
[150] See Nukhrat, *Ka*, 1, 1928, p. 53.

was all the more so because the party's *prime* organizational network at the grassroots, especially in the countryside, was unreliable and weak, to the extent that its authority, as distinguished from its power in the traditional milieu, was in many cases nonexistent. Under the circumstances, it was senseless to hamstring auxiliary organizational forms for women on the *a priori* grounds that they were overly "[unorthodox and] special . . . superstructures." Indeed, the party could not afford to be choosy: in many cases, these structures were literally *the sole foci* of political contact and influence the party had in the Central Asian hinterland. This meant that here they were "demanded by reality . . . by life itself." For that matter, in such a situation, "any forms and methods of [mass] work . . . that [responded to local needs and were] conducive to spreading the party's influence," beginning with carefully adapted "seedbeds of elementary culture," could be considered *ipso facto* "good."[151]

The criterion of selective and segregated cadre formation. Issues raised in connection with the functional diversity, practicality, and

---

[151] See Liubimova, *Ka*, 7, 1926, p. 70 (italics added); Niurina, *Ka*, 4, 1925, p. 80; V. K., *Ka*, 9, 1925, pp. 67-68; Ross, *Ka*, 8, 1926, pp. 57-58; A. N., *Ka*, 9, 1926, pp. 34-36; Nukhrat, *Ka*, 11, 1928, pp. 57-59.

Some of the reasons for Soviet difficulties in establishing a genuinely influential network in the countryside are discussed in Maiorova, *Ka*, 6, 1928, p. 88; and Pravda, *SS*, 12(41), 1929, pp. 105 ff. The role of mobile units for women in such a context, especially on the nomadic range, is discussed in some detail by Khairova, *Ka*, 1, 1928, pp. 68-70; Burlova, *Ka*, 8, 1928, p. 90; I. Ch., *KP*, 2-3, 1928, pp. 254-62; Gelis, *KP*, 6, 1929, pp. 35-36.

The requisites of regularized and trust-inspiring contacts in the process of political socialization are explicitly examined by Ross, *Ka*, 8, 1926, pp. 57-58. Cf. Prishchepchik, *Ka*, 9, 1926, pp. 76-77.

For Soviet expectations concerning the utilization of cultural, vocational, and medical services (among others) for political purposes, see, e.g., Kasparova, *Ka*, 7, 1925, p. 90; Prishchepchik, *Ka*, 12, 1925, p. 63, and *Ka*, 9, 1926, pp. 76-78; Shirman, *Ka*, 4, 1927, pp. 73, 80; Gubaidullina, *Ka*, 6, 1927, p. 58; Ar-na, *Ka*, 1, 1928, p. 60; Minina, *KP*, 1, 1930, pp. 46-48; Moskalev, *Uzbechka*, pp. 39-40. Cf. Pal'vanova, *DSV*, pp. 68-70, 73.

On most of these issues, explicit discussions are found primarily in publications that appeared between 1925 and 1927. All public documents dated later than this make largely the same argument, but only implicitly. It is a safe assumption that this was due to the obvious political sensitivity of the matter, especially at a time when the regime was attempting to formulate a policy of retrenchment in a highly volatile situation in Central Asia, and when there was a growing need to allay the suspicions of Moslem males concerning Soviet plans for mobilizing native women.

political utility of the infrastructure (as well as those pertaining to voluntarism, and to a mass- rather than class-approach) clearly denoted this matter of necessity: in order to succeed in its assigned tasks, the auxiliary network had to stress specialized and selective cadre formation rather than general social mobilization. This meant not only selective recruitment of indigenous female personnel but also its training in protected cultural islands. It also entailed the preservation, where necessary, of segregated facilities for Moslem women, even if this served to perpetuate for a time sexual segregation in most spheres of Central Asian life.

As Nukhrat put it (with the clear concurrence of authoritative party personnel), a sexually segregated institutional network for Moslem women, no matter how unorthodox it seemed, was indispensable in a milieu where a host of traditional taboos "separated people into [distinct] male and female worlds. . . ." While such arrangements under Soviet auspices could indeed be viewed as temporary, they could be needed as long as it would take for the "ancient [socio-cultural] traditions . . . to atrophy."[152] Until then, it was necessary not merely to discourage male participation in the women's units, but (in especially sensitive circumstances) to exclude men altogether[153]—thus, in effect, "isolating" the process of women's socialization from the male population.[154] This was required in order to reduce a woman's deeply embedded fears about violating traditional taboos. It was also essential for precluding the immediate enragement of male sensibilities: husbands and kinsmen who felt reassured that female participation in extra-familial activities did not involve contacts with other men were less likely to stand in their women's way. Moreover, in segregated situations women were more likely to create and to partake of a mutually supportive atmosphere and collectivity; they could share their emotional experiences—grievances as well as confidences—with each other and with female party personnel; they could play new roles

---

[152] See Nukhrat, *VMV*, p. 18, *Ka*, 12, 1927, pp. 41-44, *Ka*, 11, 1928, pp. 57-59, and *Ka*, 1, 1929, pp. 24-25. Cf. Yesova, "Protiv Parandzhi," in *ZVR*, pp. 372-73; Pal'vanova, *DSV*, pp. 66-67; Kasparova, *Ka*, 10, 1925, pp. 85-86; Ross, *Ka*, 8, 1926, pp. 57-58; Zavarian, *Ka*, 6, 1926, pp. 69-70; Liubimova, *Ka*, 11, 1927, pp. 74-75, and *Ka*, 2, 1928, p. 84; Sudakov, *Ka*, 8, 1927, p. 23; Khairova, *Ka*, 6, 1928, pp. 86-87; Smirnova, *Ka*, 8, 1928, pp. 82-83; Safadri, *Ka*, 11, 1928, p. 31; L'vov, *PN*, 4, 1935, pp. 54-60.

[153] See Nukhrat, *RN*, 3, 1933, p. 47. Cf. *BSE*, Vol. 25, 1932, p. 255; Kunitz, *Dawn Over Samarkand*, pp. 289 ff.

[154] See Yesova, "Protiv Parandzhi," in *ZVR*, p. 373.

and perform new functions with confidence; in short, they were more likely to become conscious of themselves as a separate and politically significant stratum.[155]

The regime's decision to encourage separate facilities for Moslem women within the special auxiliary network also found expression in related spheres. Between late 1928 and early 1931, exclusively female collective farm brigades were formed, as well as various workshops, domestic craft cooperatives, primary, secondary, and nursing schools, teachers' institutes, electoral facilities, and even Komsomol and Pioneer units.[156] Concurrently, the allocation of female labor and the training of female technical cadres in Central Asia assumed a definite pattern which received growing official encouragement in the early 1930's. This pattern clearly emphasized heavy (often exclusive) concentration of native women in cotton-growing, in rug-, silk-, textile-, clothing-, and food-production, and in health-, education-, and welfare-oriented professions.[157] In effect, then, a high degree of interdependence was established between associational forms and labor and professional recruitment patterns among Moslem women.

The training of selected female personnel in isolated and protected cultural islands became especially important in two contexts. First, beginning in 1929, small but apparently firm preferential quotas were officially established for preparing a nucleus of skilled industrial, administrative, and cultural cadres among native women —in effect, regardless of immediate need and cost.[158] This prepara-

[155] Various facets of this reasoning are explicitly or implicitly suggested in the preceding two footnotes as well as in Nukhrat, *OZV*, pp. 58-60; Butuzova, *Ka*, 9, 1927, p. 62; Nasurullin, *NKK*, 11-12, 1928, p. 273; Minina, *KP*, 1, 1931, p. 46. Cf. Kunitz, *Dawn Over Samarkand*, pp. 289 ff.

[156] See Sulaimanova, *ISGPU*, Vol. 2, pp. 238, 440-41; Vagabov, *Islam i Zhenshchina*, pp. 114-15; *ZVR*, pp. 373 ff.; M. P. Kim, *et al.*, eds. *Kul'turnaia Revoliutsiia v S.S.S.R., 1917-1965* (Moscow, 1967), p. 358; Liubimova, *VPG*, pp. 60-61; Pal'vanova, *DSV*, pp. 99-100; Karpov, *SS*, 11(28), 1928, pp. 61-69 (esp. p. 66), and *SS*, 6(35), 1929, pp. 64-68 (esp. p. 67); Karimova, *Ka*, 3, 1929, p. 43; Gladkovskii, *SS*, 5(34), 1929, pp. 166-69; Amosov, *Ka*, 14, 1929, pp. 26-27; Krylov, *SS*, 5(70), 1932, pp. 113, 115. See also Note 119 in this chapter, *supra*.

[157] The development of this pattern will be discussed in some detail in the context of a subsequent study (see Note 19, Chapter Six).

[158] The quotas were never clearly specified in public. See the Resolution of the Central Executive Committee of Uzbekistan (December, 1928) in "V Tsentral'nykh . . . ," *SS*, 4(33), 1929, pp. 157-58.

tion was to take place in suitably tailored programs in Tashkent and in large Russian industrial and urban centers, including Moscow and Leningrad, under the auspices of appropriate state commissariats. It seems to have been taken for granted that recruitment for such programs—involving departure for many months of training, often thousands of miles away from home and in a totally alien milieu—would have to concentrate on urban and relatively unattached women, since those who left under these circumstances could not hope to be taken back into the fold of traditional families and communities.[159]

Second, arrangements were quietly made to draw carefully selected Moslem girls and young women into special training centers and political schools run by the party. Available evidence suggests that these institutions, organized as boarding schools in or near Central Asia's largest cities, and completely isolated from traditionalist influences and threats, were designed to train females who were most disaffected from tradition or who were otherwise politically reliable and promising. This included orphans, young widows, runaway child brides, children (some apparently illegitimate) of native female communists whose duties made care of their offspring difficult, as well as children whose parents had been murdered in the course of the traditionalist backlash accompanying *khudzhum*. It would seem that special emphasis was placed in these schools on preparing party cadres not only for organizational and propaganda work among women but also for service in the judicial and police apparatuses of Central Asian republics.[160]

[159] For early Soviet experience in such cases, see, e.g., Liubimova, *VPG*, pp. 40-41. Cf. Nukhrat, *VMV*, pp. 17-20.

[160] For explicit and implicit indications of this trend, including its earliest manifestations, see Gurko-Kriazhin, *NV*, 7, 1925, pp. 369-75; Kasparova, *Ka*, 7, 1925, pp. 91-92; Zavarian, *Ka*, 6, 1926, p. 66; Ross, *Ka*, 8, 1926, pp. 57-58; Moskalev, *Uzbechka*, p. 47; Liubimova, *Ka*, 2, 1927, pp. 50-51, and *VPG*, pp. 40-42, 49; Nukhrat, *OZV*, pp. 78-79, 83; Balaban, *VS*, 40-41, 1928, pp. 15-17; Digurov, *SS*, 2(19), 1928, p. 60; "Golos Kursantki . . . ," *KP*, 12, 1929, pp. 68-69; Akopov, *RN*, 4-5, 1930, pp. 68-69; Sulaimanova, *ISGPU*, Vol. 2, p. 638. Cf. Pal'vanova, *DSV*, pp. 59-60, 64-65, 79-80, 84, 148; Kunitz, *Dawn Over Samarkand*, pp. 283 ff., 295 ff., 300; Halle, *Women*, pp. 135, 219-31.

The party's long-term commitment to train native female organizers, in socio-cultural as well as political spheres, was reflected in a new comprehensive training program adopted in mid-1929. See "Proekt Programmy po perepodgotovke zhenorgov Vostoka i natsmen," in *Ka*, 10, 1929, pp. 53-64.

This latter purpose became clearly apparent during the first great purges in the region (in 1929-1930, and throughout the 1930's) when a number of young female communists emerged as members of the party's purge commissions, as high-level administrators in commissariats of justice, and as public prosecutors, "people's assessors," and special state witnesses in court. Their assigned tasks included the public denigration and "unmasking" of local officials designated by party and security organs as "enemies of the people."[161] In this fashion, the party obviously hoped to recruit, over the long term, what may be viewed as an elite of political janissaries. Composed of uniquely amenable human material, removed early in life from the traditional milieu, and educated entirely under the party's aegis, this elite was evidently expected to serve as the regime's highly devoted phalanx in gradually destroying the old order and in systematically ferreting out and denouncing the regime's real or imagined enemies in the new Soviet apparatus.

Retreat to selective and segregated cadre formation signified the party's inclination to believe that investment in long-term recruitment and intensive indoctrination of a nucleus of revolutionary and innovative cadres in Central Asia was more feasible and desirable than immediate social revolution. As suggested by a number of communist analysts in the latter 1920's, this was an approach that would permit the party's policies to be really "flexible," "practical," "well articulated," "highly systematic," as well as "congruent with the overall plans [of transformation and development]."[162]

The criterion of graduated mobilization and socialization. Those directly involved in Central Asian politics made it abundantly clear that, ideally, the mobilization and socialization of native women

---

Cf. Amosov, *Ka*, 14, 1929, p. 23 (citing the new resolution of the party's Central Committee on May 25, 1929, concerning the issue as a whole).

For some reviews of the state of training party leaders, including women, among non-Russian nationalities, see Kozlovskii, *SS*, 11(64), 1931, pp. 86-106; Vel'tner, *RN*, 12, 1931, pp. 36-38; Karneev, *RN*, 7(40), 1933, pp. 39-43; *PV*, 4.9.1934, p. 4. For some early statistics on female membership in the party, see F.R., *Ka*, 4, 1925, pp. 11-14; Smitten, *Ka*, 11, 1925, pp. 46-52; Samokhvalova, *Ka*, 9, 1926, pp. 20-28.

[161] I discuss this development in a separate study, now in preparation (see Note 19, Chapter Six).

[162] See, e.g., Shimko, *Ka*, 12, 1925, p. 67; Zavarian, *Ka*, 12, 1925, p. 31; Nukhrat, *Ka*, 10, 1928, pp. 75-78, and *Ka*, 19, 1929, pp. 34-38; Smirnova, *Ka*, 10, 1928, pp. 81-82; Kozlovskii, *SS*, 11(64), 1931, pp. 97-98.

had to be not only gradual but purposively graduated. By this they meant essentially three things. First, the enterprises comprising the new infrastructure had to be sufficiently varied to accommodate the participation of women with widely differing degrees of preparation for new practices and norms, that is, with widely differing levels of revolutionary consciousness. Second, it was important for mobilizational approaches to individuals and groups to be, when necessary, sequential. Finally, a modicum of coordination was needed among various levels of participation, to facilitate the movement of people from less to more complex spheres of socialization and performance —in effect, from lower to higher stages of collaboration and involvement in the Soviet fold.

The more sophisticated party analysts proposed to make some careful distinctions on this account, and they visualized these distinctions in rather suggestive terms. Some referred to various degrees of "primitivity" in modes of approaching Moslem women. Some projected "lower [as well as] higher forms of mass-work," "[more as well as less] complex . . . ways of spreading the party's influence," "[more as well as less] elementary . . . seedbeds of Soviet culture." Most of them stressed the need for "preliminary stages" in establishing contacts between "[women still] living in a tribal-patriarchal milieu" and "[the agencies of] the Communist Party and of Soviet modernity." Likewise, they emphasized the need to provide traditional women with "preliminary forms" of associational experience which would nurture in them the requisite "modes and habits [of participation and] . . . the comprehension of duties and responsibilities [connected with various] social functions," thus preparing them for more demanding arrangements in "higher forms." Commensurately, all these forms were consciously visualized as more or less advanced *schools* of attitudinal and behavioral change, schools of collective involvement and learning, of economic and organizational performance, of political consciousness, participation, and experience. In these schools, the exposure to new roles, values, and beliefs, the acquisition of new habits and skills and the engagement in productive work were to be fused into a single continuous process.[163]

[163] For variants of this reasoning preceding and accompanying the buildup of the infrastructure, including specific illustrations, see Niurina, *Ka*, 4, 1925, pp. 80-81; V.K., *Ka*, 9, 1925, pp. 68-70; Prishchepchik, *Ka*, 12, 1925, p. 63, and *Ka*, 9, 1926, p. 77; Zavarian, *Ka*, 7, 1926, pp. 35-40; Nukhrat, *Ka*, 7, 1927, pp. 35-36; Chernysheva, *Ka*, 8, 1928, pp. 84-86; *BSE*, Vol. 25,

While party organizers were quite explicit in stressing such guidelines for graduated mobilization, they tended to shy away from rigidly linking specific operational requirements with particular, concrete conditions and structures. Certainly, they were reticent, at least at the outset, to deal with this matter in terms of iron-clad institutional and participatory categories. In part, this may have been due to the obvious political sensitivity of this issue: it was surely difficult to discuss in public (and in great detail) the assignment of people to particular activities on the grounds that they were too "primitive" to be assigned elsewhere. At the same time, responsible communist cadres seemed well aware that it would not be easy, in any case, to differentiate precisely between various spheres of action, and to draw sharp boundaries between various institutional arrangements. Accordingly, at least in public, official proposals emphasized the *principle* of a differentiated and sequential approach rather more consistently than its concrete manifestations. They made it quite clear, for example, that some components of the organizational network (such as women's clubs, legal aid units, literacy, drama, and hygiene circles, garden, handicraft, and consumers' cooperatives) were to be viewed as definitely peripheral, or "elementary," in nature, while others (beginning with the party itself) were unquestionably central, or "advanced." However, what constituted the intermediate forms and stages of popular involvement was, at least at this point, not clearly specified. Neither was it formally spelled out how various components of the network were to be related to one another, and how a person would "pass" from lower to higher ones.[164]

But this much is certain. Soviet policies in Central Asia in the late 1920's marked an attempt to develop in practice an organizational and participatory ladder.[165] In this, they were clearly predi-

---

1932, p. 255. While some of the more explicitly stated desiderata are dated before 1929, their comparison with official pronouncements and actions between 1929 and 1932 shows that the earlier proposals indeed came to serve as guidelines for official policy in this sphere. This and related issues will be discussed in a separate study (see Note 19, Chapter Six).

[164] In practice, though, Soviet actions in the 1930's, especially in Central Asia, did involve some suggestive attempts to differentiate clearly between a great variety of participatory spheres. These will be dealt with in a subsequent study (see Note 19, Chapter Six).

[165] Samuel Huntington uses the term "organizational ladder" in discussing Leninist organizational theory rather than specific Soviet policies (see his *Political Order in Changing Societies*, p. 340). My reference to an organ-

cated on Lenin's notions about the predominant role of the Communist Party in society, and about the modalities of the party's relationship with the masses in the revolutionary process. But they went beyond these notions in proposing to build a specifically adapted and consciously graded framework wherein the process of mass-participation would be not only politicized but carefully (even minutely) institutionalized. Having been made acutely aware of the implications of uncontrolled mobilization, the regime proposed to leave little or nothing to chance. It proposed to attune a great variety of auxiliary institutions to diverse human capacities, sensibilities, and needs, so as to maximize participation in Soviet-sponsored enterprises while minimizing the risks of political destabilization. In effect, it set out to deliberately manage the movement of masses of people along a continuum away from traditional and towards what were conceived to be Soviet norms, activities, and ties. In the context of such management, graduated mobilization and socialization may be said to have entailed the introduction of a complex *tracking system* in society which was to be a crucial component of systematic social engineering.

The criterion of self-liquidation. If one were to point to a single official proviso invariably accompanying all of the stated operational criteria, it would certainly relate to the infrastructure's strictly transitory nature. As we have seen,[166] the party leadership made it quite clear towards the end of the 1920's that it would not permit the emancipation of Moslem women to become an end in itself.[167] It was made equally clear that the female-oriented network would be tolerated only if its units were strictly auxiliary in nature and served as useful transmission belts between the party and the masses.[168] By mid-1930, the language of official admonitions was both harsher and more explicit. The new specialized units were to steer clear of preoccupations with tasks and issues involving merely "good-for-nothing . . . feminine . . . trivia." They were to serve only "concrete [developmental] needs." They had to be "organically connected with [and controlled by]" Soviet state agencies, thus "[fulfilling] those aims of the party . . . which [were] most urgent"

---

izational and participatory ladder is derived independently and directly from the analysis of Soviet actions and experience.

[166] See the introductory sections (esp. "The Danger of Subversive Superstructures") in Chapter Six, *supra.*

[167] See, e.g., Amosov, *Ka,* 14, 1929, p. 26.

[168] See the first six sections of this chapter.

at any given time. These aims included, first and foremost, "the conscription of a skilled . . . disciplined . . . female labor army" for factories and fields. Such being the case, units of the new social infrastructure would be tolerated only as long as the traditional system they were designed to combat showed signs of vitality. Accordingly, they were to be viewed as purely temporary and, indeed, "self-liquidating" in nature, as merely emergency devices scheduled "gradually to dissolve in the overall [stream] of Soviet work" when their designated job was done.[169]

REASSESSMENT AND RETRENCHMENT: GENERAL IMPLICATIONS[170]

To recapitulate: the series of compromises marking Soviet retrenchment in Central Asia involved at least a partial retreat from

---

[169] See Brutser, *KP*, 4-5, 1930, pp. 91-93; V.K., *Ka*, 9, 1925, pp. 70-72. Cf. Nukhrat, *Ka*, 1, 1928, p. 55, and *VMV*, p. 18; Karpov, *Ka*, 9, 1928, pp. 82-84; Safadri, *Ka*, 11, 1928, p. 34.

It may seem unwarranted to quote, simultaneously, notions publicized in 1930 (Brutser) and in 1925 (V.K.—the initials standing either for V. Kasparova or for V. Karpych, both of them important party analysts of Central Asian affairs at that time). But a careful juxtaposition of official and semi-official views published between 1928 and 1930 (and cited in this footnote, *supra*) will show that V.K.'s position in this matter clearly reflected the thinking of the party's high command—perhaps even more so in 1930 than in 1925. Moreover, it should be remembered that the temporary and self-liquidating nature of the network could be discussed more openly in 1925-26 than in 1929-30: in the first instance, those who pressed for *khudzhum* justified it, in part, on the grounds that it would permit the party to dispense with special intermediate structures altogether; in the second instance, the buildup of the infrastructure (as a dimension of "systematic work") had just commenced in earnest, partly in response to the failure of *khudzhum,* and it would have been politically awkward to publicize the tentative and transitory quality of the entire effort at just that time. All the same, while official statements on this subject may have been less direct in the late 1920's, the regime's determination to dispose of the unorthodox units at the right time was, if anything, stronger than before.

[170] For some specific implications of the role of legalism and assault in engineered revolution, see Chapter Ten, *infra*. I have attempted elsewhere to develop a framework for comparative inquiry into the determinants of revolutionary acceleration and retrenchment under authoritarian auspices; see my "Family Law and Social Mobilization: A Comparative Analysis of Soviet Central Asia and Communist China," in David C. Buxbaum, ed., *Chinese Family Law and Social Change in Historical and Comparative Perspective* (University of Washington Press, forthcoming).

expectations of an attitudinal and behavioral revolution on command from above. Commensurately, they indicated a renewed emphasis on some of the elementary Marxist suppositions concerning the relationship between base and superstructure:[171] human beliefs, values, practices, and ties were to a large extent dependent on the economic base; fundamental changes in the former could take place primarily as a consequence of significant shifts in the latter. Dimanshtein (for a time, one of the party's chief strategists in dealing with minority nationalities and cultures) alluded to this new emphasis in 1930. While his formulation of the issues was (necessarily) circumspect, the implications were unmistakable:

> [It is a fundamental] Marxist proposition that, in the present period of reconstruction, the national question changes its nature to the extent that a change occurs in the economic base of the Soviet Union as a whole and in the economies of [our] national regions [in particular. Such a reconstruction of the base] induces basic changes in the class relations among the people [inhabiting our] national republics.
>
> At the same time, [however,] it is necessary to keep in mind the teachings of Marxism regarding the relationship between the base and the superstructure, [namely] that an economy does not influence the superstructure *automatically,* like some sort of wound-up mechanism, but a certain period of time is required, even if not a very long one, for the superstructure itself to change. From a historic point of view we are, of course, at the [very] beginning of the reconstruction-process, but, given our *conscious influence* upon historical processes, and given our deep understanding of the tendencies [implicit in them], we can to a certain extent *speed up* their influence upon the changes in the ideological forms of a society, especially since, at the same time, work is also being done to change the superstructure [directly].[172]

Such a formulation not only reaffirmed the continuing dependence of socio-cultural and psychological superstructures on the base. It specifically anticipated a significant *lag* of the former behind the latter, especially in the traditional societies of the Soviet East. Such a lag was now seen as justified on the basis of both doctrine and

---

[171] See, e.g., the reasoning in Mokrinskii, *SP,* 3 (27), 1927, pp. 106-107.
[172] Dimanshtein, *RN,* 1, 1930, p. 9 (italics supplied).

reality, as a dialectical relationship that was not subject to sudden modification or reversal by mere sleight of hand.[173]

Given such authoritative redefinition of Soviet goals—amounting, in effect, to a new official perception of the scale of priorities— in Central Asia, proponents of "systematic work" could now project long-term directed social change as a relatively undramatic task of correlating the buildup of Soviet institutions with the erosion of traditional relationships and orientations. Three prime forces were clearly expected to facilitate this task: the inexorable grinding of the wheels of industrialization and of overall economic development;[174] the unspectacular but steady organizing, socializing, and model-setting operation of the new social infrastructure for women;[175] and the steady trickle of the most disaffected female elements —the "pioneers of emancipation"[176]—from the hinterland to special Soviet reception and training centers in Central Asian and Russian cities.[177]

[173] It is safe to assume that Dimanshtein, as well as others—including Krupskaia—who shared his views in this case, could now hark back to what Stalin himself had said in 1920 in about early Soviet attempts to wipe out the traditional life styles in Central Asia and in the Caucasus. At that time, Stalin (as Commissar for Nationalities) had likened Soviet tactics (including forcible closure of mosques) to mindless "cavalry attacks," and explicitly warned military and party personnel against such actions:

... cavalry raids with the object of "immediately communizing" the backward masses of the people must be discarded for a cautious and well-conceived policy of gradually drawing these masses into the general stream of Soviet development.

See Stalin, "The Policy of the Soviet Government on the National Question in Russia," *Pravda*, October 10, 1920, as quoted in J. Stalin, *Marxism and the National Question* (New York, 1942), p. 85.

[174] For an indication of Stalin's early hopes on this account, see Stalin, "K postanovke nats. voprosa," *Soch.*, Vol. 5, 1946, pp. 56-58. Cf. Stalin, "The Soviet Republics of the East" in *Marxism and the National Question*, pp. 193-94; and Lenin, "A Great Beginning," *Selected Works*, Vol. 9 (London, 1937), pp. 441, 496, 501. See also Dimanshtein, *RN*, 1, 1930, p. 9; Perimova, *Ka*, 9, 1929, p. 38; Nukhrat, *RN*, 3, 1933, p. 50; Pal'vanova, *DSV*, p. 59.

[175] See, e.g., Nukhrat, *Ka*, 1, 1928, pp. 53-56; Khodzhaev, *SS*(35), 1929, p. 59; Dimanshtein, *RN*, 12(58), 1934, pp. 27-28; Pal'vanova, *DSV*, pp. 66-70.

[176] For some early uses of this term, see Gurko-Kriazhin, *NV*, 7, 1925, pp. 369-75. Cf. Halle, *Women*, p. 135; Kunitz, *Dawn Over Samarkand*, p. 300.

[177] See the preceding section, "The Criterion of Selective and Segregated Cadre Formation," in this chapter. Cf. Kunitz, ibid., pp. 283 ff., and 295 ff.

From this perspective, then, the main road to the transformation of a traditional system lay *via* purposive and systematic endowment of people with what were, in their social context, extrasystemic roles and opportunities. This meant gradually involving the traditionalist population in new (Soviet) structures, procedures, and responsibilities, and thus drawing them away from traditional practices, obligations, and ties. Thus, the direction of the main thrust of Soviet actions now seemed self-evident: to bring about the disintegration of a traditional way of life, while safeguarding the stability of the revolutionary regime, required not attacking the traditional system head-on but sapping that system's vitality and relevance, thus inducing atrophy in its institutions. In other words, the tasks of a revolutionary modernizer were not those of all-out collision and war in society but those of infiltration and subversion.

Needless to say, ideally such an approach called for careful balancing of changes in societies and cultures against changes in economic patterns and political institutions. Certainly, it entailed a commitment to long-term, comprehensive, substantially pragmatic planning—including piecemeal and incremental change in some social sectors, if necessary—wherein the process of social transformation could be subject to close control, and could be consciously guided in a direction and at a rate considered desirable and safe from the Soviet point of view. Khoziat Markulanova, one of the first Tadzhik female party organizers, and one intimately involved in the attempted "cultural revolution" in Central Asia, reflected this awareness quite precisely when she explained the Soviet decision to abandon *khudzhum*:

> . . . we Bolsheviks, while intransigent in our aims, are yet, when necessary, patient in pursuing them. We gamble only when we are fairly certain of our chances. And, . . . in dealing with cultural and psychological "superstructures," we often resort to Fabian tactics. . . . This may not be as romantic as you first imagined, but it is more certain.[178]

[178] As quoted in Kunitz, ibid., p. 300. Compare Samuel Huntington's argument concerning "Fabianism" and "blitzkrieg" as strategies of social change, in his *Political Order in Changing Societies* (New Haven, 1968), pp. 344 ff.

389

TEN · *Summary and Conclusion:*
Reflections on the Limits of
Legalism and Assault
as Revolutionary Strategies

THE substance and circumstances of Soviet reassessment of revolutionary means and potentialities make it possible to evaluate the limits of legalism and assault from a broader perspective. These limits, as suggested by Soviet experience in Central Asia, may now be summed up as follows:

(1) The realization through Soviet law and administrative command of new ideal norms in Central Asia tended to be inversely related to the degree of force in attempts to apply them in reality. This is not to say that a simple, one-to-one relationship may be posited between the realization of these norms and the mode of their implementation, i.e., that the less coercive the policy the greater the possibility for revolutionary change. What Soviet experience does permit us to infer is that coercion, even in the hands of a determined and powerful regime which was both authoritarian and revolutionary, could not be an autonomous and decisive factor in inducing significant change. By the same token, the amount of coercion in the process of enforcement constituted only one of many determinants in the success or failure of laws and decrees as instruments of revolutionary change.

Although Herbert Packer has considered this problem in a very different context, his conclusions are quite applicable here: "The criminal sanction . . . becomes largely inefficacious when it is used to enforce morality rather than to deal with conduct that is generally seen as harmful. Efficacy aside, the less threatening the conduct with which it is called upon to deal, the greater the social costs that enforcement incurs." Just as enforcement authorities are thereby driven to ever more extreme measures of intrusion and coercion, so are masses of individuals driven towards growing alienation from constituted authority.[1]

[1] H. L. Packer, *The Limits of the Criminal Sanction* (Stanford, 1968), p. 365.

390

Of course, the regime's first clear-cut recognition of this problem was expressed in its decision not to apply the new criminal sanctions retroactively. As Lon Fuller would see it, this decision implied the realization that it would be dangerous, even absurd, to "[command] a man today to do something yesterday,"[2] and to prosecute him for failing to do so.

In fact, Soviet arguments in favor of reassessment and retrenchment implied the desirability of both a negative and a positive perspective in this matter. In *negative* terms, just as sudden, indiscriminate, and draconic application of force in the sacred realms of human existence tended to trigger a variety of forms of resistance and hence of hindrances to overall change, so could the de-emphasis of coercive measures serve to remove these specific hindrances. On the other hand, the *positive* factors in effecting radical social change were assumed to be a function not so much of relatively permissive policies as of the correlation of such policies with a network of requisite supportive attitudes, actions, and structures that would serve as a tangible and acceptable underpinning for an alternative way of life.

(2) Statute law, while perhaps a suitable parental surrogate (to paraphrase Harold Berman[3]) in the Russian milieu, lacked the cultural underpinnings for such a role in Central Asia, and therefore could not be easily transplanted in its specific Soviet-Russian forms. In the Russian context, the state could indeed seek, through law, to play the role of guardian, while the individual before the law could play the role of ward. Thus, the subject of law could be treated as a "dependent member of the collective group, a youth, whom the law must not only protect against the consequences of his own ignorance but must also guide and train and discipline. . . . The parent or guardian or teacher may be cruel or benevolent, angry or calm, bad or good. He may dislike the child. But he is responsible for the child's upbringing."[4]

Such a relationship between state, law, and the individual could not be easily duplicated in the Moslem traditional milieu of Central Asia. Here, the constraints of a collective group—a tribe, clan, religious sect, or village community—were often utilized to deflect and evade the controls of an overarching political community, such as the state. At the same time, these constraints tended to be them-

[2] See L. L. Fuller, *The Morality of Law* (New Haven, 1964), p. 59.

[3] See his *Justice in the U.S.S.R.: An Interpretation of Soviet Law* (rev. ed., 1963), esp. Section 3.

[4] Berman, ibid., pp. 423, 283-84.

selves counterbalanced by the personalistic and patriarchal self-assertion of heads of families, supported by kinship networks acting on the basis of perceived self-interest. Concomitantly, the influence of judicial institutions was dependent to a large extent not only on the personal qualities of judicial personnel but on their connectedness with religion and custom. Both of the latter certainly antedated whatever formal arrangements existed in the judicial realm, and both carried prescriptions and sanctions considered to be fruits of divine revelation, and thus, as a rule, not subject to manipulation by secular (not to speak of foreign) authorities from above, certainly not in intimate realms of interpersonal relationships.[5] To the extent that such manipulation did take place and had to be at least overtly accepted by believers, it went hand in hand with persistent attempts by individuals and families to turn judicial proceedings to personal advantage, and to deal with the law not as wards, dependents, and errant youths but as essentially sovereign men and kin-groups inclined to bargain and maneuver for maximum returns.

It is safe to assume that, in order to overcome such socio-cultural patterns, a special kind of "parental" mediation was necessary. As Almond and Powell have pointed out, "It is the nature of traditionalism to resist the very idea of rule making, since this grants legitimacy to the 'changing of the rules.' As a consequence, one of the most important mechanisms of change in political structure and in public policy in traditional systems is the charismatic mechanism."[6] Yet it is precisely this mechanism that was conspicuously absent from the Central Asian scene at the time of *khudzhum*. No figure comparable to Mao or Atatürk emerged—or could emerge—here and manage a "cultural revolution."[7] Strenuous Soviet attempts to

[5] See, e.g., I. S. Qureshi, "The Background of Some Trends in Islamic Political Thought," in J. J. Spengler, *et al.* (eds.), *Tradition, Values, and Socio-Economic Development* (Durham, N.C., 1961), pp. 189-95; M. Berger, *The Arab World Today* (Garden City, N.Y., 1964), pp. 163-64; Levy, *The Social Structure of Islam*, Ch. 6.

[6] G. A. Almond and G. B. Powell, *Comparative Politics: A Developmental Approach* (Boston, 1966), p. 136.

[7] For a comparative analysis of some facets of attempted cultural revolutions in Soviet Central Asia and Communist China, see my "Family Law and Social Mobilization in Soviet Central Asia: Some Comparisons with Communist China," a paper delivered at the Annual Meeting of the Association for Asian Studies, Boston, Mass., March 28-30, 1969; to be published in slightly amended form in David C. Buxbaum, ed., *Chinese Family Law and*

392

promote the largely distant, impersonal, and ethnically alien images of Lenin and Stalin for this purpose were quite inadequate here. At the same time, if there were some opportunities for Central Asians to identify with locally relevant figures of requisite stature—to respond to the will of, and transfer emotional allegiance to, a potently patriarchal, palpably heroic and charismatic, and ethnically akin figure of a supreme leader—such opportunities were deliberately and systematically undermined by the Soviet regime itself.

This had to do primarily with Moscow's fears of incipient nationalism and separatism in the region, which left none of the emerging local leaders above suspicion. For that matter, we have here a paradoxical situation: it would seem that the more intimate and effective was a man's involvement with his countrymen at the grassroots, and the greater the popular respect accorded to him in the process, the more suspect was he in Moscow's—and certainly in Stalin's—eyes, regardless of actual autonomist or nationalist proclivities on his part. As a result, we find in Central Asia a well-nigh constant erosion of actual or potential leadership—and a persistent gulf between the party and the masses—as, one after another, the most brilliant, admired, and authoritative of Central Asia's emerging native communist leaders were politically constrained, publicly disgraced, and physically liquidated on Moscow's orders.

(3) The functioning of law and administrative command as instruments of mobilization (as both repositories of ideal norms and foci of grievances), while powerful in its revolutionizing impact, tended to be directly related to the degree that extra-legal integrative and supportive arrangements were provided for and coordinated with the mobilizational thrust. Thus, while there can be little doubt that legal and administrative intervention successfully elicited, reinforced, and focused grievances, they tended to be dysfunctional to the extent that they encouraged hopes—certainly among women—they could not satisfy. More specifically—as Samuel Huntington would visualize this—a high rate of induced social mobilization, unaccompanied by requisite institutionalization of political and other relevant organizations and procedures, and

---

Social Change in Historical and Comparative Perspective (University of Washington Press, forthcoming). For a discussion of Atatürk's role in imposing a new legal code in Turkey, see I. E. Postacioglu, "The Technique of Reception of a Foreign Code of Law," *International Social Science Bulletin*, IX, 1, 1957, pp. 54-55.

hence greatly exceeding the system's ability to assimilate and absorb newly mobile people, entailed the perennial (and growing) threat of political instability.[8]

In Central Asia, the cumulative effects of such a mobilizational process tended, of course, to be especially pronounced. While legalism and assault spurred here what might have been, from the Soviet point of view, positive aspects of female mobilization, they also served to mobilize into politics, albeit for profoundly negative reasons, large numbers of traditionalist males. Huntington's general conclusions about the consequences of an equivalent process help to bring this problem into sharp focus:

> The nature of the demands and the nature of the issues formulated by the reformer in large part shape the allies and the opponents who will play roles in the political process. . . . The reformer who attempts to do everything all at once ends up accomplishing little or nothing . . . [since he attempts] simultaneously to push a large number of reforms on a wide variety of fronts, in order to change comprehensively the existing traditional order. He fails because his efforts to attempt so much mobilize so many opponents. . . . Virtually all the social groups and political forces with a stake in the existing society [feel] themselves threatened; the blitzkrieg or all-out attack simply [serves] to alert and activate the potential opposition. Here then is the reason why comprehensive reform, in the sense of a dramatic and rapid "revolution from above," never succeeds. It mobilizes into politics the wrong groups at the wrong time on the wrong issues.[9]

[8] See S. P. Huntington, "Political Development and Political Decay," *World Politics*, April, 1965, pp. 386-430, *passim*. For an equivalent argument about the relation of rapid economic growth to political instability, see Mancur Olson, Jr., "Rapid Growth as a Destabilizing Force," *The Journal of Economic History*, 23, 4, 1963, pp. 529-52.

[9] *Political Order in Changing Societies*, pp. 346-47. It should be noted that Huntington seems to equate blitzkrieg with a comprehensive strategy of social change. In the context of Soviet experience, this makes sense only if it refers to the comprehensiveness of revolutionary *goals*, i.e., to a transformer's ambition to change everything at once. It makes less sense if it defines *techniques* and *means* as well. As we have seen, *khudzhum*—by and large, Huntington's blitzkrieg—while indeed intended to produce a vast upheaval in Moslem societies, was quite narrowly focused both in its chosen means and in the target-sectors of its thrust. It is partly on these grounds— as we have seen in Chapter Nine—that Soviet proponents of an altogether

394

(4) Given its vivid imagery of justice and of equality of the sexes before the law, as well as the imagery of instant liberation and potency in mass-demonstrations in the course of *khudzhum*, the operation of the Soviet legal system and of administrative assault as instruments of recruitment unquestionably made a highly important contribution to Soviet revolutionary objectives. Recruitment through these channels evidently tended to net female cadres that were the toughest, the most disaffected from tradition, the most vengeful, and hence politically the most reliable from the Soviet point of view. But the impact of the Soviet system through these vehicles tended to be diluted to the extent that the manipulations of its native male personnel made female judicial and administrative roles purely honorary or menial. The impact of Soviet actions was also relatively narrow in that they seemed to appeal primarily to female personalities with authoritarian (aggressive as well as submissive), but not necessarily cooperative, imaginative, and creative, characteristics.

Moreover, as experience has shown, many of these women could withdraw from the Soviet fold just as suddenly as they had entered. In many cases, they evidently did this when frustrated by the perceived discrepancy between the promise and reality of Soviet initiatives, or when subjected to intolerable moral pressure of their communities. But it may also be surmised that they could leave (or avoid) the Soviet fold for other than purely negative reasons. Even if institutionalized female inferiority and segregation were important facts of life in the traditional order, they were not necessarily the *only* determining characteristics of male-female relationships in that world. While the masculine-feminine dichotomy there was sharp, and while men indeed retained formal authority, women occupied, albeit informally, important positions in the kinship system, and thus, indirectly, in society at large. They could exert in-

---

different strategic emphasis ("systematic work"), while continuing to look forward to radical and ultimately total change, came to stress, precisely, a comprehensive, multifaceted approach to social engineering. By this they meant long-term, planned coordination and interlocking of a variety of mobilizational and integrative means. They were consciously willing to trade what they viewed as a sweeping (and dangerous) assault on a few crucial sectors of social life for a multidimensional (hence slower, but safer and more broadly conceived) program of action. As we have also seen in the preceding chapter, they were willing to pay the price of pronounced unevenness in the modes and pace of socio-cultural change in the U.S.S.R.

395

fluence by exercising what Daniel Lerner refers to as "relay" functions in family and community—involving, among other things, clear-cut dominance in childrearing and often crucial mediatory roles in relations within and between families and clans.[10]

In short, as Robert Levine has pointed out, it would be a mistake to view women's roles even in patriarchal and patrilineal traditional societies as invariably set and monolithic:

> Roles may be differentiated by sex within each of the major institutional aspects of the social system: the family, the economy, the political system, the religious systems, etc., and the patterns in one aspect may not be consistent with those of another.[11]

This means that, in the diverse world of Central Asian communities, women's roles could be superordinate as well as subordinate, and could bring satisfactions as well as engender frustrations and tensions.

At the same time, married life itself as well as membership in traditional communities and adherence to ritual and custom could evidently fulfill deeply felt needs (of women as well as men) by providing elements of spiritual, material, and existential security, of intimacy and affiliation—in effect, elements of *certainty*. It is no wonder, then, that many Moslem women chose to remain in (or return to) the traditional fold, especially when Soviet recruitment efforts brought with them the realization of the palpable insecurity and uncertainty characterizing the proffered new world.

(5) Deliberately fashioned and used as instruments of class struggle—instruments dispensing distinctly political justice,[12] and initiating a direct political assault on status, religion, and custom—Soviet laws and decrees tended to be eufunctional (from the Soviet point of view) only if "class enemies" could be readily detected and safely indicted, but tended to be dysfunctional to the extent that the local traditional milieu was alienated in the course of the regime's

[10] See D. Lerner, *The Passing of Traditional Society* (Glencoe, Ill., 1958), pp. 196 ff.

[11] See R. A. Levine, "Sex Roles and Economic Change in Africa," *Ethnology*, 4, 2, 1966, p. 186. For a broader theoretical perspective on this issue, see W. N. Goodenough, "Rethinking 'Status' and 'Role': Toward a General Model of the Cultural Organization of Social Relationships," in M. Banton, ed., *The Relevance of Models for Social Anthropology* (London, 1965).

[12] The term is Otto Kirchheimer's. See his *Political Justice* (1961).

396

crude and indiscriminate attempts to identify and apprehend such enemies. Indeed, if the Soviet revolutionary effort should be likened to a purposive re-education campaign, one of its basic flaws could best be defined in Gordon Allport's terms: "It is an axiom that people cannot be taught who feel that they are at the same time being attacked."[13]

While this may be said to have applied primarily to men, it would seem to have been pertinent in the case of women, too, though for somewhat different reasons. By definition, a class-approach to social tensions, with women cast in the role of a consistently deprived class, could be meaningful if inequalities and divisions based on sex could indeed be made consistently synonymous with those based on class. But this task proved to be far more complex and difficult than it may have been envisaged. For the most part, women may be said to have failed to function as a social class, a stratum with a sense of shared identity, with a distinct, clearly perceived community of experience, interest, purpose, and action. Their connections with men, no less than with each other and with established social institutions, proved to be both manifold and varied. The imperatives of interdependence between the sexes, based on affect as well as function and need, proved to be more potent than the appeals of self-assertion as a social class. In short, sexual roles proved to be less susceptible to polarization than class roles; sexual identity could not readily serve as a basis for class identity; sexual politics could not be reduced to class politics.

(6) Having to function not only as conveyors of new norms but also as instruments to extirpate the entire antecedent legal and customary system, Soviet initiatives enjoyed the advantages of (a) a formal monopoly of the legal universe; (b) a formal monopoly and overwhelming superiority of brute force; (c) a centralized and potentially efficient bureaucratic apparatus; and (d) the backing of an authoritarian party-state committed to an overarching ideology and uninhibited by moral and democratic constraints. They could indeed, at a minimum (as Morroe Berger would see it), withdraw the formal-legal machinery from the support of discriminatory patterns, "withhold [established] privileges from the discriminators," and "put the state's influence and power on the side of

[13] Gordon Allport as quoted by Kurt Lewin and Paul Grabble in "Principles of Re-Education," in W. G. Bennis, *et al.*, eds., *The Planning of Change* (New York, 1961), pp. 508-509.

397

those who [were] discriminated against and give them effective means for defending themselves."[14]

They were at a disadvantage, however, and hence were congenitally unattractive, or at least not immediately useful, in that (a) they lacked the sacred qualities and personalities of the antecedent system; (b) they tended to be abstract, rigid, incipiently coercive, and impersonal; (c) they could not easily gain access to traditional communities either because the latter were physically distant, or nomadic-pastoral (hence elusive), or because they were governed by a combination of religious and customary law and in accordance with kin-oriented solidarities.

In such a context, various legal functions were not significantly differentiated from each other and from other functions of the socio-cultural milieu.[15] Moreover, primordial customary laws—deeply habituated, normatively justified, and conditioned by implicit or explicit sanctions of peers and kin—were never tied up with the formal machinery of a court.[16] Traditional communities could thus be significantly independent of, and elusive from, formal legal structures as well as administrative commands. In such communities (to paraphrase Galanter) even the demise of traditional law did not necessarily and automatically lead to the demise of traditional society.[17]

(7) To the extent that Soviet legislation and decrees were intended to be a warning system (a network of "tripwires," in Stanley Hoffman's terms) designed to mark rigid frontiers of permissible action and thus prevent transgressions and resulting conflicts, they tended to be relatively useless (since they were regarded as irrelevant, or disregarded altogether, by traditionalist males) and decidedly dysfunctional (in that, far from preventing conflicts, they helped to trigger and aggravate them).[18] The radicalizing trigger-

[14] See M. Berger, *Equality by Statute* (New York, 1952), p. 192.

[15] Cf. Y. Dror, "Law and Social Change," *Tulane Law Review*, 33, 1959, p. 790.

[16] M. Rheinstein makes this argument in a different context; see C. Geertz (ed.), *Old Societies and New States* (New York, 1963), pp. 241-42. Cf. P. Stirling, "Land, Marriage, and the Law in Turkish Villages," *International Social Science Bulletin*, 9, 1, 1957, p. 21.

[17] See M. Galanter's discussion of law and change in traditional milieus, in M. Weiner (ed.), *Modernization: The Dynamics of Growth* (New York, 1966), p. 162.

[18] This is very much in line with Stanley Hoffman's conclusion in another context. See his "The Study of International Law and the Theory of Inter-

effect might have been especially strong, in this case, not only because the new arrangements were being imposed in a quintessentially "dynamic" rather than "static" period (one involving dramatic changes in positions and stakes),[19] but because the kind of conflict they engendered could indeed very easily ". . . [bring] into the conscious awareness of the contenders, and of the community at large, norms and rules that were dormant before the particular conflict."[20]

(8) To the extent that Soviet laws and administrative commands had to function as a protective shield for revolutionary agents and converts, they tended to be not only useless (in that they could do little or nothing to protect defecting Moslem women from violent retribution), but decidedly dysfunctional (to the extent that they obliged the Soviet regime to risk the lives of valuable and scarce political activists in the impossible task of protecting the rights and lives of masses of individuals scattered in an extremely hostile milieu).[21]

(9) In their role as heretical models, Soviet legal and administrative arrangements were bound to have an exceptionally great impact on the traditional milieu.[22] Perhaps no other instruments could hold out to the traditional community, and especially its women, revolutionary standards of human relationships and potentialities as palpably, consistently, and authoritatively as Soviet initiatives did. Perhaps no other instruments could, in the short run, be as powerful catalysts of systematic alienation in, and fundamental transformation of, the traditional milieu.

But Soviet initiatives as heretical models tended also to be dys-

---

national Relations," in *Proceedings of the American Society of International Law*, 57th Annual Meeting, 1963, pp. 26-35. Cf. B.V.A. Rölling, "The Role of Law in Conflict Resolution," in A. de Reuck *et al.* (eds.), *Conflict in Society* (Boston, 1966), pp. 328-50; and L. Pye, *Aspects of Political Development* (Boston, 1966), pp. 121-22.

[19] See Rölling, ibid., p. 335.

[20] This is Coser's variant of Simmel's and Durkheim's propositions in a different context. See L. Coser, *The Functions of Social Conflict* (London, 1956), p. 127.

[21] This calls for some significant qualifications in Arnold Rose's proposition regarding the role of law as a shield protecting innovators and daring minorities. See his "The Use of Law to Induce Social Change," *Transactions of the Third World Congress of Sociology*, 6, 1956, pp. 52-63.

[22] For a discussion of the potential functions of heretical models in this context, see "Introduction" to Part Four, *supra*.

functional to the extent that (a) they were felt to be forced upon traditional communities by men who were ethnically or ideologically outsiders; (b) they not only posed a threat to the traditional unities and values, but impinged directly upon the most intimate and sacred realms of local life-styles; (c) they stimulated the self-assertion of both Soviet-oriented heresy and traditionalist orthodoxy; (d) they put a discipline-oriented, implicitly authoritarian system in the paradoxical position of encouraging iconoclastic and libertarian propensities that showed themselves capable of turning —even in women, the prime beneficiaries of Soviet policies—just as easily against the Soviet regime as against the traditional order. Ironically, then, the revolutionary potential of a surrogate proletariat turned out to be as problematic and elusive as history has shown the political moods of the real proletariat itself to be.

It can be said, moreover, that in the broadest sense of the term— at least in the Central Asian context—heresy meant, quite literally, unprecedented choice. Indeed, in terms of Shapley's and Shubik's analysis of the feudal system,[23] Soviet-sponsored female mobilization in the course of *khudzhum* may be said to have constituted the introduction of *strategic choices* in a world of *predetermined duties.*[24] What Soviet heretical initiatives threatened to do was to transform an essentially closed system, quite suddenly, into an open one.

In being closed as well as segmentary and small in scale, local socio-cultural systems may be said to have been highly integrated, in the sense that there was a high degree of interdependence and mutual sensitivity of at least some of these systems' important norms, relationships, statuses, and roles. It would seem that the most critically important (and hence most sensitive) dimensions

[23] Although their analysis is devised for a different context and from a different perspective, its conceptualization seems quite applicable here. See their "Ownership and the Production Function," *Quarterly Journal of Economics*, 1, 1967, p. 93.

[24] To be sure, as Manfred Halpern has proposed, Moslem women (though to a lesser extent than men) had choices, which grouped themselves around a number of what he calls tension-managing polarities. But these choices may be said to have been only tactical ones, and operative within an essentially closed system. It is in this sense that Soviet heretical initiatives threatened to transform this system into an open one. See Halpern, "Patterns of Continuity and Change, Collaboration and Conflict in Traditional Islamic Society," a paper presented to the Plenary Session of the Annual Meeting, Middle East Studies Association, November 15, 1968, Austin, Texas.

in the interdependence of these component parts concerned precisely women.

Thus, Soviet initiatives constituted not merely an attack on sacred as against secular aspects of life (as Kenneth Boulding would visualize it),[25] or on consummatory as against instrumental values, or on expressive and evaluative as against emotionally neutral areas of activity, or on covert and private as against overt and public behavior.[26] They constituted, first and foremost, an assault on a role that was the most distinctly ascribed rather than achieved one in the entire system, and that was functionally highly diffuse rather than specific. This role was diffuse in the sense that its functions tended to be critically interdependent with more (and more emotionally charged) roles, values, and meanings than was probably true in any other case. In other words, an attack on female positions in a Moslem milieu meant an attack on a highly interlocking set of roles with a very wide spectrum. A significant departure in one of its components seemed to imply the collapse of the entire system. For, in this context (in what David Riesman calls a typical example of a "male vanity culture"),[27] men's roles may be said to have been to an extraordinary extent defined by apposition to female roles; maleness seems to have been, in effect, negatively defined with respect to the very concept of woman. Thus, to drastically alter this concept threatened to dissolve the boundaries defining maleness itself, and hence not just a man's superordinate position vis-à-vis women, but in effect his self-image, self-definition, self-esteem, and ego-identity. This, it would seem, might be the

[25] See his *The Impact of the Social Sciences* (New Brunswick, 1966), pp. 78-101.

[26] For discussions of the potentialities and limits of imposed rules in dealing with these attitudes, relationships, and actions, see Roscoe Pound, *Social Control Through Law* (New Haven, 1942), pp. 54 ff.; Morroe Berger, *Equality by Statute* (New York, 1952), pp. 171 ff.; Dror, "Law and Social Change," pp. 800-801; Boulding, *The Impact*, Ch. 4; Stirling, "Land, Marriage . . . ," p. 32; and C. G. Howard and R. S. Summers, *Law, Its Nature, Functions, and Limits* (Englewood Cliffs, N.J., 1965), pp. 403-50. For some very useful reviews of the literature on law and (evolutionary) social change, accompanied by some highly incisive propositions on the relationship between law and the social process, see Lawrence Friedman and Jack Ladinsky, "Law as an Instrument of Incremental Social Change," Sept. 8, 1967 (a paper read at the Annual Meeting of the American Political Science Association, Chicago, Ill.), and the special issue of the *American Behavioral Scientists*, 13, 4, 1970, devoted to law and social change.

[27] As quoted in Lerner, *The Passing of Traditional Society*, p. 197.

ultimate implication of the concept of *'ird* (honor) in Islam, the extraordinary degree of interlocking and interdependence between male and family honor on the one hand, and the role and concept of woman on the other in Moslem imagination.[28]

These inferences become all the more relevant when viewed in the light of George De Vos's analysis of human systems of segregation and exploitation. De Vos finds significant parallels between the stratification patterns of caste societies and of those based on institutionalized female inferiority. In both cases he sees the dynamics of domination and segregation as related not so much to "instrumental" exploitation (one that is rationally utilitarian and goal-directed and that characterizes a class society in the Marxist sense), as to what he terms "expressive" exploitation (deriving from irrational and unconscious psychological processes and motives). Accordingly, the tensions prevalent in societies stratified on the basis of caste and male superiority are very different from those that characterize a class society, making Marxist notions about class struggle not quite pertinent in such cases. As De Vos points out (largely on the basis of Durkheim's analysis of religious forms of life), in cases involving expressive exploitation social hierarchy is defined in sacred rather than secular terms; typically there is a need to elevate those "who deal with the supernatural" and to separate them from those "whose behavior personifies the reprehensible or unclean, the polluting or dangerous." In such cases out-caste groups or women (or both) serve in scapegoating and projective functions; and the dominant individuals have a continuing feeling of dependency toward the degraded social segments and toward the

---

[28] In attempting to clarify this matter, I have benefited enormously from discussions with Mohammed Guessous and Allen Kassof, friends, and colleagues at Princeton University. Some anthropological and sociological investigations in other Islamic societies would seem to support such an assessment. See, e.g., H. M. Miner and G. De Vos, *Oasis and Casbah: Algerian Culture and Personality in Change* (Ann Arbor, 1960); J. G. Peristiany (ed.), *Honour and Shame: The Values of Mediterranean Society* (London, 1965), esp. essays by Bourdieu and Abou-Zeid. For a very interesting case-study, including an excellent bibliography, see David C. Gordon, *Women of Algeria: An Essay on Change* (Cambridge, Mass., 1968). Cf. W. J. Goode, *World Revolution and Family Patterns* (New York, 1963), esp. Ch. III; J. Berque, *The Arabs: Their History and Future* (New York, 1964), esp. Ch. IX; and R. N. Bellah, *Beyond Belief: Essays on Religion in a Post-Traditional World* (New York, 1970), Ch. 8, esp. p. 164.

functions they perform. Thus, for high-status individuals who feel insecure in their role, "a sense of threat is countered by some symbolic affirmation of their status demanded of those in the legally or socially subordinate group. . . ."

Under normal circumstances, when there are no significant challenges to established norms and ties, this does not present a problem. Indeed, as De Vos emphasizes, " . . . expressive gratification [is] derived from social stratification by *both* the dominant and the subordinate groups . . . based on divisions made for the realization of mutual obligations as well as an alleviation [*in everyone*] of feelings of dependency and helplessness." This means, though, that dominant men can gain relief from inner tensions only as long as their individual psychic structures are sustained by collectively held and socially reinforced representations, and as long as requisite status affirmations are forthcoming from those considered inferior. This also means that such men live in a perennially precarious psychic equilibrium:

> Being sensitive to some inner awareness of the motivations attributable to socially submerged groups, it is difficult for men in dominant positions to avoid feelings of possible retribution from exploited segments of their own society. . . . [To wit:] the greater the political dominance of men over women, the greater the fear of women, and consequently the greater the need to maintain barriers securing the social status of men. Generally, the greater the exploitation of subordinate groups, the greater the social need to maintain external symbols of status differentiation.

In turn, the more a man's ego integration is dependent on rigid distinctions between male and female roles, the greater the perception of inner stress when the barriers are threatened, and the less manageable the resultant inner conflicts. In these circumstances, then,

> Any diminution in deference can result in immediate sensitivity, and in the use of coercion or even violence to reaffirm dominance. . . . [Thus,] man's capacity to identify brings human conflict within him. . . . Potentially permeable to the feelings and experiences of others, given also to the projection of his feelings into objects and beings about him, he . . . [finds himself espe-

403

cially insecure] in situations in which a pronounced continuous dependence upon an exploited group cannot be resolved. . . . [In such situations] man experiences conflict intra-psychically.[29]

Accordingly, while most other Soviet initiatives in Central Asia could be perceived and handled as, by and large, challenges *ab extra*, female mobilization through legal prescriptions and administrative commands constituted an *ab intra* challenge par excellence, and hence was on all counts far more threatening than anything else. That is why, when confronted with such a challenge, Moslem communities in general and men in particular showed themselves to be so vulnerable, and why a sharp shift in female status, critically affecting the nexus of authority relations in the most intimate circles of a man's life, served to provide the vehicle for a most violent and widespread reaction.

In such a context, then, it proved to be far from a simple matter to adopt what Karl Deutsch considers the most efficient approach to social innovation and change: the manipulation of social segments that are characterized by a "highly unstable equilibrium," and are thus a society's "[most] promising instabilities."[30] In a Moslem traditional milieu, such an approach turned out to be distinctly double-edged in its effects. In other words, deliberate and direct manipulation of familial/sexual roles in Central Asia, while engendering exceptionally potent heretical models, and exploiting the greatest vulnerability of Moslem societies, also engendered their most determined efforts to resist.

This makes Harry Eckstein's hypotheses about the conditions of a society's lability under a variety of stimuli—that is, in his terms, its proneness to change or, concomitantly, weakness to resist modification—highly pertinent here.[31] In exploring the spectrum of relationships and values in society that might be most or least sensitive to deliberate political manipulation, he comes to the following conclusion:

[29] See George De Vos, "Conflict, Dominance and Exploitation in Human Systems of Social Segregation . . . ," in de Reuck, *Conflict in Society*, esp. pp. 68, 70-71, 77-80, and pp. 60-80, *passim* (italics supplied).

[30] See Karl W. Deutsch, *The Nerves of Government* (New York, 1963), p. 147.

[31] For some of Eckstein's formal hypotheses that are most relevant here, see his *Authority Relations and Governmental Performance: A Theoretical Framework* (Center of International Studies, Princeton University, September, 1968, mimeo), esp. pp. 53-57.

. . . lability increases with accessibility to direct engineering, especially that which may result from prescriptive rules. In general, . . . strongly institutionalized family, tribal, ethnic, and status structures [are] highly inaccessible to direct manipulation. . . . Moreover, . . . the more intimate, spontaneous, and simple relations, among men—e.g. friendships or amorous relations— are far less susceptible to external manipulation, least of all by formally prescribed directives, than more public, standardized, and complex relations. . . . [This] tells us something about the frequent animus of revolutionary transformers against intimate and atomized relations, their frequent obsession with the legal transformation of such social relations, and their equally frequent failure actually to accomplish it.[32]

(10) It follows that, as a regulative mechanism in a revolutionary situation, Soviet law in particular was at one especially pronounced disadvantage, apart from all those already mentioned. It turned out to be exceedingly difficult, if not impossible, to distinguish friend from foe in any meaningful or reliable way. First, as we have seen, the perceptions and responses of the women themselves turned out to be far from homogeneous in intensity, orientation, and value. Second, the attitudes and behavior of male clients turned out to be determined at least as much by old unities based on kinship, custom, and belief as by new, legally ensured considerations of property, bureaucratic status, and sex. Third, and perhaps most important in the short run, the performance of the new Soviet apparatus—the "sponsor system"—composed in the lower echelons of largely native cadres was itself subject to the same complex parallelogram of loyalties. Needless to say, this meant that the sponsor groups could contain at least as many self-perceiving beneficiaries and adversaries, in this case, as the client groups, and that the challenge-and-response flows between them could not be as simply drawn as in a one-to-one relationship. In other words, it was found to be difficult to replicate in reality the simple, "rational" dichotomy between "we" and "they," between "sponsors" and "targets" of action, between the worlds of "revolutionary agents" and "traditional clients."

Thus, contrary to James Coleman's expectations in this general realm, it proved to be far from easy to achieve a direct and effective correlation between legal and social change—even though (to cite

[32] Ibid., pp. 54, 56.

some of Coleman's stated conditions of directed social transformation) "those who [had to] implement the change [were] in a direct line of authority below those who [were] responsible for the change," and even though "there [were] individuals [and] organizations already prepared to make use of the formal authority created by the legal change."[33]

In sum, a revolutionary instrument that was itself not easily controllable, and was itself seeking legitimation in a traditional world, could not very well control tensions as widespread, pervasive, and corrosive as those induced by the heretical model, and hence could not ensure order in that world while it was enforcing with all the power at its command the very quintessence of illegitimacy: heresy.

(11) Therefore, in its role as a specialized tension-management system designed to induce and control revolutionary change, the combination of legalism and assault turned out to be an exceedingly volatile, imperfect, inexpedient, and, in certain circumstances, dangerous instrument. It tended to be volatile in the sense that it could just as easily go too far as not far enough in inducing and managing change. It was imperfect in the sense that, if devoid of supportive institutions and arrangements that would permit the translation of legal rights into real roles and opportunities, it tended to define new goals while failing to supply the means to reach them. It was inexpedient in the sense that it could undermine the traditional *status quo*, but could not really transform it. It tended also to be dangerous in that, as a heretical model, it maximized undesirable as well as desirable tensions, while, as a regulative mechanism, it could not minimize the impact of those tensions on the political structures and developmental objectives of the incumbent Soviet regime.

(12) Revolutionary legalism and administrative assault as strategic approaches to social engineering could be self-delusory to their sponsor as well as dangerous. Their perfectionist emphasis on adherence to uncompromising, if seemingly rational, rules, and their heavy stress, on the one hand, on rationally devised legal machinery and, on the other hand, on coerced, massive, and public violation of traditional taboos, served to arrest or derail more broadly conceived transformationist programs. To wit, they served to de-emphasize to the point of neglect or exclusion precisely those

[33] See J. S. Coleman, "Conflicting Theories of Social Change," *American Behavioral Scientist*, 14, 5, 1971, pp. 637-38.

initiatives that were needed most for the attainment of revolutionary and developmental objectives, and for the legitimation of the Soviet system itself, initiatives involving comprehensive, systematic, and coordinated social action whereby human needs, potentialities, and expectations would find a reasonable chance to be fulfilled. Given such omission, revolutionary legalism and administrative assault, intended to induce a strategic conflict in a traditional milieu for the purpose of changing it, tended instead to precipitate cataclysmic conflict verging on civil war.

This goes a long way to explain why the same decade (1929-39) that saw a vast intensification, largely by administrative *fiat*, of pressures for economic production and political conformity (including purges of "enemies of the people") throughout the Soviet Union, was also marked by growing caution, retreat, and deliberate reduction of tensions in matters affecting tribal, communal, and family relations—especially male-female relations—particularly and first of all in Central Asia.[34] The conclusion seems to have been reached that, in Moslem traditional milieus, Soviet revolutionary actions had approached dangerously close the outer limits of human adaptability to the stresses and strains imposed by rapid, uncontrolled social change. In effect, Soviet authority could not successfully legitimate itself and pursue its developmental objectives while it was destroying and drastically transforming the social bases on which legitimacy had to rest. At the same time, an authoritarian system could not consistently encourage libertarian propensities in the process of mobilization, since these could turn just as easily against the new regime as against the traditional order. Certainly, political elites whose notions of mass mobilization were profoundly (indeed, increasingly) instrumental—considering people primarily as means to serve the ends of the regime—could not very well tolerate the possibility of female emancipation becoming an end in itself. Thus, as I have pointed out earlier,[35] in a situation where Soviet revolutionary actions were analogous to insurgency by an incumbent, it turned out to be of fundamental importance that the imperatives of insurgency could not be easily reconciled with the

[34] I will deal with some of these issues in two separate but related studies, now in preparation: *Systematic Social Engineering in Soviet Central Asia: Tactics, Problems, and Achievements*; and *Nomadic Tribes and Revolutionary Politics in Soviet Central Asia*.

[35] See "Introduction" to Part Three of this study, *supra*.

imperatives of incumbency, since both sets of imperatives were generated, and needed to be weighed, by one and the same party— the incumbent Soviet regime.

From every point of view, then, a revolution in social relations and cultural patterns evidently could not be managed concurrently with large-scale political, organizational, and economic change. While it was clear to Soviet leadership that congruence between these two sets of processes was extremely important for success in both, it was equally clear that some of the consequences of the former constituted an immediate, direct threat to the overarching goals of the latter. In short, political institutionalization and stability as well as a modicum of economic growth[36] had to be purchased

[36] On the face of it, it might seem inconsistent to refer simultaneously to political stability and economic growth. Mancur Olson and others (see Olson's "Rapid Growth as a Destabilizing Force," *The Journal of Economic History*, 23, 4, 1963, pp. 529-52, have convincingly shown that certain modes and rates of economic growth can become important factors in political destabilization. But it should be kept in mind that Stalinist schemes for economic development, while grandiose for the U.S.S.R. as a whole, turned out to be quite selective in emphasis.

In some of Russia's peripheries, and especially in Central Asia, both the mode and the rate of economic growth seem to have been deliberately linked with a number of locally important considerations. Unlike in European Russia, Central Asian industrial development tended to be by and large confined to mining and processing rather than manufacturing industries. Moreover, industrial development to a large extent tended to be concentrated in urbanized (hence heavily European, especially Slavic) locales, and tended also to be accompanied by an accelerating influx of European (especially Slavic) technical and managerial personnel brought in to staff the new enterprises. At the same time, relatively the greatest developmental emphasis was placed on the region's agriculture, especially cotton growing (and correlated irrigation) and the production of silk, fruit, and meat (the latter based on the region's great cattle herds).

Thus, it may be said that, at the height of Moscow's draconic pressures for economic growth in the Soviet Union (1930's), Central Asia's economic development tended to be compartmentalized in such a way as, in effect, to minimize the impact on local population: the new industrial segments happened to be strongly correlated with non-native population; and the agricultural segments happened, by and large, to fit the relatively long-established production patterns in the area, thus providing a modicum of continuity in the midst of generally quickening change.

It might be added that even in the agricultural sector itself Moscow chose to make some adjustments (for reasons we have discussed, and for other reasons with which I shall deal in a separate study) that were unusual in the broader Soviet context. For example, Central Asia was the only major region in the U.S.S.R. where (after initial disasters) the pace of collectiviza-

at the price of revolutionary and ideological purity and of a lower rate of social transformation. This implied a willingness, on the part of the regime, to tolerate distinctly uneven development in political, economic, and socio-cultural spheres—indeed, a willingness to leave pockets of antecedent life-styles relatively undisturbed, if necessary, for an indefinite period of time.

Thus, within two and a half years of the beginning of the intensive phase of their experiment in Central Asia, Soviet authorities reversed their emphasis: from precipitate legalistic and administrative pressures for the sake of drastic social change to long-term social rebuilding for the sake, in part, of meaningful legal change, administrative development, and political legitimation.

Can this be regarded as a valid general maxim about the relation of law and administrative intervention to revolutionary social change? After all, neither Soviet experience in Central Asia nor the lessons derived therefrom may be literally applicable in other milieus. They do not tell us, for example, to what extent other methods of legal codification and judicial organization, applied under other political auspices, might have been more effective than the ones used; or whether legal and administrative means might have been more effective when focusing on less explosive issues than sexual and generational relationships; or whether social engineering through law and administrative command might be more effective in societies where supra-communal agencies (for example, those of a modern state) are collectively expected to play (by way of political manipulations in general and legal engineering in particular) a more powerful regulative and transforming role than is evidently the case in relatively intact traditional Islamic milieus. It is also true that Soviet objectives were unusually large, and Soviet

---

tion was perceptibly slackened (in 1930-31), and where some of the central organizational features associated with collective farms were quietly dropped or adapted to the structure and sensibilities of local social units.

If we also consider that Soviet elites came to view (quite rightly, in my judgment) economic development itself as having an indirect rather than direct impact on social relations and customs, and a gradual and extended effect rather than a concentrated and immediate one—especially when contrasted with legal and administrative intervention in society and culture—then there are grounds to suppose that, in Soviet Central Asia, it was indeed feasible to expect that economic growth could be purchased at the price of a lower rate of socio-cultural change, thus also minimizing the potential for political destabilization.

Central Asian societies especially distant from these objectives. Yet one wonders whether this very fact does not permit one to see, enlarged and accentuated, what is less apparent, but nonetheless true, in all confrontations between legally and politically expressed ideals and social actualities.

In fact, if we consider that the Soviet campaign took place under almost "ideal" conditions—a determined commitment to revolutionary purposes by a radical modernizing elite; the incumbent's undisputed and centralized political power, overwhelming superiority of force, and authoritarian dispositions coupled with the absence of democratic constraints; isolated and small target populations denuded, in large part, of their traditional elites; the incapacity or unwillingness of neighboring states to intervene in the affairs of their ethnic brethren; and, therefore, the sponsor-regime's relative freedom both to *initiate* and to *retreat* from a revolutionary experiment—then there are grave questions about the utility of law and administrative command as autonomous strategic instruments of rapid, administered social change under less favorable circumstances.

This is not to suggest that the third major operational alternative envisaged by the Soviet regime—"systematic work"—was destined to be automatically more successful as a revolutionary strategy. Its insights and initiatives were not necessarily consistent with each other. Nor could they be implemented to achieve quickly and effectively the general social transformation of Soviet Central Asia. The Stalinist regime was in fact inclined to use them more for maximizing economic production and social control than for effecting genuine (and genuinely emancipatory) individual and sociocultural transformation. At the same time, even the maturation of Stalinism as the dominant totalitarian force in Soviet politics failed to obscure completely the choices perceived in the 1920's: Stalinism only, up to a point, perverted their meaning and application. While many of the original proponents of gradualism and pragmatic innovation in Central Asia were silenced or eliminated in the 1930's, some of their most salient proposals were incorporated by the regime in its policies in Soviet Asia. Concomitantly, a host of unanticipated problems and needs, pertaining not only to female mobilization, but also to nomadism and tribal organizations, to kin and communal structures, to collective forms in agriculture, and to Islam as a religion, asserted themselves strongly enough to com-

410

mand definite, if grudging, adjustments in the regime's expectations and actions.

These adjustments in what was supposed to be a coherent pattern of "systematic work" were frequently made with palpable uncertainty, illogic, and misleading rationalizations, leaving unsolved or creating as many problems as they were intended to tackle. In short, the years that followed the first decade of Soviet revolutionary experiments in Moslem milieus were destined to be characterized not by the unfolding of a grand, well-calibrated strategy of social engineering in action, but by a protracted, feverish, and far from conclusive quest for optimal techniques conducive to modernization as well as stable rule. Thus, contrary to earlier communist expectations, no magic wand for social change was to be found in Soviet Central Asia, and no easily applicable model for the benefit of impatient revolutionary modernizers elsewhere.

BIBLIOGRAPHY

BOOKS

Agabekov, G., *OGPU*. New York, 1931.

Allworth, Edward, *Uzbek Literary Politics*. The Hague, 1964.

———, ed., *Central Asia*: *A Century of Russian Rule*. New York, 1967.

Almond, G. A., and Powell, G. B., *Comparative Politics*: *A Developmental Approach*. Boston, 1966.

Anderson, T., *Masters of Russian Marxism*. New York, 1963.

Arsharuni, A., and Gabidullin, Kh., *Ocherki panislamizma i pantiurkizma v Rossii*. Moscow, 1931.

Bacon, E. E., *Central Asians under Russian Rule*: *A Study in Culture Change*. Ithaca, New York, 1966.

Bailey, F. M., *Mission to Tashkent*. London, 1946.

Baker, G., and Cottrell, L. S., eds., *Behavioral Science and Civil Defense Disaster Research Group*, Study No. 16, 1962.

Barghoorn, F. C., *Soviet Russian Nationalism*. New York, 1956.

Bartol'd, V. V., *Istoriia Kul'turnoi Zhizni Turkestana*. Leningrad, 1927.

Becker, S., *Russia's Protectorates in Central Asia*: *Bukhara and Khiva, 1865–1924*. Cambridge, Mass., 1968.

Bellah, R. N., *Beyond Belief*: *Essays on Religion in a Post-Traditional World*. New York, 1970.

Bennigsen, A., and Lemercier-Quelquejay, C., *Islam in the Soviet Union*. New York, 1967.

Bennis, W. G. (*et al.*, eds.), *The Planning of Change*. New York, 1961.

Berger, M., *Equality by Statute*, New York, 1952.

———, *The Arab World Today*. Garden City, New York, 1964.

Berman, H., *Justice in the USSR*: *An Interpretation of Soviet Law*. Revised edition. Cambridge, Mass., 1963.

Berque, J., *The Arabs*: *Their History and Future*. New York, 1964.

Bil'shai, V., *Reshenie Zhenskogo Voprosa v S.S.S.R. Moscow*, 1959.

412

Bol'shaia Sovetskaia Entsiklopediia. Moscow, 1926-47. Second edition, Moscow, 1949-58.

Borodin, George, *Cradle of Splendor: The Song of Samarkand.* London, 1945.

Boulding, K., *The Impact of the Social Sciences.* New Brunswick, N.J., 1966.

Bozhko, F., *Oktiabr'skaia Revoliutsiia v Srednei Azii.* Tashkent, 1932.

Brown, D. R., ed., *Women in the Soviet Union.* New York, 1968.

Brzezinski, Z., *The Permanent Purge.* Cambridge, Mass., 1956.

Buslov, K., *Problemy Sotsial'nogo Progressa v Trudakh V. I. Lenina (1917–1923 gg).* Minsk, 1963.

Caroe, Sir Olaf, *Soviet Empire: The Turks of Central Asia and Stalinism.* London, 1953. Revised edition. New York, 1967.

Carr, Edward Hallett, *A History of Soviet Russia: The Bolshevik Revolution, 1917–1923.* New York, 1951-53. *The Interregnum, 1923–1924.* New York, 1954. *Socialism in One Country.* New York, 1964.

Carrère d'Encausse, H., *Réforme et Révolution chez les Musulmans de l'Empire Russe.* Paris, 1966.

Coates, W. P., and Zelda, *Soviets in Central Asia.* London, 1951.

Conolly, V., *Beyond the Urals: Economic Developments in Soviet Asia.* London, 1967.

Czaplicka, M. A., *The Turks of Central Asia in History and at the Present Day.* London, 1918.

Daniels, Robert V., *The Conscience of the Revolution.* Cambridge, Mass., 1960.

———, *A Documentary History of Communism from Lenin to Mao.* New York, 1960.

De Reuck, A. (*et al.*, eds.), *Conflict in Society.* Boston, 1966.

Desiatyi Vserosiiskii S'ezd Sovetov . . . 23–27 dekabria 1922 goda. Moscow, 1923.

Deutsch, Karl W., *The Nerves of Government.* New York, 1963.

Deutscher, Isaac, *Stalin, a Political Biography.* New York, 1949.

Eckstein, Harry, *Authority Relations and Governmental Performance: A Theoretical Framework.* Center of International Studies, Princeton University, September, 1968, mimeographed.

———, *Pressure Group Politics.* Stanford, 1960.

Engels, Frederick, *The Origin of the Family, Private Property and the State.* New York, 1942.

413

Erickson, John, *The Soviet High Command, 1918–1941*. London, 1962.

Erlich, Alexander, *The Soviet Industrialization Debate, 1924–1928*. Cambridge, Mass., 1960.

Evans-Pritchard, E. E., *The Position of Women in Primitive Societies and Other Essays in Social Anthropology*. New York, 1965.

Fainsod, Merle, *How Russia Is Ruled*. Revised edition. Cambridge, Mass., 1963.

Fedorov, E. G., ed., *Uchreditelnyi S'ezd Sovetov Kirgizskoi (Kazakhskoi) A.S.S.R., 4–12 oktiabria 1920 g; protokoly*. In VKP (b) Kazakhskii Krayevoi Komitet, *Iz istorii partiinogo stroitel'stva v Kazakhstane*. Alma-Ata, 1936.

Fleron, Jr., F. J., ed., *Communist Studies and the Social Sciences: Essays on Methodology and Empirical Theory*. Chicago, 1969.

Fuller, L. L., *The Morality of Law*. New Haven, 1964.

Geertz, C., *Islam Observed*. New Haven, 1968.

———, ed., *Old Societies and New States*. New York, 1963.

Geiger, H. K., *The Family in Soviet Russia*. Cambridge, Mass., 1968.

Goode, William J., *World Revolution and Family Patterns*. London, 1963.

Gordon, David C., *Women of Algeria: An Essay on Change*. Harvard, 1968.

Gurvitch, G., *Sociology of Law*. New York, 1942.

Halle, Fannina W., *Women in the Soviet East*. New York, 1938.

———, *Women in Soviet Russia*. New York, 1934.

Halpern, Manfred, *The Politics of Social Change in the Middle East and North Africa*. Princeton, N.J., 1963.

Hayit, Baymirza, *Turkestan im XX Jahrhundert*. Darmstadt, 1956.

Hirschman, A. O., *The Strategy of Economic Development*. New Haven, 1958.

Hudson, A. E., *Kazakh Social Structure*. New Haven, 1938.

Huntington, Samuel P., *Political Order in Changing Societies*. New Haven, 1968.

Huxley, J. S., *Evolution in Action*. New York, 1953.

Juviler, P. H., and Morton, H. W., *Soviet Policy-Making*. New York, 1967.

Kassof, A., ed., *Prospects for Soviet Society*. New York, 1968.

Kastelianskii, A. I., ed., *Formy Natsional'nogo Dvizheniia v Sovremennykh Gosudarstvakh*. St. Petersburg, 1910.

414

Kim, M. P. (*et al.*, eds.), *Kul'turnaia Revoliutsiia v S.S.S.R., 1917–1965.* Moscow, 1967.

Kish, Egon Erwin, *Changing Asia.* New York, 1935.

Klimovich, Liutsian, *Islam v Tsarskoi Rossii.* Moscow, 1936.

Kommunisticheskii Internatsional v Dokumentakh. Moscow, 1963.

Kommunisticheskaia partiia Sovetskogo Soiuza, *Protokoly i Stenograficheskiye Otchety S'ezdov i Konferentsii Kommunisticheskoi Partii Sovetskogo Soiuza.*

————, *Protokoly Desyatogo S'ezda RKP(b).* Held in Moscow, March 29-April 4, 1920. Moscow, 1960.

————, *Protokoly Desyatogo S'ezda RKP(b).* Held in Moscow, March 8-16, 1921. Moscow, 1963.

————, *Odinadtsatyi S'ezd RKP(b), Stenograficheskii Otchet.* Held in Moscow, March 27-April 2, 1922. Moscow, 1961.

————, *Dvenadtsatyi S'ezd RKP(b), Stenograficheskii Otchet.* Held in Moscow, April 17-25, 1923. Moscow, 1923.

————, *Trinadtsatyi S'ezd RKP(b), Stenograficheskii Otchet.* Held in Moscow, May 23-31, 1924. Moscow, 1924.

————, *XIV S'ezd VKP(b), Stenograficheskii Otchet.* Held in Moscow, December 18-31, 1925. Moscow-Leningrad, 1926.

————, *XV S'ezd VKP(b), Stenograficheskii Otchet.* Held in Moscow, December 2-19, 1927. Moscow-Leningrad, 1928.

————, *XVI S'ezd VKP(b), Stenograficheskii Otchet.* Held in Moscow, June 26-July 13, 1930. Moscow-Leningrad, 1931.

Kommunisticheskaia Partiia Sovetskogo Soiuza v Rezoliutsiiakh i Resheniiakh S'ezdov, Konferentsii i Plenumov Ts.K. Seventh edition, Part I, 1898-1925; Part II, 1925-53. Moscow, 1953.

Krader, Lawrence, *Peoples of Central Asia.* The Hague, 1963.

————, ed., *Handbook of Soviet Central Asia.* 3 volumes. New Haven, 1956.

Kraskin, I. S., ed., *Zemel'no-Vodnaya Reforma v Srednei Azii.* Moscow, 1927.

Kraval', I. A., ed., *Zhenshchina v S.S.S.R.*, statisticheskii sbornik. Second edition. Moscow, 1937.

Krupskaia, N. K., *O Rabote Sredi Zhenshchin.* Moscow, 1926.

————, *Zhenshchina v Strane Sotsializma.* Moscow, 1938.

Kuchkin, A. P., *Sovetizatsiia Kazakhskogo Aula, 1926–1929 gg.* Moscow, 1962.

Kunitz, Joshua, *Dawn Over Samarkand.* New York, 1935.

Laqueur, Walter, *The Soviet Union and the Middle East.* New York, 1959.

415

Lenin, V. I., *Lenin o Druzhbe s Narodami Vostoka*. Compiled by I. I. Kul'kov. Moscow, 1961.

——, *Lenin o Natsional'nom i Natsional'no-Kolonial'nom Voprose*. Compiled by Institut Marksizma-Leninizma pri Ts.K. K.P.S.S. Moscow, 1956.

——, *O Rabote Sovetov*. Moscow, 1963.

——, *Natsional'nyi Vopros*. Moscow, 1936.

——, *Selected Works*. London, 1937.

——, *Sochineniia*. Second edition. Moscow, 1926–32.

——, and Stalin, I. V., *Statii i Rechi o Srednei Azii i Uzbekistane*. Tashkent, 1940.

Lerner, D. *The Passing of Traditional Society*. Glencoe, Ill., 1958.

Levy, Reuben, *The Social Structure of Islam*. Cambridge, 1962.

Liubimova, S., *V Pervye Gody*. Moscow, 1958.

Low, Alfred D., *Lenin on the Question of Nationality*. New York, 1958.

MacLean, Fitzroy, *Back to Bokhara*. London, 1959.

Mandel, William, *The Soviet Far East and Central Asia*. New York, 1944.

Marx, Karl, *Capital, A Critique of Political Economy*. New York, n.d.

Masal'skii, V. I., *Turkestanskii Kray*. Volume 19 in Semenov-Tianshanskii, ed., *Rossiia*. St. Petersburg, 1913.

Melnikov, G. N., *Oktiabr' v Kazakhstanie*. Alma-Ata, 1930.

Merton, R. K., *Social Theory and Social Structure*. Glencoe, Ill., 1957.

Meyer, Alfred G., *Leninism*. Cambridge, Mass., 1957.

——, *Marxism: The Unity of Theory and Practice*. Cambridge, Mass., 1954.

Miner, H. M., and De Vos, G., *Oasis and Casbah*: *Algerian Culture and Personality in Change*. Ann Arbor, 1960.

Moore, Barrington, Jr., *Soviet Politics—The Dilemma of Power, The Role of Ideas in Social Change*. Cambridge, Mass., 1950.

Moskalev, V., *Uzbechka*. Moscow, 1928.

Nalivkin, V., and Nalivkina, M., *Ocherk Byta Tuzemnoi Zhenshchiny Fergany*. Kazan', 1886.

Niurina, Fanni Efimova, *Parandzha*. Moscow, 1928.

——, *Trudiashchiesia zhenshchiny v oborone S.S.S.R.* Moscow-Leningrad, 1927.

Nove, A., and Newth, J. A., *The Soviet Middle East: A Communist Model for Development*. New York, 1967.

Nukhrat, A., *Iurty-Kochevki* (*K Rabote Zhenskikh "Krasnykh Iurt"*). Moscow, 1929.

————, *Oktiabr' i Zhenshchina Vostoka*. Moscow, 1927.

————, *Stepnoi Skaz*. Moscow, 1928.

————, *Vos'moe Marta na Vostoke*. Moscow, 1928.

Packer, H. L., *The Limits of the Criminal Sanction*. Stanford, 1968.

Pal'vanova, B., *Docheri Sovetskogo Vostoka*. Moscow, 1961.

Park, Alexander G., *Bolshevism in Turkestan, 1917–1927*. New York, 1957.

Pavlenko, Petr Andreevich, *Puteshestvie v Turkmenistan*. Moscow, 1932.

Peristiany, J. G., ed., *Honour and Shame: The Values of Mediterranean Society*. London, 1965.

Pervyi S'ezd Narodov Vostoka, Baku, 1–8 sent. 1920g., Stenograficheskie Otchety. Petrograd, 1920.

Pierce, Richard A., *Russian Central Asia, 1867–1917*. Berkeley, Calif., 1960.

Pipes, Richard, *The Formation of the Soviet Union: Communism and Nationalism, 1917–1923*. Revised edition. Cambridge, Mass., 1964.

Pound, Roscoe, *Social Control Through Law*. New Haven, 1942.

Pye, Lucian, *Aspects of Political Development*. Boston, 1966.

Rakowska-Harmstone, T., *Russia and Nationalism in Central Asia: The Case of Tadzhikistan*. Baltimore, 1970.

Ryskulov, T. R., *Kirgizstan*. Moscow, 1935.

Rywkin, Michael, *Russia in Central Asia*. New York, 1963.

Schapiro, Leonard, *The Communist Party of the Soviet Union*. New York, 1960.

Schlesinger, Rudolf, *Changing Attitudes in Soviet Russia—The Family in the U.S.S.R.*; documents and readings. London, 1949.

————, *The Nationalities Problem and Soviet Administration*. Selected readings on the development of Soviet Nationalities Policies. London, 1956.

Shikhmuradov, O. O., and Rosliakov, A. A., eds., *Ocherki Istorii Kommunisticheskoi Partii Turkmenistana*. Ashkabad, 1961.

Shklar, J., *Legalism*. Cambridge, Mass., 1964.

Shteinberg, E. L., *Ocherki Istorii Turkmenii*. Moscow, 1934.

Skrine, F. H., *The Heart of Asia*. London, 1899.

Sokol, E., *The Revolt of 1916 in Russian Central Asia*. Baltimore, 1954.

Spengler, J. J. (*et al.*, eds.), *Tradition, Values, and Socio-Economic Development*. Durham, N.C., 1961.

Stalin, J., *Marxism and the National Question*. New York, 1942.

———, *Sochineniia*. Moscow, 1946-1951.

Strong, Anna Louise, *Red Star in Samarkand*. New York, 1929.

Sukhareva, O. A., *Islam v Uzbekistane*. Tashkent, 1960.

Sulaimanova, Kh. S., and Ishanov, A. I., *Istoriia Sovetskogo Gosudarstva i Prava Uzbekistana*, 2 vols., Tashkent, 1960 and 1963.

Trotsky, Leon, *The History of the Russian Revolution*. Ann Arbor, 1932.

Uchastnitsy Velikogo Sozidaniia. Compiled by A. V. Artiukhina, *et al*. Moscow, 1962.

Ugolovnyi Kodeks R.S.F.S.R. Moscow, 1957 [Includes, among others, Chapter X (*On Crimes Constituting the Relics of the Tribal Order*) added to the Criminal Code of the R.S.F.S.R. on April 6, 1928 (pp. 100-103)].

Ulam, Adam B., *The Bolsheviks*. New York, 1965.

Vagabov, M. V., *Islam i Zhenshchina*. Moscow, 1968.

Vambery, Arminius, *Western Culture in Eastern Lands*. New York, 1906.

Weiner, M., ed., *Modernization: The Dynamics of Growth*. New York, 1966.

Wheeler, Geoffrey, *The Modern History of Soviet Central Asia*. London, 1964.

Wilber, C. K., *The Soviet Model and Underdeveloped Countries*. Chapel Hill, 1969.

Winner, Thomas G., *The Oral Art and Literature of the Kazakhs of Russian Central Asia*. Durham, N.C., 1958.

Zenkovsky, Serge A., *Pan-Turkism and Islam in Russia*. Cambridge, Mass., 1960.

Zhenshchiny v Revoliutsii. Compiled by A. V. Artiukhina, A. I. Vakurova, A. I. Nukhrat, E. A. Popova. Moscow, 1959.

ARTICLES

Abidova, Dzhakhan, "Zhenshchina Uzbekistana v bor'be za svoe raskreposhcheniie," *Revoliutsiia i Natsional'nosti,* 3(73), 1936, pp. 46-50.

Abramzon, S. M., "Manapstvo i Religiia," *Sovetskaia Etnografiia,* 2, 1932, pp. 82-97.

418

Aitakov, N., "Itogi II Turkmenskogo s'ezda Sovetov," *Sovetskoe Stroitel'stvo*, (10-11), 1927, pp. 71-77.

————, "III S'ezd Sovetov Turkmenskoi S.S.R.," *Sovetskoe Stroitel'stvo*, (35), 1929, pp. 60-63.

Akhun-Babaev, "Put' bor'by i pobed uzbekskogo naroda," *Sovetskoe Stroitel'stvo*, (12), 1937, pp. 84-90.

Akopov, S., "Bor'ba s bytovymi prestupleniiami," *Revoliutsiia i Natsional'nosti*, 4-5, 1930, pp. 58-69.

Amosov, M., "Shire organizuite massy," *Kommunistka*, 14, 1929, pp. 23-30.

A-na, "Ocherednye zadachi komissii po uluchsheniiu truda i byta zhenshchin Vostoka," *Kommunistka*, 3, 1928, pp. 18-24.

Anisimova, S., "Dom krest'ianki (dekhkahki) v Turkmenistane," *Kommunisticheskoe Prosveshchenie*, 1, 1927, pp. 75-77.

————, "K itogam raskreposhcheniia zhenshchin Uzbekistana," *Kommunistka*, 8, 1927, pp. 54-56.

Arkhincheev, I., "Korenizatsiia kak sotsial'no-politicheskaia problema," *Sovetskoe Stroitel'stvo*, (43), 1930, pp. 98-113.

Ar-na, A., "Ot 'nastupleniia' k sistematicheskoi rabote (k obsledovaniiu raboty v Srednei Azii)," *Kommunistka*, 1, 1928, pp. 57-63.

Artiukhina, A., "Pervye itogi uchastiia zhenshchin v perevyborakh sovetov," *Kommunistka*, 5, 1927, pp. 1-8.

Arykova, "Obshchestvo 'Doloi kalym i mnogozhenstvo,' " *Kommunistka*, 6, 1928, pp. 81-83.

Balaban, N., "Organizatsionno-massovaia rabota sovetov i bor'ba s bytovymi prestupleniiami," *Vlast' Sovetov*, 40-41, 1928, pp. 15-17.

Berin, T., and Ioshpe, Ie., "Narodnoe zdravookhranenie v Turkmenskoi S.S.R.," *Revoliutsiia i Natsional'nosti*, (85), 1937, pp. 67-70.

Bogacheva, "O chadre," *Kommunistka,* 11, 1928, p. 66.

Bol'shakov, V., "Kooperirovanie zhenshchin v vostochnykh natsional'nykh raionakh," *Kommunistka*, 5, 1927, pp. 53-56.

Broido, G., "Materialy dlia istorii vosstaniia Kirghiz v 1916 godu," *Novyi Vostok*, 6, 1924, pp. 407-34.

Brullova-Shaskol'skaia, N. V., "Na Amu-Dar'ye: etnograficheskaya ekspeditsiia v T.S.S.R.," *Novyi Vostok*, 16-17, 1927, pp. 290-303.

Brutser, L., "Politprosvet rabota sredi zhenshchin vostoka (itogi II Vsesoiuznogo Soveshchaniia zhenskikh klubov, krasnykh iurt i kibitok)," *Kommunisticheskoe Prosveshchenie*, 4-5, 1930, pp. 90-93.

Burlova, "Nachinaem rabotat'," *Kommunistka*, 8, 1928, pp. 89-90.

Burshtina, L. B., "Ordenonsnyie kolkhoznitsy khlopkovykh polei," *Revoliutsiia i Natsional'nosti*, (75), 1936, pp. 34-39.

Butuzova, E., "Zhenskie lavki v Uzbekistane," *Kommunistka*, 9, 1927, pp. 62-67.

Byzov, E., "Iskra kul'tury v Turkmenskom aule," *Za Sotsialisticheskii Turkmenistan*, 12, 1928, pp. 57-61.

Ch., I., "I Vsekazakhskoe soveshchanie Politprosvetov," *Kommunisticheskoe Prosveshchenie*, 2-3, 1928, pp. 254-62.

Chernysheva, A., "Kakim dolzhen byt' zhenskii zhurnal," *Kommunistka*, 8, 1928, pp. 84-86.

Davydova, "Zhenskii trud v promyshlennosti Uzbekistana," *Kommunistka*, 11, 1928, pp. 67-68.

Digurov, K., "Natsional'naya politika v oblasti sudebnogo stroitel'stva v. R.S.F.S.R.," *Sovetskoe Stroitel'stvo*, 2(19), 1928, pp. 56-60.

Dimanshtein, F., "Protiv mull i ishanov," *Kommunistka*, 5-6, 1929, pp. 49-51.

Dimanshtein, S., "Bor'ba na ideologicheskom fronte v Srednei Azii," *Revoliutsiia i Natsional'nosti*, 12(58), 1934, pp. 21-35.

————, "Natsional'naia politika sovetskoi vlasti i M. I. Kalinin," *Revoliutsiia i Natsional'nosti*, (50), 1934, pp. 1-20.

————, "Ocherednye zadachi natsional'noi raboty," *Revoliutsiia i Natsional'nosti*, 10-11, 1931, pp. 27-41.

————, "Rekonstruktivnyi period i rabota sredi natsional'nostei S.S.S.R.," *Revoliutsiia i Natsional'nosti*, 1, 1930, pp. 9-19.

————, "XVI let Oktiabria," *Revoliutsiia i Natsional'nosti*, (45), 1933, pp. 1-11.

Dinerstein, H. S., "The Sovietization of Uzbekistan," *Harvard Slavic Studies*, 4, 1957, pp. 499-513.

Dosov, A., "Bor'ba s bytovymi prestupleniiami," *Kommunistka*, 5, 1928, pp. 29-32.

————, "Bytovye sektsii pri sovetakh i ispolkomakh," *Vlast' Sovetov*, 38, 1929, p. 13.

Dror, Y., "Law and Social Change," *Tulane Law Review*, 33, 1959.

Dubiia, B., "V Turkmenii ne vedut dostatochnoi bor'by s feodal'-nymi perezhytkami," *Partiinoe Stroitel'stvo*, 14, 1939, pp. 46-47.

Dunn, S. P., and Dunn, E., "Soviet Regime and Native Culture in Central Asia and Kazakhstan," *Current Anthropology*, Vol. 8, No. 3, 1967.

Dzasokhov, V., "Sovetskaia vlast' na dzhailiau," *Revoliutsiia i Natsional'nosti*, 2-3, 1931, pp. 65-71.

Fat'ianov, "Itogi perevyborov Sovetov v Kirgizstane," *Vlast' Sovetov*, 19, 1927, p. 18.

Fioletov, N. N., "Sudoproizvodstvo v Musul'manskikh sudakh (sudy Kaziev) Srednei Azii," *Novyi Vostok*, 23-24, 1928, pp. 204-15.

————, "Sudy Kaziev v Sredne-Aziatskikh respublikakh," *Sovetskoe Pravo*, 1(25), 1927, pp. 132-46.

Fominov, A., "Komsomol na dzhailiau," *Revoliutsiia i Natsional'nosti*, 6, 1930, pp. 69-79.

Gelis, I., "Krasnye Iurti v Kazakhskom aule," *Kommunisticheskoe Prosveshchenie*, 6, 1929, pp. 35-36.

Gershenovich, R. S., "Chem vredny parandzha i chachvan," *Bezbozhnik* (ill.), 12, 1938, p. 7.

Gladovskii, F., "Izbiratel'naia kampaniia 1929g. v Uzbekskoi S.S.R.," *Sovetskoe Stroitel'stvo*, (34), 1929, pp. 166-69.

"Golos kursantki . . . ," *Kommunisticheskoe Prosveshchenie*, 12, 1929, pp. 68-69.

Golubeva, V., "O zadachakh i rabote komissii po uluchsheniiu truda i byta zhenshchin," *Kommunistka*, 3, 1927, pp. 35-37.

Griaznov, I. S., "Zdravookhranenie v natsional'nykh respublikakh," *Revoliutsiia i Natsional'nosti*, (40), 1933, pp. 73-78.

Gubaidullina, Z., "V dalekikh ugolkakh Kazakhstana," *Kommunistka*, 6, 1927, pp. 58-60.

Guber, A., "O prigranichnykh plemenakh Kushkinskogo raiona," *Revoliutsionnyi Vostok*, 8, 1930, pp. 267-81.

Gurko-Kriazhin, V. A., "Poezdka po . . . Srednei Azii," *Novyi Vostok*, 7, 1925, pp. 369-75.

Huntington, S. P., "Political Development and Political Decay," *World Politics*, April, 1965, pp. 386-430.

Ibragimov, Gali, "Iz obsledovaniia Semipalatinskoi gubernii," *Kommunistka*, 10, 1925, pp. 87-89.

————, "Natsionalki na proizvodstve," *Kommunistka*, 9, 1928, pp. 88-90.

Ishkova, K., "Nuzhen li dekret, zapreshchaiushchii noshenie chadry," *Kommunistka*, 11, 1928, pp. 59-62.

Ivetova, "Pamiati ushedshei ot nas Enne Kulievoi," *Kommunistka*, 8, 1925, pp. 64-65.

K., "Osobyi poriadok osushehestvleniia sudebnykh funktsii v nekotorykh mestnostiakh Kaz. A.S.S.R.," *Vlast' Sovetov*, 46, 1928, pp. 19-20.

K., V., "Formy i metody massovoi raboty sredi zhenshchin vostochnykh narodnostei," *Kommunistka*, 9, 1925, pp. 67-75.

"K narodnostiam Sovetskogo Vostoka: Obrashchenie k narodnostiam, naseliaiushchim natsional'nye respubliki i oblasti Sovetskogo Vostoka," *Kommunistka*, 2, 1925, pp. 3-5.

Kalachev, P., "Kazakhskaia zhenshchina v osveshchenii statisticheskikh tsyfr," *Kommunistka*, 8, 1927, pp. 56-60.

Karimova, Sh., "Na bor'bu s bytovymi perezhitkami," *Kommunistka*, 3, 1929, pp. 43-45.

Karneev, I., "Podgotovka partiino-sovetskikh kadrov v natsrespublikakh i oblastiakh," *Revoliutsiia i Natsional'nosti*, 7(40), 1933, pp. 39-43.

Karpov, G., "Nuzhno li obshchestvo 'Doloi Kalym i Mnogozhenstvo'? (k st. Arykovoi v #6 'Kommunistki'—1928g.)," *Kommunistka*, 9, 1928, pp. 82-84.

————, "Perevybory Sovetov 1929g. po Turkmenskoi respublike," *Sovetskoe Stroitel'stvo*, 6(35), 1929, pp. 64-68.

————, "Predstoiashchiie perevybory sovetov v Turkmenskoi respublike," *Sovetskoe Stroitel'stvo*, 11(28), 1928, pp. 61-69.

Karpych, V., "O teoreticheskikh problemakh sovetskogo Vostoka i postanovke ikh izucheniia," *Revoliutsiia i Natsional'nosti*, 1, 1930, pp. 101-105.

Kasparova, V., "Formy i metody massovoi raboty sredi zhenshchin —vostochnits," *Kommunistka*, 10, 1925, pp. 84-86.

————, "Zadacha partii v oblasti raboty sredi zhenshchin vostochnykh narodnostei," *Kommunistka*, 7, 1925, pp. 85-92.

Khairova, "Krasnye iurty (opyt Syr-Dar'inskoi gubernii)," *Kommunistka*, 1, 1928, pp. 68-70.

————, "K voprosu o zhenskom obrazovanii na Vostoke," *Kommunistka*, 6, 1928, pp. 86-87.

Kharchenko, I., "Razvitiie fizkul'tury v natsional'nykh respublikakh Srednei Azii," *Revoliutsiia i Natsional'nosti*, (77), 1936, pp. 58-60.

Khodzhaev, F., "Vazhneishyie voprosy stroilel'stva Uzbekskoi S.S.R.," *Sovetskoe Stroitel'stvo*, (2), 1926, pp. 118-21.

————, "Piatiletiie Uzbekskoi respubliki," *Sovetskoe Stroitel'stvo,* 1(42), 1930, pp. 15-23.

————, "III S'ezd Sovetov Uz.S.S.R.," *Sovetskoe Stroitel'stvo,* (35), 1929, pp. 50-60.

Kliuchnikov, S., "Kto kogo? (iz opyta anti-religioznoi propagandy v Bashkirii)," *Kommunisticheskoe Prosveshchenie*, 5, 1929, pp. 60-61.

————, "Propaganda bezbozhiia v Bashkirii," *Kommunisticheskoe Prosveshchenie*, 12, 1929, pp. 64-68.

Kobetskii, M., "K 10-letiiu soiuza voinstvuiushchikh bezbozhnikov," *Revoliutsiia i Natsional'nosti*, 5(63), 1935, pp. 71-74.

Kolychev, I., "Aral-raion sploshnoi kollektivizatsii," *Revoliutsiia i Natsional'nosti*, 4-5, 1930, pp. 116-24.

————, "Tadzhikistan (po materialam obsledovaniia instruktorov Ts.I.K. S.S.S.R.)," *Sovetskoe Stroitel'stvo*, (50), 1930, pp. 117-28.

Kovynev, Boris, "Osvobozhdennaia Gairam," *Bezbozhnik* (ill.), 2-3, 1940, pp. 12-13.

Kozlovskii, Yu., "Podgotovka i perepodgotovka rabotnikov Sovetskogo stroitel'stva v natsional'nykh respublikakh," *Sovetskoe Stroitel'stvo*, 11(64), 1931, pp. 86-106.

Krupnikova, "Trebuem proizvodstvennoi podgotovki," *Kommunistka*, 10, 1928, p. 85.

Krupskaia, N., "Puti raskreposhcheniia zhenshchiny Vostoka (rech' . . . na Vsesoiuznom Soveshchanii rabotnits sredi zhenshchin Vostoka, 10 dekabria 1928g.)," *Kommunistka*, 12, 1928, pp. 5-12.

Krylov, V., "Sovetskoe stroitel'stvo v Turkmenskoi S.S.R.," *Sovetskoe Stroitel'stvo*, (70), 1932, pp. 111-19.

Kryl'tsov, I. I., "Zakonodalel'stvo Sr.-Aziatskikh sovetskikh respublik," *Sovetskoe Pravo*, 5(29), 1927, pp. 130-38.

Kuchkin, A., "Sovetizatsiia Kazakhskogo Aula (1926-1929gg.)," *Voprosy Istorii*, 10, 1946, pp. 3-23.

Kushner, P., "Manapstvo v gornoi Kirgizii," *Revoliutsionnyi Vostok*, (2), 1927, pp. 150-82.

Lakhuti, "Tadzhikskaia literatura—iz doklada na s'ezde pisatelei," *Revoliutsiia i Natsional'nosti*, (55), 1934, pp. 69-72.

423

Bibliography

Lebedev, N., and Avksentievskaia, Ye., "Fond fol'klornykh materialov Turkmenskogo instituta iazyka i literatury," *Revoliutsiia i Natsional'nosti*, (90), 1937, pp. 51-53.

Leontiev, B., "Krasnaia armiia—internatsional'naia armiia," *Revoliutsiia i Natsional'nosti*, (84), 1937, pp. 48-54.

Levine, R. A. "Sex Roles and Economic Change in Africa," *Ethnology*, 4, 2, 1966.

Limanovskii, G. A., "V riadakh stakhanovtsev—raskreposhchennye zhenshchiny," *Sovetskii Khlopok*, 11-12, 1937, pp. 91-95.

Liubimova, S., "Bor'ba na ideologicheskom fronte," *Kommunistka*, 9, 1926, pp. 74-75.

———, "Dekret o chadre i obshchestvo 'Doloi kalym i mnogozhenstvo,'" *Kommunistka*, 8, 1928, pp. 73-78.

———, "Na nekotorye temy k soveshchaniiu," *Kommunistka*, 9, 1928, pp. 78-82.

———, "O kooperirovanii zhenshchin vostochnykh narodnostei," *Kommunistka*, 5, 1927, pp. 51-53.

———, "Po Srednei Azii (k itogam raboty Sredi zhenshchin)," *Kommunistka*, 4, 1926, pp. 56-59.

———, "Vos'moe marta na Vostoke," *Kommunistka*, 2, 1927, pp. 50-52.

———, "8 marta na Vostoke," *Kommunistka*, 2, 1928, pp. 83-86.

———, "Vostok k desiatiletiiu Oktiabria," *Kommunistka*, 10, 1927, pp. 55-61.

———, "Vsesoiuznyi s'ezd rabotnits i krest'ianok i rabota sredi zhenshchin Vostoka," *Kommunistka*, 11, 1927, pp. 73-77.

———, "Vsesoiuznoe soveshchanie komissii po uluchsheniiu truda i byta zhenshchin," *Kommunistka*, 3, 1928, pp. 58-61.

———, "Zhenskie lavki v Srednei Azii," *Kommunistka*, 7, 1926, pp. 70-72.

L'vov, K. I., "Iz ekspeditsionnogo bloknota (putevye zametki)," *Prosveshchenie Natsional'nostei*, 4, 1935, pp. 54-60.

Maiorova, "Peredvizhnye krasnye kibitki," *Kommunistka*, 6, 1928, pp. 88-90.

Maksimova, M., "Krest'ianka-vostochnitsa v pereustroistve sel'skogo khoziaistva," *Kommunistka*, 6, 1928, pp. 93-95.

Massell, G., "Law as an Instrument of Revolutionary Change in a Traditional Milieu: The Case of Soviet Central Asia," *Law and Society Review*, 2, 2, 1968, pp. 179-228.

424

"Mestnye rabotniki—ob izdanii dekreta (iz rechei na Vsesoiuznom soveshchanii rabotnikov sredi vostochnits)," *Kommunistka*, 1, 1929, pp. 32-35.

Michurina, T., "Pravovoe polozhenie zhenshchiny v Turkmenii," *Kommunistka*, 10-11, 1926, pp. 80-83.

Minina, Ye., "Politprosvetrabota sredi kochevnits," *Kommunisticheskoe Prosveshchenie*, 1, 1931, pp. 46-48.

Mitrofanov, A., "K itogam partchistki v natsrespublikakh i oblastiakh," *Revoliutsiia i Natsional'nosti*, 1, 1930, pp. 29-36.

————, "K itogam partchistki v natsrespublikakh i oblastiakh," *Revoliutsiia i Natsional'nosti*, 2, 1930, pp. 35-49.

Mokrinskii, S., "Prestupleniia sostavliaiushchiye perezhitki rodovogo byta," *Sovetskoe Pravo*, 3(27), 1927, pp. 103-17.

Mostovaia, Ye., "Natsionalka na vyborakh," *Kommunistka*, 2, 1929, pp. 33-35.

————, "Pervoe vsesoiuznoe soveshchanie komissii po uluchsheniiu truda i byta zhenshchin vostochnits," *Vlast' Sovetov*, 9, 1928, pp. 7-8.

Mukhitdinova, Ye., "Na zashchitu truzhenitsy Vostoka," *Kommunistka*, 9, 1929, pp. 39-41.

Mulakov, G., "Organizatsiia otkhodnichestva v natsional'nykh kolkhozakh," *Revoliutsiia i Natsional'nosti*, 10-11, 1931, pp. 92-97.

N., A., "O fondakh na rabotu sredi vostochnykh truzhenits," *Kommunistka*, 9, 1926, pp. 34-36.

Nasurullin, "Skotovodstvo i kochevanie v byvshei Ural'skoi gubernii," *Narodnoie Khoziaistvo Kazakhstana*, 11-12, 1928, p. 273.

Nikiforov, I., "Biurokraty iskrivliaiut liniiu partii," *Kommunistka*, 15, 1929, pp. 45-46.

Nikolaeva, A., "Pervye itogi (Tashkentskii okrug)," *Kommunistka*, 8, 1927, pp. 52-54.

Niurina, F., "Usilit' podgotovku kul'turnykh kadrov Vostoka," *Kommunistka*, 5-6, 1929, pp. 22-25.

————, "V Srednei Azii," *Kommunistka*, 4, 1925, pp. 78-83.

Nukhrat, A., "Bytovye kruzhki (k resheniiu Otdela rabotnits pri Ts.K.)," *Kommunistka*, 8, 1927, pp. 19-22.

————, "Delegatskie sobraniia na Vostoke," *Kommunistka*, 7, 1927, pp. 31-37.

————, "Itogi diskussii," *Kommunistka*, 11, 1928, pp. 57-59.

425

Nukhrat, A., "Kul'tpokhod v Turkmenistane," *Kommunistka*, 9, 1929, pp. 32-35.

——, "Na vazhneishem uchastke nashei raboty," *Kommunistka*, 19, 1929, pp. 34-38.

——, "O rabote v Kazakhstane," *Kommunistka*, 10-11, 1926, pp. 77-80.

——, "Osnovnye voprosy soveshchaniia," *Kommunistka*, 6, 1928, pp. 77-80.

——, "Ot zatvornichestva k proizvodstvu," *Kommunistka*, 1, 1929, pp. 24-27.

——, "Perevybory v sovety i zhenshchiny Vostoka," *Kommunistka*, 12, 1927, pp. 41-44.

——, "XV s'ezd i zadachi raboty sredi vostochnits-krest'ianok," *Kommunistka*, 1, 1928, pp. 53-56.

——, "Podgotovka rabotnikov sredi zhenshchin korennogo naseleniia," *Kommunistka*, 3, 1927, pp. 50-54.

——, "Podniat' novye plasty vostochnits," *Kommunistka*, 17-18, 1929, pp. 17-22.

——, "Pora gotovitsia," *Kommunistka*, 7, 1928, pp. 55-61.

——, "Smotr natsional'noi kul'tmassovoi raboty," *Sovetskoe Stroitel'stvo*, (65), 1931, pp. 96-109.

——, "Usilim podgotovku aktiva," *Kommunistka*, 10, 1928, pp. 75-78.

——, "Usilit' klassovuiu bditel'nost' i proizvodstvennuiu aktivnost'," *Revoliutsiia i Natsional'nosti*, 3(36), 1933, pp. 46-59.

——, "Usilit' massovuiu rabotu Sovetov sredi natsionalok," *Vlast' Sovetov*, 6, 1933, pp. 8-9.

——, "Vostochnitsu—v sovety," *Vlast' Sovetov*, 1, 1929, pp. 5-7.

——, "Vsesoiuznaia komissiia," *Kommunistka*, 4, 1928, pp. 68-69.

"Nuzhno li izdat' dekret zapreshchaiushchii noshenie chadry (iz stenogrammy Zakavkazskogo soveshchaniia rabotnikov sredi zhenshchin 16 iiunia 1928g.)," *Kommunistka*, 8, 1928, pp. 79-81.

"Ob uvelichenii zhenskogo truda v khlopkovom khoziaistve," *Khlopokoe Delo*, 9, 1930, pp. 1125-26.

"Obzor osnovnykh zakonodatel'nykh aktov Soiuza S.S.R. . . . ," *Revoliutsiia i Natsional'nosti*, 4-5, 1930, pp. 136-39.

Olson, M., "Rapid Growth as a Destabilizing Force," *The Journal of Economic History*, XXIII, 4, 1963, pp. 529-52.

P., Z., "Dobrovol'noe obshchestvo 'Za novyi byt,' " *Kommunistka*, 6, 1928, pp. 84-85.

Perimova, "Protiv primirenchestva v bytu (Turkmenistan)," *Kommunistka*, 9, 1929, pp. 37-38.

Petrova, V. N., "Na novom etape kul'turnoi revoliutsii," *Bor'ba za Khlopok*, 1-2, 1934, pp. 34-37.

Petukhov, P., "Na podstupakh k polnoi likvidatsii natsional'noi otstalosti," *Revoliutsiia i Natsional'nosti*, (48), 1934, pp. 37-45.

Pis'mennyi, S., "O nekotorykh osnovnykh momentakh kul'turnoi revoliutsii v natsrespublikakh Srednei Azii," *Revoliutsiia i Kul'tura*, 10, 1928, pp. 11-20.

Polianskaia, A., "Rabota po uluchsheniiu truda i byta zhenshchin," *Revoliutsiia i Natsional'nosti*, 3, 1930, pp. 91-96.

Popova, Ye., "Zadachi raboty sovetov sredi zhenshchin natsional'-nykh respublik i oblastei," *Revoliutsiia i Natsional'nosti*, 3(36), 1933, pp. 60-64.

"Postanovleniie plenuma Ts.K. RKP(b)—Po dokladu t. Nikolaevoi 'Ob ocherednykh zadachakh partii v rabote sredi rabotnits, krest'ianok i truzhenits Vostoka,' " *Kommunistka*, 2, 1925, p. 45.

"Postanovleniie Presidiuma Soveta Natsional'nostei Ts.I.K. S.S.S.R.—O meropriiatsiiakh po dal'neishemu razvitiiu fiz-kul'tury i sporta v Uzbekskoi, Turkmenskoi, i Tadzhikskoi, S.S.R.," *Revoliutsiia i Natsional'nosti*, (80), 1936, pp. 95-96.

Potekhin, Yu., "Nekotoryie zadachi izbiratel'noi kampanii i vybory 1927 goda," *Sovetskoe Stroitel'stvo*, (28), 1928, pp. 69-87.

Pravda, M., "Sovetizatsiia kochevii," *Sovetskoe Stroitel'stvo*, 12, (41), 1929, pp. 105-14.

Prishchepchik, Z., "Itogi raboty partii sredi zhenshchin Uzbekistana ot I do II kurultaia (S'ezda)," *Kommunistka*, 12, 1925, pp. 63-65.

————, "Ob uchastii trudiashchikhsia zhenshchin v perevyborakh i rabote sovetov v Uzbekistane," *Kommunistka*, 7, 1927, pp. 77-79.

————, "Opyt raboty klubov v Srednei Azii," *Kommunistka*, 9, 1926, pp. 76-78.

"Proekt programmy po perepodgotovke zhenorgov Vostoka i natsmen—Zadachi i organizatsiia raboty sredi vostochnits i natsmenok," *Kommunistka*, 10, 1929, pp. 53-64.

R., F., "Zhenshchiny v RKP v tsyfrakh," *Kommunistka*, 4, 1925, pp. 11-14.

Rigin, I., "Pod znakom bor'by s parandzhoi (Kirgiziia)," *Kommunistka*, 5-6, 1929, pp. 58-59.

Rose, Arnold M., "The Use of Law to Induce Social Change" in *Transactions of the Third World Congress of Sociology*. London, 1954, Vol. VI, pp. 52-63.

Ross, Ye., "Turkmenki v kovrovom proizvodstve," *Kommunistka*, 3, 1926, pp. 73-75.

————, "Kak rabotaet dom dekhkanki (opyt Turkmenistana)," *Kommunistka*, 8, 1926, pp. 57-58.

Ryskulov, T. R., "Sovremennyi Kazakhstan," *Novyi Vostok*, 12, 1926, pp. 105-20.

Safadri, A., "Perevybory sovetov na Vostoke," *Kommunistka*, 11, 1928, pp. 30-34.

Safudri, A., "Za reformu natsional'nogo zhenskogo kostiuma," *Kommunistka*, 13, 1929, pp. 42-44.

Sakhudri, A., "Vovlechenie vostochnits na proizvodstvo," *Kommunistka*, 4, 1928, pp. 70-73.

Salim, "Musul'manskaia Religiia i Zhenshchina," *Bezbozhnik* (news.), 10, 1928, p. 6.

Samokhvalova, G., "Sostav kommunistok (po dannym statotdela Ts.K. VKP(b))," *Kommunistka*, 9, 1926, pp. 20-28.

Sannikov, G., "Literaturnyi praznik Turkmenistana," *Revoliutsiia i Natsional'nosti*, (54), 1934, pp. 43-47.

Sazonova, P., and Chernova, K., "Vnimanie ias'liam natsional'nykh raionov," *Revoliutsiia i Natsional'nosti*, (49), 1934, pp. 49-57.

Seifi, M., "Na pomoshch zhenskim promyslam na Vostoke," *Kommunistka*, 9, 1925, pp. 75-79.

————, "O rabote na Vostoke i nashem kadre," *Kommunistka*, 4, 1925, pp. 73-78.

S----i, M., "Rabota sredi zhenshchin natsmen," *Kommunistka*, 9, 1925, pp. 25-28.

Sev, "Zametki o Turkmenskom dukhovenstve," *Turkmenovedenie*, 3-4 (7-8), 1928, pp. 5-20.

Sevast'ianova, T., "Rukovodstvo zhenrabotoi v aule-kishlake (Kirgizskaia respublika)," *Kommunistka*, 1, 1928, pp. 63-65.

Shatskaia, O. I., "Turkmenskaia koliadnaia pesnia v sviazi s bytom i religioznymi verovaniami," *Sovetskaia Etnografiia*, 1, 1936, pp. 45-54.

Shimko, S., "Rabota sredi zhenshchin Kirgizstana," *Kommunistka*, 12, 1925, pp. 66-68.

Shirman, T., "Politprosvetrabota sredi krestianok natsmen," *Komunisticheskoe Prosveshchenie*, 4, 1927, pp. 73-80.

Shokhor, V., "Religiozno-bytovyie sudy v R.S.F.S.R.," *Sovetskoe Stroitel'stvo*, 8-9 (13-14), 1927, pp. 94-114.

———, "Zaveshchanie Magometa," *Bezbozhnik* (news.), 20, 1929, p. 10.

Smirnova, "Udachnyi opyt po podgotovke aktiva," *Kommunistka*, 10, 1928, pp. 81-82.

Smirnova, A., "Pochin po bor'be s religiei na Vostoke," *Kommunistka*, 8, 1929, p. 27.

———, "Zhenskoe obrazovaniie v Uzbekistane," *Kommunistka*, 8, 1928, pp. 82-83.

Smitten, Ye., "K voprosu o regulirovanii rosta i sostava zhenskoi chasti partii," *Kommunistka*, 11, 1925, pp. 46-52.

Sokolova, A., "8 Marta na Sovestskom Vostoke," *Kommunistka*, 2-3, 1930, pp. 40-42.

Sudakov, V., "Devushka Vostoka i komsomol," *Kommunistka*, 8, 1927, pp. 22-27.

"Suleiman Gora (Pismo iz Srednei Azii)," *Bezbozhnik* (news.), 34, 1929, p. 2.

Suleimanova, Kh., "Istoricheskii ocherk o sozdanii Sovetskikh sudov v Uzbekistane," *Sovetskoe Gosudarstvo i Pravo*, 3, 1949, pp. 61-69.

———, "Zarozhdenie Sovetskogo ugolovnogo prava v Uzbekistanie," *Sovetskoe Gosudarstvo i Pravo*, 10, 1948, pp. 65-69.

Tabolov, K., "K voprosu o natsional'noi kul'ture," *Revoliutsiia i Kul'tura*, 8, 1928, pp. 22-29.

Tarantaeva, V., "Opyt nedavnego proshlogo (obzor po mestnym materialam)," *Kommunistka*, 11, 1928, pp. 43-47.

Tiurakulov, N., "K voprosu o latynskom alfavitie sredi Turkov S.S.S.R.," *Zhizn' Natsional'nostei*, 1(6), 1924, pp. 38-40.

Trainin, I., "Bor'ba za ravenstvo byvshikh ugnetennykh natsional'-nostei," *Sovetskoe Stroitel'stvo*, 8(21), 1936, pp. 19-36.

Tunik, M., "Rabota sredi zhenshchin v potrebkooperatsii Uzbekistana," *Kommunistka*, 5, 1927, pp. 56-58.

Uspenskaia, "Meropriiatiia po uluchsheniiu truda i byta kazachki-skotovodki (opyt Kazakhstana)," *Kommunistka*, 1, 1928, pp. 66-68.

"V Presidiume Ts.I.K. Turkmenskoi S.S.R.," *Sovetsokoe Stroitel'-stvo*, (91), 1934, p. 109.

"V Sovete Natsional'nostei Ts.I.K. Soiuza S.S.R.," *Revoliutsiia i Natsional'nosti*, 11(81), 1936, p. 76.

"V Tsentral'nykh Ispolnitsel'nykh Komitetakh Soiuznykh Respublik," *Sovetskoe Stroitel'stvo*, (5), 1926, pp. 141-61.

"V Tsentral'nykh Ispolnitsel'nykh Komitetakh Soiuznykh Respublik," *Sovetskoe Stroitel'stvo*, (12), 1927, 138-65.

"V Tsentral'nykh Ispolnitsel'nykh Komitetakh Soiuznykh Respublik," *Sovetskoe Stroitel'stvo*, (33), 1929, pp. 149-59.

"V Tsentral'nykh Ispolnitsel'nykh Komitetakh Soiuznykh Respublik," *Sovetskoe Stroitel'stvo*, (44), 1930, pp. 132-39.

"V Tsentral'nykh Ispolnitsel'nykh Komitetakh Soiuznykh Respublik," *Sovetskoe Stroitel'stvo*, (53), 1930, pp. 141-45.

Vasilieva, G. P., "Voprosy Turkmenskoi Etnografii v Literature v 1950-1952gg.," *Sovetskaia Etnografiia*, 3, 1953, pp. 221-25.

Vel'tner, A., "Protiv putanitsy i oshibok v voprosakh natsional'-no-kolonial'noi revoliutsii," *Revoliutsiia i Natsional'nosti*, 4, 1932, pp. 82-96.

————, "Nekotorye problemy bol'shevizatsii KP(b) Turkmenii," *Revoliutsiia i Natsional'nosti*, 12, 1931, pp. 29-38.

Vinogradov, B., "Obzor postanovlenii o sovetskom stroitel'stve," *Revoliutsiia i Natsional'nosti*, 4-5, 1930, pp. 135-39.

Vorshev, V., "Osnovnyie etapy razvitiia partorganizatsii Turkmenistana," *Revoliutsiia i Natsional'nosti*, 12(58), 1934, pp. 68-80.

Yakubovskaia, S. I., "Ustranenie deistvitel'nogo neravenstva narodov; na primere istorii narodov Srednei Azii i Kazakhstana," *Istoricheskie Zapiski*, 48, 1954, pp. 156-201.

Yaroslavsky, "Reshitel'nee udarim po bytovym perezhitkam," *Kommunistka*, 1, 1929, pp. 28-31.

Z., A., "Turkmenistan nakanune perevyborov," *Vlast' Sovetov*, 52, 1928, pp. 15-16.

Zade, Osman Dzhuma, "Shire razvernut' raziasnitel'nuiu kampaniiu," *Kommunistka*, 7, 1929, pp. 48-49.

Zaitsev, P., "O bytovykh sektsiiagh," *Vlast' Sovetov*, 4, 1928, pp. 9-10.

Zakharian, Ye., "Brachnoe i semeinoe pravo na Vostoke," *Kommunistka*, 3, 1926, pp. 42-45.

Zasukhin, V., "Kirgizskii aul," *Revoliutsiia i Natsional'nosti*, 12 (46), 1933, pp. 38-40.

————, "Usloviia raboty v kochevykh sovetakh Kirgizii," *Vlast' Sovetov*, 8, 1931, p. 27.

Zavarian, N., "Delegatskie sobraniia na Vostoke," *Kommunistka*, 7, 1926, pp. 35-40.

————, "Nekotorye momenty iz raboty sredi zhenshchin Srednei Azii (iz zapisnoi knizhki obsledovatelia)," *Kommunistka*, 6, 1926, pp. 66-70.

————, "Rabota na Sovetskom Vostoke," *Kommunistka*, 12, 1925, pp. 25-31.

Zhukova, "Novoe uvlechenie staroi ideei," *Kommunistka*, 10, 1928, pp. 79-80.

INDEX

Abidova, D., 149

action "from above," xxii, 45-48, 74, 75ff; and radical impatience, 75f, 253f; political reductionism (*shablonizatsiia*) as, 45-48, 362ff

action "in depth," xxii, 84-87, 189f, 362ff; time perspective in, 84ff, 359ff

activists, local, *see* communist administrative personnel

adat (customary law), *see* law and religion, traditional

administrative assault, xxiii, 186-91, 213-46; as direct strategy, 57n, 186; as obeying "heroic" ethic, 189; as heretical model, 249-53; and Leninism, 213, 215, 216f; and Stalinism, 217, 222, 228n, 229n; and time perspective, 188 (table), 189, 214ff, 311f; Soviet arguments for and against, 189, 213-26, 249-53, 295-302; Soviet assessment and reassessment of, 253-55, 322-35, 346-53; limits of, 390-411. *See also khudzhum*

administrative personnel, communist, *see* communist administrative personnel

Afghanistan, 218-20, 340, 341n

Aitakov, N., xxxiii, 316

Akhun-Babaev, Yo., 350ff

Akopov, S., 195, 333, 341f

Aksentovich, Anna, 134, 151, 358

Alash Orda, 8, 23f, 30ff

Allport, Gordon, 397

Allworth, Edward, xxvii

Almond, G. A., 392

Amosov, N., 311

Andreev, A. A., 71, 72

Arkhimcheev, A. T., 143, 174-78

Armand, Inessa, 135

Ar-na, *see* Artiukhina, Alexandra

Artiukhina (Ar-na), Alexandra, 159, 159n, 189n, 236n, 283f, 319, 331, 343, 346ff, 361

arts, *see* theater and arts

assault, *see* administrative assault

Assemblies of Women's Delegates (Delegatskiie Sobraniia), 213, 261, 301, 328, 355ff

Association of Clergymen (Uema-Dzhemieti), *see* Turko-Islamic nationalism

Atatürk, 219f, 392f

authority, Soviet, *see* insurgency by an incumbent; legitimation of Soviet authority

authority, traditional, attempted breakdown of: legalism and assault as direct attacks on traditional elites, 76-83, 251-53, 311-21, 317f, 341; disruption of family unit by means of female mobilization and inducement of sexual/generational tensions, 85-89, 141-49, 251-53; and role of bride-price, as central to authority structure, 195; retrenchment, modes of, to isolate elite, 340-43; limits of, 390-92. *See also* elites, religious; elites, traditional political; solidarity, traditional; traditionalization

authority, traditional, persistence of, 253, 256ff, 266-84, 283f, 391ff, 398, 399-405; and continuity of personnel in elite role through kin succession, 83; traditionalization of judicial system, 305-8; scarcity of native Soviet personnel, 282f, 322f; collective responsibility and retaliation, 258f, 267, 269-

433

during, 76n. *See also* conquest of Central Asia, Soviet

revolutionary legalism, xxiii, 186-91, 192-212; as direct strategy, 57n, 186; as supplanting traditional legal structures, 187-89, 196-200; as enforcing equality of sexes, 187-89, 200ff; and time perspective, 187-89 (incl. table, 188), 196ff, 334f; Soviet arguments for and against, 187-89, 193f, 193-96, 210-12, 249-53; assessment and reassessment of, 253-55, 322-35, 335ff; limits of, 390-411. *See also* law, Soviet

revolutionary strategies, *see* revolutionary transformation, strategies of

revolutionary transformation, strategies of: comparative study of, xixf; evolution of, as alternatives and stages, xxiii-xxiv, 186-91 (incl. table, 188), 196-98; as direct or indirect, 57, 57n, 409n; initiatives in, as heretical models, 249-53; as tangible models, 250f. *See also* tension management, revolutionary action as; *and individual strategies*

Riesman, David, 401

Rose, Arnold, 399n

Ross, Yevstaliia, 134

rural locales, *see* urban/rural locales

Russian chauvinism, *see* chauvinism, Great Russian

Rykov, A. I., 44

Rywkin, M., xxviii

Safarov, G., 43ff, 51f, 55ff, 71n

Samarkand, 6

seclusion and veiling, *see* administrative assault; *khudzhum*; sexual roles and statuses, women, traditional; women, Soviet policy toward

Second All-Russian Congress of Communist Organizations of

Peoples of the East, 1919, Lenin's address to, 42f, 42n

Second Congress of Asian Communists, 1919, *see* Second All-Russian Congress of Communist Organizations of Peoples of the East, 1919

Second International Conference of Communist Women, 1921, 135f

Sections for [Dealing with the Local] Way of Life (Bytovye Sektsii), 357ff, 370

secular elites, native, *see* elites, native secular

sedentary societies, 5ff:

sexual roles in: division of labor, 98f; seclusion of women, 101; and veiling, 110f, 116f

accessibility to manipulation of, 305ff; and urbanism, 57ff, 60f, 74, 233ff, 261n, 262n, 330; and *khudzhum*, 231, 236ff, 261ff

See also khudzhum; law and religion, traditional; political structures, traditional; Tadzhiks; Uzbeks; urban/rural locales

sexual roles and statuses, men, traditional: value placed on sons, and perpetuation of kin group, 99, 293, 337; monopoly on "heroism," 99, 153; economic role of, 169f; male dominance and dependence on inferior status of women, 401ff. *See also* authority, traditional; tension management, revolutionary action as

sexual roles and statuses, women, traditional:

as inferior, 97, 109f; as dangerous, 102f, 110; as transient (in natal family), 111; as stranger (in husband's family), 103, 115; in death, 108f

and seclusion, 101f, 116f, 137f, 229f; and veiling, 110f, 138,

Book Written Under the Auspices of the Center of International Studies
Princeton University

Gabriel A. Almond, *The Appeals of Communism* (Princeton University Press 1954)

William W. Kaufmann, ed., *Military Policy and National Security* (Princeton University Press 1956)

Klaus Knorr, *The War Potential of Nations* (Princeton University Press 1956)

Lucian W. Pye, *Guerrilla Communism in Malaya* (Princeton University Press 1956)

Charles De Visscher, *Theory and Reality in Public International Law*, trans. by P. E. Corbett (Princeton University Press 1957; rev. ed. 1968)

Bernard C. Cohen, *The Political Process and Foreign Policy: The Making of the Japanese Peace Settlement* (Princeton University Press 1959)

Myron Weiner, *Party Politics in India: The Development of a Multi-Party System* (Princeton University Press 1957)

Percy E. Corbett, *Law in Diplomacy* (Princeton University Press 1959)

Rolf Sannwald and Jacques Stohler, *Economic Integration: Theoretical Assumptions and Consequences of European Unification*, trans. by Herman Karreman (Princeton University Press 1959)

Klaus Knorr, ed., *NATO and American Security* (Princeton University Press 1959)

Gabriel A. Almond and James S. Coleman, eds., *The Politics of the Developing Areas* (Princeton University Press 1960)

Herman Kahn, *On Thermonuclear War* (Princeton University Press 1960)

Sidney Verba, *Small Groups and Political Behavior: A Study of Leadership* (Princeton University Press 1961)

Robert J. C. Butow, *Tojo and the Coming of the War* (Princeton University Press 1961)

Glenn H. Snyder, *Deterrence and Defense: Toward a Theory of National Security* (Princeton University Press 1961)

Klaus Knorr and Sidney Verba, eds., *The International System: Theoretical Essays* (Princeton University Press 1961)

Peter Paret and John W. Shy, *Guerrillas in the 1960's* (Praeger 1962)

George Modelski, *A Theory of Foreign Policy* (Praeger 1962)

Klaus Knorr and Thornton Read, eds., *Limited Strategic War* (Praeger 1963)

Frederick S. Dunn, *Peace-Making and the Settlement with Japan* (Princeton University Press 1963)

Arthur L. Burns and Nina Heathcote, *Peace-Keeping by United Nations Forces* (Praeger 1963)

Richard A. Falk, *Law, Morality, and War in the Contemporary World* (Praeger 1963)

James N. Rosenau, *National Leadership and Foreign Policy: A Case Study in the Mobilization of Public Support* (Princeton University Press 1963)

Gabriel A. Almond and Sidney Verba, *The Civic Culture: Political Attitudes and Democracy in Five Nations* (Princeton University Press 1963)

Bernard C. Cohen, *The Press and Foreign Policy* (Princeton University Press 1963)

Richard L. Sklar, *Nigerian Political Parties: Power in an Emergent African Nation* (Princeton University Press 1963)

Peter Paret, *French Revolutionary Warfare from Indochina to Algeria: The Analysis of a Political and Military Doctrine* (Praeger 1964)

Harry Eckstein, ed., *Internal War: Problems and Approaches* (Free Press 1964)

Cyril E. Black and Thomas P. Thornton, eds., *Communism and Revolution: The Strategic Uses of Political Violence* (Princeton University Press 1964)

Miriam Camps, *Britain and the European Community 1955-1963* (Princeton University Press 1964)

Thomas P. Thornton, ed., *The Third World in Soviet Perspective: by Soviet Writers on the Developing Areas* (Princeton University Press 1964)

James N. Rosenau, ed., *International Aspects of Civil Strife* (Princeton University Press 1964)

Sidney I. Ploss, *Conflict and Decision-Making in Soviet Russia: A Case Study of Agricultural Policy, 1953-1963* (Princeton University Press 1965)

Richard A. Falk and Richard J. Barnet, eds., *Security in Disarmament* (Princeton University Press 1965)

Karl von Vorys, *Political Development in Pakistan* (Princeton University Press 1965)

Harold and Margaret Sprout, *The Ecological Perspective on Human Affairs, With Special Reference to International Politics* (Princeton University Press 1965)

Klaus Knorr, *On the Uses of Military Power in the Nuclear Age* (Princeton University Press 1966)

Harry Eckstein, *Division and Cohesion in Democracy: A Study of Norway* (Princeton University Press 1966)

Cyril E. Black, *The Dynamics of Modernization: A Study in Comparative History* (Harper and Row 1966)

Peter Kunstadter, ed., *Southeast Asian Tribes, Minorities, and Nations* (Princeton University Press 1967)

E. Victor Wolfenstein, *The Revolutionary Personality: Lenin, Trotsky, Gandhi* (Princeton University Press 1967)

Leon Gordenker, *The UN Secretary-General and the Maintenance of Peace* (Columbia University Press 1967)

Oran R. Young, *The Intermediaries: Third Parties in International Crises* (Princeton University Press 1967)

James N. Rosenau, ed., *Domestic Sources of Foreign Policy* (Free Press 1967)

Richard F. Hamilton, *Affluence and the French Worker in the Fourth Republic* (Princeton University Press 1967)

Linda B. Miller, *World Order and Local Disorder: The United Nations and Internal Conflicts* (Princeton University Press 1967)

Wolfram F. Hanrieder, *West German Foreign Policy, 1949-1963: International Pressures and Domestic Response* (Stanford University Press 1967)

Richard H. Ullman, *Britain and the Russian Civil War: November 1918-February 1920* (Princeton University Press 1968)

Robert Gilpin, *France in the Age of the Scientific State* (Princeton University Press 1968)

William B. Bader, *The United States and the Spread of Nuclear Weapons* (Pegasus 1968)

Richard A. Falk, *Legal Order in a Violent World* (Princeton University Press 1968)

Cyril E. Black, Richard A. Falk, Klaus Knorr, and Oran R. Young, *Neutralization and World Politics* (Princeton University Press 1968)

Oran R. Young, *The Politics of Force: Bargaining During International Crises* (Princeton University Press 1969)

Klaus Knorr and James N. Rosenau, eds., *Contending Approaches to International Politics* (Princeton University Press 1969)

James N. Rosenau, ed., *Linkage Politics: Essays on the Convergence of National and International Systems* (Free Press 1969)

John T. McAlister, Jr., *Viet Nam: The Origins of Revolution* (Knopf 1969)

Jean Edward Smith, *Germany Beyond the Wall: People, Politics and Prosperity* (Little, Brown 1969)

James Barros, *Betrayal from Within: Joseph Avenol, Secretary-General of the League of Nations, 1933-1940* (Yale University Press 1969)

Charles Hermann, *Crises in Foreign Policy: A Simulation Analysis* (Bobbs-Merrill 1969)

Robert C. Tucker, *The Marxian Revolutionary Idea: Essays on Marxist Thought and Its Impact on Radical Movements* (W. W. Norton 1969)

Harvey Waterman, *Political Change in Contemporary France: The Politics of an Industrial Democracy* (Charles E. Merrill 1969)

Richard A. Falk and Cyril E. Black, eds., *The Future of the International Legal Order*, Vol. I, *Trends and Patterns* (Princeton University Press 1969)

Ted Robert Gurr, *Why Men Rebel* (Princeton University Press 1969)

C. S. Whitaker, Jr., *The Politics of Tradition: Continuity and Change in Northern Nigeria, 1946-1966* (Princeton University Press 1970)

Richard A. Falk, *The Status of Law in International Society* (Princeton University Press 1970)

Henry Bienen, *Tanzania: Party Transformation and Economic Development* (Princeton University Press 1967, rev. edn. 1970)

Klaus Knorr, *Military Power and Potential* (D. C. Heath 1970)

Richard A. Falk and Cyril E. Black, eds., *The Future of the International Legal Order*, Vol. II, *Wealth and Resources* (Princeton University Press 1970)

Leon Gordenker, ed., *The United Nations and International Politics* (Princeton University Press 1971)

Cyril E. Black and Richard A. Falk, eds., *The Future of the International Legal Order*, Vol. III, *Conflict Management* (Princeton University Press 1971)

Harold and Margaret Sprout, *Toward a Politics of the Planet Earth* (Van Nostrand Reinhold Co. 1971)

Francine R. Frankel, *India's Green Revolution: Economic Gains and Political Cost* (Princeton University Press 1971)

Richard H. Ullman, *The Anglo-Soviet Accord* (Princeton University Press, 1972)

Library of Congress Cataloging in Publication Data

Massell, Gregory J   1925-
   The surrogate proletariat; Moslem women and revolutionary
   strategies in Soviet Central Asia, 1919-1929.

   Bibliography: p.
   1. Women, Muslim.   2. Women in Soviet Central Asia.
   3. Communism and Islam.   4. Soviet Central Asia—
   Politics and government.   I. Title.
HQ1774.C45M33   301.41′2′09584   73-16047
ISBN 0-691-07562-X